METHUEN LIBRARY REPRINTS

GERMAN DIPLOMATIC
DOCUMENTS
1871-1914
IN FOUR VOLUMES

GERMAN DIPLOMATIC DOCUMENTS
1871-1914

IN FOUR VOLUMES

SELECTED AND TRANSLATED BY

E. T. S. DUGDALE

VOLUME III
THE GROWING ANTAGONISM 1898-1910

WITH A PREFACE BY THE RT. HON.

Sir MAURICE DE BUNSEN, Bart., G.C.M.G.

FORMER BRITISH AMBASSADOR IN SPAIN AND AUSTRIA-HUNGARY

BARNES & NOBLE, Inc.
New York
METHUEN & CO. Ltd
London

This Translation First Published in 1930

Reprinted, 1969
by
Barnes & Noble, Inc., New York
and
Methuen & Co. Ltd, London

This work is based upon *Die Grosse Politik der Europäischen Kabinette 1871–1914 : Sammlung der Diplomatischen Akten des Auswärtigen Amtes,* edited by Johannes Lepsius, Albrecht Mendelssohn Bartholdy and Friedrich Thimme. Berlin : Deutsche Verlags gesellschaft für Politik und Geschichte m.b.H. 1922–1927

Barnes & Noble SBN 389 01067 7
Methuen SBN 416 15620 7

Printed in the United States of America

TRANSLATOR'S NOTE

THE present volume is a selection from Vols. XIV–XXVIII of *Die Grosse Politik der Europäischen Mächte, 1871–1914*. The Translator's aim has been to produce, with the help of references to other works, notably Gooch and Temperley's *British Documents on the Origins of the War*, a true picture of events and motives. Indeed the limited space which has had to be allotted to the period covered by the four volumes of this work makes it essential that readers shall keep ' G. & T.' on the table by them, in order to fill in the gaps in the picture of each subject.

The Translator wishes to thank Mrs. Edgar Dugdale and others who have helped in the revision of the work done in this volume ; also to add a word of deep regret for the loss of the help and advice of the late Sir James Headlam Morley, K.B.E., which so greatly enhanced the value of the first two volumes. His wide knowledge of recent German history and the illuminating suggestions which fell from his lips were an inspiration when he was there, and will be missed acutely during the remainder of the work. The Translator wishes also to thank Mr. H. Wickham Steed for information on the subject of Austro-Hungarian policy, especially with reference to the great collection of Austrian documents which was published too late for much use to be made of them in this volume.

The previous volumes of this present work are:
Vol. I. The Bismarck Period, 1875–1889; and
Vol. II. The Nineties. 1889–1898.

WORKS REFERRED TO

P. Joseph : *Foreign Diplomacy in China.*
W. Goetz : *Briefe Wilhelms II an den Zaren.*
A. Zimmermann : *Geschichte der Deutschen Kolonialpolitik.*
Sir L. Mitchell : *Life of Cecil Rhodes.*
R. B. Mowat : *Life of Lord Pauncefote.*
W. T. Stead : *La Chronique de la Conférence de la Haye.*
Captain A. F. Mahan : *Armaments and Arbitration.*
Andrew D. White : *Autobiography.*
Count Münster : *Autobiography.*
' The Times ' History of the Boer War.
Worsfold : *Lord Milner's Work in South Africa.*
Sir A. Hardinge : *A Diplomatist in the East.*
M. J. Bau : *The Open Door Doctrine.*
United States Foreign Relations.
Rev. R. Allen : *The Siege of the Pekin Legations.*
Lord Cromer : *Modern Egypt.*
Weigall : *Egypt.*
E. D. Morel : *Morocco in Diplomacy.*
Sir S. Lee : *King Edward VII.*
Dennis : *Adventures in American Diplomacy.*
Sir R. Bacon : *Lord Fisher.*
Brandenburg : *From Bismarck to the World War.*
J. A. Cramb : *Germany and England.*
Mrs. Edgar Dugdale and T. de Bille : *Treitschke's Politik* (Transl.).
H. W. Wilson : *The War Guilt.*
H. W. C. Davis : *Political Thought of H. von Treitschke.*
Lord d'Abernon : *An Ambassador of Peace.*
S. Gwynn : *Letters and Friendships of Cecil Spring-Rice.*
H. Wickham Steed : *Through Thirty Years.*
Gooch and Temperley : *British Documents on the Origins of the War.*
    Vols. I–VI.
Eckardstein : *Ten Years at the Court of St. James.*
Lord Grey of Fallodon : *Twenty-five Years.*
J. A. Spender : *Life of Sir H. Campbell-Bannerman.*
Lord Haldane : *Before the War.*
British Parliamentary Papers : Accounts and Papers.
Eyre Crowe's Minutes, given in G. & T.
British Blue Books : *Turkey,* Nos. 1 and 3. *Samoa. Russia,* 1905.
    Africa, 1900. *Morocco,* 1904.
Staatsarchiv. Various references.
Hayashi's *Memoirs.*
O. Franke : *Die Grossmächte in Ostasien,* 1894–1914.
Tirpitz : *Die Aufbau der Deutschen Weltmacht,* and *Die Aufbau der Deutschen Flotte.*
Lord Fisher's *Memories.*

Raymond : *Life of D. Lloyd George.*
O. Hammann : *Bilder aus der letzten Kaiserzeit,* and *Um den Kaiser.*
Schulthess : *Europäischer Geschichtskalender.*
H. H. Asquith : *The Genesis of the War.*
Rt. Hon. Winston Churchill : *The World Crisis.*
Sir Valentine Chirol : *Fifty Years in a Changing World.*
Lord Newton : *Lord Lansdowne.*
British and Foreign State Papers.   (B.F.S.P.)
W. S. Blunt : *Diaries.*
B. Huldermann : *Albert Ballin.*

PREFACE

BY

THE RIGHT HONBLE SIR MAURICE DE BUNSEN, BART.,
G.C.M.G.

THE third volume of 'German Diplomatic Documents' selected and translated from *Die Grosse Politik*, by Mr. E. T. S. Dugdale, covers the period from 1898 to 1911. It opens with some earlier selections bearing on the situation created by the victory of Japan over China in 1904 which opened a new epoch in the history of the Far East. It includes two momentous conflicts affecting profoundly international relations, the Boer War and the Russo-Japanese War. It touches at many points on the long discussions aiming at a naval agreement, with or without some form of general understanding, between England and Germany. Through the Alliance with Japan and the Entente with France it leads up to the separation of Europe into two rival camps, in the course of an evolution in which crisis followed crisis with increasing and often alarming intensity. On these stirring times much light is thrown in the volume under review, which has the advantage over its predecessors of enabling comparison to be made, from the date of the seizure of Kiao Chów (1897) onwards, with the six opening volumes of *British Documents on the Origins of the War*. Each work helps at many points to explain the other, and it is to be regretted that eight volumes of Austrian documents lately published should have appeared too late to enable useful reference to be made to them. Among other works frequently cited in elucidation of the German dispatches Professor Brandenburg's well-known summary of German Foreign Policy *From Bismarck to the World War* takes a prominent place. The Documents presuppose of course a general knowledge of the period with which they deal, and they do not in themselves profess to tell the whole story. Useful notes, however, are inserted which enable the reader to refresh his memory on the general sequence of events.

On the War of 1894 between Japan and China Brandenburg remarks (pages 53, 65, of above quoted work) that it 'gave the impetus to a far-reaching revolution in international relations

and in the whole political system of the world ', and he adds
that 'undoubtedly Japan's attitude at the outbreak of the
World War was largely due to Germany's behaviour at the
Peace of Shimonoseki ', when her Minister in Japan assumed a
threatening tone in presenting, together with his Russian and
French colleagues,. the joint demand of the three Powers that
Japan should retire from her conquests in the Liaotung peninsula.
The action of Baron von Gutschmidt was never forgiven by
Japan, although it was disavowed later on by his own Government (page 13).   England, in refusing to join this hostile combination, paved the way which led to her alliance with Japan
in 1902.   She had already shown her friendly leaning towards
that country by consenting, in a Treaty negotiated in the year
1894, to the abolition of the extra-territorial rights which British
subjects, in common with nationals of other Western countries,
had till then enjoyed in Japan.   For the first time an Eastern
country had succeeded in asserting its right to exercise juris-
diction over the Westerners.   The example set in London was
followed within the next few years by all the other leading
Powers, but Japan never forgot that she owed her liberation
from the ancient Treaties in the first instance to British good-
will.   The Emperor William shows by his letter to the Czar of
April 26, 1895 (page 1), only a few days after the signature of
the Peace of Shimonoseki, that in taking joint-action with Russia
to curtail the Japanese reward for her victories, he was moved
largely by his well-known sense of the imminence of the ' Yellow
Peril ', from which he hoped Russia would help him to defend
the Western World.   He had also in mind, perhaps not un-
naturally, the intention, which was subsequently realised, of
participating in the spoils to be extorted from a grateful China.
Japan gave way and it was not till after her victorious war with
Russia in 1904–5 that she finally took possession of the Liaotung
peninsula.   Meanwhile Germany, Russia and England had
occupied in turn respectively Kiao-Chau (November 1897), Port
Arthur (March 1898), and Weihaiwei (July 1898).   The buoyant
spirit in which the Kaiser embarked on the Kiao-Chau enterprise
is shown in his letter to Bülow of November 7, 1897 (page 15).
The Chancellor, Hohenlohe, feared the prize would have to be
surrendered (page 17) owing to Russian opposition, in which
case some other place would have to be selected for occupation.
   Vol. I of the British Despatches disclosed (G. and T., I, 5)
the interesting fact that in January 1898 Lord Salisbury proposed
to Russia a partition of China into spheres of influence, British
in the Yangtse territory, and Russian from the Hoangho northwards.   The British record shows that Russia at first responded
not unfavourably to this suggestion which was only abandoned

when she moved into Port Arthur. The Czar, however, in his letter to the Kaiser of June 3, 1898, claims to have rejected the idea 'without thinking twice over it'. In any case the project soon fell through, and it was followed soon after by the first intimation to Berlin that England seriously desired to come to an understanding with Germany.

So began a long series of efforts for better relations between the two countries which, though frequently interrupted, are shown in these pages (see especially Chapters IV, IX, XVII, XXII, XXVII and XXXI) to have been never definitely abandoned during the period dealt with. Indeed later records will undoubtedly refer to the far-reaching negotiations, completed on the very eve of the Great War, for a settlement of the main questions at issue with Germany in Mesopotamia, the Persian Gulf and South Africa. The Entente with France was not found at first to be a serious obstacle in the way of taking up the conversations afresh. It had implicitly embodied the idea that the settlement of outstanding differences was perhaps as good a way as any of creating a friendly atmosphere. The difficulty in the case of Germany was that there existed no obvious list of questions in dispute such as had stood in the way of good relations with France. In his notable memorandum of January 1, 1907, Sir Eyre Crowe states that 'it is as true to-day as it has been at any time since 1884, in the intervals of successive incidents and their settlements, that, practically every known German demand having been met, there is not just now any cause troubling the serenity of Anglo-German relations' (G. and T., III, 413). Again and again the discussions broke down on the realisation in this country that it was impossible to work out any scheme of harmonious co-operation so long as no abatement was procurable in the relentless process of expansion which the German fleet was undergoing through the operation of the German Navy Law.

Messrs. Gooch and Temperley, in their Foreword to Vols. I and II of the 'British Documents' remark that 'there is practically no evidence in our official records as to the first Anglo-German *rapprochement* which began in March 1898'. Mr. Joseph Chamberlain made the overture, but the precise way in which he conceived it cannot be accurately known till the publication of Mr. Garvin's promised biography. In the meantime the gap is now partly bridged over by Mr. Dugdale's selected despatches from *Die Grosse Politik*. Count Hatzfeldt, then German Ambassador in London, reported on March 29, 1898, that Mr. Chamberlain had approached him on the subject of a political understanding with Germany (page 21). England was about to abandon her policy of isolation ; she was looking around

for an ally, and a decision would have to be taken within the
next few days. The Ambassador states that 'throughout the
conversation Chamberlain spoke calmly and decidedly, and
demonstrated very frankly the desire for a binding agreement
between England and the Triple Alliance'. Bülow discouraged
the idea (page 23). 'Any such agreement', he believed, 'would
only bind the British Government for the time being.' Two
days later Count Hatzfeldt reported that an understanding with
Germany for the maintenance of the integrity of what remained
of China was now the chief preoccupation in London. The
attitude of Bülow being regarded as more or less of a rebuff, a
short period followed of closer relations with France, marked
chiefly by the conclusion of the Niger Protocol on June 14.
There was no serious breach however with Germany, with which
Power three important arrangements were come to in the course
of the next two and a half years, namely the South African
Convention of August 30, 1898, relating to the Portuguese
Colonies, the Samoa Treaty of November 19, 1899, and the so-
called Yangtse Treaty of October 16, 1900. As regards the first
of these it was always ardently hoped in England that the bankruptcy of Portugal, which was to be followed by the partition
of the colonies, would never take place. Only the second achieved
a lasting settlement. During the South African War, so universally condemned by public opinion on the Continent, apprehension
was sometimes felt that the temptation to form a European
block against England might prove too strong to be resisted.
That no such project matured may have been due, as Lord
Salisbury hinted, to the reluctance of hostile Powers to risk
losing their fleets. There was also the difficulty of securing
French co-operation without a guarantee, of course unobtainable,
of the provisions of the Treaty of Frankfurt. The Kaiser takes
credit for having unhesitatingly rejected a proposal from St.
Petersburg that he should join with Russia and France in a
collective intervention (page 124).

Soon after the outbreak of the war the Kaiser paid a visit
to Windsor which was fruitful in conversations on Mr. Chamberlain's projects. The visit is related in a long Memorandum
written by Bülow while still at Windsor (page 108). He sum-
marises the various conversations in which the English desire
for a general understanding with Germany is expressed by
Chamberlain and Balfour, the German view, generally favourable,
by the Emperor and Count von Bülow. The Queen, the Prince
of Wales and other members of the Royal Family are represented
as having also taken a lively interest in the prospect of happier
relations with Germany. Bülow found feeling in England to
be far less anti-German than German feeling was anti-British.

He devotes considerable space to an appreciation of British
characteristics, considered socially as well as politically. ' Both
physically and morally it is a very healthy country.' ' The
country breathes wealth, comfort, contentment and confidence.
. . .' More follows in the same strain, but instead of leading
up to a recommendation that German policy should be framed
with a view to joining forces with so admirable a people, the
Count concludes with the reflection ' that Germany's future task
will be, whilst preserving a strong fleet and maintaining good
relations on the side of Russia as well as of England, to await
the further development of events patiently and collectedly '.
It was indeed strictly on these lines that the German ship of
state continued to be steered. Chamberlain, however, was
encouraged by the Windsor conversations to propound his views
in clear and forcible language in his famous speech at Leicester
on November 30, 1899. His advocacy of something in the nature
of an alliance with both Germany and America met with a cold
response in Berlin, where public opinion, in sympa͟ͅny with the
Boers, was too hostile to admit of the Government taking up
an attitude favourable to the negotiations desired in England.

More than a year passed before the endeavours to reach an
understanding were resumed. The South African War was
running its course. German military opinion expected a British
defeat ; at all events it seemed certain at Berlin that a British
army would never reach Pretoria (page 118). Conversations
were, however, renewed, as reported by Hatzfeldt, on March 22,
1901 (page 141). Their failure was largely due to the efforts of
the German Government to include not only Germany but the
Triple Alliance as a whole within the purview of the negotiations,
which it was even suggested might be usefully continued at
Vienna (page 144). This would involve, in Lord Salisbury's
opinion, the liability to be called upon to defend the German
and Austrian frontiers against Russia. His objections to any
' alliance ' are forcibly put in a Memorandum given in the ' British
Documents ' (G. and T., II, 68). The discussions, which had
proceeded to the point of the Draft of a Convention being drawn
up by the Foreign Office (G. and T., II, 66) were abruptly broken
off by the effects produced in Germany of Chamberlain's speech
on October 15, 1901, expressing the indignation felt in England
at the wild aspersions cast in the German Press on the methods
of warfare employed by the British army in South Africa.

There are many signs that Bülow wished for good relations
with England, but he points out to the Emperor at the end of
1904 (p. 213), that ' everything depends on Germany getting
through the next few years with patience, avoiding incidents
and giving no obvious reason for annoyance '. Early in the

following year (page 214), Metternich thought the situation in England much improved. He was no longer in doubt that ' the climax is behind us'. The Press had dropped its ugly tone.

But by this time the Morocco question had raised its head and for the next few years it tended to draw closer the new ties between England and France. The German Minister at Tangier had reported in April 1904 (page 219) that the opportunity seemed a good one for forcible intervention, in the form of German occupation of a point such as Agadir on the Morocco coast. Baron von Holstein, in June, produced a Memorandum (page 220) to show that Germany had a good case for taking a hand in the game. France, he pointed out, had not attempted to come to terms with the Powers other than England and Spain having interests in Morocco in the way that England had prudently done in Egypt. Germany would be materially injured by the absorption of Morocco by France. Holstein's influence prevailed and the Memorandum referred to became the starting point of German intervention leading to the fall of Delcassé (page 228) and the Algeciras Conference. Holstein, however, had badly failed to realise the true significance of the Entente, as he showed by remarking towards the end of his Memorandum that ' the British diplomatic support promised to France under Article IX of the Morocco Convention will remain platonic '.

Reviewing the situation in its early phase Metternich holds that ' the Morocco question has brought us a step nearer to war with England ' (page 233).

I myself had the advantage of seeing the advent of the French Entente from the Embassy in Paris where I was Counsellor at the time, and, though the Entente was negotiated in London and not in Paris, much of what was going on was of course known at the Embassy. France was feeling that her Alliance with Russia needed another partner, and I was struck by open admissions of the expediency of drawing closer to England which were made in the French Chamber of Deputies as early as the latter months of 1902. Then came King Edward's visit in May 1903. As His Majesty passed through the Paris streets many cries of ' Vive les Boers ' were audible in the midst of the more polite acclamations of ' Vive l'Angleterre'. The popular enthusiasm was not really stirred till His Majesty's visit to the Hotel de Ville, where there were risks of an adverse style of reception. A few happy phrases in the King's unprepared French speech and His Majesty's demeanour of friendly greeting completely turned the tide which then continued to flow strongly on the side of a real popular welcome. By this time Lord Lansdowne's conversations with Monsieur Cambon were beginning to take their ultimate shape of a general settlement of outstanding differences without anything in the nature of an alliance. Soon after the published terms of the understanding became known Bülow declared in the Reichstag that Germany had no objection to offer. I can remember, however, individual German voices complaining that an agreement which could not fail to have an important bearing on international relations should have been concluded without a word of consultation with Germany. Possibly some of the acuteness of Germany's hostility to the Moroccan portion of the Agreement might have been disarmed by communicating more openly with her while the negotiations were proceeding, and thus trouble and even the dangerous crisis which ensued might have been forestalled. There was however the risk that consultation with her might have hampered the conclusion of any Entente whatever. M. Delcassé, it will be seen on page 188, did indeed give the German Ambassador in Paris a fairly full account of the main points which were being settled. The result of the Entente settlement is summed up pithily by Kühlmann in a Memorandum drawn up at Tangier on October 1 in the words : ' The Egyptian question is dead, the Moroccan question very much alive ' (page 198).

Amongst its other consequences the Entente certainly brought in its train a close association between the two Entente Powers and Spain. The latter country did not fail to take advantage of the opportunity thus offered of securing her position as a Mediterranean Power. On April 8, 1907, King Edward paid an official visit to the King of Spain at Carthagena, the *Victoria and Albert* with His Majesty on board being met in the Spanish port by a portion of the British Mediterranean Fleet. I had the honour to be present as His Majesty's Ambassador at Madrid. After a brief conversation conducted by Sir Charles Hardinge on board the Spanish Royal Yacht with King Alfonso's Ministers the latter readily fell in with the suggestion that a tripartite arrangement in the form of an exchange of notes should be agreed to between Spain, France and England declaring that they were united in the policy of the maintenance of the *status quo* in the Mediterranean Sea and Atlantic Ocean adjoining their respective possessions. Shortly after the tripartite arrangement became known Radowitz, the German Ambassador at Madrid, complained to me of Germany having been again left out in the cold as had happened before in the Entente negotiations. Baron Aehrenthal made a similar complaint at Ischl to Sir Charles Hardinge, accompanying the King on a visit to the Emperor Francis Joseph (August 1907), on the ground that the agreement appeared to him to be directed against Germany, Austria's ally, with a view to completing her isolation in Europe. It was easy to show that no slight to Germany was involved (see G. and T.,

V, 208–9). She suspected, no doubt, that Spain had now been made a partner in the Entente with France. No such partnership was involved in the exchange of Notes, which actually took place in June 1907, but it was of course true that the existence of the Entente between France and England made it natural that the Spanish Government should adapt her policy as far as possible to that of the Western Powers.

After reading the warnings contained in the reports to Berlin of the able representatives of Germany in London and elsewhere —warnings that, as matters were tending, England would assuredly be included, when the final decision had to be faced, among the Powers hostile to Germany—it is difficult to understand the surprise with which England's attitude, so often foretold, was viewed in Berlin in 1914.

Thus in a secret report to Bülow by Moltke, Chief of the General Staff, in February 1909 (page 239), the latter gives ' from a sure source ' some of the reasons which must compel England to take part in a continental war against Germany from mere motives of self-preservation.

Metternich repeatedly pointed out the danger. It arose, as he reported again and again, not from mere commercial rivalry, not from the bitter outbursts of animosity which from time to time marked the tone of the Press in both countries, not from hostile public opinion ; these were obstacles to agreement which the underlying desire of each of the two countries to live on friendly terms with the other would assuredly be able to surmount ; but from the ever-present and yearly increasing menace of the German shipbuilding programme. In Sir Eyre Crowe's Memorandum of June 1907, in which many instances are enumerated of action by Germany bearing, in his opinion, a consistently unfriendly aspect, little weight is assigned to the naval peril. Germany had a full right to build to the extent of what she conceived to be her national needs. No complaint is made in the Memorandum on this score. But, Metternich was quick to realise that in the unrestrained fulfilment of the German Navy Law would lie an insurmountable obstacle to any useful agreement with Germany on the lines of the Anglo-French Entente. Chapters XXII and XXIII contain many of his Reports in which this conviction is clearly set forth together with his judgment on the true state of British feeling, anxious always to improve relations with Germany but frustrated above all by the determination of the Emperor to admit no discussion on naval matters.

The petulant tone of many of the Kaiser's minutes so carefully preserved in *Die Grosse Politik* has long been well known, but it is fair to admit that when these outpourings exceed the limits of mere ejaculations they are often striking and illuminating. An interesting Imperial comment appears on page 306 showing that His Majesty agreed entirely with the view taken by the British Government of Aehrenthal's hasty and ill-considered procedure in the annexation of Bosnia and the Herzegovina. He describes as ' incontestable and really after my own heart ' the arguments based on International Law on which British policy was based. Von Marschall and many other influential Germans are believed to have agreed with His Majesty. Bülow, however, caused his own view to prevail, namely that loyalty to Austria, the only friend left to Germany, demanded compliance with any action taken by Austria in the Balkans (page 305). Thus was the blank cheque given, and thenceforward it remained in the power of Austria to impose, in the last resort, the policy which she held to be in accordance with her interests, upon her great Ally. Aehrenthal writing to Bülow on December 8, 1908 (page 317), refers gratefully to the latter's assurance ' that you would leave it to my judgment to decide how to deal with these (conditions in Serbia) if they continue '.

The chapters (XXIV–VI) on the dangerous annexation crisis of 1908–9 open with a Memorandum by the Austro-Hungarian Ambassador in Berlin (page 301) which should dispel, once for all, the illusion that during his visits to the Emperor Francis Joseph in 1907–8 King Edward employed his powers of persuasion to divert Austria from her Alliance with Germany. Baron Aehrenthal enabled the Ambassador to state that on the occasion of the visit in 1908, Sir Charles Hardinge ' quite thought it natural for Austria to cling to the Alliance with Germany. . . . From the British point of view and also for the maintenance of peace the rupture of this Alliance would be a great misfortune '. King Edward had used identical language.

The Young Turk revolution (July 1908) was well received in England, although it put an end to the negotiations between the Powers for the introduction of a reformed administration in Macedonia. The Young Turks were to be given a chance of achieving results which had been attempted, with little success, by the Powers. The movement had restored much of the lost prestige of England at Constantinople. This was one of the reasons which had caused the outburst of anger in England, where Turkey had become popular, when the annexation of Bosnia and the Herzegovina on October 6, 1908, became known. There was of course the manifest breach of Article 25 of the Treaty of Berlin on which Sir E. Grey's protests were chiefly based. Metternich explains the British attitude quite correctly in his report to Berlin (page 318). But the injury done to Turkey was no less deeply resented, and when in February 1909 the

Sublime Porte recognised the annexations in consideration of the payment of £2½ million, one of the chief causes of offence was removed. A Conference to sanction the infringement of the Berlin Treaty continued, however, to be persistently demanded by what was coming to be called the Triple Entente, Austria refusing to agree to the summoning of the Conference except on condition that the Powers would promise beforehand to accept the revocation of Article 25 when it met. By a step partaking of the nature of an ultimatum Germany obtained at St. Petersburg the reluctant consent of Iswolsky to giving the required undertaking. Her intervention, described by Bülow (page 323) as 'a friendly discussion', though gratefully accepted by the Czar who wired his thanks to the Kaiser, was taken by Iswolsky as an insult involving deep humiliation to Russia whose weakness compelled her to submit to it. It did perhaps more than anything else to fortify the Triple Entente, and to invest it thenceforth with more of the compactness and unity of front which it had so conspicuously lacked during the annexation crisis. England refused to follow suit but continued to press forward what proved to be the much more helpful effort to bring about the Mediation of the Powers at Belgrade. Metternich had agreed (page 320) that the line taken by Grey promised well. Serbia had placed herself badly in the wrong by the terms of an offensive note to Austria on March 14, 1909.

An Austro-Serbian war could now only be averted if Serbia could be induced to address a sufficiently submissive note to Vienna. Mainly by the efforts of Sir Edward Grey a form of words was devised which, though humiliating enough to satisfy Aehrenthal, was adopted by Serbia under the united pressure at Belgrade of the Representatives of England, France, Italy and Russia. Grey had in the end given the ardently desired undertaking that if asked he would accept the abrogation of Article 25 without reserves 'after Serbia has written the note in the terms agreed and Austria has accepted it as satisfactory' (G. and T., V, page 750). The mediation of the Powers had been initiated by Grey on March 17 (G. and T., V, 695). It matured in the nick of time, for on March 29, that is two days before the Serbian note was presented to Aehrenthal, a Council of Ministers at Vienna had ordered mobilisation of the Army. and War on Serbia was imminent. Had it not been headed off by the timely mediation at Belgrade, it can hardly be doubted that Serbia would have been crushed by Austria beyond possibility of recovery for a generation. The story is well told in Sir F. Cartwright's despatch of March 29 (G. and T., V, 758). Conrad von Hötzendorf's strong wish to take this apparently easy opportunity of stamping out the Southern Slav movement for the creation of a greater Serbia was frustrated at the moment when it appeared to be on the point of realisation. Russia was impotent, France largely indifferent, and England not likely single-handed to intervene. There was a good chance of the war, if it came, being localised, as it could not be localised, with a revived Russia, in 1914.

The Central Powers had shown, in the course of the annexation crisis, that the balance of power at this time inclined manifestly in their favour. The following years were to show the growing intimacy and strength of the Entente Powers, which continued until they, in their turn, achieved, as a consequence of the Balkan Wars (1912–13), a predominance corresponding to that which had accrued to the Triple Alliance in 1908–9. The earlier crisis presented many features similar to those which marked the later one. They are well summarised by Brandenburg (page 335 of his above quoted work). The fundamental difference in the two situations lay in the weakness of Russia in 1908–9. There was also at the earlier date a much less overpowering motive for united action between the Entente Powers than was afforded by the menace to their very existence of which they were conscious in 1914.

Much can be learned in these pages of the personal character and political leanings of some of the leading public men of Germany at home and abroad. Reference has been made to the parts played by Bülow and Metternich. In Chapters XVI and XXI Baron Speck von Sternburg, Ambassador at Washington, is shown in intimate relations with President Roosevelt which must have rivalled for a time even the personal touch never lost between the latter and Sir Cecil Spring Rice. The President expresses himself rather contemptuously on the subject of the British and French Statesmen of the day (page 200). He was evidently attracted by Speck's personality as well as by the views to which the latter was instructed to give expression on the maintenance of the ' open door ' in China. Speck spoke to Roosevelt in the strain of the Kaiser on the danger of victorious Japan aiming at the control of the Pacific Ocean and thus becoming a practical exemplification of the Yellow Peril (page 262). Suggestions also came from Peking for combinations between Germany and other Powers in defence of China, but on these Bülow threw cold water (page 265) and the President a year later (December 1908) concluded a *status quo* and ' open door ' Treaty, not with Germany but directly with Japan (page 297, and G. and T., V, 511).

The policy of Germany in Turkey during the discussions concerning Crete is illustrated in the despatches of Baron von Marschall, German Ambassador at Constantinople and later in

London.   In his despatch of May 30, 1910 (page 390), he draws
conclusions from his estimate of the true nature of British policy
in the Near East which had come to find its centre of gravity
no longer in Turkey but, since the British occupation, in Egypt,
a change of attitude on England's part which, he held, had
proved detrimental to the interests of Turkey in a manner giving
opportunities for the Triple Alliance to regain the position which
the Turkish revolution had destroyed for a moment.

CONTENTS

GERMAN
DIPLOMATIC DOCUMENTS

CHAPTER I

THE CHINO-JAPANESE WAR, AND THE EAST-ASIATIC TRIPLE ALLIANCE. JULY, 1894, TO MAY, 1895

In October, 1894, when the Chino-Japanese War [1] was practically decided in Japan's favour, the British Government invited the rest of the Powers to intervene between the belligerents. The idea was, however, considered premature, and the interests of the others were not sufficiently considerable in the Far East for it to take root at that moment. In the following year, however, Russia, alarmed for her pet scheme of obtaining a warm-water terminus for the Trans-Siberian Railway, invited France, her ally, and Germany to join her in preventing Japan from securing a foothold on the mainland of China.

The Emperor, William II, was possibly not solely responsible for the adoption of an anti-Japanese policy directed against the ' Yellow Peril ' ; but it is certain that he was deeply obsessed by it. There was, at all events, in him a determination that Germany should have her share of any advantages to be gained by intervention.

The negotiations, from which England was deliberately excluded, were successful in their object, and Japan was prevented from acquiring permanent possessions on the mainland.

IX. 359

THE EMPEROR WILLIAM TO THE TSAR, *April 26th*, 1895

Private letter.   Extract (written in English).

. . . For that is clearly the great task of the future for Russia to cultivate the Asian Continent and to defend Europa from the inroads of the Great Yellow Race. In this you will always find me at your side ready to help you as best I can. You have well understood that call of Providence and have quickly grasped the moment ; it is of immense political and historical value, and much good will come of it. I shall with interest await the future development of our action and hope that, just as I will gladly help you settle the question of eventual annexations of portions

---

[1] Cf. P. Joseph, *Foreign Diplomacy in China*, Chap. III ; Brandenburg, p. 53 et seq.

1

of territory for Russia, you will see that Germany may also be able to acquire a port somewhere where it does not ' gêne ' you.[1]

IX. 241

BARON VON ROTENHAN, GERMAN FOREIGN OFFICE, TO HERR VON KIDERLEN, ON THE EMPEROR'S STAFF AT MEROK, IN NORWAY, *July 16th,* 1894

As is known, owing to a rising which took place in Southern Korea, China and Japan sent troops to that country to restore order. When this task was accomplished, the Japanese Government refused to withdraw until the Korean Government should have introduced reforms there, which might prevent the recurrence of similar disturbances. China is ready to withdraw her troops simultaneously with Japan, but refuses so far to associate herself with the Japanese pressure for reform. Tension has thus arisen between the two East Asiatic Powers, and there is danger, for the Japanese are now in occupation of the capital, Seoul, whilst the Chinese troops, which remained up to the present in the South, are approaching the capital in order to resist any attempt by Japan at gaining a dominant influence with the Court and to maintain China's more nominal than actual suzerainty over Korea.

This being the situation, the Chinese Government has appealed to us to mediate and to persuade Japan to withdraw from Korea. Before this, the British Government also approached us with the request to join in intervention by the Powers in favour of a peaceful settlement of the differences that have arisen.

In consideration that England and Russia are deeply interested in the question of Korea's existence and that this affair might lead to a clash of interests between the two Powers, we have replied that it is not our business to intervene. Nevertheless it appears, as far as this clash is not imminent, that if the other European Powers are working for peace, we ought to take part in these joint efforts in consideration for our trade interests in Eastern Asia.

The Imperial Ministers in Pekin and Tokio have received instructions by telegram (copy enclosed).

You will please prepare a statement for His Majesty the Emperor in the sense indicated above after the pattern of the enclosed telegrams.

Minute by KIDERLEN.

His Majesty, to whom I communicated the contents of the despatch, was fully in favour of refusing our intervention in a matter which interested Russia and England alone, apart from China and Japan.

[1] *Briefe Wilhelms II an den Zaren,* Walter Goetz, p. 291.

German Note.

The substance of these instructions (July 11th, 1894) was for the Ministers to associate themselves with the joint efforts of the other Ministers of the Great Powers for a peaceful settlement of the differences between China and Japan. The Minister in Tokio was further instructed to maintain reserve in the event of a clash of interests arising between England and Russia.

War was declared by Japan against China on August 1st, 1894.

IX. 244

BARON VON MARSCHALL TO THE GERMAN MINISTERS IN PEKING AND TOKIO, *October 14th*, 1894

On October 7th the British Ambassador, under instructions from his Government, wrote proposing intervention in the Chino-Japanese War. The basis was to be the independence of Korea under the guarantee of the Foreign Powers and an indemnity to be paid by China. An identical invitation was sent to St. Petersburg, Paris, Rome and Washington. We at once indicated the objections against such action and said further that at present intervention appeared scarcely opportune. In all probability Japan would reject it. What method should then be adopted? Was it intended to resort to action in that case? The result of these objections, which had been raised elsewhere also, is that we are informed that in London they merely contemplate some sort of offer of ' advice ' to the belligerent Powers.

German Note.

A telegram sent by Count von Metternich, Chargé d'Affaires in London, stated that Lord Rosebery, the Prime Minister, also inclined to the German view—that intervention was premature and would not be well received by Japan. He was therefore ready to give up intervention for the present.

Russia has indeed declared herself in favour of the idea of mediation as a ' principle ', but makes her agreement depend on the Tsar's consent, which does not seem to have been obtained so far.

I tell you this for your personal guidance. I shall be interested to learn the impression made in Pekin (and Tokio) by the British *démarche,* which is no doubt known of.

German Note.

At the end of November Japan did in fact reject an offer of mediation by the United States. The Emperor William II wrote on October 30th to the Chancellor that Viscount Aoki, Japanese Minister in Berlin, had expressed grateful thanks for the ' loyal German attitude '.

IX. 248
BARON VON MARSCHALL TO COUNT HATZFELDT,
February 1st, 1895

Secret.

Our Minister in Peking very lately suggested that, if other Great Powers used the Chino-Japanese War to acquire territorial possessions at China's expense, we too might well consider obtaining a firm *point d'appui* for our fleet and commerce in Eastern Asia. He suggests first Kiao-Chow bay and after it the Pescadores Islands, which are on the line from Formosa, as points worthy of our consideration.

It must be admitted that it would make an impression to the disadvantage of German policy, if, when other Powers were tearing off pieces of the Chinese Empire, Germany alone went empty away.

On the other hand, the two points indicated by the Minister do not seem especially worth coveting. The possession of Kiao-Chau offers at present no trade advantages. There would be no question of these, until a branch of the Chinese Railway system reached that bay. A seizure of land there, i.e., on the Chinese mainland, might entail fortifying the place, and might under given circumstances draw a hostile attack on itself. The Pescadores are quite worthless ; they offer no support for trade, and it seems very doubtful if they possess good enough harbours.

Even Formosa Island,[1] for the possession of which there has for decades been a certain feeling in Germany, must be left out of consideration, for the subjection of the inhabitants, who are Chinese subjects in name only, and the defence of the Island against those Powers (France in particular) which are asserting a claim on the island, would demand sacrifices from us which we can scarcely afford.

It would best suit us, as far as can be seen now, to possess the Island of Chusan at the entrance of the Bay of Hangchow, South of Wusung. As early as 1869 and 1870 Professor von Richthofen, the authority on China, strongly recommended the acquisition of this island in detailed memorials addressed to Prince Bismarck. He praises it as having a good harbour, easy to protect and fortify, and still believes that it would be easy by suitable measures, such as establishing a Free Port there, to make it into an emporium, which would not only attract the trade of the neighbouring Ningpo,[2] but would soon supersede the river-port, Shanghai, which is difficult of access, as a centre for the trade of all those districts.

Now, as you know, M. Hanotaux spoke not long ago of a

---

[1] Formosa was eventually acquired by Japan.
[2] Cf. Joseph, *Foreign Diplomacy in China*, p. 76.

right of possession of the Chusan Islands, which England claimed under certain conditions from China by a secret Treaty after the Opium War. With this corresponds the intelligence, which has frequently appeared in the papers lately, that England intends to occupy these islands very soon. At the end of December last year the London Correspondent of the *Novoye Vremya* claimed to have heard not only that British naval circles were taking a lively interest in the strategic importance of the islands, but that the China firms in the City were confidently awaiting the occupation, in order to establish factories and depôts on the largest island.

If any fact underlay these rumours, and if England really had secured a right to Chusan by treaty, of which nothing definite is known, we should naturally have to drop all thoughts of acquiring it. In the opposite event it might be asked if we cannot take a hand in the affair. It would then, as far as we can see now, be a matter of entering with the least possible delay, at any rate before the conclusion of peace, into secret negotiations for the purchase of Chusan Island and to complete them as quickly as possible. China might not be very willing to hand the island over to an unpleasant neighbour, without getting any return for it, as indeed she might easily be obliged to do, but she might do so more willingly to Germany from whom she has no injury to fear, in return for a suitable price.

In order to find out whether Baron von Richthofen's views on the subject are unchanged, I have asked the Imperial Consul General at Shanghai for a telegraphic statement as to the importance commercially which would accrue to the island of Chusan in European hands.

Meanwhile I should like, before deciding on any further steps, to hear your views also, particularly on its probable reactions on politics in general.

Perhaps the news mentioned above as to the hopes of the City merchants may serve as an indication of the circles in which, among others, information on the true intentions of the British Government may be gathered.

I shall peruse your report with interest.

IX. 252–3

BARON SCHENCK VON SCHWEINSBERG, MINISTER IN PEKING, TO
    THE GERMAN FOREIGN OFFICE, *March 3rd*, 1895
Cipher telegram.

In the name of the Chinese Government Li Hung Chang begs for a confidential application to Japan for moderate peace-terms. He considers it impossible to make concessions on the mainland, which would threaten China's existence. In view of Li Hung Chang's proved friendship, I promised to lay his request before

Your Highness.   Japan indicates Shimonoseki as the place for negotiations.

IX. 255

MEMORANDUM BY KLEHMET, OF THE GERMAN FOREIGN OFFICE,
February 20th, 1895

Extract.

As long ago as the beginning of the sixties we felt the need of a naval station of our own on the Chinese coast, and only lately His Majesty said the same.   More than 30 years ago detailed enquiries were made on points touching the same question.   The island of Chusan was shown to be the most suitable for the purpose, as it has a safe harbour, Tinghai, in a good position for trade, but hard to approach.   The spots also mentioned, such as Mirs Bay, near Hong Kong, and the little Island of Ku Lang Su, near Amoy, are hardly worth mentioning now, as, apart from other objections, they are too insignificant for us ;   also the places recently suggested by our Minister in Peking, the Pescadores Islands, off Formosa, and the Bay of Kiao Chow, South of the Shan Tung range.   Professor von Richthofen, the well-known expert on China, has already warned us against the Island of Formosa, which was also proposed, saying that it has not one serviceable harbour. . . .

If we really contemplate claiming Chusan for ourselves, we shall certainly have to face a protest from England, who appears to have acquired rights over this island by a secret compact with China some time ago; whereas, if we demanded Formosa, we should come into collision with Japan and also with France, both of whom are aiming at this island.

In reference to a former report His Majesty stated that when dealing with causes of quarrel between England and France, and between England and Russia, our policy must be kept perfectly free and independent,[1] so that when the moment arrives when England absolutely needs us and begs for our help, we can exact proper payment, and if a conflict takes place without our being involved in it, we can take what we want for ourselves.[2]

IX. 253–4

THE CHANCELLOR, PRINCE VON HOHENLOHE, TO THE EMPEROR,
March 19th, 1895

Extract.

In reference to the telegram which has been submitted to Your Majesty, and in which the Emperor of China solicits Your

---

[1] Cf. Joseph, *Foreign Diplomacy in China,* p. 81.
[2] Cf. *Briefe Wilhelms II an den Zaren,* 1894–1914 (Walter Goetz), p. 290 et seq.

Majesty's support in bringing about peace with Japan, I beg leave to submit the following statement of our position towards the Chino-Japanese conflict.

In accordance with Your Majesty's decision at the time, our attitude so far has been one of strict neutrality. Even before the struggle actually began, Your Majesty's representatives in Peking and Tokio were empowered to take part in any steps taken jointly by the representatives of the other Great Powers towards a peaceful settlement. . . . After hostilities broke out, we declared our readiness to join in common action by the Powers, so far as this was confined to the protection of persons and property.

On the other hand the repeated suggestions made both by England and China in favour of intervention and of our taking part in it, have been rejected by us on the grounds that we considered such a step taken beforehand to be premature.

The following considerations lay at the bottom of this : England and Russia are especially interested in the development of affairs in Eastern Asia, and England wishes to keep China as far as possible unharmed as a buffer State to protect India against a Russian advance, whilst Russia does not wish to see her alleged claims to Korea, or at least a part of it, prejudiced by further Japanese progress. But Germany on the other hand has no such great interests at stake, at least for the present, in the Far East. German trade has not noticeably suffered from the state of war up to now. On the contrary, our manufacturers, merchants and shippers have found good openings for profit by supplying and delivering war material. . . . . By joint intervention with England and Russia, aimed solely at restoring peace, we should first and foremost be helping the affairs of these States, probably with considerable sacrifice to ourselves ; for it is quite likely that nothing would be successful in dealing with a victorious Japan but armed intervention or at least a demonstration of absolutely superior force at the theatre of war itself.

It follows from these considerations that our attitude would have to be altered if there were to be prospect of special advantages in compensation for the sacrifices we should offer. And first of all we should expect to acquire certain points of the coast of China to serve as stations for our fleet and commerce. We have felt the need of these for decades past.[1]

It is naturally no business of Germany's, as the Power least directly interested in proportion, to give the signal for the partition of the Chinese Empire by coming forward with claims of this kind. We ought rather to wait until other Powers show signs of intending to realise similar aims.

[1] Cf. preceding document.

All this will depend on the course of the coming peace negotiations. Japan still withholds the conditions, which she means to impose, and seems to wish only to produce her final demands gradually. But there are indications that these will bear very hardly on China. A few days ago the Japanese Minister here communicated in strict confidence and with a request for secrecy, the fact that at the end of last month his and the Russian Governments held a conference, and that Japan agreed to the Russian demand of complete independence for Korea, whilst Russia promised to support Japan at the peace negotiations in the matters of indemnity, territorial concession and readjustment of the commercial relations between Japan and China. The above agrees with the Report of Your Majesty's Ambassador in London —that Russia and England have agreed that Korea's independence must be maintained.

To this Mr. Aoki added in confidence that the Japanese military authorities regard the cession of Port Arthur with a part of the country behind it as indispensable, whilst in their eyes the cession of an island, e.g., Formosa, is of the first importance. (The EMPEROR : ' We could then claim it.')

Now I consider that Port Arthur in Japanese hands would mean Japanese control of the Gulf of Chi-li, and with it a permanent menace to the Chinese Capital. It is therefore probable that the Chinese will resist this cession to the utmost.

China's military situation is well-nigh hopeless. In reply to a telegraphic enquiry Your Majesty's Minister in Peking has stated that he does not believe that the Chinese forces could hold the Japanese back from Peking. The seizure of the Capital would certainly not be followed precisely by a general collapse of the Government organisation, but Li Hung Chang does not think it possible to remove the Court from Peking now. On the other hand, Baron von Gutschmid telegraphs from Tokio that Japan could carry on the war till next winter without fear of exhausting her man-power, money or war-material, and that the war-spirit of the Japanese nation is as high as ever.

Up to now the Chinese Statesmen have shown a tendency towards self-deception as to the true state of affairs, and it seems that if Japan does not give up her claim to Port Arthur and content herself with Formosa, it is not impossible that they will renew the unequal struggle.

If so, it might well come to intervention by the Powers in spite of their divergent interests, and the Chinese question might have to be dealt with by us also.

I humbly consider that the right line for our policy would be to avoid being drawn into any action which would serve foreign interests in the first place, but on the other hand to be open to take part in any enterprises which might lead to delays in establishing the influence of the Great European Powers in the Far East. (The EMPEROR : ' *Correct.*')

I request Your Majesty's authority to instruct the Imperial Ambassador in London, who has been given provisionally a general idea of the above point of view, to indicate to the Government there orally, and without committing us, that Your Majesty's Government is not by way of rejecting in advance the idea of joint intervention, and will not hesitate to fight for German Interests (The EMPEROR : ' *Yes, but not Chinese.*') with all energy, if the settlement in the Far East is really delayed.

According to utterances by British Statesmen up to the present, England appears to wish earnestly to draw us in as a makeweight against France and Russia and will certainly meet our wishes to some extent. (The EMPEROR : ' *We must make our price a dear one.*')

We can hardly tell now what and how much we shall demand for our co-operation. It will depend partly on what the other Powers claim for themselves. As regards this, a remark by Sir Frank Lascelles, the British Ambassador in St. Petersburg, as reported by our Ambassador, indicates that England would raise no objection if Russia were to annex a part of Northern China for the sake of her railway and some port in Korea. What England would take for herself is unknown ; (The EMPEROR : ' *Shanghai !* ') but former experience causes one to think of the islands of Chusan opposite Ning-po, amongst other places. . . .

IX. 262

COUNT HATZFELDT TO THE GERMAN FOREIGN OFFICE,
April 4th, 1895

Cipher telegram

Lord Kimberley shares the view personally that the cession of Port Arthur would result in a Japanese protectorate over China and endanger its existence, and also lead to seizure of territory by other Powers. But so far he is not at all convinced that Russia will look on the collapse of China as a serious menace to her own interests and would not prefer to let things run their course. He anticipates that France would not mind seeing China weakened.

My impression that there is so far no arrangement between England, Russia and France, either about acquisitions or an agreed joint attitude.

If they agree in St. Petersburg to urge moderation on Japan and to treat the acquisition of Port Arthur as out of the question, they will not leave themselves out here, as far as I can judge. But if they show indifference in St. Petersburg, it is very doubtful if the British Government will act alone. All that would remain would be an understanding between the interested Powers on the acquisitions they mean to make.

IX. 265

BARON VON MARSCHALL TO TSCHIRSCHKY, CHARGÉ D'AFFAIRES IN ST. PETERSBURG, *April 8th*, 1895
Telegram.

Under instructions from his Government the Russian Chargé d'Affaires proposed that the views of the European Powers (The EMPEROR : ' *Possibly without England.*') should be communicated to Japan in a friendly form—to the effect that ' the annexation of Port Arthur is a permanent hindrance to the establishment of good relations between China and Japan and a standing menace to peace in the Far East.' On receiving His Majesty's commands, the Imperial Government is ready to instruct its representative at Tokio to deliver this declaration jointly with the Russian representative. Inform Prince Lobanoff of the above. (The EMPEROR : ' *Yes.*')

Minute by the EMPEROR on a Report by Count Hatzfeldt, April 13th. IX. 267 :

The present wish for non-intervention is caused by the fear of Russia and the movement for an alliance with Japan. Last summer England tried for no reason to force Europe, and especially Russia, to intervene, because she thought that her own interests were being threatened by Japan. This way of protecting interests may be all very well for England by herself, but continental policy, with consistency and tradition in mind, will not be bound by this.

IX. 268

COUNT MUNSTER, IN PARIS, TO THE GERMAN FOREIGN OFFICE, *April 10th*, 1895
Cipher telegram.

Lord Dufferin informed me confidentially, that yesterday, under instructions from Lord Kimberley, he had stated to M. Hanotaux that the British Cabinet considered the Japanese peace terms favourable to European interests (The EMPEROR : ' *British !* ') and would not intervene. (The EMPEROR : ' *That means that the British have made themselves secure by a secret private Treaty with Japan. The above alters nothing of my directions. The British want of foresight will cost them dear.*')

[On April 13th Count Hatzfeldt telegraphed :
. . . ' In a telegram which Baron de Courcel read to me M. Hanotaux again expressed his readiness, supposing England persisted in her refusal, to come to an understanding with the other two Powers on the treatment of the affair.']

IX. 269

TSCHIRSCHKY, IN ST. PETERSBURG, TO THE GERMAN FOREIGN
OFFICE, *April 17th*, 1895

Cipher telegram.

Prince Lobanoff made me the following proposal:
England's defection makes it Russia's duty to take in hand
the protection of her own interests in the Far East. These
coincide with those of Europe. The Russian Government has
decided to request Japan, first in a friendly form, to abstain from
occupying the Chinese mainland in permanence. He distinctly
hopes that Germany and France will associate themselves with
this démarche, and he has instructed the Russian representatives
in Paris and Berlin to this effect. If Japan should reject this
friendly advice, Russia contemplates joint war-like operations of
the three Powers by sea against Japan, the first aim being to
isolate the Japanese forces on the mainland by cutting off their
home communications.

IX. 270

BARON VON MARSCHALL TO BARON VON GUTSCHMID, MINISTER
AT TOKIO, *April 17th*, 1895

Telegram.

For your guidance. Germany rejected the British proposal
of October 7th, 1894,[1] to intervene in the Chino-Japanese dispute
out of friendship for Japan.

But the present Japanese peace terms are too stringent.
They injure European interests, including Germany's, though in
a lesser degree.

We have cause, therefore, to join in protesting and shall, if
necessary, do so with sufficient force.

Japan must give in, as a struggle against three Powers is
objectless. If the Japanese Government regards a Conference
as the only non-humiliating form of submission, telegraph here
at once.

German Note.

The Peace of Shimonoseki was concluded on April 17th, 1895. This
fact did not, however, affect the intentions of Russia, Germany and France.

IX. 271

TSCHIRSCHKY, IN ST. PETERSBURG, TO THE GERMAN FOREIGN
OFFICE, *April 20th*, 1895

Cipher telegram.

The Count of Montebello told me that yesterday morning
he had communicated officially to Prince Lobanoff France's

----

[1] Cf. p. 1; also Joseph, *Foreign Diplomacy in China*, p. 117.

adherence to the Russian programme. A joint démarche at Tokio is to follow to-day. Baron de Courcel's most recent reports mention Lord Kimberley as being very nervous and irritable at England's complete isolation ; it seems also that public opinion in England is about to swing round.

Last evening Sir Frank Lascelles, under instructions from his Government, made Prince Lobanoff the following proposal : ' In consideration of the Entente hitherto existing between the European Powers, England proposes to Russia to request Japan to communicate the authentic text of the peace conditions to the Cabinets. Prince Lobanoff replied that he sees no reason for this démarche, which would gain nothing and only waste time. The main points of the text are quite sufficiently known to him through the Russian representative at Tokio and the Japanese Minister here. Now that Russia has adopted an attitude in agreement with France and Germany, she could not enter into a discussion of the peace terms. If England would join with them, he and the other two Powers would certainly welcome it with pleasure.

Sir Frank Lascelles returned no reply to the above.

Prince Lobanoff and Count Montebello think that England is beginning to realise that she has made a mistake in her judgment of the economic results of the peace terms and that, if the three Powers remain firm, she will finally return to her original programme.

[Germany urged the impropriety of excluding England from a Conference on Far Eastern affairs.]

IX. 294

PRINCE VON RADOLIN, IN ST. PETERSBURG, TO THE GERMAN FOREIGN OFFICE, *May 12th*, 1895

Cipher telegram. Extract.

Prince Lobanoff would regret the plan of including England. What he had wished to avoid was additional participation, and for this reason he had only spoken of propounding an Article. England retired when she might have been useful. Prince Lobanoff thinks it desirable that as the three Powers have achieved the success without England, they alone should reap the fruits of it.[1] So far England has not claimed to participate ; if she does so, the matter can be discussed again. Moreover the prestige of the three Powers would suffer in the East, if England were let in in addition. Japan would conclude that the Powers can do nothing without England. The British Press is trying to create this impression.

[1] Cf. Joseph, *Foreign Diplomacy in China*, p. 129.

IX. 295
BARON VON MARSCHALL TO PRINCE VON RADOLIN, *May 12th*, 1895
Telegram. Extract.

This further action on a changed and extended basis (the demand that the Pescadores should not be fortified) would be impossible without the participation of other Powers. It was out of respect for Prince Lobanoff's objections against England's participation that it appeared essential to drop this point, and all the more so because even to combine temporarily the Liao-tung question with that of the fortifying of the Pescadores was enough to endanger anew what has been achieved.

IX. 331
BARON MUMM VON SCHWARTZENSTEIN, AT TOKIO, TO THE CHANCELLOR, PRINCE VON BÜLOW, *June 13th*, 1907
Extract.

In the course of conversation Viscount Hayashi told me that the feeling in Japan against Germany dated from the time of Germany's joint intervention with France and Russia in 1895. It was a misfortune that Baron Gutschmid, with his violent character, was the German representative just then. He enjoyed the opportunity for humiliating Japan. He, Hayashi, had been Vice-Minister for Foreign Affairs, and had received the declarations from the three Ministers, as representative of the sick Count Mutsu. The declarations were identical in form, but the French Minister, Harmand, and even the Russian, Hitrovo, had used conciliatory expressions throughout, when they delivered their declarations, whilst Baron Gutschmid added to his own a long written statement, in which he—and he alone—baldly threatened war. (The CHANCELLOR : *'Was Gutschmid ordered to do this ? Were his instructions as harsh as this ? I wish to see the records.'*) When he, Hayashi, called Baron Gutschmid's attention to this variation from the declarations of his colleagues, he finally declared his readiness to withdraw formally that expression—the threat of war. He, Hayashi, however had said that the oral declaration of readiness to withdraw was quite sufficient. The document was in the Foreign Office Records, but in the interests of friendly relations with Germany, the Japanese Government had always taken care to keep it secret. (The CHANCELLOR : *'Gutschmid remains in my memory as an irritable and rather incompetent agent. It would be well to let Hayashi know that Gutschmid exceeded his instructions.'*)

CHAPTER II

THE KIAO - CHAU OCCUPATION AND MR. CHAMBERLAIN'S ALLIANCE PROPOSAL. NOVEMBER, 1897, TO APRIL, 1898

[In recompense for the services done to China in forcing Japan to reduce her demands following on her victory over China, Russia and France received large concessions in the North and South of China respectively. Germany alone was offered no advantages. When the chance came, however, she was not slow to seize it. Cf. G. & T., II, p. 1.]

[The German Government first thought of Kiao-chau as a possible base on the coast of China in November, 1894.[1] In August, 1897, Bernhard von Bülow, writing from St. Petersburg, drew up a statement, which he showed to the Russian Foreign Minister, as follows :]

XIV. 58

BERNHARD VON BÜLOW TO THE GERMAN FOREIGN OFFICE,
August 11th, 1897

Extract.

Sa Majesté l'Empereur d'Allemagne ayant demandé à Sa Majesté l'Empereur de Russie, si la Russie avait des vues sur la baie de Kiautchou, Sa Majesté répondit qu'effectivement la Russie avait intérêt d'assurer l'accès de la dite baie jusqu'à ce qu'elle ait obtenu un port plus septentrional qu'elle avait déjà en vue (Petchili). L'Empereur d'Allemagne ayant demandé si l'Empereur Nicolas voyait un inconvénient à ce que les navires allemands en cas de besoin et après avoir pris le consentement des autorités navales russes, mouillent dans la baie de Kiautchou, Sa Majesté l'Empereur de la Russie répondit négativement.

[For Count Muravieff's interpretation of this arrangement see p. 18.

News having been received of the murder of two German Missionaries in Shantung Province, the Emperor William on November 6th ordered the German Squadron in China to seize Kiau-chau without delay.]

---

[1] Cf. p. 4.

14

XIV. 69

The Emperor William to Bernhard von Bülow,
November 7th, 1897

Telegram.

Our conversation about Kiao-chau on the day of my departure for Piesdorf, at the end of which you said that it was high time to stiffen up our tepid and vacillating policy in the Far East, has had a quick result, quicker than we imagined. Yesterday I received official information of an attack, with murder and robbery, on the German missionary station at Yen-chu-fu in Shantung. So the Chinese have at last given us the grounds and the 'incident' which your predecessor, Marschall, so long desired. I decided to lay on at once. For all reports, whether in writing, officially or privately, or orally from travellers returning from the Far East, leave it in no doubt that we have reached a turning point as regards our whole prestige, influence, and hopes of trade development. All eyes, both of Asiatics and of Europeans living there, are turned upon us, and everyone is asking if we will stand this or not.

The message to the Admiral contains instructions to proceed at once to Kiao-chau and seize it, threaten reprisals and act with energy. To-day the Chancellor informed me that this intention would be a breach of the Peterhof Agreements [1], and that it must first be ascertained how the Russian Government would feel towards this enterprise. One might eventually occupy the island of Chang-tau and clarify the position in St. Petersburg in the meantime. However humiliating it may be for the German Empire to be obliged almost to obtain permission in St. Petersburg to protect and avenge the Christians in China who are committed to its care, and also to help itself to a spot which it refrained from occupying three years ago out of excessive modesty—and to which there could have been no objection—I did nevertheless not hesitate a moment in taking this step for the good of my country. I telegraphed in person to the Tsar :

' Chinese attacked German missions, Shantung, inflicting loss of life and property. I trust you approve according to our conversation Peterhof my sending German squadron to Kiau-tschou, as it is the only port available to operate from as a base against Marauders. I am under obligations to Catholic party in Germany to show that their missions are really safe under my protectorate. [2]

The Tsar answered me immediately :

' I am very grateful that you informed me personally.

---

[1] With Russia.   [2] English in text.

Regret attack by Chinese on German Catholic missions under
your protectorate. Cannot approve nor disapprove your sending German squadron to Kiao-chau as I lately learned that this
harbour only had been temporarily ours in 1895–1896.[1] I feel
anxious lest perhaps severity may cause unrest and insecurity
in Eastern China and widen the breach between Chinese and
Christians.' [2]

I do not share this anxiety. Thousands of German Christians
will breathe again, when they know that the German Emperor's
ships are near them. Hundreds of German merchants will
rejoice at the realisation that the German Empire has at last
won a firm footing in Asia. Hundreds of thousands of Chinamen
will tremble when they feel the iron fist of the German Empire
heavy on their necks, and the whole German people will be
glad that their Government has done a manly act. I have
forwarded the Tsar's answer to the Chancellor by the first post,
and at the same time ordered the Admiral to proceed at once
to Kiao-chau, which will now become ours in spite of Li Hung
Chang's intrigues and Cassini's [3] lies ;—on Cassini, by the way,
the Crown Order, 1st class, which he has long desired but will
only receive in return for Kiao-chau, apparently has not failed
to have its influence. From this it is evident that Russia sets
great store on having us on her side in the Far East and on
keeping us in a good humour. Let the world, once for all,
draw from this incident the moral that my motto is ' *Nemo
me impune lacessit*'.

XIV. 74

BARON VON ROTENHAN IN BERLIN, TO THE EMPEROR WILLIAM,
November 10*th*, 1897

Cipher telegram.   Extract.

. . . Your Majesty's Chargé d'affaires in St. Petersburg has
just telegraphed that Count Muravieff said to him :

' As regards Russia's right to Kiao-chau Bay, he had at the
time (during 1895–96) received from China not only the right
to use the harbour, but also the *droit du premier mouillage*, i.e.,
a promise that if the harbour was to be handed over to a foreign
Power, Russia should under all circumstances be assured of
the preference. (The EMPEROR : ' *He hid this from us and
apparently his Emperor ! Li Hung Chang quite recently declared
that Russia had nothing to say at Kiao-chau.*') For the safeguarding of these rights the Russian Commander of the squadron
in the Far East had been commanded to send Russian ships

---

[1] Cf. Joseph, *Foreign Diplomacy in China*, p. 200.
[2] Re-translated from the German.   [3] Russian Minister in Peking.

into that harbour, the moment that any German ships entered it. But the Russian ships would not participate in our action in obtaining satisfaction for the murder of the missionaries. He, Count Muravieff, deplored the Imperial Government's step. The result would be that the British, and perhaps even the French, would send ships into Kiao-chau Bay, and this could not be prevented ; (The EMPEROR : ' *But only if Russia invites them.*') so that what would happen would just be what least suited both our interests ; the harbour would become open first to England, and then to all nations. (The EMPEROR : '*!* ') Moreover it was an open question what China's attitude would be towards a forcible seizure of the harbour. Finally Count Muravieff said that so far he had discussed the matter with no one. (The EMPEROR : ' *He is sure to have spoken to Hanotaux.*')

The Russian Minister thus declares clearly enough that the Emperor Nicholas' Government has no intention of letting any other Power have Kiao-chau, but wishes to take it itself, supposing China loses it. (The EMPEROR : ' *The direct contrary of what he and his Master both said to me at Peterhof.*')

XIV. 83

THE CHANCELLOR, PRINCE VON HOHENLOHE, TO COUNT HATZFELDT, *November 13th*, 1897

Extract.

. . . It is possible that Count Muravieff [1] ventured to speak as singularly as he did in consideration of our bad relations with England. In the matter before us, therefore, it would be well if his confidence in that direction could be shaken a little. Of course an improvement of our relations with the island kingdom cannot be realised in twenty-four hours, though we never allow ourselves to lose sight of it. Nevertheless the road might be prepared for it by some step, which could be turned to account abroad.[2]

Please examine the matter from this point of view and give me your opinion on it.

The methods above mentioned are to be recommended from still another point of view in reference to the same matter. If, as I am bound to fear, we are forced to retire from Kiao-chau after having exacted atonement, there will be an urgent desire to select for occupation one of the other places in China recommended by the navy, all of which lie nearer to the British sphere of interest. Thus the question would then be what attitude

---

[1] Cf. G. & T , I, p. 5.
[2] Cf. Joseph, *Foreign Diplomacy in China*, p. 201.

the British would adopt. The Navy is in favour of taking Tsing-tau, which might, however, not be without objection owing to its nearness to Chusan.

Please give me your opinion of this aspect of the question also.

XIV. 83

Count Muravieff, in St. Petersburg, to Count Osten-Sacken, in Berlin, *November 13th*, 1897

Telegram.

Voici l'explication de la teneur de mes deux derniers télégrammes : Nous devons considérer la baie de Kiautchou comme fermée aux termes des déclarations qui nous ont été faites par le Gouvernement chinois. Mais, il ne nous saurait évidemment être contesté le droit de faire entrer nos escadres dans la baie du moment que des excadres étrangères pénétreraient dans ce port, la priorité de mouillage étant été obtenu en premier lieu pour nos bâtiments en 1895. Cette situation a été clairement reconnu dans la lettre que le Prince de Hohenlohe m'a adressée en date de Peterhof le 10 août,[1] et dans la notice secrète qui m'a été remise le 4 septembre par le Prince de Radolin.[2] Les deux pièces subordonnent à une entente préalable avec les autorités navales russes l'entrée éventuelle des navires de guerre allemands dans la baie en question.

XIV. 86

The Chancellor, Prince von Hohenlohe, to Count Hatzfeldt, *November 16th*, 1897

Telegram. Secret.

A stiffening, if only temporary, of our relations with Russia is to be expected, since His Majesty the Emperor is not disposed to let Kiao-chau go, whilst the exchange of views between here and St. Petersburg, of which you know, show that Russia takes a lively interest in that spot. . . . I naturally do not contemplate the possibility of England's supporting us ; but any recognisable mark of British consideration—e.g., if only in connection with Samoa—would at the present moment greatly influence feeling here as well as in Russia. To me the danger in the near future is not so much a conflict with Russia as the price to be paid for an understanding with her.

From this stand-point I give you full freedom, if you see a chance of using it, to indicate to the Prime Minister in your own fashion (as from yourself) the appropriateness of his being ready to meet our wishes.

[1] See p. 14.   [2] Not in the German records.

[Samoa was also a special subject of the Emperor's. Cf. p. 67. In a year's time all Germany's dealings with England were made subordinate to it.

XIV. 124

BERNHARD VON BÜLOW TO BARON VON HEYKING, AT PEKIN, December 17th, 1897

Telegram. Extract.

Inform the British Minister that, in consideration for our relations with England, we have hesitated to accept China's recommendation to occupy a port in the South. Our consideration for Great Britain would prove mistaken if England now stood in our way at Kiao-chau, especially as our claims there are confined to narrow limits . . .

XIV. 142

BERNHARD VON BÜLOW TO COUNT HATZFELDT, *January 8th*, 1898

Extract.

Your Excellency stated recently that Lord Salisbury would probably wish that the declaration of our intention to make Kiao-chau into a port open for world trade should be made not confidentially, but in a universally recognisable form, perhaps through the *Reichsanzeiger*. For reasons already made known to you, this publication will only be postponed until the German-Chinese agreement is complete in every part. But even then its form must be such as shall not bind us for the future ; so that Kiao-chau will be declared a Free Port ' until further notice '. Reliable connoisseurs of local business conditions in China are firmly convinced that only as a Free Port can Kiao-chau attain that commercial development, which is the main object of our settling there. But this conviction is at present only a theory ; we must await the results of experience. In any case, *German* interests alone can govern future developments regarding our new settlement. We must therefore avoid and avert every thing likely to force us to show greater consideration to other nations. . . .

The standpoint which Russian statesmen, in the first phase of our action at Kiao-chau, tried to adopt, namely, that Kiao-chau was well inside the Russian so-called sphere of interest, has never been recognised by us, but a glance at the map shows that we have approached nearer to the Russian sphere with our settlement than to any other. This fact lays on us—so long as the maintenance of good relations with Russia seems to us worth an effort—the duty of satisfying Russia that she has no need to fear any invasion of her sphere of interests on *Germany's* part. . . .

[In January, 1898, the British Government approached the Russian Government with a view to agreed action in the question of China. Negociations began,[1] but it soon became evident that Russia did not desire any definite agreement with England. The Emperor Nicholas' comment (xiv. 250) on the matter in a letter, written in English on June 3rd, 1898, to the Emperor William, points clearly to this fact:

' Three months ago, in the midst of our negotiations with China, England handed us over a memorandum containing many tempting proposals trying to induce us to come to full agreement upon all the points in which our interests clashed with hers. These proposals were of such a new character, that I must say we were quite amazed, and yet—their very nature seemed suspicious to us, never before had England made such offers to Russia. This showed us clearly that England needed our friendship at that time, to be able to check our development in a masked way in the Far East. Without thinking twice over it, their proposals were refused. Two weeks later Port Arthur was ours. As you know we have arrived at an understanding with Japan upon Corea and we have been since a long time on the best of terms with North America.

' I really do not see any reason why the latter should suddenly turn against old friends—only for the *beaux yeux* of England. . . .'

Since it was evident that there was no hope of inducing Russia to come to any agreement, the British Government turned to Germany. It was an unfortunate moment, for, although Lord Salisbury had stated that a German settlement at Kiao-chau would mean no injury to British interests he had not meant to include all forms of German activity in China.]

German Note. XIV. 193.

After the conclusion of the German-Chinese Agreement about Kiao-chau of March 6th, 1898, the British Minister at Peking protested against the decision promising to German contractors and capitalists a prior right to build railways in the Shantung Province. The British action, which was hardly in consonance with Lord Salisbury's repeated assurances that no British interests were injured by the Germans settling down at Kiao-chau, was bound to strike Berlin all the more, since the seizure by Russia of Port Arthur which had happened meanwhile and her intention to bring Talien-wan also into her possession in the form of a long lease seemed to indicate for England a rapprochement with Germany.

XIV. 146

COUNT HATZFELDT TO THE GERMAN FOREIGN OFFICE,
January 12th, 1898

Cipher telegram.

To-day Lord Salisbury again declared that no British interest would be injured by our settling down at Kiao-chau. . . . He remarked that he had from the first objected not so much to the fact of our occupation of Kiao-chau, as to the form in which it had been done, chiefly because he regarded it as a dangerous precedent, which *others* might imitate. I replied that I did not share this view and that no other way had been open to us, for the Chinese Government had clearly refused to understand

---

[1] G. & T., I. p. 5 et seq. ; also Joseph, *Foreign Diplomacy in China,* Chap. X.

that it was the duty of gratitude, as well as to their own interests to place at our disposal the coaling station, which will be indispensable to us in future ; the Minister admitted that there was no other way of obtaining this object.

XIV. 196
COUNT HATZFELDT, IN LONDON, TO THE GERMAN FOREIGN OFFICE, *March 29th*, 1898

Very secret.   Private for the Secretary of State.

Mr. Chamberlain, whom I met to-day, explained to me in detail and *strictly confidentially* that a turn had come in the political situation, which no longer permitted England to continue her policy, hitherto traditionally one of isolation. The British Government was faced with the need of soon making far-reaching decisions and would now be able to count on the support of public opinion if it gave up its policy of isolation and looked round for alliances, which would assist it in maintaining the peace which it desired. The situation was critical not only on account of the China question, about which the British Government must very promptly decide on the points intended to be debated in the House next Tuesday, but also serious complications were to be feared with France on the subject of West Africa. M. Hanotaux's statements, according to which the negotiations in Paris were going on satisfactorily,[1] had in reality no foundation. So far no basis had been found on which an understanding could be expected, and he, Chamberlain, was quite determined to give way no further.

German Note.

On March 26th the French Foreign Minister, Hanotaux, had stated in the Chamber of Deputies, regarding the Anglo-French negotiations about West Africa, that in Africa the Government had a very ticklish question to deal with with Great Britain, but the examination of it was being carried out on both sides with skill and good will and without incidents ; the points of difference, which had up till then delayed a final agreement, were already fewer.

The Minister then turned to Anglo-German relations and went shortly over the reasons which had led to their late estrangement, and he remarked finally that in his opinion both countries possessed the same political interests, and that the few little colonial differences that existed could be settled, if only *at the same time* agreement could be obtained on the great political issues. He added that the occupation of Kiao-chau had only been unwelcome here, because it was foreseen that Russia and France would do likewise, only more extensively, and that

[1] Cf. G. & T., I, p. 132 et seq. 147.

serious difficulties would result from it. For the rest, he fully recognised that our action there threatened no British interests. If friendly relations between England and Germany were restored and a political understanding, such as he had in mind, followed, England would not only not oppose us in China, but would help us there with all her power.

In answer to the above I argued that we had settled our business in China by our own initiative and without foreign help, so that, as far as I knew, we owed no one thanks or anything else. We had shown friendly consideration to England by refusing the offer which was, as I knew for certain, made to us to occupy points lying more to the South. It was therefore to England's interest not to make difficulties for us at Kiao-chau, as this, so far as I could judge personally, was bound in the end to force us to turn towards Russia. I could of course merely express my own personal views and suppositions.

Chamberlain answered that he quite agreed with this, and that we might consider our conversation as simply an exchange of ideas between two private persons. But if it was to lead to any satisfactory result at all, the first condition must be that we should deal with each other quite frankly. From this standpoint he would inform me quite honestly and freely that the British Government, as he had said at the beginning, was under the absolute necessity of taking serious decisions during the days immediately following and that it wished to renounce its policy of isolation and to reach an understanding with us and our friends. In other words, if we would be on England's side now, England would be on Germany's supposing she were attacked. This would be equivalent to England's accession to the Triple Alliance and require confirmation by a treaty, for which we should have to formulate our conditions.

At this point, without expressing a view regarding the proposal, I indicated that England always sent others into the fire and wished to stay out of it, just as now, with injury to herself, she had tried to do with Japan. Chamberlain replied that it was Japan's fault, if she had not received sufficient enlightenment regarding England's intentions. If the Japanese had simply asked how far, if at all, England would support them in practice, a frank reply would have been given to them.

Finally I mentioned conversationally the rumours current here regarding the intended movements of the British squadron in Chinese waters and named Wei-hai-wei; Chamberlain answered with a smile that he had heard tell of more serious matters, naturally also only by report,—for in his character of Minister he could not say what was known to him officially. When I pressed him a little, he said that there seemed to be talk of sending the British ships to Talien-wan. He thought it questionable whether the Russians would not protest against this. When I said it was not clear to me whether merely a naval visit or a landing were intended, Chamberlain answered merely that, as it appeared now, the harbour of Port Arthur could be entirely dominated from high ground near Talien-wan, so that if the British occupied this high ground, they would control it both by land and water.

Throughout this conversation Chamberlain spoke calmly and decidedly and demonstrated very frankly the desire for a binding agreement between England and the Triple Alliance. He repeated several times that there was no time to be lost in the matter, as a decision must be taken in the next few days.

If Your Excellency considers that an official report on this conversation is called for, I beg you to treat the foregoing as an official telegram and to number it as such.

I request that Chamberlain's words be treated with strict discretion, for if ever it becomes known, especially in St. Petersburg, it would undoubtedly destroy all the British Minister's confidence in myself.[1]

XIV. 199

BERNHARD VON BÜLOW, IN BERLIN, TO COUNT HATZFELDT, March 30th, 1898

Telegram. Very secret. Private.

I beg Your Excellency to thank Mr. Chamberlain for his confidential overtures and say to him the following, which will show him that we also entirely trust his personal reliability and discretion.

Mr. Chamberlain desires to avert the threat to England's peace by making England, in alliance with Germany, stronger than her rivals and so to force them to renounce their hostile intentions against her. But the weak point of such an Anglo-German treaty would be that any such agreement would only bind the British Government for the time being. If the enemies of the Anglo-German group wished, after the ancient principle of the Horatii, to fight their rivals singly, and fell first upon Germany, I must certainly say that at present I have no faith that the British party to the treaty would in this case spring to our assistance. It would be more in the spirit of British policy up to the present for the Government, which had engaged itself to us by treaty, simply to go out of power and be followed

---

[1] Cf. Eckardstein, *Ten Years at the Court of St. James*, p. 93 ; Dennis, *Adventures in American Diplomacy*, p. 387 ; H. W. Wilson, *The War Guilt*. p. 61 ; Brandenburg, p. 103, et seq.

by one which, mindful of the warning received, would obey public opinion and confine itself to its usual role of looker-on. This procedure by a vote in Parliament enables England to disavow any inconvenient foreign treaty at the psychological moment ; so that in consideration of this ever open back-door, no German statesman, however great his sympathies for England and however sure he might be that the maintenance of England's power is needed for upholding the world balance, would be likely to assume responsibility for the consequences which an Anglo-German treaty, entered into with an eye to future events, would entail for Germany. . . .

Finally, time is against England. In ten years, if the Siberian Railway and the Russian war preparations on the Indian frontier are completed, and the Emperor of Russia may perhaps have become more proof against female influences in his family, it may humanly speaking be less easy to deter Russia from taking part in an Anglo-French war than at present ; whereas in ten years' time British feeling will still present the same obstacle to a British alliance with continental Powers as it does to-day. Thus the injurious influence will continue, and the favourable influences will shrink or disappear.

[On April 1st Mr. Chamberlain came forward with fresh proposals.]

XIV. 203

COUNT HATZFELDT TO THE GERMAN FOREIGN OFFICE,
April 1st, 1898

Extract.

. . . Your Highness will see that the object of an Anglo-German understanding about China would be quite different from that suggested by Chamberlain on March 29th. Then the idea was to involve us in an aggressive attitude towards Russia's recent acquisitions ; whereas to-day it seems certain that the idea of seriously protesting against or resisting these, if it ever existed, is practically given up. On the other hand, with our help the rest of China would be saved and kept open for world trade, in return for which England would grant us special privileges in China. In fact, Mr. Chamberlain indicated that a further extension of our sphere of interests in the hinterland of Kiao-chau would certainly be welcomed by us. . . .

XIV. 211

COUNT HATZFELDT TO THE CHANCELLOR, PRINCE VON HOHENLOHE,
April 7th, 1898

Extract.

. . . On April 5th I had other business reasons for calling on Mr. Balfour, and he took occasion to mention my conversation with Mr. Chamberlain which the latter had evidently reported to him. When I described the considerations forbidding us at present to enter into so sudden and far-reaching a proposal as that formulated by Mr. Chamberlain, I found Mr. Balfour somewhat unexpectedly ready to admit the weight of our arguments. He confessed that it could not be foreseen with certainty how Parliament would accept a treaty of alliance with the Triple Alliance, for which public opinion had been so little prepared. He did not deny that the leader of German policy would be undertaking an immense responsibility if, in view of this parliamentary uncertainty, he was ready to conclude a treaty which, if rejected by Parliament, would almost inevitably result in an attack by France combined with Russia against Germany. (The EMPEROR: ' Correct.') Another remark added by Mr. Balfour that Mr. Chamberlain sometimes wished to advance too quickly gave me the impression that this *personal* ill-success of Mr. Chamberlain's in this matter was not altogether unwelcome to him.

Finally we agreed in the view that now above all it was important gradually to remove the ill-feeling which still existed between the two countries by an accommodating attitude of both Governments in small questions and to prepare public opinion both here and in Germany for a possible future political rapprochement. (The EMPEROR: ' Yes.')

I consider it certain that all the members of the Cabinet were informed of Mr. Balfour's and Mr. Chamberlain's respective utterances and proposals to me and were agreed as to the object in view. I am assured that this was especially so with the Duke of Devonshire, and I hear a rumour that Sir William Harcourt and Lord Rosebery declared that if the Government were to seek an understanding with Germany, they would not oppose it in any way. (The EMPEROR: ' Good.')

XIV. 226

Minute by the EMPEROR to a despatch of April 26th, 1898 :

The gist of the matter is : by occupying Wei-hai-wei in a temper and so shaking her fist in front of Russia's nose, England suddenly finds herself in a very uncomfortable position. Russia has not so far struck at the fist, but is keeping that for later on ; this is beginning to dawn on John Bull, and he wants someone to get him out of his dilemma. I certainly shall not do this merely on Chamberlain's promises ! We shall see what may happen later on.

[See also G. & T., I, p. 100–104.]

XIV. 217

German Note.

The rejection of Chamberlain's alliance feeler by the German Government at once produced an attitude of greater friendliness towards France, especially in the Colonial Secretary, and made the Anglo-French negotiations concerning West Africa easier.[1]   On April 6th Count Münster reported from Paris that Chamberlain, who had at first stood in the way of an Anglo-French understanding, had suddenly became more favourable to it.   On May 25th Lord Salisbury admitted to Count Hatzfeldt that England and France were drawing nearer together month by month in the Niger negotiations and that a satisfactory conclusion could now be counted on.   The Protocol was signed on June 14th, 1898, [by the British and French Niger Commissioners—cf. G. & T., I, p. 157.]   Soon however the friendly relations which were thus growing between England and France suffered a severe blow owing to the dispute about Fashoda.

[On April 30th, 1898, Bernhard von Bülow wrote to Count Hatzfeldt (XIV. 228) : I do not share Mr. Chamberlain's opinion, but think rather that to-day France will not be induced by any price that England can pay to consider an alliance against Russia, even of the most platonic and defensive kind . . .

In August, Sir Frank Lascelles, then on leave in London, found that Mr. Chamberlain was now advocating a defensive alliance with Germany in the event of attack by two Powers at the same time.   On his return to Germany he held a conversation with the Emperor (G. & T., I, p. 68 ; also this volume, p. 38).   The Emperor summed up his impressions as follows :]

XIV. 338

MEMORANDUM BY THE EMPEROR WILLIAM, *August 22nd*, 1898

Extract.

. . . Throughout my conversation with the British Ambassador I made it clear that I should enter into no arrangement directed against Russia.   The practical implication of Chamberlain's proposal, if it ever takes a more definite shape, is that if England is attacked by France and Russia at the same time, we should have to engage one opponent, the French ; whilst in the alternative case the British must help us.   As long as the Franco-Russian alliance exists, any reasonable Russian policy cannot begrudge our trying to protect ourselves against France in the event of a double attack, if we explain clearly that we in no way desire to disturb Russia's schemes :—Reinsurance !—Anglo-Russian antagonism *by itself* cannot draw us into any complication arising out of a *defensive* alliance with England with the condition that *two* opponents must be attacking one of the parties in order to bring the *casus foederis* into action.

[1] Cf. p. 21 ; also G. & T., I, p. 132 et seq.

CHAPTER III

THE ANGLO - GERMAN CONVENTIONS OF AUGUST 30TH, 1898. JUNE – SEPTEMBER, 1898

[This chapter should be read closely with Gooch and Temperley, Volume I, Chapter II (II).]

German Note.

On June 6th Count von Tattenbach telegraphed from Lisbon that Luiz de Soveral, the Portuguese Minister in London, had been sent to England with instructions to obtain money by mortgaging the revenues of Mozambique, Angola, and other Portuguese colonies. (Cf. Brandenburg, p. 155 et seq.)

The German Government at once decided to bring pressure so as to be admitted as joint lender to Portugal, and introduced a condition that no other country should be permitted to offer a loan.

The motives prompting England and Germany in so doing were opposed to each other. The German Government pressed for a speedy conclusion of an agreement forcing a loan secured on Portugal's colonies in the thinly disguised hope of being certainly able to foreclose on the share of them which was to fall to Germany. The British Government, on the other hand, was genuinely anxious for Portugal's finances to recover to the extent of removing all danger of her losing her African possessions. (Cf. G. & T., I, p. 75, 94–5.) The length of time occupied by the Anglo-German negociations, and possibly also the fact that measures were in progress for the relief of Portugal's finances contributed towards their recovery. In July, 1899, Count Tattenbach admitted (cf. G. & T., I, p. 86) 'that a marked improvement had lately taken place', and 'that a loan under the Anglo-German Agreement was now out of the question'.]

XIV. 259

BERNHARD VON BÜLOW, IN BERLIN, TO COUNT HATZFELDT,
June 8th, 1898

Very confidential.

In your report of June 3rd [1] you mentioned that—if it was of moment to us to receive concessions from England on the colonial side—you would be able to indicate the points which can in your opinion be discussed in London with hopes of success.

I beg you to furnish me with a report on the subject.

The colonial party here has very confidentially expressed certain desires in that direction, which are given in detail in the

[1] Not given.

enclosure. I beg you to pay special attention in your report to the *desiderata* described in it.

Just now especially we must watch the development suffered as a consequence of the financial situation in Portugal [1] by the Portuguese colonial question, upon which the enclosed copy of a telegram from Lisbon will give you further information. . . .

You will see from His Majesty's marginal notes to your report of June 3rd that His Majesty holds that our objects for compensation against British territorial expansion in Africa do not themselves lie necessarily in Africa. (The EMPEROR : ' *Agreed.*')

Enclosure.

In West Africa :
  1. A naval station in the Canaries or Cape Verde islands ;
  2. Fernando Po ;
  3. The Volta down to its mouth as the frontier between Togoland and the Gold Coast Colony ;
  4. Angola, including the southern part of Mossamedes and Benguella ;
  5. Walfisch Bay.

In East Africa :
  1. Zanzibar with Pemba ;
  2. The Zambezi and Shire as southern frontier of German East Africa.

In Asia :
  1. Portuguese Timor ;
  2. The Sulu Archipelago ;
  3. At least one of the Philippine Islands (Mindanao).

In the Pacific :
  1. The Caroline Islands ;
  2. The Samoan Islands.

XIV. 261

COUNT HATZFELDT TO THE GERMAN FOREIGN OFFICE,
June 14th, 1898

Cipher telegram.

I wrote down Lord Salisbury's reply to my communication of to-day in French, in order to avoid any misunderstanding, and it was admitted by him to be correct. It is as follows :

' Lord Salisbury m'a répondu que M. Soveral est revenu de Lisbonne pour chercher des ressources et lui en a parlé en exprimant le désir de faire un emprunt. Lord Salisbury ignore

[1] G. & T., I, p. 44.

(The EMPEROR : ' *!* ') les conditions que le Portugal offrirait et il a engagé M. Soveral à s'entretenir à ce sujet avec Mr. Chamberlain." (The EMPEROR : ' *It is always the same game. He wants to be taken by surprise by Chamberlain. He knows perfectly well what is demanded. Salisbury, and not Chamberlain, must decide this question, for it is a political one.*') . . .

At the start of our conversation the Prime Minister once again declared that England was not only bound by old treaties, to which Lisbon was now appealing, to guarantee Portugal in her possessions,[1] (The EMPEROR : ' *That will hardly have been done in a Portuguese sense !*') but is also greatly interested in preventing a collapse there. But he had declared to M. Soveral that the Chancellor of the Exchequer (Sir Michael Hicks-Beach) would hardly be ready to meet his wishes without quite substantial money guarantees, and had begged him to discuss the details of his proposals with Chamberlain. He added that this discussion was probably taking place to-day.

When I explained in friendly but emphatic terms that one-sided action in the matter here, involving actual or contemplated passing of Portugal's sovereign rights in those colonies into British hands, would make a very bad impression with us and also would not tend to produce the improvement in our relations which we both desired, and that the question was a political one, which he, Salisbury, and not Chamberlain, would have to decide (The EMPEROR : ' *Very true* ') the Prime Minister answered that he continued to wish for the best relations with us, which was why he wished to tell me quite frankly and in good time everything that was done in the matter. But he could not, as I required of him, admit in principle that the British Government would not be justified in assisting the Portuguese Government financially without our previous consent. (The EMPEROR : *It is the method and the form that matter ! Those interest us greatly !* ')

During our conversation Lord Salisbury said that there was no interest here in Angola, but only in the Portuguese colonies in East Africa. He also indicated *very confidentially* that Chamberlain's desire to conclude a financial bargain with Portugal must be ascribed to the fear that we were intending to take possession of Delagoa Bay. (The EMPEROR : ' *!* ')

My impression from Lord Salisbury's whole attitude to-day is that he is leaving this affair also for Mr. Chamberlain and wishes to avoid getting in his way. He made me the curious proposal that I should myself talk to Chamberlain. (The EMPEROR : ' *!* ') and agree with him direct, but he withdrew this later on. His observations made it clear that a mortgage on the Portuguese revenue from these colonies is in the wind.

[1] Cf. G. & T., I, pp. 48, 94–5 ; also H. W. Wilson, *The War Guilt*, p. 64.

I believe that Lord Salisbury will keep his word and inform me of any *formal* agreement negotiated here, but am not at all sure whether he will not merely communicate to me a decision taken here after its completion, (The EMPEROR : ' *Yes* ') without making the carrying of it into effect dependent on our previous consent. (The EMPEROR : ' *I decline anything of the sort ! and it would be unloyal and contrary to the agreements.—This report and especially the last sentence, is evidence of the false and unreliable game Lord Salisbury is playing against us ; this is not the way to lure us into an alliance !* Dieu nous en garde ! ')

XIV. 266

BERNHARD VON BÜLOW, IN BERLIN, TO COUNT HATZFELDT, *June 17th, 1898*

Telegram.

The French Ambassador [1] informed me that he had heard very confidentially from Paris that ' suspicious negociations ' were in progress between England and Portugal. Apparently England was promising financial assistance and protection against dangers at home and abroad in the event of a mortgage on Delagoa Bay.

I answered the Ambassador in a deprecating tone, for I still at present hope that we shall attain more by negociation with England than by combining our South African interests with those of France.

Possibly, however, in the knowledge that France is looking for someone to help her against England, the British statesmen will be more accommodating towards such considerable claims as ours.

[The foregoing and following documents are an illustration of ' the peculiarity of diplomatic communication ', which ' is that it avails itself regularly of two separate lines '. Cf. R. B. Mowat. *Life of Lord Pauncefote,* p. 172.]

XIV. 266

BERNHARD VON BÜLOW TO COUNT MUNSTER, IN PARIS, *June 18th, 1898*

Telegram.

The Portuguese Minister in London, M. de Soveral, started for London on the 3rd with instructions from his Government to obtain money by mortgaging the revenue from Portuguese possessions in Africa, his country's rights of sovereignty being included in the mortgage.[2] From a confidential enquiry made

---

[1] Marquis de Noailles.
[2] Cf. H. W. Wilson, *The War Guilt,* p. 63.

to me yesterday by the French Ambassador, it is clear that the French Government has already heard of these plans and is strongly disquieted. If that Anglo-Portuguese agreement came into being, it would in fact cause a complete revolution to the disadvantage of the Powers with interests in Africa, or whose nationals are creditors of Portugal. In both these respects Germany and France possess an identical interest whether in preventing or having a say in such an alteration of the Portuguese *status quo* both in politics and business. If France is clearly still hypnotised by the *trouée des Vosges* [1] and has in consequence no eye free for observing the questions of the moment, the Russian alliance will scarcely be able to prevent England from expanding everywhere outside Europe without considering French interests.

In the above event diplomatic co-operation between Germany and France would not be against England direct, but against Portugal, whose intention to mortgage the permanent sources of revenue of her colonies will quite considerably reduce the permanent sources of her own revenue, with no guarantee that the money obtained by the mortgage will be properly applied. Therefore it will have to be put to the Portuguese Government that the German and French Governments, whose nationals unfortunately have extensive interests in Portugal, are constrained to raise the question by what means of pressure, commercial or otherwise, it might be possible to introduce international control of the Portuguese finances.

Our gracious Master, the Emperor, commands you to speak to M. Hanotaux emphatically in this sense. The main object of the conversation should, I think, be to ascertain clearly whether all practical co-operation between Germany and France in all individual questions, whatever they may be, is out of the question as a principle, as it was at the time of the Jameson Raid.[2] I need not tell you that the clearing up of this point will be of wide importance in the future shaping of our foreign policy.

German Note.

On June 14th, 1898, Méline's Ministry, in which Hanotaux was Foreign Minister, resigned and was succeeded by Brisson, with Delcassé as Foreign Minister . . . On June 30th Münster reported to Berlin : ' I fear that the new Foreign Minister Delcassé will earn our distrust. He has written much about politics and been very busy behind the scenes as an amateur. He has all along tried to work for the Russian alliance.' The German Foreign Office soon came to the conclusion that under the new Brisson-Delcassé Ministry there was no hope of practical co-operation between France and Germany. Cf. p. 40.

[The German Government was anxious to exclude France from participation in the loan to Portugal and from any benefits supposing Portugal

---

[1] I.e. the fear of a German invasion.   [2] Cf. Vol. II, Chap. XXV.

were forced to renounce some of her territory. Lord Salisbury was very unwilling to agree that any loss of territory at all was involved in the question of a loan.]

XIV. 272

BERNHARD VON BÜLOW, IN BERLIN, TO COUNT HATZFELDT,
June 22nd, 1898

Telegram. Extract.[1]

. . . For us as well as for England, in this matter as in all colonial matters in general, it is an affair not so much of provable rights, but of interests and the power available for establishing these interests, if need be. England is stronger on the water than we are. In so far as they have believed there is no need to consider Germany, British Governments have acted in the consciousness of their own maritime strength, and also in the belief that Germany will get no support from other sea Powers, for Russia favours the shifting of the British centre of gravity to South Africa, whilst for known reasons French public opinion would be disinclined for joining with Germany, as was shown at the time of the Jameson Raid.

But no proof is needed to show that the attitude of Russia and France would change at once if Germany proposed setting in order *all* African questions, *including that of Egypt*. You know quite well from your former conversations with Baron de Courcel that this statesman keenly desires to reach a general settlement of all African questions. It is equally well known that Russia considers driving the British away from the neighbourhood of the Suez Canal to be one of her most important political tasks. Austria and Italy would do little to prevent such a general settlement. Austria does not worry about Africa, and Italy could be bought off.

On Germany alone depend the measures for a general settlement in Africa, and up to now Germany alone has prevented it. And British policy banks on Germany's being inclined to consider a strong British Empire as a useful, if not indispensable element for constitutional stability in Europe and the world, and on her having hitherto formed her Egyptian policy on this basis. We saw England go into Egypt without envy and helped her to establish herself there. Since Germany is not in a position to render political services gratis, we expect a corresponding return, as the natural outcome of our action in cases where we have rendered important assistance. (The EMPEROR: 'Yes') If England, seeing that she is once again getting ready to seize silently a considerable portion of the African continent, is really disregarding the German claim for reciprocity, damage is involved

[1] Cf. G. & T., I, p. 50.

not only to German interests, but also to the prestige of the Government of His Majesty the German Emperor both at home and abroad; and against this Germany would be forced to react with energy.

Therefore England will certainly get cheaper out of this by first agreeing with Germany regarding her schemes for expansion in Africa. On our side we must now decide whether such an understanding with England is or is not possible, for Portugal's financial necessities are so great that the foreign loan, which was refused the day before yesterday, will sooner or later have to be accepted subject to territorial guarantees. After our recent experiences, however, we could not justify sitting still up to the moment when England presents us with a *fait accompli*.

I have therefore, with the approval of His Majesty, our gracious Master, to instruct you to enquire of Lord Salisbury how he views the future partition of the Portuguese colonies between England and Germany and whether he is ready to conclude a binding agreement on this question now. Germany will take account of the facts that England already possesses interests of long standing in Africa, that she is the stronger sea Power, and finally that any opposition to British policy by means of a freshly constructed continental combination would present fewer difficulties at the present than dangers for the future, and therefore ought—as we need not conceal from the British Prime Minister—to be avoided by us, on the condition that he himself does not, by the immoderation and inconsiderateness (The EMPEROR: ' *and falseness* ') of his attitude drive us in this direction. . . .

[Here follow proposals in detail regarding the partitioning of the Portuguese colonies.]

Finally there is your question whether we should consent to an Anglo-Portuguese loan and should be satisfied with concluding a binding agreement with England, whereby England definitely recognises our claim to certain portions of the Portuguese colonies, supposing Portugal loses them or gives them up. An agreement of this kind would certainly be better than none at all; but it would not offer the same security as an arrangement allowing us to share to a considerable amount in the loan to be granted to Portugal and to receive direct from Portugal certain territorial guarantees, which would have to be defined exactly and kept separate from those offered to England. The only correct means of obtaining the money needed for this purpose would be for the German Empire to guarantee it to the capitalists; but I have no doubt that in view of the important national interests involved, the Reichstag will later on grant the necessary guarantee. Up to the moment of concluding the treaty, the negociations would have to proceed secretly between Germany and England on the one side, and Portugal on the other. So long as England and Germany enjoy the prospect of agreeing together, both will do best to leave France out of it. (The EMPEROR: ' *if the Francophil Salisbury is loyal enough to keep silence* ') France is clearly pursuing her own territorial aims in South Africa. This is shown by the great anxiety felt by French diplomacy over the Anglo-Portuguese agreement, and even more clearly by M. Rouvier's dislike of the idea of international financial control, which would at one stroke put an end to Portugal's financial stress and be the only practical method of relieving her from the necessity of selling or mort-gaging her colonies. I cannot imagine that the British Prime Minister would welcome the formation of a French colonial empire opposite to Madagascar, and can therefore only repeat my conviction that England would do best through a private agreement with Germany. (The EMPEROR: ' *Yes* ')

XIV. 278

COUNT HATZFELDT TO THE GERMAN FOREIGN OFFICE, *June 24th,*
1898

Extract.

. . . I said to Lord Salisbury that under the existing circum-stances I knew of no other way of safeguarding our interests than to join in the loan, or to obtain a binding assurance from England that if a certain eventuality, by no means unwelcome to us, arose, she would adjudicate to us certain portions of the Portuguese colonies.

Lord Salisbury replied that England's participation in the Greek loan (December, 1897) had caused such unpleasantnesses, that no one here would hear of another such joint loan. He did not mean to say that we had not just as much right as England to grant a loan to Portugal. I replied that if I understood him aright, this was bringing us back to the idea of a *parallel* loan,[1] which, at our last meeting, had seemed unwelcome to him. My personal impression was that our interests could be secured by this means, assuming that the guarantees offered by Portugal (Customs) referred to the objects we should have to claim, sup-posing Portugal eventually gave up her colonies. With this in view an understanding between ourselves and England about the eventual partition would have to come first. Lord Salisbury did not deny this, although he did not definitely agree with it. (The EMPEROR: ' *He wants it all for himself* ') . . .

[1] Cf. G. & T., I, p. 52.

Count von Tattenbach, at Lisbon, to the German Foreign
Office, *June 30th*, 1898

Cipher telegram.

The King, who received me to-day, formally and emphatically
repeated his promise to conduct no negociations with other Powers
without informing us.

He considers the only possible solution of the financial question to be a loan based on territorial guarantees. He realises
completely that Germany wishes to share in this and regards
this participation as a guarantee for Portugal.

The King desired me to express his thanks for the communication.

XIV. 281

Count Hatzfeldt to the German Foreign Office, *July 6th*,
1898

Cipher telegram.

In our conversation to-day [1] Lord Salisbury himself began
again upon the Portuguese question and assured me that he was
by no means refusing to come to an understanding with us on
it. His only fear was that the situation in the Iberian Peninsula
was at the moment too uncertain [2] to pursue a definite plan on
this basis just now. Whilst he considered it advisable to await
developments in the peninsula for a while, it did not mean that
he was rejecting the understanding with us. He then asked
whether we should be inclined eventually to give up our exterritorial rights at Zanzibar and added that we might be able
to agree concerning Angola as well as Mozambique, where he
considered it natural in us to desire eventually to possess the
northern part.

Report follows by messenger.

XIV. 282

Count Hatzfeldt to the Chancellor, Prince von
Hohenlohe, *July 6th*, 1898

Extract.

I told Lord Salisbury . . . that I had never concealed from
him that the policy pursued by Sir Philip Currie in Constantinople has aroused the greatest suspicions throughout Europe as
to England's intentions. . . .

In reply to my remark about England's policy in the East
Lord Salisbury as usual tried to show that the suspicions aroused
by it were entirely groundless. But he must admit that Sir
Philip Currie's continuously unfriendly attitude had twice

[1] Cf. G. & T., I, p. 55.   [2] Cf. Vol. II, Chapter XXXII.

obliged the Porte to ask for the recall of the British Ambassador, and added of himself that British policy had aroused very deep mistrust of England's intentions in the East, even in Austria, where a more friendly judgment might have been expected. Lord Salisbury then tried to attribute the ill-feeling between England and Germany to our having favoured the Boers (The EMPEROR : '*/ /* ') and especially to our unfriendly attitude at Zanzibar, where we protected the pretender, who was hostile to England, and gave him an asylum in German territory. I did not fail to reply, representing very fitly that it was hard for German public opinion to forget the amazing personal attacks and insults which had been so often directed against His Majesty in the Press here and in public speeches and on public occasions. (The EMPEROR : ' *Good* ') . . .

XIV. 300

COUNT HATZFELDT TO THE GERMAN FOREIGN OFFICE, *July 20th*, 1898

Cipher telegram. Extract.[1]

. . . Finally, referring to the mouths of the Congo, Lord Salisbury remarked that he had only contemplated handing them to King Leopold because he thought he ought to reassure us regarding any possible British intentions at the mouth of the Congo or any special advantages that England might derive from acquiring it. He had never thought of claiming any return concession from King Leopold. Regarding the connecting strip he reminded me that an attempt to get a concession from King Leopold had been made in Lord Rosebery's time [May, 1894],[2] in direct opposition to a memorandum which he had himself left behind him in the Records, when he retired from office ; he had given his opinion that such an attempt was out of the question.

XIV. 316

COUNT HATZFELDT TO THE GERMAN FOREIGN OFFICE, *August 8th*, 1898

Extract.

. . . As our conversation [3] proceeded, I realised that the Prime Minister wishes at all costs not to appear at Lisbon in the light of an expectant heir, dividing the Portuguese heritage in advance with another ; therefore he wishes to limit the published agreement with us to the loan, and to include in an agreement— to be kept secret—all points relating to the future transference of these colonies or their customs administration to England and Germany. . . . Under present circumstances, it is not

---

[1] Cf. G. & T., I, 58–9.   [2] Cf. Vol. II, Chapter XXII.
[3] Cf. G. & T., I, 62.

impossible that France will make an attempt—very unwelcome here—to do a deal with Spain, similar to our intended one with Portugal, regarding Ceuta and the Moorish coast. With this in view we must avoid letting France know of our partition agreement, so enabling her to appeal to it as a precedent.

Although the delay caused by handing over further negociations to Mr. Balfour [1] is undesirable, yet I think we must consent to it. The last time he represented Lord Salisbury,[2] Mr. Balfour was honest and forthcoming towards us ; when we come to discuss the matter with him it will probably be soon evident whether a quicker conclusion is to be expected in this way. Lord Salisbury says that Mr. Balfour will probably start discussing the matter by next Wednesday.

[On August 11th Count Hatzfeldt handed Mr. Balfour a memorandum which was an amplification of one read by him to Lord Salisbury on August 3rd. Cf. G. & T., I, p. 62–3.]

XIV. 317
Baron von Richthofen to Count Hatzfeldt, *August 12th*, 1898

Telegram.

I consider the arrangement, as it stands now, to be quite acceptable. Free communication from the lakes to the coast on the Zambesi and Shire is a geographical necessity for us ; this right will be best acknowledged as a natural consequence of our entry into the earlier Portuguese treaties.

There is an interesting communication from Lisbon, that the Portuguese attempt to secure a loan in France was rejected on the plea that ' the Portuguese guarantees were insufficient'. This sounds very much as if France also wants to demand territorial guarantees. The Franco-Portuguese negociations are to be resumed in October—a clear sign that England and Germany ought to lose no time. There can be no doubt as to the urgent character of the Portuguese need of money. The only question is whether France or England and Germany give it.

[On August 18th Mr. Balfour handed Count Hatzfeldt two draft Declarations, A and B. Cf. G. & T., I, p. 63–5. He told him that Lord Salisbury had made no definite arrangement about Timor.]

XIV. 321
Baron von Richthofen to Count Hatzfeldt, *August 19th*, 1898

Telegram.

Please make it clear orally, direct to Mr. Balfour or through Mr. Bertie, that an arrangement without Timor is unacceptable to

---

[1] Lord Salisbury was going on leave. [2] Cf. p. 24.

us, and that we shall only continue to negociate on the understanding that the promise made to us regarding Timor from the
start by Lord Salisbury, which has never been questioned
throughout the discussions, remains untouched. Say that Mr.
Balfour's statement—which has no doubt been inspired from
without—that we do nothing but threaten and neither concede
nor promise anything, is incomprehensible at the moment when
we are letting England have South Africa and are ready to fulfil
our promises. In our eyes the agreement was the starting point
of a joint colonial policy. Our demands are the minimum for
our leaving the Boers to themselves. Failing this recompense
we should be unable promptly to justify the agreement in the
eyes of our own public opinion, and should be forced to strike
out another course and to broaden the question by introducing
other elements.

XIV. 328

COUNT HATZFELDT TO THE GERMAN FOREIGN OFFICE, *August 20th*,
1898

Cipher telegram. Private.

Timor is settled, and I am convinced that we owe it to Mr.
Balfour alone, for he urgently desires a conclusion. I beg therefore that as few difficulties as possible be made for him regarding
his draft, and that a secret note in explanation of the affair be
agreed to in the manner I recommended.

[In an account of a conversation (XIV. 334) between himself and Sir
Frank Lascelles on August 21st the Emperor wrote that he had told the
Ambassador that ' unless the negociations in progress during the last few
days between my Ambassador and Mr. Balfour lead to no more acceptable
result than they had up to the present, the continued presence of my
Ambassador in London would be superfluous just now '. (Cf. G. & T.,
I, 68 ; also Wilson, *The War Guilt*, p. 64.)]

XIV. 340

BERNHARD VON BÜLOW, AT SEMMERING, TO THE EMPEROR
WILLIAM, *August 24th*, 1898

Cipher telegram. Extract.

. . . Your Majesty's conversation with Sir Frank Lascelles
was all the more opportune, since Balfour—who fears that if in
the future France makes a protest against the Portuguese agreement, we shall buy her off with a part of the Portuguese territory
assigned to us by England and so expose England to a forward
movement on the part of the French—expressed the wish that
Germany and England should engage that neither party to the
treaty should give to France any part of the territories which
come within its scope without the consent of the other. According

to Your Majesty's directions there need be no more objection
to such an assurance than against Declaration B.(1),[1] which was
reported by Count Hatzfeldt : ' Great Britain and Germany
agree jointly to oppose the intervention of any third Power in
the Provinces of Angola and Mozambique and in Timor,[2] whether
by way of loan to Portugal on the security of the revenues of
these Provinces or by way of acquisition of territory, by grant,
cession, purchase, lease, or otherwise.' . . . (The EMPEROR :
' *Agreed* ').

XIV. 359

BERNHARD VON BÜLOW TO COUNT HATZFELDT, *September 3rd,*
1898

Telegram.

The British Government's recent dealings with Portugal are
a proof of either stupidity or over-confidence.   I prefer to assume
the latter since the Anglo-Portuguese negociations were nearly
complete when the French and German protests brought them
temporary to a standstill. If Count Tattenbach reported
rightly, the consent of the leading Portuguese was already
secured for the mortgaging of the colonies. At any rate the
British haste in giving to the world the news of the agreement
with Germany is doubly disadvantageous ; first, the French
opposition will now make itself more felt than would have been
the case after the agreement between England and Germany, on
the one hand, and Portugal, on the other, had been formally
established ; also the German Government will have difficulty
in defending its action against attacks from its own Press, for
we believe that too much publicity will prejudice the conclusion
of the agreement with Portugal.   It would therefore be to the
greatest interest of Germany—and indeed of England—to end
the uncertainty of the position by a quick settlement with
Portugal.

I leave it to you how far you can exert influence in this direction.

[For the text of the Convention, the secret Convention, and the secret
Note, signed by Mr. Balfour and Count Hatzfeldt on August 30th, 1898,
see G. & T., I, p. 68.

It never came into operation, for the finances of Portugal showed signs
of improvement, and the German efforts to force a loan on the Portuguese
Government (cf. G. & T., I, p. 86, July 22nd, 1899) in the hope of gaining
control of the Portuguese Customs came to nothing.

Having failed to interest Russia in the South African problem (cf.
p. 35), Germany turned to France.]

[1] Cf. G. & T., I, 65.
[2] The Declaration did not mention Timor.

German Note.

In spite of Germany's appeals for ' speed and silence ', the facts of the agreement were made public in England, and its carrying out was thus postponed indefinitely. The so-called Windsor Agreement of 1899 between England and Portugal which was carefully kept secret from Germany and was hardly in consonance with the Anglo-German one of 1898, makes us ask whether those indiscretions and their results were intentional . . .

XIV. 360

BERNHARD VON BÜLOW, IN BERLIN, to PRINCE VON RADOLIN, IN ST. PETERSBURG, *September 2nd,* 1898

Very confidential.

The present world situation calls on us to be ready for all kinds of surprises. Besides the possibility dealt with in my telegram of August 30th, there is another which it is my duty to discuss with you.

German Note.

This telegram (XIII. 191) discussed the possibility that Count Muravieff might offer, as ' honest broker ', to try and arrange a rapprochement between Germany and France, which could only be obtained by giving up what had been gained in 1870–71. Prince Radolin was to forestall such a possibility by explaining that a Russian attempt on these lines ' might involve a swing towards the Anglo-Saxon group not only of popular feeling, but even of German policy'.

As you know, the future of South Africa repeatedly in January, 1896, and also this summer was discussed between the German and Russian Governments. You yourself reported on January 8th, 1896, that Prince Lobanoff had spoken of South Africa without interest and had even been rather inclined to excuse England's action against the Transvaal. This summer Count Muravieff spoke out even more clearly to Herr von Tschirschky, who was charged to sound him as to the attitude the St. Petersburg Cabinet thought of adopting towards England's notorious aspiration to use Portugal's financial need for the purpose of acquiring her colonies.[1] Count Muravieff's reply was that all that left him quite cold, as Russia luckily had no colonies in Africa.[2]

In its anxiety to be informed as precisely as possible as to future prospects, the German Government also enquired regarding French diplomacy. By the French it was made clear that France was interested in the future of South Africa, but at the same time an idea came to light, which was expressed by the French Ambassador as follows : ' At present French opinion forbids the

---

[1] Cf. G. & T., I, p. 76. Minute by Lord Salisbury. 'They (the Germans) are not content to wait for events to give them their share of Portuguese territory, but wish to force the pace of destiny . . .'
[2] Cf. p. 35.

French Government to *bind* itself in respect of any joint action with Germany ; between Germany and France it could therefore only be a matter of an accidental agreement—parallel action, so to speak."[1] This idea bears a certain family resemblance with Baron de Courcel's words to Lord Salisbury at the time of the Anglo-German conflict over the Transvaal [2] : ' France has only one enemy, that is Germany. England may shape her policy on that assumption.'

Seeing that the conclusion to be drawn from our enquiries in Russia and France was that we were isolated against England in protecting German interests in South Africa, the only course left was to reach an understanding direct with England on the South African question. With this in mind we negociated with England, and have now made an arrangement having as its subject the possibility of a loan to be granted to Portugal on suitable security, and excluding intervention by a third Power. We and England stand together to protect this arrangement.

Seeing that the Russian Government, through Prince Lobanoff and Count Muravieff, declared that South Africa was a matter of indifference, this Anglo-German private arrangement is naturally not aimed, even indirectly, against Russia.

Whenever Count Muravieff mentions the Anglo-German South African agreement to you, please speak to him confidentially in the sense of the foregoing.

[1] Cf. G. & T., I, p. 86.   [2] Cf. Vol. II, p. 402.

CHAPTER IV

SAMOA, AUGUST, 1898, TO NOVEMBER, 1899

[This chapter should be read in connection with Gooch and Temperley's *British Documents on the Origins of the War*, I, 108 et seq.

King Malietoa of Samoa died in August, 1898. Whereupon, England, Germany and the United States inaugurated a joint control. Mataafa, the exiled pretender to the throne, returned however and was supported by the majority of the Chiefs. The Chief Justice, Chambers, by virtue of the right assigned to him under the Convention signed in Berlin in 1889, rejected Mataafa and chose Malietoa Tanu, the late king's son. The leading Germans [1] in the Islands, Dr. Raffel, President of Apia Municipality, and Dr. Rose, the German Consul, favoured Mataafa, whilst the British and American officials supported Malietoa Tanu. War followed, in which Mataafa triumphed and appointed a provisional Government with himself and Dr. Raffel at its head. With the help of British and American warships the authority of the Supreme Court was upheld and the provisional Government overthrown (March 13th, 1899). Fighting continued nevertheless. On April 4th the three Powers agreed to send out a joint Commission of three members, which successfully restored tranquillity. Malietoa Tanu resigned, and the administration was placed in the hands of the Consuls.]

German Note. Extract.

. . . We can only enter here into the wide-spread and complicated negociations between the three Powers, which . . . were approached by Germany from the start with an intention of partitioning Samoa amongst the parties to the Samoa Treaty, so far as they concern questions of high politics and Germany's relations with England and America. The local Samoan question is ignored as far as possible.

Further details about the events in Samoa are to be found in the documents published by the German Government—the *Denkschrift* of 1900—and in the British Blue Book, *Further Correspondence respecting the Affairs of Samoa*. A good general account is given in A. Zimmermann's *Geschichte der Deutschen Kolonialpolitik*, pp. 296 et seq.

XIV. 567

BERNHARD VON BÜLOW, IN BERLIN, TO COUNT HATZFELDT, IN LONDON, *August 31st*, 1898

Telegram.

Malietoa's death, combined with the arrangements of the United States to construct a coaling station at Pago-Pago may

[1] G. & T., I, 110, 120; Dennis, *Adventures in American Diplomacy* p. 108 et seq; Brandenburg, p. 125 et seq.

cause fresh difficulties in Samoa. We consider that there is only one way to guard against these in good time and to obtain a tolerable solution of the Samoa question. This is to embark on a plan of partition, whereby America would receive the islands of Tutuila (with Pago-Pago) and Manua, Germany Upolu (with Saluafata) and Savaii, and England the Tonga Islands.

Please sound Mr. Balfour in confidence, to see whether England would be ready to join us in proposing the foregoing in Washington.

Very confidential. Haste is urgent, for Day, the Secretary of State, leaves Washington on the 16th, and nothing can be done about the question in the near future, owing to coming changes in the State Department and the probable absence of the President. Herr von Holleben [1] also goes on leave very soon.

XIV. 569

COUNT HATZFELDT, IN LONDON, TO THE GERMAN FOREIGN OFFICE, *September 1st*, 1898

Cipher telegram.

In confidential conversation with Mr. Balfour to-day, I referred to an article in the *Morning Post* and expressed my personal fear that Malietoa's death and the American arrangements regarding Pago-Pago might cause difficulties and react upon the Samoa question. I added that for years I had repeatedly pointed out to Lord Salisbury that the best solution would be to partition Samoa and the Tonga Islands between ourselves and England. To-day the position was somewhat altered by the fact that America had to be taken into consideration as a participant.

Mr. Balfour replied that he earnestly hoped that my fears regarding fresh troubles in Samoa would not be realised, and that he really did not see why this was bound to happen. The Berlin Convention regarding Samoa had laid down exactly the procedure for choosing a new king, and moreover the whole group of islands had been declared neutral ; which being so, the Americans could not be intending to fortify Pago-Pago. I objected that the establishment of a coaling station, pointing to an American intention of settling there permanently, might lead to protests, supposing the other participants wished to make themselves strong there likewise. Balfour answered emphatically that, in this event, England and Germany would clearly have a similar right to establish coaling stations if they wished.

My impression was that Balfour was apparently determined

---

[1] German Ambassador in Washington.

not to see the real point of my remarks, and so avoided discussing the question more in detail, because he is thinking of
starting his leave in two days' time, and is expecting to hear at
any moment from Lord Salisbury, who arrives at the Schlucht [1]
to-morrow, that he will resume control of the business himself.

German Note.

Count Hatzfeldt was empowered by telegram on September 1st, 1898,
to offer concessions to England in return for her agreeing to the German
Samoa proposal. ' If, by an extension of the Egito Line [Egito, on the
coast of Angola] so as to secure a connection between Central Angola and
British Central Africa, or, if that is not enough, by our renouncing our
ex-territorial rights at Zanzibar [2] in addition, agreement could be obtained
for our Samoa proposal, I should consider it to be a clear gain.'

XIV. 570

COUNT HATZFELDT, IN LONDON, TO THE GERMAN FOREIGN
OFFICE, *September 2nd*, 1898

Cipher telegram.

To-day I returned to the Samoan question and informed
Mr. Balfour that since the understanding arrived at regarding
South Africa, and now that the parties on either side had agreed
about the railways in China,[3] nothing now remained but to
settle the Samoan question, in order to produce a lasting favourable impression in both countries and to strengthen the friendly
rapprochement which we both hoped for. I myself thought
this so desirable, that I was ready to use my whole influence
to meet his wishes regarding the line extension and ex-territoriality, if the matter could be facilitated thereby. In the
event of an agreement to make a combined enquiry in Washington, our task there ought neither to be difficult nor unwelcome,
for instead of hoping for merely a coaling station, as she did
to-day, America would be receiving two islands as a possession.

This time Mr. Balfour listened to me attentively and did not
reject the idea from the start. He said that he would write to
Lord Salisbury about my suggestions at once. His own sole
objection was that it was not clear to him what benefit England
would gain by the concession of the Tonga Islands, and why the
British had not occupied them long ago if it was desirable to
possess them.

Unluckily it is doubtful whether Mr. Balfour does not go
on leave the day after to-morrow.

Count Hatzfeldt telegraphed to Lord Salisbury in the Vosges Moun-
tains through the Foreign Office, begging for a statement on the German
scheme of partition as early as possible.

---

[1] In Alsace, where Lord Salisbury occasionally went in summer.
[2] Cf. G. & T., I, 70.   [3] Cf. G. & T., I, pp. 27, 37.

XIV. 571

COUNT HATZFELDT, IN LONDON, TO THE GERMAN FOREIGN
OFFICE, *September 8th*, 1898

Cipher telegram.

Mr. Bertie informs me confidentially that Lord Salisbury's
reply to yesterday's enquiry is substantially as follows :

He does not think that anything can be done regarding
Samoa, since Australia would object to any alteration.

From this reply of Lord Salisbury's it is, as I expected, to
be presumed that nothing is to be done on either question,
and we must await further developments. I think there is no
hope of obtaining a statement through the medium of correspondence.

[Read Gooch and Temperley (G. & T.), I, 107.]

German Note.

Lord Salisbury's negative reply caused the Samoa negotiations to rest
for a while, until a suggestion coming from America re-opened the question.

XIV. 572

BARON VON HOLSTEIN, IN BERLIN, TO COUNT HATZFELDT,
January 20th [?], 1899

Telegram.

The Secretary of State is much pleased at the success of your
efforts as described in your private telegram.[1] It occurred
to me that the *Times* article, which has made a great impression
here, was inspired by you.

Now you must help with the Samoa muddle. The two
Germans, [Rose], the Consul and [Raffel] the President of Apia
Municipality, have put themselves in the wrong ; but the
American Chief Justice [Chambers] is equally in the wrong. We
admit the *German* mistake, and now the *American* Government
must do likewise about the American, and England ought to
help in this direction, as a go-between. Official instructions in
this sense follow by telegraph.

The humour of the situation is that the American Chief
Justice based his protest against the choice of Mataafa, which
choice was endorsed by the Consuls, on a declaration placed
on record by the *German* Secretary of State at the Conference
of 1889, to the effect that the German Government would
recognise any choice but that of Mataafa. Now only the
American missionaries continue to rage against him, because
he is a Roman Catholic.

It *may* be that in the present world situation, the British

[1] Not in the German Records.

Government would not desire to see tension arise between ourselves and America.

XIV. 575

BERNHARD VON BÜLOW, IN BERLIN, TO COUNT HATZFELDT,
January 22nd, 1899

Telegram.

The *Kölnische Zeitung* has received the following important telegram from its Washington correspondent :

' It can be stated on reliable authority that, in the course of the negociations to be conducted in Berlin on the revision of the Samoa Treaty, America will entirely renounce her joint protectorate [1] and will show a most friendly spirit to Germany. Confidential. This comes from the Secretary of State ' (John Hay).

I do not wish for a conference, as I consider negociations between Cabinets more fruitful in results ; but I am gratified to note the American willingness to meet our wishes, and hope that it means an intention to grant concessions elsewhere. This is not the first time that indications coming from America have held out hopes that, in spite of occasional gruffness, there is less objection there against German expansion in Samoa than exists in England. Now that America is in this mood, British mediation will be no longer necessary. I imagine that the final result will be that England will keep the island of Savaii, and that when satisfaction has been found for America elsewhere, we shall gain the islands of Upolu and Tutuila (excluding the American port of Pago-Pago). Therefore I do not want negociations between the three Powers, for I think that England would vent her dislike to acquisitions by Germany this time, as she did ten years ago, by pressing forward America's claims. Thus, it will be best for us to negociate with America direct without letting England know anything about it.

German Note.

A telegram from Holleben in Washington (February 14th, 1899) announced that Hay, the Secretary of State, had ' in no way rejected, but had not exactly agreed ' with the Ambassador's suggestion that Rose and Chambers should be recalled simultaneously.

XIV. 577

BERNHARD VON BÜLOW, IN BERLIN, TO HOLLEBEN, IN
WASHINGTON, *February 20th*, 1899

Telegram.

I concur entirely with Your Excellency's action. I have requested the American Ambassador here [2] to press for the early

---

[1] Cf. G. and T., I, 110, 115.   [2] Mr. Andrew Dickson White.

recall of Chambers, the Chief Justice, seeing that the statement
—published in Germany—of this official who is shared by all
three Governments, betrays that his aim is to drive Germany
out of Samoa ; which aim is incompatible with his duty. It
was also explained to Mr. White that we consider that the
removal of all three Consuls would conduce still further to
restore good relations between the officials in Samoa, as then
all the five appointments in question would be held by fresh men.
I will add for your confidential information that suitable steps
are being taken with the British Government regarding the
British Consul. Finally the plan for partitioning Samoa was
touched upon. Mr. White seemed to prefer handing over
Samoa in its entirety to Germany or England, but admitted
the difficulty of buying off the Powers which would be withdrawing from it.

For you personally. Count Hatzfeldt reported on the 8th
that Lord Salisbury was dealing with the partition question
very dilatorily, and had said it would be an improvement, if
the whole administration were entrusted to some individual to
be selected by the Powers, as in the case of Crete. Count
Hatzfeldt's reply was that this did not seem to him practical.

I beg Your Excellency to work for the recall of the Chief
Justice and all the Consuls and a final settlement of the Samoan
affair.

[For Lord Salisbury's opinion, see G. and T., I, 110–11.]

German Note.

Just at this time, in the process of finishing up the Fashoda incident,
there were negociations in progress between England and France for a
compromise over Central Africa [1] which led to the Agreement of May 21st,
1899. On the other hand, a friendly reception of German war-ships in
Algerian harbours at about the same period, gave rise to much talk of a
Franco-German rapprochement. A possibility of a closer understanding
between France and Germany was offered by the Egyptian question, in
which the matters of the Mixed Tribunals and the *Commission de la Dette*
were still unsettled between France and England. On February 3rd,
1899, a detailed despatch on the subject was sent to Count Hatzfeldt,
who was instructed that he might have to demand the largest possible
compensation from England in return for the renunciation of German
rights in Egypt ; these would naturally lose a great part of their value,
supposing a general understanding was reached between France and England. Shortly after this an attempt was made to enlighten England as
to the value of German support in Egyptian matters by a show of favour to
the Franco-Russian standpoint on the two questions mentioned above. [2]

[1] Cf. G. & T., I, 206.
[2] Cf. p. 59 ; also G. and T., I, 197 et seq.

XIV. 579

COUNT HATZFELDT, IN LONDON, TO THE GERMAN FOREIGN
OFFICE, *February 23rd*, 1899

Cipher telegram.

Private for Baron von Holstein.

To-day's conversation was about alliances in general. Lord
Salisbury thought the time for these was past, and that there
could only be rapprochements between States with common or
non-contradictory interests. I gave it as my opinion that we
lived now in a time when the question of groupings of Powers
played the principal part, and when, according to events, each
one of them might change its view as to the grouping which
would suit its interests best. Hence I thought that an Anglo-
French alliance was not out of the question, whilst many people
in France were thinking of an alliance with Germany. To this
Lord Salisbury remarked that he thought it more likely that
we should conclude one with Russia. I replied : ' The decision
of this question will not be in my hands, and I do not know
how it will turn out. But I personally can assure you of one
thing ; if England made an alliance with France, I should, if
asked, decidedly advise that we should come to a firm understanding with Russia the very next day '.

Believe me this is how things are here just now. Lord
Salisbury will do nothing for us, either in Samoa, Morocco,
Zanzibar or anywhere else, and it would be a good move to
inform him quietly and calmly that if this goes on, we might
secure our interests by other means to the injury of England.
I should be very pleased if they got the impression here that a
rapprochement between ourselves and France is not an impossi-
bility.

Lord Salisbury told me that the Queen had invited His
Majesty to Cowes in August. I should be glad to learn if this
is true.

XIV. 580

HOLSTEIN, IN BERLIN, TO COUNT HATZFELDT, *February 24th*, 1899

Telegram.

I shall lay your private telegram of to-day before the Secretary of State at once ; but I will say now that Franco-German
relations are being calmly and academically discussed in the
desired sense, and that the mere fact of their being discussed
at all is to be regarded as a step in advance.

I personally should like to ask you whether there could be
no way of making use of certain of Lord Salisbury's colleagues
to get him to attend to the questions that concern us, as was

done at the time of the Fashoda incident. I should think that Chamberlain must have realised by this time the increase of prestige, freedom of action and power which England gained through the relatively unimportant private agreement regarding South Africa (i.e., the Portuguese colonies). He is quite clever enough to recognise that yet more private agreements would bring yet more strength. This is no regular suggestion by me, but merely a private enquiry. You alone are in a position to judge whether a direct application to Chamberlain might not perhaps do more harm than good.

There is another matter which I would beg you to consider. It is known that Cecil Rhodes wishes to come to Berlin. Is he a man with whom one could discuss questions of compensation on a largish scale—I mean, is his influence strong enough in England to carry points upon which he is keen, even against the *vis inertiae* of Lord Salisbury? Would he be listened to in London even on questions affecting Morocco? Could he be induced to consider giving up Zanzibar in return for railway and other concessions? Could his influence make itself felt in dealing with the Samoan question? He does not come for a fortnight, so you will have time to examine this question.

German Note.

Sir [*sic*] Cecil Rhodes, Chairman of the Chartered Company, who was in England at the beginning of 1899, in order to push his great scheme for a Cape to Cairo railway,[1] was naturally anxious to get into touch with the German Government in regard to carrying the line eventually through the territory of German East Africa. General von Liebert, the Governor of German East Africa, representing Germany was particularly in favour of coming in with Rhodes' plans. The Emperor William minuted a report by Count von Alvensleben, German Minister in Brussels (February 5th, 1899), on a visit paid by Cecil Rhodes to the King of the Belgians, as follows : ' Governor-General Liebert urges it (an exchange of notes with Cecil Rhodes on his railway scheme) in the interest of our colonies, and has begged me to get Rhodes to come here, if possible. We ought to give him facilities for his railway with the proviso that, if he promises to appoint only Germans as attendants and officials in our territory, to use German material, and to build a branch line to Tabora, we will allow him to construct his line on our land.'

Cecil Rhodes did come to Berlin on March 10th and was received on the 11th by the Emperor. Both the Emperor and Count von Bülow showed keenness to meet Rhodes' wishes, but they tried also to interest him in an agreement with England on the Samoa question. During Rhodes' visit to Berlin nothing was settled about carrying the trans-African North-South railway through German East Africa ; this was announced in the Reichstag on March 21st by Bülow. But an agreement was reached on the subject of laying the African Transcontinental Company's cable in German territory. Rhodes boasted later on of the friendly reception he had had in Berlin, and on returning to London, he took pains to further

---

[1] Cf. Sir L. Michell, *Life of Cecil J. Rhodes*, II, 248 et seq.

Germany's wishes regarding Samoa. Baron von Eckardstein's further account of the telegraph negociations is incorrect. It was Turkey and not the ' fears, short-sightedness and lack of instinct for practical politics in Berlin which wrecked the clever scheme '[1] of extending the telegraph line through Asia Minor to Constantinople and linking it up there with the German telegraph system, which was still in its infancy.

[The Agreement signed in Berlin, between Germany and the British South Africa Company contained the following provisions :
I. In the event of the Company constructing a line across its western boundary or through Bechuanaland at any point south of 14° S. latitude, such crossing of the boundary shall only take place at a point of the British-German boundary S. of the degree of latitude agreed upon ; so that the continuation of the Company's railway system to the West African coast, S. of the 14°, shall always pass through German territory.
II. Germany is bound to link up the rails, in default of which, the Company to have the right to build on German territory to the coast.
III. The B.S.A. Company not to connect with the coast N. of the 14th degree S. latitude before the other connection is carried out.
IV & V. Provisions for a transit duty.
(Michell, *Life of Cecil J. Rhodes*, II,251.)]

XIV. 582

COUNT HATZFELDT, IN LONDON, TO THE GERMAN FOREIGN OFFICE, *February 24th*, 1899

Cipher telegram.

Private for Baron von Holstein.

In reply to your telegram. I will say at once that I do not at all wish for a real understanding with France against England, but merely to produce an impression in Paris, and more particularly here, that it might come to pass, if they continue to ignore our interests in colonial matters.

I have already discussed the question how, if at all, pressure can be brought to bear on Lord Salisbury. Mr. Chamberlain is still ill, and to do business with him direct behind Lord Salisbury's back would be much open to objection. I shall perhaps send [Baron Alfred] Rothschild to him first ; I spoke to him about the situation yesterday, and he proposes that I should hand him a short memorandum on the questions at issue (Samoa, Morocco), which he could give to Mr. Balfour. There are objections even to this, supposing Mr. Balfour is not absolutely discreet in dealing with Lord Salisbury. I doubt greatly also if he could attempt to influence foreign questions, or do so successfully. My feeling is that Lord Salisbury is quite determined to enter into no special arrangements with us at present. In the Fashoda question he was constrained less by his colleagues than by public opinion, which demanded a firm stand. In questions that affect us, public opinion, knowing

[1] *Ten Years at the Court of St. James*, p. 234.

nothing about them, refuses to take a hand at all and as regards Zanzibar it would probably speak out against giving it up in any form.

I am glad that Sir [*sic*] Cecil Rhodes is to be received in Berlin, for I think good relations with him very desirable. He would understand a policy of large compensation, if concessions concerning railways etc. were to be granted to him. But I doubt whether he would try to intervene here in questions not directly involving Cape Colony or the [railway] connection with North Africa. And we ought not to overestimate his influence here, for since the Jameson Raid it has diminished considerably. In such questions Mr. Chamberlain will perhaps listen to him up to a certain point, but Lord Salisbury certainly will not. As regards Zanzibar, my opinion, as you know, is that they will never give it up voluntarily here. Hence I consider that our only chance of England's giving it up to us would be if she became so hard pressed as to be obliged to buy our friendship at any price.

XIV. 583

BERNHARD VON BÜLOW, IN BERLIN, TO COUNT HATZFELDT, *March 16th*, 1899

Telegram. Secret.

Have discussed the Samoan affair with Cecil Rhodes.[1] He has promised to use all his influence in London, and especially with Salisbury and Chamberlain, so that the British Government may agree to partition Samoa as we propose, Germany receiving Upolu, England Savaii, and America Tutuila.

I hope that you also will be able to assist Mr. Rhodes' efforts.

XIV. 583

COUNT HATZFELDT, IN LONDON, TO THE CHANCELLOR, PRINCE VON HOHENLOHE, *March 9th*, 1899

Dr. Solf (Dr. Raffel's successor as municipal President of Apia) has been in touch here with important personages, and his impression from their utterances is that the situation in Samoa is taken more seriously in England than he had expected, and that any later difficulties may perhaps originate here rather than in America. Mr. Chamberlain explained to him that Australia would hardly consent to territorial acquisitions by foreign Powers. Sir Donald MacKenzie Wallace said the same. Mr. Chamberlain also considered that the acquisitions in the

---

[1] Cf. Sir L. Michell, *Life of Cecil J. Rhodes*, II, 249 ; also G. & T., I, 118.

South Seas would not be worth the troubles they would cause. Mr. Villiers, head of the Department for Samoa in the Foreign Office, in his conversations with Dr. Solf, definitely—if only ' candidly and quite unofficially ' [1]—took the part of Messrs. Chambers and Maxse against Herren Raffel and Rose. Dr. Solf described to me a few details of this conversation :—Mr. Villiers considers a change in the Samoa Act to be essential, on account of the lack of precision in its provisions, and also because the Condominium has been proved to be wholly unsatisfactory. In principle he thought the best solution would be to partition the islands ; in practice, however, the scheme would be wrecked, because England would be unable to give up her right to Upolu in return for worthless Savaii. Besides the ' strong colonial feeling ' [1] of the British, there would have to be considered the political feelings of New Zealand. Moreover, a change in the President's functions would, ' as it has been suggested ',[1] be desirable, since this seemed inevitably to lead the occupants of this part to ' arrogate functions, as Herr Raffel appeared to have done '.[1] Mr. Villiers further touched on the possibility of using Samoa as a subject for compensation and of altering in some way the Anglo-German line of demarcation in the South Seas, and he pointed to the line on the map drawn North-east from German New Guinea to the Marshall Islands.

Dr. Solf was careful to listen to all observations and to maintain reserve, saying that he wished to enter upon his new office unprejudiced, as far as possible.

German Note.

The Final Act of Samoa, 1889, stated that unanimity between the three treaty Powers was necessary in selecting the Chief Justice, but that his removal could be obtained by a majority vote. Changes in the Act could only be effected by agreement between the three Powers. Certain decisions of the Consular Court required unanimity but about ordinary cases nothing was laid down. In the draft of a note from Count Hatzfeldt to Sanderson (sent April 4th, 1899) which discusses the question of unanimity versus majority in detail, the German point of view is argued, not on the grounds of the text of the Samoa Act, but of the fact that when the Commission appointed for the purpose fixed the conditions under which land was held, the principle of decision by unanimity was followed almost without exception.

XIV. 181.

German Note.

The memorandum [from which the following portion is extracted] was prepared for Prince Henry of Prussia, who was appointed on March 2nd, 1899, to command the German squadron in the Far East (cf. G. & T., I, p. 34). It was designed to inform him on the general political situation. . . .

---

[1] English in text.

XIV. 185

MEMORANDUM BY BERNHARD VON BÜLOW, *March 14th*, 1899
Extract.

. . . By a treaty which is not to be laid before the Spanish
Cortes for ratification for some months and must reamin *absolutely secret* until then, the Spanish Government has handed to
us the Caroline, Pellew, and Marianne Islands (without Guam)
in return for the sum of 16 million marks and certain trade
concessions. We shall thus become neighbours of the Americans
who possess the Philippines, though only nominally for the
present, and we have very great interest, therefore, in maintaining good relations with that sensitive nation which is so
difficult to deal with. The value of the American market for
our industry is immense. An aggressive Press put American
public opinion in a hostile mood against us, which was constantly nourished by existing business differences, lying reports
about our attitude in the Spanish-American War,[1] and finally
by recent events in Samoa. A conflict with the great North
American republic, whose self-confidence has been greatly
increased by the successes against Spain, would be very unwelcome to us just now. His Majesty's Government therefore
earnestly desires to settle the business differences between
Germany and the United States in a friendly manner and to
clear up the Samoa affair, at least for some time to come, for
this stands in the way of our understanding.

The ships of His Majesty's cruiser squadron are the subject
of special resentment in the United States. It is therefore of
the greatest importance to us that His Majesty's fleet should
with careful tact, but naturally preserving its dignity to the
full, aim at avoiding any conflict with the American navy and
authorities. Also for the sake of our coming occupation of the
Caroline Islands we must be assured against disturbance by the
Americans. So we must avoid any appearance of supporting
the rebellious Tagals, and especially of any intention of extending
our influence over the Philippines.

With regard to the above, the question of good relations
with the British fleet and authorities becomes of considerably
higher importance, on account of the undoubted rapprochement
which has taken place between England and the United States,
even if it has not yet reached the stage of a binding alliance.
Every disturbance of our relations with these two States would
be succeeded unfailingly by a rapprochement between them,
in spite of any differences, such as those which arose lately over
the Nicaragua Canal question and the Canadian question.

[1] Cf. Vol. II., Chapter XXXII.

XIV. 585

COUNT HATZFELDT, IN LONDON, TO THE GERMAN FOREIGN
OFFICE, *March 25th*, 1899

Cipher telegram. Extract.

In conversation with Mr. Chamberlain at the house of a
third party . . . I said that I now concluded that the American
Admiral in Samoa had been instructed to carry out majority
decisions, i.e. decisions on which the British and American
Consuls were agreed.   We should be obliged to appeal strongly
against this in Washington with a reference to the clear provisions of the Samoa Act.   I did not know what had since
happened in Samoa.   But I fully realised that we could make
no successful resistance there, if England and America meant
to join together in using force.   I also realised that in this case
it would be quite useless for me to continue my former efforts
for an Anglo-German rapprochement, and that, even if it desired
it, my Government, when faced with the inevitable irritation
of our public opinion, would be unable to continue its hitherto
friendly attitude towards England.   Under these circumstances,
I had heard with pleasure that Sir J. Pauncefote had suggested
a means of reaching a solution honourable for all parties.[1]   In
accordance with this we had formulated a proposal in Washington,
and my one earnest hope was that England would definitely
support us in this.

Mr. Chamberlain said in reply that Anglo-American relations
were just now excellent, but that England also wished to be on
the best terms with us.   There was no distrust of us here regarding Samoa, and I should have gathered from utterances in the
British Press on the subject that public opinion here was not
thinking of making us responsible for a few indiscretions of our
representatives in Samoa.   Regarding the latter he begged
leave, in the interests of the case, to speak quite frankly.   From
all he had observed, our Consul had entirely ignored the decisions
of our Government, which was correctly taking its stand on the
Samoa Act.   He had refused to agree with his colleagues at all,
and even to join with them in guaranteeing the Chief Justice's
safety, or in letting the German flag be hoisted alongside of the
British and American flags ; this had caused a crisis which it
would need special measures to relieve.

As regarded the question of partition, Mr. Chamberlain said
quite frankly that he had opposed Lord Salisbury, when the
latter asked for his opinion.   New Zealand and Australia were
almost independent states with which England was closely

[1] Cf. G. & T., I, 111 ; also *Life of Lord Pauncefote.*

allied, and whose views *must* be attended to here.   They would never accept a solution of the Samoa question which did not give Upolu, with Apia, to England.   A partition on these lines, therefore, could be accepted here.   If we would give up partition and hand the entire Samoa group to England, we should naturally be entitled to compensation ;   the Gilbert Islands, which had good harbours, would be regarded here as suitable for the purpose. As far as he knew, our interests were on the decrease at Apia, so that we had no reason for setting special store on the possession of Upolu.

I replied that this assumption was unfounded.[1]   The outstanding interests in Upolu were, on the contrary, ours, and I did not think we could give it up.   The only thing remaining was to find a solution, whereby the future efficiency of the Samoa Act might be assured, and difficulties be avoided between the three Powers ; for this object Sir J. Pauncefote's idea seemed particularly suited.   Mr. Chamberlain replied that he wished to express no definite opinion, but that he was inclined to think that if nothing else turned up, an understanding might be found on these lines. . . .

XIV. 588

BARON VON RICHTHOFEN, GERMAN FOREIGN OFFICE,
TO HOLLEBEN, IN WASHINGTON, *March 29th*, 1899

Telegram.   Extract.

The American Embassy here handed us on the 26th a memorandum about Samoa, which appears to agree with the telegram shown to you by the Secretary of State.   It is to the effect that the American Government is ready to respect not only the rights, but also the wishes of the German Government and has instructed the American representatives in Samoa by telegraph to do nothing against the Samoa Act.   Only under most pressing circumstances might a majority of the Consuls be forced to take measures in the interests of peace and order ;   such action would be purely provisional and be submitted to the three Powers for ratification.   The American Government recognises that unanimity of the three Powers is necessary for the settlement of the questions still undecided. . . .

German Note.

The American Ships before Upolu fired on the country behind Apia from March 15th to 17th continuously, during which the German Consulate received damage.[2] . . .

---

[1] Cf. G. & T., I, 110.   Cf. G. & T., I, 112–14.

XIV. 590

BERNHARD VON BÜLOW, AT KLEIN FLOTTBECK, TO THE GERMAN
FOREIGN OFFICE, *April 1st*, 1899

Cipher telegram. Extract.

For His Majesty.

In my humble opinion, the declaration given yesterday by
the American Government, that President MacKinley deplores
the latest events in Samoa and accepts our proposals to send
three Commissioners to settle the questions under dispute there,
is particularly satisfactory, since England continues to employ
her dilatory tactics regarding our suggestions.   I cannot escape
the impression that in the recent events in Samoa, it was
England who drove and America who was driven.   (The
EMPEROR :   ' *Unconsciously.*') It looks as if the British meant
to use the Americans to push us out of Samoa.   If a clash
occurred between Germany and America, England would, from
the standpoint of her commercial and colonial interests, be
delighted, as the *tertius gaudens*.   We must therefore—and also
because we possess less means for bringing diplomatic pressure
on America than on England—handle America more cautiously
than England.   (The EMPEROR :   ' *I recommended this to Richthofen also.*')   I have made it quite clear in all my instructions
to Count Hatzfeldt that Your Majesty would not be able to
continue the friendly attitude which you have shown to England
since last summer in all parts of the world and in all questions,
because of the disappointment and excitement in German public
opinion occasioned by the British attitude in Samoa,—unless
the British Government definitely and quickly showed us more
consideration in the Samoa question.   (The EMPEROR :   ' *We
cannot count on that any more.*')

I would respectfully suggest to Your Majesty to demand
from England an unambiguous declaration that she will not
make fresh arrangements in Samoa except with Germany's
consent ;   (The EMPEROR :   ' *Good.   Agreed.*') and to say that
for Your Majesty's Government the legal *status quo* in Samoa
is the situation created, as far as we know, by the latest unanimous decision of the Consuls of January 4th, until it shall be
decided unanimously to make some alteration, either by the
three Powers or by their representatives present or future.
(The EMPEROR : ' *Yes.*')   A few forcible changes, which have
been introduced in the meanwhile, cannot prejudice the decisions.
If England breaks her treaty concluded with Germany, Your
Majesty could not reply to such an act, directly illegal and
openly contemptuous, (The EMPEROR :   ' *Bravo !* ') by declaring
war, but you would withdraw your representative from England,

since business under international law would be pointless, where treaties concluded under that law are not observed. At the same time, this declaration of ours might be secretly communicated to Cecil Rhodes. (The EMPEROR : ' *Yes.*') When acknowledging the consent of the Washington Cabinet to our Commission proposal, we should inform it that we have no doubt that Germany and America will finally agree upon a legally correct settlement of the treaty obligations, since we know that for America the present crisis is not a mere pretext in order to seize upon Samoa. (The EMPEROR : ' *Good.*')

What has happened in Samoa is a fresh proof that an overseas policy can only be carried on with a sufficiently powerful navy. (The EMPEROR : ' *What I have been preaching for* 10 *years to those thick heads (Ochsen) in the Reichstag.*') The duty of the moment appears to me to be to state all this emphatically in our Press, and also to maintain our prestige in the world intact, despite all our present difficulties.

XIV. 597

COUNT HATZFELDT TO THE GERMAN FOREIGN OFFICE, *April 3rd*, 1899

Cipher telegram.

The Under-Secretary informs me in confidence that by Lord Salisbury's orders, Sir Frank Lascelles was informed yesterday evening by telegram that Lord Salisbury was ready to appoint a Commissioner [1] for Samoa—probably a diplomat—with unrestricted powers to agree with the two others on all measures requiring the consent of the other two Powers. He is to report on the causes of the present unrest in Samoa and his views as to the best means of avoiding them in future, but he is not to share in any joint report by the three Commissioners on the question.

This shows that Lord Salisbury has so far given in as to consent to abide by the joint decision of the three delegates on questions still unsettled without making them dependent on a majority. [2]

XIV. 598

BERNHARD VON BÜLOW, IN BERLIN, TO COUNT HATZFELDT, *April 5th*, 1899

Telegram.

. . . If the British Government add, in their verbal note, that each of the three Commissioners shall report separately to his own Government, I insist on my original contention—that

[1] Sir Charles N. E. Eliot, K.C.M.G. (See Preface to Vol. II.)
[2] Cf. G. & T., I, p. 115.

the Imperial Government considers it essential that the *decision* shall be arrived at unanimously, as provided by treaty, but that their methods in deliberation need in no way raise insuperable obstacles.

The British Government have declared that ' an impression exists both in Samoa and England that Germany has been attempting to force America and England out of Samoa, and such a supposition would alone seem to explain the unjustifiable action and extravagant language of the German Consul-General.' [1]

We, on our side, have never concealed from the British Government that we regarded Consul Maxse's attitude towards the President of the Municipality in the question of the correspondence between the Consuls and the Samoan Government to be unfriendly and contrary to the practice hitherto of conducting this correspondence not direct, but through the President. Similar representations regarding Mr. Maxse's tendency to start fresh disputes have been made by us to the British Government on other occasions. When we observed the increasing nervousness of Dr. Raffel, the official under the treaty, we did not fail to propose his being sent on leave and later on his dismissal. Finally in January we declared frankly that we considered that all the representatives in Samoa had acted wrongly, and Lord Salisbury had admitted this with the remark that mistakes had been made by all parties.

Our view of the object of diplomatic representation is that one Government should call the other's attention to dark points, likely to make relations more difficult, immediately they appear, and without waiting for a crisis to arise. The task of such representation is to forestall crises by calm and timely discussion. In all countries it has at times happened that a Consular official has misinterpreted the limits of his rights and duties, and it never can be prevented altogether. But the more conspicuous his behaviour is, the more clear is it that the foreign Government which thinks that its rights have been injured or threatened by the action of the official, should mention the matter in good time through diplomatic channels, and, as I said, before a crisis arises. We genuinely regret that the Government of Her Britannic Majesty did not think fit to take this course nearest to hand, by complaining of Consul-General Rose diplomatically at the proper moment. The suspicion which is now directed towards various quarters would never have existed.

I have stated the foregoing to the British Ambassador in reply to his note.

I beg you to speak in the same sense on all suitable opportunities.

[1] Cf. G. & T., I, p. 115; also Sir Charles Eliot's report G. & T., I, 120.

XIV. 600

BERNHARD VON BÜLOW, IN BERLIN, TO COUNT HATZFELDT,
April 10th, 1899

Telegram.

To-day the Russian Ambassador, Count von der Osten
Sacken, communicated to me the thanks of his Government for
the support given by the German Government for the views of
France and Russia in the question of the Egyptian Mixed
Tribunals.[1] England had given way, and this showed that
co-operation by the three Powers on other points also might
be of assistance. In our further discussion, which the Ambassador based on detailed instructions of quite recent date, he
pointed out that it would be opportune for the three Powers to
join mutually in guarding and furthering their respective interests
in Asia, e.g. in the Persian Gulf. In order to make this idea
more attractive to me, the Ambassador referred to the present
Anglo-Russian negociations on the one hand, and on the other
to the violent and arbitrary action of the British in Samoa.

The conversation was interrupted by my being summoned
to attend the Emperor, but it will probably be resumed shortly.

I leave it to your discretion to judge whether to suggest in
the right quarter in England, perhaps through Rothschild, the
idea that events in Samoa have caused the Russian Government
to suggest tentatively three-Power co-operation with France.

It shows that the St. Petersburg Cabinet does not expect
the Anglo-Russian negotiations, now in progress, to remove
the antagonism between Russia and England.

XIV. 601

COUNT HATZFELDT, IN LONDON, TO THE GERMAN FOREIGN
OFFICE, *April 10th*, 1899

Cipher telegram.

Lord Salisbury had just telegraphed in answer to the Foreign
Office that he cannot accept our proposals without substantial
modifications ; he cannot telegraph these without risk of misunderstanding.

XIV. 605

BERNHARD VON BÜLOW, IN BERLIN, TO COUNT HATZFELDT,
April 13th, 1899

Telegram.

Lord Salisbury's draft for the Commission Agreement, which,
in my opinion, expresses unconditional acceptance of the principle of unanimity, runs as follows :

[1] Cf. note, p. 47.

' In view of the troubles which have recently taken place in Samoa and for the purpose of restoring tranquillity and order therein, the three Powers, Parties to the Conference of Berlin, have appointed a Commission to undertake the provisional government of the islands.

' For this purpose they shall exercise supreme authority in the islands. Every other person or persons exercising authority therein whether acting under the provisions of the Final Act of Berlin or otherwise shall obey their orders ; and the three other Powers shall instruct their Consular and Naval officers to render similar obedience. No action taken by the Commissioners in pursuance of the above authority shall be valid unless it is acceded to by all three Commissioners. It will fall within the attribution of the Commissioners to consider the provisions which they may think necessary for the future government of the islands or for the modification of the Final Act of Berlin and to report to their Governments the conclusions to which they may come.'

Unless Your Excellency finds objection, I consider that we should at once declare our agreement in the form suggested by you,[1] and announce the appointment, approved by His Majesty, of Baron Speck von Sternburg [2] as our Commissioner, adding that the Commission will be sailing from San Francisco on the 19th, if that is possible. . . .

XIV. 609

COUNT HATZFELDT, IN LONDON, TO THE CHANCELLOR, PRINCE VON HOHENLOHE, *April* 15th, 1899

Baron von Eckardstein, Councillor of Legation, has just described to me a conversation which he had with Mr. Cecil Rhodes.

Both because time is short before the Messenger leaves, and also in consideration of Mr. Rhodes' characteristic methods of thought and expression, Your Highness may kindly allow me to report his words in *English*, as they were communicated to me by Baron Eckardstein.

About Samoa Mr. Cecil Rhodes spoke as follows :

' A few weeks ago when I returned from Berlin where I had a most kind and courteous reception by the Emperor, the Foreign Office and official world, which has given me a great encouragement in my great African scheme, I set at once to

---

[1] Count Hatzfeldt had written : ' If Germany and America agree with his draft, Lord Salisbury wishes that the agreement of the three Powers be confirmed by an exchange of notes.'

[2] First Secretary at the German Embassy in Washington.

work to induce the English Government to help Germany in
settling the Samoan difficulties in a friendly way and in accordance with the Samoa Act of 1889. The Emperor himself had
asked me to do so, and I used all my influence on the Cabinet,
the Foreign Office and the Press. I saw Lord Salisbury a day
or two before he went south, and after having had a long chat
with him about Samoa, I left him with the impression that
everything would be settled in a satisfactory way all round.
The news about the fighting in Samoa which reached us a week
afterwards was therefore quite unexpected by me, and I could
hardly understand it, because I thought after my interview
with Lord Salisbury that he had given strict instructions to the
English authorities in Samoa to abstain from any rash act.
(The EMPEROR : ' *It never occurred to him !* ')   I myself consider
the English and American action in Samoa absolutely illegal
and unfriendly to Germany. (The EMPEROR : ' *Bravo !* ')   It
is impossible for me to understand how the policy of the Foreign
Office can be so shortsighted as to offend German susceptibilities
and pride for three little islands in the Pacific, whilst English
policy is trying to come to a perfect and friendly understanding
with Germany in Africa. (The EMPEROR : ' *Yes! but not
Salisbury !* ')

' I authorise you to make use of my opinion, as stated to
you, as much as you like,—if you think fit, even to the Press
of Germany.

' What I stated above I stated to everyone I have seen in
London, and all my friends are of the same opinion.'

Later in the conversation Mr. Rhodes heartily deplored his
inability to take further steps with the Foreign Office in the
Samoan affair. He would have to wait for Lord Salisbury's
return. (The EMPEROR : ' *Very good. As I commanded before,
Rhodes with his schemes must be entirely kept apart from Samoa!
I shall certainly help him in this !* ') [1]

XIV. 611

COUNT HATZFELDT TO BARON VON HOLSTEIN, IN BERLIN,
April 22nd, 1899

Cipher telegram.

I see no sign at present that a policy of animosity is intended
here. Unless anything special happens in Samoa, it is not to
be presumed that public opinion here will become heated about
it. . . . [2]

---

[1] Cf. G. & T., I, 118.
[2] For the excited state of German opinion, cf. G. & T., 119, 126.

XIV. 612

COUNT HATZFELDT TO BARON VON HOLSTEIN, *April 22nd*, 1899

Extract.

. . . I must take this opportunity of destroying an illusion which our Press, at any rate, appears to cherish. It seems to be thought in Berlin that in the Samoa question Chamberlain is more favourable to us than Salisbury. (The EMPEROR : '*I never believed that.*') I can now most decidedly tell you that Chamberlain much more than Salisbury was against granting us unanimity for the Commission. Moreover, Eckardstein, whom I saw yesterday, tells me that he found his whole attitude and speech greatly changed in Germany's disfavour, compared with what it had been. Chamberlain made remarks like the following : 'Last year we offered you everything, and you refused ; now it is *too late* '.—You see that we cannot hope for much from this so-called friend.

[The first part of the following despatch concerns a suggestion made by the Russian Ambassador, Count von Osten Sacken, to conclude a Russo-German agreement regarding the East.]

XIV. 613

BERNHARD VON BÜLOW, IN BERLIN, TO COUNT HATZFELDT,
May 6th, 1899

Extract.

. . . I now come to Mr. Chamberlain's most recent utterances. If I have rightly understood the information which has come to me privately, he has uttered contradictory views on Anglo-German relations in quick succession. First he said it was too late for an Anglo-German alliance—which was never at any time offered directly or indirectly. A few days later he appears to have thought otherwise and to have spoken in a more accommodating spirit.

At present the main thing for Germany is not to bind herself and to wait quietly and see whether England's attitude makes our former benevolent neutrality still possible. This question is not yet decided but is still in doubt, for Mr. Chamberlain's words about 'trifling questions not worth twopence to either of us' are two-edged and might be used by us also. For England the Samoa question means much less than for Germany, and so far as I, as a party concerned, can allow myself an objective opinion, I am more and more convinced that it would be a good and profitable policy for England to be more accommodating to the German people in this very question. For England, who possesses the Fiji Islands near by with its good harbours, Samoa means very little, whilst from the start the name Samoa has meant for Germany the birth of our colonial aspirations. Instead of compliance England has shown us harsh and open hostility. I am ready to assume that this is not the fault of Mr. Chamberlain, and that events in Samoa were not in the sense of his directions. We can form our own opinion on this, if it becomes clear in the course of the Commission's deliberations what attitude the British delegate adopts, especially the question of compensation, and generally, whether his efforts are for an understanding or for wrecking the negotiations. . . .

Finally I assure you that the resumption of direct relationship with Mr. Chamberlain has greatly pleased me. Owing to his brilliant cleverness he is more susceptible to arguments appealing to reason than many another British statesman, and that you should continue to meet him in any way that you consider suitable and free from objection will entirely meet my wishes.

XIV. 615
BERNHARD VON BÜLOW, IN BERLIN, TO COUNT HATZFELDT,
May 16th, 1899
Secret.

Yesterday Mr. Holls,[1] a German-American, and a close friend of President McKinley, who is on his way to the Hague Peace Conference, came to see me. He told me in strict confidence that the American Ambassador in London, Mr. Joseph H. Choate, had given a dinner for him, at which the British Ministers (with the exception of Lord Salisbury) and certain Opposition leaders had been present. He, Holls, had made no secret of his opinion that he could not imagine what advantage England expected to gain by her abrupt treatment of Germany in a matter so unimportant as the Samoa question.

Mr. Balfour had replied, using the French expression, '*A qui le dites vous ?*', and had added that he, Balfour, had been of opinion from the start that England ought to renounce her claims to Samoa in Germany's favour. The other Ministers, including Mr. Chamberlain, had objected to this view on the grounds that Australia would not stand complete renunciation of England's rights in Samoa. The American Ambassador in London, who well knew how unsound this objection was, had answered : ' In the end you will be obliged to declare yourselves independent of your colonies, just as your greatest colony, America, declared itself independent of you.'

[A misunderstanding concerning the Emperor's reply to the Queen's invitation to him to visit Cowes in July gave rise to a long letter addressed by him to the Queen, in which he complained of Lord Salisbury's discourteous treatment of Germany's claims and protests regarding Samoa.

---

[1] Cf. p. 80.

XIV. 617

THE EMPEROR WILLIAM TO QUEEN VICTORIA, *May 22nd*, 1899

Extract.

. . . Lord Salisbury has treated Germany in the Samoan question in a way which is entirely at variance with the manners which regulate the relations between Great Powers according to European rules of civility. He not only left my Government for months without an answer to our proposals, dating from autumn last year, but he even refrained from expressing his or the Government's regrets after the first acts of violence by Commander Sturdee and the other ships had occurred at Samoa. A fact the more unintelligible, as the President of the United States of America immediately sent word to say how sorry he was that such acts had happened on the part of American officers and men. The British ships went on for weeks bombarding so-called ' positions ' of so-called ' rebels '—though no one knows against whom they rebelled—and burning plantations and houses belonging to German subjects, without even so much as an excuse being made, and that on an island which by three fourth is in German hands.

This way of treating Germany's feelings and interests has come upon the people like an electric shock ; . . . the feeling has arisen that Germany is being despised by his [Lord Salisbury's] Government, and this has stung my subjects to the quick. . . . A pleasure trip to Cowes after all that has happened, and with respect to the temperature of public opinion here, is utterly impossible now. . . .

XIV. 620

QUEEN VICTORIA, AT BALMORAL, TO THE EMPEROR WILLIAM, *June 12th*, 1899

DEAR WILLIAM,

I thank you for your letters which Uncle Arthur sent me. With regard to Coburg I think and hope everything is easily to be settled to the satisfaction of the Family and the Duchess.

Your other letter, I must say, has greatly astonished me. The tone in which you write about Lord Salisbury I can only attribute to a temporary irritation on your part, as I do not think you would otherwise have written in such a manner. And I doubt whether any Sovereign ever wrote in such terms to another Sovereign, and that Sovereign his own Grand Mother, about her Prime Minister. I never should do such a thing, and I never personally attacked or complained of Prince Bismarck, though I knew well what a bitter enemy he was to England, and all the harm he did.

I naturally at once communicated your complaints against him to Lord Salisbury, and I now enclose a Memorandum which he has written for my information, which entirely refutes the accusations and which will show you that you are under a misapprehension.

Your visit to *Osborne, not* to *Cowes* I looked upon as a visit for my *birthday*, as I was not able to receive you on the day itself. —I can only repeat that if you are able to come, I shall be happy to receive you at the end of July or in August.

I can have you and two of your sons as well as two gentlemen in at Osborne and you could leave the rest of your suite on board your Yacht.

Believe me always
Your very affectionate
Grand Mama
V.R.I.

XIV. 619

COUNT HATZFELDT, IN LONDON, TO THE CHANCELLOR, PRINCE VON HOHENLOHE, *May 25th*, 1899

Cipher.

Mr. Holls' statements concerning random utterances by British statesmen, the correctness of which I do not doubt, do not give a true picture of the situation here with regard to Samoa, about which I think I possess exact information.

In a general sense it is true that several British Ministers, including Mr. Chamberlain and Mr. Balfour, continue to regard good relations with Germany as desirable, as far as seems possible without giving up any real British interests. This is why they deplored the complications with us in Samoa ; but they do not go so far as to consider England to blame for them or to be able to have acted in any way differently. Rather are they convinced that the trouble was solely to be ascribed to Herr Rose's action, which in the matter of choosing a king was contrary to the clear provisions of the Samoa Act and evidently aimed at driving the British out of Samoa. They are completely influenced by the conviction, which I combat at every opportunity, that Australia would have consented neither to England's withdrawal at this time nor to her peacefully ceding her rights in Samoa to us, and that if the British Government did not take care, it would be involved in very great unpleasantness with that colony. However incomprehensible it may seem that it is not understood here that a political change of direction by Germany in favour of

England's rivals would mean a much greater disadvantage, we can only recognise the fact that this knowledge has not yet sunk in here, and even the German Press manifestations have so far made no difference. Every day I come across the imperfectly concealed assumption only to be explained by the incredible ignorance of German conditions to be found even in prominent British Ministers, that in Germany there is no public opinion at all in the British sense where foreign affairs are concerned, that the attitude of our Press on that subject depends, therefore, on inspiration by the Imperial Government, and that the latter, which does not particularly wish for an actual break with England, has complete power to make any policy that it favours, even in the Samoa question, acceptable to our public opinion. Even those British Ministers who are favourably disposed towards us, first and foremost Mr. Chamberlain, start with the conviction that there are now no further grounds for sensitiveness or fresh disagreement, now that England has made the great concession renouncing the majority principle for the decisions of the Samoa Commission, and that the admittedly unpleasant but really trifling incident in Samoa cannot stand in the way of further good relations between England and Germany. . . .

XIV. 621   *Enclosure.*

Memorandum by Lord Salisbury.

Referring to the German Emperor's remark that the German Government was left for months without an answer to its proposals, dating from last autumn, Lord Salisbury is unable to imagine to what proposal the Emperor refers. He has been through the papers and can find none that was left without an answer. . . .

Lord Salisbury says that the reason why the British Government did not apologise on the occasion [of the naval bombardment] was that they had done nothing to German subjects or property for which an apology could be due. The Americans, he states, did fire into the German Consulate. It was an accident and they very properly expressed their regret for it. But British fire struck no German property and no German subject. . . .

[In Samoa] everything His Imperial Majesty asked for has been, in effect, done . . .

In everything therefore Lord Salisbury considers the German Emperor has had his way, and it is quite unintelligible to him on what grounds the Emperor can maintain that British action with regard to Samoa has been in any sense unfriendly to the German Government.

XIV. 623

COUNT VON BÜLOW, AT SEMMERING, TO THE GERMAN FOREIGN
OFFICE, *July 13th,* 1899

Cipher telegram. Extract.

For His Majesty. Count Hatzfeldt telegraphs that Lord
Salisbury informed him that he would be delighted to be able,
when Your Majesty visited England, ' to remove by personal
discussion the misunderstandings which had unfortunately arisen,
since nothing was further from his wishes than to initiate a policy
hostile to Your Majesty's legitimate interests.'

In this declaration I see a fresh success for Your Majesty. . . .

At the same time Lord Salisbury not only consented to the
dismissal of Chambers, the Chief Justice, but also agreed that the
difficult question of indemnities for damage done in Samoa
should be referred to the King of Sweden for arbitration [1] (in
accordance with Art. III, section 2, of the Samoa Act) . . .

XIV. 627

COUNT VON BÜLOW, IN BERLIN, TO COUNT HATZFELDT,
August 29th, 1899

Telegram. Extract.

It appears to be an absolute necessity that the Samoa affair
should be finally settled in a form which the Imperial Government can accept, before His Majesty's contemplated autumn visit
to England. It will also be of importance to the British Government just now, in consideration of the critical situation in South
Africa, to clear up finally this dispute which continues to lie
between us. . .

[The Emperor's visit to the Queen took place in November. It was
welcomed in England as a sign that Germany had no intention of showing
active hostility in the matter of the Transvaal.

For Lord Salisbury's views on the difficulties attending arbitration and
his suggestions for solving those difficulties, see his despatch of September
15th, 1899 (G. & T., I, p. 120). At its conclusion he wrote : ' By several
expressions he (Count Hatzfeldt) dropped, I gathered that his great earnest-
ness upon this question arises, not from the intrinsic value of the islands,
or even from the vehemence of German opinion on the subject, but that
it is a question on which the Emperor himself has fixed his heart, and is
pursuing his own solution with his well-known inflexible tenacity.']

COUNT HATZFELDT, IN LONDON, TO THE GERMAN FOREIGN
OFFICE, *September 13th,* 1899

Cipher telegram. Extract.

. . . Lord Salisbury said that in settling the affairs of Samoa,
there were still other difficulties to consider, for instance, the

---

[1] Cf. G. & T., I, p. 120.

religious question and that of freedom of trade for the British. The religious question was extraordinarily important, for the religious societies, so powerful here, would never forgive him if he neglected it. . . .

German Note.

Baron Eckardstein (*Ten Years at the Court of St. James's*, p. 107) states that early in September, 1899, he was requested by Count Hatzfeldt to go to Berlin and explain the seriousness of the matter in the Wilhelmstrasse, that at the consultations in Berlin he had advocated that Germany should give up her third share of rights in Samoa in return for concessions elsewhere, and that on his return to London he had begun his negociations with Chamberlain on this basis.

XIV. 637

COUNT HATZFELDT, IN LONDON, TO THE GERMAN FOREIGN OFFICE,
September 20th, 1899

Cipher telegram.   Extract.

At to-day's meeting between Mr. Chamberlain and Baron von Eckardstein the Samoan question was discussed. I had previously provided the latter with detailed information and instructions.

Baron von Eckardstein explained to the Minister in clear terms the feeling reigning in Germany, and indicated that if England did not finally show more accommodation in this matter and consider my very moderate proposals, a change in Germany's foreign policy was inevitable, since the German Government, which had hitherto always shown itself loyal to England and tried to maintain friendly relations, would be driven in another direction by public opinion. He then enquired whether it was understood here what this would mean for England.

This exposition seemed to affect Mr. Chamberlain unpleasantly ; his calmness fell from him for the moment, and he complained bitterly that Germany wanted to make capital out of England's embarrassments in South Africa.[1] Baron von Eckardstein sharply rejected this insinuation, describing it as ridiculous, since my proposals had been made weeks before when war with the Transvaal was considered totally improbable.

When Chamberlain had considered a little and was become calmer again, he said that he recognised that good relations with Germany were more worth having than these islands in the Pacific ; but public opinion in Australia and New Zealand was making it very hard for the British Government to accept a proposal of arbitration. Nevertheless he would use every possible effort to produce a satisfactory solution of the Samoan question. . . .

[1] Cf. p. 38.

XV. 395

COUNT VON BÜLOW, AT SEMMERING, TO THE GERMAN FOREIGN OFFICE, *September 21st*, 1899

Telegram. Extract.

. . . In view of the ever increasing pressure of the Transvaal crisis, we must not let it appear as though we desire to exploit for ourselves the difficulties of the British, whether actual or presumed. As a matter of fact, however, we should be blamed for lack of diplomatic skill, if we did not now obtain a satisfactory settlement of several of the questions outstanding between ourselves and England—especially that of Samoa ! . . .

XIV. 640

COUNT VON BÜLOW, AT SEMMERING, TO THE GERMAN FOREIGN OFFICE, *September 22nd*, 1899

Cipher telegram.

It would only be possible to justify the renunciation of Upolu in the eyes of German public opinion, if we really receive full value in compensation. Otherwise giving up Upolu would produce bitterness in Germany, which would make impossible with the best will in the world that co-operation with England which the German Government has genuinely aimed at.

We cannot deny with sufficient emphasis the stupid assumption that we are making use of the Transvaal crisis to wring concessions in Samoa from England; we should point out that months before matters in South Africa came to a crisis, Germany indicated in London that for her a reasonably acceptable settlement of the Samoan question was the preliminary condition for really friendly relations between ourselves and England. Count Hatzfeldt will be able to gauge the advisability of using the argument that His Majesty's visit to England, if indeed it can come off, will not be fruitful in good results, unless the Samoan question is settled beforehand. If only in consideration of the Transvaal, the British must now desire this visit.

It is very important to keep the negociations secret until further notice, and that the result, when it comes, shall be published not by England, as in the case of the Anglo-German Agreement of two years ago, but by us, and in a manner suitable for our public opinion.

[On the same day (September 22nd) Lord Salisbury accepted ' the proposal to determine by the arbitration of the King of Sweden and Norway the question between the two Powers as to the possession of the Islands of Upolu and Savaii . . .' Cf. G. & T., I, p. 124.]

XIV. 643

COUNT VON BÜLOW, AT SEMMERING, TO THE GERMAN FOREIGN OFFICE, *September 25th*, 1899

Cipher telegram.

If hopes of peace revived amongst the British, they would make concessions to us neither in Samoa, nor on the Volta, nor anywhere else. Considering the risk of war which threatens England in South Africa, and also with regard to the Emperor's visit to England which the British desire, and the feeling in America just now, the present moment is particularly favourable to us. Therefore I consider that we must hesitate no longer in providing Count Hatzfeldt with the instructions he asks for. We must strike while the iron is hot. . . .

I think that we should combine Lord Salisbury's [1] and Chamberlain's proposals somewhat in the following form :

The King of Sweden . . . will decide to whom Upolu and, on the other hand, Savaii, Savage Island and Tonga are to belong. England promises the Arbitrator that if Germany receives Savaii and Tonga, she will hand the Gilbert Islands over to us. It would be very desirable to get the Togo question settled in our favour at this opportunity. But this should be effected in a separate agreement depending on the completion of the South Seas agreement, and in a form by which Germany receives the Volta delta and Yendi in the neutral zone, giving up to England the neutral zone and her exterritorial rights in Zanzibar. . . .

XIV. 646

COUNT HATZFELDT TO THE GERMAN FOREIGN OFFICE, *September 29th*, 1899

Cipher telegram. Extract.

Lord Salisbury's words to-day gave me the decided impression that Chamberlain [2] has already spoken to him, that the Prime Minister either does not yet agree with him, or wishes to stand out obstinately for more advantageous conditions . . .

He asked what I thought of these, and I mentioned, as my *personal* opinion, the following points :

1. Adherence to [the King of Sweden's] arbitration.

2. For us Savaii with Savage Island, Tonga and Gilbert Islands, and other small island groups in their neighbourhood.[3]

3. By a separate but dependent treaty, exchange of the

---

[1] G. & T., I, p. 124.

[2] Mr. Chamberlain had talked to Eckardstein on September 28th. Cf. *Ten Years at the Court of St. James*, p. 110 ; also G. & T., I, p. 125.

[3] Union, Ellice and Phœnix Islands.

Volta delta for the Neutral zone (I should probably refer again to Yendi later on). The Minister replied that this was far too much, for the delta was immeasurably more valuable than the neutral zone. He could not give up the Tonga Islands. On my remarking that I had always offered him Savaii with Savage *and* Tonga Islands, and that this must be worth the same to us, he returned persistently to the great value of the Volta delta and demanded of me an exact valuation of the small island groups, which I was claiming as well as the Gilbert Islands. He then asked what the position was with regard to his suggestion that Germany should renounce her exterritorial rights at Zanzibar. When I described this renunciation as very difficult for us, Lord Salisbury appeared much displeased and said that he was informed that our treaty with Zanzibar, on which our exterritorial rights were founded, was very soon to come to an end.

It was finally agreed at my suggestion that I should at once ascertain from Berlin under what conditions, if at all, the German Government would consent to give up Upolu. As soon as I know this, I must request him to discuss it again. I thought fit to consent to this, as it gives me time for a further understanding with Chamberlain.

A remark of Lord Salisbury's about buying out the German interests in Upolu is a proof that he and Chamberlain have met to-day. Recently he had refused this definitely, whereas to-day, in agreement with Chamberlain's statement of yesterday [to Eckardstein], he said that it might be considered, if we would undertake a similar engagement with regard to British interests in the Volta delta.

XIV. 648

Count Hatzfeldt to the German Foreign Office,
September 30th, 1899

Cipher telegram.   Extract.

. . . It is remarkable that to-day in confidential conversation with Baron von Eckardstein, Mr. Chamberlain said that the British Government well knew that our attitude towards England was absolutely correct, but the public in general did not know it ; on the contrary it was generally assumed that the feeling and attitude in Germany were unfriendly. Mr. Chamberlain also suggested the possibility and opportuneness of a public proof of our sympathy with England in this crisis, which would enlighten and reassure public opinion as to our attitude . . .

[This was that the German representative in Pretoria should undertake the task of protecting British interests there in the event of war with the Transvaal. Cf. pp. 69, 103.]

XIV. 650

COUNT VON BÜLOW, AT SEMMERING, TO THE GERMAN FOREIGN
OFFICE, *October 2nd*, 1899

Cipher telegram. Extract.

. . . Our attitude towards the South African crisis is strictly
neutral and absolutely loyal. Compared with that of the French
and Russians, it might be described as being remarkably friendly
to England. After the troubles in Samoa this spring, it was
extraordinarily difficult for the Imperial Government to adopt
such an attitude. We cannot overstep this line until the Samoa
question is settled in a manner acceptable to our public opinion.[1]
Any German Government which was ready for such a renunciation without tangible and sufficient compensation by England
would be tolerated neither by German public opinion nor by His
Majesty. We cannot play *le dindon de la farce.*

XIV. 656

COUNT HATZFELDT TO THE GERMAN FOREIGN OFFICE, *October 9th,*
1899

Cipher telegram. Extract.

In to-day's conversation with Chamberlain Baron von Eckardstein described our point of view in the Samoan question according to my instructions.[2] Chamberlain replied that he personally
fully understood our position, but must describe our demands
as too high, since England was giving a very valuable district,
the Volta delta, which was her property, whilst Germany could
offer nothing which actually belonged to her. He, Chamberlain,
wished most earnestly to arrive at an agreement with Germany,
but Germany must offer something which was her property, in
order to receive concessions of equal value. He then proposed
that Germany should give up to England her share of New
Guinea, as well as Upolu and the Tonga Islands, and receive
Savaii and the Gilbert and Ellice Islands. Baron von Eckardstein laughed at this and replied in joke that he, on the contrary,
had meant to demand British New Guinea as compensation for
Germany. Chamberlain then answered that it would be best
to look for a fresh basis and begged Eckardstein to make another
proposal. . .

[1] Cf. pp. 103–4.
[2] Cf. Eckardstein, *Ten Years at the Court of St. James,* p. 111.

XIV. 660

ADMIRAL VON TIRPITZ, SECRETARY OF STATE TO THE ADMIRALTY,
TO COUNT VON BÜLOW, *October 11th,* 1899

Extract. Secret.

. . . The possession of the Samoan Islands would even now be of great strategic value to the German navy, as an important stopping place on the voyage from Kiao-chau, via our possessions in the South Seas, to South America. A time will come when German control of the Samoan Islands will be still more important, since the Panama Canal will mean new routes for the world's trade, and new strategic military routes will result from it. An extension of the rights to a coaling station, which we now enjoy in the Tonga Islands (Vavau), by the cession to Germany of this island or another of the same group, would—although not quite without value—not constitute an equivalent. The already numerous and important German interests in Samoa (in comparison with Tonga) would be of inestimable assistance in the eventual conversion of a harbour in these islands into a highly valuable base.

I must not fail also to point out the extraordinarily favourable situation of Samoa as a landing place and a station for a German world-cable (South America—Samoa—New Guinea—East Africa—West Africa), which we shall have to aim at in future. . . .

[For the texts of the Convention and Declaration between England and Germany (London, November 14th, 1899) and the Convention between England, Germany and the United States (Washington, December 2nd, 1899) see *Br. & For. State Papers*, XCI, pp. 75–81. For the King of Sweden's decision (October 14th, 1902), see *B.F.S.P.*, XCII, pp. 794 and 1063.]

CHAPTER V

THE FIRST HAGUE PEACE CONFERENCE, 1899

German Note. XV. 141.

On August 24th, 1898, the Emperor Nicholas sent out his famous Peace Manifesto. (See *Staatsarchiv*, LXIV, 107 et seq.)

It greatly surprised the German Government and was in sharp contrast with Russia's attitude up to that time and with the continuous massing of troops on the German eastern frontier during the Tsar's reign . . . The frequent assertion that even early in the nineties the Emperor William thought of inviting a European Conference for peace and disarmament (cf. W. T. Stead, *La Chronique de la Conférence de la Haye*, 1899, p. 31) cannot be proved by reference to the Records. (Cf. G. & T., I, p. 215 ; *Life of Lord Pauncefote*, p. 226 ; Brandenburg, p. 129 et seq.)

XV. 149

BERNHARD VON BÜLOW TO THE EMPEROR WILLIAM,
August 28th, 1898

I lay before Your Majesty a memorandum on the statement last evening by Lord Gough, the British Chargé d'Affaires, when he heard of the Russian disarmament proposal and of the accompanying report by the British Ambassador in St. Petersburg.

It appears that the British (The EMPEROR : ' *They must have laughed hugely !* ') are anxious to avoid (The EMPEROR : ' *How naïve.*') hurting the Emperor Nicholas' feelings by a direct refusal, but that they already perceive the point chiefly interesting to England—the awkwardness of comparing land-forces with sea-forces for compensation purposes.

Regarding the question of disarmament, Prince Radolin adds that ' the Tsar hopes that the German Emperor regards with benevolent consideration (The EMPEROR : ' *Yes, but not with observance* ') the idea described in the Russian Memorandum— that of restricting excessive armaments and thus working for peace.' (The EMPEROR : ' *But it is there ! We have had 28 years of peace !—I shall consider even more closely the intended expenditure of 90 million roubles on 8 new first-class battle-ships and 6 first-class cruisers ! These are not included in the disarmament proposals !—The whole lucubration seems to me to come from Russia's grim necessity of escaping from her financial mess . . .*')

74

XV. 182

COUNT MÜNSTER, IN PARIS, TO THE GERMAN FOREIGN OFFICE, *April 4th*, 1899

Cipher telegram. Very confidential.

M. de Staal [1] wrote to me that he understood I was appointed to the Hague Conference, that he was delighted at this and was coming to Paris to talk it over with me. He arrived here yesterday.

He admits the difficulty of the task, but hopes it may be possible to get round the armament question and suggest a few alterations in International Law and the Statute of the Red Cross. We ought not to separate without some result. I agree with him in general.

Sir J. Pauncefote [2] will represent England. We both know him well and could wish for no better British representative. M. de Staal thinks the Conference will last 6 weeks ; he means to take a villa in the Hague or at Scheveningen and advises me to do the same.

German Note.

His selection by the British Government as its representative at the Hague is explained by the fact that he had already successfully conducted negociations with America for an Anglo-American Arbitration treaty and for the settlement of the Venezuela dispute by arbitration. Vice-Admiral John Fisher accompanied him as Naval Delegate, whose sovereign contempt for all arbitration and the like was displayed even at the Hague.

German Note. XV. 183

The American delegates took on the whole a progressive view of the peace question ; they had Captain A. F. Mahan [3] attached to them as Naval Delegate. [He died just at the outbreak of the Great War.] In *Armaments and Arbitration* (1912) he laid down ' that neither arbitration in a general sense nor arbitration in the more specific form of judicial decision based on a code of law, can always take the place, either practically or beneficially, of the processes and results obtained by the free play of natural forces. Of these forces national efficiency is the chief element, and armament, being the representative of national strength, is the exponent '. White, the Ambassador, in his *Autobiography* (II, 347), said of Mahan : ' He has had very little, if any, sympathy with the main purposes of the Conference, and has not hesitated to express his disbelief in some of the measures which we were specially instructed to press.'

XV. 219

COUNT HATZFELDT TO THE CHANCELLOR, PRINCE VON HOHEN-LOHE, *May 25th*, 1899

The British Government inform me in a note (copy enclosed) of May 19th that on the point of increased protection for private

---

[1] Russian Ambassador in London. He was Russian representative at the Conference and became its President.
[2] British Ambassador in Washington.   [3] G. & T., I, p. 231.

property in a naval war they see no reason at present to adopt any attitude, since the United States Government are not yet in agreement with them on the point.

They have received a resolution from the Chamber of Shipping of the United Kingdom in support of a Memorandum addressed by the New York Chamber of Commerce to the President of the United States on the subject.

According to reports from the British Ambassador in Washington, the Resolutions in question have been laid before the Senate and the House of Representatives, but no decisions have yet been taken.

On May 25th, 1899, Sir Julian Pauncefote surprised the Conference with his proposal to set up a permanent Court of Arbitration. Both Count Münster and Admiral Fisher spoke against it to Mr. Andrew White, basing their objections on similar grounds, namely that the German army and British navy were ' in a state of complete preparation for war, and that the truce afforded by arbitration proceedings would give other Powers time, which they would otherwise not have, to put themselves into complete readiness '.[1] (Cf. Mr. White's *Autobiography*, II, p. 263.) It was hinted that this was Russia's own motive in calling the Conference (p. 265). (Cf. G. & T., I, p. 227.)

XV. 222

COUNT MÜNSTER, FIRST GERMAN DELEGATE AT THE HAGUE, TO THE CHANCELLOR, *June 12th*, 1899

Mr. Andrew D. White, the American Ambassador and First Delegate, has just been with me. He said that the American Delegation was instructed to introduce a discussion on protection [inviolability] of private property at sea, and asked me what attitude my Government would adopt. It was above all things important to disarm the opposition of those who, under cover of the Russian Circular, wished to prevent a discussion. He considers that in a debate on a permanent Court of Arbitration, about which there is nothing in the Russian proposals, and by so creating a precedent, there might be a majority in the Assembly in favour of permitting the discussion. Even if—and Mr. White recognised this—no result came of it for the moment, as long as England and France entirely rejected it, it would be desirable to raise the question out of consideration for public opinion ; I might be sure that in the whole world of commerce the question of protection for private property at sea is much more important and must, in the end, be more popular than one of a permanent Court of Arbitration.

[1] This was also Mr. Goschen's opinion. (Cf. p. 80.)

I beg for immediate telegraphic instructions whether I am to support the Americans and vote for discussion on this question.

Up to now I have followed your despatch of May 27th and maintained an attitude of reserve.

Regarding this decided wish of the Americans, the point now is whether we mean to cling firmly to the already badly riddled Russian programme or to allow a discussion, and whether we are willing to go into this important question later.

As regards the other Powers, Sir Julian Pauncefote seems personally to go further than his Government, and even if public opinion in England favours protection for property at sea more than before, Lord Salisbury and the present Government are not prepared to consider an alteration.

The French are the most vehement opponents, and the Russians have promised to support them, although their Delegates here seem to hold a different opinion. All the other Powers, particularly the smaller ones, are in its favour. A discussion at the Conference cannot therefore lead to any practical result, but it may decidedly influence public opinion, and this counts for a great deal, as we saw in the Court of Arbitration question.

The negociations are dragging on because the Chairmanship lacks energy ; long speeches are made in the Committees, so I fear we may be here till the middle of July. Finally we shall have to say : ' Much ado about nothing '.

XV. 279

BERNHARD VON BÜLOW TO COUNT HATZFELDT, *June 14th,* 1899

Telegram. Extract.

. . . We should have serious objections to a permanent Court of Arbitration of this kind especially since the wish has been expressed in the discussion that the permanent Court should have the right of initiating proposals to summon a Court after hostilities between States had broken out, and that a permanent Commission of five members should be chosen, all ready to arbitrate. Even if these ideas are not pursued at once, it is in the nature of things that they will reappear again as soon as the Pauncefote proposal becomes a reality.

We think it questionable whether there would be sufficient security for independence and impartiality in a Court so formed.

Please enquire of Lord Salisbury whether Sir Julian's proposal comes from the British Government, and if not, what is the latter's attitude towards it.

XV. 279

Count Hatzfeldt, in London, to the German Foreign Office, *June 14th*, 1899

Cipher telegram.

Your telegram received.

Lord Salisbury replied that Sir J. Pauncefote's proposal was decided on when he was last here, and corresponded in essentials with a project for arbitration which had been discussed between England and America several years before. He could only explain our objections to it by some misunderstanding regarding the importance and extent of its operation. The idea here was that the permanent Court should only be entrusted with disputes of minor importance, particularly in cases dealing with claims for money compensation, and not with decisions on more important and political questions. An appeal to it was not to be obligatory, but optional. Nor was it intended here to give the Court the right of initiative or of mediation. Lord Salisbury added that he hoped this would clear up the misunderstanding. He considered it absolutely out of the question that the Court of Arbitration, as proposed by Sir J. Pauncefote, would ever be called upon to intervene in great political questions, such as Egypt or Alsace.

[On June 28th, 1899, the German Naval Delegate reported that Vice-Admiral Sir John Fisher had given him his views on the question of private property at sea, emphasising the fact that they were his own personal views, and not necessarily shared by his Government.]

XV. 226

Report by Captain Siegel, German Naval Delegate, *June 28th*, 1899

. . . Sir John Fisher believed that next to England, Germany was most interested in this question, as her merchant marine was the second largest in the world and was continually increasing. It was essential, therefore, that the two countries should be agreed about this matter. . . .

Even if property was to be held generally inviolate, contraband goods still naturally remained liable to seizure.

The decision of what was contraband depended on the strength of the belligerent, and indirectly almost anything could be declared contraband. Thus it was quite possible—and no international convention, however clear and binding, could prevent it—that the ship itself could be declared contraband ; so that one might consider the cargo and goods inviolable, and yet hold the ships which carried the goods to be contraband, on the pretext that they might be used as auxiliary cruisers, colliers, munition ships, or in any capacity however far-fetched to help in carrying on the war.

After careful study, the British Admiralty had laid it down that the war fleet was strong enough to protect the whole of the merchant shipping. As things were now therefore, shipowners, being convinced that their ships were efficiently protected by the war fleet, would calmly go on trading and have no interest in changing their flag.

But if private property were declared inviolable at sea, the natural consequence would be that the former protection would be considered more or less superfluous. Timid shipowners and shippers ('and such are proverbially timid,' said the Admiral) would certainly believe that this protection was to all intents taken away . . .

[The result would be that] the trade of a belligerent would certainly be transferred to a foreign flag, and history taught that in this event it hardly ever returned. . . .

There is still another point which we [in Germany] must consider :—If private property at sea were declared inviolable, voices would at once be heard in the land demanding a diminution of naval war material, particularly of cruisers, since the protection of trade would cease to be one of the fleet's duties ; it would be said that in future only battle-ships would be needed.

The growth of this feeling in the country must under all circumstances be combated, for it would be the greatest mistake to diminish the cruiser fleet. It is by these alone that England is able to maintain her character as the strongest Power all over the world, and holds the position she requires. . . .

America has very good reasons for proposing that private property at sea shall be inviolable.

The trade between England and America is enormous, and the Americans would like to get into their hands at a good opportunity not only this part of England's overseas trade, but also all the rest. They think this proposal offers them a good handle ; for if England was at war with another Power, probably a part of the Anglo-American trade would adopt the American flag and stay under it. . . .

I would mention as a curious fact that when a few days ago Professor Zorn and Mr. Holls [1] went to Berlin on the business of the Arbitration question, the Admiral told me it was thought at the Hague that we had made an agreement with the Americans, that they were to support us on the question of the Court of Arbitration, and we should help them in the matter of protection for private property. I did not fail to deny this suspicion with energy.

[1] Cf. p. 65.

I noticed also that the Admiral attaches no importance to the present trend of British public opinion in favour of close connection with North America and thinks their artificial friendship cannot be permanent, as there are so many points on which their interests clash.

He said characteristically that he had been summoned as a Delegate, because his requirements and his views on naval warfare were known. He had been brought from the West Indies before the termination of his command, and he had forewarned the Admiralty that he knew of only one principle : Might is right.

He had informed Mr. Goschen [1] quite clearly as to his personal opinions, when he received his new appointment, and had left him free to choose another Admiral to command the Mediterranean squadron if his views were not agreed with. . . .

German Note. XV. 298
Frederick W. Holls, the Secretary of the American Delegation, a German-American, who went with Professor Zorn to Berlin on June 17th—the mission, according to Mr. White, was arranged between Holls and Count Münster (*Autobiography*, II, p. 308)—made known to the Chancellor his wish, strongly supported by Mr. White, to be received by the Emperor. Although the Emperor was willing, this meeting did not come to pass. Even Bülow, the Foreign Secretary, to whom Holls was to deliver a detailed memorandum from White, does not seem to have seen him in spite of White's statement to the contrary (White, II, pp. 309, 317–18). But Bülow promoted a conference between the ' very influential and correct thinker politically ', Mr. Holls, and Holstein, Hellwig and other advisers in the Foreign Office, which took place on the 19th.

[Mr. Holls said that Germany's remaining out of the business of the Court of Arbitration did away with its usefulness. On another occasion he said this would not prevent the matter coming to pass, since four Great Powers (England, America, Russia and France) were for it, and it would be a great pity if Germany, and perhaps the other Triple Alliance Powers, kept aloof (XV. 299). It was very largely owing to the efforts of the American Delegation that an agreement was finally arrived at. (Cf. p. 63.)]

XV. 304

BERNHARD VON BÜLOW TO THE EMPEROR WILLIAM, *June 21st,*
1899

Extract.

Your Majesty will allow me to summarise the result that I have achieved, when all is said and done. The Arbitration Court idea is in itself utterly distasteful. Your Majesty's firm and decided attitude has nevertheless succeeded in inducing the other States to discard all the objectionable aspects of that idea. If the plan, as now arranged, ever becomes awkward, it will be

---

[1] First Lord of the Admiralty. ' A determined opponent of the proposal '.

felt by other States (The EMPEROR : ' *England above all.*') far more keenly than by Germany.   If we reject the whole idea of the Court, we shall risk again losing the fruits of Your Majesty's far-seeing policy, especially in regard to Russia (The EMPEROR : ' *It should not matter to me !   But what about these childish dreams !   What will it come to as time goes on ? '*) and the United States of America.   But if we join with the other States, I am convinced, if I may speak in all humility, that it will make a fresh leaning of the Americans towards England difficult, and the United States will rather turn towards us.   (The EMPEROR : ' *I hope so.*')   The Triple Alliance remains unshaken, and above all, Your Majesty's relations towards the Emperor Nicholas acquire a new strength, (The EMPEROR : ' *I think it more than questionable ! '*) which will not please them on the Thames and give them much to think about . . .

XV. 345

COUNT MÜNSTER, AT THE HAGUE, TO THE CHANCELLOR, PRINCE VON HOHENLOHE, *July 30th*, 1899

The Conference at last ended yesterday in a solemn meeting.

As regards disarmament and all that may diminish war strength, the badly drafted and undefended Russian proposals have been rejected.

The Brussels Convention is somewhat modified.

The Geneva Convention stipulations are to apply to naval warfare as well.

As for arbitration, a very complicated organisation has been adopted.   A net full of large holes,[1] but one in which one can get entangled nevertheless.   From the beginning the German delegation has insisted that anything implying an engagement to submit to the Court of Arbitration must be cut out, and appeal to the Court must be strictly optional.

A number of declarations have been adopted, which may be harmful.   I do not like the suggestion of further Conferences ; nor that the Conferences should be perennial, like many a weed.

Therefore I have signed neither the Convention nor the Resolutions.   (The EMPEROR : ' *Correct.*') . . .

[1] Cf. Brandenburg, p. 131.

CHAPTER VI

THE BOER WAR, 1899. PRELIMINARY CORRESPONDENCE

German Note.

From the beginning of 1899 onwards, relations between England and the Transvaal Government once again became worse. In addition to the unsatisfactory negociations about the Republic's claim for indemnity for the Jameson Raid at the end of 1895, there were also points of difference in the question of continuing the dynamite monopoly,[1] but above all, in the British Uitlanders' complaints at the withholding of political rights. On March 21st, 1899, Mr. Chamberlain, the Colonial Minister, had, in contradistinction to Lord Salisbury, from the beginning favoured an active policy with regard to the Transvaal. In a House of Commons speech he uttered bitter complaints, almost amounting to threats, against the Government of the Boer Republic. In reply to Chamberlain's speech of March 24th, President Kruger actually suggested that the Uitlanders' grievances, when viewed aright, were, at bottom, merely a pretext. ' They wanted the country to be given to England ' [English in text]. President Kruger was, as a matter of fact, not altogether unaware of the necessity of concessions in the Uitlander question. From the start the German and Dutch Governments had urged the Transvaal Government to make such concessions as were possible in this direction.

[It will be found useful to refer to the ' *Times* ' *History of the Boer War*. Vol. I. ; Worsfold, *Lord Milner's Work in South Africa*, and Sir L. Michell's *Life of Cecil J. Rhodes*, Vol. II. ' President Kruger . . . was determined not merely to set himself against all measures of reform, but to increase the disabilities under which the Uitlanders had hitherto lived.'— Worsfold, p. 103.]

XV. 367

BERNHARD VON BÜLOW, IN BERLIN, TO THE EMPEROR WILLIAM, AT URVILLE, *May 10th*, 1899

Cipher telegram.

In view of recent expressions of opinion in the British papers concerning the Transvaal, I telegraphed to Your Majesty's Ambassador in London, the head of our Consulate at Cape Town and Your Majesty's Consul at Pretoria to report by telegraph on the present state of relations between England and the Transvaal. The Ambassador in London answers :

[1] Cf. ' *Times* ' *History of the Boer War*, I, 235–275.

' The information that I have collected contains no certain symptom of any *immediate* intention on Mr. Chamberlain's part of taking action against the Transvaal. Nor do I think that, considering the present political situation in Europe, Lord Salisbury would desire it. In the opinion, moreover, of our Military Attaché (Baron von Lüttwitz), who is making a report, the British have at present not anything like sufficient military forces in South Africa to attack the Transvaal with a prospect of success, and they do not appear so far to be preparing to reinforce them. Under these circumstances, I am inclined to believe the information that Mr. Chamberlain is addressing a strongly worded note to the Transvaal Government, but wishes to send it by post so as to avoid any appearance of an ultimatum.[1] I learn that capitalists here meanwhile wish to persuade President Kruger to return a conciliatory reply and give way, and that they hope to succeed. On this and on the measure of the concessions to be granted to the Uitlanders I think that the further development of affairs will depend here. If the concessions are really insufficient, we must be prepared to see Chamberlain exploit the situation, both for exciting public opinion here and for forcing the Government to intervene in a way which may lead to a conflict. Moreover, it seems not impossible that in the event of success, England might seek to gain further advantages direct or indirect, —perhaps in connection with Delagoa Bay—which would affect our interests and be at variance with the spirit of the Anglo-German agreement.[2] If the conflict is really in sight (The EMPEROR : ' *Not until it has actually broken out.*') it might perhaps be advisable for us to approach the British Government in a suitable form with regard to due respect for our interests, as secured by treaty.'

Your Majesty's Consul at Cape Town telegraphs : ' The great tension which has existed between England and the Transvaal for several weeks is due to Chamberlain, Sir [*sic*] C. Rhodes and the jingoes, who by provocation and threats of war, are trying to induce the Transvaal Government to give way entirely on the Uitlanders question during the present session of the Volksraad.

' There is no immediate danger of war, since every reason for war is lacking. But it is clear that at bottom Mr. Chamberlain desires war with the Transvaal and is trying to lead them into some step which will give an excuse for it. The Governor, who moreover is a tool of Chamberlain's, and the Ministers here are employing their influence in England and the Transvaal

---

[1] For Mr. Chamberlain's note of May 10th, see British Blue-book (C. 9345), No. 83.
[2] Cf. Chapter III.

to prevent war, which would spread over the whole of South Africa. Feeling is quieter here owing to the news of Chamberlain's departure.'

Your Majesty's Consul at Pretoria reports :

' Government believes Chamberlain desires war, but hopes and wishes to maintain peace ; it is, meanwhile, busily preparing defences. Feeling of the Boers against England. Johannesburg evidently much excited, and reckless fighting and destruction of enemy property to be expected. Support by Dutch elements in [South] Africa possible.

'Secret. Negociations are in hand for a meeting between Kruger and Milner at Bloemfontein. I do not yet believe in war.'

German Note.

At the end of May President Kruger and Governor Milner met ; but after lasting several days the meeting broke up without result.[1] For Milner's detailed report see Staatsarchiv, LXIII, 263.

XV. 370

BERNHARD VON BÜLOW, IN BERLIN, TO COUNT HATZFELDT, IN LONDON, *July 4th,* 1899

Telegram.

In agreement with the two last sentences in your telegram of May 9th, I invited the Dutch Government very confidentially, when it was in the act of offering conciliatory advice in its own name to President Kruger at Pretoria, to add that Germany also advised all possible conciliation. This overture was made to the President, who replied as follows :

He gratefully acknowledged the Dutch Government's friendly advice ; he would give way as far as was at all possible, but could not renounce his country's independence. In the matter of the franchise he was ready to make far-reaching concessions, but could not admit that persons who were British subjects could have the right to vote in the Transvaal ; it would be equivalent to admitting the suzerainty of England. He was ready to reduce the interval for acquiring the franchise from 14 to 9 years, and would later on make it shorter still. But if need be, he was prepared to fight and trusted that now as formerly God would protect the Boers' independence.

I beg you to use your judgment to whom and how far, if at all, you communicate the foregoing in strict confidence, and whether you wish to use Baron von Eckardstein as intermediary.

[1] Worsfold, *Lord Milner's Work in South Africa,* 170 et seq ; also *' Times' History of the Boer War,* I, 259.

Such a communication—especially if made to the open-hearted Chamberlain or to him *and* Lord Salisbury—might perhaps afford a clearer insight into the final intentions of the British. Also if the matter were raised by you, it might perhaps remove any ill-temper regarding *our* motives better than if the fact of our intervention were revealed to the British by any third party.

XV. 371

COUNT HATZFELDT TO THE GERMAN FOREIGN OFFICE, *June 7th*, 1899

Cipher telegram.

In reply to the telegram of June 4th.

To-day, as on my own initiative, I informed Lord Salisbury confidentially that the Imperial Government together with the Dutch Government had advised President Kruger to show as conciliatory a spirit as possible,[1] and he begged me to thank Your Highness sincerely. Concerning the conference at Bloemfontein which has recently taken place, Lord Salisbury said that a satisfactory conclusion had not yet been reached, but the ending of the conference did not mean that negociations were broken off, and further ones would probably take place.

On the Stock Exchange the news of the break down of the conference caused a sharp fall to-day. I have good information that the position is thought serious by the Colonial Office, which is busily considering asking for *les bons offices* of Germany with President Kruger in order to avert a war with the Transvaal, to which *la haute finance* is strongly opposed.

XV. 372

MEMORANDUM BY BARON VON HOLSTEIN, BERLIN FOREIGN OFFICE, *June 8th*, 1899

We could not possibly consent to mediate between England and the Transvaal. The dispute cannot be composed, unless one party recedes considerably from its position. If we suggest to the Transvaal concessions which would make bad blood there, we should have unpleasantness with German public opinion. If we advise the British to cease to claim their position as suzerain, we should have to face acute mistrust in our dealings with England.

It would be advisable, therefore, first to wait and see whether we really are requested to mediate, and to make no statements in one sense or the other. If the request really were made, our reply should be somewhat as follows :

[1] Brandenburg, p. 135.

Once the fact is made public that Germany and England had come to an agreement [1] about territory in South Africa bordering on the Transvaal, Germany is no longer the one to act as mediator. Any decision not absolutely anti-British would be represented as partial and as the result of concessions made to us by England. It would, therefore, be better for England that we should not let ourselves be pushed into the foreground. As in nearly every other case, so here avoidance of war will most redound to the credit of German interests. As soon as we found, therefore, that the Dutch Government agreed with us on this point, we requested it to forward our friendly advice, along with its own, to Pretoria. Failing the unsuspected support of the Dutch, we might possibly have withheld our advice, in the idea that the impression produced on the Transvaal Government by our South African agreement was sure to weaken the effect of our advice considerably. We considered the North American Republic to be the most suitable mediator of all. For one thing, it stood closest to England at present amongst all civilised states. In the state and social life in America, on the other hand, the Dutch element still occupied a prominent position to-day. This circumstance, as well as the republican form of government, would naturally inspire the Boers with confidence.

So much for the draft of the reply to be returned to England, if it is asked for. It might, however, be advisable now immediately to publish in the Press the suggestion that America is the proper mediator between England and the Transvaal. Even if the idea were traced back to a German source, it is not obvious how that could hurt us. The suggestion would certainly flatter the Americans, and if it came to nothing owing to England, it would doubtless be a disappointment to them. (B. von Bülow: ' I quite agree.')

XV. 374

BERNHARD VON BÜLOW, IN BERLIN, TO FLOTOW, GERMAN
CHARGÉ D'AFFAIRES AT THE HAGUE, *June 12th*, 1899

Extract.

. . . The idea of American mediation certainly first saw the light in one or two *British* newspapers, so that it cannot be regarded as one which is unfriendly to England. But whether it was British, American or Africander *by origin* will be hard to determine. It is significant that that suggestion has not been loudly echoed in the British Press, but has been the more freely welcomed in America . . .

[1] Cf. Chapter III.

XV. 375

Flotow, Chargé d'Affaires at The Hague, to the Chancellor, Prince von Hohenlohe, *June 14th*, 1899

Secret.

At to-day's reception by the Minister de Beaufort, I was able
. . . to discuss the Transvaal question with him. M. de Beaufort spoke of the affair with the lively interest which I have
always remarked in him, and which is actually caused by his
long-standing personal friendship with President Kruger.

The Minister did not show any liking for the idea of arbitration
by America. The published declarations of British Ministers
allowed him no hope that the British Government would ever be
willing to admit arbitration by a Foreign Power on this affair.
It would force them to desert the principles they had hitherto
followed in their relations with the Transvaal and bind their
hands in all future disputes with the Republic. There would also
be a fear that, owing to its present inclination towards England,
the American Government might decide altogether in the sense
of the British claims ; even now American papers were speaking up for England and against the Transvaal Republic. He
imagined that President Kruger also shared this view with him
and would regard the idea of arbitration by the United States
with suspicion. M. de Beaufort finished by saying that he
considered that further developments must be awaited.

Directly after this conversation I was able to see the Minister's
Chef de Cabinet and reported my conversation with M. de Beaufort to him in confidence. I found him much more inclined to
entertain the idea of American arbitration. He thought the
Imperial Government's arguments very much worth considering
and pointed to the United States, as the only Power suitable
under the circumstances to act as arbitrator. In England also
they were perhaps not so likely to reject the idea, since they were
evidently embarrassed there as to what attitude to assume.
Owing to the attitude of Cape Colony, there were strong objections
against a war ; but if the British Government failed to take any
energetic steps now at once, the prestige they would lose in South
Africa would be incalculable. M. Ruyssenaers said quite spontaneously that he would not think it a bad plan if M. de Beaufort
sent for Mr. Leyds [1] and discussed the idea of American arbitration with him. He would himself in any case talk the matter
over with the Minister again.

Considering the decision with which the Minister gave his
opinion, I should not anticipate any too great success for this

[1] Minister of the South African Republic at The Hague, also accredited
to Berlin and Paris.

gentleman's attempt to turn him. Meanwhile, it may perhaps be well to give him a few days to let his suggestive influence work on the Minister.

XV. 377

FLOTOW, AT THE HAGUE, TO THE GERMAN FOREIGN OFFICE,
June 22nd, 1899

Cipher telegram.

Dutch Minister in Paris informs M. de Beaufort that Mr. Leyds called on him and informed him that President Kruger does *not* consider the present moment yet suitable for calling in American mediation.

XV. 377

COUNT VON BÜLOW, IN BERLIN, TO FLOTOW, AT THE HAGUE,
July 4th, 1899

Telegram.

Count Hatzfeldt telegraphs that he considers the prospect of peace in the Transvaal affair very doubtful, because, though the majority in the British Ministry is against war, it is tied by Mr. Chamberlain's public action which the Government permitted. In consequence of this, it is *forced* to allow certain substantial concessions to avoid the risk of being blamed for a shameful retreat. Also, any news of disturbances in Johannesburg and of their suppression would—rightly or wrongly—incline public opinion more towards war than has been the case hitherto. The present condition of relative quiet cannot last any longer, in Count Hatzfeldt's opinion.

The contents of the telegram indicate that the Ambassador thinks that the Transvaal ought to hesitate no longer with the moderate concessions necessary to prevent war; otherwise it will be too late.

Please report Count Hatzfeldt's views in the right quarter, without special instructions.

German Note.

On July 28th, 1899, the Transvaal question was debated in both Houses of Parliament. In the House of Commons Mr. Chamberlain declared outright that England's condition for not intervening was that the Transvaal Government should proceed seriously to place the indigenous Dutch population on an equal footing politically with the Uitlanders. In the Lords Lord Salisbury also protested against the differentiated legal status of the Uitlanders and Dutch. He refused to admit that the London Convention of 1884, on which the Boers based their arguments, was good for an unlimited period. Whilst England had no intention to annul such conventions so long as they were granted an honourable existence, very few Englishmen would wish now to have England's seal stamped on that Convention in its original form.

The Emperor, who was yachting in the North just then, took exception
to Lord Salisbury's theory of the Convention, as appears from a telegram,
dated Semmering, July 30th, from Count Bülow to the German Foreign
Office ; he caused Count Hatzfeldt, as well as Count Bülow, to ask for an
expression of his opinion on Lord Salisbury's speech.

XV. 378
COUNT HATZFELDT, IN LONDON, TO THE GERMAN FOREIGN OFFICE,
July 30th, 1899

Cipher telegram.

In obedience to His Majesty's command to express my opinion
on Lord Salisbury's Transvaal speech, I have telegraphed as
follows to Count zu Eulenburg at Bergen :

' When I last met Lord Salisbury (The EMPEROR : ' *The date ?
Before or after his House of Lords speech ?* ') he told me in strict
confidence that the settlement of difficulties with the Transvaal
needed still more time, and that before they were settled there
might be unpleasant explanations (The EMPEROR : ' *With or
without arms ?* '), but that he did *not* believe in the inclination
recently shown by President Kruger, to resort to war. (The
EMPEROR : ' *! Die Botschaft hört ich wohl, allein mir fehlt die
Glaube.—I heard the message, but I did not believe it.*') The speech
is thus explained by the need of convincing the Transvaal Government that the British Cabinet is united on the question, and of
not relaxing the pressure that this fact should exercise on the
councils of President Kruger. As an indication that Lord
Salisbury's peaceful tendencies continue to keep the upper hand
in the Cabinet, I think it should be pointed out that the Transvaal
Government is showing more readiness to negociate and is not
refusing unconditionally to go a step beyond its latest concessions.
Chamberlain's speech also shows that he wishes to gain time,
for in it he said that he had proposed to the Transvaal Government
a joint enquiry [1] into the question as to how far President Kruger's
latest concessions would give the Uitlanders genuine and immediate representation. (The EMPEROR : ' *As Kruger regards himself
as the President of an " independent State," such a proposal is an
insult.*') In the interests of peace it would be desirable for the
Transvaal Government to agree to this. (The EMPEROR : ' *He
cannot do this without giving away everything.*')

' Sir Frank Lascelles (on leave in England), who has been constantly meeting all the leading personages here, informed me
confidentially on his departure that he was taking away a decided
impression that the danger of war complications no longer
existed.'

[1] Cf. ' *Times* ' *History of the Boer War,* I, 309; also, Worsfold, *Lord
Milner's Work,* 229, 231, 237.

The EMPEROR : ' *I greatly regret that I cannot come to this conclusion.—Lord Salisbury put Hatzfeldt off with general phrases, because he was unwilling to lie to him directly and to have to eat his words, if after all he does go to war! He remains as obscure as before! This telegram leaves me just as wise as I was before it!* ')

XV. 379

COUNT VON BÜLOW, AT SEMMERING, TO THE GERMAN FOREIGN OFFICE, *July* 31st, 1899

Cipher telegram.

For the Emperor.

The speeches of Lord Salisbury and Mr. Chamberlain, in my humble opinion, leave no doubt that the British Government is making demands on the South African Republic over and above the measure of the concessions, already sanctioned by the Boers. It is not out of the question that, rather than endure this limitless pressure, President Kruger might finally prefer a war in which military superiority would at first be on the Boer side. This latter fact may, on the other hand, induce the British not to strain the bow too violently. On their side the Boers cannot but be aware that, in the long run, England is very much the stronger party, and that, once engaged, she must bring it to a victorious conclusion.

On the whole, therefore, I should gather from the recent Transvaal debates in the British Parliament that there will be no war, but that the speeches made at this moment may be taken as a further attempt at intimidation and part of the ' game of bluff ' [1]—especially at a moment when even President Kruger himself is not quite at one with his Volksraad. Government and Opposition in England appear to me to be following the same plan—that of making it clear to Boers and Afrikanders that all parties in England are agreed about the South African question—in order to force the Transvaal to grant further concessions. To show that the war-danger is not yet acute, I will mention that up till yesterday Consols had not fallen, indicating that the City does not believe in a war.

I hope that the theory of the Convention set up by Lord Salisbury may only be taken as meaning : ' War destroys treaty.' Otherwise, and if made to apply generally, the British Prime Minister's sentiments would effectually diminish the value of British treaty arrangements and promises.

The possibility of a serious conflict in South Africa will make the British more compliant and certainly more careful when dealing with Russia. Even in the event of war in South Africa, the British Government would be very unwilling to go as far as

[1] English in text.

to denude India, owing to the distrust of Russia so deeply rooted in England.

[THE EMPEROR WILLIAM, AT WILHELMSHÖHE, TO PRINCE VON BÜLOW, AUGUST 8TH, 1899. EXTRACT. [Published in September, 1928, by the *Berliner Tageblatt.*]

Best thanks for your interesting communication. The most astounding thing—if no longer anything like most surprising—is the doing of the fat English Premier (Lord Salisbury). Three weeks ago full of anxiety, attention, and heartfelt longing for conversation with me, now precisely the reverse. I assume it is a sign that his old woman (Seine Alte) is regaining her strength, for she directs him, and the British petticoats seem in general to house a wind which blows contrary to me and my attempts. Well, that will just have to be borne and reckoned with. Anyhow, it is very good to see what sort of impression it makes among the promenaders of Europe when we greet Madame Gallia on parade and she puts her parasol on the other side, and nods and even stops a moment and talks to us. That will do more for the peace of Europe than ten Hague Conferences and some dozens of peace-tribunal-privy-judicial-chief arbitration-appeal-conference-sheep's heads.

But La Belle France must still always be very hysterical. For that a hypocritical, energetic warrior like (General) Galliffet, for the sake of God and his post, has implored me to have no compliments for the army and its graves is the most monstrous thing that I have experienced up to the present. The reverse would have appeared to me so natural, so much a matter of course, that I could have interpreted an omission of this action only as a gross lack of tact. And now precisely not. The devil take it.

Anyhow, I beg you to instruct Le Prince de Derenburg (Muenster) to watch like a pointer for the comments which will come out on the 18th in the Paris Press. And so soon as there is only a hint that something ought to have been done in the form proposed by me—but rejected by Galliffet—he must ruthlessly come out with the truth before the public, however nasty that may be for Galliffet. My speech is decently and inoffensively enough drafted, and I won't make further alterations in it.]

XV. 380

COUNT HATZFELDT, IN LONDON, TO THE GERMAN FOREIGN OFFICE, *August 9th*, 1899

Cipher telegram.

Herr Goerz [1] sends me a copy of a telegram sent to him to-day in English by his Johannesburg agent. It is as follows :

' We hear that the Transvaal Government has not yet replied [to the British proposal for a conference on the franchise question [2] ; it is going to return a very polite answer, but will explain that the Government does not yet see what good an examination of the franchise question alone would do, and will propose a discussion of official questions. We hear that President Kruger informed V. S. Aubert, the French Consul, unofficially that the

[1] Head of the house of Goerz, in Berlin, with branches in London and Johannesburg.
[2] Cf. p. 88. For the text of the British note and the Transvaal Government's reply, see Staatsarchiv, LXIII, 310, 320.

Government will grant a Commission, if the German, French and Russian Consuls appoint delegates ; (The EMPEROR : *" No ! that would not suit us."*) otherwise the risk cannot be avoided that the British Government may interfere in the internal affairs of the South African Republic. We do not believe that the British Government will agree, or that the German Government will be prepared for this step. We have seen Consul Biermann, who said to me privately that he also was inclined to believe this, but he begs me to ascertain, through Goerz' Berlin house, the Foreign Office view of the matter.

' E. Boucher (a Johannesburg Frenchman) and the French Consul have telegraphed to Paris. If the French Government agrees, it is intended that the French in Johannesburg shall present a petition regarding a delegate to their Consul. We hear that the British Government have selected Conynghame Greene,[1] its diplomatic Agent at Pretoria, as their delegate.' . . .

(The EMPEROR: *' We keep out of it! let the Hague Peace Conference step in.'*)

XV. 381

BARON VON RICHTHOFEN, IN BERLIN, TO BIERMANN, CONSUL AT PRETORIA, *August 10th*, 1899.

Telegram.

Whenever you are invited, especially by private interested parties, to make statements about the Anglo-Transvaal conflict, and particularly about the Imperial Government's probable attitude towards this conflict, you will in future maintain the *strictest reserve.*

German Note.

After the close of the Hague Peace Conference at the end of July, M. Delcassé [French Foreign Minister] went to St. Petersburg. (Cf. p. 97.)

XV. 382

COUNT VON BÜLOW, AT SEMMERING, TO THE GERMAN FOREIGN OFFICE, *August 12th*, 1899

Cipher telegram.

With reference to the telegram of August 9th from the Imperial Ambassador in London, which quotes Herr Goerz' message, Count Hatzfeldt telegraphs privately :

' The people who are pressing Kruger to demand appointment of Russian, French and German delegates are playing straight into Chamberlain's hands. If Chamberlain says no to this

---

[1] Cf. Sir A. Hardinge, *A Diplomat in the East*, p. 242. ' Mr. Kruger seemed to be on very friendly terms with Sir Conynghame, with whom he conversed in fluent Dutch, not the Taal.'

attempt to get rid of the suzerainty claim by means of foreign arbitration, he will have British public opinion behind him and be stronger than ever.   Moreover, President Kruger will probably be proved wrong, if he imagines that Russia and France, or France alone, will espouse his cause at the risk of a serious difference with England ; and I do not think that here they are seriously worried by it or think that such will result from Delcassé's journey.   Even the suspicions against Rothschild, which I mentioned confidentially in this connection, will hardly make much difference.

'I do not yet believe in any immediate measures for using military force, even if the Transvaal Government should give an answer referring to foreign intervention, as reported by Goerz. But it might cause us to pass into the second and more dangerous phase of concentration of troops—all the more dangerous, because, after the adjournment of Parliament, the Opposition is no longer effective.   It has been Chamberlain's very clever game from the beginning gradually to warm up public opinion, which was at first very cool, in favour of the scheme, to represent himself as the champion of legitimate but extremely moderate demands, and to put the Transvaal Government apparently in the wrong as against England.   This has been continuously more and more successful up to a certain point, and neither public opinion nor the more peaceable members of the Cabinet would now seriously oppose decisive action, if Kruger really rejected all enquiry or made it dependent on foreign participation, which would be taken still worse here.   Would it not be possible, before it is too late, to make the situation clear to Kruger, either through the Dutch or directly through our Consul ?   In any case it seems to me essential to avoid all statements which could be pointed to as an intrigue out there for participation against the British proposal. If the suggestion in Goerz' telegram is a true one—that Biermann regards our participation in the appointment of European delegates as improbable, but that he *suggested* that the house of Goerz should ascertain in Berlin what was the Foreign Office view—such a statement, if it came to the ears of the British Government, would be quite enough to arouse the greatest suspicions against us.'

On the grounds of general policy and in consideration of the Anglo-German Agreement, we must naturally avoid being forced into a false position, both with England and the Transvaal, in connection with the present troubles in South Africa.   Consul Biermann's attitude seems rather an unsafe one, and it would be advisable to impress on him once again that Germany will not let herself be dragged into the Transvaal dispute in any form whatever.   Herr Biermann can, of course, only have spoken as he did, if the question of European participation in the dispute was discussed with him or in his presence. As for Count Hatzfeldt's suggestion that President Kruger should be warned by the Dutch, it would have to be considered whether, all things being taken into account, a telegram should be sent to Baron von den Brincken, our Minister at the Hague, somewhat as follows :

'The view of the Imperial Ambassador in London, which was communicated to the Dutch Government in June, that, by hesitating to comply, President Kruger would make the Transvaal's position worse and more dangerous, appears to be confirmed. British public opinion, which hitherto championed the peace idea, is beginning to regard the hesitations of the Transvaal Government as a sign of hostile intentions. Moreover, the power to oppose, which lay hitherto in the attitude of the Parliamentary Opposition, will now fall away when Parliament is adjourned. Count Hatzfeldt sees a further danger in the influence on British feeling of the idea, now apparently suggested by the Transvaal Government, to attempt to draw Germany, France and Russia into the unsettled dispute. Germany could not consent to this proposal which, if accepted, would imply German partizanship. The Russian Government has repeatedly declared that South Africa leaves it cold. That France by herself would stand up with the Transvaal against England is improbable, even though President Kruger might have received encouragement from Paris ; he certainly possesses no binding and unambiguous promise in writing of armed support by France. We are informed that the British people would regard an appeal to European Powers, who are somewhat held in suspicion in England, as a direct provocation—almost more than would be a definite rejection of the form of enquiry as proposed by England. As for ourselves, we should, out of genuine sympathy for the Boers, prevent President Kruger from playing into the hands of the war party and rushing into a war, the result of which cannot, humanly speaking, be doubtful, considering the isolation of the South African Dutch. Your Excellency will therefore communicate the foregoing to M. de Beaufort immediately and beg him to pass it on in confidence to the Transvaal Government. It would be better to telegraph it to Pretoria than to communicate it to Mr. Leyds. Count Hatzfeldt fears that a decided change in the direction of war is imminent, supposing the Transvaal Government should definitely refuse an enquiry or appeal to the great continental Powers. The Imperial Consul at Pretoria has been instructed direct concerning Germany's abstention.'

German Note.

The telegram suggested by Bülow was despatched on August 13th.

XV. 384.

BARON VON RICHTHOFEN, IN BERLIN, TO BIERMANN, CONSUL AT
PRETORIA, *August 13th*, 1899

Telegram.

Germany is not to be drawn into the Transvaal dispute *in
any form*. But you will naturally not declare this, unless you
find fully sufficient and ample reason for doing so—when the
question of intervention by the European Powers is discussed
with you or in your presence.

German Note.

The Suzerainty question [see below] was introduced by Chamberlain
in a telegram, dated July 13th, 1899, after President Kruger had met
Milner, the High Commissioner, at Bloemfontein and insisted on the South
African Republic's integrity remaining unquestioned.[1] The introduction
of this ominous question at once acted prejudicially on the negotiations.
In a telegram (August 19th), Reitz, the Secretary of State of the Republic,
rejected the British proposal of a joint Commission to settle the Uitlander
question, but of his own initiative offered further concessions, adding a
demand that the British Government should cease to assert their Suzerainty. A British note (August 28th), rejecting this demand point-blank,
was followed by the Republic's withdrawal (September 2nd) of its offer
of concessions in the Uitlander question ; whereupon the British Government threatened (September 9th) ' to treat the affair from a fresh
standpoint and make some proposals of his own, calculated to bring about
a final settlement '. For the text of the notes, see Staatsarchiv, LXIII,
322.

XV. 385

COUNT HATZFELDT, IN LONDON, TO THE EMPEROR WILLIAM,
August 27th, 1899

A few days ago it was still generally assumed that a satisfactory
answer was to be expected from the Transvaal Government, and
that peace would thus be assured. But now, since President
Kruger has placed the suzerainty question in the forefront, the
situation has become worse again. It cannot be ignored that
by doing so he has played into Mr. Chamberlain's hands, whose
efforts for some time have obviously been directed towards
exciting public opinion here in favour of energetic action against
the Transvaal. For this purpose the franchise question proved
insufficient, and I know from a sure source that after the failure
of the Bloemfontein conference, Mr. Chamberlain complained to
his friends that the public here took little interest in the question
and that this indifference had tied his hands. To-day all is
changed, for the national consciousness of the British has been
stung and wounded by the demand that England shall renounce
her suzerainty, and I believe that hardly any Englishman exists,

[1] Cf. p. 84.

whichever Party he belongs to, who would oppose the maintenance
by force of England's control of the Transvaal, if there were any
question of it.   It would make no difference whether this view
is justified by treaties of which most of the public here are probably quite ignorant, and people are satisfied with the assumption
that, even though unsupported by any title based on a treaty,
England, is 'the paramount Power' in South Africa (The
EMPEROR : ' *The old English policy of unscrupulous self-interest
and clownishness.*'), and must keep up her position under all
circumstances.   This being so, I think it was a decided mistake
of the Transvaal Government to introduce this question and to
demand a formal renunciation of suzerainty, if it is not ready to
fight at once.

In a long confidential conversation which I had yesterday
with the Prime Minister this question was touched upon, and
his observations showed that he thinks this condition demanded
by the Transvaal Government quite unacceptable, but that he
does not, on this account, think that further concessions by the
Transvaal Government are out of the question, and so far,
therefore, *he* has not given up the hope of maintaining peace.
From his whole attitude and the tone of his utterances I gained
the impression then, as indeed whenever Mr. Chamberlain is
mentioned between us in confidence, that he does not agree with
his colleague's aggressive policy in every respect, bears no great
personal good will to him, and is not particularly anxious for
him to strengthen his political position still further by a successful
coup.   We cannot, of course, conclude from this that the Prime
Minister will oppose the use of force, if the Transvaal Government
sticks to a demand which is considered unacceptable here, and
if Mr. Chamberlain uses it as a lever for pushing England into
a war.   It must also be realised that the Prime Minister cannot
raise a protest, even if he would, since in this case Mr. Chamberlain
would undoubtedly have public opinion on his side.

On the other hand, Lord Salisbury clearly assumes that the
decision whether it is to be peace or war is not yet imminent.
When I asked how he imagined matters would develop further,
he said without hesitation that they would probably drag on for
some time to come.   Then, in order to draw further remarks from
him, particularly as to Mr. Chamberlain's intentions, I said that,
as an impartial observer, it was my impression that the Colonial
Secretary had manœuvred very cleverly from his own point of
view, so as to arouse public feeling, which was at first very cool,
in favour of the energetic action which he desired.   Lord Salisbury
admitted willingly that this idea was correct and proved that
I had been following developments attentively.   He added that
even in London there had been a party inclined for war from the

beginning; whereas in the country, especially in the North, feeling had been in favour of peace.

Referring to an article which appeared recently in the *Standard*, denying the accusation that England wished to possess the Transvaal, on the ground that, apart from the mines, the country was quite valueless, I said in joke that if this assertion was true, it could hardly be brought into line with Mr. Chamberlain's keenness in endeavouring to bring this valueless country under British control in some form. The Prime Minister laughed heartily at my remark and did not deny its correctness. Nor did he deny it at all when I suggested the possibility that the Transvaal Government was perhaps under the impression that, even if it now gave way in everything, Mr. Chamberlain would sooner or later find a reason for starting a fresh discussion and for reducing its independence still further. (The EMPEROR: ' *Correct.*')

On this occasion Lord Salisbury spoke with much irritation of Schreiner,[1] the Cape Minister, who had been letting through arms and munitions for the Transvaal Government behind the back of Sir Alfred Milner. It was unheard of that this could happen in a British colony. Moreover, the Transvaal Government was already so well supplied with arms as to able to equip every Burger who would bear arms with two rifles. Of course, it might still be in want of ammunition, which explained the tactics practised at Pretoria of protracting the negociations with England in order to gain time. Hence also the irritation at the behaviour of the Portuguese, who were holding up the transport of munitions intended for the Transvaal.[2] I quietly refrained from expressing an opinion on this point.

As our conversation proceeded, M. Delcassé's journey to St. Petersburg [3] came under discussion, also England's relations towards Russia, and I consider it right to repeat Lord Salisbury's words on the subject and also an opinion he expressed regarding conditions in France, since, if I may be allowed to judge, they are not without bearing on England's present attitude in the Transvaal question.

Having said that so far he had learnt nothing definite as to the motive of this journey, but that he could not quite share in the view which, according to his information, was put about in St. Petersburg, that the journey was merely due to motives of personal vanity, he volunteered a kind of exposition of the

[1] Cf. ' *Times* ' *History of the Boer War*, I, 305.

[2] Cf. ' *Times* ' *History of the Boer War*, I, 318; also G. & T., I, p. 88 et seq.

[3] The object of this visit was to consolidate the French alliance with Russia.

relations between Count Muravieff and the British Ambassador (Sir Charles Scott), of the present attitude of the Russians towards England, and of the political situation in Russia. First he said that, as I knew, the personal relations between Sir Charles Scott and the Russian Foreign Minister were of the friendliest. Moreover, Russia's attitude towards this country had been not at all unfriendly of late, and, strange as it might seem, the Russian Emperor had been showing consideration for British interests in China. These the Minister did not describe more closely. (The EMPEROR : ' *This was done to impress us.*') Lord Salisbury then argued that Russia was now unable to undertake any great political enterprise abroad. The famine in Russia was much more serious than was generally supposed and was engaging the resources and attention of the Government. Added to this was the lack of money, for which M. Witte had so far found no cure.

The Minister now turned to conditions in France, and said emphatically and with unmistakable contempt that they could only be described as complete chaos. The present pretenders [to autocratic power] were personally so insignificant, that they clearly had no prospect of success. So far no other outstanding personality had been found in France with a prospect of taking the lead successfully. Until this happened, there could hardly be a change in the situation in France, and it could not be expected that the French, as they now were, would play a decisive part in European politics.

Though Lord Salisbury limited himself to this exposition and omitted to add any deductions from it, it is clear, if I am not mistaken, that his object was to show me that England now thinks that her hands are free and sees no reason to fear interference from Russia and France jointly, and certainly not from France alone. (The EMPEROR : ' *Correct.*')

I venture to suggest that this view of the European situation is not a pleasant one for our interests here, since the British now see no reason for making any great sacrifice for our friendship. (The EMPEROR : ' *Correct.*') The wish to be on good terms with Germany is fairly general amongst the public and is, according to my information, shared by most of the Cabinet. But the realisation that England must make appropriate sacrifices for it will not come until bad times arrive and England is forced to recognise that she has no alternative but to be friends with Germany. (The EMPEROR : ' *It is interesting that in his lecture on the upsetting of the balance between the Powers the Premier forgot India and Persia. If there is a Transvaal war, the Russians will make themselves felt there ! Then the value of our friendship will rise in the market, especially in London !* ')

An immediate outbreak of war in South Africa is hardly imaginable, unless the Transvaal Republic begins it. From all that I hear, confirmed also by the reports of Captain Baron von Lüttwitz, all measures have been prepared here for war, but once the orders are given, the carrying out of them will certainly take a longish time. The forces now in South Africa are quite insufficient to undertake an attack, and it is not at all unlikely that an attack under such circumstances would be followed by a serious defeat. Thus it may be presumed also that the negociations will continue meanwhile, and it would be desirable in the Republic's interests that the President should realise two things : firstly, that the defeat of the Republic is merely a matter of time when England's resources are considered; and, secondly, and— most important—that the inevitable result of defeat would be, if not annexation, complete loss at any rate of any sort of independence.

I have good information that Her Majesty Queen Victoria passionately desires to end her long reign in peace and not to be involved in a European war, and that she looks with anxiety and suspicion on any sign that arouses her fears that England may be involved in war with Russia and France. I think I may assume that Lord Salisbury, who stayed at Osborne two days ago to make his report, reassured the Queen during this visit and told her, as he has told me, that even in the event of war with the Transvaal, no interference by France or Russia, and therefore no conflict with them, are to be feared.

I will mention, as being curious, that at this critical moment Mr. Chamberlain is remaining at Birmingham, whilst Lord Salisbury is in residence at Walmer Castle, near Dover, and only rarely comes up to London for a few hours. He gave me a meeting yesterday, and I thought it my duty not to mention it, as he had refused appointments with the other foreign representatives. On parting he said to me that he would not come up during the whole of next week and would regard himself as being on leave. This will make my task of discussing our business with him considerably more difficult.

XV. 390

COUNT VON BÜLOW, IN BERLIN, TO BARON VON DEN BRINCKEN, AT THE HAGUE, *August 29th*, 1899

Telegram. Secret.

In a private letter, written the day before yesterday in the evening, Count Hatzfeldt writes :

' Even now I do not yet believe in war, given that they have not gone mad at Pretoria. Salisbury certainly does not want war, if he can avoid it ; but he will be driven into it, if Kruger insists on the suzerainty being definitely renounced. By so doing, he is doing Chamberlain the greatest service, whereas the latter will tumble into the gutter if Kruger renounces it. The Boers ought to be satisfied with letting existing treaties remain in force, perhaps with a reservation that any differences of opinion which may creep in should be decided by a *legal* tribunal. To-day the chances are that the Transvaal will be defeated and then lose everything.'

Please communicate the above to M. de Beaufort immediately, with a request to pass on the contents to Pretoria—but not to compromise Count Hatzfeldt.

German Note.

At the meeting of September 8th the Cabinet discussed the reply to the Transvaal Government's note of September 2nd—which reply (September 9th) was one of rejection and thereby intensified the crisis ; also, and especially, the question of military preparation for the war which now appeared highly probable. As telegraphed by Hatzfeldt on September 9th, it was decided to send 10,000 men, including 6,000 from India, to South Africa.

XV. 392

COUNT HATZFELDT, IN LONDON, TO THE GERMAN FOREIGN OFFICE, *September 8th*, 1899

Cipher telegram.

The result of to-day's Cabinet Council has been kept very secret. From words used to-day by Lord Salisbury, I have the impression that he has not quite given up hope of a peaceful settlement. He admitted freely that no ships had yet been chartered for the transport of troops and that it would take more time still to fit them out.

My present impression is that an energetically worded reply will be handed to the Transvaal Government and that a few thousand men will be sent to South Africa, in order to increase the pressure, but that negotiations will not entirely be broken off.

As regards the Queen's feelings, Lord Salisbury told me very confidentially that Her Majesty earnestly desired to urge peace upon her Government, but she had in no way forgotten nor got over the Majuba defeat in February, 1881.

I am reliably informed that in a telegram to-day to one of his political friends here Mr. Rhodes expressed a conviction that the Transvaal Government would end by giving in.

XV. 393

BARON VON RICHTHOFEN, IN BERLIN, TO THE EMPEROR WILLIAM,
AT MAGDEBURG, *September 13th*, 1899

Cipher telegram.

Your Majesty's Ambassador in London telegraphs :
' Referring to the Transvaal situation Lord Salisbury has
just told me in strict confidence that he does not even now believe
in a war. (The EMPEROR : ' *Then why all this transport of troops
from India ? '*)   He said that Chamberlain's latest note did not
mention the question of suzerainty.'[1]

XV. 394

COUNT HATZFELDT, IN LONDON, TO THE GERMAN FOREIGN OFFICE,
September 14th, 1899

Cipher telegram.

I hear from the City to-day that war is generally expected
there, and that there has been a considerable fall in prices on
the Stock Exchange. Definite grounds for this panic are not
ascertainable, for [Alfred] Rothschild, whom I have just seen,
has had no news of any refusal by the Transvaal Government.

XV. 395

COUNT HATZFELDT, IN LONDON, TO THE GERMAN FOREIGN OFFICE,
September 20th, 1899

Cipher telegram.

In confidential conversation with Baron von Eckardstein
to-day, Mr. Chamberlain described war as unavoidable now that
the Transvaal had made any peaceful compromise impossible.
England must of course now insist upon stronger conditions and
demand guarantees from the Boers ; these he did not define.
He himself did not believe that the fresh British demands, which
would be settled at the next Cabinet Council, would be accepted
by the Transvaal. Speaking of the Orange Free State, Mr.
Chamberlain showed some anxiety lest it might at the last moment
desert the Transvaal and remain neutral. He added in explanation that if this happened the Orange Free State would continue
as an independent wedge in the middle of British South Africa.
Moreover it was important strategically to send British troops
through the Free State, and this could not be done if it remained
neutral. Finally Mr. Chamberlain said that there was no
necessity to summon Parliament at present, as the Government's
reserve fund gave it sufficient means for starting the war. He

[1] Cf. Note, p. 95.

mentioned that he had met with difficulties here on all sides in his Transvaal policy, and he let me see that this had been particularly the case with Lord Salisbury.

XV. 395

COUNT VON BÜLOW, AT SEMMERING, TO THE GERMAN FOREIGN OFFICE, *September 20th*, 1899

Cipher telegram.

The language of our Press should be calm and cool about the Transvaal crisis and should confine itself to facts. Whilst the admittedly semi-official journals must carefully avoid offending large sections in Germany by conspicuous partisanship for England or spiteful attacks upon the Boers, it is also desirable that the German Press should not fall into the errors committed by it during the Spanish-American war, in championing the weaker side from the start in an unnecessarily blatant tone. It must be explained throughout the country that since France, Russia, Italy and Austria are not thinking of becoming enemies with England on account of South African questions, Germany cannot step forward and commit herself there all alone.

XV. 397

COUNT HATZFELDT, IN LONDON, TO THE GERMAN FOREIGN OFFICE, *September 30th*, 1899

Cipher telegram.

To-day's *Standard* announces from Paris that certain semi-official papers have published, treating it as inspired, a telegram from London, to the effect that the British Government is anxious concerning our attitude in the Transvaal question. It is worth nothing that in confidential conversation with Baron von Eckardstein [1] Mr. Chamberlain said that the British Government knew perfectly well that our attitude towards England would be correct throughout. But the general public did not know this; in fact it was universally assumed that our feeling and attitude was unfriendly. Mr. Chamberlain also questioned whether it might not be possible and opportune to enlighten and reassure public opinion here by a public demonstration of our sympathy with England in this crisis.

At the next opportunity I intend to inform Mr. Chamberlain through Baron von Eckardstein that it is the British Government's business to enlighten the public through the Press as to the real facts of the case, which it knows quite well. Also I felt that I had no right to recommend the Imperial Government to make a public demonstration of sympathy, whilst the conclusion of the

---

[1] Cf. *Ten Years at the Court of St. James*, p. 110.

agreement on the Samoan question, which alone stood in the way of intimate relationship between us, still met with such great obstacles here.

[Count Hatzfeldt was instructed to inform Mr. Chamberlain that the foregoing correctly represented the intentions of the German Government. (Cf. pp. 69, 101.)]

XV. 398

Sir Frank Lascelles, in Berlin, to Derenthall, German Foreign Office, *October 3rd*, 1899

I have the honour to inform Your Excellency that I have received telegraphic instructions from the Marquess of Salisbury to inquire whether the Imperial Government would allow the Imperial Representative at Pretoria to take charge of British interests in the event of its being found necessary to withdraw the British Agent in consequence of a hostile movement directed against British territory by the Boers.

I have the honour to request Your Excellency to be so good as to inform me at your earliest convenience as to what answer I may return to Her Majesty's Government.

German Note.

From telegrams despatched by Count Hatzfeldt on October 7th, 1899, it appears that he made efforts to bring influence to bear [regarding the Samoan settlement] on Lord Salisbury through Alfred Rothschild, Lord Lansdowne, Mr. Goschen, and others.

XIV. 653

Count von Bülow, in Berlin, to Count Hatzfeldt, *October 8th*, 1899

Telegram.

. . . On your side you have done all, if not directly, then by other means, to attain the object ; so that I am not giving up hope that we shall finally reach a satisfactory settlement, and I consider your method of influencing Lord Salisbury through the medium of influential Englishmen to be the one best suited to the Premier's character.

At present, however, the situation is so unfriendly in England that His Majesty's Government has been forced to renounce the idea of representing British interests in the Transvaal for the reasons already known to you.

Herr von Derenthall explained very confidentially to the British Ambassador, who came for the purpose of enquiring, that Germany's representative in the Transvaal was merely a Consul, who had only recently been transferred, and in whom we did not expect enough authority and local knowledge to be able to cope at once with all the difficult and complicated duties involved in representing British interests. The Ambassador accepted the statement with calm seriousness and offered no comment, but Herr von Derenthall's impression was that the Ambassador understood what was meant.

Having, as in duty bound, fulfilled the obligations of politeness by our formal declaration, we should now not fail to place the real motive for our refusal in its right light. I shall speak to the British Ambassador in this sense to-morrow and can confidentially leave it to your experience to decide where and how you make your explanation in London. As things are I think that neither you nor I shall find much trouble in making our listeners understand the glaring disproportion between Lord Salisbury's wide claim on our friendly support—for protection of British interests in the Transvaal would naturally have meant no mere formality—and his freely expressed unfriendly treatment of all questions which interest Germany. Even a strong Government, like the German one, must avoid challenging the legitimate criticism of public opinion at home, which would at once be aroused, if it repaid slights, such as those constantly suffered by it in the course of the Samoan question, with acts of friendship. Germany would make her position worse not only with England, but with the rest of the Powers who are looking on.

These discussions will perhaps give you an indication of the real reason for the Premier's lack of cordiality. The disapproval of the political personages mentioned in your telegrams shows me that his brusqueness is not to be explained by any material British interests ; so that there only remains the supposition that the ' personal question ' mentioned by Mr. Chamberlain, i.e., his entirely causeless irritation against the Emperor, or perhaps some suspicion whose source is unknown to us, plays a part in it. The irritation, for which just now there is no cause whatever, should be capable of being overcome by strong *British* arguments. As for the suspicion—that also must be without valid reasons, for throughout the whole course of the Transvaal crisis the German Government has observed a perfectly loyal and unfailingly correct attitude, which disappointed the Transvaal and was criticised by a large section of the German people and some of the other Powers ; the British reproaches on this count must therefore at most refer to events having no political significance. Owing to the importance of the whole affair I shall communicate with you more in detail, but now I say that they may find excuses, but not reasons, for their suspicion.

[The task of protecting British interests was, in the end, undertaken by the United States.]

XIV. 655

COUNT VON BÜLOW, IN BERLIN, TO COUNT HATZFELDT,
October 8th, 1899

Telegram.   Very secret.

The British Government's attitude of refusal in the Samoa affair may perhaps be explained by the supposition that Lord Salisbury and perhaps Mr. Chamberlain also have conceived an unfounded suspicion against our loyal attitude in the Transvaal question.

It is quite unknown here what can be brought with any justification against our absolutely loyal and correct attitude in the Transvaal affair.   In any case I will inform you confidentially that certain German business men in South-West Africa, led by Herr von Hansemann, have for some months been trying to obtain a concession to build a railway [1] through the Transvaal to connect with a line through Bechuanaland and the mining district of German South-West Africa and so on to the Atlantic coast, and a proposal was made lately to the Transvaal Government.   The news of this purely private enterprise may have come lately in some way to the knowledge of the British Government, in such a form as to arouse suspicion against us.

If, after careful enquiry, you come to the conclusion that the fact that German capitalists are pushing this Transvaal railway concession with the Transvaal Government has really aroused Lord Salisbury's suspicions and contributed to the British Government's attitude of refusal in the Samoa affair, you will explain the facts of the case so as to remove all further misunderstanding and say that the Imperial Government sets no store on obtaining such a railway concession in itself, but that it is purely a question of private German enterprise as is often observable elsewhere, especially in England.   We shall be satisfied if we are assured that Mr. Rhodes' railway across South Africa is certainly to be carried through German territory and on to the coast of the Atlantic Ocean, as was settled in the latest agreement with Mr. Davis, Mr. Rhodes' representative.   Please say also that we should unfailingly proceed with the ratification of the East African Telegraph agreement with Mr. Cecil Rhodes, as soon as the consent of the Chartered Company and of the British Government, which are required for the agreement, is in our hands.   Mr. Davis is now in London for the purpose of obtaining this consent.

[1] Cf. p. 49.

CHAPTER VII

THE SOUTH AFRICAN WAR. OCTOBER, 1899 TO NOVEMBER, 1900. THE 'BUNDESRATH' INCIDENT

[The beginning of the South African War was the signal for a storm of abuse of England in the Press in nearly every continental country, especially in Germany,[1] France and Russia. Public feeling took its cue from the papers and greatly embarrassed any Government which desired to preserve a neutral attitude.

Dr. Leyds, the chief agent in Europe of the Transvaal Government, was making a tour of the continental Capitals in the hope of obtaining a European combination against England. When it came to the point, the Emperor and the German Government showed the world that they had no intention of intervening in favour of the Transvaal. Further proof of this was the Emperor's visit to Queen Victoria in November, 1899.]

XV. 405

Count von Bülow, in Berlin, to Rücker-Jenisch, Chargé d'Affaires in Brussels, *October 16th,* 1899

Telegram.

Please do your best quietly to prevent Dr. Leyds from travelling [to Berlin], as I could not receive him. His coming here and being received would give rise to false interpretations, which it is in general our interest to avoid.

[Dr. Leyds gave up coming to Berlin.

Count Hatzfeldt was at this time very ill, and his work was done chiefly by Baron von Eckardstein, who moved in English society much more freely than his chief ever had done. The Emperor's visit and the difficulties caused by his insisting in bringing Admiral von Senden with him are described in Eckardstein's *Ten Years at the Court of St. James*, p. 120 et seq.]

XV. 410

Count Hatzfeldt to the German Foreign Office, *November 15th,* 1899

Cipher telegram. Private for Baron von Holstein.

It is my duty to describe the feeling in important circles here, and I must therefore inform you very confidentially that

[1] Brandenburg, p. 135 et seq. ; Sir Eyre Crowe's Memorandum, January 1st, 1907 (G. & T., I, 276).

I am told there is a set-back to the feeling which in high Court circles has been so far very favourable to us. The Queen and Prince of Wales are greatly annoyed to have been left so long without either news or an answer to their question regarding the details of the [Emperor's] visit. The Prince of Wales is angry because all his suggestions have been rejected, and especially because he has not yet been told whether the Admiral in question is to come, and if so, whether, in this case, he is to address the desired letter [of apology] to Sir Frank Lascelles. Finally and worse still I hear that Chamberlain has said that there is no ground for the present unexpected attitude of our Press now that our wishes regarding Samoa have been satisfied, and that under the circumstances it is impossible to continue negociating with us.

German Note.

. . . Eckardstein exaggerates the difficulties caused by the Prince's objection to the presence of Admiral von Senden in the Emperor's suite ; they were removed by a letter from the Admiral to Sir Frank Lascelles. The Emperor's visit, which at this moment was highly important to England, was only in doubt owing to England's slowness in settling the Samoan affair in a manner satisfactory to Germany. On November 12th, directly after this question was settled, Count Hatzfeldt was informed by telegraph that the visit would certainly take place at the appointed time. As the visit was unfavourably received by the German as well as by the Russian and French Press, the Emperor thought it right to emphasise its purely family character and to give up all public functions, as a visit to Cambridge University, which the Prince of Wales much desired. The Emperor also declined visiting the Duke of Devonshire, as was originally intended. He did however receive the Lord President of the Council and other influential members of the Cabinet, among them Mr. Chamberlain, at Windsor.

XV. 412

COUNT VON BÜLOW TO COUNT HATZFELDT, *November 15th*, 1899

Telegram.

I may not form an opinion on the sensibilities of Royal Families, nor on the Senden affair, etc. . . .

A not unimportant obstacle to the improvement of Anglo-German feeling is the present *Times* correspondent, Saunders. Twice or three times a week he collects bitter criticisms of England and sends them to London, omitting to say that they always come from agrarian and other trouble-making papers, i.e. those that hate their own Government more than England, and hope thus to make difficulties for it. But the British Press describes these utterances as though they came from ' authoritative sources ', and the *Times* writes sour leading articles, which are answered from here in the same tone. It may go on for a long time like this if Saunders remains here. I have already told you that Saunders' statements show that he is a personal opponent of Chamberlain. It is Chamberlain's business to remove the cause if his policy is incommoded by it. The German Government cannot do more than it has done. It has needed good nerves and strong determination to keep German policy consistently free from all anti-British ties, in spite of the constant discouragement offered by England's policy, Press and people.

I cannot see that it will do harm to bring the contents of this simple statement to Chamberlain's knowledge in undiluted form as far as possible.

I inform you personally that the Russian suggestions for a 'little private arrangement' have just lately been again put forward. I do not imagine that these discussions will lead to anything, for I see no pressing need at present for us to consider them.

[Towards the end of October, 1899, Count Muravieff toured Europe in the hope of raising a coalition against England and of effectually forcing her and Germany apart. He visited Paris and Madrid and proceeded to Berlin, arriving there on the day that the Anglo-German Samoa Agreement was published. This caused him to shorten his stay in Berlin, and he travelled straight on to St. Petersburg. (Cf. Eckardstein, *Ten Years at the Court of St. James*, pp. 127, 164–7; G. & T., I, pp. 234–5.) He tried to persuade the British that the movement for an anti-British coalition originated in Germany.]

XV. 413

MEMORANDUM BY COUNT VON BÜLOW, AT WINDSOR, *November 24th*, 1899

Very confidential.

His Majesty the Emperor honoured Mr. Chamberlain after the banquet of the 21st with a long conversation. In answer to the Colonial Secretary's remark that he desired a general understanding between Germany, England and America His Majesty said that a general rapprochement of this sort had objections for both sides. Whilst it was not in the British tradition to conclude formal alliances, definite political frontiers were drawn for Germany for some time to come by her excellent relations with Russia. But there were several points on which Germany and England might agree as they turned up. Both countries ought to follow up the method of special agreements which had been tried with success on two occasions. His Majesty added that it was to England's interest to handle carefully the sensitive, obstinate and rather sentimental German and not to make him impatient, but to show him good-will in small matters. The German was 'touchy'; the more this was borne in mind by the British the better for the relations between the two countries.

On November 22nd Mr. Balfour visited me. He said that here all parties wished for a rapprochement with us, and if possible, also with America at the same time. I answered that our wishes regarding England were more negative than positive. We had no positive requests to make of England nor any positive desires, nor did we make any positive suggestions to England. But we did wish that between England and Germany there should be in future neither misunderstanding nor friction nor needless provocation. Mr. Balfour said that no British states-man would fail to subscribe to this programme. In England there was no grudge against Germany's economic development. England was too rich and was herself making too great economic strides to fear German competition to the extent imagined both here and in Germany. Fundamentally England and Germany stood on the same economic ground, and Germans were prospering in the British colonies and Englishmen in the German colonies. Both peoples were much nearer together in business than the British were to either the French or the Russians. Mr. Balfour of himself described the African Agreement with Germany as a very useful arrangement, by the carrying out of which both parties and also the world's peace would profit. He declared that he would have no objection if German con-tractors obtained the concession for constructing the Anatolian Railway.[1] England was not thinking of putting obstacles 'in Germany's path in Asia Minor. Mr. Balfour complained of the German Press, as being much more anti-British than the British Press was anti-German.

German Note.

As a matter of fact, at the beginning of the Boer War the German Press was far less anti-British than either the French or the Russian. The French papers, especially the comic ones, were incredibly sordid and obscene in their attacks on England and the Queen. The Foreign Office records furnish very ample proof of this. Count von Bülow did all that was possible to induce a calm, cool and matter-of-fact attitude in the German Press.[2] After the British reverse at Ladysmith he telegraphed on October 31st to the Foreign Office : ' Regarding the British reverse at Ladysmith our Press should observe calm and coolness of expression. Too clear evidence of joy at the defeat and open jubilation would merely direct against us the bitterness of the British whom we are not yet strong enough to meet at sea, and at the same time cause the French and Russians to hope that we are prepared to move against England by ourselves. Whilst avoiding false sentiment for England, but also impolitic excitement against her, the Press must confine itself to expressing the point of view that (1) the British army leadership has fallen behind what was hitherto expected of it, (2) it must be shown what England will do to make good her serious set-back in Africa, (3) we must wait and see how the British reverse will react on the attitude of Russia and France '. Cf. Eckardstein, *Ten Years*, p. 143.

---

[1] Cf. Chapter XXVIII.   [2] Cf. pp. 104, 107.

I pointed out to Mr. Balfour that Saunders, the *Times* correspondent, was amusing himself by collecting every attack on England from the most obscure German papers and laying them before the British public each morning. This tendencious method of reporting made it very difficult for us to keep up the good relations with England which were desired on many sides. Mr. Balfour is ready to try whether it is not possible to effect a change in the representation of the *Times* in Berlin. He spoke of France in a tone of pitying contempt ; and he denied any belief that there was any unbridgeable antipathy between England and Russia ; Asia was big enough to hold them both. He seemed worried at the situation in Austria and asked if we would consent that, in the event of the Hapsburg monarchy breaking up, the Cis-Leithan provinces should fall under Russian control. I replied that in that case not only Cis-Leitha, but the whole Balkan Peninsula would come under Russian influence, for without Austria the Balkan States would be unable to maintain their independence. We could not, however, resist such a turn of events, since we had no interest whatever in annexing parts of Austria,—which would, in effect, amount to a return to the *status quo ante* 1866. The perspective of a Russia dominating the whole of Eastern Europe seemed to appal Mr. Balfour in view of its effect upon British trade interests there.

Mr. Balfour was received on the evening of the 22nd by His Majesty, who without going into details explained to him that we wanted nothing from England and had not come here as ' poor relations ', but on the other hand we wished to maintain calm relations with England and to avoid disturbing incidents.

On the 24th Mr. Chamberlain called upon me. He began the conversation by saying that sooner or later we should have to come to a general understanding, since we needed each other. He fully admitted that England needed Germany ; but a time might come when Germany would find herself in need of England ; I said to him that the second was so far not yet the case. We were on very good terms with Russia ; between Russia and ourselves there was no political point of difference. As for France, feeling against us there had considerably calmed down. The French were no longer thinking of staging a war of revenge against us.

German Note.

This, of course, was not Count Bülow's real opinion, for shortly after this, in the negociations about Russia's suggestion of intervention in the Boer War, he actually based his refusal on the lack of security against the French desire for revenge. If Count Bülow sought to place Germany's situation and security before Chamberlain in a good light, his reasons for this were not far to seek. Cf. p. 108.

The question was whether Fashoda was not more in their heads than Sedan. Thus, humanly speaking, our peace was not threatened ; whereas I might well imagine that, owing to the great extent of her Empire and the daring conceptions of her statesmen, England might fall into serious difficulties at more than one point. Mr. Chamberlain's answer indicated that he foresees some such difficulties in the Far East. He does not conceal from himself that Russian influence has increased in China. He sees with anxiety how well, as against the British, the Russians know how to assimilate Asiatics. He said that a time might come when hundreds of thousands of Chinamen and Tartars armed with Russian weapons and drilled and led by Russian officers would be added to the Russian army. England had nothing in the way of a land army to set against this ; she would have to turn to Germany and America for support. America had no standing army, but she had vast resources and, in case of need, would be able to set on foot great masses of men, as at the time of her own Civil War. Mr. Chamberlain thinks he is sure of American help for the Far East. He said more than once that England desired no further increase of territory in Asia. She could not control more than she now possessed there. A second India on the Yang-tsze would be beyond her strength ; but she could not submit to be driven out of Persia and China by Russia. It was to England's interest to keep China, Persia and Turkey on their feet until further notice. The question was whether this would be possible much longer. These countries were like empty sacks which could not stand upright without support. Mr. Chamberlain, who was evidently informed of our desires in Asia Minor by his friend, Cecil Rhodes,[1] volunteered the remark that our trade, and even our colonial aspirations in those parts would not be objected to by England, if only we would be friendly to her ' on other points '. Regarding America Mr. Chamberlain said that a rapprochement with this Power was one of the cardinal points of his policy ; so that he would do nothing to wound American susceptibilities. For instance, he would not reach out towards South America, although there were districts there with great future possibilities. I told Mr. Chamberlain that if his ideal really was a rapprochement between England, Germany and America, he ought to see that misunderstandings do not recur between us and the Americans. He should exercise his great political and personal influence with the Americans to show them the profitableness of conciliating Germany in politics and business. Mr. Chamberlain replied that if Germany and England were in good and trusting relationship, England would

[1] Cf. note, p. 49.

certainly be interested in preventing friction between Germany and America. Mr. Chamberlain spoke of France as of a land in a decline, with which no business could be done. He is impressed by Russia on account of her rapidly increasing population, vast natural wealth, and consistent Asiatic policy. He fears Russia, but seems less inclined than Salisbury and Balfour to make a pact with her. In Italy he sees a useful friend for England, but with a very doubtful financial position. But England cannot escape from the obligation of defending the Italian coast, because Italy would otherwise fall entirely under the influence of France. He complained also of the German Press which was attacking England so violently. . . .

The projected strengthening of our fleet did not seem much to the taste of Mr. Chamberlain. He said that Lord Salisbury did not wish for an alliance with Germany, because he did not want to bind himself at all. Lord Salisbury wished for an alliance with Germany no more than with France or Russia ; he was a very cautious statesman, and believed it was always best to keep his hands free. Mr. Balfour was more inclined to the view that a general understanding with Germany would suit British interests.

His Majesty, the Emperor, granted Mr. Chamberlain an audience on the same day. Mr. Chamberlain said much the same to His Majesty. Only on two points did he say more to His Majesty than to me.

1. He informed His Majesty that he wished British capitalists to have a share in our Anatolian Railway. He had already got into touch with Herr Siemens and would prefer to see the Germans in Asia Minor than the French or Russians ; he did not begrudge us Asia Minor.

[The scheme would have gone through but for the determined opposition of Baron von Marschall, the German Ambassador in Constantinople, against any co-operation with England. Cf. Eckardstein, *Ten Years at the Court of St. James*, p. 169.]

2. Mr. Chamberlain turned the conversation on to the Mediterranean and Morocco, and described Tangier as an object of British desires. He added that we might maintain ourselves on the Atlantic coast of Morocco without harm coming of it. His Majesty replied to this suggestion that it might be a subject for confidential discussion between his Ambassador in London and Mr. Chamberlain. Mr. Chamberlain is emphatic on the necessity of avoiding everything likely to arouse jealousy or suspicion in Lord Salisbury, but sets store on close feeling with us, and would certainly do what he could so that we and England might conclude further useful agreements.

[Mr. Chamberlain wrote to Eckardstein : ' I had two long conversations with the Emperor, which confirmed my former impression of his extraordinary grasp of questions of European politics '. Encouraged by his conversations with the Emperor and Bülow, Chamberlain, at a great meeting at Leicester on November 30th, 1899, advocated a German alliance, as the ' most natural alliance ' for England. Cf. Eckardstein, *Ten Years at the Court of St. James*, pp. 130, 135, 143. The overture was, however, received with a storm of Anglo-phobe fury in Germany and came to nothing. (Cf. p. 209.)]

In the two interviews, with which Queen Victoria honoured me, Her Majesty expressed a very lively desire that no further misunderstandings should reign between England and Germany. She was preoccupied by the language of the German Press and said it was not good to irritate the British too much with attacks in the papers. The Englishman was slow and indolent, but if abused too much he might end by losing patience. I explained to Her Majesty that the irritation of the German Press against England was due to occasions when England had not observed proper consideration and good manners towards Germany. The Prince of Wales and all the Queen's daughters declared that a rapprochement between England, Germany and America would be to the interests of all of them, and the best guarantee of world peace.

British politicians know little of the Continent. They do not know much more of continental conditions than we do of those in Peru or Siam. To our ideas they are rather naïve.[1] They are naïve in their candid self-seeking, and again in the easy way in which they give their confidence. They believe with difficulty that others have bad motives. They are very calm, very easy-going (*pomadig*), very optimistic. The South African war excites the Berliners more than it does political circles here. It is only mentioned when someone's relation has been shot. Not a soul doubts that England will come well out of the affair. Everyone agrees that the Government must be supported until the situation in Africa is cleared up. If after great British successes, the Government strung up the Boers, even the most liberal Englishmen would give it their approval. Yet if after further failures, in order to avoid excessive sacrifice and expense, the Government concluded a barely honourable peace with the South African Republic, even the jingoes would not oppose it. They will accept anything which promises a practical solution. The country breathes wealth, comfort, contentment, and confidence in its own strength and future. One observes that the people have never seen an enemy in their land, and do not believe that anything could ever really

[1] A favourite word of Holstein's. Cf. *Ten Years at the Court of St. James*, p. 108.

go wrong, either at home or abroad.   With the exception of a few ' leading men ', they work little and give themselves plenty of holiday.   Both physically and morally it is a very healthy country.   Balfour is attracted by science and philosophy ; he reminds one of German statesmen in the fifties ; he impresses one as being benevolent and honourable.   Chamberlain, the modern merchant, very decided, very shy, very scrupulous, very much aware of his own advantage, and yet sincere, for he knows that without sincerity there can be no big business. The Duke of Devonshire is a typically calm and distinguished *grand seigneur,* to whom his sport and his horses are more important than any political question ; these, however, he deals with with *bon sens,* but always with the assumption that England is superior to all other Powers and has nothing serious to fear. Mr. Goschen has the intelligent industry of a German official ; he ought to do more for the navy than any of his predecessors. He models himself naturally on the thoroughbred Englishman, but expresses, nevertheless, a strong wish for good relations with Germany.   There is no doubt that feeling in England generally is far less anti-German than German feeling is anti-British.   Therefore the most dangerous Englishmen for us are those, who, like Chirol and Saunders, know from personal observation how sharp and deep is the German dislike of England. If the British public realised the feeling reigning just now in Germany, it would cause a great change in their view of the relationship between England and that country.

I consider that Germany's future task will be, whilst possessing a strong fleet and maintaining good relations on the side of Russia as well as of England, to await the further development of events patiently and collectedly.

XV. 424

COUNT HATZFELDT TO THE CHANCELLOR, PRINCE VON HOHENLOHE,
December 2nd, 1899

Extract.

. . . In his speech at Leicester [1] on November 30th, Mr. Chamberlain frankly and directly discussed the question of an alliance with Germany.   I must refrain for the present from expressing a decided opinion as to his motives on this occasion ; so far I can only base it on suppositions, but I intend to return to it later on.   But I should like to call attention to the view often expressed to me that Mr. Chamberlain is a very shrewd, competent business man but no diplomat, and that he ties himself down by fixed rules in his dealings.   However great may be his personal ambition, I do not consider that it should be

[1] Cf. Brandenburg, p. 138.

assumed that he is entirely guided by it and not by fixed political convictions at the same time. As Your Highness will remember, his idea of an alliance with Germany and America is by no means a new one ; a considerable time ago he discussed it with me repeatedly in secret conversations which I reported at the time. His coming out with it now in public proves, in my opinion, that he believes he has most of the Cabinet behind him in that matter, and also that he thinks the moment has come for getting the British public, which so far has been frightened of alliances, used to the idea of one. I do not think it at all certain that he is trying, out of personal ambition, to push matters to a breaking with Lord Salisbury and to turn him out of the saddle in the hope of seating himself in it. I am convinced that Lord Salisbury, in spite of many complaints made of him in his own party, is not at all to be regarded as finished politically, or that the Conservatives would allow him to fall until he himself should display a wish to retire. Moreover there can be no doubts in Mr. Chamberlain's mind that if the present Prime Minister retired, it would still be quite a question whether he could regard himself with certainty as his successor. With all this in consideration, I am not disinclined to assume that when Mr. Chamberlain made his speech about the alliance, he already had Lord Salisbury's consent to it in principle in his pocket, or else was convinced that—as in the Samoan question—with the help of a majority of his colleagues he would succeed in persuading the Prime Minister to accede to his wishes.

If I may allow myself an opinion, it can only be useful for us if, without our committing ourselves to any engagement, Mr. Chamberlain clings to the hope that we shall end by being persuaded to come in with his wishes for an alliance or a close understanding. At any rate as long as he clings to this hope, he will be accommodating to us in the colonial questions which will probably continue to turn up, and will—as in the Samoa question—try to influence the Cabinet, and especially Lord Salisbury, in our favour. (The EMPEROR : ' *Correct, and that is the point.*')

XV. 426

COUNT HATZFELDT TO THE GERMAN FOREIGN OFFICE, *December 20th,* 1899

Cipher telegram.

Mr. Chamberlain has shown to Baron von Eckardstein [1] in strict confidence two telegrams from Sir Alfred Milner, in the accuracy of which he believes. The first says that the British

[1] Returned to the Diplomatic Service as First Secretary in London, November 26th, 1899.

authorities seized a letter addressed to Colonel Schiel [1] by a German officer, still in the army, who announced that he was shortly leaving to join the Boer army. (The EMPEROR: *'Give his name! Hatzfeldt should not let himself be bluffed by impudent Joe and should make short and sharp work of such general accusations with a reference to my Orders to the army.'*) The second telegram contains a report from the British Consul at Lorenzo Marquez that 12 German officers and 29 N.C.O.'s (mostly Gunners, still on the Reserve) arrived by the steamer *Königin* and proceeded to Pretoria. Mr. Chamberlain spoke with regret (The EMPEROR: *'I regret that he believes such a thing!'*) of the bad blood this will cause when it is known. (The EMPEROR: *'If it depended on him, it would not become known. It is his revenge for the failure of his speech and for Count Bülow's apparently frigid speech about England!'*)

There is in fact an idea spread abroad amongst the public, and even in the highest circles, that the Boers are led by officers of the German General Staff. (The EMPEROR: *'This has already been rebutted very cleverly and correctly through Mister Robinson [2] in an interview. Nonsense! but it could be foreseen that something of the sort would be asserted. The Ambassador must inform Mr. Chamberlain of my Order to all Army Corps, that none of their members, including even troops that have been disbanded, are permitted to go to Africa.—That is all that is required.—If we had a fleet, Chamberlain would not have dared!'*)

XV. 428

COUNT HATZFELDT TO THE GERMAN FOREIGN OFFICE,
December 21st, 1899

Cipher telegram.

Private for the Secretary of State.

Baron von Eckardstein assures me that from his latest conversations with Mr. Balfour and Mr. Chamberlain (the latter of whom he met yesterday) he has obtained a distinct impression that in Government circles here the necessity is being more and more felt of gaining some kind of control—perhaps only temporary—of Delagoa Bay,[3] and of thus cutting off the continuous flow of assistance to the enemy through this channel. It is considered in these circles—and the tone of the Press seems to confirm this expectation—that British public opinion is becoming more urgent for action in this sense, and that the Government will end by having to give in. At the same time it appears certain that leading British statesmen have become convinced that they

---

[1] Commanding the German Volunteer Corps in the Boer War.
[2] Sir Hercules Robinson.
[3] Cf. G. & T., I, p. 243; also Eckardstein, *Ten Years*, p. 152.

cannot proceed further without our previous agreement, and also that they do not know in what form eventually to deal with the matter at Lisbon. They apparently hesitate between two possibilities ; whether to offer Portugal financial help and an offensive and defensive alliance, whereby England would get control of Delagoa Bay, or to act forcibly at Delagoa Bay and to explain it at Lisbon on the ground that by letting through arms, munitions and volunteers for the Transvaal Portugal has not observed her duty of neutrality.

His conversations have given Baron von Eckardstein the impression that a strictly confidential enquiry under what conditions, if at all, we would come in with the British wishes regarding Delagoa Bay may be expected at any moment. He also considers that renunciation of Zanzibar is regarded here as quite out of the question, but that they might eventually be ready to give up Walfisch Bay. . . .

XV. 433
COUNT VON BÜLOW TO COUNT VON TATTENBACH, AT LISBON, December 25th, 1899

Telegram.

The war in South Africa, the development and duration of which cannot now be estimated, gives the possession of Lorenzo Marquez an importance both for the belligerents and also for third parties. For Germany, with her large and carefully nurtured colonial and business interests in South and East Africa, it is by no means a matter of indifference what becomes of Lorenzo Marquez and Delagoa Bay. Please therefore declare officially to the Portuguese Government that any agreement concluded by Portugal with a third Government regarding possession or control of Delagoa Bay can only be recognised by His Majesty's Government, if the latter is informed beforehand of the negociations and is able to determine whether the intended agreement can be brought into line with German interests. Any agreement regarding Delagoa Bay which ignored Germany would have to be regarded by us an an unfriendly act. You may inform your British colleague of this instruction in confidence, but you will put it to him in a form showing that it is not exclusively and obviously directed against England.

German Note.

Count Hatzfeldt telegraphed to Count Bülow : ' Agree absolutely with instruction to Lisbon. I think we must go slowly and get the British to meet us half-way. They are not yet reduced enough to think of giving up Zanzibar.'

[Regarding Dr. Leyds' activities in Paris Count Münster telegraphed XV. 430) : ' Dr. Leyds . . . obtains no hearing here. The French desire still further ill-success for the British Army.' Count Hatzfeldt telegraphed (XV. 435) : ' The British Cabinet, which seems to attach greater importance to Herr Leyds' intrigues in Paris than they really perhaps merit, is convinced, I understand, that it is due to Germany's attitude, that Delcassé abstained from entering into them, since he was unable to get Germany to join in them. They are delighted here at our attitude.']

Minute by Count Bülow to a despatch of December 26th (XV. 434).

Far the greater number of soldiers here *believe that the war in South Africa will end in a complete defeat of the British. A few of our officers think that if the British act very cautiously and send all the troops they can to South Africa, they will gradually wear down the Boers. Even these observers consider that directly the fortune of war turns to them or merely stands still, the British will make peace with the Boers on a* status quo ante bellum *basis. No one at the moment believes in a British advance on Pretoria. But,* chi lò sà !

[Acting on information which was proved later to be false, H.M.S. *Magicienne* detained the German Mail Steamer *Bundesrath* (and two others. which were, however, quickly released) and brought her before a Prize Court at Durban. The case was important in International Law, as it raised the question how far steamers carrying the mails should be immune from detention and search. Cf. Parliamentary Papers. *Africa*, 1900, No. 1 ; G. & T., p. 245 ; Eckardstein, *Ten Years*, p. 152 et seq. ; Sir A. Hardinge, *A Diplomat in the East*, p. 247 ; Brandenburg, p. 139.]

German Note. XV. 475

According to Baron von Eckardstein, detailed and exhaustive research finally proved conclusively that (*Ten Years*, p. 154) both the suggestions, which were originally made to the British representatives at Hamburg, and also the anonymous letters to the Prize Court at Durban, originated with Dr. Leyds and his agents. A search made in the Records of the Foreign Office has revealed nothing in support of this assertion. It looks very much more as if the head of the *Foreign Press Association* in London, a Russian named Vesselitski, had a hand in it. [Eckardstein reported (January 24th) that this Association maintained close relations with Leyds and the cable correspondence which Leyds subsidised.]

XV. 445

COUNT VON BÜLOW TO COUNT HATZFELDT, *January 3rd*, 1900 *Telegram.*

German East African Line [1] begs that the question of bail for the steamer may not be touched immediately, as they fear that if other steamers are detained the sum will come to too much.

We decidedly expect early news of the ship's release, for Prize Court procedure seems to us out of the question considering the nature of the case. Only proved presence of contraband

[1] The Woermann Line.

of war can justify this. Whatever the ship might contain this is impossible, for according to the recognised principles of International Law there can be no contraband in trade between neutral ports. This view corresponds with the standpoint adopted in 1863 by the British Government itself against the sentence of the American Prize Court when the *Springbok* was detained, and it is also defended by the British Admiralty in its *Manual of Naval Prize Law* (1866). In face of the rules there laid down ' A vessel's destination should be considered neutral, if both the port to which she is bound, and every intermediate port at which she is to call in the course of her voyage be neutral,' and ' the destination of the vessel is conclusive as to the destination of the goods on board '—our claim for the release of the ship without a Prize Court examination is entirely justified, and all the more so, since the ship's character as a mail steamer with a fixed voyage forbids the discharge of cargo in any other than the determined port of destination.

You will at once make use of this and yesterday's telegram [1] and apply by note for the release of the *Bundesrath* with reservation of our claim for compensation ; you will declare that the wrongful detention has already lasted more than a week, and that so far the London Cabinet has not informed us as to the reasons for this.

[Another German mail steamer, the *General*, was detained at Aden on January 4th, 1900. Count Bülow addressed a very peremptory note to London in a tone described by Eckardstein as one of ' sheer offensiveness ' (p. 152). The note and Lord Salisbury's letter of protest against its tone are printed in Blue Book, *Africa*, No. 1.]

XV. 452

COUNT VON BÜLOW TO COUNT HATZFELDT, *January 6th*, 1900

Extract.

. . . For your confidential information I will add that I am informed that Sir Arthur Hardinge, the British Consul-General at Zanzibar, travelled from Naples to Zanzibar as a passenger on the *Bundesrath*, which is surprising considering the unluxurious character of the steamer ; it gives food for thought.

From the enclosed cutting from the *Leipsiger Neureste Nachrichten* of the 3rd you will see that public opinion is excited about an order for steel grenades, apparently accepted by the Krupp Works for the British Government. I have taken occasion to write to Herr Krupp requiring him to delay delivery of

---

[1] Containing the report of the German Consul General at Cape Town and an assurance that there was no contraband in the *Bundesrath*.

war material to England till further notice, and will take care to inform you as soon as a final decision has been taken on this question. Meanwhile I beg you not to make use of this.

XV. 504

COUNT VON ALVENSLEBEN, IN BRUSSELS, TO THE CHANCELLOR, PRINCE VON HOHENLOHE, *January 10th*, 1900
Extract.

A visit to Dr. Leyds gave me an opportunity for a long discussion. He told me that the South African Consul-General in London, Montague White, whom he had requested to go to the United States, had arrived there. His instructions were to create a feeling in favour of mediation by the United States Government, and there were hopes that his efforts may be successful now that public opinion there is so decidedly in favour of the South African Republic. Dr. Leyds thought that Mr. MacKinley would only consent to mediate if he considered it would help him in the Elections, and this would chiefly depend on the attitude of the German and Irish population ; Dr. Leyds reckons confidently on their pronouncing in favour of the Boers.

In spite of his countrymen's persistent success Dr. Leyds looks on the situation as very serious and desires mediation, the basis of which must naturally be independence for the Transvaal. . . .

Regarding the possibility of the British seizing Delagoa Bay, Dr. Leyds thinks that for various reasons it would be a great injury to the Transvaal ; it would stop any possibility of bringing in munitions, food, mails, etc. There was no fear of the rifle ammunition running short, for a few years ago the stock for Mauser rifles had stood at over 30 millions, and for the Martini-Henry at over 20 millions of rounds. Since then a part had certainly been used against the Kaffirs. But the artillery ammunition would gradually be spent ; the present stock would only last a few months, and even if the shells could be made in the country, the fuses could not. . . .

XV. 468

SIR FRANK LASCELLES, IN BERLIN, TO COUNT VON BÜLOW, *January 14th*, 1900
Extract.

. . . In the opinion of Her Majesty's Government the passage cited from the Manual ' that the destination of the vessel is conclusive evidence as to the destination of the goods on board ', has no application to such circumstances as have now arisen. It is considered that it cannot apply to contraband of war on board of a neutral vessel if such contraband was at the time of seizure consigned or intended to be delivered to an agent of the enemy at a neutral port, or, in fact, destined for the enemy's country.

The true view of the latter category of goods is, as Her Majesty's Government believe, correctly stated in Paragraph 813 of Professor Bluntschli's *Droit International Codifié* as follows (the French translation of the 2nd edition of the work of this most eminent German jurist is cited) :—

' Si les navires ou marchandises ne sont expediés à destination d'un port neutre que pour mieux venir en aide à l'ennemie il y aura contrebande de guerre et la confiscation sera justifiée.' . . .

[A statement made by Lord Salisbury that ships should no longer be examined at Aden, and that the question of the consideration to be shown by British naval commanders to mail steamers was under consideration, did not satisfy the German Government. Cf. Eckardstein, *Ten Years*, p. 153 et seq.; G. & T., I, p. 246.]

XV. 471

HOLSTEIN TO BARON VON ECKARDSTEIN, IN LONDON,
January 14th, 1900

Telegram.   Drafted by Count von Bülow.

To be deciphered by yourself.

Your telegram of to-day has made the most unfavourable impression here.   The Emperor is considering whether someone should not be sent from here at once within 48 hours to ascertain by Thursday by a direct question whether we are likely to come to an understanding with England or shall be forced to meet by another method the uneasy situation in which the to me incomprehensible apathy of the British Government places us.

Please keep this from the sick Ambassador, but inform me whether we may expect satisfaction for our requirements and proper fulfilment of British promises, particularly with regard to renewed arbitrary action against mail steamers.

German Note.

There is no evidence in the records that the Emperor really proposed such a mission, nor that Holstein sent out the same type communication in a harsher form by a separate channel (not Eckardstein) to the effect that an Admiral was on the way to present the British Government with an ultimatum of 48 hours.   From what can be found in the Records the Foreign Office appears not to have laid the documents concerning the detention of the steamers before the Emperor at all, the object being to avoid unconsidered steps by him ; at any rate these documents contain none of the Emperor's marginal notes.   The only part the Emperor played in the affair, as shown in the Records, was a direction on January 7th to propose a Court of Arbitration to England.

XV. 481

HOLLEBEN, IN WASHINGTON, TO THE GERMAN FOREIGN OFFICE,
January 21st, 1900

Cipher telegram.

The *Washington Times* says that Germany's diplomatic victory over England seems to be complete. The whole civilised world owes gratitude to the German Foreign Office for the clear, irreproachable and decided way in which it settled the affair. The view held in America for more than 100 years, that private property, even that of an enemy, should be exempt from seizure at sea, will, as a result of the late friction between the United States and Germany on the one hand and England on the other, now probably be generally accepted.

XV. 510

HOLLEBEN, IN WASHINGTON, TO THE GERMAN FOREIGN OFFICE
February 2nd, 1900

Cipher telegram.

In a long conversation with me the Secretary of State again spoke with much feeling of England's unhappy situation in South Africa, and said that seizing Delagoa Bay would finally be the only means of escaping from her difficulties. He asked me whether I thought that in that event the other European Powers would depart from their reserve. Without answering the question I indicated that America's attitude would in that event probably not be without its influence on the others. He insisted that America would maintain strict neutrality and would not think of offering mediation, which, moreover, would apparently not be desired by both parties. On my saying that, seeing the strong swing over in public opinion here, especially in the Republican camp, even an appearance of too much good-will to England might endanger the President's chances of re-election, he denied this completely and said that good-will towards England, especially if her situation became worse, would be understood by every reasonable man, since England's ruin would be a world-misfortune.

The Secretary of State also thinks that the news originating in St. Petersburg that England has already threatened Lisbon with an occupation of Delagoa Bay is not correct.

XV. 518

COUNT VON METTERNICH, (TEMPORARY) AMBASSADOR IN LONDON, TO THE CHANCELLOR, *March 3rd* [?], 1900

I understand that the Prince of Wales spoke to various Members of Parliament on Anglo-German relations in the following sense :

During the South African war the Emperor and his Government had shown the greatest friendliness to England and repeatedly offered proofs of sympathy. The Emperor thoroughly understood the South African question and knew well that it was not one of the gold mines in the Transvaal, as appeared to be thought by continental public opinion, but of whether England was to remain the predominant Power in South Africa or was to be utterly driven out by an Africander republic. England could not forget that it was owing generally to the Emperor's visit to England and also to the attitude of the German Government that England's enemies had not intervened. (The EMPEROR: '*Very good and quite correct.*') As little attention as possible should be paid here to the German Press; the main thing was that the German Government was friendly disposed towards England. No one could deny that in the sad days through which England had passed that Government had proved itself a true and reliable friend. (The EMPEROR: '*Donnerwetter! That is a very great deal from the Prince of Wales; up to now he has never said a word in our favour! I owe him high thanks. The correspondence may have contributed something to his views.*')

German Note. XV. 423

After the Emperor's visit to England, there started a lively and friendly correspondence between the Emperor and the Queen and the Prince of Wales, dealing largely with the Boer War. A letter from the Prince of Wales (December 27th, 1899) shows the Emperor had already (on the 21st) sent him *A few thoughts* (Gedankensplitter) *on the war in the Transvaal,* to which his *Aphorisms* formed a second series. These earlier *Thoughts* are not in the Foreign Office records.

German Note. XV. 554

The Emperor's own account of his *Aphorisms* given in a *Daily Telegraph* interview is as follows: ' I bade one of my officers procure for me as èxact an account as he could obtain of the number of combatants in South Africa on both sides, and of the actual position of the opposing forces. With the figures before me, I worked out what I considered to be the best plan of campaign under the circumstances, and submitted it to the General Staff for their criticism. Then I despatched it to England, and that document likewise is among the State Papers at Windsor Castle awaiting the serenely impartial verdict of history. And, as a matter of curious coincidence, let me add that the plan which I formulated ran very much on the same lines as the one which was actually adopted by Lord Roberts and carried by him into successful operation.' Speaking in the Reichstag on November 10th, 1908, Prince Bülow stated that no plan of campaign or any similar work by the Emperor had been examined by the General Staff or forwarded to England. Nor is there any confirmation of it in the Records. The Emperor must only have shown it to his aide-de-camp on duty at the time, who did belong to the General Staff.

[The following private note (March 3rd, 1900) from the Emperor to Sir Frank Lascelles shows that the expression ' unmitigated noodles ' referred to by Eckardstein (*Ten Years at the Court of St. James*, p. 215) was not a new one with the Emperor. (Cf. p. 144.)

MY DEAR SIR FRANK,

I have just received to my utmost astonishment the invitation from the Imper. Russian Government to take part with them and France in a collective intervention for the Boers to bring England to make peace. *I have refused.* Intimating in my answer that I must leave it to the generous instigator of the European Peace Conference to kindly inform himself in London wether (*sic*) the British Government and People were in any mood to lend an ear to the Imperial proposals in the name of the Dual Alliance, I for my person had my serious doubts and was unable to second the movement, as I was quite sure of the nature of the answer !—*Privately* ! the British Government would be a set of unmitigated noodles if they cared a farthing ! Private information say that they expect a refus at Petersburg, and that they will DO *nothing*, as an answer to it. (Cf. p. 144; G. & T., II, 53; III, 3rd page before end.)]

XV. 521

COUNT METTERNICH, IN LONDON, TO THE GERMAN FOREIGN OFFICE, *March 7th*, 1900

Cipher telegram.

At the beginning of our conversation to-day Lord Salisbury of his own initiative mentioned the Emperor's recent conversation with Sir Frank Lascelles and begged me to express his thanks for His Majesty's very gracious sentiment for England.

The Minister added that yesterday a telegram had been received from the two Boer Republics proposing peace, but stipulating independence for both Republics.

Although he did not say it outright, his words implied that this condition could not be discussed here.

HOLSTEIN : *It must permanently injure Sir F. Lascelles' position with His Majesty, if the Emperor sees in what tone the ' Times,' which is directed by Lascelles' friend, Chirol, and Saunders, who is in almost daily touch with Lascelles, continues to write. As I do not know Lascelles, I cannot judge whether a warning would be useful.*

BULOW : *Agree entirely ; will refer to it when I next see Lascelles.*

[In answer to an appeal from Pretoria (March 10th, 1900), Count Bülow consented to mediate in the cause of peace. In a letter written by the Emperor to Bülow the next day (published by the *Berliner Tageblatt* in September, 1928), the Emperor wrote : ' . . . England the paramount Power ! That pleases Sir Frank Lascelles and pleases in London. Should, however, London be inclined to go into mediation, at any rate it knows what it has to expect from us. If it turns to us, *tant mieux*; then my goal is attained, and England receives South Africa from me ! *Voilà !* The consequences you can imagine for yourself.']

[On March 13th, 1900, the United States offered mediation.]

COUNT VON METTERNICH TO THE GERMAN FOREIGN OFFICE,
March 14th, 1900

Cipher telegram.

Lord Salisbury informed me that he had rejected with thanks the friendly offer of mediation by the United States ; the British Government did not intend to avail itself of mediation by a third party. He described the American action as an election manœuvre.

So far no other Power had taken action here on the appeal of the Boer Presidents, and he did not think it would happen. He warmly agreed with my remark that Germany's attitude was preventing a coalition for intervention.

[On a report from Count Pourtalès at The Hague discussing the advisability of a visit of Boer delegates to America the Emperor wrote ' *Yes* ' and ' *I do not wish to have the gentlemen in Berlin* '.]

XV. 544

COUNT VON BÜLOW TO COUNT VON POURTALÈS, AT THE HAGUE,
May 28th, 1900

Extract.

Herr von Holleben telegraphs from Washington that the Boer delegates intend, after their return from America, to go to Berlin in order to lay their case before the Emperor if possible.

The unfavourable course of the activities of the South African mission to America, the American Government's refusal, and the ill-success so far of the pro-Boer movement in the United States make any attempt to promote action in Europe in the Boers' favour seem more hopeless than before. The realisation that the United States, ignoring the small sister-Republics in South Africa, have taken advantage of the South African crisis to emphasise their solidarity of interests with England will probably be a warning to the European Powers, divided as they are by many private interests, to observe special care and reserve. . . .

[The Boer delegates did enjoy an enthusiastic popular reception in the States, but this did not influence the policy of the American Government. Cf. p. 131.

In November, 1900, President Kruger left his country and after staying a week in Paris he arrived at Cologne on December 1st. On the grounds put forward in the following memorandum the Emperor refused to receive him.]

XV. 549

MEMORANDUM BY LINDENAU, GERMAN FOREIGN OFFICE,
November 5th, 1900

It would be well to inform the Dutch Minister orally and confidentially that there is no intention here to answer the statement of the Boer delegates [1] which has been received here. It would perhaps have a good effect if the Emperor's marginal remark [2] were shown to the Minister in confidence.

Since the Boers apparently continue to hope to find support in Germany, it might be well to use this opportunity to say emphatically to the Dutch Minister that we never ceased offering the Boers good advice while there was yet time. But we could not promise the least advantage to ourselves in a tour by President Kruger through Germany for agitation purposes, and we consider it essential for Kruger's interests, as well as for the Dutch and German Governments, that the Dutch Government should use its undoubtedly legitimate influence on President Kruger to deter him from useless attempts at this stage of the question to get German influence to work in his favour and against England.

[1] Imputing ' methods of barbarism ' to the British in their conduct of the war.
[2] ' *Non possum !* '

CHAPTER VIII

THE BOXER REBELLION. JUNE, 1900, TO MARCH, 1901. THE YANG-TSZE AGREEMENT

[The principle of recognising that the Powers could claim spheres of interest in China for the development of their trade was mutually admitted by the end of 1897. (Cf. p. 19, also G. & T., I, p. 2.) On April 28th, 1898, Russia and England agreed formally to recognise them, and on September 9th, 1898, the British and German bankers did likewise. (Cf. M. J. Bau, *The Open Door Doctrine*.) The Powers, and especially the United States, expressed adherence with varying sincerity to the doctrine that trade in the ports within their spheres of interest should be open to all nations—in other words, the Open Door. (Cf. *U.S. Foreign Relations*, pp. 355, 373 ; Brandenburg, p. 147 et seq.)

The Yang-tsze Agreement between England and Germany was based on these lines, but its efficacy was destroyed by the German fear of annoying Russia. Count Bülow refused to admit that the principle of Chinese territorial integrity applied to the Russians in Manchuria ; where the Russians were concerned he insisted on strict German neutrality. (Cf. Sir Eyre Crowe's *Memorandum*, G. & T., II, p. 152.)

The Boxer rising against foreign influence and the peril to the foreign Legations at Pekin were practically over by the time that the European contingents under Count Waldersee arrived in China, (Cf. Eckardstein, *Ten Years*, p. 174) and Count Waldersee's duties as Commander-in-Chief largely consisted in keeping the peace between the component parts of his army. He was anti-British in sympathy, and diplomatic pressure had more than once to be applied to restrain his tendency to allow encroachments on British rights.]

XVI. 20

COUNT HATZFELDT, IN LONDON, TO THE GERMAN FOREIGN OFFICE, *June 26th,* 1900

Cipher telegram.

Lord Salisbury's telegram of to-day to Berlin, directing the British Embassy to ask for our support in St. Petersburg regarding despatch of 20,000 Japanese troops to China is the result of urgent advice by Sir Frank Lascelles,[1] as the latter informs me. The Ambassador represented to the Prime Minister, who had consulted him, that the distrust he met with in Berlin was greatly to be ascribed to the fact that he did not declare his intentions to Germany openly and frankly.

[1] On leave in England.

From St. Petersburg, whither a telegram on the same subject was despatched yesterday evening, no reply has yet been returned, and Salisbury tells me he fears that Count Lamsdorff will not have the courage to take either initiative or responsibility. He seemed to consider it settled that Japan should not send these troops to China until she received a guarantee that Russia would cause her no embarrassment on that account. When I suggested that Japan might perhaps demand another guarantee from England for the event of complications with Russia, the Prime Minister replied that I knew how unwilling England was to promise military support to another Power.

Lord Salisbury had enquired in Washington what they were prepared to do there for the protection of foreigners in China. The answer returned through the American Ambassador [1] was rather unsatisfactory, the Prime Minister said, for in Washington they wished to send no more than 300 men.

The report current here that Tientsin has been relieved rests so far only on private British information.

XVI. 21

TSCHIRSCHKY, IN ST. PETERSBURG, TO THE GERMAN FOREIGN OFFICE, *June 27th*, 1900

Cipher telegram.

I have been able to ascertain that the British Ambassador [2] invited the French Chargé d'Affaires [3] especially in order to tell him of Lord Salisbury's telegram entrusting Japan with a mandate.

I am following Anglo-French relations on the Chinese crisis with special attention, because I think it not improbable that England is trying here also to draw France to herself by means of a direct understanding on the delimitation of the Yang-tsze territory—as well as other subjects.

XVI. 27

THE EMPEROR WILLIAM, AT BRUNSBÜTTELKOOG, TO THE GERMAN FOREIGN OFFICE, *July 1st*, 1900

Telegram.

Since a regular campaign against Pekin has become necessary the commander of the cruiser squadron is asking for an Infantry division. Please observe from my telegram of a fortnight ago to the Foreign Office that I considered it necessary to order not only mobilisation of the Marines, but also the immediate equipment of an Infantry division. Your Excellency advised strongly

---

[1] Joseph H. Choate.   [2] Sir Charles Stewart Scott.
[3] Count Vauvineux.

against this ; it might have been ready to start to-day ! I had long been expecting Bendemann's [1] telegram. It was bound to turn out so.

German Note.

. . . From Brunsbüttelkoog the Emperor went on the 2nd to Wilhelms-haven, where two telegrams from the Foreign Office met him with the confirmation of the news of the murder of Baron von Ketteler,[2] German Minister at Pekin, of which rumours only had so far been received. Imme-diately under the impression of this, to which was added the news that the position of the closely besieged Ministers in Peking was well-nigh des-perate, the Emperor made to the troops before embarkation the celebrated speech demanding ' exemplary punishment and revenge ' for the deep insult suffered by Germany. ' I shall not rest until the German flag along with those of the other Powers waves victoriously over that of China and, planted on the walls of Pekin, dictates peace to the Chinese.'

XVI. 201

DERENTHALL, IN BERLIN, TO COUNT VON BÜLOW, *July 27th*, 1900

Telegram.

I may allow myself the following commentary on Count Hatzfeldt's message of to-day :

The question which governs everything is the Yang-tsze.[3] Since we cannot count on monopolising it—at least for a long time to come—we should at least aim at preventing England from doing so. In this we are on the side of the other Powers who wish the Yang-tsze to be free for all nations.

The sooner the Russians learn that this is our view, the less inclined they will be to give in about it. Neither is it to be expected that the Americans,[4] in their strongly developed egoism, will admit the Yang-tsze as a British sphere of influence, for it is obvious to assume that if too many non-British goods enter through the ' open door ' the British may one day close it.

It is clear that in order to get the Yang-tsze England will concede much to Russia, and not in the Far East alone. For this reason Germany is not interested in this agreement. I think that there can be no better way of suppressing it than to strengthen the Russian side by associating ourselves with it in this and other similar questions, *but only case by case.* . . .

German Note. XVI. 61

Baron Eckardstein's statement (*Ten Years*, pp. 173–4) [regarding the appointment of Count Waldersee as Commander-in-Chief at Pekin] is an exaggeration . . . The facts of the case were that first of all, the German Government extended an entirely personal feeler in London through Hatz-

---

[1] Commanding the cruiser squadron in the Far East.
[2] Cf. Rev. R. Allen, *The Siege of the Pekin Legations*, pp. 77, 103.
[3] Cf. G. & T., II, pp. 2, 9 et seq.
[4] Cf. *U.S. Foreign Relations*, pp. 355, 373 ; also G. & T., II, p. 200.

feldt, and then, on the strength of a British enquiry on July 21st, gave it out that Germany would accept the command in chief, if it were proposed by England.   On August 5th the Emperor William, in a personal telegram to the Tsar, enquired about handing the command to a Russian—a subject already mentioned by Germany on July 25th—and proposed the appointment of Count Waldersee in the event of a Russian refusal.   The first mention of Waldersee in the Records is in a telegram from Count Bülow to the Emperor on August 5th.   It is out of the question that from the middle of July onwards William II regarded his own choice of Count Waldersee as Commander-in-Chief as an accomplished fact, as stated by Eckardstein . . . [Cf. *British and Foreign State Papers*, XCIV–V ; also G. & T., II, p. 8.]

[The words used by the Emperor in his telegram to the Tsar on the subject of the chief command were as follows : ' The strongest corps only really worth speaking of will be the Russian, German and Japanese.   Is it your special wish that a Russian should be commander-in-chief ?   Or would you eventually wish one of my generals ?   In the latter case I place Field-Marshal Count Waldersee at your disposal . . .' (XVI. 82.)

The Tsar replied : ' Having thought much about your proposition concerning the question of one commander-in-chief, I am happy to tell you that I fully agree to the nomination of Field-Marshal Count Waldersee to that post.   I know him well ; he is certainly one of your most able and experienced generals, and his name stands high in the Russian army. With full confidence I place my troops in Petchili under his command.'

The force consisted at that moment of 14,000 men, including 2,000 British, 1,500 Americans, 500 Germans.   (Cf. Rev. R. Allen, *The Siege of the Pekin Legations*, p. 235.)]

XVI. 71

Count Hatzfeldt to the German Foreign Office,
July 27th, 1900

Cipher telegram.

Lord Salisbury's hesitation in adopting an attitude with regard to the chief command is explained, as I gather from remarks by his private secretary, Mr. Barrington, and similar ones by the Russian Chargé d'Affaires,[1] by his wish that all military operations in the Yang-tsze [2] territory should, with the consent of the Powers, especially of Russia, be reserved for England alone. This was why Lord Salisbury first proposed in St. Petersburg that each Power should act alone and independently in its own sphere of interest and that only the army destined to march on Pekin should be under one command in chief.   It is indifferent to him which Power holds this command.   If Russia agrees to his proposal of independent action in each Power's sphere of interest and thus recognises the British claim to the Yang-tsze territory, I am informed that the Prime Minister is prepared to accept a Russian or French command for the troops marching on Pekin and to recommend it to the other Powers.   If Russia does not accept his proposal, he would under certain circumstances

---

[1] P. M. Lessar.   [2] Cf. G. & T., II, p. 2.

prefer a German commander. He does not claim it for England, since he would wish, under the pretext that the British troops are needed, for the protection of southern China, to hold aloof as much as possible from the operations in the north and to leave it to the other Powers to settle the matter.

The Russian Chargé d'Affaires said confidentially that Russia would scarcely consent to the British proposal. Russia would operate more or less independently in Manchuria, whilst England hoped to obtain Russia's consent to her proposals and that Russia would recognise the Yang-tsze as exclusively a British sphere of interest. Russia would never consent to this, for she had no intention of handing the rich Yang-tsze country with its 220 million inhabitants to England alone.

XVI. 208

PRINCE VON RADOLIN, IN ST. PETERSBURG, TO THE IMPERIAL CHANCELLOR, *August 2nd*, 1900

A conversation with Count Cassini, the Russian Ambassador in Washington, at present on leave here, gave me an opportunity of learning his views on Anglo-American relations. The Count spoke very freely and said that, in spite of England occasionally currying favour with America and of Mr. Hay's predilection for England and his drawing President MacKinley along with him to some extent, there was bound in a short time to be a violent break in the relations between the two countries. A collision of interests could not be averted. England could not look on at America's enormous advance in shipbuilding without anxiety.

In the United States, says Count Cassini, there is, side by side with strongly expressed animosity against Germany on account of her great trade development,—notwithstanding the fact that they have to reckon with 10 millions of Germans—a definite and unmistakable hatred of England, which is fanned by 15 million Irish. Mr. Hay is playing a very bold game with public feeling when he gives free play to his British sympathies. The enthusiasm with which the Boer delegates were received in the States [1] was a slap in the face for England.

Another and real point in favour of discord would, in the Ambassador's opinion, be England's policy on the Yang-tsze Kiang. In spite of the apparent temporary good feeling between the British and American troops at Tientsin, America would not long stand England's supremacy on the Yang-tsze, the right to which she absolutely opposed. Material American interests on that stream were too large for them to allow them to be controlled by British financial magnates. Count Cassini's views coincide

[1] Cf. p. 125.

with those of C. Tower, my American colleague here, for as against the contested British monopoly on the Yang-tsze, he regards a virtual Russian domination of Manchuria by means of railways and fortified settlements as entirely right and proper.

[The Prince of Wales, accompanied by Sir Frank Lascelles, visited the Emperor at Wilhelmshöhe on August 21st, 1900. The Emperor then proposed that Germany and England should co-operate in maintaining the policy of the ' open door ' on the Yang-tsze. (Cf. G. & T., II, p. 7 et seq. ; also Eckardstein, *Ten Years*, p. 176.)]

XVI. 214

COUNT VON BÜLOW TO COUNT HATZFELDT, *September 1st*, 1900 *Telegram*.

The British Ambassador, who undertook to report to Lord Salisbury His Majesty's words on the Yang-tsze question, has handed in here the following reply :

' The Marquis of Salisbury fears that he has not understood rightly the expressions which the Emperor used in his recent conversation with Sir Frank Lascelles.

' If Count Bülow will be kind enough to telegraph to Sir Frank Lascelles or, should he prefer it, to Lord Salisbury the proposals regarding Chinese affairs which His Majesty desires to make, His Lordship will give them of course his most respectful consideration. Lord Salisbury is however not aware that the Emperor had proposed any course of conduct to her Majesty's Government which differs from that now being pursued and which for some time has been pursued by them.' [1]

Lord Salisbury's grudging *insouciance* may be explained by his personal feeling,[2] or by actual dislike of an agreement which would define, i.e., limit, the claims on the Yang-tsze.

I consider that the proper course now is to use the Prime Minister's general statement, which merely implies that the condition described by His Majesty as desirable is at this moment actually in force, as the starting point for a suggestion somewhat as follows :

' The Government of His Majesty the Emperor consider that the unrest and insecurity, which is now making itself felt in China's relations with the Powers and—partly also as a result of this—in those of the Powers with each other, point to the desirability of an agreement between the Powers chiefly concerned in business with China on the principle that freedom of trade on the Yang-tsze is to the permanent joint interest of all, and therefore to be jointly and permanently protected.'

We should make this proposal simultaneously in London,

---

[1] Cf. G. & T., VI, p. 10.
[2] Lord Salisbury was at this time far from well.

Paris, Washington and Tokio, but not in St. Petersburg, where they show characteristic indifference to the Yang-tsze. In England it could be argued that it is merely a matter of making permanent the existing conditions to which Lord Salisbury alluded with satisfaction.

Before going further, however, I must ask for your views on the ideas given above and on the method of carrying them out,— whether our suggestion to England should be made through you in London or to Sir Frank Lascelles.

German Note. XVI. 218

Mr. Bertie, Assistant Secretary to the Foreign Office, [cf. G. & T., II, p. 11] made certain overtures regarding the railway lines Taku-Tientsin and Tientsin-Pekin, which had fallen into the hands of the Russians, notwithstanding that both lines had been constructed with British money. [The action was authorised by Waldersee, in his quality as Commander-in-Chief.] Mr. Bertie expressed a wish to Count Hatzfeldt that Germany should join with England to seek restitution of these lines, or at least take measures to prevent the Russians from capturing the Tientsin-Pekin line. (Cf. G. & T., II, p. 19.)

XVI. 221

COUNT HATZFELDT [1] TO THE GERMAN FOREIGN OFFICE,
September 14th, 1900

Cipher telegram.

I have just spoken to Lord Salisbury on the two points communicated by Mr. Bertie. The Prime Minister replied first that the extent of the proposals communicated to him by Sir Frank Lascelles [2] was not clear to him, because the expression ' open door policy ', so often used here, was very vague and capable of various interpretations. Just because of this vagueness he had chosen in his declaration to the Americans a more precise form admitting of no misunderstanding, and he thought we should both do well to choose this or a similar form when drafting the point in question. I replied to Lord Salisbury that we considered that his declaration to the Americans was too general and unsuited to the aims which all the participants must follow— *liberté de trafic* on the Yang-tsze. The Minister remarked that this aim was quite in consonance with the policy always followed by England in connection with China, and he hoped therefore that we should be able to come to an agreement if a form could be found acceptable to both parties.

As regards the second portion—a mutual engagement to acquire no territorial advantages in China as a result of the present troubles—I said confidentially that I had laid this point before my Government in order to be able to deny the constantly

[1] Cf. Eckardstein, *Ten Years at the Court of St. James*, p. 176.
[2] Cf. G. & T., II, pp. 7-9.

recurring doubts as to German and British lack of self-seeking in China. Lord Salisbury answered that he had no objection to offer on this point, assuming that a suitable form was agreed upon. He added that such a declaration of altruism was not made easier by Russia's attitude, who had, as he understood, declared that she would take nothing unless forced to do so by other Powers. I thought it best not to discuss this charge.

As the above showed that Lord Salisbury had no objection on principle against the two points, I thought I might tell him that if an understanding about the Yang-tsze was to work properly it must apply to all interested parties and that I should eventually propose to him to invite their adherence. Again Lord Salisbury raised no objection on principle, merely remarking that this would mean France, Japan and Russia. I said only that as far as I knew Russia had shown no interest in how matters were arranged on the Yang-tzse.

Finally, in order to hasten the matter, I suggested to the Prime Minister that if he wished it I should like to submit to him a draft of the points in question to which I would first obtain my Government's consent. He was of course free to suggest modifications and changes in it. Lord Salisbury agreed with this,' and I beg Your Excellency to let me have a suitable draft, which I would translate into French for Lord Salisbury.

I do not think it impossible that Lord Salisbury may raise difficulties about the drafting or impose fresh conditions, but my impression is that at present he is inclined to agree in general with the basis outlined by us.

[For the text of the Anglo-German Yang-tzse Agreement, as finally concluded on October 18th, 1900, cf. G. & T, II, p.15. Eckardstein (*Ten Years*, p. 176) wrote : ' Unfortunately Manchuria was omitted at the express desire of Count Bülow, and consequently, as is generally the case with half-measures in politics, the agreement resulted in the opposite of what was intended.' For the irritation which the Agreement caused in St. Petersburg, see G. & T., II, pp. 16–18.]

XVI. 250

BARON VON ECKARDSTEIN, IN LONDON, TO THE GERMAN FOREIGN OFFICE, *October 22nd*, 1900

Cipher telegram.

Various Cabinet Ministers, whom I met yesterday at dinner, spoke as follows on the Chinese Agreement :

They were glad that there was a certain amount of Anglo-German co-operation in China, and the Agreement had helped considerably to clear up the situation. Unluckily it was neither comprehensive nor precise enough and left many loop-holes, so that if the parties chose they could escape from the engagements they had undertaken. They feared that in spite of the treaty Germany would never allow an energetic attitude to be adopted towards Russia, which would utterly frustrate the objects of the Agreement ; Russia would then do what she pleased in China. Count Waldersee's attitude in the railway question, which was very soon going to cause a storm in British public opinion, was a proof of this.

I had the greatest trouble in satisfying the Ministers and especially the usually well-disposed Duke of Devonshire,[1] that the British Government could rely on the Imperial Government's goodwill in producing a settlement in consonance with British wishes.

The Under-Secretary told me that Sir Charles Scott had been instructed by telegraph to hand in a very strong note in St. Petersburg on the railway question.

Statements by other Ministers give me the impression that the mistrust of Count Waldersee is greatly increasing, and I should not wonder if Russia has been and will be intriguing strongly in this respect.

Chamberlain was not against it, but his colleagues tell me he shares the opinions of the other Ministers regarding our Agreement and the railway question.

The Russian Ambassador, who was visited by Sir T. Sanderson at Lord Salisbury's desire, informed me that the Under-Secretary had come to him ' pour addoucir le choc '. Indeed the sudden publication of the Agreement had been a shock to him, especially as he had not had the slightest idea that negociations were in progress. He told the Austrian Chargé d'Affaires that his Government would make the best of a bad job. It could in fact hardly do otherwise, having already declared that it has no intention of annexing Manchuria. . . .

[In November, 1900, Lord Salisbury handed the Foreign Office over to the Marquess of Lansdowne.

On December 26th, 1900, the German and Russian authorities agreed to remove the railway from the control of Mr. Kinder and his British staff to that of Count Waldersee in his quality as Commander-in-Chief. The agreement did not ignore the fact that the line had been constructed with British capital and the rights of property which this involved. Nevertheless the greatest suspicions were aroused in England. (Cf. G. & T., II, p. 22.)]

XVI. 273

MUMM VON SCHWARZENSTEIN, IN PEKIN, TO THE GERMAN FOREIGN OFFICE, *January 9th*, 1901

Cipher telegram.

Your telegram of yesterday [2] received in time to postpone signature—to some annoyance on the Field-Marshal's part—

[1] Cf. Eckardstein, *Ten Years at the Court of St. James*, p. 177
[2] Not given.

after instructions to sign had at last been received from Kuropatkin.

R. Tower [1] is awaiting instructions from London by return as
to whether an objection is to be raised against the Agreement.

The same to the same, January 12th, 1901

Tower reports that last evening a telegram was received from
the British Government, consenting to the Russo-German Railway
Agreement, on condition that bondholders' rights are expressly
recognised by it and the Agreement still more clearly described
as being a *purely military and provisional* measure. Also an
assurance is required that the *whole* line shall be given back to
the Railway Company when the troubles are over, *including* the
Shan-hai-kuan—Niuchuang section.

[The Agreement was signed on January 17th.]

XVI. 281

Count Hatzfeldt, in London, to the German Foreign
Office, *January 24th*, 1901
Cipher telegram.

To-day the Under-Secretary showed me an instruction sent to
Sir Frank Lascelles regarding the Russian and Belgian acquisitions at Tientsin and the intentions of France and Japan to
enlarge their concessions there. . . . The Ambassador is instructed
to sound the Imperial Government as to its intentions in the
matter and to suggest a joint démarche by the Powers in the
following sense : ' The Powers should arrive at a general agreement neither to recognise the pending agreements amongst themselves nor the validity of any concessions or settlements obtained
since the outbreak of the Boxer disturbances and the siege of
the Legations '. . . .

XVI 288.

Count Hatzfeldt to the German Foreign Office,
February 1st, 1901
Cipher telegram.

For several days I have had to struggle with Lord Lansdowne
and other members of the Cabinet in order to remove a certain
annoyance with us, (Bülow : ' *After our attitude in the Boer
War !—refusing to receive Kruger, and His Majesty's visit !* ')
which I think rather serious, about the Russian acquisitions
at Tientsin, and I regret to report that I have been so far
unsuccessful.

Regarding these they still insist that in spite of all the St.

[1] British Chargé d'Affaires in Pekin.

Petersburg Cabinet's assurances to the contrary they are to be taken not as merely a concession, but as a territorial acquisition and contrary therefore to the Anglo-German Agreement. Russia, they say, who has hardly any trade in Pechili, has by private negociation with Li-Hung-Chang secured a concession nearly three miles long between the Pei-ho River and the railway, considerably larger than all the foreign settlements at Tientsin put together. There is no doubt that however innocent Russia professes to be now it is her intention (BÜLOW : ' *There is no proof of it yet.*') to use this territorial gain to bring the land and sea connections between Pekin and the sea under her control. Fortifications will very soon arise in this new concession, (BÜLOW : ' *!* ') and in a very short time Russia will attain to such a predominant position in Pechili, that it will hardly be worth while for other Powers to claim any influence in this province or in Pekin. (BÜLOW : ' *!* ')

The British Government regret that the Imperial Government did not at once join with London, as provided in Art. III of the Anglo-German Agreement, to discuss the nature of the Russian acquisitions, but got into touch instead with St. Petersburg by itself, without consulting the London Cabinet at all. (BÜLOW : ' *!!* ') The British Cabinet, which has quite enough difficulties already with its own public opinion in passing over in silence the Russian action in Manchuria, will, directly Parliament meets, have to expect very sharp attacks regarding the Russian acquisitions at Tientsin in its relation to the Anglo-German Agreement.

I shall continue my efforts to remove the annoyance which has arisen in the British Cabinet and shall report progress to Your Excellency. (BÜLOW : ' *It is all a (rather clumsy) attempt to embroil us with Russia without getting England into trouble.*')

XVI. 300

SIR FRANK LASCELLES TO THE GERMAN FOREIGN OFFICE,
March 17th, 1901

A telegram dated March 15th has been received from Sir E. Satow, reporting that on a piece of land near Tientsin, which is claimed as the property of the Chinese Northern Railway and where the British Military authorities were constructing a siding, sentries have been placed by the Russian Military authorities, in order to prevent the British from proceeding with the work. The piece of land in question forms part of a district recently appropriated as a concession by the Russians. Instructions have been issued to the General Officer Commanding to the effect that Count Waldersee as Commander-in-Chief of the Allied Forces in Chi-li, is the authority who can most conveniently settle the question of the right of the British and Russian troops to the occupation of certain points. General Gaselee has accordingly been directed to ask His Excellency to settle the immediate difference which has arisen in Tientsin between the British and Russian Military authorities, but to reserve for future examination the question of the validity of the concession as a whole or of proprietory rights within it.

The British Commander has been instructed that in the meanwhile he should not use force except to repel aggression, nor should he eject the Russian sentries.

Sir Frank Lascelles has been instructed by Lord Lansdowne to urge that immediate instructions to act in the sense proposed may be issued to Count Waldersee.

XVI. 301

COUNT VON BÜLOW TO THE EMPEROR WILLIAM, *March 19th*, 1901

I have the honour humbly to report to Your Majesty as follows :

Sir Frank Lascelles has reported that the Commander of the British troops in Chi-li has been instructed to apply to Count Waldersee in his capacity as Commander-in-Chief to settle the recent dispute that has arisen between the British and Russian troops about the *military* right to occupy certain points at Tientsin, and that *legal* question regarding the status of the Russian concession at Tientsin and the rights of private ownership inside the concession are to remain over for further examination by other methods.

The British Government asks that Your Majesty's General-Field-Marshal shall be at once instructed from here to undertake the required decision.

I humbly consider that this British application in its present form be sharply rejected. The British cannot urge without reason given that it is a purely military task, part and parcel of the attributes and duties of a Commander-in-Chief, to provide for maintaining peace and order between the contingents under him and to stop or allay open hostilities, which are incompatible with military discipline. (The EMPEROR : ' *So far the contingents have bothered very little about Waldersee. If we fulfil this wish of England's, England must favour us in the matter of indemnities !* ') If we simply reject the British application, there is a risk that the British Government may treat it as an announcement that we regard our command, at least over the British and Russians, as having expired.

For the rest, England now merely asks for the application of the principle followed by Count Waldersee in settling the question of military possession of the railway lines from Pekin to Tientsin and from Tientsin to Shan-hai-kuan.

I therefore beg to propose to Your Majesty to send to Field-Marshal Count Waldersee the telegram of which I enclose a draft.

[For Count Bülow's announcement in the Reichstag that the Anglo-German Agreement did not include Manchuria, since Germany possessed no interests there, see G. & T., II, p. 26. The German Government did offer its good offices in St. Petersburg, as the following telegram shows.]

XVI. 303
COUNT HATZFELDT TO THE GERMAN FOREIGN OFFICE,
March 20th, 1901

Lord Lansdowne showed much pleasure at my communication. He requested me to convey to Your Excellency his heartiest thanks for the efforts of His Majesty's Government in the interests of a peaceful settlement of the Tientsin incident and promised to treat as strictly confidential the step taken by the Imperial Government in St. Petersburg.

I have a decided impression that this communication will greatly stem the mistrust of German policy which has been again disseminated systematically here from various quarters.

CHAPTER IX

THE BRITISH ALLIANCE PROPOSAL, 1901

German Note. XVII. 40

According to a telegram despatched on March 8th, Lord Lansdowne. and Bertie, the Under-Secretary, sounded Count Hatzfeldt as to whether Germany would be inclined, in the event of a Russo-Japanese conflict, to make a joint declaration with England in Paris that in the interests of European peace both Powers desired such a war in the Far East to be localised and would observe strict neutrality so long as no other European Power (France) intervened in the Russo-Japanese war. The Chancellor's marginal remark was : ' We could declare this in London and Tokio, but not in Paris, and under no circumstance until the first shot had been fired.' In Holstein's private telegram of March 9th, 1901 (Cf. *Ten Years at the Court of St. James,* p. 203), Holstein [1] suggested the idea of a defensive alliance between England and Germany, but he warned Eckardstein in no case to make the suggestion himself, as it must come from the British side. ' In my personal opinion—and that is all it amounts to at present— Germany might consider such a *general defensive alliance* rather than an agreement on a special point, e.g., Morocco, where the risk is the same, but the advantage less. But as I said, you should open this subject of an alliance *now*, if only because I am sure that Lord Salisbury will let St. Petersburg know of the fact that such a suggestion was made by Germany. In another private letter to Eckardstein (*Ten Years*, p. 206) on March 17th Holstein wrote even more emphatically : ' Dear friend, I *expressly* forbid you to whisper the slightest word of alliance. The right moment has certainly not come, if it ever does.'

XVI. 350

MEMORANDUM BY BARON VON HOLSTEIN, *March 27th*, 1901.

We had best leave to England the task of urging Japan to adopt an energetic policy, i.e., in making good her claims to Korea.

For Germany, who would wish to preserve the best relations with Russia, Japan is a compromising comrade as she is pursuing openly a policy of acquisition. The Japanese know that at present no one is threatening the existence of their island Empire and thus will not easily take interest in a defensive alliance. If we talked to the Japanese to-day about an arrangement for the benefit of both parties, they would be less likely to contemplate joint defence than joint aggression. Since this mental tendency

---

[1] Brandenburg, pp. 162, 177.

of the Japanese is known—and especially in St. Petersburg—
the mere circumstance that we were commencing conversations
with them regarding a joint policy would be taken in Russia as
a sign that we were ready to desert our present purely defensive
attitude in favour of a policy of aggression.   For obvious reasons
it would not benefit us, with no other support than that of the
shaky Triple Alliance, to incur the kind of suspicion which would
bring into the foreground the chauvinistic elements and tendencies
of the Dual Alliance.

All would be quite different if England would make up her
mind to link herself at some time with the Triple Alliance, and
if Japan came in also as a pendant to England.   In this case
England, who both in Asia and Europe is genuinely for a defensive
policy, would serve as a counterweight to Japan's restlessness ;
but even if not, that new alliance would be so strong that the
feelings of the other Powers would become less important to us
than at this moment, when it is advisable to let Japan go her own
way, even in company with England.   The Japanese would reply
to any German attempt at a rapprochement by asking if we would
help them to enter Korea or get the Russians out of Manchuria.
On this basis no understanding would be possible.   We have
informed the Japanese that we have no political arrangements
of any sort with Russia, particularly about Korea, that we should
certainly remain neutral if Japan and Russia went to war, and
that humanly speaking our neutrality would carry that of France
along with it.   We could not possibly withdraw from this declaration.   (BÜLOW : ' *For Baron von Holstein.   Many thanks for this
masterly memorandum, with the conclusions of which I agree at all
points.*')

XVII. 46

COUNT HATZFELDT TO THE GERMAN FOREIGN OFFICE,
March 23rd, 1901

Cipher telegram.[1]

With reference to recent and impending questions in Parliament about the Anglo-German Agreement, Lord Lansdowne discussed with me yesterday its extent and application with regard
to the engagements undertaken by either party.   The Minister
said that he personally was very anxious to bring declarations
on the subject as fully as possible into agreement with the views
recently expressed by Your Excellency in the Reichstag.   (BÜLOW:
' *Good.*')   He admitted that Manchuria had been expressly
omitted from the negociations, also that the Agreement bound
neither party to oblige a third to observe its principles.   (BÜLOW :

---

[1] Cf. G. & T., II, p. 60.

' *Correct.*') The conversation then turned to a further academic mention of the idea of a defensive arrangement. At first the Minister hesitated to speak, (BÜLOW : ' *! !* ') but he said finally that he had composed a memorandum, which he had first discussed with Mr. Arthur Balfour and then submitted to Lord Salisbury. (BÜLOW : ' *Good.*') After closely studying the memorandum, the Prime Minister had said that in principle he was for a strictly defined defensive alliance, but that all possible eventualities must be carefully considered and also all means found to remove the difficulties due to the peculiarities of British parliamentary feeling with regard to long term agreements.

Lord Lansdowne did not tell me what the memorandum contained ; but he asked the following questions, which lead to the conclusion that he has been considering the details of such an arrangement.

1. Do you think personally that the Imperial Government will eventually consent to a binding defensive agreement with England ? (BÜLOW : ' *Best of all in the form of an agreement between the Triple Alliance and England.*') And will this be possible in the face of the acutely anti-British feeling in Germany ?

2. Assuming that the Imperial Government favours such an idea, how, in your opinion, would such an alliance be conceived ? Would an absolutely defensive alliance be preferred or one in which the *casus fœderis* would only arise when one of the parties was attacked on two or more sides ? (BÜLOW : ' *The second.*')

3. Would a secret agreement or one to be accepted by Parliament be preferred ? (BÜLOW : ' *Only the second.*')

4. Would Japan, in connection with the Far East, eventually be included ? (BÜLOW : ' *Ça dépend.*')

To this I replied that it was naturally very difficult for me to answer these questions as I did not know my Government's views. But according to my *purely personal* observation I thought I might reply to each question as follows :

1. Assuming that the agreement rested on full reciprocity, it might be taken that the Imperial Government would not be disinclined to consider it, especially if it was concluded in a form attaching England to the Triple Alliance. (BÜLOW : ' *Correct.*') The Imperial Government was always obliged to reckon with German public opinion, but in the long run only two personages counted in all questions of foreign policy, the Emperor and the Chancellor. The more England was accommodating not only in large but also in small outstanding questions, the easier would be a policy friendly to England.

2. I thought personally that supposing the Imperial Govern-

ment considered the idea of a defensive alliance it would be preferable from the German standpoint (BÜLOW : ' *Even better from the
British.*') that the *casus fœderis* should apply only when one of
the parties were attacked on two or more sides.

3. In my opinion an agreement to be accepted by Parliament
would from the German standpoint be very greatly preferable,
if not a *conditio sine qua non.*

4. I considered that the addition of Japan to this new con-
stellation would be very much to the point.

The idea that England should at once turn to Vienna I have
not yet mentioned to Lord Lansdowne, as I do not think matters
sufficiently advanced. (BÜLOW : ' *Correct.*')

When, in order to prevent any misunderstanding, I again told
Lord Lansdowne that my words did not come from the Imperial
Government but were my purely personal opinions, the Minister
replied that his own words were so far not the views and policy
of the Cabinet, but personal to himself and academic.

XVII. 48

THE CHANCELLOR, COUNT VON BÜLOW, TO COUNT HATZFELDT,
March 24th, 1901

Secret.

We approve your attitude towards Lord Lansdowne's questions. Whilst he or any other Cabinet Minister continue to discuss the matter purely academically or in the form of personal
opinions, you need not reply otherwise than with your own
personal views. With this expressly in mind, you will use the
following points as a guide, so that if the subject crops up again
in the same personal form you may so reply that the threads are
eventually gathered up again by the British.

[This did not happen at once, for Dr. Stuebel, of the German Foreign
Office (Colonial Section), was in London, demanding the raising of the
Chinese Maritime Customs duties (which were eventually fixed at 5 per
cent (cf. G. & T., II, pp. 63, 138 ; and Lee, *Edward VII*, II, p. 122) ; he
also caused much indignation in England by his demands for compensation
for destruction of German private property and loss of trade in the Transvaal ; many of these demands were considered unjustified and extravagant
(cf. Eckardstein, *Ten Years at the Court of St. James*, p. 212).]

It is our view at least as much as Lord Salisbury's that for a
defensive alliance all possible eventualities must be very closely
considered beforehand.

1. A form attaching England to the Triple Alliance would be
much the most practical for all parties and in every respect.

2. The *casus fœderis* only to apply against two or more
enemies. In an absolute defensive alliance there would have to

be too many exceptions—in particular, (*a*) for an Anglo-American war about Canada, (*b*) for an Anglo-Russian war about India, (*c*) for a Franco-German war. But if in cases (*b*) and (*c*) France or Russia, as the case may be, join in, it is no longer a question of India or Alsace-Lorraine, but of the balance of power in the world.

Supposing negociations really take place, we must be careful that the British Government are not in doubt as to our standpoint in respect of (*a*), (*b*) and (*c*).

3. The agreement must not be secret but parliamentary.

4. Japan is inclined for acquisition and may not therefore see any particular advantage to herself in a purely defensive alliance. But it would do her good in so far as it would introduce her into good political society.

[On April 9th, 1901, the Emperor held a conversation with Sir Frank Lascelles, in which he expressed friendship for England. Holstein wrote to Eckardstein on April 10th (*Ten Years*, p. 215) : ' The Kaiser referred generally to persons who gave credence to unjustified suspicions as " unmitigated noodles " (cf. p. 123). The Foreign Secretary said it was his personal impression that the Kaiser had spoken sharply but well, and had struck the right note.' During the ensuing week there was a friendly exchange of letters between the Emperor and King Edward.]

German Note.

. . . It seems impossible that shortly after the conversation with the Ambassador the Emperor could have repeated the expression in a letter to King Edward in direct reference to the British Ministers, as Eckardstein relates. . . . [*Ten Years*, p. 217 ; also G. & T., II, p. 63.]

XVII. 53

BARON VON RICHTHOFEN, IN BERLIN, TO COUNT HATZFELDT,
April 14th, 1901

Telegram.

When you discuss the alliance question again with Lord Lansdowne please make use of the idea that just now the enemies of the Triple Alliance are trying to make the Austrian dynasty and Government suspicious of Germany and are spreading a report that Germany intends, after the death of the Emperor Francis Joseph, to bring about a partition of Austria. There can be no more practical way of disarming this suspicion than by the realisation that the Austro-Hungarian Monarchy is being allotted a leading part by Germany in the formation of the projected new alliance. This is why we set so much store on making Vienna to some extent the centre for the alliance negociations.[1]

[1] Cf. Eckardstein, *Ten Years at the Court of St. James*, p. 221.

XVII. 58

COUNT HATZFELDT TO THE GERMAN FOREIGN OFFICE,
May 16th, 1901

Cipher telegram. Extract. Secret.

A few days ago I said to Lord Lansdowne that . . . between Germany and Russia there were very few points of difference, and as for China, Germany was able at any moment to withdraw from it. (BÜLOW: ' *Good.*') There was indeed a strong party in Germany in favour of this. The moment she withdrew from China, there would hardly be a single point on which German and Russian interests clashed directly, (BÜLOW: '*Correct.*') and Germany would even be able more than now to arrive at a lasting understanding with Russia.

At my [1] yesterday's conversation Lord Lansdowne began at once on the alliance question. He remarked that, as he had already said, he and some of his colleagues would much desire a defensive alliance with Germany. He had lately gone closely into the question with Lord Salisbury and had told him what I had said about Germany's relations with Russia. The Prime Minister was now inclined in principle (BÜLOW: ' *?* ') to consider a defensive arrangement by treaty with us (the *casus fœderis* being when either is attacked by two or more), but he mentioned various objections (BÜLOW: ' *Naturally.*') against the engagements to be undertaken towards *Austria and Italy.* If it was merely a matter of Germany the idea of a defensive arrangement would be quite simple, but Austria and Italy would complicate the framing of such a treaty. (BÜLOW: ' *An arrangement is only imaginable on this basis.*')

Lord Lansdowne asked the following questions amongst others :

1. In the event of Austria breaking up, which, humanly speaking, could not long be delayed after the death of the Emperor Francis Joseph, (BÜLOW: ' *? ?* ') what would England's attitude have to be ? This event, said the Minister, involved so many possible complications of all sorts, that every contingency must be considered beforehand, as for instance the case—certainly very improbable—that if a serious crisis arose Russia might intervene and at the same time tempt Turkey to regain the provinces ceded to Austria after the last Russo-Turkish War. (BÜLOW: ' *Silly.*')

2. Regarding Italy Lord Lansdowne asked—what should England's attitude be supposing Italy were attacked over the Moroccan or some other Mediterranean question by France

---

[1] Probably Eckardstein's. Cf. G. & T., II, p. 64.

and Spain—the latter of whom counted officially as a Great Power ?

May 17th.

At the end of the conversation Lord Lansdowne said that perhaps the time had now come to put a draft of a treaty in writing and then discuss the wording of the various points. I replied that, as he knew, I was not empowered to make any proposals, and the preparation of a draft would not be in accordance with my instructions. . . . Lord Lansdowne said that the objections to preparing a draft applied to him also, but there was no other way of advancing further than for *both* of us to set to work and decide to set down our academic ideas and discuss them point by point.

[The London Foreign Office prepared a draft treaty (cf. G. & T., II, p. 65) ; but Holstein was suspicious. Lord Lansdowne was asking for ' documents antérieurs ', by which Holstein understood that he wished to see the text of the Triple Alliance treaties. He wrote for a copy of the British draft, but said, ' I dislike anything in writing at the present moment.' For the German Government's note in reply, see G. & T., II, p. 71.

For Lord Salisbury's memorandum on the policy of isolation, see G. & T., II, p. 68. He questions whether ' isolation has ever constituted a serious danger for England ', and points out that the circumstance ' fatal to the proposed arrangement is that neither we nor the Germans are competent to make the suggested promises '.

On June 1st the Prussian Minister at Hamburg, Count von Metternich, wrote a long memorandum on the theme, ' Is it worth while, particularly for Germany, to draw England over to the Triple Alliance ? ' One of Count Bülow's marginal remarks runs as follows (XVII. 82) : ' The main objection to any understanding with England is that the Russians (Court and public opinion) would then direct all their disappointment and rage against us, and the British would use this to make friends with Russia in spite of the treaty and force our hand in colonial questions.'

For King Edward's visit to Germany and his conversation with the Emperor and Sir Frank Lascelles, [cf. p. 280 and Sir S. Lee, *Edward VII,* II, p. 125 et seq.]

XVII. 101

MEMORANDUM BY BARON VON HOLSTEIN, GERMAN FOREIGN OFFICE, *October 31st,* 1901

Being instructed to do so, I received Mr. Valentine Chirol to-day for the first time since January, 1896,[1] and I have put down the substance of our more than two hours' conversation.

Chirol described the internal situation of England as highly unsatisfactory owing to the apathy of the ruling classes. As for Anglo-German relations he was impressed by the general

[1] Cf. G. & T., II, p. 84 ; Chirol, *Fifty Years in a Changing World,* pp. 296–7 ; also H. W. Wilson, *The War Guilt,* p. 82.

animosity against England which showed on every occasion in German public life and the Press.

I replied that not so much antipathy, but rather mistrust, was the feeling among the small informed class in Germany and that I myself was not free from that. (BÜLOW: ' *Very good.*') I quoted practical examples to justify my point of view. Firstly I told him that on July 30th, 1895,[1] Lord Salisbury consulted Count Hatzfeldt as to whether Italy might not be fully compensated in Albania or Tripolis in return for Zeyla, which England could not let go. When the Ambassador said that Albania would probably cause a conflict between Austria and Italy and break up the Triple Alliance, Lord Salisbury had suggested that the Ambassador should himself propose a plan for partitioning Turkey. Count Hatzfeldt had reported this to Berlin, and the Foreign Office had at the eleventh hour communicated it by telegram to the Emperor, who was at Heligoland on his way to England. The Emperor and his Government were agreed that a partition of Turkey would be equivalent to a great continental war, and that Germany must keep aloof from and if possible prevent it. Directly after the Emperor's arrival Lord Salisbury had explained his scheme of partition to him, but met with a rebuff the vehemence of which may well have offended him, for when the Emperor renewed his invitation to discuss the matter again, he slipped out of it and went off to London instead. This snub to the Emperor became the subject of a long diplomatic correspondence between Berlin and London and was not without its influence on the Kaiser's attitude at the time of the Jameson Raid.[2]

Mr. Chirol said : ' This is the direct opposite of what I have always been told, which was that the proposal to partition Turkey emanated from Germany, (BÜLOW: ' *! !* ') and that Lord Salisbury had wished to avoid further discussion of this delicate subject, and so took his departure.' (BÜLOW: ' *!* ')

I had already got out the documents and read out parts of Hatzfeldt's report and the telegraphic warning sent to Herr von Kiderlen at Heligoland. Chirol said : ' This is a serious matter. We were used until now to assume that a Prime Minister's word was to be believed. Now at any rate I know.' ...

German Note.
The part omitted concerns the question of Koweit, in which Holstein definitely declared that Germany was not sufficiently interested to make a serious matter of it with England.

I came then to the Chinese Agreement and the question of Manchuria. I referred again to the records and showed that

[1] Cf. Vol. II, p. 329 et seq. [2] Cf. Vol. II, p. 339.

from the very start Lord Salisbury agreed that Manchuria was not to come within the scope of the arrangement. (BÜLOW: *' I said this recently to Deym who had suggested that we disappointed Lord Salisbury, since he imagined that we meant the agreement to include Manchuria.'*) Lord Salisbury had merely desired that Manchuria should not be mentioned by name, and so in the course of negociations had proposed Latitude 38° as the northern limit of the Agreement. This was confirmed by a declaration made by Lord Lansdowne in the House of Lords on March 30th. The answer to a question given some time later by Lord Salisbury that he knew nothing about Manchuria being excepted did not correspond with the truth.

From Chirol's remarks I held that I might assume that he accepted my statements as being fully proved by the documents. When I said that the Prime Minister's memory was severely impaired by his bodily suffering, he said that this assumption was very depressing. Concerning the facts of the Chinese question, he said that the omission of Manchuria from our Agreement had pained him deeply. I added the suggestion that England, like any other reasonable person, must make the best of the times. At the close of the Napoleonic era about a century ago and even later, England had been the paramount Power in every part of the world outside Europe. This position could not be brought back now, for besides England there were four Great Powers of the first rank, and any British attempt to play at being paramount Power would be almost sure to lead to an anti-British grouping. (BÜLOW: *' Excellent.'*) Chirol replied that only an Englishman of limited intelligence could now cling to the idea of predominance. I said that not infrequently the British Press did cling to that idea.

Regarding England's relations with individual Powers Chirol said he would ●not anticipate much from an agreement with Russia, as it would not alter the facts. Moreover it was impossible for England to exclude Japan from any arrangement with Russia, and he thought an understanding between Russia and Japan would be extremely difficult.

He thought England's most dangerous opponent to be the United States. However matters stood, he would ever and under all circumstances be in favour of a good understanding with them ; for in a conflict with America it would be England—even if, contrary to expectation, she had allies—who would always be hit the hardest. I replied that this point of view was evident to me less because of any military or naval achievements that were to be expected from America than because England was dependent on America for a considerable part of the materials of existence. Meanwhile, I added, England's situation would in any case be made easier by having allies. In a war her rear would be protected ; and moreover, the question of war would be quite different for the opponent if England formed part of a group instead of remaining isolated. (BÜLOW : ' *Very good.*')

I wished however to guard against discussing the alliance question otherwise than academically.   In the first place, I did not believe that Lord Salisbury, whilst he was in charge, ever wished to pursue any policy but that of ' chestnuts ', even though this had long been seen through by all parties concerned ; secondly, Germany had no reason to seek support, for of late years our position had greatly improved.   The German and Russian Emperors were each firmly convinced of the other's friendly intentions towards himself.   Chirol asked whether the Russian Emperor had really derived this conviction from ours. I replied yes certainly, and supported this by referring to the Tsar's frigid and reserved reply to President Loubet's toast at Compiègne, which was all for action.   I mentioned also the historical fact that the Tsar Alexander III did not decide on the French alliance until much insinuation and tendencious inter-pretation of a speech made by our Emperor on his yacht in favour of extending the Triple Alliance treaty had made him anxious lest our Emperor in the bubbling enthusiasm of youth might be planning something serious against Russia.   (BÜLOW : ' *Correct.*')   This anxiety of the Tsar's was now, as I said, allayed, and this was bringing back the realisation (which had been temporarily thrust into the background) that France was the most serious opponent of an active Russian policy with regard to the Straits.   In order to cover up this fact the members of the Dual Alliance continued to represent the Bagdad Railway as a German conspiracy against the power of Russia as well as of England ;   there was however no point in attempting to construe the Bagdad project as a political menace when its real development was considered.   On the other hand, the Straits question was still the sharp reef it was ninety years ago when the *système de Tilsit* came to grief on it.   (BÜLOW : ' *Brilliant.*')   A few years ago the French Minister, Hanotaux, had said during the Armenian troubles : J'espère que la Russie ne va pas soulever la question des Détroits, parceque cela serait trop gros pour nous.'   Russia is paying attention to her ally's feelings and is leaving the Straits question alone ; she is more or less forcibly stifling the whole Eastern question.   But the Russian leaders naturally cherish a stronger and stronger con-viction that the more France's power is strengthened and unchallenged the stronger becomes the French bar in front of the Straits.   The logical consequences follow of themselves.

Under these circumstances Germany has, as was said before, no violent inducement to seek further alliances. But I am one of those who assume that the trend of the times will gradually bring together the great common interests of Germany and England, though perhaps not in my own lifetime. This view is held in high circles in Germany, in fact, by the Emperor and the Chancellor. Policy must be judged not by words but by facts, and it is an important fact that on two separate occasions since the Boer War began Germany rejected an official suggestion to participate in so-called ' good offices ' ! (BÜLOW : ' *Very good.*') My feelings of loyalty prevented me from mentioning the source of these suggestions. If Germany had joined in, probably every State, certainly every European State great and small, would have done the same, and it was easy to calculate the influence of such an event on the population of Cape Colony.

Chirol said : ' I was not aware that the idea of ' good offices ' had taken so concrete a form, but as you say so I believe you.'

I replied that if I included the semi-official suggestions as well, twice would not be enough. Words weighed little in comparison with these facts. The ' man in the street ' had no practical influence. Sympathy for the Boers was not confined to Germany only ; many sections of humanity wished success to the Boers simply out of hostility towards the institution of standing armies. Even if the Boer War ended in England's favour I was sure that it would inflict permanent injury on her, and I wished therefore—with my presentiment that in the future England and Germany were destined to follow a common path— that England would thoroughly reorganise her land forces. As for the present relations between the two countries, I considered that the question of an alliance could not in practice be discussed whilst Lord Salisbury remained in power. The only thing to do now was to leave the future open, if this could be done.

Mr. Chirol thanked me very much for my words and said that after our discussion he took a much more hopeful view of Anglo-German relations than before it. (BÜLOW : ' *Very pleasing.*') He is coming here again before he goes away.

[The rejection of Mr. Chamberlain's repeated efforts to come to a friendly arrangement with Germany convinced him by the autumn of 1901 that Germany and her Government were definitely hostile to Great Britain. An attack by the German Press, seconded as a political piece of tactics by the Liberal Opposition in England, on the ' methods of barbarity ' attributed to the British command in South Africa aroused Mr. Chamberlain's resentment. On October 15th, 1901, he replied at Edinburgh to these attacks with references to the methods employed by the German Army in the Franco-Prussian War. This speech gave rise to further attacks on England in the German Press. (Cf. Lee, *Edward VII*, p. 133.)]

XVII. 195

THE CHANCELLOR, COUNT VON BÜLOW, TO COUNT VON METTERNICH,[1] *November 26th*, 1901

I have seen your latest reports on the political situation in England, and the course of the more important questions of the day. I have taken special note of your report of the 20th on the British attempts at a rapprochement with Russia and on Anglo-German relations.

As regards the former, it should be of no small value to us that Russia is still represented in London by an Ambassador who is friendly to Germany and thus shows no very great activity. For a long time I have known this to be the character of M. de Staal, the present Russian Ambassador, so that it will be to our interests for this well-meaning diplomat, whom age and illness has made somewhat inactive, to remain as long as possible at his London post. I beg you to try quietly to influence M. de Staal in this sense.

As regards the Anglophobia now appearing in Germany, which has drawn fresh and ample sustenance from Mr. Chamberlain's rash speech at Edinburgh, please keep your mind fixed on the following points: (1) The provocation, which cannot be denied, originates in Mr. Chamberlain and not in us. No German Minister has ever spoken on England or English affairs otherwise than reasonably and tactfully. Mr. Chamberlain has only made matters worse by his secretary's letter and the allusions in it to the ' artificial agitation ' in Germany. (2) Mr. Chamberlain's speech is making it difficult for the German Government to stick to its friendly attitude towards England in spite of the anti-British feeling aroused in Germany and all the other continental countries on account of the South African War. (3) No Minister can treat the public opinion in his own country as a *quantité négligeable* when it is a matter of injury to legitimate national and military sensibilities. We can do this no more than the British Ministry, which has always paid special attention to public opinion and its momentary currents of feeling. (4) In spite of the caution made necessary for us by circumstances, our policy towards England will remain genuinely unaltered even with regard to the war in South Africa. It should be to England's essential interest not to make it hard for us to continue this policy, especially as no other Power has

[1] Ambassador in London after Hatzfeldt's death on November 22nd.

shown anything like so benevolent an attitude towards England in the Boer war as Germany has, nor one at the same time so helpful.

You will try to use the foregoing points in your conversations with British Statesmen and other influential personages.

CHAPTER X

THE ANGLO-JAPANESE AGREEMENT, 1901–2

[In April, 1895, England supported Japan when pressure was applied to her by the other Powers to evacuate Port Arthur. (Cf. p. 11 ; also G. & T., II, p. 89.) Again in February, 1901, Lord Lansdowne joined with the Japanese in the following declaration : ' In the opinion of His Majesty's Government any such agreement as that reported to have been concluded [with Russia] with regard to Manchuria (cf. G. & T., II, p. 35) would be a source of danger to the Chinese Government and no arrangement affecting territorial rights in the Chinese Empire ought to be concluded between the Chinese Government and any one of the Powers.' To their identical declaration the Japanese added the following : ' All agreements arising out of present negotiations should be joint and China shall make no separate agreement with any Power ' (XVI, 322).

In April, 1901, Baron Hayashi, Japanese Minister in London, sounded both Lord Lansdowne (G. & T., II, p. 89) and Baron von Eckardstein (*Ten Years*, p. 218) as to ' whether Germany would eventually consent to a far-reaching arrangement along with England and Japan for the maintenance of the open door and the integrity of China, the arrangement to be based on the Anglo-German Agreement. The Minister developed the idea that these three Powers should not only engage themselves to observe the principle of integrity and the open door in China, but also, if need be, to hold others to it. In the event of such an arrangement an exception could be made in Manchuria ; there could then be no harm in letting Russia have this assuming that existing treaty rights were observed . . .' Germany showed no inclination to accede to the Japanese proposal, so England and Japan proceeded with the negociations which ripened into the Anglo-Japanese Alliance.

On July 12th, 1902, Mr. A. J. Balfour succeeded his uncle, Lord Salisbury, as Prime Minister.]

XVII. 141

BARON VON ECKARDSTEIN TO THE GERMAN FOREIGN OFFICE,
July 19th, 1901

Cipher telegram.
  Private for Baron von Holstein.

Lord Lansdowne, whose attention I have recently called in various ways to the dangers and symptoms of a Russo-Japanese rapprochement, informed me in strict confidence that yesterday he had a long conversation with the Japanese Minister, to whom he said that he would do his utmost to get the British Government to accede to any wishes of Japan. The Minister's reply was that at the moment he had no wishes to put forward for his Government, but that it was possible that he might shortly declare such wishes.

To Lord Lansdowne's question whether the Press rumour that Russia and France had offered financial help to Japan was a true one the Minister replied that quite recently Russia had again declared at Tokio that she was very ready and at any moment able to procure the Japanese Government a largish loan in Paris. As far as he, the Minister, knew, any offer of the sort had been rejected at Tokio up to the present.[1]

Lord Lansdowne said nothing as to whether England would come to Japan's assistance financially if asked, but I have a decided impression that he personally would do all he could to fulfil any wishes of the Japanese.

The telegram from Tokio which I sent recently to the *Daily Mail* has made a visible impression on political circles, but more particularly in the class which is financially interested in China.

XVII. 93

MEMORANDUM BY MÜHLBERG IN BERLIN, *August 2nd*, 1901
Extract.

. . . In order to counter an Anglo-Russian rapprochement there is only one method possible—that the German Government shall formally approve Director Siemens' conversion of the Bagdad project [2] from a German into a Franco-German one, and that we should announce it officially in St. Petersburg. This would remove the present main cause for political irritation between us and Russia.

For the consistency of the control of German policy it will be necessary for His Majesty not only to approve this point of view, but to identify himself with it, so that during the Homburg meeting he may never lose sight of the conviction that we shall ruin our relations with England the moment it is known there that we are on bad terms with Russia and France.

[The correspondence on the subject of the Alliance bears scarcely any marginal notes by the Emperor. Eckardstein (*Ten Years*, pp. 226, 231–2) shows evidence that the facts of it were kept from the Emperor's knowledge.

Late in August, 1901, King Edward visited the Emperor at Wilhelms-höhe and held with him a conversation at which Sir Frank Lascelles was present. (Cf. Lee, *King Edward VII.*, II, p. 125 et seq.)]

XVII. 97

MEMORANDUM BY THE EMPEROR WILLIAM, *August 23rd*, 1901 [3]
Extract.

. . . I said—Here am I in the middle of Europe with my

[1] G. & T., II, p. 90.   [2] Cf. Chapter X.
[3] Given in full in Lee, *King Edward VII*, II, p. 128.

strong army, and in company with my allies whom I can trust, I shall see to it that all remains quiet.

King Edward and Sir Frank Lascelles admitted the high merit earned by Germany in preserving peace.

This being so, I continued, England must shape her policy to suit it.   Business interests had brought us nearer to France,[1] and we shall always find someone as an ally to protect our trade interests against third parties.   England must have perceived that on the continent there was a strong tendency in favour of a continental business union against those who annoyed the continent in matters of trade.   England would do well to consider this.   I could not judge whether it was possible or profitable for England to maintain her ' splendid isolation ', or if it was to her interests to range herself on the side of the continent or America.   I would only suggest that America and Russia were perhaps more intimate together than people in London would consent to believe.   In America Russia had a very clever and energetic representative in Count Cassini, who knew America intimately and adopted the right tone with the people there.   America already possessed the Philippines and was constructing a cable.   This meant a step against the Yang-tsze.   Did England imagine she would be able to oppose America and Russia in the Far East by herself without Japan ?   France would certainly not help England, and Germany had no fleet for such enterprises. . . .

XVII. 98

THE CHANCELLOR, COUNT VON BÜLOW, AT NORDENEY, TO THE GERMAN FOREIGN OFFICE, *September 16th*, 1901

Cipher telegram.   Secret.

Count Metternich wrote to me from London on the 13th : ' When I was here eighteen months ago on a similar mission [2] jingoism was at its height.   Patriotic enthusiasm flamed brightly, and all the nation's nerves were on the stretch in order to win the South African war.   To-day the excitement has disappeared and depression has taken its place.   Nevertheless the great majority still cling to the cry of no peace until the independence of the Boer Republic falls, but privately everyone is sick of the war.   The excitement of the last years has been replaced by a drowsiness, which I think must be held to embrace foreign affairs also.   We have to deal with a man who is tired after the struggle and wants rest and will undertake nothing which lays duties on him requiring any fresh effort.   England's

[1] *German Note.*
    The Emperor was clearly thinking of the Bagdad Railway.
[2] Taking the place of Count Hatzfeldt, during his illness.

overdone imperialism threatens to lead her back to Gladstone's principle of non-interference. The feeling that there has been enough of trouble for the present may account for the vehement Press campaign which has been going on for some time (especially in *The Times*) in favour of a settlement between England and Russia in the Persian Gulf. What I write here rests on small indications and on what my *vox interior* tells me. I sit here in London all through September and October as though on a desert island. No one of any political importance is here with whom to talk, and the British Foreign Office clerks are not the right people to collect general political impressions from. I have not mentioned the alliance question as it seems to me too remote. I hope that at Danzig you succeeded in drawing tighter the bonds between Germany and Russia. For the more England holds aloof, the nearer must we draw to Russia in spite of all difficulties. It might become more and more difficult to tack between the two. By this I do not mean that a rapprochement with Russia must imply open enmity with England. The one does not necessarily mean the other.'

Count Metternich's strictly confidential communication given above agrees in many points with what I hear from Germans settled in England, who know the conditions there and who sympathise with England. I think correct the views expressed in his closing sentence, that in spite of continuous and careful attention to our relations with Russia we have no reason for assuming an unfriendly attitude towards England. At Danzig it was my impression that the Russians would hardly have been so accommodating if our good relations with England had not heightened our prestige in their eyes. Also for the sake of our foreign policy we must avoid anything likely to reverse the policy to which we have held in recent years, unless we must . . .

[In December, 1901, the Marquis Ito visited St. Petersburg with a view to coming to an agreement about Korea, where Japan possessed great interests. In June, 1901, it had been the Russian Government's impression that Ito ' wished by every means to avoid a conflict with Russia, but that war-like influences in Japan were constantly increasing in strength ' (XVII, 139). The visit to St. Petersburg led to no result, and Marquis Ito went first to Paris, and then to London. (Cf. G. & T., II, p. 108 ; Eckardstein, *Ten Years at the Court of St. James*, p. 226.]

XVII. 144

MEMORANDUM BY BARON VON ALVENSLEBEN, IN ST. PETERSBURG,
December 4th, 1901

Extract.

After his ten days' stay in St. Petersburg Marquis Ito left to-day. He was treated by Russian official circles with particular attention from first to last and the whole Russian Press published flattering articles about him.

Nevertheless it can hardly be assumed that the Marquis Ito's conversations here can have led to any conceivable result ; on the contrary it must have been Russia's prevailing wish to send away this statesman, who is influential at home and whose personal feelings are known, with the best possible impressions.

It appears as if the Marquis Ito's reason for coming to St. Petersburg was to ascertain how the points of difference between Japan and Russia with regard to Korea and Manchuria could be settled. . . .

[Shortly after the New Year, 1902, the Marquis Ito came to England and stayed with Lord Lansdowne at Bowood. On January 30th the Anglo-Japanese Agreement was signed. (Cf. G. & T., II, p. 115)]

XVII. 149

The Chancellor, Count von Bülow, to Count von Metternich, in London, *March 13th*, 1902

Very Confidential.

I thank you sincerely for your letter of February 21st.[1] . . .

I entirely concur with you that Chamberlain's recent and very correctly and pleasantly expressed show of friendship towards Italy respecting Malta is only to be explained by annoyance at Italy's attitude towards France, also that only the British Government's fear that Ito and Japan might end by joining hands with Russia over England's head could have brought the Anglo-Japanese Agreement into existence. The step to the ' entangling alliance ' seems to have been a hard one for your British friends.

> *So nimmt ein Kind der Mutter Brust*
> *Nicht gleich im Anfang willig an,*
> *Doch bald ernährt es sich mit Lust.*

I think that just now for us the circumstance—which you rightly mention—that the Agreement with Japan will set aside the attempts at a rapprochement between England and Russia is far the most important point, and even the A B C -politicians of the *National Review* will in consideration for their new Japanese friends try harder than ever to find arguments to convince a sober-minded Englishman that there is no point of dispute worth mentioning between England and Russia in Asia. A British understanding with Russia would in fact amount to a British declaration of bankruptcy in Asia and Europe. Time helps Russia, but not England, and every British

[1] Not in the Records.

concession to Russia hastens the ruin of British prestige in Asia and Europe. . . .

For the rest careful observation of the British Press by you (and Eckardstein) will be of especial value to us in future, as it may be important in view of our future decisions to see *against whom* the increased self-confidence, which you mention as a result of the departure from isolation, will be directed. Against Russia—France—ourselves ? And if, as you very rightly say, we must not ignore the possibility that the Anglo-Japanese group may come forward in opposition to our aspirations in the Far East, we must naturally follow every indication of such a later orientation of the Anglo-Japanese group with all the more attention, if symptoms appear in the British Press, public opinion or in Government circles that in the event of a more active Anglo-Japanese policy in the Far East they might feel assured of the sympathy or even the support of the United States.

[The French and Russian Governments prepared a joint note on the Anglo-Japanese Agreement, (cf. G. & T., II, p. 135) which was handed to the British and German Governments on March 19th and 20th respectively. The last sentence runs as follows : ' Toutefois, obligés d'envisager eux aussi, le cas où soit l'action agressive de tierces puissances, soit de nouveaux troubles en Chine, mettant en question l'intégrité et le libre développement de cette Puissance, deviendraient une menace pour leurs propres intérêts, les deux Gouvernements alliés se réservent d'aviser éventuellement aux moyens d'en assurer la sauvegarde.']

XVII. 179

MEMORANDUM BY THE CHANCELLOR, COUNT VON BÜLOW, *March 20th*, 1902

This morning the Marquis de Noailles read me the Franco-Russian declaration regarding China and handed me a copy. On paragraph 1 of this document I remarked that no Power could fail to agree with it. To paragraph 2 as far as the words ' extrême Orient ' I had no objection. To the last sentence I merely remarked that it was a case of the sting being in the tail. I confined myself to thanking the French Government for the friendly and courteous form of the communication and to acknowledging its receipt. In the course of our conversation the Marquis indicated, but only as his private opinion, that he rather disliked the idea of joining with Russia against England and Japan. France had no special interests in North China, and he urgently hoped that no complications with England and Japan about Korea and Manchuria would ensue. With much hesitation he suggested how nice it would be of us to help Russia in Korea and Manchuria against the restless Japan ; whereupon I replied to the Ambassador that our policy in the Far East was one of entire reserve and only concerned trade.

I had a long conversation with the Russian Ambassador on the same subject. He began by saying that he was only instructed to deliver the declaration without comment, since we had already declared our unwillingness to refer to the matter again. But from himself alone, *à titre d'ami*, he added the following : Count Lamsdorff was annoyed not so much at the fact of our not coming in but at the form of our refusal, for it was this which had disappointed and hurt them in St. Petersburg, particularly because Count Lamsdorff had submitted his draft to the Emperor Nicholas, naming France as the sole participant ; the Tsar had replied : ' Oui, mais avec l'Allemagne.' I repeated in a most friendly tone that we had refused to support the aspirations of England and Japan in Manchuria and Korea, and that for the same reasons, equally cogent in this case also, we could not engage ourselves for the other side in those far-off regions. I spoke in the sense of my Reichstag speech and my last telegram to Count Alvensleben,[1] and said that we perhaps had Austria-Hungary *à contre cœur* on our side, but in no case Italy. Finally Count Osten-Sacken said it was the object of both of us to see that the incident had no evil consequences, as it was more than ever the duty of the two Emperors to hold together faithfully against revolution and the insecure condition of Europe.

[1] German Ambassador in St. Petersburg.

CHAPTER XI

THE JOINT ACTION AGAINST VENEZUELA, 1902-3

German Note.

The Civil War in Venezuela of 1898–1900 had caused severe losses in money and property to German as well as to British, American and Italian settlers and businesses. In the winter of 1901–2 there were diplomatic negociations between the German and British Governments about making good these losses, but their object was not attained. In the late autumn of 1901 the German Government, whose patience was being tried by the harsh demeanour of the Venezuelan Government, which repeatedly ignored the forms of diplomacy, was forced to send a squadron to the ports of Venezuela. When it was ascertained that a blockade of these ports would not be opposed by the United States, and the British Government had indicated its readiness to act jointly with Germany, the German Foreign Office considered the moment had come to proceed seriously to blockade the Venezuelan ports.[1]

XVII. 241

THE CHANCELLOR, COUNT VON BÜLOW, TO THE EMPEROR WILLIAM, *January 20th*, 1902

The events in Venezuela have given cause for an examination of the question of the legal aspect and practical working of a blockade in peace time. The Foreign Office reports to me its conclusion that a peace blockade has been carried out with success in a number of cases. The practice, as developed at least amongst European States, is that in general a peace blockade rests on the same principles as apply to a blockade in war time. The essential difference is that ships running the blockade are not to be confiscated, but merely turned away or detained until the blockade is raised. On the other hand there is no doubt that in a peace blockade the conditions mentioned apply to the ships of neutral Powers as well. The United States of America have so far adopted no definite line regarding these questions, but their Government, having been informed of the foregoing principles by Your Majesty's Ambassador, has announced that in the present instance it has no objection against a peace blockade being declared.

[1] Cf. Dennis, *Adventures in American Diplomacy*, p. 285 et seq.; also G. & T., II, p. 153 et seq.

Thus the most important of the measures of constraint which are contemplated against Venezuela—i.e. the closing of the ports—is permissible under International Law by means of a peace blockade. It would render impossible the levying of export and import duties—almost the only revenue of the State—and the feeding of the country would be made considerably harder, and it would certainly make a declaration of war against Venezuela unnecessary. . . .

In the meantime the political situation has altered. The British Government, which has also received claims against the Venezuelan Government, has recently indicated that under certain conditions (The EMPEROR : ' *Too vague.*') it might consider joint action against Venezuela. Moreover the Italian Government has instructed de Riva, its representative at Caracas, to associate himself with all measures taken by Your Majesty's Chargé d'Affaires there.[1]

The Chargé d'Affaires' note to the Venezuelan Government, demanding payment of the German claims occasioned by the last civil wars, has been replied to to the effect that the matter will be laid before the next Congress. This reply is not satisfactory, and, as the Chargé d'Affaires states, must be regarded as a fresh attempt at evasion, seeing that owing to the present unrest there is no saying when the Congress may reassemble.

I beg respectfully to suggest to Your Majesty the idea of granting the Venezuelan Government a short term for the satisfaction of our claims. At the same time I beg to be empowered to get into touch with the British Government for the purpose of some combined action against Venezuela. (The EMPEROR : ' *If we can be sure that the Britons will not use the opportunity to make the Americans suspicious of us and so weaken the effect of my brother's visit. In any case such a step must wait till the Prince's mission is over; he can be provided with instructions—perhaps in writing—for Roosevelt when the time comes.*')

[Early in March, 1902, Prince Henry of Prussia was sent to the United States, where he visited several of the principal cities. Although the object of the visit was undoubtedly to remove the ill-feeling against Germany in America caused by the Manila incidents in 1898, it was denied that any definite political aim was being pursued. It was to be merely an assertion of the Emperor's good-will towards America.]

German Note. XVII. 243

. . . In his letter to Prince Henry of Prussia Bülow wrote : ' The events in South and Central America should not be discussed by Your Royal Highness of your own initiative, and naturally there must be no admission of German intentions in those regions. If the Americans should

---

[1] von Pilgrim-Baltazzi.

betray anxiety as to German ideas of acquisition or influence in connection with Central or South America, these should be dismissed as absurd imaginings, with a reference to His Majesty's peaceful policy and our many tasks to be done elsewhere in the world ; such ironical denial need not bear the character of a solemn declaration. Germany desires peace throughout the Western hemisphere and good friendship with the United States.'

[The question then rested, as far as Germany was concerned, until the autumn.]

XVII. 256

COUNT VON QUADT, CHARGÉ D'AFFAIRES IN WASHINGTON, TO THE GERMAN FOREIGN OFFICE, *November 25th*, 1902

Cipher telegram.

The British Ambassador, Sir Michael Herbert, who had been absent the last few days informed me that he had told Hay, the Secretary of State, orally of the intentions of his Government with regard to Venezuela. Mr. Hay had replied that his Government greatly deplored intervention by a European Power in the affairs of a South American republic, but that it understood that European Powers were bound to claim the right to defend their interests in South America.

COUNT VON METTERNICH, IN LONDON, TO THE GERMAN FOREIGN OFFICE, *November 26th*, 1902

Cipher telegram.

To-day Lord Lansdowne informed me of the Under-Secretary of State's communication to the British Chargé d'Affaires in Berlin [1] to the effect that the Venezuelan Government had tried to win us over by a promise to satisfy our claims if we would consent not to stand up for the British claims, and that we had rejected this suggestion. The Minister expressed thanks for the Imperial Government's attitude and promised that in analogous cases the British Government would act similarly.

[The attempt was repeated by Mr. Bowen, the American Minister at Caracas, in February, 1903 (cf. G. & T., II, 169). His confession to the Italian Ambassador in Washington that the main principle of his diplomacy was to create discord between Sir Michael Herbert and Baron Speck von Sternburg (G. & T., II, 171) had a large effect in maintaining the co-operation between the claiming Powers.]

XVII. 258

THE CHANCELLOR, COUNT VON BÜLOW, TO THE EMPEROR WILLIAM, *December 12th*, 1902

I respectfully inform Your Majesty that as a measure of compulsion against Venezuela England proposes a war-blockade of the Venezuelan ports instead of a peace blockade.[2] As it seems highly desirable to convince the British that in any

[1] G. W. Buchanan.   [2] Cf. G. & T., II, p. 160.

further action we move with them without reservations, I humbly venture to request Your Majesty's consent to accept the British programme. In accordance with Art. XI. Section 2 of the Constitution of the Empire the consent of the Bundesrath would then be required.

Meanwhile the situation has so far altered in that Italy has applied formally to us and in London to participate in the Anglo-German blockade with two cruisers to protect her own claims against Venezuela. Since England, so far as is known, has about 8 ships in the West Indies, the three Powers would be providing about 14 war-ships for the blockade. From the political point of view a further increase of the blockading squadron appears undesirable, because feeling in the United States, which so far has not been aroused by our action, might turn round if the three Powers transferred sea-forces from home waters to join those which are actually on the spot.

According to a Reuter cable which has just come in the British 1st Class reserve squadron at Devonport has been ordered to be ready to go to sea in 24 hours. I am instructing Your Majesty's Ambassador in London to enquire whether this news is correct and whether the squadron is intended for action against Venezuela. If this is so, I may have further proposals to make. For the present it seems best for England to continue reinforcing her squadron, so that there may not be fresh nourishment for the tendencious reports which are broadcasted everywhere in the British and American Press to the effect that Germany was the chief instigator [1] of the whole movement and of all the measures of compulsion in particular.

The leader in spreading these insinuations is again *The Times*, whose Washington correspondent, in discussing the alleged sinking of a Venezuelan war-ship by the German squadron,[2] concludes with the following sentences : ' It would be a vain attempt to deny the bad impression produced here by the events of the last two days. The main criticism of the sinking of the Venezuelan war-ships is that it has given the action against Venezuela the character of a punitive expedition. It is significant that the general inclination here is to ascribe the blame for this treatment not to the British but to the Germans.' In a leading article on this correspondence *The Times* expresses its wish and expectation that British war-ships did not take part in this sinking.

[1] Cf. German Note, p. 160.

[2] Cf. G. & T., II, 162. According to the German Note, a single British ship joined the German squadron in this action against the Venezuelan ships and the fort at Puerto Cabello, the whole proceeding being due to the fact that the Venezuelan Government ignored the joint ultimatum for the satisfaction of claims, which was presented on December 7th.

In view of this fresh attempt to revive the anti-German agitation, I hold myself bound humbly to suggest that Your Majesty may graciously abstain for the present from any extension of military preparations.

. . . (The EMPEROR : ' *Agreed ! Italy may take part at her ease, and the more ships the British send the better. Thus our action becomes less prominent, and theirs more so. Naturally we join in with the British programme. I am against sending more of our ships away from home ! Our flag is represented, so let us leave England to take the first step.*')

[The American Government was anxious not to be involved in the dispute. When the Venezuelan Government applied for a settlement by arbitration, the American Government stated that it confined itself to ' forwarding the Venezuelan proposal and would not associate itself with it. All official statements in the Press that have been received in Berlin go to prove the wish of the American Cabinet to keep clear of the whole affair.' (XVII. 261).]

XVII. 269

COUNT VON QUADT, CHARGÉ D'AFFAIRES IN WASHINGTON, TO THE GERMAN FOREIGN OFFICE, *December 18th*, 1902

Cipher telegram.

To-day Secretary Hay assured me that the President, as well as himself, reposed entire trust in us in the Venezuelan affair and were firmly decided not to be involved in it. But the Secretary of State considered it highly desirable to reach a settlement soon, for both public and Congress were nervous and excited. Hay said there might easily be a resolution moved in Congress demanding that the President should see that the Monroe Doctrine, with which the executive was familiar, had not been and should not be violated. This would be painfully felt in leading circles. . . .

[On January 17th the fort of San Carlos at Maraciabo fired on the German ship *Panther*, which promptly bombarded and destroyed the fort. (Cf. G. & T., II, p. 165.) The action was defended by Bülow as the ' justified repulse of a hostile attack. Fire was opened by the Venezuelan fort, when the *Panther* in the justifiable exercise of her functions in the blockade was steaming over the bar into the lagoon. No American or British Admiral would have done otherwise ' (XVII. 274). Nevertheless, the effect in America and England was injurious to Germany and tended to destroy faith in her protestations. The incident did not affect the course of the negociations respecting the claims against Venezuela.]

XVII. 288

COUNT VON METTERNICH, IN LONDON, TO COUNT VON BÜLOW, *February 4th*, 1903

Private letter.

The Royal Family, the King, the Queen, and the Prince of Wales were clearly opposed to the joint action in Venezuela.

I could see that we were regarded as mischief-makers, chiefly owing to the bombardment of San Carlos.

Public opinion in England clings blindly to President Castro's point of view, that the bombardment of his fort was a profanation of the sacred soil of Venezuela. The British have entirely forgotten that not so long ago they themselves bombarded Puerto Cabello. (BÜLOW: '*Could not this be published in some English newspaper?*')

It is a good sign that the British Ministers are beginning to defend their Venezuelan policy in public speeches. Mr. Austen Chamberlain, the Colonial Minister's son, has been the most successful in this.

Lord Lansdowne is a man of honour, who sticks to the promises he has made. When Parliament meets on the 17th, the situation may be dangerous for him and the Ministry, if his Venezuelan policy in the meantime causes a sharper difference of opinion between him and the United States. I consider very dangerous any public discussion of the question who first suggested joint action—England or Germany. (BÜLOW: '*We on our side must absolutely avoid such a discussion. No retrospective justifications!*') If it was proved by documents that Lord Lansdowne had suggested it, (BÜLOW: '*That will happen in no case.*') I think that he would fall, considering the feeling reigning in Parliamentary circles.

Bowen's shameless behaviour is the best means of deterring the Government here from giving way too easily. To-day Lord Lansdowne described him to me as a scamp.

If President Roosevelt loses patience, gives way to the Yellow Press, and demands, for instance, the raising of the blockade, the British Government might fall at once. They could not stand up against the American fetish in combination with the dislike of Germany. A fresh Ministry, replacing the present one as a result of its having co-operated with Germany, would mean a serious danger to official Anglo-German relations. (BÜLOW: '*Correct. Rosebery is much more dangerous than the Balfour-Chamberlain-Lansdowne Cabinet.—Please thank Metternich for his interesting and well-conceived letter and answer him in the sense of my marginal notes. Say that His Majesty also fully agrees with his attitude in the Venezuelan question.*')

[The essentials of the complicated negociations which led to the Protocol of February 13th, 1903, are given in Bluebooks, *Venezuela*, 1 and 2. See also Dennis, *Adventures in American Diplomacy*, p. 296.]

CHAPTER XII

THE WEAKENING OF THE TRIPLE ALLIANCE, 1902-3

[Since France was becoming each year on worse terms with Germany, the Franco-Italian rapprochement which culminated in an understanding reached later in 1902 was imperilling the continuance of the Triple Alliance. An attempt was however made to patch it up. (Cf. Brandenburg, p. 186 et seq.) By this mutual understanding France was to allow Italy a free hand in Tripoli, whilst Italy declared her neutrality in the event of a Franco-German war.]

XVIII. 522

COUNT KARL VON WEDEL, AMBASSADOR IN ROME, TO THE GERMAN FOREIGN OFFICE, *January 9th*, 1902

Extract.

In our conversation Signor Prinetti referred again to the renewal of the Triple Alliance. He had a free hand and had arranged everything with the King of Italy and Zanardelli. Count Bülow and Count Goluchovski had declared that political and commercial treaties bore no direct relation to each other, and he had been careful not to put forward a different opinion.

Since he had promised M. Barrère, if only in conversation, that the treaty was not to include France as an object of aggression, he would prefer, as the whole of the treaty could not be published owing to the Balkan clauses, etc. (although Count Nigra pleaded that such publication would be the best way to reassure the world), that a form of preamble should be found declaring its defensive character, which might be communicated to France. . . .

XVIII. 746

MEMORANDUM BY COUNT VON BÜLOW, *January 12th*, 1902

I invited the Italian Ambassador to see me to-day and said to him that I hoped the misunderstanding about Tripoli was now removed. Nothing was further from our intention than to begrudge the Italians their possession of Tripoli or to place difficulties in the way of their acquiring it. . . .

XVIII. 523

But about the Triple Alliance I said I had not much more to tell him than I had told him privately on January 1st and had declared publicly in the Reichstag. The treaty with Italy was no matter of life and death to us. Under certain circumstances we might very possibly find support, compensation, and a compromise elsewhere. For many reasons isolation would be less of a menace to us than for Italy. The Roman question was, in fact, more delicate and difficult than that of Alsace-Lorraine. For Germany I wanted the renewal of the Triple Alliance more as an act of piety towards a long standing arrangement, but for Italy I wanted it on account of her old friendship with this country, since for her the Triple Alliance was a question of existence, and she would otherwise fall into complete dependence on France. I was ready to renew the Alliance, but on two conditions :

(1) Italy must declare to us that she had come to no arrangements with other States, which might impair the *defensive* efficiency of the Triple Alliance treaties ;

(2) The Triple Alliance must remain *unchanged* where it touched us, whilst we should probably agree to the arrangement made by Italy with Austria-Hungary regarding the Balkans or to any changes made in their treaty. I also insinuated that I could not escape the impression that Signor Prinetti had been very weak and all too trustful in M. Barrère, and that I was beginning to believe what was whispered to us about the Italian Royal couple's liking for France.

Finally I remarked that I did not press for the conclusion of the Triple Alliance, but would warn him that if the matter was urged by Italy it might easily make the Emperor suspicious. There was no saying what, if our Gracious Master seriously mistrusted Italy, might be the consequences for the future orientation of our policy and for the future of Italy.

[Early in 1902 General von Schlieffen, the Head of the German General Staff, completed his plan for invading France through Belgium. He also approached Italy on the subject of her sending 200,000 men to help Germany in a war. (Cf. Wilson, *War Guilt*, pp. 84–6, 101).]

XVIII. 702

MEMORANDUM BY KLEHMET, GERMAN FOREIGN OFFICE,
September 7th, 1902

According to an oral statement by General Count von Schlieffen, Lieutenant-General Saletta, the Chief of the Italian General Staff, spoke and acted when he was here as though there were no change in any of the Triple Alliance arrangements and as if the military arrangements in particular were still in full force.

But—so said Count Schlieffen—General Saletta was no longer in the mood to rejoice in the Triple Alliance as formerly he had been. In particular he had spoken of the agreement whereby Italy was to throw two Army corps into Germany in the event of war, and had said that for this purpose, if the road through Austria-Hungary were not free, Italy intended when the time came to lead both corps under arms through Switzerland. He had also said that if both these Army corps were to be shut away from their homes he would have to see to obtaining the necessary munitions, etc., in Germany. Italy had deposited here the required models for the munitions. Now that these models had become out of date it would be necessary to send new ones. The boxes containing these were to be sent at once to the Italian Embassy in Berlin. General Saletta begged for provision to be made so that there might be no difficulties in the German Customs or in forwarding them to the Embassy.

[General Saletta's words, as reported in the following despatch, show that Germany's old policy of making Italy dependent on England in the Mediterranean and uniting the two against France was now turning to Germany's disadvantage.]

MAJOR VON CHELIUS, MILITARY ATTACHÉ IN ROME, TO GENERAL VON SCHLIEFFEN, *December 1st*, 1903

Extract. Secret.

I used the occasion of a visit to General Saletta for giving the conversation a political turn in order to ascertain, as I had meant to do for some time, what echo a mention of the political events of the preceding summer would find in the Chief of the Staff.

In speaking of King Victor Emanuel III's visits to Paris (October 14th–18th) and to London (November 14th–21st) I passed to the Italian third army and said that the events of the summer had left me with the impression that there was hardly any question now of the Italian army supporting the German army in the event of war against France. I gave this as my personal opinion in order to provoke a definite answer.

General Saletta was evidently disturbed by this, but he answered at once that for the King and himself nothing was altered in this matter ; the King's visits to London and Paris had not affected these arrangements in any way. The General then said : ' We are obliged to maintain good relations with France and England on account of the Mediterranean, where lie our vital interests ; I hope and believe, however, that the Triple Alliance will continue to be the basis of our foreign policy. The French friendship has been magnified incredibly by the Press in the pay of M. Barrère, and I can understand the doubts you express; but the intimacy between these two countries is far from being as it is represented in public. I always think that France merely wishes to exploit us, as for instance now in the Cuneo-Nice railway scheme, which would be built entirely for the advantage of France and which I mean to oppose with all my strength.'

On my suggesting that the former Ministry had made very extensive concessions the General said: 'I hope to reverse all that.'

I referred to the growing antagonism between Italy and Austria, and General Saletta said that in his view the only danger to the Triple Alliance came from that side and not from any Franco-Italian rapprochement; it could not be denied that the difference between Italy and Austria was growing ever more acute. . . .

XVIII. 708

General Count von Schlieffen to Baron von Richthofen, *December 14th*, 1903

In reply to Your Excellency's letter of the 11th [1] I beg to state that I am convinced that not only can we not count on the Italian third army, but that we shall have to make up our minds to face the entire French army without any reinforcements from the Alpine frontier.

Notwithstanding this, all preparations are being systematically worked out each year jointly with the Austrian General Staff, such as are necessary for that army in accordance with the terms agreed upon.

German Note. XX. 37

On February 28th, 1904, Count Monts reported from Rome that for the visit which President Loubet was to pay in April in return for Victor Emanuel's visit to Paris (October, 1903) a great programme was contemplated including a naval review of the ships of both countries at Naples, whilst for the Emperor's approaching visit (whilst on his Mediterranean cruise), when he was to meet the King of Italy at Naples (March 26–7), a much more modest programme was arranged.

XX. 45

The Chancellor, Count von Bülow, to Count Monts, in Rome, *March 15th*, 1904
Cipher telegram.

I told the Italian Ambassador this evening I did not doubt the good will of the Italian Ministers, but that I must tell him frankly that the continuity of the Italo-German alliance depended on how Loubet's visit went off. The only reason I could not

---

[1] Cf. H. Wickham Steed, *Through Thirty Years*, p. 323.

continue objecting to the naval exercises at Naples was because King Victor Emanuel seemed to be determined on them. But I presumed that all the ships, which were to greet Loubet later on, would be at Naples for the Emperor and remain on there. I considered it as a *conditio sine qua non* that the King's toast to Loubet should be very *sobre* and include the sentiment que l'Italie est fidèle à ses engagements qu'elle considère comme une garantie primordiale de la paix.

CHAPTER XIII
THE FIRST SIGNS OF THE TRIPLE ENTENTE, 1903

[The following documents show that at first the responsible authorities in Berlin were not alarmed by accounts of the preparations for an entente between England, France and Russia. To them it seemed that the British and Russian differences in the Far East, Persia, etc., were too deep-seated to admit of any genuine meeting-point. That they were wrong and Eckardstein right has been proved by events.

Even King Edward's great reception in Paris in May, 1903, did not make them fully realise which way the wind was blowing, for it seemed to them that a little careful nursing of British susceptibilities would bring back the old British desire for Germany's friendship. (Cf. H. Wickham Steed, *Through Thirty Years*, p. 206; also Mr. Eyre Crowe's important memorandum, G. & T., III, p. 397 et seq.; Brandenburg, p. 182 et seq.)]

XVII. 342
COUNT VON METTERNICH, IN LONDON, TO THE GERMAN FOREIGN OFFICE, *January 30th*, 1902

Cipher telegram. Secret.

I learn in strict confidence that for about ten days negociations have been proceeding between Chamberlain and the French Ambassador for the settlement of all outstanding differences between France and England in colonial questions. Chamberlain has proposed to the French Ambassador to handle the various colonial questions in dispute not singly, but as one whole. Newfoundland, the Niger, New Hebrides, the commercial treaties in Madagascar, the ex-territoriality question in Zanzibar—all these form part of the so-called colonial questions which Chamberlain would like to settle now once and for all. Cambon, who also seems eager to reach a definite arrangement on these questions with the British Government, according to an official closely associated with Chamberlain in the Colonial Office, mentioned the Morocco [1] question also with a reference to the last Franco-Italian agreement in the Mediterranean; he let it be seen that his Government would not be disinclined to negotiate for an Anglo-French compromise regarding Morocco. Chamberlain's reply was that he was quite prepared to discuss that question

[1] Cf. Lee, *Edward VII*, II, 219; G. & T., II, p. 256 et seq.

and to try and arrive at an arrangement satisfactory to both parties, but he would suggest treating the Morocco question separately from the other so-called colonial questions.

German Note.

On February 3rd Metternich wrote that Lord Lansdowne had denied to him that there had been an agreement with France about the old colonial questions. It was concluded in Berlin that there had at least been negociations, and enquiries were made in St. Petersburg and Madrid, whence it was reported that a closer understanding was in progress, but without definite result at the present stage. Lamsdorff, in St. Petersburg, only believed in academic discussions.

XVII. 570

THE CHANCELLOR, COUNT VON BÜLOW, TO COUNT VON ALVENS-LEBEN, IN ST. PETERSBURG, *May 13th*, 1903

I beg to enclose to you a copy of a memorandum in which the former Counsellor of Embassy, Baron von Eckardstein, argues on the grounds that he mentions the view that we shall shortly have to reckon with a British-French-Russian understanding brought about by M. Delcassé.   Herr von Eckardstein assumes that since King Edward's stay in Paris passed off without unpleasant incidents an understanding will be reached on the questions under discussion between England and France, including even Morocco.   An attempt will then be made to extend this understanding to Russia as third participant.   Baron von Eckardstein thinks that in his efforts to this end, M. Delcassé will be able to count on energetic support by the *haute finance* of France, which is perpetually disquieted by the thought that France has invested 10 milliards of francs in Russian bonds and by the possibility that an Anglo-Russian war will produce a financial catastrophe in Russia.

Up to now Baron von Eckardstein has stood alone in his anticipation of a fresh British-French-Russian grouping.   The news now received here of a general Anglo-French understanding which, according to Baron von Eckardstein, is to initiate the new Triple Entente is by no means optimistic.   Moreover last autumn the Morocco question was discussed between England and France without result.   The possession of Tangier played a large part in these discussions, but we do not know whether the French Ambassador, Cambon, under instructions from M. Delcassé, actually, as a great French paper asserted a few days ago, offered Tangier to the British, but that the French Cabinet stated that giving up Tangier was an impossible concession for France. Considering the present world-position and the state of popular feeling in France it will be difficult to solve the question of the possession of Tangier by peaceful methods for a long time to come.

An understanding between England and Russia would be still harder to attain than one between England and France. The communication from London forwarded by Your Excellency on May 5th states that the wish for such an understanding exists on the British side ; but it stated also that the British enquiry on the subject met with no favour on the Russian side.

German Note.

On April 25th, 1903, Count Bernstorff had written to St. Petersburg that it was the British Prime Minister's wish to bring about a clear-cut division between British and Russian interests in Asia, but that thése proposals had found no favour in Russia.

The British proposal seems in fact to have been to draw a line from the gulf of Alexandretta straight across Asia to the mouth of the Yang-tsze, and to cause Russia to be free and undisturbed to the North of this line and England to the South ; [1] the proposal was however not of the kind to attract Russia, for whom access to the ' warm ocean ' has acquired an importance similar to that of the possession of Hagia Sophia.   It is also not clear how far that Triple Entente, Russia-France-England, would improve the position of the Russian Empire as against its present one.   The present Dual Alliance forbids France to protest—at least openly—against Russia's schemes, whilst the experience of the last hundred years allows it to be prophesied with certainty that in the new Triple Entente France and England would agree together in questions of Eastern policy more easily than with Russia.

Moreover there has so far been no sign on the British side that a rapprochement with Russia would be bought at the price of admitting her into the ' warm ocean '.   Lord Lansdowne's recent speech . . . rejects expressly any compromise regarding conditions of sovereignty in the Persian Gulf and neighbouring waters.

German Note.

On May 5th in the House of Lords Lord Lansdowne spoke in clear terms on England's policy in the Persian Gulf : ' Should it be the intention of another Power to establish a naval station or a fortified harbour in the Persian Gulf, it would be considered to be a serious menace to British interests, and England would resist it with all the means in her power.'

For Germany the question of an Anglo-Russian understanding is of solely financial interest.   As Your Excellency knows, the Imperial Government influences the money market to a certain extent in the sense that so long as the commercial treaties are not run off, a certain reserve towards Russian money claims is advisable.   Thus the Prussian Minister of Trade recently declared his

---

[1] On this proposal the Emperor wrote : ' *Aha ! and so deprive us of the Bagdad Railway and keep the Yang-tsze.*'

intention of preventing all or part of the 72 million rouble Bonds of the Reich-Adels-Agrar Bank being placed in Germany. But if the possibility of an Anglo-Russian rapprochement is as imminent as Baron von Eckardstein makes it out to be, we shall have to consider whether it is to German interests to draw the strings so tightly, and whether a greater measure of accommodation on our part would not better suit those conditions. As I said at the beginning I still fail to see a reason why I should agree with Baron von Eckardstein's views. Nevertheless I should be unwilling to form a final judgment before learning Your Excellency's opinion. I therefore beg you to give me them, after careful consideration, by letter or telegram.

XVII. 575

COUNT BERNSTORFF, CHARGÉ D'AFFAIRES, IN LONDON, TO COUNT VON BÜLOW, *May 17th*, 1903

Extract.

. . . I might describe the aims of the Russian Embassy in London as the following : First to widen the breach existing between Germany and England, and then to place a Russian loan on the English market. The first aim is unfortunately only too easy to accomplish. Any slander against Germany launched in the Press by Russian agents finds credulous readers. It is naturally highly desirable to the St. Petersburg Government to maintain this pleasant position. In the near future co-operation between England and Germany is impossible ; so that Russia has no further need to reckon with the only political combination capable of hampering and really frightening her.

The second aim of Russian activities here is far more difficult to attain. . . . To-day the practical Briton will not take on a bad investment, especially if he knows that every shilling he spends will help in reducing British influence in Asia. Since Count Benckendorff [1] has these two objects in view, he may well be contemplating the possibility of a few Russian concessions to the British in order to lull them to sleep. But I do not think he is out for a general understanding or an alliance.

If there is any idea here of a Triple Entente coming into being, I think that there would be many more here in favour of a British-French-American combination. There would be an apparent atmosphere of freedom in this alliance, which would very greatly attract the British Philistine. Mr. Choate [2] occupies decidedly the first place among the Ambassadors in the public estimation here, as the Anglo-Saxon cousin.

In answer to the question how we are to bring to naught the

---

[1] Russian Ambassador in London.   [2] American Ambassador.

machinations of our opponents and restore tolerable relations with England, it is my humble opinion that we should leave the British Government completely at rest and postpone all disputed questions for a more convenient season. But I should recommend active manipulation of public opinion here. This concerns only one point. Everyone here regards us as endlessly ambitious and greedy of expansion. If we can succeed in gradually and carefully persuading the Britons that we are not so, all is won. They will then again begin to think of England's real opponents. I am strengthened in this opinion by the fact that since the Manchurian question came up again our friends in the Press have again raised their heads. An article like the one in yesterday's *Saturday Review* would have been impossible a few weeks ago. It would certainly make our business here easier if the German papers would refrain from discussing the strengthening of the fleet as if it was directed against England.

Postscript.

To-day's newspapers violently attack Russia for the Jewish pogrom at Kishineff. We know that the English Rothschilds are very orthodox Israelites and used for that reason to feel no friendship for Russia. This new phase of the Jewish question may very likely revive their former feelings.

XVII. 591

COUNT VON METTERNICH, IN LONDON, TO THE CHANCELLOR, COUNT VON BÜLOW, *June 2nd*, 1903

Extract.

. . . The attempts at a rapprochement with Germany came partly from fear and partly from inclination. The fear that Germany's power might be turned against England has, since the settlement of the Egyptian question and the.cementing of the Franco-Russian alliance, lessened so far as can be seen at present. Jealousy persists only in the domain of trade. The inclination died with the Boer War.

It is a great error to assume that the Englishman is merely a cold calculating egoist. He is led and misled by his feelings like any other man. The sentimentality of the German, who on a fine May night is moved to ecstasy on seeing the moon and thinks he is getting a whiff of the universe, (The EMPEROR: ' *Very good.*') is not at all the same as the Englishman's sentiment, but even he may be and often has been a sentimentalist in politics. (The EMPEROR: ' *Correct.*') Abroad this quality is usually ascribed to him as hypocrisy for selfish motives.

The Anglo-French rapprochement is a product of the general

dislike of Germany. (The EMPEROR : ' *Correct.*') In disputes between England and Germany French policy has always taken the British side, because she looks on Germany as the more dangerous rival whom she always hopes to vanquish. Without the Anglo-German estrangement an Anglophil feeling would not have been possible in France, and M. Delcassé would have had to wait long for the fulfilment of his desires. Without the feeling against Germany the British Press would not have been working for months in favour of reconciliation with France, nor could M. Cambon have made his conciliatory speeches. King Edward's visit to Paris [1] was entirely his own work, and I know for certain that it sprang from his own initiative. (The EMPEROR : ' *Yes.*') I am far from assuming that King Edward meant it to be a hit at Germany ; but as the feeling on both sides of the Channel was favourable, it was from his and his Government's point of view quite reasonable for him to do his best to remove the old tension. (The EMPEROR : ' *Correct.*')

That is how it stands. A few days ago Sir Thomas Sanderson, the Under-Secretary, voluntarily assured me that in Paris there were neither political arrangements nor a settlement of outstanding questions, and there is no sign that the statement of this cautious and experienced official represented anything but the truth. . . .

I am convinced that the British Government, by the progressive reconciliation with France which has fallen so neatly into their lap, mean no contrary implication as regards Germany. They have the satisfactory feeling of having one rival the less, without any sacrifice involved. Their prestige is increased at home and to some extent abroad also. Reconciliation with one opponent does not necessarily imply enmity with another. . . .

[1] Cf. Lee, *Edward VII*, II, p. 236 et seq. ; G. & T., II, p. 364.

CHAPTER XIV

THE RUSSO-JAPANESE WAR, 1903–5. THE DOGGERBANK INCIDENT. THE EMPEROR WILLIAM AND THE TSAR, 1904

[The Japanese Government became convinced that Russia intended to annex Manchuria and so become a permanent threat to Japan's interests in China and Korea, whose independence Russia refused formally to recognise. On February 7th, 1904, Japan declared war. (Cf. Lee, *King Edward VII*, II, p. 281 et seq.; G. & T., II, p. 251; Brandenburg, p. 199 et seq.) The American Government [1] at once telegraphed to the Ambassadors in London, Berlin and Paris (XIX, 101): ' Consult Ministers of Foreign Affairs regarding possibility and desirability of neutral Powers concurrently using good offices with Russia and Japan, in case a state of war should unfortunately be created, to induce them to respect the neutrality of China and in all possible ways her administrative entity, to localise and limit as much as possible the area of hostilities, so that undue excitement and disturbance of the Chinese people may be prevented and the least possible loss to the commerce and peaceful intercourse of the world may be occasioned.']

XIX. 12

COUNT VON BERNSTORFF, CHARGÉ D'AFFAIRES IN LONDON, TO THE CHANCELLOR, COUNT VON BÜLOW, *October 12th*, 1903

The news from the Far East, and especially the semi-official statement that the Tsar has given up his visit to Rome, are filling public opinion here with unrest and anxiety. In spite of every denial by the Japanese Legation belief in a conflict in the Far East is growing. Just now England desires war as little as can be imagined. Everyone is groaning under the still-felt financial burden of the Transvaal War, the army leadership is discredited, and the Government, which appears to be breaking up, is distrusted.

As far as can be judged from here, if Japan wishes to go to war with Russia at all, the last suitable moment for it seems to have come. They appear to have made up their minds in Tokio that England is no longer to be regarded as an absolutely reliable friend. (The EMPEROR : ' *Nothing less than that.*') The

[1] Cf. G. & T., II, p. 252.

Anglo-French negociations during M. Loubet's visit [1] here have not remained hidden from the Japanese Government. Although these involved no breach of the treaty, being aimed at maintaining peace and eventually localising the war, the Japanese must already recognise that England is now more attached to her newly acquired French friend than to her ally. (The EMPEROR : ' *Correct.*')

I hear on good authority that the proposed Anglo-French negociations led to the first disagreement between the Duke of Devonshire on the one hand and Mr. Balfour and Lord Lansdowne on the other. There was apparently a lively discussion on the subject, for the Duke already regarded the negociations as lack of loyalty to the treaty and feared that England would be accused of duplicity by Japan and would be held in less respect throughout the Far East. (The EMPEROR : ' *And quite rightly so.*')

It is hard to say how far Japan has been able to lift the veil from the Anglo-French negociations. At any rate Baron Hayashi seems to have realised that since the Alliance with Japan was concluded there has been a decided change of feeling here. The Minister must have remarked the British Government's anxiety in alternately warning Japanese statesmen to remain quiet and praising their moderation and reasonableness. If such a change of mood could occur under a Unionist Government, what can Japan expect from a Liberal one if it came into power after the next General Election ? Consideration of conditions here is therefore bound to lead the Japanese Government to begin a war with Russia soon, if it wishes to at all. Later on the British alliance might be found to be entirely illusory, (The EMPEROR : ' *Correct.*') quite apart from the fact that Russia's position in the Far East is daily gaining in strength. (The EMPEROR : ' *Yes.*') In spite of the weakening of the British Government, they would, notwithstanding all motives to the contrary, rouse themselves to an energetic attitude, supposing the United States supported Japan in any way. American journalists here assert that public opinion in the New World would be sharply in favour of taking Japan's part. (The EMPEROR : ' *?* ') How far this is true I cannot judge from here. At any rate it is to be feared that a war for the sake of Japan, which would in itself be very unpopular in America for the sake of England, would have to count on the general consent of the nation if it meant making the American alliance into a real thing. Such an opportunity of restoring its prestige would certainly not escape the Government here. Nevertheless it could only venture as far as it suited the Americans. (The EMPEROR : ' *Then our price would greatly appreciate in Russia, for Gaul is held down by England.—The Crimean War*

[1] July 6th to 9th. Cf. Lee, *King Edward VII*, II, p. 244.

combination with Japan as an ally and America in the background is not a bad idea ! ')

XIX. 107

THE CHANCELLOR, COUNT VON BÜLOW, TO COUNT VON ALVENS-
LEBEN, IN ST. PETERSBURG, *February 13th, 1904*

The idea of neutralising Chinese territory came neither from Germany nor America, but from the French Minister in Peking on February 3rd or 4th. The French proposal to neutralise the Province of Chi-li was enough to make us reflect, and the fact that it was suggested by France does not diminish our hesitation. Under ordinary circumstances a simple refusal would be our first impulse. But we had to consider that a few days before (January 28th) a great American newspaper had published in a telegram apparently from St. Petersburg the news that Germany intended to claim possession of the Province of Pechili when the inevitable partition of the Chinese Empire took place. A simple rejection of the neutralising idea would have added to this suspicion. We were therefore obliged to ascertain the extent and the reasons for this unexpected suggestion. That we did not enquire first in St. Petersburg is explained by the fact that Russia carefully avoided dragging us into a discussion of the question of the Russo-Japanese dispute. We wished not to seem to be seeking an opportunity of probing into secrets. Also the fact that the first suggestion came from France necessarily set aside the idea that the neutralisation of Chi-li could be unwelcome to the Russian Government. It was therefore obvious to suppose that the neutralisation would be unwelcome to other Powers. This supposition was strengthened when Conger, the American Minister, when questioned by Baron von Mumm as to his attitude to the affair, promptly refused to communicate the neutralisation idea to his Government. Since it was not a light matter for us to be thrust into taking a side, the Imperial Ambassador in Washington was instructed to sound the American Government as to its attitude towards the idea and to say that in principle we were in favour of it in consideration of our trade interests in the Far East, assuming that the terms were precisely defined. Then the American Government took the initiative, and its proposal arrived here a day earlier than that of the four representatives, which was suggested by France. The American proposal, which naturally excludes the war area, temporarily secures the existence of the rest of the Chinese Empire and seems to me more likely to reassure the Chinese and to keep them neutral. China cannot stand up in open battle, but she may cause inconvenience by sending guerrilla hordes, and Count Lamsdorff probably has learned more of the details than we have, namely, that Yuan-Shi-Kai is sending the regiments, formed under European officers, with all speed to the northern frontier.

The answer to Count Lamsdorff's question why the Americans do not include Korea in the neutralisation is that America merely regards the neutralisation as a practical measure of utility. They wish to exclude the war-area in order not to be bothered by questions of sovereignty. I must also add my view that this way of dealing with the matter suits Russia's interests, whilst on the other hand, Japan, as I gathered from something the Japanese Minister here said yesterday, is thinking of demanding that the Powers interested in neutralisation shall in principle assign the sovereignty of Manchuria to China. If this suggestion is formally expressed, the German Government, by categorically rejecting it, will not fail to influence the other Governments in some measure.

I consider that our attitude to the neutralisation idea is that we are quite disinterested, but now that it has been raised by the very Governments whose policy we always have to observe most carefully we are bound to give it our consideration, bearing in mind that we have always said that neutralisation can only be discussed in so far as it does not interfere with the two belligerents in the pursuance of their war aims.

I beg you to explain the attitude of the German Government to Count Lamsdorff in the sense of the foregoing.

[On January 3rd, 1904, the Emperor wrote to the Tsar urging him to go to war with Japan and to accept no arrangement. (Cf. H. W. Wilson, *War Guilt*, p. 89; W. Goerz, *Briefe Wilhelms II an den Zaren*, p. 333.) The Tsar replied : ' I am still in good hopes about a calm and peaceful understanding in the end . . . Nicky, Adm. of Pacific.'

(William II had formed the habit of signing himself ' Admiral of the Atlantic '.)]

XIX. 62

MEMORANDUM BY THE CHANCELLOR, COUNT VON BÜLOW,
February 14th, 1904

Extract.

The Emperor told me this morning that he was deeply disappointed by the Tsar's answer to his letter. He had hoped that its warmth would induce the Tsar to turn all his forces against Japan.[1] Instead of this the Emperor Nicholas' attitude was still a poor-spirited one ; he seemed not to want to fight, and it was not impossible that he would end by letting the Japanese

---

[1] Cf. H. Wickham Steed, *Through Thirty Years*, pp. 199, 211 ; also Mr. Eyre Crowe's memorandum, G. & T., III, p. 398 ; S. Gwynn, *Letters and Friendships of Cecil Spring Rice*, p. 388 et seq.

have Manchuria without a blow or only after weak resistance.
Such a turn of events must be prevented under all circumstances.
I replied that the surest means of making the Russians conclude
a hasty and empty peace with Japan would be by rash German
suggestions addressed to the Tsar. If the Tsar saw that His
Majesty wanted him to get his teeth well into Japan, it would be
enough to make him break it off on the spot.

His Majesty replied that from the point of view of a statesman I might be right. But he felt as a Sovereign, and it pained
him to see the harm the Emperor Nicholas was doing himself by
his flabby way of going on. The Tsar was compromising all great
Sovereigns. . . .

[From the start of the war with Japan Russia suffered an unbroken
series of defeats by land and sea. The old European question of the
Dardanelles was reopened, since the Russians wished to send their Black
Sea fleet to the scene of war.]

XIX. 240

COUNT VON METTERNICH, IN LONDON, TO THE GERMAN FOREIGN
OFFICE, *August 18th*, 1904

Cipher telegram. Extract.

. . . As early as February Lord Lansdowne told the Russian
Ambassador (Count Benckendorff) that England would object
to allowing the Black Sea fleet to run out [1]—a *casus belli* then,
as Count Benckendorff said to me—but would let the Baltic fleet
go without hindrance. Now the Minister had told him that
the Baltic fleet would not be allowed to coal in British ports on
the way to the Far East. When the Ambassador protested that
the British Government had promised in February to put no hin-
drances in the way of the Baltic fleet, Lord Lansdowne's answer
was that it was not their intention now, but they could not
assist the fleet to reach the scene of war. Japan would rightly
regard this as a breach of neutrality.

Count Benckendorff considers this declaration, which would be
very seriously felt in St. Petersburg, to be very stupid, since, as
he let me see, he is not fully convinced that the Baltic fleet is
really serious about sailing. I asked him if he knew how France
stood as regarded the question of coaling, as, according to what
Balfour had said, the French Government appeared to share the
British views. Count Benckendorff seemed to know nothing of
the French Government's attitude towards it. Lord Lansdowne
had told Count Benckendorff that Wei-hai-wei was closed to the
fighting ships. But if a fighting ship ran in there, the 24 hours'

[1] Cf. G. & T., II, 242 ; Wilson, *War Guilt*, p. 91 ; Lee, *King Edward
VII*, II, p. 289 ; S. Gwynn, *Letters and Friendships of Cecil Spring Rice*,
p. 414.

respite would not be given, and the ship would have to be disarmed immediately.   When Count Benckendorff appealed to the
former British declarations, the Minister had replied that the
24 hours' respite applied only to ships that were to sail straight
for home, and not to those which used neutral harbours as a
base for fresh attacks after 24 hours' rest. Wei-hai-wei lay too
near the scene of war for fighting ships to be allowed to use
it.   Lord Lansdowne had not mentioned Hong Kong. Count
Benckendorff enquired of me about admission into Tsing-tau.

German Note. XIX. 248
   . . . On August 17th the Emperor telegraphed to the Governor of
Tsing-tau: ' Russian war-ships to be allowed to remain at Tsing-tau as
long as is needed to restore their sea-worthiness with proper hastening of
repairs, and beyond this up to 24 hours at most to provide themselves with
what is needed for the voyage to their nearest harbour ! If the ships do
not leave within the time allowed them they are to be disarmed. Fighting
repairs or taking in war supplies not to be permitted. It must be understood that the repairs are only for making the ships sea-worthy.' . . .

   I told him that the Russian ships had been disarmed and the
crews interned as they had not observed the 24 hours' respite.
I replied yes to his further question whether Lord Lansdowne
had questioned me about admission into Tsing-tau, but did not
tell him that there had been a difference of opinion between the
British and Imperial Governments over the 24 hours' respite.
I also forebore to discuss whether we should regard the 24 hours'
respite as a fixed rule under all circumstances.

German Note.
   The Russian Baltic fleet left Libau on October 15th. As early as in
August the Russian Government had been warned of the danger of possible
Japanese attacks on the squadron in the North Sea.

XIX. 281

COUNT VON METTERNICH, IN LONDON, TO THE GERMAN FOREIGN
                OFFICE, *October 13th*, 1904
Cipher telegram.

   I am informed on reliable authority that if the Russian
Black Sea fleet sails, mines are to be laid in the Sound and Cattegat
by agents in Japanese employment.
   I beg that this warning may be communicated to the Russian
Government. (BÜLOW : ' *Has anything been done about this ?* ')

German Note.
   Richthofen replied : ' On A/16/288 nothing has been done by me, since
(1) the information given did not seem certain enough to be passed on, and
(2) passing it on to the Russian Government did not appear to me
compatible with our neutrality.'

[The *Army and Navy Gazette* laid the blame for the Dogger Bank incident [1] of the night of October 21st on Germany.

German Note.
The accusation is unfounded. Neither in the Records nor in the Emperor's letters to the Tsar is there proof that Germany gave any such warning. On the contrary no action was taken on Count Metternich's suggestion to warn the Russian Government against Japanese attacks— as the foregoing telegram shows—in order to avoid a breach of neutrality.

XIX. 285
COUNT VON METTERNICH, IN LONDON, TO THE GERMAN FOREIGN OFFICE, *October 27th,* 1904

Very confidential.

The Russian Ambassador has just told me that he still looks on the situation as serious, but mainly because of the excitement here. However the British Government's attitude is less stiff than it was two days ago.[2]

The only real difficulty lies in the question of punishing the guilty Russian officers. These assert that they saw two torpedo-boats and that was why they gave the order to fire. The British Government say they are ready to recognise the *bona fides* of the Russian officers, but cannot admit that there were torpedo-boats in the neighbourhood of the Russian fleet. They propose arbitration, (The EMPEROR : ' *Never been done before ! On a question of discipline and command of a foreign fleet ! What shamelessness. One cannot be judged by* foreigners *as to retention of one's own officers in the service !* ') and demand eventual punishment of the officers concerned if the enquiry establishes their guilt. Count Benckendorff has forwarded this proposal to St. Petersburg, (The EMPEROR : ' *I hope not.*') but has received no reply yet. But he openly assumes that the affair may be settled by this means. (The EMPEROR : ' *Unheard of !* ')   But it would probably be necessary to land certain Russian officers at Vigo to act as witnesses. There might be difficulties if the fleet had already proceeded on its voyage. The Russian Admiral was certainly to be blamed for not having made his report directly after the incident. (The EMPEROR : ' *As it happened at sea by night, it could only have been reported at Dover.*') Then the dangerous excitement might have been avoided.

There is no doubt that the noise in the Press is increasing. It appears that the Japanese Legation is pouring oil on the fire. (The EMPEROR : ' *Naturally ! They wish England to hold the*

[1] Cf. Lee, *Edward VII*, II, p. 301 ; Wilson, *War Guilt*, p. 92 ; British Blue Book : *Russia* (No. 3 (1905) [Cd. 2352] ; G. & T., III, p. 400 ; Dennis, *Adventures in American Diplomacy*, p. 393 ; Brandenburg, p. 213 et seq. ; Bacon, *Lord Fisher*, II, p. 59.
[2] Cf. G. & T., IV, p. 14.

Russian fleet by the throat by preventing it from continuing its voyage.')

[Since both the British and Russian Governments wished for a peaceful solution, the affair passed over without grave consequence. King Edward himself contributed largely to this result. (Cf. Lee, II, pp. 302–3.) The German fears for an Anglo-Russian entente are described by Sir S. Lee (pp. 305–6), who translates two despatches from London (XIX. 360–5, 366).

The German Emperor seized the occasion for an effort to draw nearer to Russia. It took the form of an exchange of private letters between the two Emperors with the approval of Count Bülow, who actually drafted one for the Emperor. At the end of this one William II added for himself : (XIX. 306), ' May it meet with your approval ; nobody knows anything about it, not even my Foreign Office ; the work was done by Bülow and me personally. " May God's blessing rest on the purposes of the great Rulers, and may the mighty three-fold group, Russia, Germany and France ever help to keep peace in Europe ". These were his words when we had finished . . .'

The project came to nothing, for the Russian Government was reluctant and would do nothing without France's concurrence.]

XIX. 332

MEMORANDUM BY COUNT VON METTERNICH, IN BERLIN, *December 18th*, 1904

Extract.

In England the opinion is widely spread that Germany cherishes hostile intentions against the island kingdom, whilst Germany thinks the same about England. Both are untrue. England wants no war—with anyone. She wants rest and recovery from the financial consequences of the Boer War. The position of the *Army and Navy Gazette* is not the same as that of our *Militär-Wochenblatt*. It is not official. Arnold White, the writer on naval matters, recently pleaded in a second-rate Sunday paper, the *Sun*, for a British knock at the German fleet after the fashion of Copenhagen in 1800. When Balfour, the Prime Minister, was shown this article, he said : ' Arnold White ought to be hanged.' . . .

XIX. 346

THE EMPEROR WILLIAM TO THE CHANCELLOR, COUNT VON BÜLOW, *December 28th*, 1904

DEAR BÜLOW,

Enclosed is the Tsar's answering letter.[1] It is a clear rejection of any idea of an arrangement without France's previous knowledge. An absolutely negative result after two months of honest toil and negociation ! The first personal failure of my life. I hope it is not the first of a series of similar experiences. America and Japan must now be cultivated all the more. The latter are

[1] Not given.

doubtless much piqued about England and in a gloomy mood, since all is not going as they hoped.

The French have clearly got wind of our negociations and brought them to naught. Delcassé is damnably clever and very strong. I am one in heart and soul with the Bulgarian ; he is coming for my birthday.

German Note.

The Emperor met Prince Ferdinand of Bulgaria at Coburg at the end of December. Bülow had advised him to treat the Prince in a friendly fashion and accede to his wish to be received by the Emperor in Berlin.

He has already given promises regarding the Bagdad Railway and is to try to win the French over to it. He is very angry with Austria and has been negociating secretly with the Hungarians, whose defection he thinks quite certain the moment the present Emperor dies. He says Franz Ferdinand [1] is a Czech pure and simple. He intends to make his wife Empress ! The affair of the English nurse in the Tsar's palace is glorious ! His Britannic Majesty works with the old-fashioned weapons of the Rococo period.

German Note.

The Tsar's son's English nurse was caught near the Tsar's papers in his private study.

XIX. 656

COUNT VON QUADT, GERMAN CONSUL-GENERAL AT CALCUTTA, AT SIMLA, TO COUNT VON BÜLOW, *October 26th*, 1904

The political Mission to Afghanistan,[2] which is going to Kabul with Mr. [Louis] Dane, the Indian Foreign Secretary, will start from here for Peshawar about the middle of November and proceed thence on the 25th. The Mission will be accompanied by Mr. Dobbs, of the Political Department, who returned last August from Kabul, where with Major Wanliss he was the Amir's guest for some time ; he will act as secretary to the Mission. Other members of the Mission will be Major Malleson, of the Intelligence Department, Captain Brooke, Lord Kitchener's aide-de-camp, and a doctor. Just a few native soldiers will go as orderlies ; the Amir is to provide the escort.

Besides political arrangements, there will be military discussions at Kabul. Captain Brooke, one of the cleverest of the very efficient staff collected by Lord Kitchener, told me at any rate that he was working day and night, for it was his job to be

---

[1] Cf. H. Wickham Steed, *Through Thirty Years*, p. 218.

[2] Cf. Lee, *King Edward VII*, II, pp. 354, 372 ; G. & T., II, p. 250 ; III, p. 367 ; IV, p. 512 et seq. ; p. 520, note.

familiar with all topographical details of Afghanistan and her military history before the Mission started.

The main object of the Mission seems to be to make England's influence predominant in Afghanistan and to induce the Amir to take such military measures under British advice and supervision as will make a Russian invasion through Afghanistan impossible. Moreover, Mr. Dane seems bent on promoting trade between India and Afghanistan.

Thus England has been quick in seizing the opportunity offered by the war in the Far East to secure her position in India for a long time to come. Here there is general and open delight at the annoyance the despatch of the Mission will probably cause to Russia. (The EMPEROR : ' *Who laughs last, laughs best.*')

Besides the Mission, there are going to Kabul in the next few days an engineer, a doctor for the Amir, two women doctors, and a Persian interpreter. These will remain with the Amir for three years. The Amir's doctor is Major Cleveland, who will be accompanied by his wife, a daughter of Detring, the well-known Customs Commissioner at Tientsin. (The EMPEROR : ' *A German.*')

XIX. 657

COUNT VON BERNSTORFF, IN LONDON, TO THE CHANCELLOR, COUNT VON BÜLOW, *February 27th*, 1905

Secret negociations have been going on for some time between the Indian Government and the Amir of Afghanistan. Recently King Edward said to me in joke that the Amir seemed to adopt a British or Russian complexion just as he liked, and he could not be trusted. The negociations themselves are kept strictly secret. Questions in Parliament remain unanswered.

The Russian Ambassador told me yesterday in the course of a long conversation that he had seen Lord Lansdowne four times since he returned from leave. Now the Minister had not mentioned the war in the Far East as he had before, and the words peace or war were never on his lips. But the North Sea Naval Commission was one subject, and he had to get the Minister to discuss Afghanistan. When I asked what had happened there, Count Benckendorff replied that the military movements and reinforcements on the North-West Frontier, the Curzon programme of making Afghanistan a glacis for India, the Anglo-Afghan negociations, of which he knew nothing but which were certainly intended to strengthen the British position, were engaging the serious attention of his Government. By treaty Afghanistan was a buffer State between England and Russia and must not sink to be a vassal of India.[1] The increased armaments in

[1] Cf. G. & T., I, p. 306 et seq.

India must needs be followed by a similar Russian increase in Turkestan, and he regarded this tendency to increased armaments on both sides as a serious menace for the future. He confessed that the Russian forces in Turkestan were at present very small. The Ambassador imagines that in the event of war the Amir will join the British.

[The arguments contained in the foregoing documents were used, amongst others, by the Emperor, when he extracted the Tsar's consent to the Björkö treaty, which is very fully described in Lee, *King Edward VII*, II, p. 354 et seq. It was signed on July 24th, 1905, seven weeks after Delcassé's fall,[1] quite privately by the Emperor and the Tsar, but it had to be given up, as it ran counter to the general policies of both Germany and Russia.]

[1] Cf. p. 227.

CHAPTER XV

THE ANGLO-FRENCH CONVENTION, MARCH TO JUNE, 1904

THE KHEDIVIAL DECREE

[The Anglo-French Convention of March 8th, 1904,[1] included a declaration embodied in the ' Khedivial Decree ', whereby the restrictions which were necessary when Egypt was practically bankrupt were to be removed in view of the fact that Egypt was now becoming a very rich country. The reasons for such a course are forcibly put by Lord Cromer in his *Modern Egypt* which is quoted by Lord Lansdowne in his despatch of April 8th, 1904, to Sir E. Monson. (Cf. G. & T., II, pp. 364–6). The facts were readily recognised by all the Powers concerned [2] except Germany, whose Government was not disposed to be behindhand in claiming the right to benefit fully from the brilliant administration of Egypt's finances by Lord Cromer and his British colleagues. The Anglo-French Convention had promised France special commercial privileges in Egypt for 30 years in return for her leaving England with a free hand there. England had reciprocated in Morocco. Germany had nothing to offer but mere abstention from active ill-will; nevertheless she succeeded in securing equality of rights with France in Egypt, and in particular, an assurance that the Director of the Khedive's library should continue to be a German. (Cf. Brandenburg, p. 202 et seq.; Lee, *King Edward VII*, II, p. 248 et seq.)

The Anglo-French Agreement of March 8th, 1904, was described by M. Delcassé to Prince Radolin, Ambassador in Paris, as follows :]

XX. 4

PRINCE VON RADOLIN, IN PARIS, TO THE CHANCELLOR, COUNT VON BÜLOW, *March 23rd*, 1904

M. Delcassé, with whom both at a dinner which I gave in his honour and to-day I had long conversations, spoke fairly frankly as follows about the Anglo-French Agreement which has been mentioned in the Press :

There were certain questions between France and England needing settlement. In order to prevent these disputed points from disturbing good relations the two Governments were

---

[1] For the text, cf. G. & T., II, p. 402 ; also cf. Cromer, *Modern Egypt*, p. 390 ; Weigall, *Egypt*, 1798–1914, p. 201.
[2] Cf. G. & T., IV, pp. 190–5.

trying to reach an understanding at any rate in principle and to clear up once and for all individual questions, as far as might be.

It would not be difficult to include the Newfoundland Fisheries affair in the list of those questions which were capable of settlement.

Ever since the Peace of Utrecht France had held that certain parts of the coast had been granted to her as settlements for the fishermen and as places to dry the fish. The then population of at most 5,000 souls neither used nor needed these districts. Now it was otherwise. The fish had departed, the French fishing population was greatly reduced, and their coastal settlements had no longer their former importance, whereas the Newfoundlanders had risen to two or three hundred thousand, who naturally found exclusion from the coastal districts inconvenient and hampering to their development. France was ready to renounce her old rights for suitable compensation.

It was also possible to discuss many points in the Egyptian question. The use to be made of the surplus of the *Dette publique* was an international matter and did not depend on France alone.

M. Delcassé then spoke of Morocco and again said, as he often had done before, that before everything he wished to maintain the *status quo* as long as possible. He must insist on the Algerian border being secured against invasion. The defence of this line was so costly that this intolerable situation must certainly be cleared away.

The weakness of the Morocco Government made trade so precarious for all nations that a change there also was necessary for the general interest.

The only way to attain this end just now was to give the Sultan more backbone and his Government more power. It was France's task as a neighbouring State to see to this, and he, Delcassé, believed that France would earn the gratitude of every trading nation if, by her influence, she brought about orderly or at least tolerable conditions in Morocco.

A further question was to assure for the mariners of all nations free passage through the Straits of Gibraltar. France must insist on the coast being neutralised. It would be quite justifiable to guarantee Spain's ancient rights in Morocco.[1] France wished for no special privileges in Morocco, but it was her duty to end the anarchy in the neighbouring State with all her energy in the interests of all trading nations.

M. Delcassé carefully avoided the word ' protectorate ', but this does not exclude the possibility that the influence sought by

[1] G. & T., III, p. 25 et seq.

France for restoring order in Morocco may be equivalent to a protectorate. (The EMPEROR : ' *Yes.*')

The Minister closed the conversation by saying he hoped that the Agreement now under way with England would shortly be concluded.

As a corollary to the Minister's words, I hear on good authority a communication, alleged to be from the Quai d'Orsay, that the negociations on the question outstanding between England and France are near their end. The final French draft of the documents connected with it was forwarded last Saturday to the Ambassador in London, who by now will have handed it to Lord Lansdowne.

The points about West Africa and Newfoundland [1] are settled both in principle and detail. In Newfoundland France gives up her territorial rights and the ' French shore ' and receives a small money indemnity for the four or five lobster canning factories which are there. Further, England grants a regulation of frontier in Sokoto,[2] giving France easier and quicker communications between two of her possessions on the coast of West Africa. (Instead of a 10 days' march over the desert, French troops and trading caravans will only have 2 or 3 days to travel.)

As regards Egypt and Morocco the drafting must be done with special care if difficulties are to be avoided later on.

My informant tells me that France demands that England shall renounce any rights she may claim in Morocco in return for France's renunciation of her rights in Egypt. (The EMPEROR : ' ? ')

About Siam I hear merely that two points in the Anglo-French treaty of 1896 are to be defined more precisely.[3]

I understand there is no mention of the New Hebrides in the projected agreement.

[Count Bernstorff concluded a despatch discussing the chances of improving Anglo-German relations in the following terms :]

XX. 19

COUNT BERNSTORFF, CHARGÉ D'AFFAIRES IN LONDON, TO THE CHANCELLOR, COUNT VON BÜLOW, *April 16th,* 1904

Conclusion.

. . . The Government here seem to wish to go against the tendencies of the Press. (The EMPEROR : ' *If they would! The spirit is willing !* ') Mr. Gwynne, the present very Ger-

---

[1] Cf. G. & T., III, p. 1 et seq.   [2] Cf. G. & T., II, p. 347.
[3] Cf. Vol. II., pp. 236, 402, 407.

manophil manager of Reuter's, informed me at any rate that he had lately been told in the Foreign Office that he might fight against the Press agitation as strongly as he could. Once reconciliation with France was achieved, the Government wished to begin the same work with Germany. (The EMPEROR : ' *Now I am really curious!* ') It is naturally very difficult for us to influence British public opinion, for the journalists are armed with all their old prejudices. At night in their editorial sanctums they often fail to stick to what they have promised me in the afternoon. But this may easily change if the Government is really prepared to exercise a calming influence.

In my humble opinion it would be a good beginning of improved mutual relations for us to conclude an arbitration treaty with England. (The EMPEROR : ' *I have nothing against it. Even though I dislike acting a fresh comedy!* ') Such treaties in the form now customary are quite harmless and *de facto* meaningless. But it is amazing how phrases dominate the ' practical Englishman ' in political matters. If we were prepared for an arbitration agreement, countless people would believe here that the Germans, once so greedy of conquest, had become peaceable folk. We could still go on building warships, if only not too much were said about it in public.

The papers here say that King Edward wishes to visit our gracious Master at Potsdam on his return journey from Marienbad. I cannot tell whether it is true or whether such a visit would be welcome to the Emperor ; but if correct, a visit by King Edward to Germany might turn British public opinion in our favour. His Majesty came to the throne at a moment when his people yearned for peace more than ever before. The King has known wonderfully how to adapt himself to this phase of feeling. They think of him as an apostle of peace who wishes and is able to remove all the existing dislike of England. If the German people have sufficient political sense (The EMPEROR : ' *They have not!* ') to give His Majesty a hearty reception, the British will begin to think we wish to be reconciled with our British cousins who now stupidly doubt it. Even the most rabid pan-German,[1] if he consults his intelligence, (The EMPEROR : ' *They have none! That is the great misfortune.*') must wish to conciliate British opinion. The object is now within our reach without the necessity of any political services to the Britons. If then we have to fight England for the sake of our power and expansion, (The EMPEROR : ' *Necessary it is not.*') every hour by which the struggle is postponed is a gain for us. The might of the German people is continually increasing, whilst no one can live with his eyes open amongst the island people without

[1] Cf. G. & T., III, p. 353.

realising that they have already reached their highest point. (The EMPEROR : ' *Splendidly written.*')

XX. 124

THE CHANCELLOR, COUNT VON BÜLOW, TO BARON VON RICHTHOFEN, FOREIGN SECRETARY, *April 19th*, 1904

Many thanks for your interesting lines.[1] I discussed the question with Holstein this morning, but not in connection with them, and we came to the same conclusion as yourself.

As soon as we have disposed of the Reichstag discussions, we must discuss this very important matter calmly and thoroughly. I feel that Egypt is the best nail to hang all the rest on. Yesterday Szögyényi [2] asked me what we thought of the Egyptian part of the Anglo-French Agreement. I requested him to discuss it with you as our authority on Egyptian matters. It may begin on this basis.

I quite agree that we should try and include all questions both large and small—Samoan and Transvaal indemnities, as well as Canada and preferential treatment for the mother-country. It would be well to include the arbitration matter also. A naval treaty in the sense suggested by you would certainly not be proposed by us before agreeing with England on the other subjects at least in principle, and it would have to be handled carefully and delicately. But nothing must leak out about it prematurely. With this preparation I am convinced that I can win His Majesty over to the whole transaction.

XX. 34

RÜCKER-JENISCH, GERMAN CONSUL-GENERAL AT CAIRO, TO THE GERMAN FOREIGN OFFICE, *May 31st*, 1904

Cipher telegram.

I have just visited Lord Cromer.[3] His first remark was that since our last meeting he had heard nothing of negociations in Berlin. I then informed him of Your Excellency's private negociations with the British Ambassador, but did *not* mention the conditions attached by Lord Lansdowne to the observation of Art. IV. I merely said that the only point of dispute was the granting of the same freedom of trade in Egypt to Germany as to France, and that we were still waiting for the answer from London. Lord Cromer read Art. IV again and said he saw no difficulty in granting the Germans this equality. Egypt's present and future policy was to treat all nations alike commercially. When I enquired why this right had been promised to

---

[1] Not in the Records.   [2] Austrian Ambassador in Berlin.
Cf. G. & T., II, pp. 323, 335 ; III, p. 17 et seq.

France by a special treaty, he replied that in Morocco the British had been obliged to insist on a definite assurance regarding their trade interests and for this the French had demanded its equivalent in Egypt.

I then mentioned the question of the Directorship of the Khedive's library, pointing to the services rendered by German savants since its foundation. After opposing it at first, Lord Cromer empowered me to telegraph to Your Excellency his readiness to make the desired concession to Germany (the Director to be a German) ' as soon as the other questions are settled '.

Lord Cromer assumed from my statement—and personally I agreed with him—that it seemed to imply a legal contract with us, as with the French. He did not think this the proper way of embodying the agreement mentioned above, but that another way could well be found—perhaps an exchange of notes.

Lord Cromer is evidently very keen to obtain our consent to the Decree. He said that if further difficulties cropped up he would send [Eldon] Gorst to Berlin.

He is telegraphing to London in the sense of our conversation.

XX. 142
COUNT VON METTERNICH, IN LONDON, TO THE GERMAN FOREIGN OFFICE, *June 3rd*, 1904
Cipher telegram.

The Government here fears that annoyance will be caused in France if they promise us equal rights with the French unless we undertake similar engagements to theirs.[1]

COUNT VON METTERNICH TO THE GERMAN FOREIGN OFFICE, *June 4th*, 1904
Cipher telegram.

Last evening and to-day I held conversations with Lord Lansdowne. He persists in his attitude of refusal. He said Russia,[2] Austria and Italy had consented to the Khedivial Decree at once, because it contained nothing to their disadvantage. He presumed that the same applied to Germany. Thus he could hardly defend his position before Parliament, if, in return for our consent to the Decree which was injurious to no German interest, England were to make important concessions to Germany, which, where France came into it, merely formed part of a general settlement. Art. IV mutually promised freedom of trade in Egypt and Morocco, whilst we were demanding one-sidedly freedom of trade in Egypt for 30 years and offering

[1] Cf. G. & T., III, p. 19. [2] Cf. G. & T., IV, p. 193.

nothing for it, whilst our Commercial Treaty with Egypt would lapse in 1912. I replied on the last point that we must all the more think of keeping freedom of trade in Egypt, if even now there was a doubt whether the Egyptian Government, guided by the British administration, would grant us a favourable commercial treaty in 1912.

Then he said that *after* consenting to the Khedivial Decree we could easily come to an understanding with the Egyptian Government on the schools question and the director of the library.

It would take too long to repeat all the arguments for and against ; suffice it to state that there is decided opposition in the Cabinet against letting our consent to the Decree depend on granting us the same assurances as have been made to France. I declared finally to the Minister that the British Government's attitude of refusal prevented me from going on with the matter, since we insisted on freedom of trade.

Lord Lansdowne is to speak to the Prime Minister at the beginning of next week and is to hand me a memorandum of his own views. I expressed a fear that this would hardly help on the affair. I thought he was demanding of us a policy altogether too altruistic and regretted that we now could not agree about Egypt, where we had always backed up and helped England.

[The memorandum of Lord Lansdowne's views and the ensuing negociations are given in G. & T., III, p. 19 et seq.

The Belgian Minister in Berlin had said he had reason to believe that
the Anglo-French Agreement contained clauses about the Rhine frontier.
(XX. 27).]

German Note.

Count Metternich's opinion (below) turned out to be essentially correct.
(Cf. the secret Articles of the Agreement of March 8th, 1904, published in
1911—British Blue-book, Cd. 5969 ; E. D. Morel, *Morocco in Diplomacy*
(1912), p. 234 et seq.)

XX. 29

COUNT VON METTERNICH, IN LONDON, TO THE GERMAN FOREIGN
OFFICE, *June 4th*, 1904

Cipher telegram.

In answer to your telegram.

I do not believe in Anglo-French secret arrangements regarding the Rhine frontier, but I do believe in secret arrangements
whereby France promises her support for British policy in Egypt
when the international institutions are removed later. Lord
Lansdowne told me definitely yesterday that England has
promised France *désintéressement* in Morocco, but has by no
means engaged herself to take France's part in the relations of
third parties towards Morocco. Even less will England bind

herself in advance in the event of a continental war. The Cabinet's sudden opposition to granting to Germany the assurances granted to France in Egypt [1] is very remarkable, but it may be entirely due to the fear of being represented in Parliament and the country as having been out-manœuvred by Germany. The Cabinet may also fear that it might weaken the effect of the *entente cordiale*. If there were other and sufficient reasons, Lord Lansdowne, knowing exactly the arrangements with France in advance and not till after the Cabinet Council, would have adopted an attitude of refusal regarding Egypt.

Arrangements of any sort with Germany would, considering the present feeling in the Conservative Ministry, be highly unpopular.

But it is not out of the question, although I doubt it, that the British Government may have promised France her benevolent neutrality in case France is involved in war on the Continent.

When I next see Lord Lansdowne I shall try to get precise information and telegraph it to Your Excellency.

XX. 151

COUNT VON METTERNICH, IN LONDON, TO THE GERMAN FOREIGN OFFICE, *June 9th*, 1904

Cipher telegram.

Sir Frank Lascelles, whom I met to-day and who seems to be doing his best to bring about a solution of the Egyptian difficulties, is to propose to Lord Lansdowne and also the Prime Minister to concede our requirements and to notify the other three Powers that they can accept from them the same assurances as ourselves and the French, subject to the same conditions regarding Egypt.

I consider this is the only way for the British Government to escape from the blind alley into which fear of Parliament has driven them, and as far as I can judge such a solution would not harm our interests.

I am going next Monday to a small dinner-party at Lord Lansdowne's and shall be able to make a communication, if Your Excellency wishes to instruct me further in the matter.

XX. 30

COUNT VON METTERNICH, IN LONDON, TO THE GERMAN FOREIGN OFFICE, *June 19th*, 1904

Cipher telegram.

I remarked to Lord Lansdowne to-day that it had come to my ears that there were secret arrangements between France and England for the event of European complications.

[1] Cf. G. & T., III, p. 53 et seq.

It was alleged, for instance, that England had promised neutrality in the event of France being involved in a European war.

The Minister replied that no word of these rumours was true.

When I remarked further that it was asserted that the arrangements included some rectification of the Rhine frontier, Lord Lansdowne answered that this suggestion was ' a perfect mare's nest '.

[Here see p. 214.]

XX. 31

MEMORANDUM BY KÜHLMANN, FIRST SECRETARY AT TANGIER, *October 1st*, 1904

Six months have passed since the conclusion of the Agreement between England and France. Considering the short life of earlier ' *ententes cordiales* ' between the western Powers it seems suitable to celebrate the six months' existence of the latest Entente with a look into the past and future.

From the British point of view the Entente had a double object ; first, general policy—to create a re-insurance against the risks of the Japanese alliance by settling England's relations towards at least one of the Great Powers concerned, i.e. France, and thus nipping in the bud a possible coalition between Germany, Russia and France. The facts at the time were that France was the country which best fell in with England's traditional need of attaching herself to a strong continental Power, especially as this combination seemed to flatter the lively hopes of an Anglo-Russian understanding which certain circles in England cherished. The more direct second object of the Agreement was to remove ' surfaces of friction '. England wished to obtain a sanction *de jure* for her *de facto* position in Egypt, whilst France wished to make a reality of her so far theoretic aspirations in Morocco. The rest of the stipulations—perhaps excluding Newfoundland—fall under the head of colonial agreements, which are too numerous to have much political importance attached to them.

England's complete honesty in the Agreement appears in rather a queer light when one sees the difference of treatment given to her interests in Morocco and to France's in Egypt by the otherwise so remarkably ' parallel ' provisions of the instrument. If a British interest in Morocco is injured by French action, England is not bound to stand the ' leading Power's ' action ; in Egypt England promises to protect France's existing rights, but there is no mention of the political consequences of failure to keep the promise.

France could easily have made the clause referring to evacuation by England [1] of no effect if, immediately after the Agreement was signed, she had approached the other Powers and secured the support of each one by treaty. Russia's could have been obtained at once. Reasonable guarantees would have won over Germany and Austria. Italy could not have objected on account of former agreements. It was due to the Perdicaris affair that the United States consented so unreservedly. Armed with the definite recognition of all the leading Great Powers France could have treated this British clause with indifference, and her position in Morocco would become a *fait accompli* internationally ; Spanish annoyance at this would have made no difference. Being without hope of diplomatic succour Spain would have had to surrender unconditionally ; it is probable that the present vagueness of the diplomatic situation merely extended her opposition. The result of these sins of omission is already becoming obvious. In an article in the September number of *Questions diplomatiques et coloniales* entitled *Aux difficultés de notre action au Maroc*, A. Terrier writes : ' Aux difficultés d'ordre local s'ajoutent des difficultés internationales qui entravent singulièrement elles aussi notre action et retardent l'heure de l'ouverture de Maroc.'

England on the contrary has made haste to settle the Egyptian question in her own favour. The irregularity of her position in Egypt was a worry which bore heavier than has usually been supposed. For if the Powers were awkwardly grouped Great Britain might find herself face to face with a strong combination, and this would produce a serious situation considering the weak diplomatic basis of her claims. Now she is guarded by treaty with Russia, Germany, Austria and Italy against any possible combination which the Egyptian question could give rise to. As far as the direct object of the Agreement is concerned England's advantage is concealed ; now there remain only conceptions in the domain of general politics which make it seem advisable to go on maintaining the Agreement.

The above-mentioned obvious mistakes of French foreign policy have reversed the roles ; England now holds the long arm of the lever . . .

It ought at once to be found out in Madrid how seriously England considers France's position as the ' leading Power ' in Morocco ; the British attitude, both official and non-official, towards the Franco-Spanish negociations would serve as a reliable measure for England's honesty. The personality of the

[1] De son côté le Gouvernement de la République Française déclare qu'il n'entravera pas l'action de l'Angleterre en Egypte en demandant qu'un terme soit fixé à l'occupation Britannique ou de toute autre manière . . .

new Ambassador, Sir Arthur Nicolson, ought to make the French anxious. The French Minister's wife said of him : ' Il est content, parcequ'il pense qu'il nous a fourré dans un guêpier '.

On both sides of the Channel voices are heard which do not approve of the Agreement. Too much should not be made of the protests of the Frenchman, Fischer,[1] the influence of Hanotaux's friends nor of impatient colonial enthusiasts and the nationalist excitement over Marchand and Anatole France, nor should we be upset by Rosebery, ' The Truth about Morocco ', and the *Morning Post.* . . .

In one word the result of the last six months is : The Egyptian question is dead, the Morocco question very much alive.

[1] Theobald Fischer, a writer.

CHAPTER XVI

PRESIDENT ROOSEVELT'S MEDIATION BETWEEN RUSSIA AND JAPAN, 1904–5

[The strict neutrality which the European Powers imposed on themselves in the struggle between Russia and Japan and their mutual jealousy in all that concerned the Far East tied the hands of any one of them when it became a question of mediation between the belligerents. It was left for the United States in the person of President Roosevelt to take up the task.[1] They were supposed to be in close and friendly touch with Russia, although this friendship was mostly on the side of the latter. America was anxious about the growing power of Japan. Hence she insisted that territorial ambitions should be renounced universally. The Emperor William made himself the President's confidant and acted as his agent in his communications with the Tsar throughout the whole business.

The British Government were in a difficult position owing to their alliance with Japan. Their attitude [2] was one neither of encouragement to fight nor the reverse, and they made it quite clear that no material help was to be expected. The consequence was that the full honours of the peace settlement were President Roosevelt's, and his alone.]

XIX. 534

BARON SPECK VON STERNBURG, AMBASSADOR IN WASHINGTON, TO THE GERMAN FOREIGN OFFICE, *August 12th,* 1904

Cipher telegram.

I have quietly made enquiries in Washington as to England's intentions regarding the Chusan Archipelago ; absolutely nothing seems to be known here. But the *New York Sun* states in a leading article that it is rumoured that negociations about the Yang-tsze valley are in progress between England and other European Powers with the object of securing British supremacy in the Yang-tsze province.

Owing to the scarceness of reliable journalists I consider it not at present desirable to mention the matter in the Press. If a good opportunity offers I will do so.

[See Sir Eyre Crowe's Memorandum, G. & T., II, p. 152.]

---

[1] Cf. Brandenburg, p. 217 et seq. ; S. Gwynn, *Letters and Friendships of Cecil Spring Rice,* p. 441 et seq. ; G. & T., IV, pp .71 et seq., 88 et seq. ; Lee, *King Edward VII,* II, p. 433 et seq. ; Dennis, *Adventures in American Diplomacy,* p. 389 et seq.   [2] Cf. G. & T., II, pp. 230–1.

XIX. 541

THE CHANCELLOR, COUNT VON BÜLOW, TO BARON SPECK VON
   STERNBURG, IN WASHINGTON, *September 5th,* 1904

Telegram.

Being for a short time in Berlin, I took the first opportunity
of reporting in person to the Emperor the very satisfactory
words of President Roosevelt.

His Majesty fully agrees to our maintaining the closest
possible touch with the President and the United States in the
Far East.

Like the President, the Emperor takes his stand absolutely
on the principle of the open door and is hand in hand with America
for carrying it through as completely as possible.

Finally His Majesty pointed out that Port Arthur had not
yet fallen, and the Russian army was still in the field, so that it
could not yet be known how matters would develop further.
But he inclined to the opinion that if the Russians were definitely
defeated Manchuria would most likely fall to the Chinese as
being the cradle of their dynasty, and Korea would be delivered
to the Japanese with the reservation of the open door.

In conducting this very desirable negociation with Mr.
Roosevelt you will have to bear in mind and make it your
special aim that he engages himself as strictly as possible in
favour of the open door, especially on the Yang-tsze.

I shall receive your further reports with interest.

XIX. 541

BARON SPECK VON STERNBURG TO THE GERMAN FOREIGN OFFICE,
                    September 27th, 1904

Cipher telegram.

Yesterday I handed to President Roosevelt *Education in the
German Empire.* He charged me to thank the Emperor for it
most warmly.

He then spoke on the situation in the Far East as follows :
The latest events showed that the Japanese were not such
marvels in the military sense as the world believed. The fire
of their ships in the last engagement had been especially bad.

Then on his relations towards the Powers : ' England has
not a man I can deal with. I do not think much of Balfour
and less of Lansdowne. Chamberlain is quite unreliable and
might jump into the Yang-tsze valley at any moment. And
how am I to deal with this creature of an Ambassador (Sir
Mortimer Durand) ? If I had Spring Rice here, things might
be different.

' With France I am in a similar position.

'The only man I understand and who understands me is the Kaiser.' [1]

On hearing this I communicated to the President the contents of the telegram of the 5th. He was highly pleased with it, especially at His Majesty's desire to combine as much as possible with America in establishing the open door. After his re-election Mr. Roosevelt is to return to this question with me. . . .

XIX. 546

BARON SPECK VON STERNBURG, IN WASHINGTON, TO THE GERMAN FOREIGN OFFICE, *November 17th*, 1904

Cipher telegram.

The Secretary of State, Mr. Hay, informed me that apart from the doubts expressed to me by the President regarding the German proposal there were first and foremost *constitutional* difficulties in the way. The powers of the Executive respecting international arrangements which might possibly lead to hostilities were greatly limited. An arrangement like the one thought of would have to be submitted to Congress for ratification and would without doubt be debated. According to information received the situation in China hardly demanded such drastic measures for the present. He was fully persuaded of the advantages of the German proposal, and if the situation grew more critical he was prepared to discuss it again.

[Mr. Hay had advised the President ' not to join in any action whatever in China which might be misinterpreted by either of the belligerents'. Cf. Dennis, *Adventures in American Diplomacy*, p. 391.]

XIX. 547

COUNT VON BÜLOW TO THE EMPEROR, *December 24th*, 1904

Extract.

. . . Baron Sternburg has collected the views of the American President on the world situation and on that in the Far East in the enclosed memorandum. It is evident that personally and also in consideration of the feeling reigning amongst both Republicans and Democrats in the United States he does not wish to bring America into opposition to Japan, whose expansion and growing power he does not fear (The EMPEROR : ' *Because it is directed mainly against Russia and the continent of Europe.*') and whose friendship he wishes to gain. On the other hand he feels deeply suspicious of Russia's projects of aggrandisement and prohibitive tendencies. He wishes neither China nor Korea included in the Russian system of exclusion. . . .

---

[1] All English in text ; cf. S. Gwynn, *Letters and Friendships of Cecil Spring Rice*, p. 448.

XIX. 550   *Enclosure.*

Public feeling in the United States regarding Russia and Japan.

The United States are following Russia's policy in the Far East with growing mistrust and would regard any extension of her sphere of power there as a great danger. China under Russian influence would be far more dangerous for Western civilisation than under Japanese influence. Russia's policy is entirely dishonest, and no Government can believe her word.

Russia, being still probably protected by France, would hardly listen as readily as Japan would to the other Powers' suggestions regarding abstention from territorial expansion or political measures likely to threaten their interests. Japan is a young Power and has tried to pursue an honest policy and to respect other Powers. If Japan showed signs of gratifying territorial greed on the mainland or of pursuing a policy in opposition to the interests of the Powers, joint pressure brought to bear on Japan might have more prospect of success than the same applied to Russia. The superstition that Japan was invincible on land and sea would only last a short time.

It is not true, said the President, that Russia's popularity has in recent times increased in the United States. On the contrary, amongst thinking people mistrust of Russia has been as freely expressed as ever before. The fact is that the universal enthusiasm over Japan's success in the field has been repressed. In various ways Japan has become unpopular in the Press because she treated the American War correspondents less well than Russia did. It was Alexieff's policy to allow the greatest freedom of action at the front to the American correspondents. He evidently gave orders to show them the greatest consideration everywhere and covered them with flattery and amiability. In certain quarters his policy has been successful, but it has made no impression on the Government. Those who count are convinced that if Russia wins she will pursue her crooked policy in the Far East with increased energy.

Mistrust of the Russo-German Coalition.

The President said openly that in certain circles he had observed latent mistrust of a Russo-German coalition in the Far East. He said : ' I believe absolutely your earlier assurances on this question ; I merely mention that I have come across this mistrust.'

The Government's wishes regarding arrangements after the conclusion of peace.

The desire of the United States is to acquiesce in surfaces of friction in the delimitation of frontiers between Russia and Japan after the conclusion of peace.

' The most desirable to us, said the President, would be the restoration of Manchuria to China and for the interested Powers to declare its neutrality. We should willingly see Korea under a Japanese protectorate, but we could never agree to a Russian occupation of Korea. We should like to see Port Arthur razed to the ground.'

Russo-Japanese alliance.

The Washington Government has received confidential information from Tokio that the question of a Russo-Japanese alliance has been raised there and is popular in certain influential circles in Japan. In Washington it is thought that Japan would only accept this as a last means of bringing the war to an end and for her own financial and military recovery.

XIX. 575

BARON SPECK VON STERNBURG, IN WASHINGTON, TO THE GERMAN FOREIGN OFFICE, *February 17th*, 1905

Cipher telegram.

The President tells me he has discussed the Far Eastern situation with Mr. Kaneko.[1] He first expressed satisfaction that relations between Berlin and Tokio had become more intimate. Then he told the Japanese Minister very decidedly that he was fully confident that Japan would shape her coming policy in the direction of moderation so as not to arouse suspicion amongst the European Powers by excessive demands. This could only hurt Japan. It would call a coalition into being which would mean Japan's ruin. There was no saying whether this advice would be followed, said the President. The Japanese Minister answered his question whether Japan was ready for peace negociations with a strong negative, but he said that within the next two months Japan would be taking important action. The President, who urged me to keep this information strictly private even from Mr. Hay, added that it was meant only for the Emperor ; the other Powers must on no account know of it, especially England. The President assumes that this action will not be in a military but a peaceful direction. I then showed the President your telegram of February 15th, which clearly surprised him.

[1] Special Envoy of Japan to America.

German Note.

This was to the effect that the *Figaro*, in an article inspired by Delcassé (February 14th), had demanded an alliance of European Powers against Japan with the object of dividing China into protectorates or spheres of occupation.

His first remark was : ' I am sure England is not in it.' He intends to discuss the communication with the French Ambassador as though he had it from Paris and will inform me of his reply.

So far the American Press has taken no notice of the articles in the *Figaro*.

XIX. 576

CHANCELLOR COUNT VON BÜLOW, TO BARON SPECK VON STERNBURG, IN WASHINGTON, *February 21st*, 1905

Telegram. Extract.

It is curious that in Tokio also the Imperial Ambassador has been told that a surprise is in store for him. All things considered it can only mean a peace, with Japan's accession to the Franco-Russian Alliance. Last December Count Lamsdorff said to Count Alvensleben : ' Les Français connaissent nos conditions ' ; i.e., France has Russia's mandate to prepare the peace. . . .

XIX. 590

BARON SPECK VON STERNBURG, IN WASHINGTON, TO THE GERMAN FOREIGN OFFICE, *April 2nd*, 1905

Cipher telegram.

The President said to me : ' I am genuinely grateful to you for putting me into confidential touch with the Russian Ambassador. You have done me a great service. I had a second conversation with him yesterday evening, and although I cannot quite describe the result of it as satisfactory I feel we came nearer our object. When he said that Russia could consider neither paying an indemnity nor giving up territory and talked of going on with the war, I begged him to tell his Government that I considered Russia's position hopeless unless she soon decided on peace. Russia should learn from her own history ever since Peter the Great, for it contained several examples of giving up territory which was, however, regained later. If I were in your Emperor's place, I should say the following : " I order peace in order to reorganise the army and navy completely and correct faults in the administration. If God keeps me alive I will show the world what Russia can do in 15 years." As for the indemnity question, I have approached neither Russia nor

Japan about it. I feel certain that Japan will demand one, but will confine herself within moderate limits. I have spoken out clearly regarding China's integrity. After the war Manchuria goes back to China ; Japan gets Port Arthur and Dalny and obtains suzerainty over Korea. Japan's advance on Kharbin and Vladivostock is greatly disturbing England, who foresees an active policy by Russia against India and the Persian Gulf if she is driven out of the Far East.

' I am delighted at the British refusal to have anything to do with a congress. It is a fresh brilliant result of our joint action in the Far East and shows what two Governments can do when they thoroughly understand each other. Thus France and Russia are left alone with their Congress.

' I am leaving because I feel that Russia will need at least a month to procure definite plans, if she ever does so. Meanwhile I beg you to communicate all important changes in cipher and to keep me *au courant* by letter.'

XIX. 602

BARON SPECK VON STERNBURG TO THE GERMAN FOREIGN OFFICE,
May 17th, 1905

Cipher telegram. Extract.

. . . It is extraordinary how obstinately the President and other politicians here stick to the idea that an alliance between England and Russia is quite impossible at present. The President told me that the hatred of Russia in England was far deeper than the hatred against Germany. When last evening I again indicated the signs which caused us to believe firmly that a quadruple alliance in the Far East was being formed, the President said about England : ' Then they are not liars ; they are curs.' [1]

[On June 2nd, 1905, Baron Speck von Sternburg telegraphed that ' the British Ambassador had told him that the Anglo-Japanese alliance would certainly continue '. (XIX. 607.)

Five days before that the Russian fleet had been destroyed by the Japanese in the Straits of Tshushima. On June 10th Japan accepted President Roosevelt's offer of mediation, and on August 10th the Peace Missions met at Portsmouth, in New Hampshire. Cf. Lee, *King Edward VII*, II, p. 307.]

XIX. 613

BARON SPECK VON STERNBURG, IN NEW YORK, TO THE GERMAN
FOREIGN OFFICE, *July 5th*, 1905

Secret. [2]

The President expressed much satisfaction at the way the peace negotiations were going. ' For the first time ', he said,

[1] English in text.   [2] Dennis, *Adventures in American Diplomacy*, p. 406.

'Russia seems ready to deal fairly and quickly. I have taken in hand the question of an armistice and hope soon to settle it. England is making it difficult for me by her refusal to urge moderation on Japan.[1] (The EMPEROR : ' *Aha ! Now America sees for the first time where the real disturber of the world's peace lies !* ') I have warned the British Government that they will be mistaken if they favour Russia being driven into Eastern Siberia, where she will be sure to try to keep up frontier friction with Japan after the peace. (The EMPEROR : ' *Correct.*') England's stupidity is helping to push the Russian power towards the South-west ; I am chiefly worried by Russia's internal situation. If the army joins the revolutionaries it will place us in an awkward position as regards the peace. And who will then lend money to Russia for her reforms ? Russia's curse is the ring of Grand Dukes who make the Tsar powerless.

' I intend to select for the negotiations a watering-place in the North, where troops can keep off curious intruders. I shall receive the delegates here at Oyster Bay on a war-ship.' (The EMPEROR : ' *Very good.*')

[After much modification of Japan's demands, the terms of peace were agreed by the end of August, and the Treaty of Portsmouth was signed on September 5th, 1905. In his *Autobiography* (p. 586) President Roosevelt wrote : ' During the course of the negociations I tried to enlist the aid of the Government of one nation which was friendly to Russia and of another nation which was friendly to Japan in helping bring about peace. I got no aid from either ; I did, however, receive aid from the Emperor of Germany. His Ambassador at St. Petersburg was the one Ambassador who helped the American Ambassador, Mr. Meyer, at delicate and doubtful points of the negociations.' (XIX. 628.)]

XIX. 641

THE CHANCELLOR, PRINCE VON BÜLOW,[2] TO BARON SPECK VON STERNBURG, IN WASHINGTON, *October 29th*, 1905

Telegram.

Personal for the Ambassador.

Following the Anglo-Japanese rapprochement [3] diplomatic as well as journalistic work is being done on the Anglo-Russian one,[4] and France has been sharing in this. As far as we know the Russians are so far still passive listeners, but they are being strongly pressed. There are attempts to represent the hoped for grouping to the outside world as purely defensive. Since each of the four Powers concerned has been energetically pursuing a policy of expansion in Asia, it may be presumed that

[1] Cf. G. & T., IV, p. 89.
[2] Created Prince after the resignation of Delcassé, May, 1905.
[3] Renewed August 2nd, 1905.
[4] Cf. Lee, *King Edward VII*, p. 309 ; G. & T., III, p. 364.

acting together they will not confine themselves to a simple defensive. This group, whose strength may perhaps attract other States to its side, forms, as I said before, the strongest political factor in the world as long as it lasts. We cannot be surprised that now that Delcassé's Asiatic programme, about which the *Temps* of January 13th and the *Figaro* of February 14th sufficiently informed the world,[1] has been taken up afresh, Delcassé is again taking a leading part in the discussion. Perhaps we shall see him in office again in a few months. The fact that Jaurès' paper *L'Humanité* said a few days ago that if Delcassé had remained at the helm it would have been France and not America who would have negotiated the Russo-Japanese peace shows how active is the agitation in his favour.

Until now Russia, England, France and Japan worked against each other ; now they are trying for a friendly agreement about the future of Asia. From the point of view of these four it is a seductive notion. I can trust your circumspection and experience to decide how, if at all, you wish to touch this theme in your next conversation with President Roosevelt. I should naturally be interested to hear how he thinks the Quadruple Alliance in the making will affect the American interests entrusted to his care and the portion of humanity not connected with the quadruple Trust.

German Note.

Baron Speck von Sternburg reported on November 24th, 1905, that the President did not believe a quadruple alliance in the Far East would come to pass, owing to the strong Russo-Japanese differences.

[1] Cf. p. 204.

CHAPTER XVII

ATTEMPT TO RECONCILE ENGLAND AND GERMANY, DECEMBER, 1904

[The plans for making Germany into a first-class naval Power which the Emperor, urged thereto by Admiral von Tirpitz, was pushing forward with all the energy at his command necessitated a 'war-scare' against another naval Power—obviously England—in order to make the vast expense of it popular in Germany. On the British side Admiral Sir John Fisher (Lee, II, 327 et seq.; Bacon, *Lord Fisher*) caught the ear of King Edward by his appeal for increasing the efficiency of the navy. At his advice plans for a naval base at Rosyth were initiated in order that a large squadron, available for instant use in the North Sea, could be maintained there. This added to the mutual tension until the diplomats of both countries took alarm and proceeded, as is shown in the following pages, to do their best to allay the storm which was being fanned by the Press of both countries and by the policy of the Emperor, Bülow [1] and Tirpitz. (Cf. Brandenburg, p. 211 et seq.) The discrepancy between German official policy and German popular feeling was largely due to the fact that the younger generation of Germans was deeply imbued with the teaching of Heinrich von Treitschke (1834–96). He was a lecturer of commanding personality and narrow ideas, who from his early youth had been nearly stone-deaf. He taught that only by the sacrifice of the individual to the State could Germany eventually dominate the world. The obstacle which must be overcome was England; England therefore must be reduced to submission. Then the Empire, which she had acquired more by luck than by merit, would be transferred to the more worthy Germany, who would permeate the world with her *Kultur*. (Cf. J. A. Cramb, *Germany and England*; Treitschke's *Politik*, translated by Blanche E. C. Dugdale and T. de Bille; Wilson, *War Guilt*, pp. 18, 290; H. W. C. Davis, *Political Thought of Heinrich von Treitschke*.)]

XIX. 367

MEMORANDUM BY COUNT VON METTERNICH, IN LONDON, FOR THE CHANCELLOR, COUNT VON BÜLOW, *December 25th*, 1904

Mr. Cecil Spring Rice, First Secretary at the British Embassy in St. Petersburg and Sir Frank Lascelles' son-in-law, is a sharp, wide-awake Irishman, who knows and learns much.

A few days ago I had a conversation with him in Berlin which was essentially as follows:

Mr. Spring Rice pointed to fear of the German navy as

[1] Cf. Lord d'Abernon, *An Ambassador of Peace*, I, 82.

being the principal one amongst other causes of dissension between England and Germany which I pass over for the sake of briefness as they have often been referred to.

Up till now England had maintained no fleet in home waters equal to the German one. Along with the deterioration of relations between the two countries the feeling of insecurity and fear of Germany had grown. Mainly from this feeling had arisen the mistrust which was noticeable everywhere against Germany and which had been encouraged from many quarters. Even those Englishmen who suspected the German fleet of no directly aggressive intentions against England had reflected that supposing England were entangled in a war elsewhere the German fleet could be used as a means of diplomatic pressure for obtaining British concessions to Germany. He mentioned, as an example, an Anglo-Russian war as a possibility which might easily happen owing to the irritation in Russia, and England's duty as an ally of Japan. Once England was engaged for months together in India and with her fleet in the Far East Germany might be tempted, by reason of the concentration of her fleet and with the German coast as a base, to demand a high price for her neutrality, the cession of coaling stations, for instance.

Then Mr. Spring Rice mentioned the fear felt by many of his countrymen of the ' fascination of the German Emperor ',[1] who twisted British Statesmen round his finger whenever he met them. Mr. Chamberlain, for instance, was under the influence of this extraordinary gift of fascination, when he shortly afterwards made his foolish Leicester speech,[2] which was coldly rebuffed by Germany. But for this speech Mr. Chamberlain might still have been our friend. Lord Salisbury, who, as the initiated knew, in the last years of his life always avoided meeting the Emperor, did so chiefly because he himself feared to fall under His Majesty's hypnotic power.[3] He, Mr. Spring Rice, had heard this from a son of the late statesman who was a friend of his. In short the German fleet and the fear of being overreached by German diplomacy under the influence of the Emperor had amongst other things played a large part in England during recent years. The new British naval plans had arisen mainly from the wish to be independent of Germany under all circumstances. England had weakened herself in the Mediterranean and had sunk to the rank of a second class maritime Power there so to speak, simply in order to insure her home against all eventualities. This object was now assured

[1] S. Gwynn, *Letters and Friendships of Cecil Spring Rice*, p. 467.
[2] Cf. p. 113.   [3] Cf. Vol. II, p. 339.

by the great increase of forces which England had transferred to her home ports.

Mr. Spring Rice imagines that with the feeling of security given by the new naval organisation England will be reassured as regards Germany, which should really help to improve relations between the two countries. He denied that there are any aggressive intentions in England against Germany worth mentioning. (The EMPEROR : ' *? He dares say that !* ') As soon as the present excitement in England, a consequence of the attitude of German public opinion during the Boer War, had disappeared—and there were signs that it was diminishing—it would be better realised that there were no real differences between England and Germany. Commercial rivalry even was not a disadvantage. Twenty-five years ago trade between the two countries was only a quarter of what it was now. Thus it was clear that German trade and industry had done good to England. In the domain of politics the mistake had for a long time been made in England of waiting for Germany to protect England against Russia—which never could happen. Maintenance of good relations with Russia was too valuable to us for it to be possible to help England in the matter of India ; whereas a political arrangement with profit to both countries could very well be arrived at. We needed coaling stations on our route to the East and as many places as possible where we could import freely. England might, for instance, grant by treaty to Germany undisturbed enjoyment of our coaling stations for a series of years and the treatment of German trade in India on an equal footing with British, whilst Germany might promise neutrality supposing England were involved in a war. (The EMPEROR : ' *?* ')

Mr. Spring Rice went so far as to assert that once better relations were restored England might use the Entente Cordiale to help on reconciliation between Germany and France. (The EMPEROR : ' *Thanks very much ! we would rather see to that ourselves !* ') I was struck by his mentioning the great services performed by the Italian Government in bringing about the Entente Cordiale between England and France. When I said that there were many in Germany who believed less in England's good intention of reconciling us with France and rather that she was trying to isolate us, Mr. Spring Rice replied that there was a long way to go before Germany was isolated, and a powerful empire like the German could not be isolated.

Mr. Spring Rice's pictures of the future may be very attractive, but they are of less actual interest than what he told me of his impressions of Russia.[1] He mentioned more than once

[1] Cf. G. & T., III, p. 57.

the dangerous situation created by the existing bitterness against England, (The EMPEROR : ' *Not lessened by the English nurse being caught in the Tsar's study.*' [1]) which might easily cause war complications against the wishes of England. He viewed the internal condition of Russia unfavourably. The hopes of the educated and moderate elements for more liberal administration had been destroyed by the Tsar's recent decisions. There were two parties opposed to each other, the one which hoped to reduce discontent by granting more freedom and the other which aimed at suppressing every movement towards freedom. The Grand Duke Serge led the second movement ; he hoped with the help of the moujiks to crush the moderate elements. The moujik was nothing but a barbarian and no more educated than the Chinese Boxer, and if the moderate progressive element was successfully crushed with his help, we should have the same experiences as with the Boxer rising in China—murder and offences against property and foreigners.

But he would not prophesy revolution whether by the parties of revolt or of suppression in the near future. But he feared that the recent decisions taken against the will of the moderates would force the extremist elements to the front and with the numerous discontented class lead on to an attempt against the person of the Tsar. Once the hope was again removed of independent development by peaceful means it appeared likely that the violent elements would try to get rid of the Tsar and set up a long regency under a semi-idiot—Spring Rice's expression— (The EMPEROR : ' *!* ') and so create a situation which would make a favourable foundation for their schemes in the general confusion. It was extraordinary how indifferent they were to attempts to murder in Russia. No one had mourned for Plehve's murder, even those who agreed with him, and the assassination had been universally regarded as something quite natural.

As a curious example of how things are dealt with in the Press in Russia Mr. Spring Rice told me of a case which he had been able to follow closely in all its stages. One day some news, apparently emanating from Copenhagen, which was of a kind likely to arouse suspicions in England against Germany, had been published through Reuter's Agency—whether in connection with the Doggerbank incident or something else I cannot now remember. He said that he had been able to trace to its source this report, which had since been proved false. It came from a Russian agent in Paris who had told it in a letter to General Hesse in St. Petersburg. The latter had repeated it to the St. Petersburg correspondent of the *Echo de Paris*, (The EMPEROR : ' *A nice set—the Tsar's entourage !* ') who had reported

[1] Cf. p. 185.

it to Paris. From there it had reached Copenhagen, where it saw the light in the form of a Reuter telegram.

In our conversation we touched more than once on the suspicions to which German policy was exposed owing to having been brought into contact with the Doggerbank incident. Mr. Spring Rice said that even he had suspected for some days that Germany had had a hand in it. It was known that quite at the beginning the *Novoye Vremya* had stated that an ' interested Power ' had kindly warned Russia of treacherous attacks on the Baltic fleet, whereby the Russian Admiral's suspicions had mainly been aroused.[1] The paper had not been content with this vague indication, but had in common with two or three other St. Petersburg papers, including the *Russ* if I am not mistaken, informed the British Embassy (The EMPEROR : ' *So a direct lie at our expense in order to bring us up against England. In token of gratitude for our attitude !* ') that the ' interested Power ' was Germany. Mr. Spring Rice added that most of the Russian papers were in French pay.

We had, he said, no idea how indiscreet the Russians were about us in St. Petersburg. (The EMPEROR : ' *Very probable.*') All the time they said that the German Emperor had communicated or advised this or that. (The EMPEROR : ' *A lie, like the rest.*') It was evident from the nature of these communications that they were certainly meant for Russian ears only. There was no doubt that in St. Petersburg they were proud of our Emperor's friendship and that just now he was enjoying extraordinary popularity there.

XIX. 372

THE CHANCELLOR, COUNT VON BÜLOW, TO THE EMPEROR,
December 26th, 1904

On Christmas Day I had a long conversation with Sir Frank Lascelles.[2] . . . I said that what the German Press said about foreign matters had in practice but little importance, (The EMPEROR : ' *Correct.*') for the German populace was unfortunately but little informed politically and the German Press was doctrinaire. With us only the official policy mattered, (The EMPEROR : ' *Correct.*') and this especially during the Boer War had been not merely correct and loyal to England but even outspokenly cordial. It was otherwise in England. The attitude of the big English papers was in fact a fine indication of how British policy was going, for the final decision lay with public opinion. It was also a fact that just because, unlike Germany, they had an old tradition in politics, they did not

[1] Cf. p. 182.

[2] The substance of this conversation is given in G. & T., III, p. 56.

usually write in opposition to the views of the Government on leading international questions. Thus if the British Press attacked a foreign country as vehemently as it was now attacking Germany it was bound to cause great anxiety. Besides this England was so much superior to us at sea that the possibility of a German attack on England was not to be mentioned by thinking people ; (The EMPEROR : ' *Very correct.*') but the alternative was quite conceivable.[1] Lascelles denied absolutely that the British Government, the Navy, the City and the great majority of the people desired war with us. For the moment there were great mistrust and irritation against us ; but England was seeking no conflict with us ; (The EMPEROR : ' *! ?* ') she wanted rest.

King Edward sends friendly messages to Your Majesty by Lascelles, which the latter hopes to be able to present at the reception at the New Year. The King said to him : ' I place full confidence in Count Bülow.' As Your Majesty so often rightly said, everything depends, in dealing with England, on our getting through the next few years with patience, avoiding incidents, and giving no obvious reason for annoyance. Our position is comparable with that of the Athenians when they were forced to erect the Long Walls at the Piraeus and not to let the domineering Spartans prevent the completion of this measure of protection. (The EMPEROR : ' *My dear Bülow, How often have I quoted this example during recent years ! ! ! The only answer to Lascelles' reproach (which is the general opinion among the Britons) that our fleet is designed for an attack on the English coast is that since the new British disposal of the ships 43 ships of the line and about 140 cruisers are at their disposal as against our 14 ships of the line and 20 cruisers. Who then shall make the attack ! ! ? The questions* (1) *why we built our ships and* (2) *why we keep them at home are to be answered :* (1) *because we had no more and required them and had first to replace the old ones,* (2) *because we really did not know where in the whole world to put them ! We had no Gibraltar, Malta, nor anywhere else in Europe ! ! Formerly we used to sail the Mediterranean, but we gave that up in order not to be a nuisance to the British.*')

XIX. 377

COUNT VON METTERNICH, IN LONDON, TO THE CHANCELLOR, COUNT VON BÜLOW, *January 11th*, 1905

Private letter.

Since my return to England I have become more and more convinced that suppositions regarding aggressive intentions on England's part are groundless.

---

[1] Cf. Mr. Bashford's interview with Count Bülow in the November number of the *Nineteenth Century*, 1904.

You will perhaps remember that at Homburg last autumn I thought that the time had not yet come for an attempt at reconciling England and Germany and that the hand outstretched by us would be refused here. I thought then that the time was not ripe for a successful attempt to reconcile differences which were largely fictitious. My view was based on my estimate of feeling in England, which was so embittered and wrongly directed, that any attempt to introduce a proper view of affairs would be rebuffed owing to the prejudice which reigned there. Every way we could think of for showing our good will would be misrepresented, a striking example of this being the way the visit of our squadron to Plymouth was received by the British public.

German Note. XIX. 195

On July 10th, 1904, 14 German war-ships visited Plymouth. On July 12th Count Metternich reported on the cool way in which the British Press received the German squadron : ' Most of the papers regard every step in the progress of our fleet as a menace to England. Many voices also loudly declare that the curiously frequent visits of German ships in British waters can be with no other object than to obtain information as to the dispositions of the British navy and coast defences for the benefit of the German Admiralty. The sight of the German fleet at Plymouth reminds Great Britain that she must be sufficiently armed to uphold absolutely her supremacy on the sea.' And yet it was at King Edward's desire, which he expressed at Kiel, that the Emperor ordered the visit.

[In his account of the King's visit to Kiel Sir Sidney Lee (II, 292 et seq.) does not mention that he expressed any such wish. He may however have done so conversationally.]

I was not consulted at the time as to the political advisability of the visit and am not to be held responsible for it.

You may perhaps still recollect from the many instructive conversations which we had together shortly before Christmas in Berlin that whilst I definitely denied any aggressive intentions on England's part, although, owing to the strained political atmosphere, there was a latent danger which might become acute if anything happened, I also expressed a feeling that the worst of the tension was over and that we were entering, if only *very gradually,* upon a calmer period. Since my return to England I am no longer in doubt that the climax is behind us and the *détente* is increasing—more quickly than I had expected. The Press here has on the whole dropped the ugly tone of suspicion against Germany, and articles appear here and there showing a wish for reconciliation. The same tendency is observable in the Monthly Reviews for January. I have pointed this out in my reports.

Apart from accidents our position towards England may be quite different by the end of the year. It is important, however, that our Press drops the theme of the war danger with England. It flatters the British who do not realise that we fear them, but it keeps alive the grudges on both sides.

Lord Rothschild told me yesterday it was stupid of us to believe England had war-like intentions. Such never existed here, and this Government especially wished to maintain good relations with us. Mr. Balfour had said this to him a few days before.

XIX. 570

BARON SPECK VON STERNBURG, IN WASHINGTON, TO THE CHANCELLOR, COUNT VON BÜLOW, *February 10th*, 1905

England's numerous efforts to draw closer politically to the United States have been especially active during recent months, and since my return I have been repeatedly warned by Americans to be on the *qui vive*. The British are trying to popularise the idea of a naval alliance between England and the United States.

I have already reported that after Sir Mortimer Durand was appointed Ambassador in Washington, an individual intimately connected with the British Embassy told me that the new representative's first task was to seek to establish closer relations with America and to isolate Germany.

One informant, the well-known journalist, Callan O'Laughlin,[1] who is a friend of the President's and is listened to in leading Government circles here, said to me yesterday : ' England is beginning to realise how Germany has got ahead of her in America. I can assure you that she will use every possible means to regain her lost ground. I come to warn you because there is a strong movement on.'

In the same connection some words may be of interest which were spoken to me three weeks ago by Arthur Walter, the owner of the London *Times*, and quite recently here by the British diplomat, Cecil Spring Rice.

I was on a visit in the middle of last month at the house of Mr. St. George Littledale, the well-known explorer of Tibet ; there I met Mr. Walter, amongst others of his neighbours, whose late father I had often visited at Bearwood in earlier years.

After being introduced Mr. Walter at once spoke of politics and of the relations between England and Germany. He said that in earlier years he, like his father, had often stayed in Germany with great enjoyment and that he had had much feeling for that country. And yet various causes had estranged them during recent years ; especially the unfriendly treatment suffered by one of his correspondents in Berlin [2] and the tactless

---

[1] Cf. S. Gwynn, *Letters and Friendships of Cecil Spring Rice*, p. 434.
[2] Mr. Saunders.

behaviour of one German diplomat in London towards himself.
(He meant Baron Eckardstein.)

Mr. Walter then mentioned the United States and criticised
sharply the British Ambassador in Washington and the British
Diplomatic service in general.   He told me he had recently sent
Valentine Chirol to represent him on a diplomatic mission in
Washington.   When I asked after the success of the mission,
he said : ' The future will show.'

From certain remarks of Mr. Chirol's, when he spent an
evening with me shortly before my departure for Europe, I
gathered that he can have achieved no particular success.
Walter's words strengthened me in this opinion ; he said that he
meant soon to visit the United States himself to take part in a
railway conference.   And yet I am told that Walter is little
interested in railway questions, so I assume that the chief
reason for his going is to win the American Press over to his
interests and to work here in a sense hostile to Germany.

I could gather from Walter's words and manner at Ascot
the bitter grudge that he bears against Germany.   My host
told me that Walter was a grim fanatic regarding Germany
and seemed to have made it his life's task to do her harm.   In
his eyes *The Times* was a highly dangerous weapon both at
home and abroad.

Here and in England I was assured on well-informed authority
that Walter has relations with the Foreign Office in London ;
I was able to gather this from his words.

Whilst in New York at the beginning of this month I met
Mr. Smalley, the political correspondent for *The Times* in
America, at several parties at the best houses in New York
(Whitelaw Reid, Sloane, Vanderbilt).   He has lived for many
years in New York and is intimate with the most exclusive
social circles in that city.

Soon after I returned from Europe a prominent Washington
journalist said to me : ' Chirol has had one success ; he has made
Smalley desert his soft feather-bed in New York and take up his
residence in Washington in order, as everyone says, to keep an
eye on you.'

To me personally this change is not unwelcome.   For one
thing, it removes Mr. Smalley from the strongly Anglophil
environment of the so-called Fourhundred in New York, and
then I can watch his doings in Washington better, and if he
employs dirty methods there, I can pillory him the more easily.

Mr. Spring Rice's journey to Washington is first and foremost
in answer to the President's wish, as he wants to obtain a clear
idea as to England's policy in the Far East.[1]   Spring Rice, who

[1] Cf. S. Gwynn, *Letters and Friendships of Cecil Spring Rice*, p. 434.

without doubt has received instructions from his Government, seems to have used his visit, which he lengthened considerably, in working skilfully for England's interests.

At heart Spring Rice has little sympathy with Germany, and even less with Russia. Even before being appointed to St. Petersburg it was his constant effort, in his private correspondence with the President, to represent Russia as the Arch-enemy of civilisation.

Spring Rice's lack of sympathy for Germany appeared very plainly in various conversations which I had with him, and I presume that he has spoken in like terms to his own friends. The trains of thought in the words used by Spring Rice and Walter to me were remarkably similar.

Spring Rice argued that the German Government and the parties adhering to it were entirely under the influence of Russia and were preaching war against England. The systematic agitation of the German people against England was encouraged by the Government and its parties. He had proof that in certain schools in Munich England was represented as the country with which the German navy would have to reckon in the near future.

The cause of this anti-British movement in Germany was the Boer War. . . .

I had an interesting conversation with the President yesterday on Anglo-German relations.

The President, who, as I have said before, would like to see a rapprochement between the three Protestant nations, England, Germany and America—especially the first two—in order to check the spread of Slav influence in Europe, expressed regret at the bitter animosity now existing between England and Germany. He said : ' I am continually being warned by Englishmen and friends of England that Germany's real objective for attack is America and not England. I naturally smile at this idea and think my informants blind and weak. Such strained relations between two Powers, however, are a great danger ; for both incessantly expect to be attacked. I hear, for instance, that Germany recently mobilised her fleet in order, as was supposed in England, to attack her.'

German Note. XIX. 376

. . . The *Standard* had asserted that after the Doggerbank incident the Kiel squadron was mobilised. . . . In a private letter to Count Metternich (January 18th, 1905) Count Bülow wrote : ' After the *Standard* article was telegraphed to me I inquired without delay of the Admiralty whether anything underlay this rumour, and I received an absolute assurance that the whole story was an idle invention.'

I took this opportunity of enlightening the President as to the real cause of this reported mobilisation. He then continued :

'Germany's relations with England remind me keenly of my own with the South. You know how bitterly my policy was attacked there, and how I was bespattered with mud. I ignored these attacks completely and did not allow myself to be diverted from my Southern policy. What is the result? The South is beginning to appreciate me and has suddenly discovered that after all I'm a man and a good fellow.

'Germany certainly showed little skill in dealing with England during the Boer War, especially in her attempt to brand the British soldiers as Vandals. The British soldier may be incompetent, but on the whole he is a decent good-natured fellow.'

Then I told the President of my meeting with Walter and of his deep embitterment against Germany. On my saying that Walter meant soon to come to America, he said: 'When Walter comes to Washington, I will have him and you at the White House, and he shall hear something.'

'It appears to me,' he continued, 'that the British are no longer the nation they were. They have lost much of the old manliness, self-confidence and freedom from nerves. This appears in their relations with Germany. You will recollect the *Punch* cartoons about the German navy a few years ago. I am delighted that the German navy is being strengthened, first as a counterweight in Europe, and secondly, so that Japan may be held in check. If ever Japan became dangerous to us your fleet and ours together could bottle her up. England's fleet is strong enough to do this by itself.'

About England the President said: 'The Government is to blame for this situation. England is governed by the highest social class, which is apparently becoming more and more corrupt and immoral. Its evil influence is spreading to the other classes. God shield us from such a Government!'

CHAPTER XVIII

MOROCCO. APRIL, 1904, TO JUNE, 1905

[The Anglo-French arrangement of March 8th, 1905, about Egypt and Morocco was accepted by all the Powers concerned except Germany, (cf. G. & T., III, p. 152 et seq.) who set to work to turn the Sultan of Morocco against any French monopoly of influence in his country. England was bound by the Treaty to support France, whose Foreign Minister, Delcassé, was a determined enemy of Germany. By threats and persuasion the Germans induced M. Rouvier to get rid of Delcassé and reverse his policy. Russia was, of course, temporarily out of action and unable to help. They also won Mr. Roosevelt, who personally was for letting France take charge of the affairs of Morocco, over to the idea of settling the question by means of an international Conference. By the end of June, 1905, the Conference idea was generally accepted and Germany could congratulate herself on a diplomatic victory. (Cf. Dennis, *Adventures in American Diplomacy*, p. 485 et seq.; Brandenburg, p. 208 et seq.)

In a telegram (March 22nd, 1905) to Count Metternich, in London, Count Bülow recalled the fact that ' His Majesty the Emperor last year declared to the King of Spain at Vigo that Germany desires no part of Moroccan territory, small or great, but she merely regards it as her duty to keep her commercial position there from deteriorating.' (XX. 268.)]

XX. 202

Baron von Mentzingen, Minister at Tangier, to Count von Bülow, *April 5th*, 1904

At this moment [1] when the war in the Far East and the revolt in [German] South-West Africa are attracting universal attention, I think that German action in Morocco ought to be even further from our thoughts than before. Nevertheless, in consideration of the demand of the Morocco Company, in its recent memorial to Your Excellency, for compensation for a certain strengthening of France's position in Morocco, I think it should be pointed out that the Moorish Government's slackness after Dr. Genthe's murder,[2] its arbitrary treatment of the German Mochalat, El Bernussi, and its illegal action in the case of Ben Zakur give us such a motive for forcible intervention as may not occur again. Moreover, so long as France has not advanced further than at present in extending her influence in

---

[1] Cf. G. & T., III, p. 53 et seq.; Lee, *Edward VII*, II, p. 336.

[2] Correspondent of the *Kölnische Zeitung*; murdered by Kabyles near Fez on March 8th, 1904.

Morocco, she would feel less mortified now, supposing we occupied a point on the coast—say, Agadir and its neighbourhood—than later on, when she will have consolidated her domination. The Imperial Admiralty may already have decided on the method of realising such action. I would merely remark humbly that, in addition to the ships engaged in the operation, one war-ship should be stationed at Tangier to protect Europeans, and another should be cruising along the coast. Also the Germans at Marakesh should be summoned away in good time.

XX. 207

MEMORANDUM BY BARON VON HOLSTEIN, *June 3rd*, 1904

By the Anglo-French Convention regarding Egypt and Morocco England is the gaining party in Egypt, and France in Morocco. England sought and obtained an understanding with the Powers who have legitimate interests in Egypt, whilst in acquiring Morocco France entirely ignored the justified interests of third parties, with the exception of Spain, to whom, at England's desire, she is ready to make certain territorial concessions. It is undeniable that the losses which third Powers would suffer through the gradual absorption of Morocco by France would be immensely greater than any injury or loss caused by the new arrangements in Egypt. Article IV of the Egypt-Morocco Convention stipulates that the contracting Powers shall have equal treatment in respect of Customs and railway tariffs. This closely hedged in freedom to trade would not prevent foreign trade and industry from being excluded from Morocco as they are from all French colonies and protectorates. In Morocco especially none but Frenchmen would receive attention in all official agreements in matters of railway and mining concessions. To-day Morocco is one of the few countries where Germany can compete freely in trade. Since Morocco is on the point of starting a net-work of railways, Germany would suffer great injury owing to the French monopoly. Even more alarming would be the injury to Germany's prestige, if we sat still whilst German interests were being dealt with without our taking a part. It is the duty of a Great Power not merely to protect its territorial frontiers, but also the interests lying outside them. In this sense all interests are to be held justified, which are not opposed by another and stronger right. We can never admit that France, as Morocco's neighbour, has a stronger right to Morocco than we have. A right to acquisition based on neighbourhood would, if admitted, upset International Law as conceived hitherto, and lead to remarkable consequences.

Not only for material reasons, but also in order to protect her prestige, Germany must protest against France's intention to acquire Morocco. The point to be made good is as follows : France's evident scheme to absorb Morocco finishes the free competition of foreign countries and involves sensible injury to the interests of third Powers, especially Germany, for now and later. For long we have clung to the belief that France would seek an understanding with the Powers interested. This however has not happened as far as Germany is concerned. Therefore the German Government finds itself forced to take the initiative in favour of German interests, which the Emperor summed up to the King of Spain [1] as follows : ' We demand freedom to trade and do business in Morocco.' But the fact of the French acquisition annuls this programme ; *vide* Tunis, Tonking, Madagascar, etc. With this declaration the German Government intends to oppose the wrong involved when one Power injures the interest of another in neutral territory without that Power's consent. (Here we might add what I wrote above about the rights of neighbourhood.) That there may be no doubts as to its motives, the German Government declares that the position taken up is only intended to prevent injury to its legitimate interests and dignity. Finally it declares that, supposing it is proved impossible in future to maintain the *status quo* in Morocco, it consents now in advance to the acquisition by Spain of the whole coast from Melilla to the Sebu, including hinterland.

If we merely ask that Spain shall acquire Tangier, we shall be exposed to the reproach of pulling England's chestnuts out of the fire for her. But if we say that the absorption of Morocco by France injures us materially, that the injury is done without consulting us and wounds our dignity as a Great Power, it will have to be admitted that we are acting for Germany alone. Also it is an advantage for us to be furthering two British wishes in claiming free competition and consenting to Spain's acquiring Tangier. It may be assumed that the British diplomatic support promised to France under Art. IX of the Morocco Convention will remain platonic.

If we let ourselves be trampled on in Morocco, we shall encourage them to do it again elsewhere.

XX. 189

FLOTAU, CHARGÉ D'AFFAIRES IN PARIS, TO THE CHANCELLOR, COUNT VON BÜLOW, *September 24th*, 1904

Very confidential.

I hear in strict confidence from a reliable source that the Spanish Ambassador made no progress in his latest negociations

---

[1] The Emperor met King Alphonzo XIII at Vigo on March 16th, 1904.

with M. Delcassé. France's point is that Morocco does not 'belong' to her and she has therefore no control over territory in that country. M. Delcassé has proposed to the Spanish Government not to enter into any definite arrangements for about ten years, when the nature and extent of French influence in Morocco ought to be more exactly defined. After this interval they would be ready here to satisfy Spain's claims to a certain extent. Details could be arranged later on.

The Spanish Ambassador is much ruffled by this proposal.

In diplomatic circles here there has been until now uncertainty as to how far the clause regarding the guarantee of Spain's rights in the Anglo-French Colonial Agreement is involving England in the present Franco-Spanish negociations ; also how far, if at all, the British Government is prepared to support the Spanish claims.

The British Chargé d'Affaires here, Sir Maurice de Bunsen, tells me in confidence that in London it is considered important for Spain to be properly provided for on the North coast of Morocco. Lord Lansdowne has repeatedly made suggestions in this sense to the French Ambassador in London. It was too obvious, added Sir Maurice, that Great Britain was bound to wish to see the coast lands in northern Morocco, which affected the British sea route to India, in the weaker hands of Spain.

XX. 191

BARON VON RICHTHOFEN, IN BERLIN, TO RADOWITZ, IN MADRID, *October 7th*, 1904

Telegram.

To-day the French Ambassador, M. Bihourd, informed me of the conclusion of the Franco-Spanish negociations and made me the following declaration orally :

'Le Gouvernement de la République Française et le Gouvernement de Sa Majesté le Roi d'Espagne s'étant mis d'accord pour fixer l'étendu des droits et la garantie des intérêts qui résultent pour la France de ses possessions algériennes et pour l'Espagne de ses possessions sur la côte du Maroc, et le Gouvernement de Sa Majesté le Roi d'Espagne ayant en consequence donné son adhésion à la Déclaration Franco-anglaise du 8 avril, 1904, relative au Moroc et à l'Egypte, dont communication lui a été faite par le Gouvernement de la République, déclarent qu'ils demeurent fermement attachés à l'intégrité de l'Empire Marocain sous la souveraineté du Sultan.'

It is important to us to receive as soon as possible from you the text of those decisions in the Agreement which deal with protection for the commercial activities of Spanish subjects in Morocco.

[In the spring of 1905 the Emperor took a yachting trip in the Mediterranean. Bülow and Holstein determined that he should include a visit to Tangier in order to impress the Moors with the greatness of Germany. It was greatly against the Emperor's inclination. (Cf. Lee, *King Edward VII*, II, p. 339 ; Wilson, *War Guilt*, p. 97 ; H. Wickham Steed, *Through Thirty Years*, p. 230.) But his advisers saw to it that the visit was freely announced in the Press, and sent Kühlmann from Berlin to the Legation at Tangier to organise the details of it.]

XX. 261

KÜHLMANN, AT TANGIER, TO THE CHANCELLOR, COUNT VON BÜLOW, *March 19th*, 1905

Walter Harris, the *Times* .Correspondent, visited me just now, having recently returned from a long journey on leave. He told me the contents of a long letter in which the well-known Mr. Chirol gives his views on the Morocco question and particularly on Germany's position in Morocco. It is to the effect that France made a bad mistake in thinking that the international side of the question was finally settled by the British and Spanish Agreement. It was France's business to agree with the other Powers, especially Germany, just as England had done with the Powers over the Egyptian question. Germany's interests were so important that account must in all cases be taken of her commercial guarantees, and eventual cession of the Sus district between· the High Atlas and the Wad-Nûn would have won Germany's consent to a preferential position of the French Republic. England was not called upon to pull France's Moroccan chestnuts out of the fire. Diplomatic support under the treaty meant diplomatic support in Morocco only. England ought not, by any action outside these limits, to disturb relations towards other Powers, especially Germany, in whom were remarkable signs of a more friendly feeling.

Mr. Harris promised me he would show me all telegrams of political interest before sending them off so that they might contain nothing contrary to our wishes.

XX. 262

THE CHANCELLOR, COUNT VON BÜLOW, TO THE EMPEROR, *March 20th*, 1905

I beg respectfully to enclose for Your Majesty the article published to-day by my orders in the *Nord-Deutsche Allgemeine Zeitung* on the subject of the landing at Tangier.

Your Majesty's visit to Tangier will embarrass M. Delcassé, traverse his schemes, and further our business interests in Morocco. (The EMPEROR : ' *Tant mieux.*')

[The article quoted notices in the *Kölnische Zeitung* and the *Standard* ; it also gave a long quotation from *The Times*, written in strong support of the German claims in Morocco and in deprecation of the French manœuvres at the Sultan's court.]

German Note.

The paragraph quoted from *The Times* was presumably written by the correspondent, Harris, who was in close touch with Kühlmann.

XX. 285

Schoen, in the Emperor's suite at Gibraltar, to the German Foreign Office, *March* 31st, 1905

Up to the last moment His Majesty hesitated about landing at Tangier and wanted to cancel the visit on the pretext of the difficulty in landing. With the help of my friend Scholl, who was sent on shore and returned with a perfectly encouraging report, His Majesty got over his hesitation quite suddenly and proceeded to perform the historic act, which passed off with a flourish.

XX. 296

Kühlmann, at Tangier, to the German Foreign Office, *April* 3rd, 1905

Cipher telegram.

The idea of a Conference, to be summoned by the Moorish Government, to discuss the Morocco problem is in the air, so to speak, and has frequently come up of itself in conversation with diplomats. Harris is personally sympathetic to the idea and wishes to begin a campaign in favour of it at once, but he is not quite sure. if *The Times* is prepared just now to proceed with it. He promised to show a new and interesting letter by Chirol.[1]

XX. 301

The Chancellor, Count von Bülow, to the Emperor, *April* 4th, 1905

Cipher telegram. Extract.

. . . Your Majesty's visit to Tangier has brought the Morocco question into prominence. Your Majesty's imposing demeanour, the weighty speeches, especially those to the French Chargé d'Affaires and the German colony, have as a guarantee of Moroccan independence made a deep impression both in and out of Europe. I may mention that the American Minister, under direct instructions from President Roosevelt to keep in close touch with Your Majesty's representatives, when told of the sentiments regarding the ' open door ', exclaimed : ' That is just exactly what we also want.'

[1] Cf. p. 223.

Part of the British Press still indulge in wild ideas. But even this section of the British will become more reasonable when they realise that Germany genuinely seeks no special advantages . . . and all the more so, when they see that American diplomacy is on the side of Germany's ' open door '. Fear of Roosevelt is clearly on the increase in England ; whether love of him also I do not know. M. Delcassé, hard pushed, has got round the difficult corners of the Morocco question in the Senate. In the Chamber he managed to cancel a question about Morocco, which was set down for yesterday. . . .

In order to strengthen the opposition against Delcassé I am emphasising the following points : (1) Negation of territorial claims ; (2) Demand of equal commercial rights for all States to include not merely freedom of trade or even formal most-favoured-nation treatment, but the ' open door ' in the fullest sense ; (3) a hint—and this is our trump card—that all the European Powers, with the United States, have again conferred on the affairs of Morocco and concluded treaties. The last conferences of this kind took place at Madrid in the eighties. . . .

[For President Roosevelt's point of view see G. & T., III, p. 67 ; Dennis, *Adventures in American Diplomacy*, p. 487. His main desire was to prevent friction between England and Germany. He was temporarily absent from Washington.]

XX. 342

BARON SPECK VON STERNBURG, IN WASHINGTON, TO THE GERMAN FOREIGN OFFICE, *April 25th*, 1905

Cipher telegram. Extract.

. . . It is clear that for our interests it is desirable to handle the Morocco question in the most dilatory way possible until the President's return, and to put off discussing the Conference idea until then. It would further be of advantage for the American Minister to remind his Government that attendance at a Conference would help in the development of American trade.

XX. 341

COUNT VON TATTENBACH, AT TANGIER, TO THE GERMAN FOREIGN OFFICE, *April 25th*, 1905

Cipher telegram.

At an audience which Dr. Vassel, of our Consulate at Fez, had on the 21st, the Sultan promised to make no concessions before I arrived. The Sultan said also that M. St. René, in describing the French demands, had referred to a European mandate given to France. The Sultan empowered Dr. Vassel to report this.

Mr. Harris talked recently to the owner of *The Times*, who declared that the Press had been instructed to ' roar ', whilst the British Government was to confine itself to supporting France diplomatically *pro forma.*

XX. 348

COUNT VON TATTENBACH, AT TANGIER, TO THE GERMAN FOREIGN OFFICE, *April 27th,* 1905

Cipher telegram.

The British Minister, Sir Gerard Lowther, has been ordered by his Government to go forthwith to the Sultan's Court.

The French Chargé d'Affaires informed the *Temps* correspondent that the Minister was instructed to support French policy in Morocco without reservation.[1]

Sir Gerard himself spoke to Harris as follows : Although he had no instructions on the point, his opinion was that the object of the Mission was to show the French that England meant to observe the conditions of the April treaty loyally and not to withhold diplomatic support ; in the question of Morocco itself England did not mean to be entangled. He thinks the first result of the Missions, which are paralysing each other by their efforts, will be a kind of pause, when the moment for an Anglo-French declaration will have arrived. Perhaps the grounds for an understanding will be found in deciding upon a commercial sphere of influence for Germany, perhaps in the South, with a guarantee, at the same time, of Morocco's sovereignty and independence.

I have declared and shall again declare that a separate treaty with France on the Morocco question is impossible for us.

[It appears from the Documents that Rouvier, once having yielded to German persuasion, was as anxious to get rid of Delcassé as the German Government was.]

XX. 361

PRINCE VON RADOLIN, IN PARIS, TO COUNT VON BÜLOW, *April 30th,* 1905

Extract.

. . . Rouvier then mentioned M. Delcassé and told me he disapproved much that had happened. The Foreign Minister's sole duty was to carry out the decisions of the Council of Ministers ; whereas he had secured for himself a certain independence and was going outside his own proper functions. Once he (Rouvier) became sure of this, he had cut Delcassé's wings by attending to foreign policy himself and was doing all in his power to control him.

[1] Cf. G. & T., III, p. 72 et seq.

I was rather astonished at the President's frankness about these private matters, especially when he added that he had had enough trouble in the Chamber in rescuing Delcassé, whose resignation could hardly be taken seriously (I think he used the word ' comedy ') ; but he had thought it wiser to do so.

German Note.
Delcassé offered his resignation on April 19th, but quickly withdrew it.

XX. 358

MEMORANDUM BY BARON VON HOLSTEIN, *May 2nd*, 1905

Extract.

. . . The difficulties of the present situation are two, first that we are now committed in a definite direction, and secondly, the absolute mistrust of any French policy which is led by M. Delcassé. We believe that Delcassé does not stick to the truth, and that he loses no opportunity of distorting German policy.

We are quite willing to join with France on individual questions, and have often proved this ; but in the Morocco question, in consideration of the two objections mentioned above, we see no possibility of agreeing with France to-day or to-morrow or in the near future. . . .

XX. 368

THE CHANCELLOR, COUNT VON BÜLOW, AT KARLSRUHE, TO THE GERMAN FOREIGN OFFICE, *May 5th*, 1905

Cipher telegram.

Baron von Eckardstein, who arrived here from Paris early this morning, described the situation much as Betzold did.

[Betzold, a French financier, was sent by Rouvier to Berlin to discuss a possible agreement with Germany, and Eckardstein travelled from London, via Paris, to Karlsruhe at the request of Rouvier. (Cf. his *Lebenserrine- rungen*, III, p. 100 et seq.)]

He says Delcassé's presumptuousness makes him personally unsympathetic to Rouvier and Étienne, and since Delcassé wants to direct foreign policy by himself, they wish to get rid of him ; he is also unpleasant socially. Both sides fight in the Cabinet and the Chamber. Above all we must avoid attacking Delcassé in the Press, for that would only strengthen his position in France. Even attacks against France, as a nation, would attract patriotic spirits to Delcassé's side. The British are egging on Paris as much as they can, in order to bring about a Franco-German war, which all Englishmen desire. When in Paris, King Edward had privately expressed quite anti-German sentiments. With a request for absolute discretion Baron Eckardstein told me that Rouvier had told him that those who desired a general improvement in Franco-German relations would find their task much easier, if His Majesty in a speech, I myself in the Reichstag, and the *Norddeutsche Allgemeine Zeitung* in semi-official form, would argue somewhat as follows : L'Allemagne ne pourrait pas permettre que la France la tienne en dehors de la question marocaine. Elle estime que le Gouvernement français aurait du négocier avec elle comme avec les autres Puissances, et elle poursuivra sa politique dans ce sens de façon à ce que les intérêts de l'Allemagne soient respectés. Mais il n'est pas dans l'intention de l'Allemagne de troubler la paix de l'Europe, à laquelle elle s'est toujours montrée plus attachée que n'importe quelle Puissance du monde. Elle ne demande qu'à entretenir des relations amicales avec une grande nation comme la France qui, de même que l'Allemagne, s'est toujours trouvée à la tête de la civilisation. Donc l'Empereur ne voit pas d'impossibilité à conserver de bons rapports avec la France en défendant en même temps les intérêts de l'Allemagne au Maroc. L'Empereur d'Allemagne a fait beaucoup pour l'entretien des bons rapports avec la France. Ce n'est pas de sa faute si ce pays n'a pas compris que son intérêt était de vivre dans des conditions amicales avec l'Allemagne.

Baron von Eckardstein thinks that some such declaration would bring Delcassé down. He said casually that Rouvier quite agreed with our recent proposal to conduct the Morocco question in slow time for the present. Baron von Eckardstein thinks that if a Franco-German war broke out, the British would certainly side with France. King Edward made this quite clear in Paris. The British over-estimate the French desire for action. In Eckardstein's opinion an improvement in Franco-German relations would disappoint the British as regards France, but would make them better disposed to us. From what I gather from His Majesty's entourage, the Emperor seems to have no intention at the moment to make a speech at Grave-lotte [1] or elsewhere.

[On the same day Count Bülow wrote privately to Holstein : ' With what he has been told here Baron von Eckardstein can do no mischief.'

On May 25th Prince Bülow telegraphed to Washington : ' I share the view that the decision of the Conference question actually rests with the President.']

XX. 406

FLOTOW, CHARGÉ D'AFFAIRES IN PARIS, TO THE CHANCELLOR
PRINCE [2] VON BÜLOW, *June 7th*, 1905
Confidential.

M. Rouvier's tactics have been very clever in completely isolating M. Delcassé and bringing about his fall yesterday by

---

[1] At the dedication of a War Memorial.   [2] Cf. p. 206, note.

producing a panic in the Chamber the day before. In the lobbies of the Palais Bourbon the prospects of a war were freely discussed. Moreover the absence of a telegram from the Emperor to M. Loubet after the attack [1] on May 31st was commented on in this sense.

The story of M. Delcassé's fall [2] is evidence that there is doubtless an undercurrent in France, desirous of a friendly understanding with Germany as being serviceable to French interests. Moreover it is remarkable that in the whole Press of all parties there is scarcely a paper which does not blame Delcassé's anti-German policy. If this feeling fails to come out louder and more unmistakably, the explanation must be still sought in Alsace-Lorraine. Even Frenchmen who turn away from any idea of revenge will not permit themselves openly to acknowledge the loss of territory and to treat it as irreparable ; it is on this rock that any attempt at a nearer rapprochement between the two great neighbouring *Kultur*-nations is wrecked.

XX. 625

The second interesting point in the story of the last few days is the fact that, in spite of persistent and almost pressing offers of British help,[3] in spite of immense agitation on England's part by material and moral or immoral methods, French public opinion has never shown any real inclination to accept this help. Wherever one was able to enter into touch with public feeling— in the clubs, society, the Press, and elsewhere—one met the view that England was merely trying to get the power of France on her side in her differences with Germany, and that, if it became serious, France would have to pull England's chestnuts out of the German fire. One cannot always credit the French political world with mature reflection ; but it must be said that in this case they have sensibly withstood the first impulse to throw themselves into England's arms. Through a third person I was able cautiously to sound M. Rouvier on the offer of an Anglo-French offensive and defensive alliance, as reported by M. de Cuverville.[4] M. Rouvier has declared positively that beyond the known treaty conditions and a few economic arrangements there is no question of a closer treaty relationship between the two countries.

[1] An anarchist attack on the King of Spain whilst in Paris.
[2] Cf. G. & T., III, p. 78 et seq. ; Lee, *King Edward VII*, II, p. 43 ; S. Gwynn, *Letters and Friendships of Cecil Spring Rice*, p. 503.
[3] Cf. G. & T., III, pp. 72–8.   [4] On the staff of the *Matin*.

XX. 418

THE CHANCELLOR, PRINCE VON BÜLOW, TO COUNT VON TATTENBACH, AT FEZ, *June 7th*, 1905

Telegram.

Delcassé's fall and his replacement by Rouvier ought to close the acute phase of the Morocco question, whether the Conference takes place or not. The British Press, which has done its best to bring about a Franco-German conflict, now favours the ' sphere of interests '. It will be your task to persuade the Sultan that he has acted rightly for his own interests in rejecting the French programme and proposing a Conference. By so doing he has contributed his share towards removing Delcassé and drawing French policy back to quiet paths. Whether she gets on badly or better with France, Germany will not forget that the Sultan followed her advice. Even if there is no Conference, there is still Article 17 of the Madrid Convention of 1880,[1] supposing a single Signatory Power objects to an alteration of the existing situation, contradictory to the provisions of the treaty.

XX. 421

BARON SPECK VON STERNBURG, IN WASHINGTON, TO THE GERMAN FOREIGN OFFICE, *June 8th*, 1905

Cipher telegram.

In a conversation about Morocco the President [2] said to me he could hardly take part in a Conference to settle that question without risking being sharply attacked in political circles and public opinion. Since the Perdicaris affair [3] Americans believe that the interior of Morocco is inhabited by quite lawless tribes, over whom the Sultan has no authority, and who are a constant danger to foreign traders. For this reason thinking people here would gladly see Morocco civilised by a foreign Power, just as Egypt was. I hear that Jusserand, the French Ambassador, speaks generally in this sense here. I told the President that this would be a serious outrage on the rights of the Signatory Powers,[4] of whom America was one. These Powers were mutually bound to see that the treaty was respected by all. To let France have her way would create a dangerous precedent, which would have its reactions in the Far East. I handed the President a memorandum setting forth the legal side of the

[1] Cf. G. & T., III, p. 108.

[2] Cf. G. & T., III, pp. 90, 97, 256 ; Dennis, *Adventures in American Diplomacy*, p. 492.

[3] Mr. Perdicaris, a Jewish American resident at Tangier, was kidnapped by Moorish robbers and eventually ransomed.

[4] Of the Madrid Convention of 1880.

question. He promised me a definite answer. I discussed in the State Department the contents of the German declaration of June 5th [1] and left a translation of it.

[For the reasons mentioned above, America was inclined to support the French scheme.

Lord Lansdowne's reasons for considering an international Conference an undesirable method of settling the Morocco problem are given by G. & T., III, pp. 92–3.]

XX. 442

BARON SPECK VON STERNBURG, IN WASHINGTON, TO THE GERMAN FOREIGN OFFICE, *June 17th*, 1905

Cipher telegram.

The President spoke to me as follows : ' On the basis of your memorandum about Morocco I had a long conversation with the French Ambassador a few days ago. I thought it necessary to let him know all the points to which you drew my attention. I said I well knew that his Government might regard my action as interference in their business, but as the Morocco affair threatened to cause a war between Germany and France, which would trouble the world's peace, I felt justified in doing as I did. I begged the French Ambassador to tell this to his Government and say that France could only lose by a war with Germany, and England would only gain. I thought the best way to settle the Morocco question was a Conference. Yesterday the French Ambassador thanked me . . . [2] for my efforts in the interests of peace. They [the French Government ?] would examine the question thoroughly and tell me their decision.

' I have just told the British Ambassador that I expect England to put no difficulties in the way of a peaceful solution of the question between Germany and France.'

I hear that since the King and Lord Lansdowne received Mr. Hay [3] in London there has been an exchange of telegrams between him and the President, in which Mr. Hay tried to win the President over to England's side in the Morocco question. From what the President said to-day, I gather that this has not been successful.

The President has heard that England and France are now negotiating together on the question.

We have certainly made good political capital out of Mr. Hay's absence. About the Far East, the Peace and Morocco,

---

[1] Cf. G. & T., III, p. 92.

[2] Cipher group missing in the German.

[3] Cf. Lee, *King Edward VII*, II, p. 427 ; Dennis, *Adventures in American Diplomacy*, p. 510.

the President has pursued a policy directly contrary to Hay's principles ; the Press admits it. Certain circles, which thought that the President's foreign policy would be aggressive and warlike, needing the age and experience of Mr. Hay to counteract it, have been quite reassured by the President's outstanding successes with his foreign policy, which the whole country appreciates. So that it may be hoped that this may induce Mr. Hay [1] to think about retiring.

[From now on the Conference idea was generally accepted, and preparations for it became active.]

XX. 647

COUNT VON METTERNICH, IN LONDON, TO THE CHANCELLOR, PRINCE VON BÜLOW, *July 22nd*, 1905

Private letter. Extract.

. . . There is no doubt that at the moment King Edward is strongly aroused against us and, unfortunately, against the person of the Emperor in particular.[2] I imagine that he talked several times to Delcassé, a fact which his Ministers do not know. Nothing can have angered him so much as our Moroccan policy, which ignores the Agreement with France, the great event of his reign. When at one moment it looked as if M. Rouvier, driven by fear, was ready to sacrifice the Entente, King Edward must have done his best to appear as France's firm support. As far as can be ascertained here, the French seem to have lost their first fear and to have assumed a distinctly Anglophil attitude. Since they feel surer than before of British help, our negociations with France may have to go slower and be more difficult to complete. Nevertheless, if this assumption is correct, I think quiet, continuous pressure on the French will be the best way to attain our wishes in Morocco.[3] The prospect of reaching a general agreement with France about Morocco seems unfortunately to be becoming more remote. The increase of self-confidence on the subject, which is inspired in them by England, may give rise to a serious situation before or during the Conference. A trial of strength to the point of bending or breaking would involve a greater danger to peace than the first time. But it may be assumed that fear would again grip them in Paris ; but if the French go mad and allow it to come to a war, they will, even without a treaty, find England's armed power on their side.[4] In England the Morocco question has

---

[1] Mr. Hay died on July 1st, 1905. Cf. Dennis, *Adventures in American Diplomacy*, p. 528 ; S. Gwynn, *Letters and Friendships of Cecil Spring Rice*, pp. 480, 483.

[2] Cf. Lee, *King Edward VII*, II, p. 348.

[3] Cf. G. & T., III, p. 100 et seq.　　　　[4] Cf. Lee, II, p. 363.

come to mean a fight for the friendship of France, and in order to keep this and also to prevent a predominant German hegemony over Europe they would venture on a war.

Nevertheless, I insist that neither King Edward nor his Government, nor even the British people, who are aroused against us, wish for a war with Germany. But there are causes which might lead to it. The Morocco question has brought us a step nearer to war with England. I am far from wishing to criticise our Morocco policy ; on the contrary, I think we were quite right to break down the French plot. But I consider it my duty to indicate the possible consequences as far as England is concerned.

When last December we were inclined to think that England wished to make war on us, and an English friend of the King's mentioned the ' war scare ' to him, the King broke out with the words : ' It is monstrous to pretend that I want to make war on Germany. I wouldn't declare war against Germany any more than I would make war against the Prince of Wales.' Two natures are hidden in his breast.

I would not attend too much to what the Dutch Ministers reported in Paris and London. The first is a pompous fool, and the other knows no more about England than if he lived in Batavia.

[Their report was that King Edward was heading for war with Germany and had recently expressed openly his anger against Rouvier and the Franco-German understanding. (XX. 638.) Cf. G. & T., III, p. 115 et seq.]

CHAPTER XIX

THE ALGECIRAS CONFERENCE, 1906. THE MILITARY CONVERSATIONS

[The new Liberal Government declared their intention of continuing the Moroccan policy of their predecessors and of supporting France without reserve at least until the Algeciras Conference was over. Lord Grey, in his *Twenty-five Years*, gives a very clear and complete account of the problems confronting a Minister for whom the preservation of peace stood in front of every consideration save that of the nation's honour. When pressed by the French and Belgians to promise support even in the event of war with Germany, he had to limit himself to consenting to conversations between the military authorities of the two nations (cf. G. & T., III, p. 170 et seq.) in which the Cabinet was not to be officially involved. To the German questions on the subject he had but one answer, as the following pages show. Mr. Eyre Crowe's memorandum (G. & T., III, p. 397 et seq.) gives an account of the German pressure on France during 1905–6.

The general feeling of the Powers represented at Algeciras, including America, was that all of them ought to have a greater share in the control of Morocco than France was prepared to offer them, and Sir Arthur Nicolson did his best to persuade his French colleague of this. (Cf. Brandenburg, p. 244 et seq.)

The German Minister at Tangier was Friedrich Rosen. For the American point of view see Dennis, *Adventures in American Diplomacy*, p. 497 et seq. The difficulty in negociating with foreign Powers, due to the right of the Senate under the Constitution to refuse to ratify any treaty, is described by Dennis, p. 524 et seq.]

XXI. 45

COUNT VON METTERNICH, IN LONDON, TO THE CHANCELLOR, PRINCE VON BÜLOW, *January 3rd*, 1906

To-day I had an important conversation about Morocco with Sir Edward Grey.[1] Since my recent conversation with him [2] I have been careful not to mention it to him ; but to-day he began upon it himself.

I will first say that Sir Edward Grey gives me the impression of being a frank, straightforward man, and that one knows where one is with him.

He said that the approaching Morocco Conference [3] filled

[1] Foreign Secretary in Sir H. Campbell-Bannerman's Liberal Government.　　　　　　　　　　[2] Not given.

[3] Cf. Lord Grey of Fallodon, *Twenty-five Years*, p. 71 et seq. ; G. & T., III, p. 170 ; J. A. Spender, *Life of Sir H. Campbell-Bannerman*, I, p. 249 et seq.

him with anxiety ; to which I replied that I could not escape the same feeling. Since our last meeting he had further examined the Morocco question, which was his reason for referring to it again with me. The Entente with France and the removal of the old quarrels were very greatly welcomed in England, and they wished to keep to it and run no risks with it. The feeling was general here that England must not leave the French Government in the lurch in a question arising out of the Anglo-French Agreement. This was the standpoint of the British Government, whether Liberal or Conservative. He thought it right to tell me his views frankly before the Conference met, for differences might arise at it between Germany and France which would make it harder for him, as a British Minister, to discuss it with me thus unconstrainedly, and for me to listen to his views. It was his earnest wish that no such differences should arise at the Conference of Algeciras and that the negotiations should pass off quietly. But just because by the Agreement of April, 1904, the British Government had undertaken to support France in carrying out this Agreement and because they were to support her at the Conference of Algeciras also, he looked forward to it with anxiety since England might be brought into opposition to Germany against her wish. The British Government desired to enter into friendly relations with Germany and also to put an end to the tension between France and Germany, and they would do their best to help it on once the Conference was happily over. But there they must support the French standpoint.

I replied . . . that we also wished the Morocco Conference to pass off smoothly, even as he did. . . . The point was to make sure at the Conference that the reforms considered necessary should be carried out under international and not purely French control. By this means alone did we feel that our business interests in Morocco would be safe. The police (with the exception of frontier defence) and the finances must be under international control.

To Sir Edward Grey's remark that commercial equality was already stipulated in the French Agreement, and therefore commercial exclusion could not ensue as it had in Tunis and Madagascar where treaties with other Powers had been annulled, I replied that the Agreement of April, 1904, only provided for freedom of trade for 30 years, and that this limited recognition of the ' open door ' principle did not imply entire equality in commerce. In a country like Morocco it meant not only importing goods under equal conditions for all, but—perhaps even more so—free competition for State concessions or loans. Whereas if a single Power controlled police and finance Morocco must do whatever suited that single Power, and for others there could be no question of free competition.

The Minister replied that, as far as he knew, the French Government had, by its private arrangement with Germany regarding the Conference programme,[1] arranged that Germany was to share with France in establishing the State Bank which was to control Morocco financially. I replied that I did not think that the reform of the Moorish finances would present serious difficulty at the Conference, if it was placed under international control.

Later in the conversation Sir Edward Grey said he had found among his predecessor's memoranda a conversation with me of the previous summer, in which Lord Lansdowne indicated that if there was war between Germany and France on account of Morocco public feeling would force the Government to fight for France. He, Grey, believed that the British people would not stand France being involved in war with Germany on account of the Anglo-French Agreement, and that, if it happened, any British Government, whether Conservative or Liberal, would be forced to help France.[2]

I replied that Lord Lansdowne had said this to me in the summer but with the addition : ' in the event of an unprovoked attack by Germany on France.' This, I said, was unthinkable. Personally however I had been very sure last summer that after 24 hours any Franco-German complication would be represented here as a German provocation, even if France led off with a sudden raid into German territory. This state of affairs was naturally very dangerous. The more the German public observed that England was ready to offer military as well as the diplomatic help promised under the treaty with France, the more would they agitate in favour of rejecting France's unjust claims. In German eyes it was a matter of defending our rights. Unluckily the Morocco question had swelled into one of prestige. If it again looked as if France, jointly with England, was ready to resort to arms in the settlement of it, we should be absolutely forced to oppose the French demands even more bluntly. To France alone we could make certain concessions, but we felt too strong as a nation to give up our rights in Morocco under pressure from England *and* France. German resistance would stiffen in proportion as the British help appeared to be gaining strength.

The Minister replied that feeling in England was not hostile

[1] Cf. G. & T., III, p. 143 et seq.
[2] Cf. his speech of August 3rd, 1914, in *Parliamentary Debates*, 1914, Vol. VIII, p. 1811 et seq.

to Germany. There was but the wish to stand by France supposing she got into difficulties owing to her agreement with England. This explained the attitude of a part of the British Press in siding against Germany in the Morocco question. Once the Conference was happily over without displaying sharp differences between France and Germany, there would be a distinct calming down in public opinion and, he thought, in the Press also. I had recently said to him that the British Government ought to adopt an attitude of conciliation between France and Germany. This was both his wish and that of the Government ; but they were bound to support the French at Algeciras on the basis of the Franco-German Conference programme ; which was his sole reason for pointing out the dangers with which this situation might threaten England also. As soon as the Conference was over he would work loyally to reconcile France and Germany. It was to his interest and to that of the Government and the country to clear away the Franco-German dispute, because then the Anglo-French Entente would rest on a more tranquil and assured foundation. Also, after it was over he would co-operate in reconciling British and German public opinion. He knew that we in Berlin complained of the British Press. The Government had no power over the Press ; but he believed that if the Foreign Minister of England spoke publicly in favour of friendly relations with Germany it would make its impression on the Press. He was ready for this, but not till after the Conference ; before it his hands were tied.

I answered that frank expression of opinion was always useful, even if it brought opposing views to light, and I thanked him for speaking quite openly to me.

I hear from a mutual acquaintance that Sir Arthur Nicolson, the British representative at Algeciras, declared that the Conference was to work out a plan for international control of the import duties at the ports of Morocco, which would be a fine introduction for the work of reform. If it effected this it would have scored a considerable success. One should not include too much all at once in the way of reforms in a country like Morocco.

[On the following day Count Metternich wrote : ' Here the Morocco question is generally regarded as a test of the Anglo-French Entente, and our Morocco policy as an attempt to smash it up.' (XXI. 52.)

For the attitude of the American Government cf. G. & T., III, pp. 97, 217. President Roosevelt was urged personally by the Emperor to support the German contention about Morocco, and he sent Mr. Henry White to Algeciras less as a delegate than an observer. Cf. p. 244.]

XXI. 102

RADOWITZ, AT ALGECIRAS, TO THE GERMAN FOREIGN OFFICE, January 21st, 1906

Extract.

. . . White, the American Ambassador,[1] has declared to me that he holds our standpoint in the mandate question to be the only correct one and intends to combine with the Marquis Visconti Venosta in bringing about a reasonable compromise with the French.

XXI. 74

LIEUTENANT-GENERAL VON MOLTKE, CHIEF OF THE GENERAL STAFF, TO PRINCE VON BÜLOW, January 23rd, 1906

I beg to submit to Your Highness my views on the military measures recently adopted by the French.

The alarming rumours in the Press regarding French preparations for mobilisation have proved false or at any rate greatly exaggerated. Especially the calling up of the Reserves of several years, as reported in the telegram from the 16th Corps, has not taken place ; neither has the Army Corps on the frontier been reinforced by secret drafts from the interior.

The actual measures taken in France are as follows :

The fortresses on the Eastern frontier are being strengthened and made fit for defence ; the stock of munitions and provisions is being completed. The troops for frontier protection are being brought nearly up to their normal peace strength by drafts from the interior. Reservists in small numbers are being called up for their regular training here and there.

The formation and preparation of the troops on the frontier is being pushed forward in every way. To this end several trial mobilisations by garrisons and field exercises of the frontier troops by night and day are being held.

All these preparations, however, are not to be regarded as preparations for an intended mobilisation, but as easily explained measures of precaution.[2]

In my opinion the French consider that to yield further now in the Morocco question would not befit the dignity of their country, seeing that they have already given way and allowed M. Delcassé to fall.

Nevertheless they fear that, as a result of their firm attitude, the Conference may not only be unsuccessful, but may even lead to war complications. They desire no war and are not themselves dreaming of attacking ; but they wish to be armed against a German attack.

---

[1] In Rome.   [2] Cf. Grey, *Twenty-five Years*, p. 90.

Up till now France was, in fact, not sufficiently prepared for a war against Germany. It is now known that last summer a Parliamentary Commission examined the condition of the Eastern fortresses with the result that considerable defects were discovered.

The frontier troops were never up to their normal peace strength and were further weakened perpetually by leave granted for the sake of economy.

As a result of the Commission's findings a special grant (200 million [1]) was placed at the Minister of War's disposal.

The measures for removing these defects have not yet been completed. . . .

XXI. 119

RADOWITZ, AT ALGECIRAS, TO THE CHANCELLOR, PRINCE VON
BÜLOW, *January 26th*, 1906

Extract.

. . . Sir Arthur Nicolson, the sole representative of his Government here, was, as is known, an opponent of the Conference idea from the start and took it as a personal matter that it came into being in spite of his opposition. He certainly came here with the intention of sticking to the French through thick and thin even if it meant wrecking the Conference. His behaviour at recent meetings and the words of some of my colleagues who are intimate with him lead me to suppose that Sir Arthur has recently become more accommodating, and perhaps even wishes that the result of the Conference may bring satisfaction to Germany as well as to France. (The EMPEROR : '*Wallace is making himself felt here.*') In the negociations he shows great knowledge of detail—having been Minister at Tangier for ten years. . . .

[Sir Donald Mackenzie Wallace was received by King Edward, before going out to represent *The Times* at Algerciras. He was urged by the King ' to use every effort to bridge over the differences between Germany and France ' (XXI. 95).]

XXI. 525

LIEUTENANT-GENERAL VON MOLTKE, CHIEF OF THE GENERAL
STAFF, TO PRINCE VON BÜLOW, *February 23rd*, 1906

Secret.

I beg to communicate to Your Highness the following information, which has come to me from a sure source, on England's attitude in the event of a Franco-German War :

The change in the distribution of political power which a victorious Germany would occasion in Europe would be so great

[1] Cf. Grey, *Twenty-five Years*, p. 93.

a national danger for England, that she would be forced to relinquish the neutrality 'which she desires, and which is the intention of the Government'.

It may naturally be presumed that Belgium would out of sympathy be drawn into a Franco-German war and would fight on the French side.

It is held that it would not be to the interest of victorious Germany to reduce France to a third-class Power. On the contrary it is thought certain that in consideration for the pride of the French nation Germany would try to attract France by a display of generosity. In return for this Germany would get Belgium for nothing and eventually seize upon Holland also.

If Germany were in possession of the Belgian coast, Holland would be forced to join Germany unconditionally, even though Germany might allow her an appearance of political independence as a reward for remaining neutral.

Especially black would be the prospect of commercial injury which England would suffer—particularly on her East and South coasts—if the Belgian and eventually the Dutch coasts fell into German hands. Indeed it is thought that even now Antwerp has taken away much of the trade of London.

It is argued also that Germany, if fixed on the Belgian-Dutch coast, must mean a perpetual risk of invasion for England, and that this urgently demands an increase of the army and a thorough strengthening of the coast defences, since the works of the South and East coasts are no longer good against modern heavy artillery. Such measures as these, however, must lead to an increase of expenditure beyond England's ability for which no Government could assume responsibility.

Also such a change in the conditions of continental power would make England unable to use her home army for the defence of India, which would become necessary eventually.

Even with this revision of the coast defences and increased efficiency of the fighting forces the homeland could not be denuded of troops, as it was in the South African War. A German invasion would always have to be reckoned with.

The fleet, however strong, could not help to remove these difficulties. Most of it was needed to protect the long route to India. Thus sufficient forces could not be kept in home waters to guard against the danger of a German invasion. Thus also, England's need of self-preservation demanded her taking part in a continental war to prevent any such predominance of Germany. The German Government should therefore declare its readiness to guarantee unconditionally the independence of Belgium and Holland, even if Belgium, driven by circumstances, should join France.

It would be out of the question to expect a victorious Germany to carry out such a demand.

If Germany refused the guarantee of Belgian and Dutch independence if demanded at the beginning of a war, it would be the duty of any British Government to range itself on the side of France in order to protect Belgium's independence.

This final aim could not be attained by merely throwing in the fleet. The land army would have to be thrown in as well.

The plans to be followed by the land army were either, after the German fleet had been destroyed, to land on the coast of Jutland or Schleswig—or, if the German fleet had not been successfully destroyed, to land on the Belgian or Dutch coasts.

German Note.

The foregoing is clearly the result of the conversations after the middle of January which took place between Colonel Barnardiston, the British Military Attaché at Brussels and The Hague, and General Ducarne, the Chief of the Belgian General Staff, on the question of military co-operation between England and Belgium in case Belgium were attacked by Germany . . . [Cf. G. & T., III, p. 187 et seq. ; Grey, *Twenty-five Years*, p. 68 et seq. ; J. A. Spender, *Life of Sir Henry Campbell-Bannerman*, II, p. 251 et seq.]

XXI. 83

Report by Captain Count von der Schulenburg, Military Attaché in London, *January* 31st, 1906

Extract.

. . . The British army leaders have for years been aiming at making the organisation for mobilisation better than it was before the Boer War. Both Brodrick and Arnold-Forster [1] have worked indefatigably at providing and perfecting the necessary war material. Though the work is not yet complete, each year means a step forward.

Naturally mobilisation will involve friction of many kinds ; the times laid down will not always be adhered to and the remount difficulty will be great. At mobilisation 102,000 fresh horses will have to be procured for the army, and these are by no means a certainty in the island, since the motor is diminishing the use of horses more and more. I assume therefore that horses for transport will be bought abroad, probably in Holland and Belgium, and that these will be sent not to England, but wherever the British army requires them.

The question so often asked for months past, ' Will England take part in a Franco-German war and use her army against Germany ? ' I answer in the affirmative.

The rapprochement with France is very popular here and will remain so in the new Liberal era.

[1] War Secretaries in the Balfour Cabinet.

If war breaks out between Germany and France, England will be all on France's side, and hatred of Germany will once again flame up brightly, with the probable result that England will take part in the war. Anything else is hardly conceivable. . . .

XXI. 79

Count von Metternich, in London, to the Chancellor, Prince von Bülow, *February 4th*, 1906

Private letter.

. . . The King told me in confidence something of Captain Allenby's [1] memorandum on his Audience with the Emperor.

The Emperor had mentioned to the Captain the French war preparations. The King said that after their experiences of last year (The Emperor: '*Which ? Fashoda was a long time ago.*') it could not be wondered at if they were trying to prepare for war.

At this point I may say that Sir Edward Grey recently told me he was hearing much from various quarters about military preparations which we were making. (The Emperor: '*False ! France is making preparations, and we not even " precautions ".*') He said he thought little of this news and substituted the word ' precautions ' for ' preparations '. Every State had a right to do this so as to be prepared for unforeseen events. [2] I replied to the Minister that I knew nothing of special military preparations on our part. We were always ready. For a standing army of 500,000 men stores of war material on a large scale were continually necessary. Since our army was always ready for striking we needed to make no sudden preparations ; whereas I had heard that ever since last summer the French had been arming energetically. (The Emperor: '*Over 200 million marks.*') Sir Edward replied that the German army certainly had the reputation of being always ready for war. . . .

[The Algeciras Conference began on January 16th, 1906. The first serious difference was over the policing of the ports. The French maintained that it should be done by France and Spain (Spain being, according to Speck von Sternburg (XXI. 103), ' entirely dependent on France both financially and also in other ways'). The German contention was that the police organisation should be made the Sultan's affair alone ; it was ' the most important point in the Conference programme, since it means re-forming the armed power of Morocco under European leadership, whilst the newly formed police troops will probably be the only reliable support of the administration ' (XXI. 99). In courting the Sultan's good graces the Germans hoped to secure the officering of these troops for themselves. Révoil, the French representative, however, stood out on this point. The Germans tried to detach Spain from her allegiance to France (Cf. G. & T.,

---

[1] Naval Attaché in Berlin.
[2] Cf. Lord Haldane, *Before the War*, p. 21 et seq.

III, p. 244) by suggesting that she should control the policing of Casablanca and Mogador, but in vain.

Germany secured unconditional support from Austria, and the Austrian delegate at Algeciras produced a proposal regarding the police question particularly at Casablanca, which was an exact expression of the German desires. (For the text cf. G. & T., III, p. 290.)]

XXI. 140
COUNT KARL VON WEDEL, IN VIENNA, TO THE GERMAN FOREIGN OFFICE, *February 5th*, 1906

Cipher telegram.

Immediately after receiving the telegrams which arrived yesterday and to-day I had a detailed conversation with Count Goluchovski. He declared to me that in the Bank question and that of the police organisation (in which he thought it possible to carry through the third point only) Austria-Hungary would go with us ' through thick and thin '. He was prepared to support throwing open the coastal trade and the ports if proposals to that effect were made by a third party, but he thought it would be unsuitable for Austria-Hungary to make them, if only to avoid arousing the suspicion that Germany was behind them. The question of the frontier zone might perhaps be settled by drawing a line from the coast to mark the boundary of the zone.

Finally the Minister told me that Count Welsersheimb was already provided with instructions, but that he would forward him to-day further precise ones.

[For the details of the Austrian scheme see G. & T., III, pp. 290–1. Sir Arthur Nicolson, the British delegate, did his best to induce M. Révoil and, through him, the French Government to accept the Austrian proposals (or, as Mr. Eyre Crowe styled them, ' the German (so-called Austrian) proposals ' (III. p. 299)) with modifications. On March 12th, however, it became evident that the French delegation meant to resist any modification of their own plan of policing the ports with officers from France and Spain only.]

XXI. 187
COUNT VON METTERNICH TO THE GERMAN FOREIGN OFFICE, *February 20th*, 1906

Cipher telegram.

Mr. Edgar Speyer told me that at a dinner he had had a conversation with the Secretary for War and the First Lord of the Admiralty about the Morocco question. Mr. Haldane had said the British Government fully intended to adopt the French standpoint and thought the French claims moderate. (The EMPEROR : ' *Very British !* ') Germany ought to produce her demands, for it seemed to him that she was keeping some in the background. If Germany brought them forward openly, an agreement would be easily arrived at.

Lord Tweedmouth [First Lord] here put in that Germany evidently wished to plant herself on the Atlantic coast of Morocco and to obtain a coaling station or a port there.

Under certain circumstances the British Government would not oppose this. He, Lord Tweedmouth, had recently discussed it with Admiral Sir John Fisher, who had said that he had no objection to Germany acquiring a port on the Atlantic coast, adding ' If we really ever had a war with Germany we should have something to bombard.' (The EMPEROR : ' *Fisher all over !* ')

XXI. 259

BARON SPECK VON STERNBURG, IN WASHINGTON, TO THE GERMAN FOREIGN OFFICE, *March 7th*, 1906

Cipher telegram.

The Secretary of State sends me the following note : ' May I ask you to transmit to the German Emperor message from the President, which is as follows :

' I have given most earnest thought to Your Majesty's comments on the suggestion contained in Mr. Root's letter of February 19th,[1] but I cannot bring myself to feel that I ought to ask France to make further concessions than the arrangement suggested in that letter would require. This being so, I would gladly drop the subject in which our traditional policy of abstention from the political affairs of Europe forbids the United States to take sides. I feel, however, that the events which led to the Conference at Algeciras forbid me to omit any effort within my power to promote a settlement of differences.

' By the request of Germany I urged France to consent to the Conference, giving her very strong assurances of my belief that a decision would be reached, consonant with an impartial view of what is most fair and most practical. The nature, the strength and the justification of these assurances may be realised by referring to the terms of Baron Sternburg's letter to me of June 28th, 1905,[2] which said : " The Emperor has requested me to tell you that, in case, during the coming Conference, differences of opinion should arise between France and Germany, he, in every case, will be ready to back up the decision which you should consider the most fair and the most practical. In doing this he wants to prove that the assistance which you have rendered to Germany has been rendered in the interest of peace alone, and without any selfish motives."

[1] Not given. Cf. Dennis, *Adventures in American Diplomacy*, pp. 502-3.
[2] Not given.

' Under these circumstances I feel bound to state to Your Majesty that I think the arrangement indicated in the above mentioned letter of February 19th is a reasonable one, and most earnestly to urge Your Majesty to accept it. I do not know whether France would accept it or not. I think she ought to do so ; I do not think that she ought to be expected to go further ; if that arrangement is made, the Conference will have resulted in an abandonment by France of her claim to the right of sole control in Morocco, answerable to the two Powers with whom she made treaties and without responsibility to the rest of the world, and she will have accepted jointly with Spain a mandate from all the Powers, under responsibility to all of them for the maintenance of equal rights and opportunities. And the due observance of these obligations will be safeguarded by having vested in another representative of all the Powers a right to have on their behalf full and complete reports of the performance of the trust, with the further right of verification and inspection.

' I feel that if this arrangement is made, Germany will have accomplished the declared object for her intervention in the affairs of Morocco and for the Conference. I feel that such an arrangement would be in very fact the evidence of the triumph of German diplomacy in this matter. . . . '

XXI. 272

RADOWITZ, AT ALGECIRAS, TO THE GERMAN FOREIGN OFFICE,
March 11th, 1906

Cipher telegram.

At to-day's session of the Commission the questions of the censors and the French share were still disputed points in spite of yesterday's full session having raised the expectation that the French now meant to give way on that main point.

The French wish the choice of one censor to be left to each of the four great Banks of England, Germany, France and Spain ; the censors' report to be communicated to their own Banks. We demanded absolutely that the four Governments should each appoint a censor out of its own National Bank and that the Signatory Powers should receive copies of the censors' reports, as being the only way of assuring the international State character of the right of control, a point of view, in our opinion, to be observed under all circumstances.

The French demand also, in return for renouncing their rights under Arts. 32 & 33 of the Loan Agreement of 1904, two founders' shares, and one extra for handing over the service of the loan and the rights of control under Arts. 15 & 16 of the same Agreement. We have definitely rejected this demand. In our opinion it could only be considered if the German group of banks was given a share in the loan service to the State Bank [of Morocco]. Then France would have four founders' shares in the joint loan combination, and Germany two, as against three to one which up to now was conceded by us. The French banks' participation in the business of advancing money would not be out of harmony with such an arrangement, as far as can be judged from here.

May we make this proposal and stick to our standpoint in other respects?

On all other points there is agreement. To-morrow the Commission is to discuss the police question, which was not touched on to-day.

The obstinacy shown to-day by the French delegate, in comparison with his attitude of yesterday, seems to be caused by the attempt to force a concession from us on the police question (giving up the appointment of an inspection officer at Casablanca) in return for giving up a share in the Bank. It is clear that since yesterday Révoil expects more reserve on the part of the new Paris Ministry, supposing he meets with a stiffer attitude here. French journalists here are urging him strongly in this sense. All my colleagues, including the British, tell me that, after our attitude at the general session, they now think the French no longer justified in sticking to the points which we described as definitely unacceptable, and have said this to Révoil.[1]

German Note. XXI. 274

On March 12th the *Lokalanzeiger* published a telegram from Algeciras, commenting drastically on Révoil's unexpectedly accommodating attitude on the 11th and the change of feeling in the other delegates. According to the clearly exaggerated report in that newspaper, the French had themselves brought about their own total isolation in the Commission. The further course of events showed that this was not at all the case. The rash report in the *Lokalanzeiger*, which the French naturally exploited cleverly and used against the German Government, contributed not a little towards the turn of events at Algeciras in Germany's disfavour. Cf. note, p. 243.

XXI. 302

BARON SPECK VON STERNBURG, IN WASHINGTON, TO THE GERMAN FOREIGN OFFICE, *March 18th,* 1906

Cipher telegram.

I have just discussed your telegram of March 16th [2] with the President. He replied that he could only adhere to his point and that, in spite of the declarations he regarded the

[1] Cf. G. & T., III, pp. 297–8.　　　　[2] Not given.

Austro-Hungarian proposal as a foolish one and not in consonance with the principles of the Conference.[1] The seed it
would sow already contained that evil ; the plant which would
spring from it in a few years could bear only evil fruits. The
proposal paved the way for spheres of interest which might
later on develop into possession. He quoted examples in
history and said he could not understand how the Powers could
support such a proposal, and he doubted whether France would
accept it. He said that his proposal [2] was a much better one
and paid full attention to the international character. He had
not the slightest intention of countering the Austrian proposal
with a fresh one, and if it was accepted he would agree to it.
Only in the event of the Conference coming to nothing would he
see cause to publish the correspondence between himself and
certain Powers on the subject in order to demonstrate the part
the United States had played.

I then had a conversation with the Secretary of State [3] who
also sharply attacked the Austrian proposal in spite of the
declarations, adding that the United States would abstain from
making proposals.

With regard to Austria's representations here regarding
Germany's exorbitant demands, the President said that these
were very emphatic and expressed very definitely. I hear in
confidence that to-day the Secretary of State described Germany's
attitude at the Conference as pettifogging and unworthy of a
great nation, and that Germany had quite lost her original strong
position at Algeciras and was on the point of losing the world's
confidence.[4]

XXI. 309
THE CHANCELLOR, PRINCE VON BÜLOW, TO BARON SPECK VON STERNBURG, *March 19th*, 1906

Telegram.

By your latest communications I see with astonishment that
it is suspected in America that Germany is working for her
own advantage and would not shrink from a war with France
to attain her own private ends. Actually Germany is thinking
neither of special advantages nor of war. The Emperor has
never dreamed of war on account of Morocco nor would the
German people understand it. Our only object was the principle
of the ' open door ', i.e., to secure equal trading rights in Morocco,
and we proposed the Conference because it seemed to us the
best way of settling the Morocco question suitably and peacefully. Germany has no more object in setting up spheres of

---

[1] Cf. G. & T., III, p. 313.   [2] Cf. p. 244.   [3] Mr. Root.
[4] Cf. Dennis, *Adventures in American Diplomacy*, p. 505.

interest than most of the other Signatory States. We therefore respect the principle underlying the American proposal,—
co-operation by French and Spanish officers in fairly equal
shares at each port. We would adhere to that proposal at the
Conference, as it includes this mixed system as well as the
Inspector-General—eventually without military powers—as
already conceded in principle by the French. We renounce
all individual points, in order thus to avoid blurring the broad
lines as has hitherto appeared to be the case to some extent.
In consideration of the various great political successes won by
German-American co-operation during the last two years—in
localising the Russo-Japanese war, preservation of international
order, and finally in restoring peace—I think that maintenance
of the mutual trust between Berlin and Washington and immediate removal of all cause of misunderstanding are more important
than the whole matter of Morocco.[1]

XXI. 311

BARON SPECK VON STERNBURG TO THE GERMAN FOREIGN OFFICE,
March 21st, 1906

Cipher telegram. Extract.

Yesterday I found the President in very high spirits. He
said : ' Inform His Majesty the Emperor of my heartiest congratulations on this epoch-making political success at Algeciras.[2]
His Majesty's policy in the Morocco question has been masterly
from beginning to end. The Emperor has done all he wished
to do at the Conference, and the world must be deeply grateful
to him for it. Tell His Majesty that I shall forward to him
through you my congratulations in writing.'

Even though the foregoing does not appear to agree with
the facts,[3] I am firmly convinced that the words spoken by the
President came entirely from the heart. . . .

[The last meeting of the Conference was on March 31st, 1906. For the
Acte Général d'Algeciras see *British Parliamentary Papers, Accounts and
Papers,* (1906) CXXXVI, (Cd. 3087) p. 331 et seq.

The main result in Europe of the Conference was an increased suspicion
of German aims and motives, and a tightening of the bonds between England and France. The American President also became more friendly
towards England and towards King Edward in particular. Cf. Lee, *King
Edward VII*, II, 437.

On April 4th, 1906, Baron von Holstein, partly as the result of intrigues,
found himself obliged to resign from the German Foreign Office. (Cf.

---

[1] Cf. Grey, *Twenty-five Years*, pp. 112, 121 ; Dennis, *Adventures in
American Diplomacy*, p. 504 et seq. ; G. & T., III, pp. 312 et seq. ; p. 315.
[2] Cf. Dennis, *Adventures in American Diplomacy*, p. 505.
[3] Cf. Lee, *King Edward VII*, II, p. 362.

G. & T., III, p. 322, and Mr. Eyre Crowe's Minute, p. 334 ; Wilson, *War Guilt*, p. 106.)]

Minute by the EMPEROR to a despatch of April 17th, 1907, by Stumm, Chargé d'Affaires in London. XXI. 567.

Herr von Holstein in his clever way twisted my perfectly definite orders and arrangements with the Chancellor in such a manner that the opposite was the final outcome.[1] *He constantly stirred up the poison against France anew and pressed so heavily on the Chancellor*[2] *that the latter in his garden to my great astonishment repeatedly asked me the same question—whether I wished or desired war with France! Whereas my instructions to Madrid and Richthofen said expressly : ' Algeciras is to be the stepping-stone of the beginning of the agreement between France and Germany !'*

German Note. XXI. 320

In April, 1906, General Palizyn, the Chief of the Russian General Staff, came to Paris, and on the 21st a Protocol was signed, by which France and Russia agreed ' to mobilise all their forces immediately and simultaneously' at the first news of a German mobilisation.   Count Khevenhüller, the Austro-Hungarian Ambassador in Paris, stated that Palizyn was then strongly urged by the Chief of the French General Staff to strengthen the Russian garrisons on the German and Austrian frontiers, since otherwise France could not carry out her obligations.   (Cf. report by Lieut.-Col. von Bülow, German Military Attaché in Vienna, May 22nd, 1906 ; also Wilson, *War Guilt*, p. 106.)

---

[1] Cf. G. & T., III, p. 365.
[2] At the time of Holstein's fall the Chancellor had a breakdown from overwork.

CHAPTER XX

MACEDONIAN REFORM PROPOSALS, 1907–8

[Knowing that the Liberal Government in England was continuing to press for reforms in Macedonia and that Russia was indifferent about them, Aehrenthal hoped in the spring of 1907 to induce the Russians and perhaps the French also to stand by whilst he took measures to wreck any hope of their being carried out. This of course would loosen the Anglo-Russian entente. Fortunately however Isvolsky refused to do anything without consulting England, and this was the first open sign of the disagreement between him and Aehrenthal, which in the end, in combination with the Austrian determination to chastise Servia, was one of the more direct ' causes of the War '.

The Servian Government produced a scheme for linking Servia with the Adriatic by a railway. There was deep-seated hostility in Austria against Servia, and Baron Aehrenthal, the Austrian Foreign Minister, conceived a rival scheme. (Cf. G. & T., V, p. 321 et seq. ; H. Wickham Steed, *Through Thirty Years*, I, p. 269 ; Brandenburg, p. 303 et seq.)]

XXV. 289

COUNT KARL VON WEDEL, IN VIENNA, TO THE CHANCELLOR, PRINCE VON BÜLOW, *January 21st*, 1907

To-day during my conversation with Baron Aehrenthal, the Servian railway scheme, and with it the scheme for a so-called Trans-Balkanic railway, were discussed. The Minister, who does not appear to have yet given much attention to these questions, said that there were two plans under consideration. One concerned the Servian Timok Valley line from Nish to a point South of Mitrovitza and so on to the Adriatic. The other, which found more sympathy here, contemplated connecting the Servian railway system with the Bosnian at Vishegrad, whereby Servia's communication with the Adriatic would run through Dalmatia. Austria would then construct the necessary link—Priboi-Mitrovitza—through the Sanjak of Novi-Bazar. In that case he admitted that there would be a great drawback, in that the Bosnian railways were of the narrow and not the normal gauge, which would mean transferring goods at Mitrovitza.

XXII. 410

COUNT KARL VON WEDEL, IN VIENNA, TO THE GERMAN FOREIGN OFFICE, *April 30th*, 1907

Cipher telegram.

Before departing for Berlin to-day Baron Aehrenthal told me he wished to talk to Your Highness about the Macedonian judicial reforms. England was beginning to press harder and harder in this direction, and he considered it very desirable that the Powers who pursued a conservative policy in the Balkans and favoured Turkish integrity should combine together. Amongst these he counted first of all Germany, and we must win Russia and France over to the same object.

Austria-Hungary could not bear the burden by herself, which would mean that he would have to pursue a different policy in Macedonia.

I have thought fit to prepare Your Highness by informing you of what the Baron said to me.

[The foregoing should be compared with G. & T., V, p. 204. Baron Aehrenthal denied in London that he had any such aim.]

XXII. 411

COUNT KARL VON WEDEL, IN VIENNA, TO THE CHANCELLOR, PRINCE VON BÜLOW, *June 3rd*, 1907

Very confidential.

In strict confidence Baron Aehrenthal told me he had had an unpleasant experience. I should remember, he said, that he had mentioned to me that he could not carry out reforms in Macedonia by himself, especially those of the Justiciary, and that he needed the support of those Powers who, being equally interested with Austria-Hungary, were pursuing a conservative policy in the Balkans, based on the maintenance of the *status quo* ; he meant Germany first of all and then France and Russia.

He had spoken in this sense during his stay in Berlin [1] and had then gone on to make enquiries in St. Petersburg. The sole object of these was to ascertain how far Russia would be inclined, in carrying out reforms in the Justiciary, to draw the limits rendered advisable out of consideration for Turkey and beyond which they did not wish to be dragged—he had, of course, been thinking of England and Italy.

M. Isvolsky had returned a very ambiguous answer.

Now it had transpired that this enquiry had come to the ears of the British Cabinet. King Edward [2] had said twice to Count Mensdorff that he greatly regretted that Austria-Hungary

[1] May 1st and 2nd, 1907.   [2] Cf. G. & T., V, p. 204.

showed such mistrust of England, who had always supported the Austrian Government's Balkan policy. Sir Edward Grey and Sir Charles Hardinge had spoken in similar terms to the Austrian Ambassador. In fact, they were very much annoyed with him in London.

He did not know how this had come about, but was inclined to assume that M. Poklevsky, the very unreliable First Secretary in the Russian Embassy in London, who had been on leave in St. Petersburg shortly before and was intimate with M. Isvolsky, had perhaps been told about it by him and had committed a grave indiscretion.

He, Aehrenthal, would have it declared in London that he had never aimed at England the communication which was imputed to him. Count Berchtold [1] had also been instructed to ask M. Isvolsky for an explanation and to request him to speak in the same sense in London.

Baron Aehrenthal added that the excitement in England was an obvious proof of a bad conscience.

But, as he had always told me, he had never properly trusted M. Isvolsky. He had long known that one could say nothing in Paris which was not immediately repeated in London ; but this, if it was not due to an indiscretion on M. Poklevsky's part, showed that one must be prepared for the same danger from St. Petersburg, and this was to be regretted. (MÜHLBERG : '*We unfortunately have had to assume this for a long time.*')

[On August 15th, 1907, King Edward ended his visit to the Emperor William at Wilhelmshöhe and travelled to Ischl to visit the Emperor Francis Joseph. (Cf. Lee, *King Edward VII*, II, p. 549.)]

XXIV. 7

THE CHANCELLOR, PRINCE VON BÜLOW, AT WILHELMSHÖHE, TO THE GERMAN FOREIGN OFFICE, *August 15th*, 1907

Cipher telegram. Extract.

. . . The position in Macedonia seemed to cause anxiety to Sir Charles Hardinge. He mentioned an intention to propose to the Vienna Cabinet that the Powers should make joint representations in Athens regarding the despatch of Greek bands into Macedonia.[2] I replied that in the East we should agree absolutely with all measures considered necessary by our Austrian ally and Russia, the friend of ourselves and Austria-Hungary. It would be a genuine satisfaction to us if the point of view of these two Powers, who had agreed on the Mürsteg

[1] Austrian Ambassador in St. Petersburg.
[2] Cf. G. & T., V, p. 119.

programme [of October 2nd, 1903],[1] met with the approval of the other Powers, especially England.

XXIV. 8

COUNT BROCKDORFF-RANTZAU, CHARGÉ D'AFFAIRES IN VIENNA,
    TO THE GERMAN FOREIGN OFFICE, *August 17th*, 1907
Cipher telegram. Extract.

. . . At Ischl [2] the question of disarmament was not touched upon, but both King Edward and the Under-Secretary declared regarding the unrest in Morocco that France would respect the Act of Algeciras to the fullest extent.

Conditions in Macedonia were discussed in detail. Baron Aehrenthal referred to the official *communiqué* in the *Fremdenblatt* [3] of August 16th which you know of, and added that he could affirm with satisfaction that England really appeared to have decided to alter her Balkan policy. Sir Charles Hardinge had given him an absolutely binding assurance [4] that the London Cabinet desired a peaceful development and maintenance of the *status quo* in the Balkans.

Your Highness' declaration to Sir Charles Hardinge seems to have made a visible impression on him, namely that we two consent absolutely to all measures in the East which Russia and Austria think suitable ; he said he considered it highly important to inform the Imperial Government at once and in detail of all steps which he would be called upon to take in the Balkans.

He meant at once to address a despatch jointly with Russia to the civil agents, extending the interpretation of Art. 3 of the Mürsteg programme in the sense that the Entente Powers contemplated producing not a temporary peace, but *permanent* orderly conditions in Macedonia.

[Article 3. Aussitôt qu'un apaisement du pays sera constaté, demander au Gouvernement ottoman une modification dans la délimitation territoriale des unités administratives en vue d'un groupement plus régulier des différentes nationalités. (Cf. G. & T., V, p. 212.)]

Baron Aehrenthal expects a good result from this despatch, which he will communicate to the Cabinets of Athens, Belgrade and Sofia. He said that the Greeks especially were disturbers of the peace, and that any violent modification of national *groupements* could not be permitted.

To-morrow Count Berchtold will receive instructions to make suitable proposals to M. Isvolsky ; meanwhile Baron Aehrenthal

---

[1] Cf. G. & T., V, pp. 49–66 ; H. Wickham Steed, *Through Thirty Years*, I, 209 et seq. ; Lee, *King Edward VII*, II, p. 266.
[2] Cf. G. & T., V, p. 208.   [3] Cf. G. & T., V, p. 213.
[4] Cf. Sir C. Hardinge's account, G. & T., V, p. 210.

begs that the foregoing be kept secret until he has assured himself of Russia's agreement.

[Germany was on the horns of a dilemma. As a European Power she had to be in favour of reforms in the Turkish Empire ; as a friend of Turkey she could not afford to bring pressure on the Sultan and his advisers.]

XXII. 421

TSCHIRSCHKY, OF THE GERMAN FOREIGN OFFICE, TO PRINCE VON BÜLOW, AT NORDERNEY, *August* 30*th*, 1907

The Ambassadors of the Entente Powers in Constantinople recently informed their colleagues of the Austro-Russian proposals for reforms of the Justiciary in Macedonia.[1] Among the Turks there is already observable violent opposition to the scheme, which is still under examination by the Powers. According to Herr von Kiderlen the Sultan shows special personal dislike of it. The Turkish Chargé d'Affaires here has, under direct orders from the Sultan and the Porte, repeatedly and urgently requested that the Emperor shall show fresh proof of his genuine friendship for the Sultan by influencing the Powers in favour of abandoning the plans for reforming the Justiciary.

I should advise against the Emperor granting this request, in order that His Majesty may not be interested in a step which is almost hopeless. A complete refusal of the Turkish request would, moreover, greatly prejudice our relations towards the Sultan and the Porte. In order at least to show our good will to Turkey, we might consider the following démarche with the Cabinets of Vienna and St. Petersburg :

' The Sultan has repeatedly and urgently requested us that the Emperor should urge the Powers to abandon the plan for reforming the Justiciary, on the grounds that he has already initiated these reforms and will himself see to their being carried out. He is therefore obliged to refuse the step contemplated by the Powers.

' The standpoint of the Imperial Government continues to be that they agree absolutely with all measures considered necessary by Austria-Hungary and Russia in the Near East. They therefore intend to place no difficulties in the way of the reforms of the Justiciary proposed by the Entente Powers. The Imperial Government believe themselves to be in full agreement with your Governments when, in the interests of the Sultan's authority and of maintaining the *status quo* in the Balkans, they state that it is desirable that the reforms should be carried out as far as possible in conjunction with the Porte and without the use of coercion. The Turkish declarations which are before

[1] Cf. G. & T., V, p. 196 et seq.

them leave no doubt that the Sultan is obstinately determined on opposition all the more since he has himself already started on the reforms. Therefore the Imperial Government suggest that it might be desirable, out of proper respect for the Sultan's sovereign rights and in order to avoid a conflict with Turkey, for the representatives of the Entente Powers first to enter into contact confidentially with the Porte so as to hear its views on the desirability and practicability of the planned reforms in their relation to the financial situation in Macedonia.'

Postscript for Vienna only :

' The Imperial Government would be ready in the meanwhile to work in Constantinople in the sense of Baron Aehrenthal's suggestion ; he explained on December 3rd, 1906, to Count Wedel that it would be desirable for Hilmi Pacha to come forward on his own initiative with suggestions for improving the Macedonian Justiciary.'

Herr von Kiderlen has been informed accordingly and telegraphs that in his opinion the démarche in Vienna and St. Petersburg will be regarded in Constantinople as a great service of friendship and that if it succeeds it will do our position good there, especially as the Turkish Government would see in it a new proof of our influence in the councils of the Powers.

I beg Your Highness to telegraph whether the Ambassadors in Vienna and St. Petersburg may be instructed in the foregoing sense.

XXII. 423

PRINCE VON BÜLOW, AT NORDERNEY, TO THE GERMAN FOREIGN OFFICE, *August 31st,* 1907

Cipher telegram. Extract.

I agree to the démarche with the Cabinets of Vienna and St. Petersburg. I think it desirable, however, that the telegrams sent there be dealt with by our representatives cautiously and delicately. Otherwise Russia and Austria might group themselves in the East with England, France and Italy against us. . . .

[The Anglo-Russian Convention of August 31st, 1907 (cf. G. & T., IV, p. 618 et seq. ; Lee, *King Edward VII*, II, p. 571 ; H. Wickham Steed, *Through Thirty Years*, I, p. 255), was taken by the Germans to be the work mainly of M. Isvolsky, the Russian Foreign Minister. Writing on January 16th, 1908, Count von Pourtalès, German Ambassador in St. Petersburg, said : ' In conversation with my colleagues here I find it generally thought that the comparatively quick completion of the Anglo-Russian Convention was very largely due to the Russian Minister's British sympathies, and one may assume that in other matters besides those included in the Convention M. Isvolsky desires to seek an understanding with England.' (XXV. 385.)]

German Note.

Baron Aehrenthal met Signor Tittoni, the Italian Foreign Minister, at Desio, on July 15th and on the Semmering on August 23rd, 1907. (Cf. H. Wickham Steed, *Through Thirty Years*, I, p. 265.)

XXII. 427

Baron von Ritter zu Grünstein, in Rome, to Prince von Bülow, *September 7th*, 1907

From a reliable source I have learnt the following about Baron Aehrenthal's meetings with Signor Tittoni at Desio and on the Semmering :

M. Zinovieff, the Russian Ambassador in Constantinople and the originator of the Macedonian reform proposals, from the first desired co-operation by all the Great Powers in the work of reform. But Austria had made difficulties and caused delays and postponements. At the time of the Desio meeting Austria's opposition was still to the fore. It was not till shortly before the Semmering meeting that the understanding between Austria and Russia came into being.

It almost looks as though at Desio Signor Tittoni played the part of mediator and brought about the change in the Austrian attitude towards the Macedonian question. If this is so, the Italian Government may have played the ' good boy ' with England also, who apparently has long wished to quicken the pace of the Macedonian reforms. The attitude of the Italian Press strengthens me in this opinion, for it cannot say emphatically enough that England has been first in insisting on the reforms with the other Great Powers.

My informant said that at any rate Italy's prompt agreement with the Austrian and Russian proposals would genuinely hasten on the Macedonian reforms.

The main result of the Semmering meeting was the change in public feeling in Italy, which would not henceforth be so easily excited against Austria as heretofore. This has been shown in an interview with the Republican and Irredentist deputy, Barzilai, who spoke in favour of removing all differences between Italy and Austria. Barzilai was born at Trieste and is one of the keenest champions of Irredentism. The Press thinks itself therefore free to mark a noticeable change in the attitude of the extreme Left towards Austria. My informant added that before the Semmering meeting such expressions by a Republican deputy would have been impossible.

The new friendship had to stand its first test a few days ago when news came of the excesses of the Slovenes at Trieste, where the Italian Vice-Consul was injured. The Italian Press has maintained a thoroughly dignified attitude, saying that there was no intention to hurt the Italian Consul. He had got quite by accident into the crowd in his motor and was hurt by a chance missile as were others.

Signor Tittoni also looks at the future with confidence, as I gathered from his expressions. He said England had already agreed in principle to the reform proposals when Sir Charles Hardinge met Baron Aehrenthal at Ischl. Count Goluchovski had always refused to consider participation by all the Great Powers in the work of reform.

This time there had been no mention of Albania, since there existed earlier arrangements for maintaining the *status quo.* Nor had there been talk of a meeting between King Victor Emanuel and the Emperor Francis Joseph.

[Sir N. O'Conor, writing from Constantinople on December 25th, to Sir Edward Grey (cf. G. & T., V, p. 221), said : ' . . . I do not as yet know what answer the Government have made to your proposals (for more effective control for the gendarmerie in Macedonia and the reduction of the Turkish garrison there), but I have not the least doubt that the Austrians will reply—at the very least—that the proposal is premature and that it would not be well to overload the coach while we are driving on the judicial path. Baron d'Erenthal takes his cue from Berlin far more than Goluchovsky, and the Austro-Russian understanding is being proportionately weakened. The Kaiser will not be persuaded to worry the Sultan so long as he gains such distinct advantages by his present complacent policy, or at any rate before He sees a distinct gain either by an understanding with us or in the shape of some positive *quid pro quo* . . .']

XXII. 477

BARON VON MARSCHALL, IN CONSTANTINOPLE, TO PRINCE VON BÜLOW, *December 24th,* 1907

Extract.

. . . Recognition that the reforms are useless [1] is visibly gaining ground. Here and there the full truth is becoming clearer that the set-back in Macedonia is connected with the reforms ; in other words, the reform action is the cause and the sanguinary racial conflicts are the effect. I have always said this. (The EMPEROR : ' *Yes, for years !* ') One need only examine the interconnection of the facts. The Bulgarians, Servians and Greeks in Macedonia look on themselves as the heirs in the event of a collapse of the Turkish domination. On ethnographical grounds each of these populations claim the greater part of the country. Whilst the Turkish domination stood fast this heritage idea was a dream for the future, similar to the French passion for revenge. The fight was carried on mainly with statistics, each party proving that the majority of the population belonged to its own race. In accordance with the custom of the country there were murders and outrages, and

[1] Cf. G. & T., V, p. 223.

bands were formed ; but these were only sporadic in character. Not until attacks on the Turkish domination began did the idea of its collapse leave the domain of dreams for that of more or less near realisation.   Then the Christian-international breaking of heads became a system of practical politics with a conscious object.   For in the event of the Turkish domination collapsing each of the rival nations means to secure for itself the largest possible ethnographical zone.   There is no doubt that the reform action of the Powers has shattered the Turkish domination, first through the civil agents, then by the international gendarmerie, and finally by the financial control.   The struggle became bloodier and more embittered.[1]   Now comes the reform of justice !   Turkish justice may be bad, and here and there its effects have been horrible.   Now the idea is to set aside the Turkish judicial authority in favour of arrangements bound to produce disorganisation and to upset the whole of the law and criminal justice above all.   Its effect on the fighting Balkan populations can be foreseen. . . .

The distaste of some of my colleagues for recent developments in the Conference of Ambassadors seems to me well-founded.   I see in them a serious political danger.   When they touch on a political question the Ambassadors naturally require a lead from instructions from home.   With this guidance we have so far regularly agreed over very difficult questions after full discussion of the essentials.   Then is the moment for the Cabinets to exchange their ideas.   This time, however, England supported by Russia has introduced in the midst of the discussion of essentials certain questions of detail coming from the Cabinets and has brought pressure to bear, thus making it impossible to discuss what is essential at the conference.   If it is England's intention to establish the principle of *avilir, puis démolir*, she could have found no better means of doing so.   Now this would do great political harm ; for our conferences have hitherto been a most important factor in producing agreement amongst the Powers themselves about very delicate and complicated matters.   (The EMPEROR :   ' *Splendid.*')

[On December 18th, 1907, Sir Edward Grey addressed a Circular Note to the Powers demanding more effective control of the Gendarmerie.   (Cf. *Brit. Parl. Papers, Accounts and Papers* (1908), CXXV [Cd. 3958], pp. 589–90).   The Powers were very reluctant to act upon it (G. & T., V, p. 226 et seq.).

In a letter to Sir N. O'Conor on February 10th, 1908, Sir Edward Grey said :   ' It appeared to me, even before I got your private letter, that Austria had played the mean game of driving a bargain with the Porte in

---

[1] Cf. Blue Books.   *Turkey*, No. 1 (1907) [Cd. 3454] and No. 3 (1908) [Cd. 4076].

favour of her railway scheme at the expense of Macedonian reform. It seems now that we are to be in the position of having all the odium at Constantinople of pressing reforms, while other members of the Concert curry favour with the Porte by obstructing them. . . .' (Cf. G. & T., V, p. 228.)

On February 18th, 1908, Sir N. O'Conor reported from St. Petersburg that there was strong feeling in Russia that ' Russia should now abandon her co-operation with Austria-Hungary and range herself on the side of the Western Powers in the question of Macedonian reforms' and that there was ' a deep-rooted conviction that a continued co-operation with Austria-Hungary and Germany—for these two Powers are considered as identical—in Balkan questions must inevitably lead to a sacrifice of Slav interests and that Russia would then have played the unworthy part of a dupe.' (Cf. G. & T., V, p. 232 ; H. Wickham Steed, *Through Thirty Years*, I, pp. 270, 290.)]

XXII. 513

Baron von Marschall, in Constantinople, to the German Foreign Office, *February 17th*, 1908

Cipher telegram. Extract.

. . . Sir E. Grey's object is quite different from Baron Aehrenthal's. He wishes, after handing in the Note about ' delays and modifications in the control of justice', to speak under the condition that the British proposals regarding increase of the gendarmerie and decrease of the Turkish troops are to be adopted. So in British eyes the Note about the Justiciary is merely a weapon against the Turks, to induce them to enter the path which Baron Aehrenthal and M. Isvolsky do not desire to tread. Sir N. O'Conor is already working in this sense. He says he is less uncompromising on the justice question than his colleagues, and he presses for the suggested measures all the more strenuously. . . .

[On February 25th, 1908, Sir Edward Grey stated in the House of Commons that the British Government would continue to work in concert with the other Powers for Macedonian reforms. (Cf. G. & T., V, p. 348, 234 ; Lee, *King Edward VII*, II, p. 624 et seq. ; Grey, *Twenty-five Years*, p. 172 et seq. ; H. Wickham Steed, *Through Thirty Years*, I, Chapter VII.) He proposed that in future the Governor of Macedonia should be a Christian.]

XXV. 388

Count Monts, in Rome, to the Chancellor, Prince von Bülow, *February 29th*, 1908

To-day Signor Tittoni [1] spoke about Sir Edward Grey's latest utterance as follows :

It is much to be regretted that just now when there is already so much political unrest the British Minister, by his new idea

---

[1] Italian Foreign Minister. Cf. H. Wickham Steed, *Through Thirty Years*, I, pp. 246–8.

of a Governor-General, is diverting the diplomatic arrangement about Macedonia from its set course. (The EMPEROR : ' *Correct.*') It is possible that internal politics first and foremost were the cause of Sir Edward's speech. One should not forget that Balkan sympathisers exercise great influence inside the body of the Government's supporters. Mainly to please these the Minister spoke as he did. For even in England no one can doubt that Turkey will never consent to a Governor except under strong coercion. The fact however is that England having brought forward this new idea involves serious risk to the Concert of Europe which has been maintained with so much effort.

Finally Signor Tittoni compared the fresh British project with the disarmament idea advanced by England.[1] Then as now considerations of internal politics (The EMPEROR: ' *Not altogether.*') gave the impetus for an act which in the end turned out to be a magnificent piece of political bluff. From another point of view it was questionable whether it was decent or good policy to subordinate international affairs so recklessly to the needs of internal politics and to play with fire, considering how critical was the present Balkan situation. (The EMPEROR : ' *Good.*')

[During King Edward's visit to the Tsar at Reval in June, 1908 (cf. G. & T., V, p. 232 et seq. ; Lee, p. 591 et seq.), the question of Macedonian reforms was fully discussed between Isvolsky, the Russian Foreign Minister, and Sir Charles Hardinge. (Cf. G. & T., V, p. 238 ; H. Wickham Steed, *Through Thirty Years*, I, p. 277.

For an account of the Constitutional movement in Turkey, which culminated in the Young Turkish Revolution and ended in Abdul Hamid's deposition in April, 1909, cf. G. & T., V, pp. 249, 268, 313.

On July 23rd, 1908, the Council of Ministers met and forced the Sultan to re-grant the Constitution of 1876. (Cf. Vol. I, p. 20 et seq.) The Sultan's inner Camarilla fled for their lives. (Cf. G. & T., V, pp. 250–1.)

The Emperor William's attitude towards these events is exemplified by the following Minute to a despatch of July 27th, 1908, (XXV. 577) :]

The EMPEROR : *La Turquie à elle même! That has always been the basic idea of my policy. It is being fulfilled at last with the summoning of the Turkish Parliament, the members of which will, I hope, take in hand the regulation of conditions in Turkey and do the ' Reforms ' themselves, so that once for all a stop will be put to the longings of intriguing European Great Powers to intervene. It is just as good for the Turkish Christians as the Musulmans, and it is what I have always tried for. I am very much pleased with the solution.*[2]

[Sir Edward Grey's declaration of February 25th, 1908,[3] and the whole movement for reform in Macedonia incensed Baron Aehrenthal (cf. G. & T.,

---

[1] Cf. p. 326.　　　[2] Cf. G. & T., V, p. 310.　　　[3] Cf. p. 259.

V, p. 234 ; H. Wickham Steed, I, p. 241), since it interfered with his scheme for a railway through the Sanjak of Novi-Bazar.[1] (Cf. G. & T., V, p. 238 et seq.) In July he said that he was ' firmly determined to adhere to the principle of non-intervention in anything that happened in Turkey . . . Let us ', he said, ' go forward calmly, and will you beg the Chancellor in my name to influence the German Press, so that the papers may not underline the diplomatic difficulties in which events in Turkey have doubtless placed England and Russia ; it would be very dangerous and would give rise to most perfidious misrepresentation of German and Austrian policy. If our Press declared that all reforms are now super-fluous, it would again be said that we had agreed secretly with the Sultan and had promised *sub rosa* to relieve him of anxiety regarding the reform question in return for commercial advantages.' (XXV. 575.)]

XXV. 575

COUNT BROCKDORFF-RANTZAU, IN VIENNA, TO THE GERMAN FOREIGN OFFICE, *July 27th*, 1908

Cipher telegram. Extract.

. . . The Minister has already given the necessary orders to the Press here. At the end of our conversation he said he was quite determined to reject the British proposal to deal with the reform proposals between the Cabinets, and to insist on its being entrusted to the Ambassadors in Constantinople ; this would be the best way of sparing the Sultan's feelings to the utmost, which was urgently necessary.

SCHOEN, OF THE GERMAN FOREIGN OFFICE, TO COUNT BROCK-DORFF-RANTZAU, *July 28th*, 1908

Telegram.

We fully share Baron Aehrenthal's point of view. The Press shall be influenced in his sense as far as possible.

[In the second week of March, 1908, the Sultan gave in to the demand for an extension of the European mandate. There was however little prospect of his sudden compliance having any effect, since the Young Turk agitation was near the bursting point and, in fact, became a revolution in the third week of July, when all idea of reform had to be abandoned.]

[1] Of this H. Wickham Steed wrote : ' At the end of January, Aehrenthal's Novi-Bazar railway scheme had destroyed the Concert of Europe ' (*Through Thirty Years*, I, p. 277).

CHAPTER XXI

GERMANY, AMERICA AND CHINA, 1907–8

[In October, 1907, the Chinese Government, encouraged by the German representative in Peking, approached President Roosevelt on the subject of a German-American arrangement to protect China against Japan. The German Emperor was attracted by the idea, being under the impression that President Roosevelt would do anything that he asked him to do. Bülow was aware that the President was not entirely a free agent in foreign affairs, but he was not averse to suggesting that Germany and the United States should interpret the 'open door' principle in their own way, virtually shutting it in the face of other nations. The scheme was not acceptable to the Americans, who were making their own arrangements for an Agreement with Japan.]

XXV. 72

BARON SPECK VON STERNBURG, IN WASHINGTON, TO PRINCE VON BÜLOW, *September 9th*, 1907

Secret.

At President Roosevelt's desire I went to see him on August 10th for a detailed conversation about Japan and the Far East. After discussing the Japanese question I said that for an indefinite time there could be no question of war between Japan and the United States, if the President could keep the anti-Japanese outbursts in the West of America under control.

German Note.

Ever since the summer of 1906 there had been strong feeling, especially in California, against the Japanese immigration, which was getting out of control.

Japan was doubtless aiming at control of the Pacific Ocean, extension of her territory southwards, and domination in China. (The EMPEROR: '*Correct.*') Symptoms of this were observable directly after the war with China, but aggressive action on Japan's part was not to be expected until she had settled her large international questions, recovered from the heavy consequences of the Russian war and was ready again for another great war. Leading military authorities considered that many years must pass (The EMPEROR: '*?*') before Japan could be ready for such a war. They said that the great danger of

Japanese expansion would affect not only the United States but also Japan's allies in an equal degree—England and France. His Majesty the Emperor had for years recognised this danger which threatened the Christian nations of the world and had urged them strongly (The EMPEROR: ' Aha! ') to forget old quarrels and combine closely together. By this means alone would these Powers be able to destroy the enemy of the world. Anyone who remained neutral and withdrew from this combination would be responsible if the Christian Powers were destroyed. (The EMPEROR: ' Good.')

At this the President handed me in strict confidence the naval programme prepared by Admiral Evans and begged me to study it and give my opinion. After perusing the document I said that if anti-Japanese outbursts in connection with the despatch of the fleet could be stopped this ought not to irritate Japan and might increase the fighting efficiency of the American Navy by 50 per cent.

German Note.

Early in July, 1907, the Press announced that a strong American squadron was to be sent to the Pacific. This did not take place until after the turn of the year.

The President replied that with regard to the Navy an insoluble problem was before him—the lack of a fortified harbour in the Far East as a base in the event of a great war with Japan. Even the best fleet must fail if after an engagement it had no such harbour to repair to.

He then mentioned the attitude of China in the event of the great war in the future, and I referred to conversations which I had had in 1884 in Washington with Liang Cheng. He was now China's cleverest diplomat and when I was in Peking he was first favourite with the Empress and continued his intimacy with myself. He was now returning to take up a post of influence in Peking. Whilst here he had seen through Japan's intentions regarding China and had discussed them thoroughly with me ; which led me to believe that this important official would make every effort to see that his policy of suspicion of Japan should be followed. It was not impossible that he might succeed in preventing Japan from combining with China, or China from remaining neutral in the event of such a war. The death of the Empress-mother and the internal unrest resulting from it would constitute a danger.

The President mentioned the possibility of a Japanese invasion of the United States in the event of a war. At the close of our conversation, after a long silence he spoke as follows :

' On my return from Cuba with the Cavalry Brigade I took

you straight to Montauk Camp for a thorough inspection of all the forces. I remember your words, " Even the best racehorse will surely fail in a big race for the want of thorough training." Since those days you know that it has been my main effort to introduce the best system of training in the Army. I have failed. I tried to force the system, and what was the result ? The soldier deserted because he refused to subject. (The EMPEROR : ' *Anglo-Saxon ! It is the same in England.*') If Japan invades America using powerful forces, our army will first suffer a crushing blow. This lesson will produce a thorough military reorganisation ; (The EMPEROR : ' *That is no good in a war.*') after this has been achieved, Japan's army will be annihilated if she has left it in America, and America will take her revenge. (The EMPEROR : ' *Very optimistic.*') I still have sincere confidence in our people.—I have discussed with you the deeply confidential sides of these great questions of vast importance, because in the history of America no foreign representative has ever held the trust of her people as you do, and in the future no foreign representative can hold this trust. (The EMPEROR : ' *Bravo.*') This is owing to peculiar circumstances. The advice you gave us during and after the war between China and Japan has in all cases proved to be the best advice the country received. I remember your letter to me from Manchuria clearly pointing out the qualities of the Japanese army, and your letter from Talienwan where you closely studied the highly important tasks of the Japanese navy there. They have not been forgotten.'

On the following day the President sent for Root, the Secretary of State, and Taft, the War Minister, in order to settle on the decisions based on his conversations with me. (The EMPEROR : ' *Bravo, Sternburg ! telegraph my thanks to him.*')

XXV. 81

COUNT VON REX, IN PEKING, TO PRINCE VON BÜLOW,
December 7th, 1907

Extract. Secret.

. . . In October I received private and reliable information that the Chinese representatives in Berlin and Washington had actually been instructed to sound the respective Governments as to an alliance. I now find that this instruction was merely to report on the general feeling in Germany and America towards China with reference to the possibility of an alliance. . . .

The object best worth our while to strive for seems to me to be the following :

1. A treaty between Germany, America and China guaranteeing China's integrity (The EMPEROR : ' *Right ! I suggested*

this a year ago.') and granting the first named Powers compensation in the form of certain trading rights to be kept secret. (The EMPEROR : ' *Is that possible ?* ') Among these might be discussed giving to Germans (The EMPEROR : ' *? ?* ') and Americans all orders for arms, and possibly a general option on all Chinese State loans which are to be placed abroad.

2. Separate from this if possible, a treaty—to be kept secret from China—between Germany, America and Russia, whereby these three Powers agree to act jointly against Japan, in the event of her seizing on territory in China itself North of the former course of the Hoang Ho or attacking the German district of Kiao-Chau. In return for this, Russia might have her present possessions in the Far East guaranteed against a Japanese attack and receive a promise of a free hand not only in Mongolia and Eastern Turkestan, but also in Manchuria and Korea, after a successful war with Japan. She would thus receive much more than the Japanese-French-British group could ever offer her.

To meet the desires of American trade Russia might promise to raise the Customs duties in Manchuria, when recovered, no higher than they are by law in China itself. . . .   (The EMPEROR : ' *Correct—Splendid! The very views I expressed to Yin Cheng!* [Chinese Minister in Berlin] *Not only Yuan Shi Kai but also Yin Cheng asked us this question on the grounds of the suggestion of an entente with us which I made direct to Her Majesty! That was a year ago, and we have done nothing since! Now something will be set going! At once,* subito ! ')

[The Emperor wrote to Bülow : ' To-day I read Rex's secret report, which I have waited for so long, with interest and pleasure . . .' (XXV. 87.)]

XXV. 89

PRINCE VON BÜLOW TO COUNT VON REX, IN PEKING,
January 3rd, 1908

Telegram.

A treaty of alliance between Germany, China and the United States is impossible owing to the United States, since the latter would not obtain the necessary consent of the Senate. The object of the negociations for a rapprochement, which we greatly desire, must be confined to an exchange of declarations in which China must ask us and the United States to support her policy, which should be that of granting territorial concessions to no Power whatever and keeping the door open for all nations ; whilst Germany and the United States would have to declare their consent to this policy and at the same time assure China that it would be their policy to maintain her complete integrity and independence. This might probably be carried in Washington and would be unobjectionable to third Powers, now that lately France and Japan, China's participation not being invited, have again come to a similar agreement ; it would also satisfy China, since our exchange of Notes informs the other Powers that the interest shared by Germany and the United States in perpetuating China is the *whole* gist of the matter. China ought to prefer a declaration of this sort to a treaty of alliance expressly confined to the 18 Provinces of the Empire, since the treaty would expose Chinese outside the Empire to aggression by third parties.

We must under all circumstances avoid the secret arrangements suggested by Your Excellency regarding privileges to be granted by China to us, for they contravene the principle of the ' open door ' and would be kept strictly secret neither in China nor Washington. In strict confidence and for your own personal guidance I add that the impression must be avoided that we are specially interested in the exchange of declarations. The initiative must come rather from China, who must aim at gaining America's support for the idea, so that for all the world the United States and not Germany shall appear to be the driving force. This will be easy to manage, if in her démarche in Washington, in which we naturally shall support her to the best of our ability, China pays sufficient attention to President Roosevelt's characteristics, especially his self-esteem and desire for action.

Please quietly urge the Chinese, perhaps through Yin Cheng, to start the negociations as soon as possible ; they must of course be kept strictly secret by the Chinese also, until they are concluded.

It is not yet time to talk about a further understanding between Germany, Russia and the United States at present.

XXV. 92

SCHOEN, GERMAN FOREIGN OFFICE, TO BARON SPECK VON STERNBURG, IN WASHINGTON, *January* 20th, 1908

Secret.

For your confidential information.

Count Rex reports that ' The question of a political understanding between Germany, the United States and China is to be submitted in the desired form to the Empress by Yuan Shi Kai and Prince Ching. It is intended to send a Special Envoy to Washington to thank for the remission of the Indemnity and also to discuss the affair.'

German Note.

In 1907 the United States let the Chinese Government off practically the whole of the ' Boxer Indemnity ' which was fixed in 1901.

[Writing on December 15th, 1908, from Peking, Count Rex said :
' The American-Japanese Declaration of December 1st has been a surprise
for the diplomatic corps here '.]

German Note. XXV. 97

For the text of the American-Japanese exchange of Notes of November
30th, 1908, see *Staatsarchiv*, LXXVI, pp. 329 et seq. ; Hayashi, pp. 236,
325 et seq. ; O. Franke, *Die Grossmächte in Ostasien von* 1894–1914, p. 300
et seq.

The American-Japanese Agreement [1] may well have surprised the
German Government, who had hoped that Tang Sho Yi's Mission to
Washington, which they had helped to bring about, would lead to a Ger-
man-American-Chinese declaration, and they were by no means prepared
to find that the States were concluding an Agreement with Japan instead.
On December 31st, 1908, President Roosevelt said to Count Bernstorff,
Sternburg's successor, as reported by him on January 2nd, 1909 : ' My
predecessor had often discussed with him the idea of a joint guarantee of
China's integrity by Germany and America in conjunction with China.
He had been unable to go into it, because it might have driven China into
a policy hostile to Japan.   A Chino-Japanese conflict would have found
China totally unarmed, in which case neither Germany nor America were
prepared to defend her against Japan.   We could not send our fleet into
the Pacific, and America could not fight for China, because her public
opinion would not have permitted it.   If there had to be an American-
Japanese war, it could only be for purely American interests.   The American people would then willingly put forward its strength and also be
certain of victory.   He had explained this idea quite frankly to the Chinese
Ambassador, Tang Sho Yi as far as it concerned America, for complete
frankness was the right policy.   Lies had short legs.   ' One is always
found out.'   The President drew an instance from Russian policy before
the Japanese war.

---

[1] Cf. G. & T., V, p. 511.

CHAPTER XXII

THE GERMAN NAVY BILL, 1908. THE TWEEDMOUTH LETTER

[The enthusiasm stimulated in Germany in favour of a large navy enabled the German Government to pass the Naval Bill of 1906, providing for a large increase of the fleet and for enlarging the Kiel Canal. (Lee, *King Edward VII*, II, p. 331). In 1907 (November 11th to 18th) the Emperor visited the King at Windsor,[1] and the visit might have had very beneficial effects but for the fact that the day after he left Windsor the German Government announced their intention of replacing battleships after a life of 20 instead of 25 years. This scheme went by the name of *Flottennovelle*, i.e., supplementary programme. After the cordial reception of the Emperor and Empress in this country the news came as a cold douche to any further confidence in German intentions, and the naval rivalry thenceforward became far more acute. (Cf. Lee, II, p. 563 ; Wilson, *War Guilt*, p. 111 ; G. & T., Vol. VI.)

The German Emperor's letter to Lord Tweedmouth (cf. p. 273) did not improve matters, and his persistence in imputing to King Edward hostile intentions towards Germany added to the resentment felt throughout England. (Cf. Brandenburg, p. 278 et seq.)]

XXIV. 21

STUMM, CHARGÉ D'AFFAIRES IN LONDON, TO THE GERMAN FOREIGN OFFICE, *November 25th*, 1907

Extract.

. . . It is doubtless correct to describe the visit of the Imperial couple to the Court here as having been very successful in every respect and free from discord of any sort and likely to give most effective support to the efforts which have been directed towards removing the tension in Anglo-German relations due to political events of recent years. But indulgence in far-reaching illusions in this connection would, in my humble opinion, be a mistake. Two factors stand in the way of a higher degree of warmth from now onward in these relations : consideration for France and the building of the German fleet. The Press here has not failed during the visit to point out repeatedly that paving the way towards better Anglo-German relations ought not to prejudice England's relations towards

[1] Cf. Haldane, *Before the War*, p. 47.

France. It has more or less expressed a view that the Emperor's visit indicates that Germany acquiesces in England's Entente policy. But as regards German naval policy, the new naval programme which became known a few days since has again produced strong disquietude. That this disquietude has not yet been more openly evident than it was before is, in my opinion, directly due to the recent visit. Even the most convinced adherents of a pro-German policy in England argue that for every new German ship two British ones must be built. That this view is argued calmly and dispassionately can only be to the good; for the certain though still latent dangers contained in present conditions cannot be considered as finally removed, until the British have got used to the idea of Germany having a strong fleet and until Germans are equally used to the idea that the British fleet will always be superior to theirs. Once this idea has lost its horror for the British imagination the French friendship will lose value in the eyes of British statesmen, and it will be possible to lift Anglo-German relations out of the condition of strict politeness which marks them at present. . . .

XXIV. 25

COUNT VON METTERNICH, IN LONDON, TO THE CHANCELLOR, PRINCE VON BÜLOW, *December 14th*, 1907

There are again to-day some articles in the British Press on the German Naval Programme. Yesterday the *Westminster Gazette* published a letter from the President of the Navy League (R. A. Yerburgh) referring to the coming increase of the German fleet and warning the British Government to maintain the British fleet in sufficient strength to be able to destroy any foreign coalition at sea. It should be done as in 1898, when the British Government, on learning of the increase of the Russian fleet, at once increased the programme of the year by 4 battleships and 4 armoured cruisers. This measure kept within its own hearth the fire which soon afterwards broke out in the Far East.

The *Daily Graphic* to-day fully agrees with this expression of opinion by the Navy League and asks why Germany considers this enormous increase necessary just when strong efforts are being made to produce friendly relations between England and Germany. (The EMPEROR : 'Navy Bill published 10 years ago.') England must observe this and act accordingly. Whatever the expense of assuring England's position on the sea England must and will see to it.

To-day's *Standard* quotes an article by Mr. Stead on the German programme, which appeared in the *Review of Reviews*.

The writer takes the same view as the Navy League and considers a corresponding increase of the British fleet as absolutely necessary. Maintenance of England's supremacy at sea is a matter of life and death ; therefore England cannot allow it to be endangered for a moment.

[In August, 1906, Mr. Haldane, the War Secretary, went to Berlin at the Emperor's invitation. Some awkwardness was caused by the fact that his visit would coincide with the anniversary of the victory at Sedan. (Cf. G. & T., III, 357, 373 et seq. ; Lee, *King Edward VII*, II, 531 ; Haldane, *Before the War*, Ch. II ; Grey, *Twenty-five Years*, p. 116.) He came back from Berlin with the impression that the Emperor and his advisers were not thinking of making war on England. This however did not deter him from pushing forward the work of reorganising the British army.]

XXIV. 26

Count von Metternich to the Chancellor, Prince von Bülow, *December 17th*, 1907

Mr. Haldane spoke yesterday at Hanley on the Two-Power standard amongst other subjects. He said it would not always be easy for England to maintain this, since the populations of Germany and America were increasing apace and placing England at a disadvantage as regards numbers. For this reason England would have to strengthen her army and land defences, since she could not rely on her fleet alone.

The *Globe* commented by hoping that the full meaning of the War Secretary's words would be understood in England. If one assumed that a time would come when it would hardly be possible to maintain the Two-Power standard, there was but one other alternative—universal military service. If people disliked this the only course was to maintain the Two-Power standard at any price.

The same. December 19th, 1906.

At Hull Mr. Haldane urged that England must not be behindhand at this moment in increasing her armaments. He said : ' I believe there is no man who desires peace in the world more sincerely than the Emperor. His Majesty thinks, however, that peace is only assured for him who is armed, and he is spending more not only on his fleet, but also on his army.'

[The *Outlook* of January 4th, 1908, drew attention to the growth of the German Navy.]

German Note.

The German Navy League, led by General Keim, started a violent agitation against the alleged insufficiency of the Navy Bill. As a result of this, Prince Rupprecht of Bavaria decided to withdraw his patronage from the Bavarian branch of the League.

XXIV. 27

STUMM, CHARGÉ D'AFFAIRES IN LONDON, TO PRINCE VON BÜLOW,
January 4th, 1908

Extract. 29.

. . . The *Outlook* only says what everyone here is thinking. If the Germanophobia has lately decreased in intensity under the influence of the Emperor's visit, it has on the other hand broadened. The introduction of the new Navy Bill, and more especially what has gone on in the Navy League in connection with General Keim's election, has had the result that even the Liberal Press—e.g. the *Westminster Gazette*—now joins in the *caveant consules* with regard to Germany's naval plans. There is a general feeling here that in 1911 Germany will surprise the world with a fresh great Navy Bill. Sir Edward Grey's recent utterances (at Berwick on December 19th) show that he shares these views. This has revivified the demand for a public enquiry into the state of the navy, which originally arose through the antagonism of Sir John Fisher and Lord Charles Beresford.[1] Now however the general nervousness which all England is feeling owing to the growth of German sea-power is being fed afresh. The question is exercising all minds so intensely that the Government can hardly remain passive in face of it ; and it may become a source of great embarrassment to the Liberal Cabinet. Much will depend on how matters go in the German Navy League. If chauvinism in Germany retires into the background, it is probable that tranquillity will return here to some extent, and it may be possible to build on the foundations which the year 1907 prepared for the improvement of Anglo-German relations. Otherwise it is to be feared that soon the tone of moderation will again disappear from public discussion of the good relations towards Germany which were the most evident result of developments in former years.

XXIV. 29.

CAPTAIN WIDENMANN, GERMAN NAVAL ATTACHÉ IN LONDON, TO
ADMIRAL VON TIRPITZ, *January 24th*, 1908

At a Liberal meeting a few days ago at Alnwick Sir Edward Grey spoke of increased expenditure for naval purposes. He justified this on the grounds of the growing armaments of foreign nations and England's dependence on her supremacy at sea.

Yesterday Lord Tweedmouth spoke at Newcastle in the same strain. He argued that it would be wrong to act hastily ; it was rather the duty of those responsible to observe the armaments of other navies and set the British programme by them.

[1] Cf. Lee, *King Edward VII*, II, p. 598 et seq. ; Bacon, *Lord Fisher*.

England did not desire to set the pace in naval increase, but she must maintain the present ratio of strength.

In connection with these official announcements *The Times* leading article to-day concludes that besides the cruisers and torpedo-boats which are demanded it would be desirable to add 2 or 3 *Dreadnoughts* to the programme for 1908–9.

The paper explains that the right ratio could be produced at any time by supplementary orders, if this programme proved insufficient ; the example of Lord Goschen is quoted.

It is hard to say whether these expressions are a reliable indication of this year's naval policy. But if a paper like *The Times* does this so shortly before the opening of Parliament we are perhaps justified in taking it as some indication. The Admiralty, which may be attacked by those who support the navy for presenting a Bill containing only a restricted recommendation, may perhaps have prepared additional ones—as in the case of the *Rodney* after the Hague Conference—for production after our Bill has been passed by the Reichstag.

German Note.

In a speech in the Reichstag (January 28th, 1908) Tirpitz said that the German Naval Bill ought not to produce anxiety in England. . . . ' England is actually more than three times as strong as we are, and she is in a position to build much faster than we can . . .' Baron Greindl, the Belgian Minister in Berlin, reported to his Government (March 28th) : ' Personne n'a jamais eu ici l'idée absurde et irréalisable d'une aggression contre l'Angleterre ; mais tout le monde éprouve la crainte d'une aggression anglaise. C'est la raison pour laquelle le Reichstag a voté sans sourciller une énorme augmentation de dépenses pour la marine de guerre quoique le budget de l'Empire souffre d'un déficit qu'on ne sait pas comment combler et que les finances de la Prusse soient en tout aussi mauvais état.'

XXIV. 30

Count von Metternich, in London, to the Chancellor, Prince von Bülow, *February 3rd*, 1908

Extract.

In to-day's *Times* there is a leading article against Admiral von Tirpitz's statement that the German naval programme has caused no disturbance in England. It says that perhaps disturbance is the wrong word to describe the impression it has produced, but it has made an impression. In order to be sure of this, one has only to look at half a dozen of the leading British papers. There can be no mistake that the German naval programme has awakened the vigilance of the British in the highest degree, and that England intends to maintain her supremacy at sea without question. It is to the interest of good Anglo-German relations, that there should be no illusion about this in Germany. . . .

XXIV. 31

COUNT VON METTERNICH TO THE CHANCELLOR, PRINCE VON
BÜLOW, *February 14th*, 1908

In answer to a question in the House of Commons Sir Edward
Grey said that according to a declaration by the British First
Delegate at the Hague Conference on August 17th the British
Government was prepared each year to communicate the number
and cost of war-ships which were to be constructed to those
Powers who were willing to do the same. (The EMPEROR :
' *Rubbish ! They know it already from our Novelle.*') Before
other Powers were ready to make such a communication, there
was, however, no reason for one Power to communicate its
naval programme to another in advance.

[On February 16th, 1908, the Emperor wrote privately to Lord Tweedmouth a letter protesting against the anti-German Press campaign in
England and denying emphatically that the increase in the German navy
was directed against England. Cf. Lee, *King Edward VII*, II, 605 ;
Wilson, *War Guilt*, p. 113 ; G. & T., Vol. VI.]
German Note.
    The Emperor's letter, which, according to a private letter of March 3rd
from Schoen, Secretary of State, to Count Metternich, was written without
the foreknowledge of either himself or Prince Bülow only appears in the
Records in the form of a copy by the hand of Admiral von Müller, the head
of the Admiralty Council. The letter was first published in the *Morning
Post* of October 30th, 1914, and more recently by Admiral von Tirpitz in
Der Aufbau der Deutschen Weltmacht, p. 58 et seq.
    [In his private reply acknowledging the Emperor's letter Lord Tweed-
mouth did not enter into details, but referred His Majesty to a memorandum which had already been prepared in the Foreign Office for Sir Frank
Lascelles to ' hand to Prince Bülow for Your Majesty's information'.]

XXIV. 36

MEMORANDUM PRESENTED BY SIR FRANK LASCELLES ON
February 28th, 1908

His Majesty's Government have never claimed the right to
criticise the German or any other Government in determining
the extent of their naval or military requirements. They
frankly recognise that this is a matter which every independent
State must settle for itself. Sir Edward Grey has himself recently
given public utterance to this view in unmistakable terms with
particular reference to the new German naval programme, and
the German Secretary of State for the Navy, when introducing
the naval estimates into the Reichstag, specially alluded to the
dispassionate and friendly tone in which the Press and public
speakers in England had discussed the German proposals.

It is however alleged that certain English newspapers have
' made attacks on the German programme', by calling attention
to the great expense which this country must necessarily incur

if compelled to build so many more ships in consequence of the increase of the German naval forces. But as the Emperor has suggested that something should be done to counteract this 'anti-German tendency', it seems requisite to explain that His Majesty's Government cannot regard as just cause for irritation in Germany an expression of regret by an independent British newspaper at the growth of expenditure inevitably imposed upon England by the increase of German naval armaments.

The organs of the German Navy League frequently use the British Navy as an illustration of the need for increasing the German Navy, and it is not unnatural that the section of the British Press which is always afraid that the Government, especially a Liberal Government, will let the navy fall behind-hand, should make similar use of the German navy to enforce its point.

The independence and very existence of the British Empire depend on the preservation of its supremacy at sea, and the British Government is bound to organise and keep up such naval forces as are essential for that purpose. It would be futile to pretend that the increase of the German fleet is not one of the factors which has to be taken into account in any calculation of the strength at which the British Navy must be maintained. To prevent the British Press from freely stating and commenting on so obvious a fact would be neither equitable nor possible.

His Majesty's Government regret as much as anyone that the newspaper Press should at times be utilised as the vehicle for international recriminations. But even if they had the power to interfere—which it is of course well known that they have not—they would not feel called upon to restrain the public but courteous expression of views which reflect the actual situation. This situation, viewed from the standpoint of the British Government, is that whilst there is no thought of attributing hostile intentions to Germany or any of Great Britain's neighbours nor of calling in question their right to build what ships they please, the supreme interest of the security of the British Empire requires that the standard and proportion of the British Navy to those of European countries, which has been upheld by successive British Governments, must be maintained.

XXIV. 39

The Chancellor, Prince von Bülow, to the Emperor, *March 6th*, 1908

The Times of to-day publishes a letter from its Military correspondent, Colonel A'Court Repington,[1] directing public

[1] Described by Metternich as ' one of the most dangerous and cleverest agitators against Germany ' (XXIV. 42).

attention to a matter alleged to be of great importance. The correspondent states that it has come to his knowledge that the German Emperor wrote a letter to Lord Tweedmouth on the subject of British and German naval policy. The Emperor's letter, which he says is undoubtedly genuine and has been replied to, points to an attempt to influence in German interests the Minister responsible for the British Naval Estimates, and the letter, along with the reply to it, ought immediately to be laid before Parliament, since the affair is an open secret.

I beg Your Majesty for a copy of the letter to Lord Tweedmouth, so that we may be armed against all eventualities, and that I may be able, after Your Majesty's return, to report on the further course of events.

XXIV. 39

THE CHANCELLOR, PRINCE VON BÜLOW, TO THE EMPEROR,
March 6th, 1908

Cipher telegram.

Count Metternich telegraphs : ' If it is possible I consider publication of the Emperor's letter to Lord Tweedmouth the best way to repair to some extent the mischief which *The Times* article has caused. If not, false insinuations will be readily believed. There will certainly be questions in Parliament. The matter may cause Lord Tweedmouth's fall and deal a severe blow to the Liberal Government which is friendly to us. All the elements favourable to us will be weakened and the Jingoes strengthened. Moreover His Majesty's popularity in England will suffer, and mistrust of our policy will increase.'

Without knowing the text of Your Majesty's letter I cannot judge finally whether publication is advisable, but I beg permission in principle for its publication by us, perhaps cutting out personal allusions, as for instance those about Lord Esher. (The EMPEROR : ' *I do not share Metternich's fears. The British have not yet gone so completely mad.* The Times *action comes from the King, who fears lest the letter should produce too tranquillising an impression.*[1] *I consent to publication.*')

XXIV. 42

THE CHANCELLOR, PRINCE VON BÜLOW, TO THE EMPEROR,
March 8th, 1908

Telegram.

I thank Your Majesty most respectfully for sending me the correspondence.

The text of Your Majesty's letter being what it is, I consider

---

[1] Cf. Lee, *King Edward VII*, 608.

that publication would in itself be all to the good. But this would not be possible without also making known Lord Tweedmouth's answer, which contains a premature communication about the British Navy Bill; it might also cause awkward attacks against the present Government, whose strength we do not wish to see impaired. It would moreover prejudice discussion and exchange of ideas between the British Admiralty and ours, and Your Majesty's relations towards the British Admiralty would be disturbed.

Thus we could publish nothing without first conferring with the British Government. We must first await to-morrow's statements in Parliament.

The British Press condemns almost unanimously the attitude of *The Times*. To-day Count Matternich telegraphs : ' Although most of to-day's papers demand publication of the correspondence, they do not follow *The Times*, but write moderately. *The Times* attempt to give the matter the importance of an international question has fallen flat.

With some exceptions, our Press behaves with dignity and calm.

[For the annoyance felt by King Edward about the correspondence, see Lee, *King Edward VII*, II, p. 604.]

XXIV. 47

COUNT VON METTERNICH TO THE GERMAN FOREIGN OFFICE, *March 9th*, 1908

Cipher telegram.

To-day's debates in the Lords and Commons show clearly the wish of the leaders of both Parties to give the letter affair its proper proportion and to prevent the Press from poisoning public opinion any further. Lord Rosebery's serious warning to the Press will not fail in its effect.

Of his own accord Sir E. Grey said to me he considered publication inadvisable on account of the certainly witty but colloquial expressions in the Emperor's letter, which would offer the Press fresh opportunities for undesirable comment. (I think the same.) When Lord Tweedmouth showed him the letter he, Grey, had, in consideration of its non-official character, been of opinion that it should not be answered by the Foreign Office but that Lord Tweedmouth should return an equally non-official reply.

When I asked if he would not think it advisable to state in Parliament that the Emperor had informed the King of his letter to Lord Tweedmouth,[1] the Minister replied that he had

[1] Cf. Lee, *King Edward VII*, p. 606.

thought it over, but it could not be done without the King's consent.

Finally the Minister said that the memorandum handed to Your Highness [1] by Sir Frank Lascelles, following the conversation with the Emperor, had been sent off before His Majesty's letter to Tweedmouth was received.

The attitude of leading British statesmen in the affair has been dignified and well conceived ; our public opinion should be satisfied with it. (BÜLOW : *I think it is better for us for the British Government to stick to this version. It would be awkward for us to have to confess that the British Government had complained to us about His Majesty's letter.*)

[It was considered that Lord Tweedmouth had not observed sufficient discretion in the affair. In September, 1908, he resigned his office ; a year later he died.]

XXIV. 48

COUNT VON METTERNICH, IN LONDON, TO THE CHANCELLOR, PRINCE VON BÜLOW, *March 10th*, 1908

Extract.

. . . As shown in the enclosed *Times* report of the debate in Parliament, the Parliamentary Under-Secretary for the Admiralty (E. Robertson) was repeatedly forced in debate to suppress comparisons with the German fleet. (The EMPEROR : ' *All caused by the articles (including Lord Esher's letter) published and discussed in January. It is the policy of the Opposition and the Jingoes always to ride in front of us !* ') They were also a good foundation for the criticism which Mr. Balfour, the leader of the Opposition, applied to the Liberal Cabinet's naval policy. Ministers appeared embarrassed by the question whether by the end of 1911 Germany would have 13 ships of the Dreadnought class as against England's 12. . . .

[Sir Frank Lascelles retired from the Diplomatic Service in June, 1908, and was succeeded in August by Sir Edward Goschen, British Ambassador in Vienna. The latter was succeeded in Vienna by Sir Fairfax Cartwright. Cf. Lee, *King Edward VII*, II, pp. 612, 619.

On May 28th, 1908, President Fallières paid a state visit to London. He was received with tremendous enthusiasm and with King Edward opened the Franco-British Exhibition at Shepherd's Bush.]

XXIV. 68

COUNT VON METTERNICH TO THE CHANCELLOR, PRINCE VON BÜLOW, *June 5th*, 1908

The hearty understanding between France and England existed before the visit of the President of the French Republic

[1] Cf. p. 273.

in London. The rejoicings on the days of festivity gave it an impulse, which still continues now that they are all over. I do not consider that a new situation has been created. For a long time it has been evident to all that the Entente which stood the fire of the Morocco crisis is desired on both sides and will be adhered to. The French doubts regarding it have died away with a few exceptions. On the British side there have been absolutely no objectors ever since it came into being. What was already there received fresh loud expression during the President's visit. There is nothing more in it, in my opinion. Nevertheless I would not underestimate the importance of the Entente. Formerly we could count at least on England's benevolent neutrality in a war with France, whereas now we must count on her malevolent neutrality at least, and very probably—in fact, fairly certainly—on open hostility. . . .

The strangest tales are told here about our navy, and—strangest of all—they are believed. We are said to have built our fleet with borrowed money—to be recovered later by a war-contribution in London. (The EMPEROR: ' / ') Our naval officers are in the habit of drinking ' to the Great Day ! ', i.e., to the battle with the British fleet. None of this, however, has anything to do with the President's visit. . . .

England will never go to war again with the United States. She depends on them for trade and importation of food and can do them no injury. She knows that under these circumstances the Americans will never attack England, and she is never certain that we shall not attack her. She regards us as dangerous neighbours and the Americans as distant friends. Nevertheless, the ruling desire here is to live on a good footing with us. . . .

It is indisputable that we have more friends among the Liberals than among their opponents. A few days ago I had a long conversation with Mr. Austen Chamberlain, the son of the well-known Statesman (now incurably ill), who was formerly Chancellor of the Exchequer and now is the leader of the Protectionist movement, about the past and future of Anglo-German relations. Perhaps our strongest opponents are in the camp of his father. Mr. Austen Chamberlain does not take a rosy view of the Anglo-German future. He agreed with me that no national necessity need lead to an armed conflict between the two countries. But he considers the political atmosphere full of electricity and that feeling in England is very bad about us. But he hopes that careful leadership on both sides will prevent any rise of excitement, and that something good will turn up (The EMPEROR: ' *Micawber* ! ') to bring the two nations together in future. No aggressive tendency was to be observed in him. . . .

The British people are less solid behind their Government

than the French are with regard to the three-sided reciprocity. They agree without reserve to the Entente with France, but not altogether to one with Russia. The Conservatives and the leading politicians of both Parties are quite in favour of a political rapprochement with Russia, but merely as a cool political suggestion and not from any sympathy. The paper under-standing in Asia is naturally strengthened by being connected with the European policy of the two Powers. The collapse of Russia has turned British policy more decisively against us ; we seem to England too powerful, and she looks on the rapproche-ment with Russia, combined with the close friendship with France, as a useful counterweight to the power of central Europe. On the other hand, the Franco-Russian Alliance is supported not only for State reasons, but also to some extent by mutual popular feeling, for French and Slav characters have much in common, e.g., quickness in apprehension and easily aroused excitement. But the Englishman and the Russian have nothing in common. This is clearly shown when feeling gets the better of cool judgment, as in the vote upon the King's journey to Reval.

[On June 7th, 1908, the King and Queen arrived at Reval on a visit to the Tsar and Tsarina (Lee, *King Edward VII*, II, p. 586 et seq. ; G. & T., V, p. 232 et seq.). The visit was violently condemned by the Independent Labour Party, led by Mr. Ramsay Macdonald, who attacked Russia and the Tsar in the *Labour Leader* at the end of May. The visit greatly contributed to improve Anglo-Russian relations.]

In the House of Commons yesterday 59 members (half Labour, half Radical) voted against King Edward's state visit, and 225 voted for it ; but these figures do not express the real feeling of the House, still less that of the country. The English-man is too well self-disciplined in politics—not by orders from outside—to make difficulties for the Government in important foreign matters having to do with the Empire's power. One of these questions is the relationship towards Russia. This silences many to whom the King's journey is distasteful. The partial opposition in the Commons rests on other grounds.

Among his people King Edward has acquired a great reputa-tion for skilled diplomacy and peacemaking. The people con-ceive his role of ' peacemaker ' literally and without *arrière pensée*, whilst those who think politically treat his Entente policy as a safeguard against possible dangers. . . .

CHAPTER XXIII

THE ATTEMPT TO SECURE A NAVAL UNDERSTANDING. JULY TO SEPTEMBER, 1908

[To Count Bülow on August 20th, 1901 (XVIII. 15), the Emperor wrote (in reference to the growing Anglo-Russian rapprochement) : ' We may be indifferent and cool about this, but we must rebuild our forts on the Rhine and establish a number of fresh garrisons in Posen and West Prussia for which I have already given the order to the War Minister. Moreover the building of our fleet must be speeded up as much as possible. It will give a good fright to the British, and perhaps it is got up against them I have mentioned the news casually in a reply to King Edward, as being something long known of. I am curious to see the faces of the King and Lascelles, who wish to lunch with me on Friday. . . .' (Cf. p. 146.)

A succession of Bills for increasing the power of the German Navy had excited remark in England, but it was not until the Liberal Government, from 1906 onward, showed signs of moderation in their naval programme that the German Government decided to speed up their plans, at the same time attempting to persuade the British that what they are doing was in no way directed against England.[1] During 1908 a strenuous effort was made by the British Government, to which King Edward added his personal support, to obtain Germany's consent to a mutual agreement to limit naval armaments. The correspondence shows that something of the sort might have been possible but for the Emperor's determined opposition to even a discussion of it. But even so it may be doubted whether the course of events would have been altered in any respect. (Cf. Brandenburg, p. 266 et seq.)]

XXIV. 93

Count von Metternich, in London, to the Chancellor,
Prince von Bülow, *July 10th*, 1908

Extract.

. . . Two days ago I had a long conversation with Mr. Balfour, the former Prime Minister, of which I give a part only for the sake of brevity. He said that Anglo-German relations caused him much anxiety. He was constantly informed by those who knew Germany (The Emperor : ' *? ! ! Vesselitsky* [2] *etc. !* ') that amongst us the doctrine was wide-spread and deeply rooted that England stood in the way of German expansion, and that our efforts must be directed towards beating England. (The Emperor : ' *Nobody in Germany thinks anything so silly.*')

[1] Cf. p. 275.   [2] Russian journalist in London.

280

I replied that this doctrine was unknown to me, but I had heard that the Chief of the British Admiralty was himself in favour of attacking the German fleet.[1] In Germany no one was planning to attack England. We were peaceably inclined, having won our unity a generation before, and we wished to hurt nobody. But it was correct that the British policy of insurance, as interpreted by our many rivals, was causing ever deeper anxiety. (The EMPEROR : '*Everywhere! not only with us.*') ' An insurance policy', I continued, 'does not prevent a fire. It is costly, uncertain and no safeguard. The more efficient and much cheaper means of preventing a fire consists in taking away combustible materials.'[2] (The EMPEROR : '*Very good.*')

Mr. Balfour sharply condemned ' the loose talk of attacking the German fleet '. Quite apart from the immorality of such action, it would call down on England the German people's lasting hatred, and do Germany no lasting injury. . . .

When I asked him how it happened that British policy had now changed completely towards Germany, though the latter was already powerful before the change, the former Prime Minister said : ' Yes, but then you had no fleet.' (The EMPEROR : '*Aha! then why not an entente with us?*') Even to-day our position in Europe, based on our population, industry and the army, caused him no anxiety. Nor did even the often expressed view that the growth of our power, combined with Russia's impotence and France's relative weakness, was endangering the balance of power in Europe. There never had been an absolute balance of power in Europe. One side had always been the stronger, and he had always preferred that this one should be the hitherto peace-loving German rather than the restless Frenchman. But the fleet ! That was what caused the anxiety and fear in England of the German danger. (The EMPEROR : '*!*') . . .

We went on to talk of the spy scare. I told him that now-a-days his compatriots were in front of the French even in smelling out spies. (The EMPEROR : '*Undoubtedly!*') Mr. Balfour said he did not think that very important. Everyone knew that large States tried to gather military information however and wherever they could. He was astounded when I told him that the German spy-system in England was simply a dream picture in the minds of frightened Englishmen. . . .

From his words it is clear that any aggressive intentions against Germany are far from his thoughts, and he does not believe that such exist in the British people. But he fears that

---

[1] Cf. Lord Fisher's *Memories*, p. 18 et seq. ; Lee, *King Edward VII*, p. 604, etc.   [2] English in text.

the teachings of Treitschke [1] and many others have educated the German people into thinking that England is standing in the way of Germany's expansion and must be defeated with the help of a strong fleet. (The EMPEROR : ' *We shall never be so stupid. It would be Hari-kiri !* ') I contested this and said that the ideas which British policy learned from our rivals were bound to infect British intentions with mistrust of Germany, and that the insurance policy did not protect against a fire. . . .

XXIV. 96

THE CHANCELLOR, PRINCE VON BÜLOW, AT NORDEZNEY, TO THE EMPEROR, (*circa*) *July 15th,* 1908

Very Secret.

I am grateful to Your Majesty for having caused Ballin [2] to visit me here. My conversation with him was highly interesting, for Ballin gave me a full account of Your Majesty's relations with King Edward. Evidently the King's aim is to irritate Your Majesty with every kind of pin-prick. Ballin says nothing amuses the King more than for us to show bad temper. He regards it as proof that he has gained his object. He would like the world to imagine that he has been irritated by Your Majesty, and he carries out these tactics with deliberation and skill. It must be our tactics not to expose any weak side and to make it impossible for the King to find reason for complaint against us either in fact or in form. This applies especially to the question of the visit. The King would be delighted if annoyance was shown by us over the failure so far to return Your Majesty's visit to England of last year. It would be a pleasure to him to find he had succeeded in making us angry. Moreover for grave political reasons we must wish the English visit to Berlin [3] to take place. To this end Ballin also thinks that Your Majesty should soon meet the King in preparation for the Berlin visit, in order to discuss its details. He thinks it would be best if the meeting took place during the King's journey to Marienbad. If this is impossible, it would have to be arranged for the return journey from that place. The King will not come to Strasburg or Metz. It would be mistaken policy to propose meeting him there, for a refusal, which is certainly to be expected, would merely increase the King's popularity in France. Could it take place at Homburg,

---

[1] Cf. p. 208.

[2] Chairman of the Hamburg-America Line. Again in 1911 he pressed for a naval understanding with England. At the end of the Great War he committed suicide.

[3] Cf. p. 319. It took place in February, 1909.

Cronberg or Baden-Baden, if it cannot be arranged for the journey out ?

Ballin is convinced that it is to Germany's interests to avoid a clash with England during the next few years, naturally whilst maintaining our dignity to the full, not only because time is on our side for increasing our population, strengthening our forces and for the hoped-for improvement of our finances, but also in consideration that King Edward is beginning to age, the element of unrest will, humanly speaking, cease to form part of the British scheme. Ballin believes that after his Majesty dies the former correct attitude will reign again in England, and foreign policy will be controlled by Ministers in agreement with Parliament, cutting out the Sovereign's likes and dislikes. Thus it is so important for us to get through the next few years. ' If thou art not caught to-day, thou shalt have escaped a thousand times.' Ballin considers that the Anglo-German tension is due, first and foremost, to Germany's naval construction and especially the speed at which we are building. If we keep on trying to justify it, British public opinion will only become more suspicious. We should therefore not draw attention by ceremonies and speeches when launching the ships. An Englishman is not like a German, who gets his impressions from books and tables (if not from the depths of his intelligence) ; John Bull is moved by what he sees in front of him. The measure of our financial strength prevents our ship-building being extensive enough to mean a danger of aggression not imaginary, but really fatal, for England. We cannot have a great army and a great navy at the same time. We certainly cannot compete in Dreadnoughts with England with her much greater wealth. The difference between us and England in fighting ships will remain about the same for a long time. Ballin suggested again and again whether it might not be possible to reach an understanding with England regarding extent and ratio of naval armaments. He thinks it would be easier with the Liberals than the Conservatives, so that it is urgently desirable to come to terms with the former, if possible.

Ballin does not believe the Russians will get much money in England, but that King Edward would apply himself, and successfully, in France to getting a fresh Russian loan placed there.

He is greatly concerned at Prince Albert of Schleswig-Holstein [1] being included in Your Majesty's suite. All the London Clubs know that the Prince is indiscreet and sends to England any confidential information which comes to his knowledge.

---

[1] Son of Prince Christian and Princess Helena of England.

Anglo-German relations are, however, of too serious a nature to be exposed to the risk of indiscretion.

What Ballin said about the general depression in trade was very interesting. Money is now as scarce in England and America as it is in Germany; it is only to be found in France, because they have not overdone themselves in industry, and because of the thrifty nature of the people. The British have got into a proper mess with the Japanese loans.

Ballin made some wise remarks about reforming our Imperial finances. He admits that, in the present state of business and German party spirit, it will be difficult to realise them. He said they were one of the very hardest tasks ever imposed. Even the new taxes would only stop the huge hole, if at the same time greater economy was practised in all departments and directions. Throughout Germany there was now a spirit of extravagance. We had everywhere gradually slipped into extravagant ways in life and business, which could not be surpassed. We must become more economical and simpler. . . .

XXIV. 99
COUNT VON METTERNICH TO THE CHANCELLOR, PRINCE VON BÜLOW, *July 16th,* 1908

Secret.

The day before yesterday Sir Edward Grey invited me to luncheon at his house to meet Mr. Lloyd George.[1] The conversation soon turned to foreign politics. From being an ultra-Radical Welsh solicitor, the Chancellor of the Exchequer has quickly become a leading and respected personage in his party and the Ministry. Being Imperialist in thought, he is well considered by the Unionists also. When in opposition a few years ago, he permitted himself, if I remember rightly, to hit in a Jingo tone at Germany now and then; but as responsible Minister I found him inclined to be conciliatory.

When I mentioned the question in Parliament about espionage, he agreed with me that unluckily any nonsense was believed here whenever it concerned Germany.

I said it was a pity that British policy seemed to wish to exchange German enmity for French friendship, and that the Entente's policy had produced anxiety in Europe. Sir Edward Grey replied more or less as follows : In the course of the last decade England had been several times in danger of a war with France and Russia. Failing some arrangement in each case, there would probably have been war. Neither of the above had been aimed against Germany. There was at present only the Entente with France ; nothing with Russia. On the other

[1] Cf. Lee, *King Edward VII*, II, p. 611.

side, Germany had the Triple Alliance. It was incomprehensible how there could be talk of a policy of isolating Germany.

Mr. Lloyd George put in that it was England's diplomatic support of France that was annoying Germany. (The EMPEROR : ' *Yes.*') Sir Edward Grey replied that so far as Morocco was concerned, England was obliged to support France.

I said that France was perfectly safe as long as she recognised the *status quo* in Europe. (The EMPEROR :. ' *Reichsland.*') By herself she would not try to shake it ; but with England's support the revenge idea might one day come to life again. (The EMPEROR : ' *Well said.*') For instance, the article in the *Temps*, recommending to England a strong army in order to make her efficient as an ally.

When Mr. Lloyd George opined that he did not believe France had war-like intentions, although the French might not yet be able to make up their minds to acquiesce in what was past, I replied that these were not my views about the French. Moreover there was nothing to remind me that England swept aside disputes with other nations. On the contrary, in the public Press the friends and defenders of British foreign policy were careful to spread abroad the conviction that it was England's object not only to compose disputes, but at the same time to raise a bulwark against the power of Germany.[1] This was not the result of a friendly tendency and could not be regarded as such in Germany ; it was, in fact, bound rather to produce anxiety in Europe. (The EMPEROR : ' *Correct.*')

Sir Edward Grey said that the unpleasant part of the situation was that each imputed hostile intentions to the other. In Germany they believed the British meant to attack them, and the British believed the German fleet was being built to threaten England.[2]

Both Ministers considered that the situation between England and Germany turned on the fleet question. Expenditure on the British navy had risen as a result of the German programme, (The EMPEROR : ' *False! as a result of British greed for Power and their seeing bogies.*') and in proportion to the increased speed of construction, (The EMPEROR : ' *There has been no increase.*') and the sense of the danger from Germany would also increase, so that relations between the countries could not improve whilst naval competition on each side rose higher and higher. (The EMPEROR : ' *There is none. Ours is limited by law !* ' [3]) Every Englishman would spend his last penny to maintain naval superiority, (The EMPEROR : ' *According to* Nauticus *they have*

---

[1] Grey, *Twenty-five Years*, p. 151 ; Lee, *King Edward VII*, II, *passim*.
[2] Cf. Grey, *Twenty-five Years*, p. 120.
[3] Cf. Lee, *King Edward VII*, II, p. 616.

it threefold.') on which not only England's position in the world, but her existence, depended as an independent State. The ruinous cost of naval competition made trustful relations between the two nations impossible. (The EMPEROR : ' *Even in the days of sharpest tension with Russia over Afghanistan England never used such arrogant language! She never came to the point of insisting on Russia withdrawing her troops from the frontier or ceasing to strengthen her garrisons.'*) Anybody with any knowledge of England knew that there was no intention here of threatening or attacking Germany with the British fleet. (The EMPEROR : ' *?! They have threatened continuously!*') Considering the size, etc., of the British army a landing was quite out of the question. Mr. Lloyd George remarked in joke that whenever mention was made of a British landing on German soil, Prince Bismarck used to say that if that happened he would leave it to the police to take up the British landing force. It was the same to-day in the matter of any British threat to Germany. But for England a powerful German navy (The EMPEROR : ' *After my Guildhall speech this is absolutely shameless!*') backed by an even more powerful army constituted a real danger.

I replied that a ' German invasion ' existed only in the British imagination. No reasonable being in Germany thought of it. (The EMPEROR : ' *Very good.*') The invention of the *Dreadnought* had unluckily made ship-building dearer and had caused England to forfeit her immense advantage ; it also committed other seafaring nations to the same large type of ship and to expenditure to match it. But, *à qui la faute?* In the Commons these days there had been mention of a new and still larger type of ship, a floating fortress. Until the British policy of insurance ceased to cause anxiety in Germany, I considered a reduction of sea armaments out of the question. (The EMPEROR : ' *Correct.*') Sir Edward Grey must first cause a slackening of the tension between the two countries and, by his policy in Central Europe, restore confidence so that his ententes could not be misused against us one day ; (The EMPEROR : ' *Very good.*') not till then would the way be prepared for a discussion on the reduction of sea armaments. (The EMPEROR : ' *Wrong! We must not talk of that at all! We will never submit to dictation as to how our armaments are to be arranged.*') Mr. Lloyd George, who was taking a lively part in the naval discussion, answered that a slow down in our naval construction would have a more reassuring effect than any political action. (The EMPEROR : ' *We are not speeding up, and have built no ' secret ' Dreadnoughts for other States—which would then be bought by England—nor have we dressed up any as armed*

cruisers, to be suddenly stripped as ships of the line.') He said
that here we should find the utmost readiness to agree on a
common basis for mutual reduction in building. (The EMPEROR :
*'The British Minister should first make this quite unheard-of
suggestion to Roosevelt, Clemenceau, Mirabello, [Italy] or Japan.
The answers would be amusing! Why only to us? Because they
think my diplomacy has its work cut out and will be taken in by
a cry of war.'*) It was a great mistake of England's to introduce
the *Dreadnought* type. The British Government would give
every possible guarantee (The EMPEROR : *'We need none.'*) that
no new type should be introduced, (The EMPEROR : *'We don't
care.'*) if that would help on an understanding. He had regretted
at the time that the Tweedmouth correspondence [1] was not
published. It would have demonstrated to the public the
Emperor's friendly feelings towards England, and he would
have taken His Majesty's letter as a means for entering into
confidential discussion with us on naval expenditure. (The
EMPEROR : *'He would have got a wonderful answer from me!
It would not have succeeded.'*) If he had been responsible then
for the State finances, he would have pressed in Cabinet for
publishing the correspondence. (The EMPEROR : *'Aha!'*) A
Hague Conference was not the right way to attain reduction of
expenditure on the Navy. (The EMPEROR : *'Correct.'*) If that
was ever attained, as he urgently hoped, it might be tried not
officially, but perhaps by an exchange of notes. (The EMPEROR :
'I should reply with grenades.') The object would be best
attained by non-official, confidential, and secret discussion, if
an understanding on the subject was to be at all possible between
England and ourselves. (The EMPEROR : *'Secret! So that the
German people may not rise up and break the Minister's windows
with paving-stones.—No!'*)

Sir Edward Grey supported all his colleague's arguments
except one in favour of publishing the correspondence.

I agreed with Mr. Lloyd George that a Hague Conference, and
still more so an official suggestion by note (The EMPEROR :
'That would be a declaration of war!') from the British to the
German Government, would fail to settle the question of reducing naval expenditure. (The EMPEROR : *'Agreed!'*) I indicated
that official action (The EMPEROR : *'We should take it as a
declaration of war.'*) in this direction would be very questionable,
(The EMPEROR : *'War for a certainty.'*) cumbrous and dangerous,
and I refused to shift from the sure ground of my demand :
first a reassuring policy, then we can talk about the Navy.
(The EMPEROR : *'No! no word at all about that!'*)

In reporting this conversation I have left out much and

[1] Cf. p. 273.

given only the essentials for brevity's sake. But the minor points help to give the picture its right tone. I venture therefore to complete it with the following final remarks, in order to leave no room for misunderstanding.

Your Excellency knows that for a long time the British Government has desired to come to an understanding with us over naval expenditure. (The EMPEROR: '*Nothing doing. They should first settle it with the other Powers.*') Before and during the second Hague Conference an abortive attempt was made in this direction. If I was rightly informed, it was already feared in Germany that the British Government, alone or with others, might formally propose to us a reduction of our naval programme, and that immediate danger of war would be the result. (The EMPEROR: '*Yes.*') I am convinced that it is far from the intention of the present Government (The EMPEROR: '*? ?*') to offer us, in the form of an ultimatum, the alternatives of compliance or war. They have no sort of wish to ask a question in the form of a threat. (The EMPEROR: '*The Minister's words contain a hidden threat, as it is! Let them settle it with America first! They are much stronger than we are!*') They wish rather to prevent the possibility of war later on by means of an agreement while there is yet time. If I reject a request, I am not at once obliged to fight the man who asks it. This does not come unless I see that the other looks like forcing his wishes on me. (The EMPEROR: '*That is what he is doing.*')

I told the two Ministers that the fulfilment of their wishes depended on a condition to be set by us. I should have narrowed future chances and embarrassed the situation unnecessarily if I had given them to understand that we should never in any circumstances be prepared to come to an understanding about naval expenditure. The price I named will not so soon be paid by Sir Edward Grey.

The EMPEROR: '*Bravo, Metternich! He did his work well up to the main point of all. The Ambassador quite overlooked the fact that it is not his business to agree, even by a private and unprejudiced expression of opinion, with the British Minister's shameless suggestion that their peaceableness should depend on our reducing our naval strength.*[1] *He has thus started down a steep slope! I am sorry for him. It must be explained to him that I do not wish for good relations with England at the price of not building the German fleet. If England means only to show us her favour on condition of our reducing the fleet, it is impertinence without limit and a deep insult to the German people and their Emperor, which the Ambassador must repel at the very start! France and Russia might equally well demand a reduction of our*

[1] Cf. Wilson, *War Guilt*, p. 114.

*land armaments.   As soon as other States are allowed under any
pretext whatever to interfere in one's armaments, one abdicates,
like Spain and Portugal.   The German fleet is built against nobody,
and so not against England.   It is governed by our own needs.
This is clearly laid down in the Naval Law and has been unchallenged
for 11 years.   The Law will be carried out to the last tittle, whether
the Britons like it or not ; it is the same to us.   If they want war
let them begin it ; we are not afraid of it.'*

XXIV. 107

COUNT VON METTERNICH TO THE CHANCELLOR, PRINCE VON
BÜLOW, *August 1st*, 1908

Secret.

The most disturbing symptom recently for Anglo-German
relations has been Lord Cromer's speech in the House of Lords,[1]
in which he warned his countrymen of the coming danger and
prophesied a probability of war.   No one doubts that the warning contained an allusion to Germany.   The speech has made
a deep impression not only abroad, but here as well.   So long
as such warnings came from newspapers and extremists, it was
more or less possible to ignore them.   But it is quite another
thing if people of Lord Cromer's importance and prestige express
them in public.   In that debate in the House of Lords Lord
Lansdowne agreed with Lord Cromer's words.   Mr. Austen
Chamberlain repeated them in the Commons, and Mr. Wyndham,
the former Irish Secretary, spoke similarly at a public meeting.
Two years ago this gentleman discussed with me the possibility
of a compromise with Germany and was in favour of England
renouncing her opposition to the Bagdad Railway.   Thus much
has feeling turned round. . . .

Lord Cromer is not the stamp of man to make party capital
out of international questions.   He means what he says, which
makes his words of deeper importance and stronger influence. . . .

Sir Edward Grey, whom I feel to be an honourable and peaceable opponent, but still an opponent, said to me it had appeared
for some time that the British Press was less aggressive against
Germany.   I admitted that this was correct, but attributed it
not to a more friendly feeling for Germany, but to a consciousness that the work of incitement was complete and that there
was no longer any fear of a swing round in Germany's favour,
but especially that the papers were becoming frightened at
what they had done and were beginning to look on the situation
with anxiety.   (The EMPEROR : ' *So much the better !* ')

The Minister replied that there was the same feeling here
about our Navy League which also seemed to be quieter, now

[1] Cf. Lee, *King Edward VII*, p. 654.

that it had thoroughly excited public opinion against England. (The EMPEROR : ' ! ')

Last Sunday I had a long conversation with Mr. Lloyd George, in whom I have won an important co-adjutor. . . . He, like all the political world here, was impressed by Lord Cromer's speech, though he did not agree with it. But he expects a favourable reaction from it, of such a kind as to warn political circles that the situation is too serious for playing with war and danger of war any longer, and that the time has come for thinking of ways to relieve the tension. . . .

Mr. Lloyd George now came to his favourite idea of slowing down the speed of naval construction, (The EMPEROR : ' *That is unheard-of ! It comes from the fact that Metternich recently consented to discuss it.*') and urged me to make use of the time at my disposal whilst the peaceful Liberal Government was in power. This he estimated at 3 to 4 years. He quite understood that we must have a navy which inspired respect ; also that the present ratio between the British and German fleets would not do and that we wished to approach nearer the British fleet. (The EMPEROR : ' *Nonsense ! it has nothing to do with it.*') There could be no objection to this, since German overseas interests had increased to the point of needing a strong navy to protect them.

German Note.

Was the Chancellor of the Exchequer expressing merely his own personal views in advocating a ratio of 2 : 3 for the navies of the two countries ? At Leeds on October 10th [1] Asquith, the Prime Minister, certainly spoke against any diminution of the British Navy's present superiority. He referred to his words in the Commons (of March 2nd) : ' Our naval position is at this moment one of unassailable supremacy, and such it must remain.' . . . It was not till 1912 that the British Admiralty proposed a ratio of 16 : 10,—not essentially differing from Lloyd George's idea ; it was promptly accepted by Tirpitz at the time. (Cf. his *Erinnerungen*, p. 178.) That even in 1908 Tirpitz did not reject the idea of a naval understanding with England in principle as absolutely as the Emperor did, seems to be proved by a letter from Sir John Fisher to Lord Esher, of February 21st, 1908 : ' Secret. Tirpitz asked a mutual civilian friend living in Berlin to inquire very privately of me whether I would agree to limiting size of guns and size of ships, as this is vital to the Germans, who can't go bigger than the *Dreadnought* in guns or size. I wrote back by return of post yesterday morning : " Tell him I'll see him d—d first " ! I wonder what Wilhelm will say to that if Tirpitz shows him the letter.' (Cf. Fisher's *Memories*, p. 184.)

In his book, *Der Aufbau der Deutschen Flotte* (p. 145), Admiral von Tirpitz referred to Fisher's letter and denied ever having made such a suggestion. [But according to his *Memories* (p. 208), it would seem that he wished for a naval agreement. (Cf. p. 298.)]

---

[1] Cf. *The Times*, October 12th, 1908.

The present Government's interpretation of the Two-Power-Standard was that the British navy must be equal to any two foreign navies, (The EMPEROR : ' *It has unsuspectingly reached a Three-Power standard already.*') but not so as to be double the strongest foreign navy ; (The EMPEROR : ' *Jesuitical casuistry !* ') that is, the German navy and another, not twice the German Navy. He thought that the ratio between the British and German navies should be fixed at something like 3 : 2. (The EMPEROR : ' *He has got that far, has he ?* ') Considering the more vital importance of the navy for England than for Germany, the British Navy must always be a good bit stronger than ours, in order to give that feeling of safety which England demanded of it, and also powerful enough to prevent her being exposed to any wanton attack. (The EMPEROR : ' *That is language to be used only to China or Italy, or similar creatures! Unheard of !!*') . . .

The EMPEROR : ' *Conversations like that between Lloyd George and Metternich are very undignified and a provocation to Germany ! I must beg that in future he repels such expectorations unconditionally. In this case he has patiently listened to and been ready to fall in with the views and orders of British Statesmen, merely vainly protesting. He must give a rough answer to gentlemen who are not prepared to put up with " our mischievous longing to aggression ". Then these people will be reasonable for the first time. That Lloyd George dared to come out with a command to tie down our building speed is nothing, but that, after it, Metternich at the first conversation should have gone down the slope with a " possibility not quite excluded " ! The clever Britons hook on to this, and sooner or later they will present him with something to which he will agree ; in spite of " private conversation ", " expressions of opinion not binding ", etc. ! He ought to have refused* ab ovo *and said, " no State allows another to prescribe the amount and nature of its armaments ; I refuse to take part in such a discussion " ! Besides —our naval law, known for* 11 *years, and let them read* Nauticus *!* '

[King Edward's meeting with the Emperor, which was being prepared for with such care,[1] took place at Cronberg in Taunus on August 11th, 1908, for just one day. The King studiously avoided discussing the naval problem during his stay, as soon as he discovered that any mention of it would destroy the harmony of the visit. Sir Charles Hardinge, however, had a full discussion with the Emperor.] (Cf. G. & T., VI, p. 173 et seq.)

XXIV. 125

THE EMPEROR, AT PADERBORN, TO PRINCE VON BÜLOW,
August 12th, 1908

Cipher telegram.

. . . Talk with Sir Charles Hardinge.[2] After dinner Sir Charles spoke to me about our military arrangements and soon

[1] Cf. p. 282.   [2] Cf. Wilson, *War Guilt*, p. 115.

came to the army and the naval question. He spoke of 'grave apprehension', which everyone in England felt about our ship-building. To my astonished questions why, seeing it was limited by law and the law had been published for 11 years, he replied that the fleet was always concentrated at home. I replied that we needed our fleet owing to the rapid growth of our trade.

He: It is always kept at Kiel or Wilhelmshaven and the North Sea.

I: Because we have no colonies or coaling stations, that is our base ; we have no Gibraltar or Malta.

He: Your trade cannot be protected from your base. Why do you not sail further afield ?

I: Because the London Embassy and our Foreign Office thought that the less the Britons see our fleet the better ; its appearance in the Channel would cause annoyance.

He: Are you trying to make a bad joke ?

I: I am deeply in earnest. My men have suffered enough from having to do their service in northern waters.

He: That is quite incredible. In England it is understood quite differently.

I: This summer I sent my fleet abroad during your grand manœuvres in the North Sea—an obvious token of my wish for peace and my trust in England.

He: It was fine and did a great deal of good ; send your fleet away often, and then our people will really be reassured. It would be still more desirable to remove our anxiety about the ship-building, for in a few years you will be as strong as we are. (!)

I: That is absolute nonsense ; besides you have begun to build *Dreadnoughts* and compelled the world to build them. Every State is building them.

He: That was a bad mistake on our part.

I: When the *Dreadnought* was launched your Press described the ship as the best instrument for destroying the German fleet.

He: That was another bad mistake.

Continuation, August 13th, 1908

He: But you are making such rapid progress in building *Dreadnoughts* that in a few years, say 1912, you will be equal and even superior to us in strength. That is what excites and disturbs the British people.

I: It is absolute folly ; who has made you believe that nonsense ?

He: It is not nonsense ; it is authentic information from the British Admiralty.

I : It is still nonsense, even if your Admiralty says it—and also a proof of how badly informed British statesmen and people are on naval affairs and your own strength, if they imagine any such thing. You have without knowing it long passed the Two-Power standard and have already reached the Three-Power standard.

He : That is quite impossible. Our Admiralty says it can hardly maintain the Two-Power standard because of the menacing nature of German ship-building.

I : Your Admiralty must know better than that ; it is amusing itself with frightening you and your people with bogies. I can prove I am right by referring to Nauticus.

He : You can get no more authentic data than what the Admiralty has given me.

I : Your data are wrong ; I am an Admiral of the British Navy, and know all about it and understand it better than you, who are a civilian and know nothing about it.

I sent for Nauticus and showed Sir Charles the tables with the ship curves which Your Highness knows of. Speechless amazement was printed on his features, whilst Sir Frank Lascelles, who was watching us from a distance and with whom I had had a similar conversation the day before, based on a copy of Nauticus which I handed to him, could hardly contain his mirth. (Sir Frank is enthusiastic about Nauticus and accepts its views without question.)

He (after a long silence) : Who is this Nauticus ? I have never heard of him.

I : It is a set of gentlemen of high capacity in every profession and station, who have authentic information at their disposal.

He : Such gentlemen cannot claim to know more than our Admiralty. These tables are quite arbitrary, and I attach no importance to them (closing the book with a bang) ; I shall show it to the Admiralty at once.

I : You can do me no greater pleasure.

He : An end must be put to this ship-building competition ; an arrangement must be arrived at for slowing it down. For our Government will have to bring in a big programme of fresh naval construction in the next few years, for which fresh taxes will have to be raised owing to lack of resources. It will be very unpopular, the people will grumble, and the Government may be turned out.

I : If you will accept the Nauticus tables as correct instead of assuming they are imaginary, you will see that an additional programme is quite superfluous for the maintenance of your superiority. We are *not* trying to compete, our speed is fixed by law, the number of ships also, and you know it. You are entering into a competition which is one-sidedly British and is an invention of your Admiralty.

He : Can't you put a stop to your building ? or build less ships ? [1]

I : Germany determines the proportion of her naval armaments according to her own interests and alliances ; [2] it is defensive and is aimed at no nation, certainly not England. It is not a threat against you, who are all just now scared of bogies.

He : But an arrangement ought to be found for diminishing the construction. You must stop or build slower. [1]

I : Then we shall fight, for it is a question of national honour and dignity. [1]

Then I looked him straight in the eye. Sir Charles became scarlet, made me a bow, begged pardon for his words and urged me expressly to forgive and forget and treat them as remarks inadvertently made in private conversation. He conducted the conversation in an irritated and almost dictatorial tone. I am sure that his instructions and marching orders came from Fisher. I resumed the conversation with him in the evening, when he was quite another man, pleasant, cheerful, telling anecdotes. He noticed with satisfaction the changes in Turkey which had, ' thank goodness ', made the Macedonian reforms unnecessary ; a weight had fallen from his breast. He was delighted that his Government and ours were agreed about developing the Balkans with railways in all directions. It was the best plan to hand the lines not to individual Great Powers, but to non-political companies. As we talked he mentioned all the points where British and German policy could act jointly throughout the world. When after dinner, with the King's permission, I conferred on him the Order of the Red Eagle, First Class, [3] he was ready to eat out of my hand. He said his grandfather had been detached from Wellington's Staff to serve under Blücher and had lost his arm near Ligny, and for this Friedrich William III had honoured him with the Order of the Red Eagle. The insignia were kept in his house as a sacred possession. My frank words when I showed him my teeth had not failed in their effect. You must always treat Englishmen thus. It is

[1] English in text.
[2] *German Note.* Probably wrongly deciphered for ' necessities '.
[3] Cf. Lee, *King Edward VII*, II, p. 618.

very clear that Ballin's talk with Sir Ernest Cassel [1] did good, and that he succeeded in preventing the King from discussing the subject.

Before the King left for Germany, Fisher had a private audience with him. He evidently primed Hardinge. Before he left I spoke to him again of my Guildhall speech.[2] I said it was a programme proclaimed in the name of my Government and my whole nation. He and his Government could depend on that. When the Emperor speaks they are not empty words ; ' he speaks what he means.' He replied : ' We have an absolute confidence in Your Majesty.'

The King proposed a visit to Berlin next year,[3] the time to be settled later on. He will greet the Emperor Francis Joseph from me. He does not think much of Aehrenthal : ' He is a poor man and not very capable.' . . .

After the King's departure I discussed my Hardinge conversation with Lascelles.[4] He was annoyed at his fellow-countryman and exclaimed : ' This comes of their not believing my reports about Germany in the Foreign Office. Hardinge is just as mad about the naval affair and as ill-informed as any of his loud-voiced compatriots.' He was pleased to see that the King had taken the best impressions away with him. The whole situation between the two countries had genuinely improved, and most reasonable Englishmen would agree with him, especially the whole City and the industrial and working classes. He said : ' They won't hear of war, and I am perfectly convinced the two countries will never meet in war.'

[King Edward's visit to the Emperor Francis Joseph at Ischl did nothing to help on the British wishes regarding a naval agreement. Though it could not affect Austria in any way, the aged Emperor turned a deaf ear to the British appeal.]

XXIV. 134
COUNT BROCKDORFF-RANTZAU, IN VIENNA, TO PRINCE VON BÜLOW, *August 19th*, 1908

Extract. Very confidential.

. . . Whether the British Statesmen acted with the intention of preparing for an Anglo-Austrian rapprochement at the expense of Austro-German relations, is beyond my knowledge. (The

---

[1] Ballin went to London in the first week of July with the object of persuading the King, through Cassel, that the Tsar was trying to embroil him with the Emperor William.

[2] Cf. p. 268.

[3] Cf. Lee, *King Edward VII*, I, p. 672 et seq. On leaving Cronberg the King went to stay with the Emperor Francis Joseph at Ischl. Cf. G. & T., VI, p. 184.

[4] Cf. G. & T., VI, p. 181.

EMPEROR : ' *Yes, surely !* ') That the Austrians not only reckoned on this possibility, but were actually prepared for it, is proved by the serious tone used by the Emperor and also his Minister [Aehrenthal] to the British guests. In order to forestall any discussion on the subject, the Emperor Francis Joseph at the very start of the conversations declared sharply that his policy for all future time was based on an unshakable alliance with Germany. Baron Aehrenthal made this declaration emphatically to Sir Charles Hardinge and indicated to him so unmistakably his determination to allow no disturbance from *any* quarter of his hearty and trusting relations with the German Empire, that Sir Charles, impressed by the utterance which he might have expected in a less categorical form, answered with embarrassment (The EMPEROR : ' *Good ! That has put a stop to his impertinence.*') that no one in London had ever doubted it and they considered this policy very natural for Austria-Hungary.[1] . . .

[In August, 1908, Mr. Lloyd George made a tour in Germany for the purpose of studying the German system of Old Age Pensions. (Cf. Lee, *King Edward VII*, II, p. 654.)]

German Note. XXIV. 137

In an article of August 18th in the *Berliner Tageblatt* it was stated : ' The object of Lloyd George's visit to Germany is, according to a statement by a member of the Cabinet, less to study the Old Age Pension system than to lay the foundation for an understanding about diminution of naval armaments. Lloyd George has often said that the Budget, which will be heavily burdened by the Old Age Pension scheme, can only be balanced by a reduction in the Navy Estimates, since any further financial measures, such as increased taxation, are out of the question. Lloyd George is held in the Cabinet to be the best man to investigate feeling in Germany and even to arrive at an agreement, if there is no objection in principle in Berlin against the British Cabinet's naval ideas.'

[According to the German Note the Emperor himself suggested receiving Mr. Lloyd George.]

XXIV. 138

THE CHANCELLOR, PRINCE VON BÜLOW, AT NORDERNEY, TO THE GERMAN FOREIGN OFFICE, *August 21st*, 1908

Cipher telegram.

For your personal information.

Count Metternich considers that if under present circumstances the Emperor received Mr. Lloyd George it would rather make it harder for His Majesty to favour the rapprochement between us and England. This being so, I beg you to dissuade His Majesty from making this suggestion on the part of Germany. Count Metternich will be seeing His Majesty on Monday.

[1] Cf. G. & T., V, p. 208 et seq. 827 et seq. ; H. Wickham Steed, *Through Thirty Years*, pp. 282–3.

STEMRICH, GERMAN FOREIGN OFFICE, TO PRINCE VON BÜLOW,
August 21st, 1908

Telegram.

In the office of the *Frankfürter Zeitung* Mr. Lloyd George
said that he would like to meet Your Highness quietly, making
an excursion from Hamburg ; he goes there by car on Tuesday.
August Stein,[1] whom he wishes to see here, will cautiously
advise him against it. If Lloyd George's wish came to Your
Highness direct it would be impossible to refuse him.

XXIV. 139

PRINCE VON BÜLOW, AT NORDERNEY, TO THE GERMAN FOREIGN
OFFICE, *August 22nd*, 1908

Cipher telegram.

Please inform August Stein in confidence at once that he
should advise Lloyd George, as from himself and not in connection with the Foreign Office, against trying to see me. The
reasons : His visit would naturally be known and connected on
both sides of the Channel with the Naval programme. The
question of slowing down naval construction is not yet ripe.
German public opinion not yet prepared. A visit from him
would arouse hopes in England incapable of fulfilment at present,
and react badly on public opinion. It would probably also
injure his prestige in England, especially with the Opposition,
for it would mean that his efforts with the German Government
had been unsuccessful.

Request Stein, immediately after his interview with Lloyd
George, to inform the Foreign Office whether he succeeded in
putting the British Minister off the visit, and telegraph the
result to me.

German Note.

On August 22nd Stemrich telegraphed that on Stein's advice Lloyd
George had given up the idea of going to Norderney.

[Raymond, in his *Life of Lloyd George* (p. 109), quotes Harold Spender's
account of the visit, and says that though ' almost a teetotaller ', he drank
glasses of ' foaming beer ' with Prince Bülow.]

XXIV. 161

THE CHANCELLOR, PRINCE VON BÜLOW, TO COUNT VON METTER-
NICH, IN LONDON, *September 22nd*, 1908

His Majesty the Emperor related to me his conversation
with Sir Charles Hardinge, but much more calmly than in his
telegrams.[2] What seems to have aroused him was that Hardinge
commented direct to him and with some sharpness on our ship-

---

[1] Berlin correspondent of the *Frankfürter Zeitung*.
[2] Cf. p. 291 et seq.

building. I must say that it would have been more in accordance with constitutional and diplomatic custom if Hardinge had expressed his wishes and proposals not to the Monarch, who is not responsible, but to the Imperial Government direct or through Sir Frank Lascelles. Much asperity would have been avoided. Confronted with these delicate matters, the Emperor replied more bluntly than would otherwise have happened. His Majesty told me especially, as you already know from his marginal remarks, that we.do not wish to build beyond our present naval programme, and for military and financial reasons could not do so, and that this programme really meant no danger for England.

Tirpitz personally would not be unwilling to discuss the naval question with the British experts ; [1] but he does not know how he can go to England without exciting remark. He told me between ourselves most definitely with reference to his responsibility to the country and to history that it was quite incomprehensible that the British could fear a German attack, seeing that we could not attain, far less shake, their supremacy at sea. To me he seemed not absolutely disinclined for an understanding with the British about ship-building. He said merely that the present naval programme, as fixed by law, could scarcely be modified, as all the popular parties in the Reichstag and public opinion would not understand it. British policy also would have to turn over a new and more friendly leaf in diplomacy and the Press, for the German people would consent to nothing which might be attributed to pressure from outside. Not till there was less tension between Germany and England was it worth while discussing the question or perhaps possible to decide whether the two countries could agree about their ship-building, thus doing away with their fears of each other.

German Note.

Cf. O. Hammann, *Bilder aus der letzten Kaiserzeit*, p. 59 et seq. Prince Bülow commented sympathetically on a paper by Vice-Admiral Gaister (retired), entitled *What Naval Armaments does Germany need ?* as follows : ' If in our naval armaments we lay more stress on defensive coastal forts, submarines, mines, etc., the main reason for tension with England falls away, and moreover it is perhaps better for our own military (and financial) security.' It is thus clear that personally the Chancellor was disposed in favour of an understanding with England about naval construction ; the only question was how successfully to get over the Emperor's blunt opposition . . . Cf. Lee, *King Edward VII*, II, 604, 682.

---

[1] Cf. p. 290.

CHAPTER XXIV

BOSNIA-HERZEGOVINA AND BULGARIAN INDEPENDENCE, AUGUST TO OCTOBER, 1908

[The centre of mid-European intrigue was now no longer Berlin. Holstein was gone, and Aehrenthal, the *protégé* of the Archduke Francis Ferdinand (cf. Brandenburg, p. 304) in Vienna, focused in himself the attention and suspicions of all Europe. It was symbolical of the new situation when Bülow on October 30th, 1908, wrote to Aehrenthal : ' I have complete confidence in your judgment ; in this special case I will add that you are in a better position to judge the Servian situation and the circumstances depending on it than we can at this distance. I shall therefore regard the decision at which you finally arrive as being that best suited to the circumstances.' (XXVI. 227.) Aehrenthal's policy, as described in the following pages, brought to an acute head the irreconcilable differences between the Germanic and Slav points of view. He placed Germany in a position of great embarrassment and discredit, duped and alienated Russia for good and generally destroyed any belief in Austrian good faith which might still exist, which was not what the Archduke, his patron, desired. The duplicity which accompanied his policy and that of his successor, Count Berchtold, occupies a prominent place amongst the more immediate causes of the World War.

Early in August King Edward paid a visit to the German Emperor at Cronberg and thence travelled to Ischl for the Jubilee of the Emperor Francis Joseph's reign. (Cf. pp. 291, 295 ; H. Wickham Steed, *Through Thirty Years*, p. 281 et seq. ; Lee, II, p. 625 ; G. & T., V, p. 827.) Although Balkan affairs were discussed, no mention was made of the Emperor's determination to annex Bosnia and Herzegovina, which was definitely settled on his birthday, August 18th.

For the influence exercised by the Archduke Francis Ferdinand, cf. Brandenburg, p. 304.]

XXV. 551

Memorandum handed in by the Austro-Hungarian Ambassador in Berlin on August 20th, 1908

The Ischl interview gave Baron Aehrenthal an opportunity for discussing political questions with King Edward and Sir Charles Hardinge. To sum up the conversation with King Edward—the King expects that the new situation in Turkey, which has produced a *détente* in the relations between the Powers, will bring about friendly co-operation between England and Austria in Constantinople. His permanent desire is that the two Empires may maintain the best possible relations with each other and that peace, which is so much needed, may be secured.

Baron Aehrenthal wished to use his meeting with Sir Charles Hardinge to describe the standpoint which had guided the Vienna Cabinet with regard to the misunderstandings and difficulties which had arisen during the last months.

Austria-Hungary, he said, in all her efforts to further and secure the reforms initiated by the Monarchy in combination with Russia, had always pointed out that the Sultan's sovereignty and the susceptibilities of the Mohammedans must be respected. The leading idea of the Mürsteg programme was to improve the condition of the Christians 'with the Sultan and not against him'.

Austria-Hungary during the last months raised certain objections to the British proposals because the foregoing standpoint had not always received sufficient attention. The Vienna Cabinet was convinced that, even on the assumption of complete agreement amongst the Powers and of energetic action by their representatives in Constantinople, the Sultan had been unable to consent to these proposals because his compliance would have been resented by the Mohammedans. Some of the British proposals would have led to the loss of these provinces or would have been equivalent to it, and to this the Sultan could not submit without a fight, even if all the Cabinets were agreed together.

Recent events have justified this view.

Austria-Hungary will still bear in mind the reform of Turkish administration. She will be ready to resume the action in Constantinople at a moment to be selected *by agreement*. Until then the Vienna Government maintains that we must wait to see what happens in the Young Turkish movement.

Austria-Hungary seeks no political advantage in the three vilayets, and in accordance with this she will pursue a policy of non-intervention. The Monarchy is Turkey's nearest neighbour in Europe. Vienna expects England, whose relations with Austria-Hungary have always been friendly, to bear this in mind.

Now, as always, the Vienna Government has no regular agreements with that of the Sultan. But there are specifically Austrian interests, which the Monarchy is absolutely determined to defend. The Government will cling steadfastly to the German alliance, because this makes for the good of Austria-Hungary and peace in Europe.

Sir Charles Hardinge thanked Baron Aehrenthal for his frankness and assured him that in consideration of the altered situation in Turkey he truly hoped that British and Austrian policy would follow the same path there. He quite thought it natural for Austria to cling to the alliance with Germany, as the Minister had said. From the British point of view and also for the maintenance of peace the rupture of this alliance would be a great misfortune. King Edward spoke to the Foreign Minister about Austro-German relations in identical terms. Since both Sir Charles and Baron Aehrenthal consider that waiting is the only right course in the present situation, future eventualities in Turkey were not discussed. The Foreign Minister merely suggested that the change which had taken place in Turkey might help on a rapprochement between England and Germany in the Eastern question and in time improve generally the relations between the two States.

[Having already fully discussed the details with Aehrenthal on March 13th and 14th, 1908, Prince Ferdinand of Bulgaria, at his own request (XXVI. 67), was received at the beginning of August by the Austrian Emperor at Ischl, and there it was arranged that Bulgaria (cf. G. & T., V, p. 381) should proclaim her independence of Turkey the day before the formal annexation of Bosnia and Herzegovina. (Cf. H. Wickham Steed, *Through Thirty Years*, I, p. 292 ; Brandenburg, p. 300 et seq. ; Grey, *Twenty-five Years*, p. 191 et seq. ; *Oesterreich-Ungarns Aussenpolitik*, Vienna, 1930, Vol. I, p. 97.

After King Edward left Ischl he went to Marienbad, where he saw both M. Isvolsky and M. Clemenceau (Lee, II, p. 628, 634 ; Steed, I, p. 284). Isvolsky then went to Austria and met Aehrenthal on September 15th (G. & T., V, p. 366). On September 5th Schoen, writing from Berchtesgaden, reported Aehrenthal's account of the interview. The latter had said to Isvolsky that ' Austria would certainly be obliged in time to consider a final settlement of the position of Bosnia and Herzegovina, and the solution could and would be no other than annexation '. Schoen concluded as follows :]

XXVI. 28

SCHOEN TO THE CHANCELLOR, PRINCE VON BÜLOW,
September 5th, 1908

Extract.

. . . I avoided giving any definite opinion on these plans, and merely said that Austria-Hungary would always find us ready to consider her interests and wishes in the Near East in a loyal and most friendly spirit. The Straits question [1] seemed to me to present many dangers, (The EMPEROR : ' *Very much so !* ') but we had no reason to discountenance it beforehand. If it meant conceding to Russia freedom of passage we would rather join with Austria in granting it than leave it for the western Powers to give as an afterthought. (The EMPEROR : ' *Yes.*')

Finally with some nervousness and with a prayer for strict secrecy Baron Aehrenthal explained to me that a further aim

[1] Cf. G. & T., V, pp. 383, 608.

of his Balkan policy was 'complete destruction of the Servian nest of revolutionaries', for which he hoped for our support.[1] Servia might be given up to Bulgaria, with the important advantage to Austria-Hungary of having as neighbour a State with a fixed ethnographic frontier.

German Note.

Aehrenthal soon gave up the idea of partitioning Servia. (Cf. p. 317.)

' I thought fit to add a comment on these cold-blooded plans. I just said we had no special sympathy for Servia, but I thought there was danger in permitting a greater Bulgaria to arise. Neither the Roumanians nor the Greeks nor even the Turks would probably take it calmly. (The EMPEROR : '*Correct.*') This alarmed Baron Aehrenthal less. He said the Bulgarians had the material for building up a quiet and orderly State existence, which in spite of all racial relationship would be a wall against any Russo-Slav flooding of the Balkans ; also Roumania was on Bulgaria's flank, which would make her cautious about adventures. . . .

[On September 16th Isvolsky met Aehrenthal at Buchlau, Count Berchtold's country residence, where Isvolsky was made fully cognizant of what was intended. Aehrenthal promised to give him ample notice before the actual date of annexation. His neglect to do this when the time came was never forgiven by Isvolsky, and the history of mid-Europe for the next few years was coloured by the enmity between these two men. (Cf. pp. 384–397.)

The translator is indebted to Mr. H. Wickham Steed for certain points from the Austrian publication of documents (*Oesterreich-Ungarns Aussenpolitik*, 1930), which came out whilst this volume was in proof. The Buchlau meeting is dealt with at length ; also the articles in the *Fortnightly Review*, that by Dr. Dillon, written under Aehrenthal's inspiration, and the second, *Vox et praeterea nihil*, which, as Mr. Steed states, was written by Prince Elim Demidoff, the First Secretary of the Russian Embassy in Vienna. Mr. Steed also writes : ' The story that Aehrenthal tried to diminish Anglo-German friction is pure moonshine. His press ran a most villainous personal campaign against King Edward both during and after the annexation crisis.' (Cf. p. 398.)

Prince Ferdinand of Bulgaria visited the Emperor Francis Joseph again on September 23rd, 1908, to make final arrangements for his declaration of independence. The Emperor William chose to consider the Bulgarian action as a deep-laid plot of King Edward's. (Cf. Lee, *King Edward VII*, II, p. 634.)]

XXVI. 79

COUNT VON METTERNICH, IN LONDON, TO THE GERMAN FOREIGN OFFICE, *September 29th*, 1908

Cipher telegram.

The Press publishes a *communiqué* according to which the British Government have declared to the Bulgarian Government

---

[1] *Cf.* Wilson, *War Guilt*, p. 117.

that there is no justification for continuing to occupy the Orient railway line.[1] (The EMPEROR : ' *Good.*')

Sir Charles Hardinge is highly incensed at the Bulgarian action which is contrary to International Law and may alienate British sympathies from Bulgaria, and that may mean much. (The EMPEROR : ' *Aha! The King's crown ?* ') It would eventually be necessary to bring strong pressure to bear at Sofia.[2] The Bulgarian agent here, Minchovitch, has excused the recent interview to the Foreign Office as being attributable to indiscretion. The explanation has given satisfaction here.

The Press is unanimous against Bulgaria, which further prejudices the attitude of Austria-Hungary and——.[3]

[On October 4th Aehrenthal told the British Ambassador in Vienna that he was unaware of any impending changes in Bulgaria. (Cf. G. & T., V, p. 379.)]

XXVI. 89

TSCHIRSCHKY, IN VIENNA, TO THE GERMAN FOREIGN OFFICE,
October 6th, 1908

Cipher telegram.

M. K. Saravov, the Bulgarian representative, has to-day officially informed Baron Aehrenthal of Bulgaria's declaration of independence. On receiving the communication the Minister said that he would at once place himself in agreement with the rest of the Powers.

At the same time he told the Bulgarian representative emphatically that there could be no question of recognising independence until the railway matter was settled. He said : ' Now we and Germany have Bulgaria in our hands.' He added that what mattered now above all was that before settlement of all the complications involved in the seizure of the railway Bulgaria should consider the ensuing negotiations and arrange with the railway company that the latter should be effectively guaranteed by a suitable indemnity. Bulgaria should engage to pay the company a fixed weekly sum.

Baron Aehrenthal said that he set store on going hand in hand with us in this question as hitherto, and he would be grateful to be informed whether Germany intended to give similar instructions to her representative at Sofia.[4] He intended to lodge another emphatic protest at Sofia the next day. To the representative here he had described the methods employed by Bulgaria as pure robbery.

[1] The line through Eastern Roumelia. (Cf. G. & T., V, p. 364.)
[2] Cf. G. & T., V, p. 595. [3] Cipher group missing.
[4] Cf. G. & T., V, p. 380. The British and German Governments urged strongly that the railway should be restored to the Company.

the next day (October 7th) the annexation of Bosnia and Herze-
was officially announced. Aehrenthal admitted later on that the
ineousness of the two events was a 'cardinal blunder'. (Cf.
nburg, p. 318.) The decree had been issued in Vienna on the
id dated October 5th.

The British Government and Sir Edward Grey in particular were
sympathetic with the Young Turk movement and indeed went so far as
to urge the Porte to strengthen the defences of the Bosphorus—which
eventually were used against England. (Cf. Brandenburg, p. 319.)]

XXVI. 107

BARON VON MARSCHALL, IN CONSTANTINOPLE, TO THE GERMAN
FOREIGN OFFICE, *October 6th,* 1908

Cipher telegram. Extract.

The Grand Vizir informed me that . . . Sir E. Grey had
invited Rifaat Bey to come and see him and said England
regretted the Bulgarian declaration of independence and the
annexation of Bosnia and Herzegovina. Though these measures
would not greatly injure Turkey materially they would do harm
to the new *régime.* 'La Turquie est maltraitée.' The object
of both measures was to handicap and discredit from outside
the new *régime* in its efforts for internal reform and consolidation.
But England was not admitting that the terms of the Treaty
of Berlin might be modified without an exchange of ideas between
the Powers or without the Porte's consent. The King's Government would therefore recognise neither the annexation nor
Bulgarian independence. But they advised Turkey 'd'exclure
le plus longtemps possible la guerre en présence "; she should
turn confidentially to the Signatory Powers. As regarded the
loss of Eastern Roumelia she would get nothing altered, but
England was prepared to urge that Turkey should receive compensation for this loss and a money indemnity, and eventually
a new congress might be summoned.

He, Grey, begged the Ambassador to ask his Government
of what in their opinion the compensation might consist. He
said that there was no confirmation of the report that Russia,
Italy and Germany had given their consent to the annexation.

Tewfik Pacha wished to speak to the Grand Vizir about the
question of compensation and the reply to be given to England.
I said nothing, but should like to suggest that we might advise
the Porte to ask the Powers to confirm Turkey in her European
possessions in general or in the possession of Macedonia and
the vilayet of Adrianople in particular, and to suggest an
indemnity both for the railway and the tribute from Eastern
Roumelia.

Over the Turkish question an Anglo-Russo-French group [1] is

[1] Cf. p. 306.

clearly in process of formation, which will strongly attract Italy. It is to our interests not to remain outside this and to draw Austria-Hungary into it along with us.

XXVI. 110

PRINCE VON BÜLOW, AT NORDERNEY, TO BARON VON JENISCH, IN THE EMPEROR'S SUITE AT ROMINTEN, *October 7th*, 1908

Cipher telegram. Extract.

I fully understand His Majesty's annoyance at Austria not having communicated her plan of annexation to us earlier. (The EMPEROR: '*Did not Szögyenyi report that Aehrenthal gave indications to Schoen on September 3rd or 4th?*'[1]) On the other hand we might truly tell the Turks as well as the Powers that we only received knowledge of the Austrian plans after the Russians and Italians and at the same time as the other Powers.

A genuine reason for the Austrian action might be found in the anxiety felt in Vienna at the Serbo-Croatian national aspirations. (The EMPEROR: '*Right! that appeared as early as April. But if it had been held then that " something " was bound to happen, there would have been time up till August to find out what and how!*') which, when I was in Vienna in April, I found not only in Aehrenthal and Beck, but also in the Archduke Francis Ferdinand and the Austrian Emperor. The Austrians believe that in the Balkans they must play off the Servians against the Bulgarians or else the Bulgarians against the Serbs. (The EMPEROR: '*If these choose to play up.*') They prefer the latter alternative, since they think that the Bulgarians attract the Austrian Slavs less than the Serbs would, and they hope that an independent Bulgaria would be against Russia, just as Roumania was when she was emancipated. (The EMPEROR: '*I don't believe she would ever gravitate towards* St. Petersburg *and London combined.*') The future alone can show whether this calculation is right, or whether the Austrians are not driving out Satan through Beelzebub. (The EMPEROR: '*Yes.*') Representations by us would not help much now, as the Austrians think they know more about Balkan conditions than we do, since it is first and foremost a matter of saving their skin there.

In my opinion it would be certainly better for us and probably for Austria also if they would rely on the Turks in the Balkans, and not on the Serbs or the Bulgarians. . . .

I consider that in politics reliability pays not only on ethical grounds, but also on those of prudence. Austria-Hungary behaved loyally towards us not only at Algeciras but also this summer in the naval question.[2] Like should be paid for with

---

[1] The Emperor saw this despatch. Cf. p. 301.   [2] Cf. pp. 243, 295.

like. . . .   (The EMPEROR.: ' *The arguments are correct!   I only
regret that Aehrenthal's fearful stupidity has brought us into the
dilemma of being unable to protect and stand by the Turks who
are our friends, seeing that my own ally has injured them.   And
now I must look on at England taking my place in Turkey with
her advice and protection, and doing so with arguments based on
International Law, which are incontestable and really after my own
heart.   Thus my Turkish policy, so carefully built up for 20 years.
is thrown away!   A great triumph over us for Edward VII!* [1]
Soon the Turkish reactionaries will declare that all this loss of land
is a result of the committees with their constitution, and that really
it is the " German " officers;   at one blow these will all be dismissed or murdered, and Englishmen and Frenchmen will take
their places.*)*

[On October 10th Baron von Marschall reported from Constantinople
that according to his impressions ' secret negotiations have been in progress
for some days between Kiamil Pacha and Sir Gerard Lowther for an
Anglo-Turkish treaty.   There is other evidence of this.   My British colleague goes daily to the Porte and remains an hour with Kiamil Pacha,
accompanied by his First Dragoman, G. H. Fitzmaurice . . .' (XXVI.
142).   In G. & T., V, p. 419, it is stated that there is no evidence in the
British records of such negociations.

On October 9th, 1908, Isvolsky arrived in London.   His object was to
obtain support for his idea of a European Conference on the Balkans and
to get the Dardanelles opened for Russian ships.   (Cf. Lee, *King Edward
VII*, II, p. 639;   G. & T., V, pp. 412, 434;   Steed, *Through Thirty Years*,
I, p. 294;   Brandenburg, p. 318).   For the part played by Germany in
March, 1909, in preventing a Conference, cf. *Oesterreich-Ungarns Aussenpolitik* (Vienna, 1930).]

COUNT VON METTERNICH TO THE GERMAN FOREIGN OFFICE,
October 9th, 1908

Cipher telegram.

To-day I spoke to Sir E. Grey [2] in the sense of your telegram
of October 7th. [3]   He was serious and reserved and spoke sharply
of Austria's action which had reopened the whole question of
the Treaty of Berlin.   Confidence in international treaties must
disappear if one Great Power tore them up.   Hence the British
Government could recognise neither the Austrian annexation
nor the Bulgarian declaration of independence. He asked
whether we had sent an answer agreeing to the Austrian notification about annexation.   I replied that I had no information,
but I made it quite clear that we could not leave our ally in
the lurch since she had stood by us in international disputes.
(BÜLOW: ' *Correct.*') . . .

[1] Cf. p. 363; Brandenburg, p. 322; Lee, II, p. 638.
[2] Cf. G. & T., V, p. 419; Grey, *Twenty-five Years*, I, pp. 190–1.
[3] Not given.

Finally I mentioned Isvolsky, who is expected here to-day, and asked if, as the papers stated, he had already announced his idea for a Conference. His interview with André Tardieu [1] seemed to show proof of this.

On this Sir E. Grey spoke with reserve at first. He wished to wait for what Isvolsky's suggestions would bring forth. It was conceivable that the Austrian action might cause dissatisfaction in Russia with regard to the Treaty of Berlin. . . .

Meanwhile Isvolsky, who is by no means trusted here, will be fêted and flattered—to-morrow at dinner in the King's elegant circle of ladies and gentlemen, at dinner on Sunday at Buckingham Palace (an engagement made at Marienbad), and on Monday at dinner with Sir E. Grey. The next days will show whether the Anglo-Russian entente will survive the Dardanelles question. . . . [2]

I shall try to see Sir E. Grey to-morrow, as I consider it important now while Isvolsky is here to induce in him confidence in our Eastern policy, (BÜLOW: ' Very right.') in order to keep him from yielding to the Russian pressure, whilst naturally avoiding getting between his wishes and Isvolsky's.

XXVI. 61

TSCHIRSCHKY, IN VIENNA, TO PRINCE VON BÜLOW,
October 12th, 1908

Very confidential.

Regarding the preliminaries of the annexation question, the Duke of Avarna [3] told me that, during his short stay in Rome, Tittoni [4] had informed him that at Salzburg Aehrenthal had said no word of annexation to him nor had he even given him to understand that it had been decided on in principle. (The EMPEROR : ' Donnerwetter ! ')

[On the other hand, Stemrich stated that the Italian Ambassador had handed him an Italian memorandum (XXVI. 57) containing the following words : ' . . . When Aehrenthal was with Tittoni and the latter hinted at plans of annexation, he had answered that in any case this was an affair of the Monarchy's internal politics. (The EMPEROR : ' False ! very much external.') He had added that if annexation took place, the Austrian Government would withdraw its garrisons from the Sanjak of Novi-Bazar and renounce its rights under Art. 25 of the Berlin Treaty. Isvolsky said to Tittoni that such action would be of eminently international character and that annexation could only happen with the consent of the Signatory Powers. He said, moreover, that Russia would not oppose it if certain conditions were fulfilled :—Besides the offered renunciation of Art. 25, Art. 29 restricting the sovereignty of Montenegro should be deleted ; and also free passage through the Straits should be restored to the States on the

---

[1] French journalist. Cf. G. & T., V, pp. 407–8.
[2] Cf. Lee, *King Edward VII*, II, p. 639.
[3] Italian Ambassador in Vienna.   [4] Cf. G. & T., V, p. 393.

shores of the Black Sea. (The EMPEROR : ' *With necessary reservations regarding Stamboul, Sultan and Turkey !* ') . . .]

Baron Aehrenthal had only mentioned the occupied provinces question in general terms, hinting that the settlement of affairs there was a matter for Austria-Hungary and Turkey only. (The EMPEROR : ' *Absurd !* ') Since the Austro-Hungarian Minister had only spoken in general terms Tittoni had not mentioned the matter again. His talk with Isvolsky [1] was the first occasion of his hearing of the intended annexation. Aehrenthal had at first only mentioned the Bosnian question quite generally and later in the conversation, when the Russian Minister asked further about the Austrian plans, he admitted that annexation was intended, but there was no mention of a date. The Russian Minister then brought forward his demand about the Straits but only in general terms ' supposing annexation came about '.

When, as I said, the Duke of Avarna handed Signor Tittoni's letter to Baron Aehrenthal proposing, as compensation, an entente in Balkan matters with Russia and Austria-Hungary (The EMPEROR : ' *Without us !* ') he also represented to him that his Chief had been much astonished on receiving by letter a bare announcement of the annexation which was to be expected a few days later. The Minister had made no protestation on this but had merely replied : ' Comment, Monsieur Tittoni n'a pas compris ce que je lui ai dit à Salzbourg ? ' (The EMPEROR : ' *Very convenient !* ')

The Italian Ambassador did not conceal from me that Baron Aehrenthal's methods had made an unpleasant impression both on him and also in Rome. (The EMPEROR : ' *On all of us.*')

[Both King Edward and the Emperor William were highly incensed at the deception which had been practised on them (cf. Lee, pp. 636–8), though it cannot be said that the Emperor was ignorant of the Austrian intentions. German policy was, however, gravely embarrassed by the injury done by Austria to Turkey, both of them being Germany's allies.]

XXVI. 169

MIQUEL, IN ST. PETERSBURG, TO PRINCE VON BÜLOW,
October 12th, 1908

Extract. Very confidential.

M. Tcharikov asked me to see him to-day and read me a telegram from M. Isvolsky about his conversation with King Edward. According to it the King said that, after all that had happened in the Balkans, still greater difficulties could only be avoided by calling a Conference. In order to bring this about M. Isvolsky might, whilst in Berlin, try to convince the Imperial

[1] Cf. G. & T., V, pp. 407, 807–8.

Government of the necessity of a Conference (The EMPEROR : ' *No.*') and to induce them to use their influence in Vienna so that Austria-Hungary should cease her opposition to it. (The EMPEROR : ' *No ! decidedly not.*') . . .

[The Conference Idea came to nothing,[1] for, as Bülow put it in a nut-shell : ' It won't come off ! we shall have nothing to do with it ! Austria won't have Bosnia included and Russia won't admit the Straits, so what is the good of a Conference ? ' (XXVI. 169.) Moreover Isvolsky failed to obtain the concessions regarding free passage through the Dardanelles, Russia being clearly too weak to enforce any such demand. (Cf. Lee, II, p. 645.)]

XXVI. 368

BARON VON MARSCHALL IN CONSTANTINOPLE, TO THE GERMAN FOREIGN OFFICE, *October 25th*, 1908

Cipher telegram.

Tewfik Pacha told me yesterday that Sir E. Grey had declared to the Turkish Ambassador, Rifaat Pacha, that with regard to negociations with Russia about the Straits question England was letting the Porte have an entirely free hand and would exercise no pressure, but she reserved the right of claiming for herself also whatever privileges were accorded to Russia.

XXVI. 129

THE EMPEROR WILLIAM TO THE EMPEROR FRANCIS JOSEPH, *October 14th*, 1908

MY DEAR FRIEND,

I thank you heartily for the friendly letter telling me of the incorporation of Bosnia and Herzegovina. The reasons you adduce for this important step I can well appreciate. In this question you can rely on my unchanging personal friendship and respect, as well as on the close alliance which binds us together. The incorporation will certainly be a blessing to the two provinces which have developed so remarkably under your administration.

I consider it a wise measure, which I can only agree with, that you have decided to withdraw your troops garrisoned in

---

[1] Cf. Wilfred S. Blunt, *My Diaries*, II, p. 219 : ' Oct. 21st, 1908. Rum-bold, whom I called on in the afternoon, thinks with George Wyndham and me that the Conference proposal will be dropped. But he is very positive that the annexation of Bosnia had nothing to do with the Ottoman revo-lution. It had been decided on to his knowledge as much as three years ago, and the only thing that delayed it was the difficulty of settling whether Bosnia should belong to Austria or to Hungary. As to Bulgaria he could not explain how it had come about that Prince Ferdinand had been so well received by the Emperor of Austria, for the Emperor had often talked to him, Rumbold, of Ferdinand as an intriguer and a scoundrel, who had connived at the murder of Stambouloff.'

the Sanjak of Novi-Bazar and to renounce in future the rights over this Sanjak which you won under the Treaty of Berlin. This step will certainly have a good effect, as it proclaims the peacefulness of your intentions and will make it easy for Turkey, to spare and strengthen whom is to the interests of both our allied Empires in equal measure, to get used to the new order of things.

XXVI. 222

MEMORANDUM BY PRINCE VON BÜLOW, *October 28th,* 1908

1. Friedjung's [1] insinuations in to-day's *Vossische Zeitung,* to the effect that England's bitterness against Austria is merely the result of the Cronberg meeting and is directed against her simply as an ally of Germany and that the differences and conflicts are not between England and Austria but England and Germany—are perfidious and unpleasant. But *at present* we must under no circumstances enter into a Press-feud with Austria ! It would be the greatest mistake we could make just now. It would demoralise and repel Austria, and would cement still more firmly the Entente of the Western Powers with Russia and Italy. Influence all the papers to which you have access, so that they may avoid all such polemics and, if possible, even academic references to the value and extent of our alliance with Austria. At present the word is to wait quietly and give no opening for misconstruction. I beg Herr von Loebell to speak to the *Deutsche Tageszeitung, Täglicher Rundschau,* etc., with an appeal to their patriotism.

2. We had best refer direct to Vienna any mediation proposals coming from England, France or Russia. We should say we wish to avoid any appearance of pressing upon our ally— which would be the case if we passed on proposals. The result of Isvolsky's discussions on London and Paris strengthens my conviction that it will suit us best for all participants to settle with each other direct, and not use us (or Europe) as a buffer. We cannot shout this from the house-tops but it must be our private *ligne de conduite.* If they try to use us as a buffer, we say simply : ' Settle it amongst yourselves ; we shall make no difficulties '.

3. Any agreement between England and France in Constantinople with the object of strengthening Turkey and the Young Turk *régime* is useful to us, since it divides both from Russia, who cannot honestly join in such a policy for any length of time. We cannot say this openly either, nor can we oppose such an agreement in the Press, but we must treat it as some-

[1] Described in the German index as an Austrian historian and journalist.

thing quite natural and legitimate for France (who holds 4 milliards of Turkish Bonds) to look after her own interests in Turkey and for England to emphasise her traditional rôle, as protector of Turkey and especially of a Liberal Turkey. We may not show anxieties or feelings regarding our own influence in Constantinople. It will do no harm if our Press says that France can be proved by statistics to have much greater financial interests in the East than we have, and that there is room enough there for British as well as German trade.

4. I beg you to inform those whom it may concern of this and to let me have a copy of these instructions.

CHAPTER XXV

THE 'DAILY TELEGRAPH' ARTICLE, OCTOBER, 1908

German Note. XXIV. 167

Colonel Stuart Wortley, a friend and admirer of the Emperor William, was impressed by the latter's repeatedly expressed wish that the British public should be as completely as possibly informed of his friendly feelings towards England in spite of the naval question. To this end Colonel Stuart Wortley, on the strength of the Emperor's utterances in the autumn of 1907 and the summer of 1908, prepared the draft of an article, which apparently received its final form in the offices of the *Daily Telegraph* with the help of the journalist, Harold Spender. The whole was submitted to the Emperor on September 23rd, 1908. (Cf. Brandenburg, p. 290 ; Chirol, *Fifty Years in a Changing World*, p. 302; G. & T., Vol. VI.)

The Emperor, who received Colonel Stuart Wortley's letter and enclosure at Rominten, was pleased at the attention showed to him. He at once sent the article to the Foreign Office for perusal with orders that it should be clearly typed out. Schoen, the Foreign Secretary, was away on leave, but Stemrich sent the original and the typed copy to Bülow at Norderney along with suggestions for modification of the article in three places on the ground that offence might be occasioned abroad, if certain sentences remained unaltered. Bülow apparently did not read the draft himself or at least only cursorily ; he sent it instead to the Foreign Office for careful revision. There no one ventured to make any drastic alterations, and the article appeared in the *Daily Telegraph* on October 27th, 1908 (q.v.).

The article was received with derision in England. In the German Press it raised a storm of indignation against the Emperor.]

XXIV. 178

PRINCE VON BÜLOW to MUMM VON SCHWARZENSTEIN, AT TOKIO, *October 29th*, 1908

Telegram.

Daily Telegraph publishes a conversation of His Majesty with an English private person with an allusion to future developments in the Pacific and the necessity for a strong Navy.

Please make it clear at Tokio that the utterance is in no way directed against Japan. The context shows that it only concerns the increase of our commercial interests in the Pacific and the need of protecting them.

XXIV. 179
PRINCE VON BÜLOW TO THE EMPEROR WILLIAM, *October 30th*, 1908

I enclose for Your Majesty a number of newspaper articles about the interview published by Colonel Stuart Wortley concerning the conversation with Your Majesty. The British papers discuss it with scepticism, disparagement and scorn. Important Englishmen such as Lord Roberts and Sir Edward Grey refuse to say anything about it. The French and Russian papers are using the occasion for strong attacks on Your Majesty and on German policy. Above all, the German Press, with few exceptions, considers that the interview has deeply injured our policy and our country. The attacks by the German papers are unjust ; for Your Majesty was so gracious as to send me through Baron von Jenisch the English writer's composition for examination. At the time I was at Norderney overwhelmed with serious questions (Eastern crisis, reform of Imperial finances, and other internal matters) and so did not myself read Colonel Wortley's long elaboration, which was very illegible and written on bad paper,[1] but I merely sent it to the Foreign Office for examination. I also gave strict orders to consider its probable effects most carefully and report to me where alterations, additions or omissions appeared advisable. The Foreign Office sent back the English manuscript with a report suggesting a few small alterations but offering no objection against publication. The Foreign Office official who was with me wrote in this sense to Baron von Jenisch.

If I myself had had personal knowledge of the manuscript, I should have begged Your Majesty not to permit its publication, at any rate at the present moment. If Your Majesty is displeased with my having failed under pressure of business to go through the English manuscript in person and blames me for the carelessness shown by the Foreign Office, I humbly beg to be allowed to retire. But if I have not lost Your Majesty's confidence, (The EMPEROR : ' *No.*') my sole object in remaining will be to counter, so far as I can, the unjust attacks on my Imperial Master publicly and emphatically. I must therefore crave permission to say officially in the *Norddeutsche Allgemeine Zeitung* (The EMPEROR : ' *Yes.*') that the attacks on Your Majesty by a great section of the Press are totally unjustified, that Your Majesty sent me the English author's manuscript and that I forwarded it to the Foreign Office, which suggested only minor alterations in it.

[The Emperor refused to accept Bülow's offer of resignation, and also Schoen's, who fell seriously ill owing to mental disturbance and overwork. Stemrich also was away ill, and at Schoen's desire Kiderlen-Waechter assumed charge of the Foreign Office until Schoen's return on December 1st.]

---

[1] He cannot have seen the typed copy.

XXIV. 183

MEMORANDUM BY KLEHMET OF THE GERMAN FOREIGN OFFICE, *November 6th*, 1908

Late one evening Stemrich, the Under-Secretary, appeared in my room and handed me a file which had come from Norderney, saying that as he thought there was something shaky about it I might take charge of it and see what could be done with it. That was all I had to guide me.

As far as I remember, the documents were as follows :

1. A type-written draft in English of the *Daily Telegraph* article.

2. A letter from Colonel Stuart Wortley to His Majesty asking for leave to demonstrate His Majesty's friendship for England by publishing the article.

3. A letter from Jenisch to His Highness calling attention to the importance of the matter. This letter informed me that His Majesty was insisting that the article should be published, and that the object of his telling the Chancellor of it beforehand was merely to give us the chance of altering individual passages if we thought fit. It was clear from the letter that His Majesty was extremely anxious that we should make use of the Colonel's welcome offer.

4. A slip written in blue pencil by the Chancellor, with orders to examine the matter carefully and write the alterations and erasures which we might think necessary on the margin of a copy which was to be prepared.

According to Jenisch's letter His Majesty did not wish the Foreign Office to be informed of the affair, and the Chancellor indicated that he wished it kept quite secret, and I did not consider myself justified in taking the advice of anyone else or of the Head of the Press Department, or in letting them look into the document. . . .

German Note. XXIV. 188

In his speech in the Reichstag on November 10th, 1908, Bülow did justice to the good intentions of the Emperor, who, he said, in his conversations with his English friends merely wished to show that he was misjudged in England ; but he admitted the great harm done by the publication in the *Daily Telegraph* with the inclusion of the Emperor's very much too strongly expressed sentiments, and said he was convinced that henceforward the Emperor would even in private conversation observe the restraint necessary for unity of policy and the authority of the Crown. Bülow's original intention seems to have been to cover the Emperor's action much more thoroughly than he did later owing to the excitement throughout large sections of the German people, which found its echo on that day in the Reichstag. In the *Roter Tag* of May 3rd, 1922, Hammann wrote that before the Reichstag debate of November 11th there was, in fact, a draft for a speech by the Chancellor ' defending and not excusing ' the publication. In the Records there is no trace of any such draft for a speech, which would certainly not have been like the one actually pronounced, for the latter only half cleared the Emperor. (Cf. Schulthess, *Europäischer Geschichtskalender*, 1908, p. 181 et seq.; O. Hammann, *Um den Kaiser*, p. 105 et seq.)

[In a speech at the Guildhall on November 9th, Mr. Asquith did his best to remove the bad impression caused by the article.]

XXIV. 188

COUNT VON METTERNICH, IN LONDON, TO THE GERMAN FOREIGN OFFICE, *November 10th*, 1908

The instructions in your telegram [1] carried out.

Sir E. Grey expressed pleasure at my communication and said confidentially that he hoped the Prime Minister's Guildhall speech would help to lessen the difficulties of the situation in the Reichstag. Yesterday before the speech he had spoken in this sense to Asquith and described my conversation with him. Neither of them thought it right to refer directly to the *Daily Telegraph* article, but the speech was so arranged as to make clear its connection with recent events.

I replied that I considered that the Prime Minister's kindly intentions had been happily expressed.

[The Emperor never forgave Bülow for the lukewarmness of his defence of the article. (Brandenburg, p. 348.) It was on the question of financial reform that Bülow fell in the end. He resigned on May 14th, 1909.]

---

[1] Not given.

CHAPTER XXVI

THE AUSTRO-SERVIAN WAR DANGER, 1909

[In 1908–9 military feeling in Austria was strongly in favour of reducing Servia to abject submission by a war of annihilation. Aehrenthal placed his talents at the disposal of this party. Prince Bülow also committed his country to a policy of supporting Aehrenthal in any scheme which he might conceive. Hence the task of averting war was left to the Entente Powers and Italy, with England as their most determined member. At the eleventh hour in spite of Isvolsky's vacillations Russia took her proper place by their side, once it was clear there was no actual danger of war.

Early in October, 1908, Turkey declared a boycott of all Austrian goods (cf. G. & T., V, p. 424) as a consequence of negociations between Austria and Turkey being broken off.]

XXVI. 455

BARON VON MARSCHALL, IN CONSTANTINOPLE, TO THE GERMAN FOREIGN OFFICE, *December 5th*, 1908

Cipher telegram.

I am informed that . . . the boycott continues to increase and the Government is powerless against it. Just as a few weeks ago the Committees and Kiamil Pacha could have nipped the boycott in the bud it is equally certain to-day that any attempt to intervene with police or troops would lead to sanguinary excesses with incalculable results. To-day even England could alter nothing by her advice ; so that I understand my Austrian colleague's hopelessness and his wish to depart.[1]

In my opinion there would be objections to such a step. It is easy to break a thread but difficult to join it up again. The Ambassador's departure would not frighten but only embitter. The boycott might take a form obliging the Austrian Government to adopt the most serious measures. The position here is quite abnormal. The feverish state of national feeling prevents any true perspective of facts as they are. In Young Turk circles they talk of war with Austria as though Turkey stood a chance of winning. They calculate that the British fleet will protect the coasts, that Albania will rise and that not only Servia and Montenegro, but the Bulgarians also, will side with Turkey the moment

---

[1] Cf. G. & T., V, p. 523.

Austrian troops enter Turkish territory,—in other words—that the Balkan Alliance under Anglo-Russian patronage, will spring into life against Austria-Hungary and against Germany also, who is Austria's ally. The Serbs and the well-known Mr. Noel Buxton,[1] the Chairman of the Balkan Committee, who let himself be fêted here as a Turkish national hero, are agitating in the same sense. Such diseased imaginings require careful handling. Baron Aehrenthal would therefore do well not to stick too obstinately to the principle of ' no negociation before the boycott is removed ' ; for he is making for an inevitable breach with incalculable complications. Once the Porte has, even if unsuccessfully, ordered Austrian ships to be unloaded Vienna can always return to the principle that ' no one can do more than he can '. Then is the time for negociation if the Turkish demands are at all reasonable. The resulting *détente* would immediately relieve the boycott. . . .

[The answer returned from Berlin was that ' owing to the powerlessness of the Turkish Government there was no chance that an order from above would produce a sudden complete cessation of the boycott; the Ambassador's departure might possibly be followed by it '. (XXVI. 457.)]

XXVI. 282

BARON VON AEHRENTHAL, IN VIENNA, TO PRINCE VON BÜLOW,
December 8th, 1908

Private letter. Extract.

As regards Servia, Forgách, our Minister at Belgrade, has been reporting for some time a visible diminution of war feeling. He considers that internal questions and faction quarrels are now more in the foreground and will cause a diversion to some extent.[2] But this will not restrain the gentlemen at Belgrade, whether the conference takes place or not, from looking for another way out of the situation which they themselves created,—some desperate step or at least a repetition of provocative acts, which we shall have to ward off. It worries me that the unbridled agitation of the British and Russian Press, and especially the presence of so many unauthorised politicians from England and Russia in the Balkans may cause further confusion and resultant conflicts. . . . In your letter of October 30th you mention ' the distasteful conditions in Servia ', as you aptly describe them. You also had the kindness to say that you would leave it to my judgment to decide how to deal with them if they continue. I can but thank you most warmly and genuinely for this new proof of friendly . confidence. Our policy is now governed by the wish not to seek a conflict with Servia. We shall continue our past attitude for

---

[1] Cf. G. & T., V, p. 536, etc.   [2] Cf. G. & T., V, p. 271, 522.

present and hope thus to help on the peace which is so gen-
ly needed, bearing in mind the desire that the Conference
ll meet. But we are not prepared to carry on this policy of
patience *ad infinitum*. If in the course of the next two months
Servia's attitude gives us cause again for serious complaint, we
should have then to make a final decision. You may be assured,
honoured friend, that I should inform you of this in good time.
If this happens I intend, in order to prevent a further extension of
the conflict, to declare definitely to the other Powers that we are
merely performing an act of clear necessity, but that we do not
mean to attack the independence and territorial integrity of
Servia and Montenegro. I may hope that a quick military
action combined with this declaration will prevent the dangers
of which I have spoken.

XXVI. 520

MEMORANDUM BY THE CHANCELLOR, PRINCE VON BÜLOW, *December 27th*, 1908

The essential point of Isvolsky's speech [1] in the Duma on the
25th is clearly his contemplated Balkan alliance directed against
Austria. Not till Russia (and England and France) succeed in
bringing about this alliance, will Austria's position become really
bad. Isvolsky's very benevolent tone towards Bulgaria shows
that the Russians hope to include the Turks and Bulgarians in
their anti-Austrian group.

Austria must come to an agreement with the Bulgarians,
and soon, i.e., before the Russians and their friends filch the latter
away. I do not think it impossible that the Russians (etc.) may
offer the Bulgarians their mediation in Constantinople on condition that Bulgaria joins the anti-Austrian group.

We have repeatedly advised the Austrians to come to an
understanding with Bulgaria. I think we ought to repeat this
advice with a reference to Isvolsky's speech and the plans and
hopes expressed in it. I beg to have a despatch submitted to me
as soon as possible, drafted so as to be read aloud in Vienna.

XXVI. 393

COUNT VON METTERNICH, IN LONDON, TO PRINCE VON BÜLOW, *January 7th*, 1909

The Austrian and German Press are again clamouring insinuations against British policy as a cause of unrest in the Balkans. [2]
Even Baron Aehrenthal is full of suspicions and inclined to credit
the British Government with the unpleasantnesses which his
policy has brought upon him. It would be interesting to learn
whether he or anyone else could show definite proof in any given

[1] Cf. G. & T., V, p. 543. [2] Cf. G. & T., V, p. 557.

case. British policy is clear and open. Its standpoint is that a treaty cannot be altered by one party, but that the consent of all the parties is necessary to legalise a one-sided alteration, and it demands an indemnity for the losing side, i.e. Turkey.[1] British policy objects neither to the method of adjusting the treaty nor to an indemnity, but leaves it for the Austrian Government to reach an understanding with the Porte, and it refuses to bring pressure on the latter until an acceptable offer is made to the Turkish Government. This attitude is unambiguous, not friendly to Austria, as ours is, but it does not indulge in intrigue. The rumours of British gold in the Balkans, of more or less secret encouragement to oppose Austria,—of intentional prevention of an understanding between Austria and Turkey, of inciting the boycott,[2] of stirring up passions in Belgrade, and the like are, to my knowledge, perfectly unfounded accusations.

British policy is shown even more clearly by the following circumstances : Baron Aehrenthal's action is regarded and condemned here not only by the Government but by all public opinion down to the working classes (I have proof of this) as a bad breach of the treaty, and all the more at a moment when exuberant though thoroughly genuine sympathy is being felt for the Young Turks. The moment chosen by Austria is taken here as a blow at the Young Turks, and her action is all the more severely condemned . . .

[King Edward, whose health was already failing, went to Berlin on February 8th, 1909, to pay a state visit to the Emperor in the hope of improving Anglo-German relations. (Cf. Lee, *King Edward VII*, II, p. 672 et seq. ; also Sir Charles Hardinge's conversation with Prince Bülow, G. & T., V, p. 608.) It appeared that Bülow was not altogether opposed to a Conference.]

XXVI. 598

THE EMPEROR WILLIAM TO THE EMPEROR FRANCIS JOSEPH, *February 12th*, 1909

Telegram.

After a visit of nearly four days, which went off well in every way, the King and Queen of England have left us. In my conversations with the King I found no sort of feeling against your Government or its policy. Whilst we alluded to politics only in general terms, we agreed in desiring a peaceful solution of all questions. I hope that this visit, with all its consequences, will not only influence for good Anglo-German relations, but also work for unity between the nations.

---

[1] H. H. Asquith, *The Genesis of the War*, p. 6 et seq.
[2] Cf. p. 316.

February 19th, 1909, Sir Edward Grey addressed a Circular Note
~~~~nany, France and Italy, inviting their co-operation in dissuading
~~~ from making war on Servia. (Cf. G. & T., V, p. 610.) Count
Metternich's comment on its being handed to him was as follows :]

XXVI. 601

COUNT VON METTERNICH TO THE GERMAN FOREIGN OFFICE,
February 18th, 1909

Cipher telegram. Extract.

. . . I told Sir E. Grey the danger lay at Belgrade, not in
Vienna. Servia had been provoking Austria for months. Pressure must be exercised on Servia and peace must be maintained.
Servia and Montenegro had not been injured and so had no right
to compensation. But if Austria wished to make presents to
these two countries it was her affair alone. Territorial indemnities were cut out from the start. I did not believe that my
Government would offer any advice unwelcome to Austria, either
by itself or jointly with others. It certainly would not take part
in any *démarche* which might be interpreted as pressure.

The Minister declared that he wished to exercise no pressure
on Austria, but merely to start a friendly discussion in Vienna on
the menace of the Servian question. But if nothing was done
anywhere and matters were left to take their course, the relations
between Austria and Servia could only end in war.

I replied that the cause of peace would be best served by a
declaration made at Belgrade that Servia had everything to lose
and nothing to gain by a war with Austria.

If in default of friendly intervention war between Austria
and Servia is really imminent, it may be advisable for us to
mention the Grey proposal confidentially in Vienna, in order to
ascertain under what conditions, if at all, Baron Aehrenthal is
prepared to discuss the Servian question. We might say that
the sentence in the Note, ' You should explain this view to Baron
Aehrenthal, etc. . .' and the following one offer a basis for
supporting Austria's policy at Belgrade. Please instruct me.

XXVI. 628

COUNT VON METTERNICH TO THE GERMAN FOREIGN OFFICE,
February 25th, 1909

Cipher telegram.

In conversation yesterday Sir E. Grey made a remark which
caused me to conclude that if no other means could be found for
allaying the Austro-Servian menace he wishes to thrust the
Conference idea forward again. (The EMPEROR : ' *Heaven defend
us from this ! The Press and above all, the Pan-Slavists will have
time to renew their agitation, and Europe won't be free from unrest
the whole summer long !* ')

[On March 10th, 1909, the Servian Government circulated a Note protesting that the annexation question was one for the Signatory Powers of the Treaty of Berlin to deal with and not merely a domestic question for Austria. It did not satisfy Austria. (Cf. G. & T., V, p. 666.) The same applies to a further Note sent by the Servian Government on March 15th. (Cf. G. & T., V, 679.)]

XXVI. 679

COUNT VON METTERNICH, IN LONDON, TO THE GERMAN FOREIGN OFFICE, *March 16th*, 1909

Cipher telegram.

Mr. Tyrrell, Sir Edward Grey's Private Secretary, tells me that Sir Edward does not regard the situation as unfavourable. There is an impression here that Servia's answer was purposely uncompliant in order to provoke a fresh *démarche* by the Powers at Belgrade ; the Serbs meant then to give way to pressure from them. (The EMPEROR : '*!*')

He says further that Austria is preparing a Circular Note for the Powers. This would give the Powers another opportunity for action at Belgrade. (The EMPEROR : ' ? *If, as is supposed, Belgrade is being beared on the market—on the assumption of the fact of annexation—démarches by the Powers will do no good and will only make them ridiculous.*')

XXVI. 678

COUNT VON METTERNICH TO THE GERMAN FOREIGN OFFICE, *March 16th*, 1909

Cipher telegram.

Mr. Tyrrell, the Foreign Minister's Private Secretary, considers the last Servian Note unsatisfactory. This astonishes him all the more since he knew for certain that St. Petersburg had advised moderation and compliance at Belgrade. (The EMPEROR : ' *And all the time they are passing in war material through Bulgaria.*') Russia could not make war ; internal conditions were so unsafe that they had to fear recrudescence of revolution and a threat to the dynasty. (The EMPEROR : ' *Yes.*') It now depended on whether Austria continued the conversation alone with Servia or appealed to the Powers to bring strong pressure to bear at Belgrade. (The EMPEROR : ' *!* ') Servia's Note could be defended neither for its form nor its contents. Its publication now, or at any rate before it had gone to Baron Aehrenthal, would be at least discourteous, especially since, by Count Forgách's last *démarche* at Belgrade, Baron Aehrenthal had shown a wish to conciliate. It was not believed here that the Minister desired war. By her action Servia had made all sympathy impossible and would have to bear the consequences of her stupid policy. (The EMPEROR : ' *Good.*') Europe's sympathy had cooled off so much that even in the lamentable event of a collision there was reason to hope that the conflict might be localised. (The EMPEROR : ' *Good*.')

Mr. Louis Mallet, the Under-Secretary, spoke to me in similar terms. When I pointed to the danger of the Servian preparations, he said that, according to information received in London, the Serbs had no more than 30,000 to 35,000 men under arms. (The EMPEROR : ' *Wrong! About* 200,000.')

XXVI. 692

COUNT VON POURTALÈS, IN ST. PETERSBURG, TO THE GERMAN FOREIGN OFFICE, *March 20th*, 1909

Cipher telegram.

Isvolsky mentions another suggestion made by Sir Edward Grey.[1] Sir A. Nicolson had told him to-day that the London Cabinet had forwarded to him a draft for a declaration to be made by the Servian to the Austro-Hungarian Government. The EMPEROR : ' *Already rejected*.') Provisional enquiry discloses that the draft has impressed the Vienna Cabinet favourably.[2] (The EMPEROR : ' *?* ') Sir E. Grey's proposal is that if the Vienna Cabinet finally accepts the Powers should combine at Belgrade to urge the Servian Government to submit a declaration in the sense of the draft. Isvolsky said that eventually (The EMPEROR : ' *Always vague!* ') Russia would be prepared to join in this *démarche* at Belgrade. The Minister did not tell me the exact wording of the draft. But he expressed fear that the passage in it about Bosnia would be used by Baron Aehrenthal as an excuse for making fresh difficulties. (The EMPEROR : ' *!* ') The Baron would probably demand absolute recognition of the Austro-Turkish Protocol,[3] (The EMPEROR : ' *Naturally*.') whereas by Sir Edward's proposal the Belgrade Cabinet was only required to confess that the Bosnian question was no affair of Servia's. (The EMPEROR : ' *Playing with words*.')

XXVI. 698

COUNT VON POURTALÈS IN ST. PETERSBURG, TO THE GERMAN FOREIGN OFFICE, *March 21st*, 1909

Cipher telegram.

M. Isvolsky asked me to come and see him and told me that he had received confirmation of the fears he had expressed yesterday. The Russian Chargé d'Affaires in Vienna had reported

---

[1] Cf. G. & T., V, pp. 695–6 ; Brandenburg, p. 331.
[2] *German Note*. This was far from being the case.
[3] Cf. G. & T., V, pp. 638–40.

hearing from Sir Fairfax Cartwright [1] that Baron Aehrenthal, who was not satisfied with Sir E. Grey's formula, was demanding another one, much more severe for Servia.   In this M. Isvolsky sees a fresh proof that the increased demands against Servia mean that Baron Aehrenthal wishes to make a peaceful solution of the dispute impossible.[2]   (The EMPEROR: '*The Tsar's telegram contains a similar sentence.*')   On my remarking that according to my impression it merely meant that there had been *pourparlers* in Vienna between Baron Aehrenthal and the British Ambassador, and that nothing had been finally settled, M. Isvolsky replied that when Sir E. Grey's formula was communicated to him he had declared his readiness to join the Powers in their *démarche* at Belgrade.   This would be made much harder for him if Baron Aehrenthal stiffened the declaration to be demanded from Servia still further.   Only a few days previously Sir Edward Grey's version had seemed to be getting a favourable reception in Vienna. (The EMPEROR :   ' *No.*')

M. Isvolsky complained bitterly of the unfair treatment he had recently suffered at the hands of the German Press.   (The EMPEROR : *'It is good for him!'*)

XXVI. 703

PRINCE VON BÜLOW TO COUNT VON METTERNICH, IN LONDON,
March 24th, 1909

Telegram.

The main obstacle to a successful *démarche* by the Powers at Belgrade seems to us to lie in the fact that Servia can always point out that the annexation question is still unsettled amongst them.

We therefore engaged in a friendly discussion with the St. Petersburg Cabinet as to whether it was prepared to express consent by Note to the Austro-Hungarian request that Art. 25 of the Treaty of Berlin [3] should be expunged in order to allow of freer and more determined speech at Belgrade.   On receiving his orders from the Tsar M. Isvolsky declared that, in the event of the Vienna Cabinet addressing a request to the Powers for their sanction to expunge Art. 25 by reason of the Austro-Turkish Agreement, the Russian Government would give its consent without reserve.   Austria-Hungary has declared her readiness to do this.

Please inform the British Government of the foregoing and ask whether they will reply to an Austrian request in the same terms

---

[1] Cf. G. & T., V, pp. 714–16 ; H. Wickham Steed, *Through Thirty Years,* I, p. 297.   By this time Cartwright was a close friend of Aehrenthal and interpreted his views to the British Foreign Office.

[2] Brandenburg, pp. 326, 330.   [3] Cf. G. & T., V, p. 412.

as Russia has done.   Telegraph the answer you receive at once.
Say that we consider M. Isvolsky's decision to be an important
stage in the peaceful solution of the crisis and that the action
which we propose will add special force to the *démarche* at
Belgrade, which was planned by British initiative.

[Sir Edward Grey refused absolutely to consent to the foregoing proposition (cf. G. & T., V, 739; Lee, II, p. 647; Brandenburg, p. 331).
The German Ambassador, after reading through Sir Edward's reply,
' said to him that he had endangered peace.   Grey denied this, saying that
if the annexation were sanctioned to-morrow Baron Aehrenthal could
easily begin the Servian war the day after.   He was ready to help in any
peaceful solution, but would not give way to pressure implying that Baron
Aehrenthal was demanding a sanction for the annexation under threat of
an ultimatum to Servia.   (The EMPEROR : ' *Servia's behaviour gives him
the right to do this.*')   I replied that I knew nothing about any pressure.
I should be grateful to hear by telegraph whether Italy and France accept
our proposal.'   (The EMPEROR : ' *Yes.—This is the first occasion on which
London has set itself in direct opposition to St. Petersburg—unless, indeed,
the coup was not secretly concerted with Isvolsky so as to make (apparent)
agreement easier for him.*'   (XXVI. 707–8.)]

XXVI. 714
COUNT VON METTERNICH TO THE GERMAN FOREIGN OFFICE,
March 26th, 1909

Cipher telegram.

To-day Sir E. Grey telegraphed to Sir F. Cartwright [1] instructions to explain to Baron Aehrenthal the reasons for his refusal.
(The EMPEROR : ' *So responsibility for the war danger is England's
alone.*')

He let it be seen that if agreement about the text of the
Servian Note were obtained and war thus averted the British
opposition to expunging Art 25 would disappear.   He was not
very definite as to whether the question respecting Art. 29 [2] must
be settled first.

The Cabinet had agreed that the sanction to expunge Art. 25
would not be given until danger of war with Servia was removed.
(The EMPEROR : ' *Bullying Vienna and endangering peace.*')

No reply has been received here from Vienna as to whether
Baron Aehrenthal accepts the alterations in the text, as proposed
by England.

The French Ambassador here says that neither Italy, (The
EMPEROR : ' *They have already accepted it.*') France nor England
could accept our proposal.   (The EMPEROR : ' *This for all our
politeness to Paris.   That unreliable rabble follow absolutely in
London's train!*')

[Sir Edward Grey's firm stand was largely responsible for the peaceful
ending of the dispute.   Although the danger of war was really past (cf.

---

[1] Cf. G. & T., V, p. 743.   [2] Cf. G. & T., V, p. 412.

Steed, I, p. 300 ; Lee, *King Edward VII*, II, p. 648), a formal settlement was necessary.   On March 30th the Ministers at Belgrade of England, Italy, France and Russia presented a joint Note urging the Servian Government to sign the admission demanded by Austria.

Isvolsky's vacillations (cf. G. & T., V, p. 763) were one of the main obstacles to a satisfactory solution.]

XXVI. 737

COUNT VON POURTALÈS, IN ST. PETERSBURG, TO PRINCE VON BÜLOW, *April 1st*, 1909

Several days before Russia's consent to the annexation was known of, my Austro-Hungarian colleague and I could observe clear signs of annoyance in the British Embassy, where they had got wind—but nothing positive—that German action was in progress.   Indeed I must testify that M. Isvolsky remained faithful to the promise I asked of him not to let news of my *démarche* leak out in any quarter.

After the Russian decision was known, Sir Arthur Nicolson made no secret of his disgust at M. Isvolsky not having maintained touch with the Entente Ambassadors.   From a short remark by the Ambassador, who is very reserved with me, it is clear that he hoped that the London Cabinet's attitude towards our proposal would make its path difficult even at the eleventh hour.

Recently my British colleague has been most openly expressing in all the drawing-rooms his disappointment at the way things have gone.

CHAPTER XXVII

PRINCE BÜLOW'S STRUGGLE FOR A NAVAL UNDERSTANDING, 1908–9

[The following chapter displays the differences of opinion between the Chancellor, Prince Bülow,[1] and practically all the authorities—including General von Moltke (p. 357)—who in theory were for a naval agreement with England, and Admiral von Tirpitz, backed up by the Emperor and with the Navy League (cf. G. & T., VI, p. 280) as a ready instrument for exciting public opinion, who was determined to connect his name with the rise of a great German Navy regardless of consequences. (Cf. G. & T., VI, p. 237 et seq.) The strong personality of Tirpitz carried the day and repeatedly nipped in the bud several attempts to discuss a naval understanding with England. Count Metternich never ceased to advocate an understanding; whilst the Emperor, prompted by Tirpitz, blamed him for misinterpreting his policy. (Cf. p. 362, however.)

The suspicions of the British Government that the Germans were building and preparing to build at a rate faster than they at any time admitted is fully discussed in G. & T., Vol. VI.

Within a few months after coming in power the Liberal Government announced that disarmament would occupy a prominent position in their policy, but the other Powers had war on the brain and were naturally inclined to increase rather than diminish their armies and navies.]

XXIII. 30

Stumm, Chargé d'Affaires in London, to the Chancellor, Prince von Bülow, *June 8th*, 1906

In reference to the news in the Press that at a meeting of the Inter-parliamentary Union which was planned to take place very shortly in London the question of disarmament was to be discussed I asked Mr. Haldane, the Secretary for War, what were the intentions of the British Government. He replied that the Liberal Government, supported by their great majority in the country, had seriously decided to take the initiative in attacking the question of disarmament at the next Hague Conference. As far as England was concerned, the Government were fully determined not to extend their naval programme but merely to complete the organisation of the Army. Whatever else might then happen must naturally depend on the attitude of the other

[1] Lord d'Abernon, in *An Ambassador of Peace*, I, pp. 82, 174, states that Bülow prevented any naval agreement being made with England. (Cf. p. 406.)

Powers. He said that the German fleet, whose duty it was to give police protection to German trade, was not yet quite completed. As far as Germany was concerned, therefore, there could only be a question of the possibility of considering some reduction in the land army.

I told Mr. Haldane that owing to our geographical position and in consideration of the superiority of the British and French navies the question was a particularly difficult one for us. I did not know my Government's views about this. But I thought I might conclude from certain statements in our Press that we should not refuse straight off to take part in a discussion of it. Mr. Haldane said that even this much would be a great gain, and then went on to give his opinions on the question of peace, which displayed his idealistic views about the world.

[The anxiety felt by the Conservative Opposition in England regarding the naval supremacy of Great Britain was expressed in a question in Parliament addressed by Mr. A. Lee [1] to the Prime Minister on November 12th, 1908. He asked 'whether the Government accepts the Two-Power Standard of naval strength as meaning a preponderance of 10 per cent over the combined strength, in capital ships, of the two next strongest Powers; and if not, could he state the definition of the Two-Power Standard which is accepted by the Government?' Mr. Asquith replied: 'The answer to the first part of the question is in the affirmative.' (Hansard, Vol. CXCVI, p. 560.) This was followed by important debates in the House of Lords.]

XXVIII. 4

CAPTAIN WIDENMANN, NAVAL ATTACHÉ IN LONDON, TO ADMIRAL
VON TIRPITZ, SECRETARY OF STATE TO THE ADMIRALTY,
November 13th, 1908

For the first time since they came into power three years ago, the Liberal Government has confessed before the world that their view of the ratio of strength for the British Navy corresponds with that of the Opposition.

As was hardly to be expected otherwise, the British people's healthy feeling for great national questions has again shown that when Imperial interests are at stake party is not considered.

This statement by the responsible leader of the British World Empire will reassure Germany also to some extent. For years the Two-Power Standard was a conception, the rightness of which no German naval politician ever dreamed of questioning. If the official declaration of its justification draws the United States Navy into the discussion, and the ' two to one German ' standard becomes merely a phrase used by a few naval fanatics, the declaration can only have a reassuring effect.

The question is now what, in practice, it means.

If one counts only the ships of the Dreadnought period, which

---
[1] Afterwards Lord Lee of Fareham.

the three leading naval Powers have so far settled to build (the 1908 programme), the result is as follows :

	England	U.S.	Germany
Dreadnoughts . . .	8	6	7
Invincibles . . .	4	–	2
	12	6 +	9 = 15

Thus England's Two-Power standard in Dreadnoughts is no longer maintained.

If we add the three additional ships of the line decided upon under the German Naval Law for 1909, the figures are :

England	12
Germany and U.S.	18
British minority	6

Reckoning in the 10 per cent. addition, England will be forced to decide on a programme of at least 7 Dreadnoughts and Invincibles for the year 1909. America's programme of new ships for 1909 is omitted from this calculation ; I do not know the figures for this.

Thus Mr. McKenna was justified in saying at the end of his Guildhall speech on Lord Mayor's Day : ' I make no apology for saying in the City of London that the charge for maintaining the supremacy of our Navy is necessarily a heavy one.'

It is still an open question whether the Government hopes to get along without a loan for 1909. Next Monday may possibly clear this up, when Lord Cawdor is to ask for a Government statement, similar to that asked for by Mr. Lee in the House of Commons yesterday.

XXVIII. 13
ADMIRAL VON TIRPITZ TO THE CHANCELLOR, PRINCE VON BÜLOW, November 25th, 1908

I beg to send Your Highness a cutting from an article in the *Saturday Review* of September 11th, 1897,[1] as I consider it very good proof that it is not our naval programme, but the commercial situation which is the *final* reason for the Anglo-German tension, even as it was with Holland at another period. I imagine that Your Highness and I are equally interested in opposing the forging of legends, which, I regret to say, the Ambassador, Count Metternich, helps on at every opportunity, as though the increase of the German Navy were the sole cause for the increasing friction in our political relations with England. In a military sense that is nonsense, because the British Navy is to-day not twice, but at least three times as strong as we are.

[1] Note the date,—11 years earlier.

The increase of our fleet must be merely a cloak for the wire-pullers in England, under which the Conservatives are pushing their political interests against the Liberals, and all the parties interested in an extensive increase of the fleet are working up public opinion.

XXVIII. 17

COUNT VON METTERNICH, IN LONDON, TO THE CHANCELLOR, PRINCE VON BÜLOW, *November 26th*, 1908

Questions of the Defence of the Realm have been occupying general attention here in increasing measure. Up to the present, anxiety regarding the maintenance of England's supremacy at sea has been principally to the fore. The wish for a strong army existed modestly in comparison with it. With the speech by the old Field Marshal, Lord Roberts,[1] the mask dropped, and the struggle for universal service entered a new stage. The Field Marshal, long a believer in it, has been thrust into the foreground by a clique, in the hope that his authority may cover the scheme for universal service, which in itself is not popular. Amongst those who are behind him are Lord Lovat and the retired Colonel A'Court Repington.[2] They are members of the National Service League, which aims at founding a strong army after the continental pattern. This league has recently acquired a large accretion of fresh members. It is necessary that the German danger should play a part in order to popularise the idea of universal service. I will add, with a prayer for secrecy, that before his recent speech in the House of Lords, Lord Roberts was requested by leading members of the Government not to exemplify it by a reference to Germany. He did not pay attention to this request, being rightly convinced that, unless Germany were dragged in, his warnings would be ignored.

Political circles here recognise that Lord Roberts is holding the danger of a German invasion before his horrified fellow-country-men in order to win them over to his pet scheme. His speech therefore will scarcely make any lasting impression. Measures for dealing with education and drink, which at this moment are being violently debated in Parliament, interest the obedient politicians far more than universal service. In spite of this Lord Roberts' words have contributed to increase public anxiety for the moment. A year ago the old Field Marshal's speech would hardly have been possible. It would have been held to be such a violent exaggeration that it would have left no impression whatever. To-day it is taken more seriously ; at any rate, it is not laughed at, and the exaggeration is not remarked upon.

[1] On November 23rd in the House of Lords.
[2] For long Military Correspondent of *The Times*.

The propaganda for strengthening the British Navy and for increasing the Army, the growth of the Protectionist movement, now that fresh taxes must be introduced to cover the Naval Budget, the growing anxiety about the German danger, and the perpetual postponement of an arrangement between Germany and England are to be ascribed, on the whole, to the same cause.

I doubt whether any impartial observer, after a stay of only a few months in England, could have any opinion but that the cardinal point of our relations with England is the growth of our fleet. It may not be pleasant hearing for us, but I see no good in hiding the truth, nor do I think it compatible with my duty.

XXVIII. 25

COUNT VON METTERNICH, IN LONDON, TO PRINCE VON BÜLOW, *December 11th, 1908*

I again had an unconstrained after-dinner talk with Mr. McKenna, the First Lord of the Admiralty. In his tone there was evident what I have remarked lately in other leading personages, namely that in circles high up they have got used to our naval programme, and that there will be an attempt to preserve the British ascendancy by fresh naval construction. They hold our shipbuilding responsible for the efforts they are making here.

German Note.

On December 8th President Roosevelt sent a Message to Congress on questions of finance and social and foreign policy. It concluded as follows : ' It is desirable to complete as soon as possible a squadron of eight battle-ships of the best type existing. The Navy should be treated as a purely military organisation, and everything should be subordinated to the one aim of assuring military efficiency.' (Cf. Schulthess, *Europäischer Geschichtskalender*, 1908, p. 435.)

When I reminded Mr. McKenna of President Roosevelt's recent Message, demanding speedy provision of 8 Dreadnoughts, he went so far as to say it was merely because of us that the Americans were forced into the building competition, and that the American fleet would count for nothing as an enemy on the coasts of England. The British navy need not even offer battle, but merely stay in harbour for a fortnight, after which lack of coal would drive the American fleet home with nothing done. Nor could they do anything in the open trading ports ; torpedo-boats and mines would see to that.

I again said that there was nothing laid down in our programme about competition, and we did not mean to be drawn into it. Your Highness' speech in the Reichstag of December 10th was not known of here last night. The First Lord will find in it a confirmation of my words.

He said that, with his experience of the new type of ship and all connected with it, we should find our ships coming much dearer than was stated in the Naval Estimates. He was not frightened at present at the prospect of Air-ships, nor of the danger from them for ships on the sea. They could see nothing by night, and by day they would be shot down or would have to stay so high up as to make accuracy of aim impossible.

He did not share Roberts' fears of invasion, but thought the fleet quite adequate for protecting England. I said that there was now much talk here of the German danger and German invasion, and there was active propaganda for an army of a million men. The danger of aggression lay elsewhere than in Germany. England with an overwhelmingly strong navy and an army of a million meant a danger for Europe, since her troops could land under the protection of her fleet. The British papers treated the agitation for a strong army mainly from this standpoint, and the French Press was asking for universal service in England, so that England might be an efficient ally, naturally for a war on the Continent. Mr. McKenna entirely agreed with me and said the Navy was for defensive purposes, and that a big army was not needed to protect England and was bound, therefore, to be regarded on the Continent as a step towards aggression. But there was not the least prospect of England having an army of a million.

This may or may not be so. The agitation for universal service continues to spread.

At our last meeting the Minister expressed the view to me that our conveniences for building big ships were further developed than they were in England.

Our Naval Attaché, whom I told of this, has furnished me with particulars, of which I made use with Mr. McKenna yesterday ; besides which, I have arranged for Captain Widenmann to see the Minister early next week in order to give him fuller information.

XXVIII. 38

THE CHANCELLOR, PRINCE VON BÜLOW, TO ADMIRAL VON TIRPITZ,
December 25th, 1908

Secret.

In your Memorandum of the 17th[1] you said no to the question whether Germany and the German people could look forward with equanimity to an attack by England. Also you indicated the creation of a strong battle fleet as the best means of keeping England from attacking us. But you do not discuss whether, in consideration of the then great superiority of the British sea forces over ours (a subject introduced by yourself),—a superiority,

[1] Not given.

moreover, which the British people appear determined to maintain in all future circumstances—our battleships could possibly go into action decisively in the event of war with England. But if we are justified in fearing that our fleet, at its present strength, might be held up in our harbours by a blockade of England's overwhelming sea-forces, we must expect that, in a naval war with England, we should at first have to act on the defensive. Hence the question whether the best course would not be to specialise on improving our coast defences, increasing our stock of sea-mines, and creating a strong fleet of submarines, instead of concentrating exclusively on increasing the number of battleships, which, as long as we continue in a state of recognised inferiority to England, may possibly never be used, never inflict injury on the enemy, and so fail to help in bringing about a favourable issue in the war. I am far from claiming an opinion on the technicalities of the subject. I merely offer a suggestion, as it strikes an unprofessional mind, which has often come into mine of late.

Whilst our primal interest in having our coasts in a thorough state of defence may appear to emphasise the importance of the defensive measures described above, I hold, on the other hand, that political considerations may lead us to reflect whether a slowing down in the carrying out of our present naval programme should not be seriously discussed. The reports lying before us show that there is no doubt that the feeling towards us in England, which you yourself describe as hostile, may well cause serious anxiety. Whether this feeling is entirely due to our naval preparations, or whether it is the natural result of competition between two great *Kultur* nations, as you take it to be, seems to me of secondary importance. But certain it is that it will, as your reports state, be some years before our fleet is so powerful that even England would run a great risk in attacking it. Hence it is our duty to seize every possible means consistent with our dignity for reducing British nervousness, so that we ourselves may get safely through the years in which our armaments are not yet complete.[1]

It has been repeatedly indicated in influential quarters in England that slowing down the pace in carrying out our present naval programme would really bring re-assurance there. There is no need to discuss how far compliance with British wishes in this respect would permanently influence our political relations with England. In this present transition period at any rate, it is highly important for us to prevent the idea of a preventive war against Germany from taking root in the British people, with a British attack on our fleet to follow. If war takes place nevertheless, in consideration of the great superiority of the

[1] Cf. *War Guilt*, p. 119.

British Navy, the fact of our entering the fight with one or two battle-ships less, owing to having slowed down our construction, would not make much difference to the result which is to be feared in this conflict.

Our Naval Law provides four new ships for each of the years 1909, '10 and '11, and two large ships for each of the years 1912 to 1917. By the end of 1911 we should possess 13 such ships, and in England they look on it now with great anxiety, for according to present British calculations the British Navy will only possess 12 ships of a corresponding class at that date. If we may assume that, under pressure of public opinion, the British Admiralty will not fail to recover the superiority in good time, which we, according to them, shall have had temporarily, I, by reason of the foregoing, would ask you whether technical military grounds of urgent character would forbid our slowing down our construction for the next three years, so as to build three instead of four large ships and fill up the deficiency during 1912, '13 and '14. We should then be building 3 large ships each year from 1909 to 1914, and laying down two each year from 1915 to 1917. Thus we should be removing a powerful instrument of agitation from our British rivals, without weakening the general result.

Finally I consider it right to indicate that recently financial and technical doubts have repeatedly been expressed as to whether it is advisable to undertake to construct that large number of capital ships all at once for which the present Acts provide. Therefore its prospects seem so much the better, and the people's representatives are more likely to consent to slow down our construction as proposed, if, at the same time, the measures suggested above for the protection of our coasts receive increased attention.

XXVIII. 40

COUNT VON METTERNICH, IN LONDON, TO PRINCE VON BÜLOW, *December 29th*, 1908

Private letter.

I beg to reply to your letter of the 25th.[1] First I should say that I have arranged with Mr. McKenna to send Captain Widenmann to him to explain our view of certain technical questions regarding our ship-building which are of interest to the Minister. It is not the custom here for the First Lord of the Admiralty to discuss naval questions with foreign Naval Attachés, and I first arranged with Mr. McKenna to invite him and Captain Widenmann to dine with me alone, so that our discussion of the naval question should be undisturbed. But the various engagements of the First Lord made the little dinner impossible, and Mr.

[1] Not given.

McKenna, whom I met again, declared his readiness to receive Captain Widenmann at the Office for this talk. Meanwhile the Naval Attaché obtained the necessary material from his superiors. His statements to the First Lord were therefore made at my suggestion.

You draw my attention further to an article in the *Kreuzzeitung*, which reports the views of Sir William White, formerly Director of naval construction to the Admiralty. This eminent naval constructor, who retired several years ago, is in opposition on many subjects to those who now control the Admiralty under Sir John Fisher.[1] The question whether the Dreadnought really represents such a step in advance of the types preceding it as her defenders make out is strongly denied by him. There are certain Admirals on the active list who say they would prefer a squadron of the Nelson type to the Dreadnought in a battle. But far the most of the sailors by profession prefer the Dreadnought. All leaders of thought and the whole nation are agreed that England must not be overtaken by any other Power in the building of Dreadnoughts. Apart from these, the British fleet is held here to be now greatly superior to any other, even without great fresh outlay. But now that the Dreadnought has been introduced— by England herself—which many think to be a mistake,—it is generally felt in all circles, professional and political, that England must make fresh great and costly efforts by reason of our shipbuilding, if she is not to be overtaken in Dreadnoughts in a few years. No one is prepared to face this ; hence the anxiety and the finger pointed at Germany.

Our Law contemplates a fleet of 38 battleships of the best modern sort, to be kept up to the mark by renewals determined by law. Each year we draw nearer the object, which according to the Law, should be reached in 1920. To an Englishman this means a danger and a call for competition, and it is useless to try and dissuade him of this. British policy is for the present determined to take up the challenge in building Dreadnoughts in order to maintain the Two-Power Standard in this class also. . . .

To return to the fresh arrangements for our ship-building from 1909–1914, I doubt whether this will greatly influence British public opinion in our favour. It would hardly make a deep impression anywhere whether in the next six years we build first four and then two, or three Dreadnoughts each year ; nor would it form a basis for obtaining a British promise of guarantees in the politics of Europe. It would be quite another thing—I say it only for the sake of argument—if we were prepared to extend the period of building, say from 1920 to 1925. . . .

Any indication of momentary slowing down in the rate of

[1] Bacon, *Lord Fisher*, II, p. 120.

German construction will be greeted here with joy, as a sign
that England also may economise.   But if the slowing down were
extended over a longer period, something might be done with it,
but not if we stick to the present programme of 18 capital ships
in the next 6 years.

Last summer was the psychological moment.   Then a little
compliance might have gained much.   But hardly so now.   At
that time the British Government was hesitating and doubtful.
Now they are determined to meet us in the Dreadnought competition on the basis of the Two-Power Standard.[1]   Moreover
they will not have failed to observe that a feeling was recently
prominent in the Reichstag in favour of an understanding with
England about naval construction.   This must arouse hopes here
extending further than merely a fresh distribution of 18 over the
next 6 years.   But this practical nation will say to itself : ' It has
not come to that yet ; let us go on arming '.   I suppose we must
do the same.   If there is to be an understanding about the Navy,
it can be made to comprise a great deal more than is foreseen
now.   It is quite possible that circumstances may lead on either
to an understanding or a war.   At present, as a direct consequence
of our naval construction, we have not the latter to fear.

It seems that in building a fleet there come critical moments,
as for instance for us, as you no doubt gather from our Admiralty,
during the next autumn and winter.   Unless something unforeseen happens, we ought to get through this period undisturbed as
far as England is concerned.

Finally with regard to Sir Edgar Speyer's statement, I would
mention that it is highly improbable that the Elections will take
place in the spring.   The critical moment is next autumn, supposing the Lords throw out the Budget.   This, however, is very
unlikely, for the risk of it is too great for the Lords.   A Party
which has been out of power for 20 years does not lightly cut
short its natural term unless it sees a prospect of re-election.
Just now this is small.   Sir Edgar is not in specially close touch
with the leaders, although he is trying hard to gain it.

XXVIII. 51

ADMIRAL VON TIRPITZ TO THE CHANCELLOR, PRINCE VON BÜLOW,
January 4th, 1909

Very secret.

I beg to acknowledge Your Highness' memorandum of
December 25th.

You recommend that, whilst maintaining our dignity, we
should do all possible to lessen the British nervousness regarding

---

[1] Cf. Brandenburg, p. 295.

us, and you consider the best means would be to reduce our annual construction of capital ships, as provided under the two last supplementary Acts (*Novellen*) of 1906 and 1908, from 4 to 3 for the next few years.

My strong objection against this is that such action would be taken both at home and abroad, as a retreat before England's threats, and that no explanation could remove this impression.

Even if British Ministers personally were prepared to dismiss it with kind words, there are too many interested parties in England ready to characterise our renunciation as humiliation. By this I mean that even the Liberal Party could only profit by our reduction of speed in building, if it appeared as a humiliation. This is how our action will be represented in England regardless of consequences. Now, as Your Highness states in your memorandum, this alteration in the speed of building is not to mean giving up the creation of a strong German navy, but it postpones its completion for some years. But the British look on the existence of our navy as their great future stumbling-block ; for the mere fact of its existence must force England to pay more attention to Germany in future than has been the case hitherto. All the naval interests in England which promoted this momentary ' navy scare ', all the Imperialists and the whole Conservative Party will continue to work up excitement, and when they see the success of their threats, they will proceed to a further humiliation of Germany. Thus the war danger with England will become greater and not less. Moreover I consider there can be no doubt that, when the present violent demand for economy at any price has died down again in Germany, the real significance of reducing our speed of construction will be properly understood, and our people will react strongly against any retreat before the British threats. This also would only increase the risk of a clash with England.

As I informed Your Highness, it is not my opinion that there is more danger now than formerly of a British preventive war. The British naval propaganda will cease the moment that the Conservative Party and the naval interests have attained their object, which is to force the Liberal Government against their will to make a big demand in Parliament for the Navy. If the British really wanted war they would first wish to complete the ships estimated for 1909, which would reinstate the British superiority. When one is preparing for a preventive war one spends money on military objects other than capital ships, which take three years to build. It is not the British view that the so-called ' critical year ' 1911 arose because we should then possess too many Dreadnoughts (9, and not 13 as you imagine and Lord Granard asserts[1]),

[1] In the House of Lords, November 24th, 1908.

but because the naval propaganda, which unluckily found its way into the Reichstag at the time of last year's *Novelle* [supplementary naval estimates], aroused very natural suspicions in England that we should promote a further increase of our Navy in 1911. We have renounced this increase and so shown remarkable readiness to meet England's wishes. Count Metternich moved in this sense before Your Highness made your declaration in the Reichstag, on the basis of which he might well have demanded positive concessions in return ; but nothing was done. Mr. McKenna acknowledged it with satisfaction and soon came forward with further requirements ; which shows how mistaken it is to slide down the steep slope of concession. I have always realised that our position with regard to England is very serious, and for twelve years have not failed to express it to Your Highness orally and in writing. But I think that ' carrying on ' means the less danger of war for us and that concession only increases the danger whilst at the same time involving humiliation for Germany.

Decreased speed in building, as Your Highness suggests, could not follow by the ordinary course, as the replacement of the ships is fixed by law. Thus a supplementary Act would be necessary, which would have to be sanctioned by the allied Governments and submitted by you to the Reichstag in the Emperor's name.

To resume—reduction of speed in construction from 4 to 3 in each year would be taken and felt at home and abroad as a humiliation for Germany, a humiliation which, in my opinion, is not *necessary*, since either there is no threat of war, or, if this proves to be an error of judgment, it is *useless*, since to postpone building 3 ships from 1909/11 to 1912/14 would not cause England to reconsider any decision in favour of a preventive war, if once resolved upon. In view of my opinion of the situation Your Highness will agree with me that I cannot undertake to defend the fresh naval *Novelle* in the Reichstag, quite apart from the fact that the same Minister cannot defend in 1909 the opposite of what he advocated with all his authority in 1908 and which was passed by the present Reichstag by an overwhelming majority. The position would be quite untenable politically.

Your memorandum of December 25th is my first information of Your Highness' views as to the political necessity of reducing the speed of building, and I could not have presumed them from your statement in the Reichstag when the Bill was first read. If these views must perforce be carried out, I must beg you to submit to the Emperor my request to be allowed to retire. I object to applying direct to His Majesty, first because it is a question of politics, and secondly because Your Highness will wish to report on the matter in person to His Majesty without his being forewarned by my request to retire, which I could not present without giving a motive.

Since your memorandum of December 25th hints at a doubt whether on technical military grounds our action is the correct one, I beg leave to add a few words on the subject. You suggest that it might be well to concentrate our attention on coastal defence and on strengthening our submarine protection instead of specialising on increasing our capital ships.

As regards the local defence of our coasts, the sums spent in recent years have attained an amount never before equalled. Improvements could naturally be added ; but I consider that in their present condition our coastal forts are well able to stand a British attack. A further sum of 62,000,000 marks has already been voted by the Reichstag and will be earmarked chiefly for the completion of the Heligoland defences, which alone are urgent.

The *Novelle* of 1906 doubled in principle the annual supply of torpedo-boats and greatly increased their size and efficiency. There is no point in creating personnel quicker than is justified by the increase of material.

As many submarines are being built as Germany can supply oil-engines for. Two are ready, and ten are under construction. 10,000,000 marks for 1909, and 15,000,000 marks annually from 1910 onwards are earmarked for submarines and have been voted in principle by the Reichstag. Before 1907 no State possessed a submarine suited to the North Sea. In this respect we shall be ready for a war with England in a short time. This hope would receive a blow if the action of the secretary to the Treasury,[1] in announcing to the Reichstag deductions of 50,000,000, and more in prospect, from the sums needed by the Navy for the next five years were successful. Hitherto I had allowed myself to hope that considering the dangerous position of our State a way out of this difficulty might have been found by the Secretary to the Treasury.

The smaller fighting craft, which form no part of the Naval Law and are therefore less in evidence, are either completed or in full construction. Their place in our armaments is relatively higher than that of the battle fleet. Taken together these are our fighting forces at sea. Small craft without a battle fleet are unthinkable ; nor would the battle fleet meet our requirements without small craft. From this Your Highness will gather that ' concentrating our attention solely on increasing the battle fleet ' does not at all represent what we are doing.

There are no grounds for the fear expressed by Your Highness that our fleet would be immediately held up in our harbours by a

[1] Sydow.

close blockade of England's overwhelming sea-forces now. We with full certainty—and it is in accordance with the reasonable handling of modern sea warfare—that the British main fleet stays in the neighbourhood of England behind the Dogger Bank, and that only smaller ships, with supports, are sent forward as a blockading line. Without a battle fleet our torpedo-boats and submarines would be unable to get at their objectives, i.e., the enemy's capital ships ; for nothing but battleships can open the way to the enemy's main concentration. In other words—if Germany has no sufficient battle fleet the war would cost England practically nothing and mean no risk to her. The backbone of our whole naval policy from its inception has always been to create such a risk for other States in our military and also, above all, our political relationship with them. The preamble of the Naval Law of 1900 states : ' Germany must possess so strong a battle fleet that a war would involve such risk for the opponent with the most powerful navy as to make the retention of his predominant position doubtful.' With every new ship that is added to it not only our battle fleet alone, but with it our highly developed torpedo-boats, will weigh heavier in the balance, and from year to year England will risk more in attacking us. Thus the object of the Naval Law, which is to assure peace for ourselves, will be more and more attained.

We might double and treble our torpedo-boats and submarines, we might cram our coasts with cannon, but this part of our sea-power would in no way assist our efforts for peace. Without a battle fleet we should be helpless against any injury which England might inflict.

The British Admiralty and Navy do not contemplate our fleet taking the aggressive against England either now or for a long time to come. Any British naval officer would be laughed at if he said any such thing seriously. Nevertheless the Admiralty's ill-temper is directed against our battle fleet, because it supplies the only means of making a success of the defensive war against England.

It is natural that an unprepared sea-power—and ours is that —should show gaps in all directions, if compared with the British Navy of to-day. Superficial critics can easily hit upon such gaps and impress the ignorant. I will say no more about that. Our sharpest critic, England, has seen clearly that our sea-power is being developed, with careful balancing of the numeral ratios of the various components of naval warfare, in a way which she has never seen before. That this rational development has still further increased the British ill-temper cannot be helped.

Not much good is to be expected from a fresh Bill for the strengthening of our coasts, such as Your Highness suggests, since the essentials are being fully carried out.   If there were an idea of bringing one in, which—as against reducing the speed of building by one ship—was really to be any good against an acute danger of war in 1909 or 1910, it could only be done by a demand for calling up many more men for service.   There is, however, no doubt that such a measure would be taken as a more direct threat of war than if we stick to our well-digested plan for developing our Navy.

[For Sir E. Grey's conversation of January 4th, 1909, with Count Metternich, cf. G. & T., VI, p. 237.
Prince Bülow ceased for a time to press for a more conciliatory policy towards England.   His position was weakened owing to the Emperor's growing dislike of him occasioned by his treatment of the *Daily Telegraph* affair.[1]]

XXVIII. 59
PRINCE BÜLOW TO COUNT VON METTERNICH, IN LONDON, *January 11th*, 1909

Private letter.   Extract.

. . . Since it is your opinion that slowing down speed of construction in the next three years will make but little impression in England, I beg you to refrain from discussing the question of altering our plans during 1909–11 with leading British statesmen in the sense of my suggestion sent to you for your opinion on December 25th.   But if Sir Edward Grey should again speak to you about the reduction of our naval armaments, I beg you to try and make him understand that nothing is gained by merely offering a limitation of British ship-building in payment for one of our own.

In England they seem, as it appears from your conversations with British statesmen, to imagine that diminution of their ship-building would be a favour to us, and that we ought to be pleased if they bind themselves to restrict their building, provided we do likewise (compare Grey, e.g., in your letter of December 20th).[2] This is not so.   We are quite indifferent how many ships England wants to build.   We build simply for purposes of defence in accordance with our general administrative and political needs, and not in order to compete with England.

So far as I can judge from your letters and reports, you have never touched on this side of the question with British statesmen.   I consider that it should be put to the leading statesmen on the other side of the Channel that we can only depart from our naval programme, which is laid down by law, if England is prepared to accommodate us in other parts of

[1] Cf. Ch. XXV; cf. G. & T., VI, p. 224.   [2] Not given.

the world,[1] as I said at the end of my letter of December 25th.

BÜLOW.

Postscript (in Bülow's handwriting).

I have done all in my power to ensure that our Press maintains great reserve about England and avoids attacking her. As far as I can tell, the German Press seems to be writing calmly about England just now. Continue writing to me everything that may help in making the visit of King Edward and Queen Alexandra a success and avoiding all discord, both material and personal.

[On January 27th, 1909, Prince Bülow wrote to Admiral von Tirpitz urging that England would certainly build up to the Two-Power Standard and might, if further exasperated by Germany's determination to go on with her programme, actually make an attack on Germany, before the latter was ready to fight her at sea.]

XXVIII. 78

ADMIRAL VON TIRPITZ TO PRINCE VON BÜLOW, *February 4th*, 1909

Very secret.

I consider that I must conclude from Your Highness' letter of the 29th [27th ?] that the arguments in my letter of January 20th,[2] were not expressed very clearly, and I hold myself bound by the special importance of the question to explain my military standpoint to you once again.

In your letter you wrote : ' that we have England against us at every step, which very greatly restricts our policy and makes it difficult ' ; and again, ' England is against us all over the world and makes difficulties for us everywhere ' ; and, ' the growing anti-German feeling in England is a danger for Germany '. (BÜLOW : ' *And the reason for all this ?* ')

In this situation, (BÜLOW : ' *How did it arise ?* ') combined with a concentration of an overwhelmingly strong fleet against our coasts (BÜLOW : ' *And for what reason ?* '), I must, as Secretary of State to the Admiralty, declare that it is our duty to arm with all our might. (BÜLOW : ' *No ;* propter vitam vivendi perdere causas ! ')

In my view we cannot desist from this arming—and even then only a little—unless we receive security, in a military sense, against a British attack by a treaty engagement on England's part to restrict her own armaments.

In the present difficult situation I consider it out of the question for us to promise to diminish our *war* preparations in return for *political* concessions. Such political concessions might easily be considered as merely a pretext.

---

[1] Bagdad Railway, Persia.   [2] Not given.

But apart from this serious objection on principle, I humbly consider that a promise from England to remain neutral ' in the event of war breaking out elsewhere ' would have no great political meaning. (BÜLOW : ' ? ') For if England declares war against us—a promise does not exclude this—and France and Russia join her, the British assurance will be objectless, whilst our restriction of armaments, undertaken in the meanwhile, will have a very real meaning; whereas a military agreement with England respecting *mutual* restriction of armaments might be followed by a change in British policy more in our favour.

I think that the formula for a military agreement, as proposed by Your Highness, would be most acceptable to England. (BÜLOW : ' *Unfortunately the British think otherwise.*') The British will not admit it at once, but they might perhaps consider it in the course of negociations later, (BÜLOW : ' *Tirpitz ought to try it himself.*') because I am convinced that they cannot stick to a Two-Power Standard plus 10 per cent. for ever.[1]

Finally I would repeat that I am convinced of the value of a *military* agreement with England, such as we could accept.

As long as we think this possible of attainment—and I myself think so—(BÜLOW : ' *Then he ought to take it in hand himself! Let him try his luck with the British and see what he can get !* ') we ought to try all we can to get the trumps into our own hand and not play them out prematurely. I should therefore think it desirable for Your Highness, as you suggest at the end of your letter, to indicate to the Party leaders (BÜLOW : ' *Certainly! When is the debate to begin ?* ') that German interests will be prejudiced if too much pressure is brought to bear in the Reichstag in favour of reduction of armaments and if too much is said about it. (BÜLOW : ' *Correct.*')

I think it is to our interests for the British to get the impression that we could get more out of the Reichstag than is demanded at present. (BÜLOW : ' *Correct.*')

I need not assure you that I shall work in the same sense and try to prevent any violent naval agitation.

[In reference to King Edward's coming visit to Berlin, Count Metternich wrote : ' I urge strongly against discussing an understanding with the British even in principle, so long as His Majesty and Tirpitz, on the one hand, and the Imperial Chancellor, on the other, fail to agree among themselves.' (XXVIII. 80.)

King Edward and Queen Alexandra, accompanied by the Earl of Crewe (Colonial Secretary) and Sir Charles Hardinge, spent three days in Berlin from February 9th to 12th, 1909. (Cf. p. 319 ; Tirpitz, *Der Aufbau der Deutschen Weltmacht* ; Lee, *King Edward VII*, II, p. 673 ; Wilson, *War Guilt*, p. 122 ; G. & T., VI, p. 227 et seq.) The journey was under-

---

[1] Cf. Brandenburg, p. 298.

taken by King Edward, in spite of his failing health, in his anxiety to preserve good relations with Germany.

For Sir Charles Hardinge's conversation with Prince Bülow, cf. G. & T., VI, p. 230.]

XXVIII. 87

MEMORANDUM BY PRINCE VON BÜLOW, *February 11th*, 1909

Lord Crewe, who came to see me to-day, expressed a warm wish for good relations between ourselves and England, as did also Sir Charles Hardinge yesterday. He hopes that King Edward's visit will have removed many causes of misunderstanding and may have a good influence on the relations between the two Empires.

In the course of our conversation Lord Crewe began of his own accord upon the naval question. He said that naturally England was not thinking of dictating to us in any way about our naval construction. But since the existence and future of the British Empire depended on its strength at sea, England was obliged to do what was necessary for her own security.

I replied that we had never dreamed of bearing a grudge against England on that account. But England should not look for dark and perfidious schemes behind our ship-building, as these were far from our thoughts. We could not understand how an intelligent people like the British could believe in Germany's intention to invade them. Lord Crewe replied that not the present Government, but a great portion of the British people were disturbed at our preferring to build battleships. We had announced, as the reason for our sea-armaments, the necessity of protecting our commerce ; cruisers could do this better. I replied that no one in Germany was thinking of building a fleet stronger than the British one. Our geographical position, which obliged us to keep a very large army, and also the measure of our financial and economic strength showed that it was quite out of the question for us to beat the British in ship-building or even approach them. Our preponderance must always be in the Army. But the German nation desired and was simply obliged to be so strong at sea that no other Power could out-class it on the ocean. The British were wrong in thinking that we were building the fleet against England. There were other countries as well against which we had to be able to protect ourselves at sea.

Lord Crewe, who conducted the conversation in the most friendly tone, quite took in this point of view. He said, by the way, that sooner or later England would come over to universal service.

I replied that if this came to pass, I should consider it fortunate for us also, since universal service made nations inclined for peace.

XXVIII. 91

MEMORANDUM BY BARON VON BUSSCHE-HADDENHAUSEN, OF THE BERLIN FOREIGN OFFICE, *February* 19*th*, 1909

In spite of the Royal visit having gone off well, I am firmly convinced, as are most of those who know England, that directly the British Naval Bill [1] is brought in the Anglo-German atmosphere will quickly cloud over again. The effect of the visit and also of the Morocco Agreement will fade from the British mind, unless we arrive at a clear understanding about the naval question. The atmosphere which has been created for the moment would be especially favourable for it, because *now* it would not look as if we were doing it under British pressure, whereas we should have *later on* to give way to it, with the sacrifice of our prestige, *if war were to be avoided.*

On economic grounds, moreover, and quite apart from the fact that our fleet will never be strong enough to crush the British, we have every economic reason for coming to an understanding with England. Protection will come more quickly in England if she is forced to find further sources of revenue for ship-building, and it cannot be delayed for long unless the British are relieved of their fear of us. The loose bonds of the British Empire, whose colonies desire independence, would be drawn closer by the introduction of Protection and by the possibility of establishing a system of Empire Preference ; this would not suit us, since an England with fewer or no colonies would not be a dangerous rival to us. But if England could meet her public opinion with proposals to diminish the ship-building, she would have less inducement to find new revenue by means of Customs duties, and this could only benefit our trade. Moreover, if there is no longer fear of us, another bond between the Mother country and the colonies would be snapped. Our Navy will be of little help to us in a crisis ; only our Army can do this, and now we are treating it rather more like a step-daughter on account of the Navy than we should if relieved of the heavy naval expenses. In peace-time our Navy injures our trade and our policy—particularly in colonial questions, in which we have so often depended on the good will of England and her colonies,—for it is on account of them that England shows an unfriendly countenance. I would mention, by the way, that even in Turkey we shall need England's good will. [2]

---

[1] Cf. Lee, *King Edward VII*, II, p. 678 ; Winston Churchill, *World Crisis*, p. 36 ; G. & T., VI, p. 241.　　　　[2] Cf. p. 363.

If we fail to come to an understanding with England—and this I consider possible now that we are tackling the naval question—all our other political aspirations may largely be ruined.

XXVIII. 101

ADMIRAL VON TIRPITZ TO THE EMPEROR WILLIAM, *March 8th*, 1909

On the despatch of March 3rd [1] from the Ambassador in London I report to Your Majesty as follows :

His view that in leading political circles, including the Government, deep anxiety has taken hold regarding the alleged intention of Germany to hasten the speed of building and to finish the capital ships more quickly than has been publicly admitted, seems to me to go too far. The Conservative wire-pullers and naval interests have certainly succeeded in inspiring the public with a naval panic, but I think that the Government realise that the idea, secretly and very cleverly disseminated by the Admiralty, that we are increasing our speed, is incorrect, but at the same time a very convenient and therefore welcome method for the Liberal Cabinet to shelter itself against the Conservative attack by largely increasing the Navy, and to justify to their own Liberal and Radical following the earmarking of large sums for armament purposes.

Individual Ministers are obliged by their own former political professions to oppose it in public, but this will hardly alter the policy of the Cabinet as a whole.

I think that in the eyes of the British Cabinet it is not a matter of foreign politics (England-Germany), but of internal politics (Conservative-Liberal). I fear, therefore, that correcting this false idea of our rate of building would neither produce an alteration in British naval strength nor prevent the dissemination of these ideas amongst the public. The Liberal Cabinet will neither wish nor be able to do without this wonderful invention for defending their large Naval Estimates for 1909. Nevertheless, in order to strengthen the elements opposed to it and with a view to unforeseen developments, I recommend that the Ambassador be empowered at once to inform the Prime Minister at lunch on the 10th officially once more that by February, 1912, not 13 Dreadnoughts, but only the ships ordered in 1909 will be ready for commission, and then not till the end of 1912 ; also that no authority in Germany contemplates any other speeding up than that which is settled according to programme.[2] If assertions to the contrary are made in Parliament or Press, we probably should not fail to correct these misstatements in the German Reichstag. On the other hand, I think it would be going too far to accede to the Prime Minister's desire for official inspection of our ship-

---

[1] Not given.   [2] Cf. Bacon, *Lord Fisher*, II, p. 87.

building programme up to 1920, as the Ambassador suggests. I see no reason for this.

Captain Widenmann has sufficient information as to the laying down and completion of the ships for 1906–9 and has his orders to inform Count Metternich. (The EMPEROR : ' *To be shown to the Chancellor.'*—' *For the information of the Ambassador in London—I agree fully with the foregoing, which represents the facts. I cannot help being amazed that, in spite of all that I said to him in Berlin and in spite of much detailed information given him by the Naval Attaché, Count Metternich clings to his false opinions. He is entirely under the thumb of the British scaremongers and lets himself be influenced by them too much. He is therefore to be informed of my serious displeasure at the position he continues to take up with regard to our Navy and he is to be told to take his stand, once and for all, on the contents of this report, which I order to be forwarded to him. He is to frame his replies to the British after consultation with the Naval Attaché. Detailed programmes of construction are not to be handed out.'*

XXVIII. 107

ADMIRAL VON TIRPITZ [1] TO PRINCE VON BÜLOW, *March 17th*, 1909
Statement of fact

Two ships for 1909 have been allotted to two private ship-yards by contract, pending the sanction of the Reichstag, in order to obtain cheaper prices and to prevent the possibility of a ring being formed. Tenders for the other two ships for 1909 will not be issued till the autumn.

I beg Your Highness to inform me how much of the foregoing statement is to be communicated to Count Metternich. (Cf. His Majesty's marginal remarks.[2]) For myself I should have no objection to telegraphing the whole of the facts to the Ambassador. (SCHOEN : ' *Admiral Tirpitz informs me that, in spite of the Emperor's marginal remarks on the duplicate of Metternich's telegram,[3] it is his view the information should be given to Metternich.'*)

German Note.

On March 17th Metternich was instructed in the sense of Tirpitz's memorandum. On the next day Count Metternich was empowered to declare to Sir E. Grey that ' 3 Invincibles are included among the 13 Dreadnoughts, which should be ready by the end of 1912 '.

---

[1] Cf. G. & T., VI, p. 250.

[2] These remarks are not in the Records. According to Tirpitz (p. 134) they were : ' I refuse to be let in for this ; ' and ' I think it would be best that Metternich should hold his tongue at last. He is hopeless ! '

[3] Asking leave to state that the British Admiralty's information that Germany had materials ready and the keels laid for the ships for 1909–10 in various ship-yards was incorrect.

XXVIII. 110

COUNT VON METTERNICH, IN LONDON, TO PRINCE VON BÜLOW,
March 17th, 1909

The seriousness with which yesterday's debate [1] on the state of the Navy was conducted shows the immense importance attached to it on both sides of the House of Commons.

As was to be expected, the centre of the debate was the German Navy and its swift growth, (The EMPEROR: '*!*') even though both Mr. McKenna, the First Lord, and the Prime Minister stated that this was not due to any unfriendly intention towards Germany. Mr. Asquith added that it would be wrong to talk of the comparison between the British and German navies as though diplomatic relations between England and Germany were now unsatisfactory or likely to be so. He was glad to say, on the contrary, that the tendency of late had been towards removing and not stiffening certain bars which had stood between England and Germany. Diplomatic correspondence between the two countries had become more open and friendly, and it was the wish and intention of the Government that it should continue to be so.

In Mr. McKenna's and Mr. Asquith's speeches, as in that of Mr. Balfour, the leader of the Opposition, could be observed a desire to raise the question of naval armaments above the level of Party politics.

The Government admitted that they had reckoned wrongly in two points and that they had to face a new situation.

Firstly, they had not expected (The EMPEROR: '*?!*') that Germany would build at the rate laid down in the German naval programme. (The EMPEROR: '*Donkey! Why not?*') This view had proved incorrect; it was reported that Germany had exceeded this rate. (The EMPEROR: '*False.*') It had also been thought (The EMPEROR: '*Where?*') that Germany's shipyards would be unable to compete with the British ones in the speed of building the Dreadnought type. This view was also proved to be incorrect. (The EMPEROR: '*!!*') The German yards could build as quickly as the British ones. (The EMPEROR: '*Childish reasons.*')

The Prime Minister stated that it was fair to say to the German Government that the British Government had received an absolute declaration that it was not its intention to speed up the completion of its programme. In view of this declaration, the British Government could not introduce a naval programme embodying an assumption that action would take place not in accordance with the declaration. There was no character of an

[1] Cf. Hansard, *Parliamentary Debates*, for this date.

agreement in this promise. He would in no way imply that the German Government was acting in bad faith in altering its plans. But the British Government had to form their programme so as to provide for all possibilities, and they had asked for powers to lay down an additional four ships if necessary.

Mr. McKenna stated that the Government's difficulty was that they did not know the rate at which German ship-building was proceeding. (The EMPEROR : ' *Last year's laying down and the orders given show that clearly.*') The First Lord then gave various data showing the numbers of British and German Dreadnoughts in 1911 and in the spring and autumn of 1912. He argued that before long only this class of ships would be worth considering, since the building and greater fighting capacity of the Dreadnought type would gradually destroy the value of such ships as the *King Edward, Formidable* and *Lord Nelson*. (The EMPEROR : ' *But only very gradually at first.*') The British superiority in cruisers did not come into it, (The EMPEROR : ' 45 *armoured cruisers against* 6 *! ! !* ') since owing to her trade England could not withdraw these from service abroad. This was a vital interest for England ; for other countries temporary loss of freedom of trade on the sea would be merely an inconvenience.

Mr. McKenna reckoned that Germany would possess 13 Dreadnoughts to England's 16 in 1911. (The EMPEROR : ' *At the end of* 1912.') By speeding up the building Germany might have 17 in April, 1912. (The EMPEROR : ' *Wrong.*') But even if there was no speeding up before April, 1910, 17 would be ready by the autumn of 1912. (The EMPEROR : ' *Wrong.*') England must make ready to have 20 Dreadnoughts by then.[1]

The figures mentioned by Mr. Balfour painted England's position even blacker. He said it was no longer a question whether England could maintain the Two-Power Standard ; the *One-Power* Standard was in danger. He was glad relations with Germany were friendly, and he would not say that Germany was overstepping her rights in building her fleet ; it was for England to ensure her own security. The Liberal Government had restricted construction, whilst Germany had not only laid down ships, but had also enormously developed her capacity for ship-building. The leader of the Opposition reckoned that by the end of March, 1911, England would have 10 and Germany 13 Dreadnoughts. By April 1st, 1912, Germany might have 21 Dreadnoughts, and in the course of that year 25. (The EMPEROR : ' *The fellow is a liar—or utterly mad.*') He said it was extra-

---

[1] Mr. McKenna did in fact overestimate the speed at which the German Dreadnoughts were destined to be completed. Two years later (February 9th, 1911) he gave replies in the Commons showing that his estimate of 1909 was 6 months to a year earlier than actually turned out to be the fact.

ordinarily difficult to find out what was going on in the German ship-yards. For the first time England was in so dangerous a position that it was difficult to measure its extent.

Mr. Asquith estimates March, 1912, as the critical moment, but that England will then have 20 Dreadnoughts as against Germany's 17, supposing the latter speeds up her construction.

In reply to Mr. Balfour's accusations Mr. McKenna said that he did not like to discuss a friendly nation's naval programme. (The EMPEROR : ' *That has already been done enough !* ') But it was desirable that he should tell the House everything. All he could say about the four ships indicated as being the programme for the following year was that two had not yet been laid down ; he believed, however, that material for them had been assembled and the armament was on the spot. About the two others he knew that one had been laid down, but he knew nothing of the state of the fourth. The ones which were not yet laid down could not be completed before August, 1911. (The EMPEROR : ' 1912 ! ')

Both Ministers, as well as the leader of the Opposition, declared themselves resolved to maintain England's supremacy at sea.

Mr. Balfour said that the next three days would settle England's fate for the next three or four years.

XXVIII. 114

PRINCE VON BÜLOW TO COUNT VON METTERNICH, *March 19th, 1909*

You will please not again offer to discuss Sir E. Grey's suggestion of a periodical exchange of information as to the state of naval construction. If the Minister should refer to it please tell him that seeing that the experience of these last days has shown that even the repeated, clear and definite statements, which we have communicated to the British Government on matters relating to our naval armaments, have not been believed by the naval authorities we are unable to promise to entertain the measures he proposes.[1]

[Cf. Gwynn, *Letters and Friendships of Cecil Spring Rice*, II, pp. 136–7. ' On the one side is England . . . not building ; on the other side is Germany steadily carrying out a programme conceived in 1897—twelve years ago, and steadily developed since then with as little fuss as possible, in a business-like programme which enabled the firms concerned to make their plant and borrow money in the security and certainty that the Government would pay over a certain sum yearly. When the time comes for the yearly sum to be paid, the Reichstag votes it without comment. . . .' Letter of April 8th, 1909, to Lady Helen Ferguson. (Spring Rice was at the Berlin Embassy from 1895 to 1897.)]

---

[1] Cf. Bacon, *Lord Fisher*, II, p. 87.

XXVIII. 115
COUNT VON METTERNICH, IN LONDON, TO THE GERMAN FOREIGN
OFFICE, *March* 19*th*, 1909

Cipher telegram.

We cannot deny that the British Government has repeatedly shown willingness to come to an agreement on the naval question, especially with regard to keeping down expenses, although no formal proposal has been put forward.[1] If we fail to admit this openly the British Government will furnish Parliament with the proofs, which they are well able to do. Sir E. Grey told me yesterday that they would not make mention of the Emperor in person (Friedrichshof—Sir Charles Hardinge).[2]

Considering the parliamentary situation on both sides, I recommend a declaration in the Reichstag to the effect that the British Government have admittedly proved willingness to arrive at an agreement over the naval programme and the subject of expenditure, but has made no formal offer. (This is not at variance with the Chancellor's statement in the winter.) When doing business together friendly States should avoid making formal offers if it was doubtful how they would be received. We can only be grateful to the British Government for not having forced us into the position of having to refuse. Although our shipbuilding does not mean a threat to any other nation, it is yet obvious that we could not consider entering into negotiations about mutual limitation of the size and cost of the fleet at a moment when ours is in the first stages of completion and when we possess none of the powerful ships which all the world is building in imitation of the standard set by the greatest sea-power; we shall, moreover, not have completed 13 capital ships until 1912 or 1913; and I should certainly avoid paying further attention to the British debates. Three days ago the Prime Minister quite rightly described Anglo-German relations as being perfectly friendly, and with a view to general policy and in consideration for the relations between Germany and England I should not let it be known what we have replied to England's informal suggestions. (SCHOEN : ' *The draft.*')

[On March 29th, 1909, Sir Edward Grey made an important speech in the House of Commons, in which he strongly urged the necessity of a naval agreement with Germany. Schoen reported on April 13th to Bülow that Grey had put forward three possibilities :

(1) A general agreement about limitation or diminution of naval expenditure ;

(2) An understanding regarding the naval Budgets year by year ;

(3) Exchange of information regarding ship-building, including mutual inspection. (XXVIII. 141. Cf. G. & T., VI, p. 255.)]

---

[1] Cf. G. & T., VI, p. 249.   [2] Cf. p. 299 et seq.

Two days earlier Sir Edward wrote to Count Metternich as follows:

XXVIII. 130

SIR EDWARD GREY TO COUNT VON METTERNICH, *March 27th*, 1909
Private letter.[1]

I want to be quite sure that what I may say in Parliament on Monday does not go beyond what your Government has itself stated in public or intended that I should be free to say.

I propose to say that we have been informed verbally but quite definitely that Germany will not accelerate her naval programme of construction and will not have thirteen ships of the Dreadnought type (including cruisers) till the end of 1912.

This has been told not in the form of an undertaking, but as a declaration of intention from the most authoritative source.

I understand this to mean that thirteen ships will or may be ready for Commission as distinct from trials by the end of 1912.

We have also been told that contracts for two ships of the financial year 1909–10 are promised in advance to certain firms, *provided the money shall be granted by the Reichstag.*[2]

I shall probably point out, as a necessary inference from all these statements, that it is intended that the construction of the two ships last referred to shall proceed at a comparatively slow rate or, at any rate, not at an accelerated rate.

You have told me in addition that these two ships will be ready for trial trips at earliest in April 1912 and will not be ready for Commission before October 1912.

You have also told me that as regards the remaining two ships of financial year 1909–10, tenders will be called for only (in the autumn) *late in summer. Orders two or three months later.*

But these two last statements I understood were not for general, and therefore not of course for public use.

There are naturally some points not covered by these statements, which our Admiralty must for its own purposes take into account, but my object in writing is not to ask for more information, but to make sure that whatever I say in public is accurate in form, and in substance does not go beyond what was told me by you for general use.

E. GREY.

I return to London on Monday morning.

[The words in *italics* are corrections which Metternich inserted before he was able to inform Sir Edward Grey that his statements were entirely correct.

On April 29th Stumm was sent to London by the German Foreign Office armed with a series of drafts of political and other agreements and with orders to sound the London Foreign Office. He met with no encourage-

---

[1] Cf. G. & T., VI, p. 253.   [2] Cf. p. 346.

ment whatever.   On his return to Berlin Stumm wrote his report (XXVIII. 158).   Sir Charles Hardinge had insisted that until Germany reassured England about the construction of her fleet, no agreement on other subjects was possible.   On receipt of Stumm's suggestion of an alliance, ' Sir Edward Grey fell into a long meditative silence, which he broke by saying that Europe was divided into two camps ; the balance of power might not be disturbed, but it would be very difficult to unite all the Powers in one camp.'   And again : ' The Minister was silent for an interval and then said there was nothing to be done for the present, and the Governments must be content with dealing with each other as frankly as possible . . .' (Cf. Brandenburg, p. 345 ; Sir Charles Hardinge's Memorandum, G. & T., V, p. 824.)

As a result of Grey's speech Prince Bülow made one more effort to induce the Emperor and Tirpitz to consider the idea of a naval understanding with England.   He called a meeting of the leading authorities, including Bethmann-Hollweg, Tirpitz, Moltke, Admiral von Müller, Metternich and Schoen, very early in June, 1909, of which the Minutes are given below.   Tirpitz made his own emendations to these Minutes, and his version is on the right half of the page where it occurs, whilst the original version is on the left.]

XXVIII. 168

MINUTES OF THE DISCUSSION ON THE QUESTION OF AN UNDERSTANDING WITH ENGLAND, *June 3rd,* 1909

The Chancellor opened the discussion with a short reference to the high importance of the subject and read a letter written to him by the Emperor on April 3rd.   In it His Majesty expressed his agreement with the views submitted to him by Admiral von Tirpitz on an eventual understanding with England, and ordered him to instruct the Secretary of State to the Admiralty, Admiral von Müller, to draw up a formula as a basis for negociations. The letter blamed Count von Metternich for not having obtained from the British statesmen compensation for any renunciation on our part of a supplementary naval programme [1] and for failing to demand atonement for Sir Charles Hardinge's unconstitutional action at Cronberg.[2]   The Chancellor showed also a copy of Count Metternich's report of June 2nd,[3] in which he defended his attitude.

The Chancellor said that among those present there neither should nor could be any question of personal feelings.   They were united in the endeavour to serve Emperor and Empire to the best of their ability.   But on one point he wished to leave no doubt. The first duty of a representative of His Majesty abroad was to report the truth and to describe circumstances as they actually were. He, the Chancellor, would always support an Ambassador who did this, whether or not the unvarnished truth was unpleasant to hear. It was no good abusing the barometer when the weather was bad.[4]

---

[1] Cf. p. 336.   [2] Cf. p. 291.   [3] Not given.
[4] Cf. G. & T., VI, p. 231.

The first matter for discussion was whether Admiral von Tirpitz's proposal of a 3 : 4 ratio, which involved dropping the renunciation of a supplementary programme, could be taken as a basis for an understanding with England. The Ambassador's view was that such a suggestion to England would lead to war in a very short while. The Chancellor gave his opinion that from the reports he had received British feeling towards us was very serious. They were dominated by the fear of the danger of our approaching them in naval construction. Influenced by this anxiety, England had lately shown hostility to us all over the world ; she was even trying to drive other Powers into conflict with us ; we had many recent proofs of this. Serious-minded people in England saw war with Germany approaching. The question now was what would be our chances in such a war. The expressed opinion of Admiral von Tirpitz was that for the next few years we could not contemplate a clash with England with confidence. The next question then was whether an understanding with England might not be possible. Diplomatic methods appeared no longer sufficient to reassure England ; but we might perhaps reach an understanding with her on the naval question on the basis of mutual slowing down of the rate of building. This would be best done in combination with an understanding on other questions, e.g., the colonies, trade or general policy,—perhaps in the form of an agreement of neutrality. Our relations with England were the only cloud on the horizon of our foreign politics, which in other respects was brighter than it had been for many years. It was 20 years since we had been so much feared and respected as now. But our relations with England darkened our future prospects.

At the Chancellor's invitation Count Metternich described feeling in England. He said that 20 years ago this had been favourable to us and the Triple Alliance. The Kruger telegram and the attitude of German public opinion during the Boer War had undoubtedly disturbed it. But it had not become deeply blackened until our naval construction and the agitation in its favour convinced the British in an ever increasing measure that our Navy meant a serious menace to England, and that absolute security and superiority were now a matter of life and death. It was not Germany's competition in the world market, even though they might not welcome it, which had produced the deep dislike, but simply her naval policy.

Admiral von Tirpitz said that lack of understanding might perhaps be found in the Emperor's letter and the inter-	Admiral von Tirpitz said that lack of understanding might perhaps be found in the Emperor's letter and the interpreta-

pretation of it. He himself had always been careful to support an understanding with England in his dealings with His Majesty. Thus last August he had made his proposal of a 3 : 4 ratio. At that time there was every prospect that England would accept it, for the British wanted to build only 4 new ships. It was different now.˙ He could not just yet promise to renounce a supplementary programme. The danger of a clash with England was less threatening than Count Metternich made out. His, Tirpitz's, information was that the annoyance of the British was rooted in their dislike of our trade competition ; the present excitement, however, was mainly the work of Lord Fisher, who was using every method of perfidiousness against Germany. The stronger we made our fleet, the more would England be careful about picking a quarrel with us. Moreover in 1912 our new construction was to go from 4 to 2 ships, a fact which already implied a slowing down of the rate of building and must be represented as such to the British. He considered it injudicious, in fact dangerous, for Germany to take the initiative for an understanding with England. England ought to come forward first with proposals. In no case could we consider an understanding with England without ample reciprocity. On

tion of it. He had always been careful to persuade His Majesty that it was wrong to refuse right off to discuss a mutual understanding about naval armaments. His, Tirpitz's, report to the Emperor of April 3rd,[1] to which His Highness referred and which had been presented at his suggestion, had only dealt with the past, and he had mentioned to His Majesty that there might have been an opportunity in the autumn of 1908 to suggest to England a 3 : 4 ratio for new construction as a basis for negociation. At that time there was a prospect of its being accepted by England, for the British only wanted to build 4 new ships. Now it was different. For such negociations it would have been right not to promise to give up a supplementary programme for 1912, but rather to use it as an instrument for negociation. In his opinion the danger of a clash with England was not as great as Count Metternich made out ; according to his, Tirpitz's, information, the annoyance of the British was rooted in their dislike of our commercial and political competition ; the present excitement, however, was mainly the work of Lord Fisher, who represented the British Admiralty and was using every method of perfidiousness against Germany. The stronger we made our fleet, the more England would be careful about

the whole he was for quietly waiting at this juncture.

picking a quarrel with us. He believed that the navy scare was over in England, and he could only regret once again that Count Metternich had promised, without a mention of return concessions, that no supplementary programme was intended for 1912 ; but he, the Secretary of State, had not been consulted regarding the instructions given to Count Metternich. He considered it injudicious, in fact dangerous, to take the initiative 'for an understanding with England considering the British Government's attitude in the spring. England ought to come forward first with proposals ; then we should learn what was offered and could make our return offer to suit hers. Moreover in 1912 our new construction was to drop from 4 to 2 ships, a fact which already implied a slowing down of the rate of building and should have been represented as such to the British. This fact, in his opinion, indicated that a fresh attempt at an agreement was not at all to be expected. In no case could we consider an understanding with England without ample military reciprocity on her part. On the whole he was for quietly waiting at this juncture.

Count Metternich again said that he had received distinct instructions from the Emperor to tell the British it was not His Majesty's intention to exceed the naval programme. He had only been told of a supplementary programme a few days before.

Admiral von Tirpitz maintained that it was known generally,

also by the British, that 1911 was a critical year, in which a supplementary programme was to be expected.[1]

The British fear that there would be an additional supplementary programme in a few years had already been clearly described by the Ambassador in his report of June 30th, 1908, on the conversation with Sir Charles Hardinge.

The Chancellor represented that hitherto in his oral and written discussions with the Secretary to the Admiralty he had never gained the impression that he desired an understanding with England on the naval question. He was astounded to hear now that in the preceding autumn the Secretary of State had thought such an understanding possible and worth trying for ; [2] it was the first he had heard of it. He could not rightly understand, however, why what then appeared to the Secretary of State possible and useful was now regarded with horror by him. The disquietude in England was not the work of Lord Fisher, but sprang unfortunately from the people's deep and firm conviction that the rise of our sea-power threatened the very foundations of the Empire. We ought to make no mistake about this. There were different kinds of policy ; the worst of all was that of the ostrich. In spite of all the recognised and admired activity of our Navy we were in Admiral von Tirpitz's opinion not yet in a position to stand a war with England and beat her. An understanding with England was desirable in order to get through the dangerous period between now and the completion of our fleet. Of course such an understanding could only be based on reciprocity. There was no need for him, the Chancellor, to protest that he would accept no solution and recommend no step which was not fully in harmony with the nation's dignity. The way in which he had conducted the country's foreign policy for the last twelve years was a pledge of this.

Admiral von Tirpitz said that he was quite aware of the danger existing to which he had earlier called attention. His realisation of it had caused him to disapprove of the Navy League under General Keim. He also was in favour of bringing about a *détente*.

His proposal based on a ratio of 3 : 4 in 10 years would still assure to the British their Two-

With regard to this and the Chancellor's exposition, he would refer them to his written

Power Standard, i.e. a ratio of 2 : 3. 6.

report of January 20th, 1909, in which he had maintained that he was entirely with the Chancellor in considering that we ought to wait for a fresh invitation from England to discuss *mutual* diminution by treaty of the navies of both countries and not to reject it from the start, so as to avoid the odium of such rejection. His report had said further that as early as the end of September, 1908, he had taken trouble to lay this point of view clearly before the Emperor. The proposal which he made in that report was based on a ratio of 3 : 4 and would in ten years have given the British almost their Two-Power Standard, i.e., a ratio of 2 : 3. 6.

Herr von Bethmann-Hollweg did not consider that initiative on our part for an understanding advisable unless we were able to formulate a definite proposal. We had not reached this point at to-day's meeting. Perhaps some *détente* with England might be attained in the domain of colonial politics or that of commercial politics. But he thought that the conditions for this—i.e., the adoption of Protection by England—were lacking.

Count Metternich considered an understanding over colonial and trade questions very desirable, but insufficient to reassure England. Only a naval understanding could effect this. If this was impossible, why not concede something to England by slowing down the rate of building?

Admiral von Tirpitz pointed to the advance in this direction in that in 1912 it would sink from 4 to 2.

The Chancellor suggested that Count Metternich might be empowered to say orally to the British that we were prepared to be approached about naval questions ; he should make no concrete proposal, but merely hint that our concessions would consist in slowing down the rate of building and abstaining from supplementary programmes.

Herr von Bethmann then asked whether slowing down was possible without altering the Naval Law.

General von Moltke was of opinion that we had no chance of

fighting through a war successfully against England. He therefore considered it worth while to try for an honourable understanding. At the same time it should be realised that the failure
of an attempt at an understanding might mean war.

The Chancellor again referred to the dangers of the situation.
The only black cloud at present hung over the North Sea, but it
was heavy with thunder.

Admiral von Tirpitz argued that the value of our Navy was
increasing year by year, and the reserve was being built up.
Taking anything out of the building programme for 5 years, as
Count Metternich seemed to contemplate, would mean a loss to us
of 15 capital ships. If such a slowing down were insisted upon,
the whole naval programme would be worthless.

Herr von Bethmann : ' The strengthening of our fleet is just
what the British have seen and what has so greatly disturbed
them. What could our Navy offer if England made a friendly
suggestion to renew the discussion ? '

Admiral von Tirpitz : ' Any offer by us can only be made after
a proposal has been made by the British, and cannot be formulated
beforehand.'

Herr von Bethmann : ' Cannot there be a slowing down in
the sense that we build 3 and not 4 ships next year, if the British
restrict themselves to 4 new ships—meaning only capital ships ? '

Admiral von Tirpitz said yes to this question. There was no necessity to alter the Naval Law. Slowing down from 4 to 3 could be effected in the ordinary course.	Admiral von Tirpitz said there was no necessity to alter the Naval Law for such a slowing down of the rate of building. Slowing down from 4 to 3 could be effected in the ordinary course.

The Chancellor stated that it was possible then to slow down
without its leading to debates in the Reichstag or even becoming
very publicly known.

Admiral von Müller said that it ought to be made quite clear
that an understanding with England on the basis of slowing down
could only come into being on condition England offered reciprocity of the same kind, i.e., by slowing down her own construction.

All those present were agreed that reciprocity was an absolute
condition for an understanding with England. The Chancellor
insisted strongly that England must not only give full reciprocity
on the technical military side, but a political assurance also.

Admiral von Tirpitz was cer- tain that in 5 or 6 years, per- haps in 1915, when the Kaiser	Admiral von Tirpitz said that in his opinion the dangerous period in our relations with

Wilhelm Canal was widened and Heligoland fortified, the menace from England would be at an end. It would be less even in two years' time.

England would have passed by in 5 or 6 years, i.e. by 1915, when the Kaiser Wilhelm Canal was widened and Heligoland fortified. It would be less even in two years' time.

[Cf. Brandenburg, p. 299 : ' It is difficult to understand how Tirpitz, the Kaiser, and to a certain extent also Prince Bülow, could believe that it was merely a matter of passing through a definitely limited period of danger. The truth was that the period was unlimited as long as England was in a position to keep up the competition, protected by the old standard of power. At no time in future should we be relatively stronger with regard to England than we were then. It was a purely arbitrary assertion when Tirpitz stated, as he once did, that by 1915, when the reconstruction of the Kiel Canal and the fortifications of Heligoland had been completed, we should be through the danger period. Important as these two measures were for the effectiveness of our fleet they left untouched the question of its relative strength compared with that of England . . .'

Cf. Bacon, *Lord Fisher*, II, p. 75. If Tirpitz thought the danger period would close when the Kiel Canal was completed, Fisher's opinion was that it would mark its beginning. ' Fisher, who was always looking ahead, foresaw that when the German programme of ship-building, whereby they hoped to rival our Fleet, was completed, the German Government would declare war on us. He even fixed the exact date to almost within one month. September or October, 1914, was his forecast. This was made almost entirely from a consideration of the date on which the alterations to the Kiel Canal would be finished and the German harvest got in.']

The Chancellor : ' That is all very well ; but the question is still—how are we going to surmount that menace ? '

Admiral von Tirpitz thought it could be surmounted by an understanding about new construction in the ratio of 3 : 4.

The Chancellor begged the Secretary to the Admiralty to obtain the Emperor's leave to work out a formula for an understanding. He pointed out, however, that no diplomacy in the world could induce England to accept a formula which looked like a threat to her existence.

Admiral von Tirpitz declared his readiness in principle to work out a formula. But he must first have concrete British proposals before him, extracted by the Imperial Ambassador in discussion with leading British personages.

Admiral von Tirpitz could see no advantage just now in drawing up a formula, especially as misunderstandings could easily creep in when it was applied by someone else in negociation with the British. Such a formula could only be taken as a preparation for the event of England actually making a move towards a rapprochement with us with a view to an agreement on armaments. Nothing but the measure of the British willingness could help us to judge what shape a formula was to take. The Admiral repeated his earlier remarks, and said that, considering the British Government's attitude in the spring, the initiative ought not to come from us.

The Chancellor begged finally that the subject of this discussion should be kept strictly secret.

BÜLOW. v. BETHMANN-HOLLWEG v. MOLTKE.

Passed on the assumption that the additions and emend-ations on the right side of the page are accepted.

I agree with the Secretary of State to the Admiralty.
v. Müller.

v. TIRPITZ.

P. METTERNICH.

v. SCHOEN.

[On June 23rd, 1909, Prince Bülow wrote to Count Metternich a private letter marked ' Very secret ', in which he said : ' . . . I should say yes to the question whether it is advisable to let it be known by a hint in the right quarter that we should not be disinclined under fair conditions to admit discussion on the naval question. I am firmly convinced that with good will on both sides, and if the British would avoid all appearance of threat or pressure, an understanding could well be arrived at about ship-building, if included in a general rapprochement. As soon, therefore, as we have cleared up the question of finance, I beg you not to force a discussion of the naval question on leading political personages, but at every available opportunity to make it clear that a naval understanding with England is not outside the domain of possibility, so far as it is bound up with a more friendly direction of British policy in general . . . XXVIII. 181.]

XXVIII. 182

ADMIRAL VON TIRPITZ, AT KIEL, TO BARON VON SCHOEN,
June 27th, 1909

Confidential.

It is reported to me from Berlin that Your Excellency intends to instruct the Ambassador in London to represent once again our intentions regarding our naval construction as remaining within the bounds of the Naval Law and to state in particular that we have so far no sort of plan for speeding it up.

I would urgently advise against the latter step, for we have already repeatedly made similar declarations, and so far British

Ministers have refused to listen ; on the contrary they announce cautiously, it is true, but on every possible occasion that they lack sufficient data regarding our naval construction. Party politics are no doubt responsible for this. Whilst these conditions endure, fresh assurances by us will fail, as before, to draw British public opinion over to our point of view.

I cannot help feeling that a fresh official statement by us would but damage our political position with regard to England. It would probably be attributed to fear and in my opinion it would be beneath our dignity.[1]

[On the following day Baron von Schoen replied in a private letter : ' The idea that I intend to empower our Ambassador in London to make a fresh statement regarding our not speeding up the rate of building the fleet must be due to a misunderstanding. No such instruction was either issued or even contemplated . . .' XXVIII. 183.]

XXVIII. 184
COUNT VON METTERNICH, IN LONDON, TO PRINCE VON BÜLOW,
June 29th, 1909

Extract. Secret.

. . . What actually happened [2] at the discussion was different. In his argument the Admiral tried repeatedly to give the impression that it had been long known that a supplementary programme was to be expected in 1912. He went so far as to assert that I had reported it. On my definitely denying this, he read a passage out of my report of June 30th, 1909, in order to back up his assertion. My answer was that my report contained nothing about a supplementary programme for 1912. The passage runs as follows : ' Sir Charles Hardinge said that the German journalists, pastors, burgo-masters, etc., must have persuaded themselves that the British people were dominated by nothing but peaceful and friendly feelings towards the Germans, but ever so many royal visits would be insufficient to remove the deep resentment which the quick building of the German fleet was causing in England. (The EMPEROR : ' ! ') I told him that other nations also built fleets, that our programme had long been known publicly, that it was not to be exceeded, and that England could build all the ships she liked so as to maintain in future the superiority which she possessed now. He replied—what guarantee was there, even if there was no intention of doing so at the moment, that after a number of years a further extension of our naval programme would not be undertaken, (The EMPEROR : ' *Our money-bags ! We can only build as many as our Naval Law provides for !* ') as had undoubtedly happened last winter, for instance ? '

[1] Cf. G. & T., VI, pp. 276–7.   [2] Cf. p. 355.

I declare once again that I was charged by His Majesty in person to declare here that there was no intention to extend the building of our fleet. Moreover Captain Widenmann, the Naval Attaché, has always assured me that the Admiralty authorities never intended to increase the fleet beyond what was fixed by the programme, and that we had not to reckon with a fresh supplementary one. It may be that the Secretary to the Admiralty has long been contemplating a supplementary programme for 1912. If it is so it is a pity that he did not tell the Imperial Chancellor of it in good time so that I might have had proper instructions. But the Admiral's assertion that I ought to have counted on a supplementary programme for 1912 and to have used our possible renunciation of it as an object for compensation in my negociations with the British statesmen is a perversion of the facts, which I absolutely controvert.

[MR. JAMES BRYCE, BRITISH AMBASSADOR IN WASHINGTON, TO SIR EDWARD GREY, *July 12th*, 1909. (Cf. G. & T., VI, p. 278.)

Confidential.

In a conversation I had with the President on July 8th the subject of the attitude of the German Government was mentioned. The President observed that, though the German Emperor was an erratic personage and had written to President Roosevelt some extraordinary letters full of alarms and wild suggestions, he did not believe he had any war-like designs, but was animated more by a sort of megalomania and by a desire to have the glory of possessing a splendid navy. So too he did not believe that the German nation was otherwise than pacific in its intentions. He did not see what would be the end of this incessant increase in armaments, but thought the weight of taxation must arrest their progress.

He had some little while before told me that people had approached him wishing him to take some action in the way of proposing a reduction in the armaments of the Great Powers but that he had not seen his way to such a step.

I gathered that much as he regretted the disquietude these preparations cause, the reports he received from his Representative in Berlin did not make him apprehensive of any disturbance of the peace of the world.

BRITISH FOREIGN OFFICE MINUTES.

But still however pacific the German Emperor and German nation may be at present, the danger lies in the fact that their possessing a Navy strong enough to enable them to go in for a war-like policy at any moment, when they may feel less pacific. There is the risk that when they have got their big fleet they will be strongly tempted to try and make somebody else pay for it.
G. S. S.   W. L.   C. H.

Yes ; and it is natural that till they have a big navy they should quiet apprehensions. E. GREY.]

[Prince von Bülow was succeeded by Bethmann-Hollweg as Imperial Chancellor on July 14th, 1909. (Cf. Chirol, *Fifty Years in a Changing World*, p. 302.)]

CHAPTER XXVIII

THE BAGDAD RAILWAY, 1908–11

[A British scheme for a railway up the Euphrates valley was successfully opposed in 1899 [1] by the Germans, on the grounds that the fact that
they controlled the line to Konia in Asia Minor gave them prior rights.
In 1902 a German Company obtained an iradé from the Sultan who had
fallen entirely under German influence. Much anxiety was felt in England
because the line would shorten the way to India and yet not be controlled
in any way by England. In 1904 the line was completed as far as Bulgurli.
The annexation of Bosnia and Herzegovina by Germany's ally, Austria,
caused Turkey to turn away from Germany in the hope of obtaining
British support.[2] This change was short-lived, but it made the German
Government realise that England was a factor which could not be ignored
in the final arrangements about the Bagdad Railway. (Cf. Lord Newton,
Lord Lansdowne, p. 249 et seq.; G. & T., V, 178; VI, p. 325 et seq.]

XXVII. 559

MEMORANDUM BY SCHOEN, IN BERLIN, *December 8th,* 1908

In the enclosed letter to Gwinner, the director of the Deutsche
Bank, Herr Helfferich [3] has reason for stating that the British
have promoted Turkish Parliamentary action for the purpose
of annulling the last Bagdad Railway agreements.

German Note.

The Convention between Germany and the Porte of June 2nd, 1908,
which sanctioned the construction of the Bagdad Railway from the rail-
head at Bulgurlu to Helif, 840 kilometres further on, and also the necessary
financial measures. (Cf. G. & T., V, p. 284; VI, p. 366; B.F.S.P., II,
pp. 884–6.)]

Herr Helfferich fears that this may entirely prejudice Germany's interests in the Railway and is in favour of an understanding with the British.

Herr von Gwinner shares Helfferich's anxiety and is inclined
for a cautious sounding of his British business friends regarding
handing the section of the line from Bagdad to Basra over to
England, Germany retaining a 30 per cent. share.

According to his telegram of yesterday Marschall has no
objection against this, assuming that such an agreement is not

---

[1] Cf. pp. 110, 112.　　　[2] Cf. p. 306.
[3] Of the Deutsche Bank in Constantinople.

to be carried out until we have constructed as far as Bagdad or are quite certain to be doing so.

Just now feeling in Turkey is doubtless unfavourable to the Deutsche Bank's enterprises. Seeing that the last Railway Convention was chiefly brought about by means of the baksheesh customary under the old régime, a discussion of this Convention in the Turkish Parliament would give our enemies a good opportunity for an attack on German business methods. For this reason and because of the constant British intrigues against us it is not unlikely that the Turkish Parliament may submit the Bagdad Railway Agreements to an unwelcome criticism and ask us to cancel them. This painful situation might be averted by an understanding with England. Formerly on account of the Sultan, such an understanding was out of the question for us. This factor is no longer there now that England has become the most intimate friend of Turkey. But whether this friendship will go so far as to hand the line as far as Bagdad to the British is a doubtful question. The new friends will have to settle it amongst themselves. We need not be more Turkish than the Turks. (BÜLOW : ' *Correct.*')

On these grounds there may be no objection against the step planned by Herr von Gwinner, assuming that attention is paid to the very natural point of view expressed by Baron von Marschall. May Herr von Gwinner be advised in this sense ? (BÜLOW : ' *Agreed.*')

XXVII. 560

Enclosure.

HELFFERICH TO GWINNER, *November 30th*, 1908
Extract.

. . . We have a difficult period before us. My impression from all that I see and hear is that we shall have to build our position here afresh in important respects ; and this impression receives strength each day that passes. We evidently much overestimated our position under the old régime. Many who pretended to be our real friends only did so because the Sultan was the declared friend of Germany.[1] Under the new régime these are on the other side. England is trumps ; and this will be so for a long time to come. In all processions and manifestations, such as during the Elections, one saw flags of all nations excepting those of Austria and Germany. There is bitterness against Austria,[2] and for ourselves indifference or

---

[1] Cf. Brandenburg, p. 313.
[2] On account of Bosnia and Herzegovina.

suspicion. The officers of high rank who were trained in the German school form the only exception. . . .

[Metternich was equally alarmed.]

German Note.

He went further than Helfferich who proposed that England should share in the Bagdad Railway. The only cure Metternich could see was to try and remove the tension between England and Germany by some concession in the question of naval construction. ' Then England would look differently at the Bagdad Railway, for she would no longer have to fear Germany in Constantinople if she was friendly to her, and would have no further inducement to struggle against her '. . . The Emperor minuted this despatch by Metternich as follows : ' The revolution is not the work of " Young Turks " from Paris and London, but by the army alone and, in fact, by the so-called " German " officers who were trained in Germany. A purely military revolution. These officers have everything in their hands and are thoroughly germanised. In the long run Russia will not stand Turkey being strengthened by England's help ; and this is where serious differences ought to occur in future.' Events justified the Emperor, for directly after the Counter-revolution of April, 1909, the newly established British influence in Turkey gave way before Germany's again.

Further we should, in my opinion, seek to protect ourselves if at all possible by an understanding with the British. The dream of a Bagdad Railway, German down to the Gulf, is over. Many large perspectives, but many obstacles also, arise from the change in German-Turkish and Anglo-Turkish relations. We can to-day grant the British the control over the Bagdad-Basra section without the Turks casting us out as betrayers of their country. We can stand it if our pan-Germans cry out about betrayal.

We must adapt ourselves to the new situation before it is too late. I am therefore making a point here of friendship for England and saying everywhere that we have always tried to strengthen Turkey's commerce and finances, and if the British cease to be the opponents, but become friends of the progressive Turkey, we shall meet on the road to the same object and be delighted to co-operate with them.

I beg you to consider how, if at all, a speedy understanding over the Bagdad Railway is possible with England—of course in consonance with our interests. The key to the whole situation lies in the solution of this question. . . .

XXVII. 566

MEMORANDUM BY STUMM, FIRST SECRETARY IN LONDON, *December 11th*, 1908

On my taking leave of Sir E. Grey he made mention of affairs in the East. He said that he hoped greatly for an early understanding between Turkey and Austria,[1] and that he was quite wrongly reproached with having worked against it. The difficulty was that Austria, who was entirely in the wrong, was unwilling to make an offer to Turkey, but was demanding that she should accept all that had happened *tel quel* without compensation.

He then said that leading financial circles in England were thinking of extending their activities to Turkey in future.[2] This did not mean any interference with German interests. On the contrary he wished for Anglo-German co-operation in Turkey. It was certain that England could no longer approve the existing system of kilometric guarantees which had been developed under the old régime and were a consequence of the evils which had characterised it.

I replied that I imagined I could assure him that nothing could be more desired by us than commercial co-operation with England in Turkey. As for political questions, our freedom of movement was somewhat restricted by considerations for our allies.[3]

I may mention that a reliable friend in the Foreign Office gave me the same information and described an Anglo-German understanding over the Bagdad Railway as desirable. He told me that the kilometric guarantees for the Bagdad Railway were disliked in England, as they meant much financial injury to Turkey because the enterprise had been greatly over-capitalised in order to assure greater profits for the banks which were finding the money. My informant further told me in strict confidence that Sir E. Grey had refused his support to various British financiers, who had approached him with railway projects in Turkey, on the ground that he wished to avoid conflicting with German commercial interests there.

[After the Counter-revolution in April, 1909, the Turks began to apply to Germany for support against the terms proposed by British financiers for railway and other concessions in the Turkish dominions.]

XXVII. 574

BARON VON MARSCHALL, IN CONSTANTINOPLE, TO THE GERMAN FOREIGN OFFICE, *October 4th*, 1909

Cipher telegram.

Rifaat Pacha told me confidentially that the British Government accepts the raising of the Customs duties [from 11 per cent.] to 15 per cent. on the following conditions :

[1] Cf. Brandenburg, p. 325.
[2] Cf. G. & T., V, p. 261 ; VI, pp. 384, 407.
[3] Cf. G. & T., V, pp. 678–9.

1. Erection of Customs offices and other buildings for the convenience of trade at certain spots.

2. Admission of the English market into the larger Turkish loans.

3. The effects of raising the tariff not to apply in carrying out contracts which were concluded under the old régime, e.g., that of the Bagdad Railway.

When the Minister asked how the Porte should act with regard to the third point I replied that it concerned the agreement concluded with the Bagdad Railway, and I begged him to get into communication with that Company. . . .

XXVII. 576

BARON VON MARSCHALL IN CONSTANTINOPLE, TO THE GERMAN FOREIGN OFFICE, *October 25th*, 1909

Cipher telegram.

The Grand Vizir tells me very confidentially that during our army manœuvres Winston Churchill, the President of the Board of Trade, and General Sir Ian Hamilton declared to Mahmoud Shevket [1] that a British syndicate was shortly about to ask for a concession for a railway from the Persian Gulf (Koweit) through Basra to Bagdad, and without any guarantee. Both of them tried to win Mahmoud Shevket over to this scheme, which they alleged would be highly advantageous for Turkey. In the meantime Tewfik Pacha has telegraphed from London that similar overtures have been made to him [2] with the observation that the works could begin at once.

Hilmi Pacha continued : ' This question puts us between the hammer and the anvil. For political reasons I cannot grant this concession to the British ; I would rather pay a million or two pounds a year than open the way into the interior of our country to England and British influence by means of a great commercial enterprise controlled exclusively by England. On the other hand it is very difficult for us to reject the British desire merely on the grounds of the railway concession already granted to Germany. It would seriously offend England, who is on a friendly footing at present and whose help we depend on in various questions. Moreover our Parliament would not understand such an attitude ; it would merely consider the financial side and fail to take in the political aspect. Besides it is impossible to explain, even in a secret session, the real reasons which make rejection necessary. In the end the British would spring every mine to win the support of the majority.

[1] Turkish Minister for War. Cf. G. & T., VI, p. 378.
[2] Cf. G. & T., VI, p. 376.

Under these circumstances I appeal to Germany for help. If the British demand for a concession is made I should like to reply that the concession for this line has already been granted to the German Bagdad Railway Company, but that in order to meet the British wishes the Porte would consider allowing British capitalists to participate in the Persian Gulf-Bagdad section in equal shares with the Germans and eventually the French, and that control of this line should be shared between the three of them. But I cannot give this answer to the British before I am sure of the Imperial Government and eventually the Bagdad Railway Company. I beg you to telegraph in this sense to Berlin.'

XXVII. 579

BARON VON MARSCHALL TO THE GERMAN FOREIGN OFFICE,
October 26th, 1909

The Grand Vizir's words of yesterday, spoken evidently in great excitement, are of considerable political importance. They show first the intensity with which the British are now pursuing their aims regarding Mesopotamia and the vilayet of Bagdad, and also how the Turks are at last realising that behind the demonstrative British friendship for Turkey is a policy of self-interest. The National Bank founded by Sir Ernest Cassel, the handing of the coastal navigation over to a British company, the pursuit of a concession for that of the Tigris and Euphrates,[1] the irrigation of Mesopotamia, and finally the desire to build an unguaranteed railway from Koweit to Bagdad have caused intelligent Turks to open their eyes. The Grand Vizir, in particular, now sees that the reason for the British opposition to our Bagdad railway is that a rail connection between the Capital and the vilayet of Bagdad would strengthen the authority of the Turkish State in the South and disturb the British aim of expansion northwards from the Persian Gulf. Being convinced that this realisation was bound to come of itself, I have maintained the greatest reserve, but I have managed by indirect means, and without betraying the source, to have the Turks warned of the danger with which their newest friends threaten them.

Hilmi Pacha informed me that one of the conditions set by England for raising the Customs tariff was as follows : ' British capital shall have a third share of any loan based on the new Customs revenue.' The Grand Vizir considers this totally unacceptable.

German Note.

The beginning and end of the following letter refer to the naval question.

---

[1] Cf. p. 385.

XXVII. 580

COUNT VON METTERNICH, IN LONDON, TO THE CHANCELLOR,
BETHMANN-HOLLWEG, *October 28th*, 1909
Private letter.

. . . Sir Edward Grey [1] said that frankness above all and
open declaration of political motives were essential for maintaining mutual confidence. He wished therefore to explain to
me his point of view regarding the raising of the Turkish
Customs tariff by 4 per cent., which our Foreign Minister had
recently mentioned to Sir E. Goschen. It was calculated that
British trade would have to bear a considerable proportion of
it. The trade of Mesopotamia up to now had been mainly in
British hands through the Lynch line [2] of steamers. A railway
line controlled by a foreign Power (SCHOEN: ' *Control ? We
exercise no control.*') was likely to divert trade and transfer it
into other hands. It was therefore contemplated here to build
a railway in the Euphrates territory, in order to make British
trade independent of the Bagdad Railway. (SCHOEN: ' *Strong
pepper !* ') But it was only contemplated for the event of our
not arriving at an agreement about the Bagdad Railway. He,
Grey, would prefer an agreement. (SCHOEN: ' *Je le crois !* ')
As things were no British Foreign Minister could, in face of the
country and Parliament, consent to the 4 per cent. increase
without first receiving an assurance from the Turkish Government that the increase of revenue from it was not to be used
for extending the Bagdad Railway. (SCHOEN: ' *It is already
promised.*') [3] No British Minister could consent to let the
burden laid on British trade by the 4 per cent. go to benefit the
building of a railway line.

I explained that the Bagdad Railway was not in the hands
of a foreign Power but in Turkey's, and that the management
only was to be mainly German. . . .

Sir Edward said he did not oppose the Bagdad Railway in
principle, indeed he thought that in time it would be built, and
he considered it wrong to be against opening up a country with
a railway. His opposition was merely against this connection
with the Persian Gulf—and so with India—falling exclusively
into the hands of a single nationality. (SCHOEN: ' *No one
wishes it.*') [4] . . .

I beg to suggest that an understanding about the Bagdad
Railway should not be attempted unless preceded by a general
political, plus a naval, understanding. [5] Then private agree-

---

[1] Cf. G. & T., VI, p. 378.   [2] Cf. p. 385; G. & T., VI, p. 421.
[3] Cf. G. & T., VI, p. 433.   [4] Cf. p. 365.   [5] Cf. pp. 372–4.

ments with us will not, as hitherto, be any more attacked in Parliament and the Press.

[Sir Ernest Cassel went to Berlin, and on December 13th he began a series of meetings with Herr von Gwinner, of the Deutsche Bank. Schoen wrote (December 15th): ' Gwinner says that Sir Ernest Cassel evidently intended to get the whole Bagdad Railway scheme away from the Deutsche Bank as much as he could. Gwinner did not let him come out with that, but formulated his own ideas *in extenso* about the railway and tried to cut the ground from under any objections that Sir Ernest might have to suggest (expense of wide gauge, advantages of the narrow gauge). Sir Ernest said : " I see that our views lie far asunder ". . . . You know, of course, that Sir Ernest Cassel is an intimate friend of King Edward and was invited to meet our Emperor at Windsor, where he was treated with much consideration.' XXVII, 604 (cf. Brandenburg, p. 362 ; G. & T., VI, p. 380 et seq.)]

Memorandum [1] *of Herr von Gwinner's proposals, December 5th, 1909.*

Mr. Gwinner formulated his ideas on behalf of the Bagdad Company as follows :

With the consent of the Ottoman Government a separate Company, English or Ottoman, to be formed to take over that part of the concession of the Bagdad Company which relates to the line from Bagdad to the Persian Gulf.

The capital of the new Company to be £300,000 nominal (£150,000 paid up), or a less amount as may appear sufficient for working the line.

A Construction Company to be formed, in Switzerland or elsewhere, upon lines similar to those of the construction companies formed by the Bagdad Railway.

In both these companies an interest of 50 per cent. is claimed, which is to be distributed as follows :

    30 per cent. for the Bagdad Company,
    10 per cent. for the Anatolian Railway, and
    10 per cent. for the Turkish Government.

The rest of the Memorandum contains Herr von Gwinner's statement what he had already arranged with the Turkish Government.]

XXVII. 609

SIR ERNEST CASSEL, IN LONDON, TO HERR VON GWINNER, *December 22nd*, 1909

On my return from Berlin I found rather disquieting telegrams from Cairo relating to my daughter's health, and I have decided to leave to-morrow for Egypt in order to join her there. This unavoidable change in my plans is highly inconvenient from many points of view, but I hope that, with regard to our Bagdad discussions, it will not be a serious drawback, inasmuch as Sir Henry Babington Smith will be here until after the beginning of the New Year, and when he has to go back to Constantinople no doubt an efficient representative—probably Lord Revelstoke or Mr. Sidney Peel—will be found to deal with any question that may arise. Meanwhile will you be good enough to address

[1] Cf. G. & T., VI, p. 410.

your reply to Sir Henry Babington Smith, c/o National Bank
of Turkey, 50 Cornhill, London, E.C., and perhaps you will
indicate to him what is the next step you propose to take in
the matter.

I have had an opportunity of discussing with my friends
here the views expressed, as embodied in the Memorandum of
our conversations. As I expected, nothing short of absolute
control of both the construction and the working companies
would be satisfactory to us, and the maximum interest we could
allow to other parties would be 40 per cent. The manner in
which that 40 per cent. is distributed would be immaterial to
us.

A great deal of discussion took place about the £2,000 per
kilometre, but finally the view prevailed that from the British
standpoint the proposal to let this amount revert to the Bagdad
Company was fair and reasonable and that under the circumstances it should be accepted without bargain or barter. This
would of course be subject to a provisional examination of the
cost of construction the result of which, I have no doubt, would
not differ materially from the figures given me confidentially by
you.

I am pleased to add that the suggestion which we discussed
in Berlin of a 25 per cent. interest for you in anything we might
undertake in Mesopotamia, subject to reciprocity to the same
extent in anything you might undertake on your part of the
line, is also favourably entertained.

XXVII. 608

SCHOEN, IN BERLIN, TO COUNT VON METTERNICH, IN LONDON,
December 31st, 1909

For Your Excellency's confidential information.

Director von Gwinner has sent the enclosed copy of Sir
Ernest Cassel's letter, according to which the British financiers
agree in general with the German views expressed in the Memorandum of December 15th. They merely demand that their
share of the section from Bagdad to Koweit shall be 60 per cent.
and not 50 per cent. Herr von Gwinner rejected this demand
in a letter of December 27th in consideration of the Turkish
standpoint explained to him by Hilmi Pacha, adding that he
could only request that the British should eventually address
themselves to the Turks.

According to the enclosed report from our Ambassador in
St. Petersburg [1] of the 27th, Sir Ernest Cassel's visit to Berlin
has not escaped the notice of M. Isvolsky.[2] It is also clear

---

[1] Not given.   [2] Cf. G. & T., VI, p. 418.

from the debates in the French Chamber that M. Pichon [1] is closely observing the affair. There is no need to stress the fact that, now that St. Petersburg and Paris have just expressed a wish for negotiations *à quatre*, we shall continue to hold to our attitude of refusal in the Bagdad Railway question. It is obvious that, for the reasons we know of, we cannot entertain these negotiations nor any formal internationalisation of the German enterprise.

[On January 10th, 1910, the *Daily Graphic* published an article including the sentence : ' At one time we were actually disposed to come to terms with Germany, but in deference to Russian wishes the negociations were broken off . . . Since then the Entente has become a reality, and among the points established in that understanding is an Anglo-Russian community of interests in the Middle East which virtually places their attitude towards the Bagdad Railway on a common basis.' (Cf. Brandenburg, p. 363 ; Grey, I, p. 254.)

In commenting on this article on February 3rd Count Metternich wrote : ' From conversations with influential members of the Press I gather that the conviction is growing that British interests would best be served by a policy of maintaining and strengthening Turkey.' (XXVII. 668.)

On January 15th, 1910, Sir Edward Goschen handed a Memorandum [2] to the German Foreign Office, stating the point of view of the British Government.]

XXVII. 623

COUNT VON METTERNICH, IN LONDON, TO THE CHANCELLOR, BETHMANN-HOLLWEG, *February* 10*th*, 1910

Private letter.

It is quite true that Sir Edward Grey wishes to make the railway question independent of the naval negotiations.[3] He definitely said so in November—and I reported on it or wrote about it to you—when he explained to me that owing to the Elections the naval negotiations must rest for a while. He hoped that an understanding over the Bagdad Railway would pave the way for a further political and naval agreement.

According to the British Memorandum, which you brought to my knowledge in your letter January 21st,[4] the British Government's view is that the fact of the British group sharing in the construction of the line from Bagdad to the Persian Gulf will benefit the existence of the whole railway, and therefore no compensation can be demanded by us for letting in the British group.[5] Also that England's consent to the raising of the Turkish tariff by 4 per cent., which would follow the agreement about the Bagdad Railway, is—seeing that British trade would be the chief sufferer—a sacrifice which the British Govern-

---

[1] Cf. G. & T., VI, pp. 424–5.   [2] Cf. G. & T., VI, p. 422.
[3] Cf. pp. 365, 369.   [4] Not in the German Records.   [5] Grey, I, p. 254.

ment is making to the railway. Moreover the British section would cut through a district into which the steamers of the Lynch Company have long since introduced British interests. Sir Edward Grey most definitely refuses us any compensation, once the group of financiers who represent German interests has made its agreement with the British group.

This being so, I see no prospect at all of getting compensation from the British Government. Apart from this, it is my opinion that there can be no question at all of Walfisch Bay,[1] since England would probably lose South Africa if her Government insisted on ceding Walfisch Bay to us.

Several times during recent years the German financial group was prepared to give the southern section of the railway up to England, in the form that England should have control, i.e., at least half of the shares and the management of the Bagdad-Gulf section. England argues, from a purely business point of view, that by taking a share British capital will lighten the burden, which our group does in fact feel oppressive.

We, that is the German Government, cannot, as you very truly say, ignore the political standpoint, nor can you, as you say in your letter, represent to our public opinion that giving up the Bagdad-Gulf section to England is in itself a sufficient help to the Railway enterprise for us to agree to it without further compensation from England ; the Bagdad Railway has been too much involved in politics all these years by the opposition of other Powers for that.[2] From the purely business point of view Herr von Gwinner is probably quite right. The Chancellor has also to take account of the grumbling in the German Empire of to-day. The concession for the whole railway is German ; so that we cannot give another country control of an important section of it without compensation. It is a different matter with the Chinese railways. There several groups backed by their Governments have been in competition for concessions, construction or control, and must divide the spoil as best they can. But the Bagdad Railway concession is purely German, and since England is interested in not being elbowed out in Mesopotamia down to the Gulf, she ought to pay or let Germany have the control. Generously taking over a railway, which is another's property, has never so far been considered as a concession made to the original owner.

But Sir Edward Grey's clear and definite refusal makes me feel that we can never get compensation, and I think we can do nothing but wait and see whether the naval negotiations produce a good result, when there might be an agreement about the Bagdad Railway on the lines proposed by Herr von Gwinner.

[1] Cf. G. & T., VI, 271–2.   [2] Cf. p. 419.

If the British Government press for a decision, I think we can calmly reply that in the existing state of German public opinion we could not propose to give up the Bagdad-Gulf section to England without compensation, but that if we could achieve a general clearing of the political situation between England and Germany matters would be different.

XXVII. 668

THE CHANCELLOR, BETHMANN-HOLLWEG, TO COUNT VON METTER-NICH IN LONDON, *February 3rd*, 1911

Private letter.

Sir Edgar Speyer,[1] who was here for a few days, came to see me yesterday and expressed a wish that an understanding with England about the Bagdad Railway might be brought about. I gave him the following information.

In this, as in the Persian question,[2] we are ready to come to an understanding with England.   In both cases, especially the Bagdad one, we are *beati possidentes*.[3]   The completion of the line as far as Bagdad is promised ; we hold a concession as far as the Gulf.   Thus it would be for England to make proposals to us on a basis taking account of the fact that we should be giving the British something that we possess.   Turkey's consent is also necessary.   Any suggestion not in accordance with this is bound to be a failure from the start.   A discussion *à quatre*, such as England has always desired, is out of the question.

Sir Edgar agreed.   He hinted that he greatly regretted that I had not sought an exchange of opinions with Sir Edward Grey in person.   In the Foreign Office there were many anti-German elements—he mentioned Nicolson—whose point of view was different from Grey's.   I replied that I could desire nothing better than to meet Grey.

I venture to tell you the foregoing, although materially it contains nothing new.   I thought it not impossible that Speyer might tell Asquith or Grey of this conversation.

The same, February 14th, 1911.

. . . You may say to Sir Edgar Speyer that it is desirable that England should clearly realise that we are still ready for an understanding over the Bagdad Railway, but only on the basis of *do ut des*. . . .

---

[1] A London financier.   [2] Cf. Brandenburg, p. 361.
[3] Cf. G. & T., VI, p. 427.

XXVII. 670

BARON VON MARSCHALL, IN CONSTANTINOPLE, TO THE GERMAN
    FOREIGN OFFICE, *February 10th*, 1911

Cipher telegram. Extract.

The Grand Vizir informs me that he intends shortly to
negociate with England about the Gulf section of the Bagdad
Railway, and at the same time about arrangements regarding the
Persian Gulf, and especially Koweit. His idea is to form a new
company for the Gulf line—Turkey's share to be 40 per cent.,
and that of the Germans, French and British to be 20 per cent.
each. The Chairman of the Board is always to be a Turk. . . .

XXVII. 672. *The same, February 24th*, 1911

Rifaat Pacha said to me, regarding the Anglo-Turkish conversations, that at his first one with Sir Gerard Lowther he had
said : It was his impression that recently ' les relations entre
l'Angleterre et la Turquie étaient un peu tendues ', and he
thought he was not wrong in imagining that the reason for this
was the undefined position regarding the Gulf section and also
on the Persian Gulf itself. Negociations were just now going
on with the Bagdad Railway Company with the object of
settling about the line to Bagdad. At these negociations, which
would soon be over, the Company had declared its readiness
to renounce the revenue from the 4 per cent. increase of the
Customs tariff unconditionally. The original idea of constructing the Gulf line under the Turkish government had been given
up. The present plan was to form the new Company with British,
Turkish, German and French capital in proportions to be agreed
upon. The first point to be considered was Koweit. The
Porte was obliged to stress the point that the terminus of the
line must be under its control, i.e., a Turkish Custom House
and Turkish police to be installed there. After Koweit, Basra,
as terminus, would have to be considered. The Porte wished
for an exchange of opinions on all these points.

Having accepted this communication *ad referendum* Sir
Gerard Lowther handed the Minister Sir E. Grey's answer two
days ago. It was to the effect that the British Government was
prepared to discuss the points indicated with the Porte and
requested detailed proposals as to the contemplated formation of
the new Company.

The Minister, who described the tone of the reply as thoroughly
friendly, now wishes, after consultation with his colleagues, to
work out a scheme for setting up the new Company and the
proportionate shares in particular, and to hand it to Sir G.
Lowther in the form of an Aide-mémoire.

Rifaat Pacha also discussed the matter with M. Bompard,[1] but he experienced a rather cool reception. The Ambassador said that there was no particular advantage for France in taking a share in the Gulf line, since she was mainly interested in the construction of the Syrian railway system. The Minister's reply to him was that there could be no question at present of a railway from Tripoli, via Homs, to Bagdad. Building two lines to Bagdad would be a luxury which the Porte's present financial position would not admit of.

XXVII. 625

THE CHANCELLOR, BETHMANN-HOLLWEG, TO COUNT VON METTER-NICH, *February 21st,* 1910

I do not agree with the views expressed in your letter of the 10th [2] and am not inclined to regard Sir E. Grey's refusal to offer us compensation for handing over the Bagdad Railway from Bagdad to the Persian Gulf to British capital as final and immutable. The language of the Memorandum seems to me so little categoric and the arguments in it so open to attack, that skilful persuasion might convince the Minister that the British Government both should and can sacrifice something for the great advantages they gain from our assistance on political matters, without falling foul of their own public opinion. I must therefore postpone a final decision, and I now beg you, but only if Sir E. Grey approaches you on the subject, merely to tell him as from yourself that in consideration of our own public opinion we should be unable to sanction Sir Ernest Cassel's and Herr von Gwinner's arrangements unconditionally. It will be best not to refer to the intended general political under-standing, so as to avoid the appearance of wishing to bring pressure on the decisions of the British Government by any such hint. . . .

XXVII. 673

COUNT VON METTERNICH, IN LONDON, TO THE CHANCELLOR, BETHMANN-HOLLWEG, *February 26th,* 1911

The French Ambassador, Paul Cambon, told me he had recently seen his brother, Jules, before the latter's return to Berlin. He then discussed the Bagdad Railway question, intend-ing to give the impression that his brother was going to discuss it in Berlin. M. Paul Cambon expressed a wish for a speedy settle-ment of the Bagdad affair, and, as far as France is concerned, he thinks it might be solved by our supporting France's railway interests in Syria with the Turkish Government and by France

---

[1] French Ambassador in Constantinople.   [2] Cf. p. 372.

liberating French capital for the Bagdad Railway in return. The Ambassador did not say definitely that his Government would be ready to agree with us on this basis ; but he would hardly have mentioned this plan unless he was sure of the support of his Government, which keeps him informed on all important questions.

As regards England, his view is that the British Government's consent to raising the Customs tariff by 4 per cent. represents a concession in return for which we might grant her a share in the Gulf section—how much he does not say—since this would release capital for building the final portion.

[In March, 1911, the obstacles to the completion of the railway seemed to be clearing away. A large Austro-German loan to Turkey had induced the Porte to authorise the final stages of construction, and the British Government appeared to be ready to withdraw much of their opposition. (Cf. Brandenburg, p. 368 ; W. S. Blunt's *Diaries*, II, p. 342.)]

XXVII. 682

KIDERLEN, IN BERLIN, TO BARON VON MARSCHALL, IN CONSTANTINOPLE, *March* 10*th*, 1911

Telegram.

Please discuss Sir Edward Grey's speech yesterday in the House of Commons about the Bagdad Railway with the Grand Vizir. The following remark by the Minister seems specially important : ' We have neither right nor claim to protest against the completion of the Bagdad Railway by German concessionaires and the Turks in accordance with the terms of the concession.'

This undisguised confession will make it easier for the Grand Vizir to realise that his anxiety regarding British susceptibilities is exaggerated. Sir Edward Grey's intelligent view of the matter offers hope of a universally satisfactory conclusion to the Bagdad Railway question.

XXVII. 682

BARON VON MARSCHALL TO THE GERMAN FOREIGN OFFICE, *March* 11*th*, 1911

Cipher telegram.

The Grand Vizir, Hakki Pacha, to whom I spoke as instructed about Sir E. Grey's speech, replied that he also had been pleased by the passage declaring that England had no right to object to the carrying out of the railway concessions in Turkey. But unfortunately there were certain remarks to follow which washed out the favourable impression. Sir E. Grey declared definitely that, as the railway was competing with British concessionaires —meaning Lynch and his Tigris navigation—England would not consent to the 4 per cent. increase. Sir E. Grey had also spoken with suspicious vagueness of reciprocity in the form of a concession for railways with British capital. More objectionable than all, however, was a part of the speech referring to the Koweit question, which drew a sharp distinction between Koweit [1] and Turkish territory. On the whole, Sir Edward Grey's words made the following impression : ' You Turks may let the Bagdad Railway be built, which you have conceded to the Germans, but England will take care to protect her own interests.' This indirect threat showed that the opening sentence of the speech was not honestly meant. . . .

[The Conventions by which the Porte gave leave to continue the Bagdad Railway were signed in Constantinople on March 21st, 1911. The Bagdad end was included in the agreements, but no work was possible there until the other nations concerned were satisfied. In the final effort to keep the peace between Germany and England (July, 1914) the Agreement settling the terms was signed, France having been previously satisfied in February of the same year. (Cf. Brandenburg, pp. 467-8.)]]

XXVII. 686

Baron von Marschall, in Constantinople, to the German Foreign Office, *March 19th*, 1911

Cipher telegram.

Rifaat Pacha . . . told me that the French were suddenly showing excitement about the approaching signature of the Conventions. The French Chargé d'Affaires, A. Boppe, had been with him and had said that in Paris it was held that the German Bagdad question would only be settled simultaneously with the French railway requirements. If Germany was granted priority of rights here, it would make a bad impression in France. Rifaat Pacha's answer was that the Porte had never given reason for the supposition that the Bagdad question would only be settled in conjunction with the new French railway schemes, which were only in their initial stages.

It is the first time in my recollection that the French have taken a step officially to interfere with our arrangements regarding the Bagdad Railway. Perhaps Delcassé's spirit is already making itself felt.[2] The French action will not be successful.

[The British Government's policy in Mesopotamia (now Iraq) during and after the war was much criticised at the time as adding to our problems and obligations without sufficient reason. The previous history of the whole question shows how generally the future importance of controlling Mesopotamia was realised. It included, moreover, control of a portion of the world's supply of oil.]

---

[1] Cf. G. & T., I, p. 333 ; II, pp. 94, 96.
[2] He joined Monis' Cabinet as Minister for the Navy.

CHAPTER XXIX

THE EASTERN QUESTION AND CRETE, 1909–10

[In 1898 Germany and Austria withdrew from the problem of Crete and left it to the other four Great Powers, England, France, Italy and Russia to settle it. They hoped thus to be free to retain the Porte's confidence whilst their rivals were releasing the island from the clutches of Turkey. But the Cretan affair became inextricably involved in the whole question of the Turkish Empire, and Germany found that her repeated declarations of *désintéressement* were impairing her influence in Constantinople in such questions as the Bagdad Railway and the shipping on the rivers of Mesopotamia.

England's hands were more or less tied for a time by the desire to give the Young Turks every chance of making good their progressive professions. (Cf. G. & T., V, p. 279.)

On October 12th, 1908, the Cretan Chamber voted in favour of union with Greece. For ten years the four Powers entrusted with the administration of the island had kept contingents in Canea and Candia, and the time fixed for their withdrawal was approaching. The British Consul and Vice-Consul at Canea were Mr. A. Peel and Mr. E. Wyldbore-Smith. (Cf. Vol. II, p. 464 ; G. & T., V, pp. 418, 437, 440, 503 ; Lee, *King Edward VII*, II, p. 518.]

German Note. XXVII. 27

On the attitude of the British Government Count Metternich reported on October 11th : ' M. Romanos, the Greek Minister, informed me yesterday that he had asked Sir E. Grey in the name of his Government to submit the Cretan question to the Conference, in order to help the Greek Government out of the undeservedly difficult situation into which Crete's inopportune action had brought it. Sir Edward met this with a refusal. On being asked whether the British Government would at least refuse to recognise the Bulgarian declaration of independence and the annexation of Bosnia the British Minister again said no.'

[On January 22nd, 1909, the German Chargé d'Affaires at Athens wrote that the report that England intended to add to her force in Crete was now confirmed. (XXVII. 36.) From now on there was a Company of British, French, and Italian soldiers and a few men from the Russian army at Canea, and two companies of British troops on the walls overlooking Candia.]

XXVII. 49

BARON VON WANGENHEIM, AT ATHENS, TO THE GERMAN FOREIGN OFFICE, *May 26th*, 1909

Cipher telegram.

The Foreign Minister, Baltazzi, made the following communication to my Italian colleague about Sir Charles Hardinge's conversation with Romanos, the Greek Minister in London, about Crete :

Hardinge declared that after the withdrawal of the foreign contingents ships of the protecting Powers were to be stationed off Crete—one ship from each for two months. M. Romanos answered in amazement that this would mean prolonging the occupation. Indeed the new situation would be worse than the old one, which had at any rate held out hopes for the future. Hardinge replied that Greece's proper course was to enter into direct negociations with Turkey. He warned Greece against violent measures. If Cretan deputies appeared in the Greek Chamber at Athens, Turkey's answer would be a declaration of war. He asked what Power would then be in a position to help Greece.

With a prayer for strict discretion Baltazzi added that as a result of the British Government's uncompromising attitude a family council had been held yesterday at the Palace, when His Majesty hinted at a possibility of his abdication.

Naby Bey told me to-day that in Constantinople they set much store on good relations with the Triple Alliance. But conditions might be altered by the initiative taken by Germany in the Cretan question, which was equivalent to a *noli me tangere* for the new régime. (BÜLOW : ' *The Turks must be left in no doubt that we are not thinking of being unpleasant to them in the Cretan question or of mixing in it at all.*')

XXVII. 53

BARON VON WANGENHEIM, IN ATHENS, TO THE GERMAN FOREIGN OFFICE, *June 2nd*, 1909

Cipher telegram.

The British Minister told me he did not believe his Government's opposition to a union of Crete with Greece was unsurmountable. The only question was how Turkey was to be satisfied. Apart from a money payment, Greece could make her substantial concessions, e.g. in the extradition question of remittances. If the Powers acted with decision, they might convince Turkey that her interests lay in renouncing Crete and arriving at a definite understanding with Greece.

XXVII. 56

PRINCE VON BÜLOW TO BARON VON WANGENHEIM, AT ATHENS, *June 8th*, 1909

Telegram.

You know that in the Cretan question we are, as hitherto, maintaining the strictest reserve. Thus we have no inducement to help the protecting Powers (i.e. the Triple Entente) out of the dilemma between hurting Turkish self-esteem and disappointing Greek aspirations.

In this matter I beg you to be restrained in what you say and keep up your rôle of a cool observer, which is best suited to our political interests.

XXVII. 59

BARON VON WANGENHEIM, AT ATHENS, TO PRINCE VON BÜLOW,
June 6th, 1909

Extract.

. . . We must seek another explanation for England's opposition. Respect for Turkey cannot have been the British Government's deciding motive, although they said it was so in a telegram to the British Minister here. For if the Powers were acting in concert, no one of them would have to fear any loss to its own interests as against the countries working along with them. (BÜLOW: '*Aha!*') But the moral reason, as stated by Sir E. Grey in his telegram—that delivering Crete to Greece would mean a breach of confidence with Turkey—must be judged side by side with the fact that England has often enriched herself at Turkey's expense. In the search for the British Government's motives one comes finally upon the old British longing for Suda Bay.[1] (BÜLOW: '*Possibly.*')

That this goes on has been shown during the occupation of Crete by the fact that the British troops have always tried to treat this bay as a part of the Cretan coast entrusted to their special protection and to keep the troops of the other Powers away from it. Of course England cannot demand Suda Bay openly before Europe as her commission for agreeing to deliver Crete up to Greece. Thus she has little inducement to hurry on with the Cretan question so long as there is no prospect of material gain for herself out of it. She is perhaps waiting to see what price Greece will offer her for changing her attitude. The Greeks are already declaring quite openly that they would give up Suda Bay to any Power that would let them have Crete. They would therefore doubtless be ready at once to give up their rights to the bay by a secret treaty with England. It should not be forgotten that England could easily cloak the transaction later on by taking Suda Bay in exchange for Cyprus, which is useless for British purposes and has long been yearning for union with Greece. (BÜLOW: '*?*') So far there are no signs of any negociations between England and Greece having taken place ; but many of the diplomats here have the impression that England does not wish to show her cards for the present and does not consider the moment come for playing out her

[1] Cf. Vol. II, pp. 454, 465.

last trumps. Up to now, however, it has been felt by the Greeks that England's opposition has been mainly caused by the alleged initiative of the Triple Alliance, and that it can be surmounted by persuasion, now that the Triple Alliance has made its disavowal. King George has written to the Queen of England asking for help, as her relation, in his own and his country's difficulties. The Greek efforts to influence England are, as I have before reported, seconded by France. Whereupon the British Government somewhat modified their expressions and sent word here that they would be pleased if Greece would come to an agreement with Turkey. At the same time England made it known that Turkey would at once approach the Cabinets on the subject, when there would be an opportunity for discussing the Greek wishes. This being so, it appears as if England would so far give in to French influence as to subscribe to a programme for the coming *pourparlers* with Turkey. . . .

Thanks to the far-sighted policy initiated by Your Highness in 1897 Germany is not directly interested in the Cretan question. Our self-restraint has also established our position on the Bosphorus. It will help us over the difficulties that are still before us here. (BÜLOW : ' *Then let us stick to this " self-restraint ".*')

XXVII. 73

COUNT BROCKDORFF-RANTZAU, IN VIENNA, TO BARON VON SCHOEN, *July 23rd*, 1909

Private letter. Extract.

. . . Baron Aehrenthal was extraordinarily forthcoming and frank in our conversation to-day ; I am quite convinced that he sets great value on going closely hand in hand with us now in the Cretan question and would be very thankful for guidance from Berlin. I have telegraphed about it and would only add here—which I carefully avoided doing officially—that, when he said repeatedly that we and Austria-Hungary were together in being only partially interested in the Cretan question, I replied that I fully agreed with him in the main, but that it was of no small interest to *us* that the question should be solved without involving serious danger to the Greek dynasty. Baron Aehrenthal agreed with me absolutely. . . .

German Note. XXVII. 95

On July 27th, 1909, the protecting Powers withdrew their troops. The Greek flag was hoisted on the citadel of Canea immediately afterwards, and was replaced the next day by one with a white cross, without the crown, on a blue ground. The Turks were unable to get this flag removed. On August 14th the Cretan Government informed the Consuls-General of the protecting Powers that its demand had been made in vain. On the

same day a party of Cretans seized the citadel of Canea in order to protect
the flag. On the 18th the protecting Powers landed sailors, who took
down the flag-staff and left a detachment in charge.

XXVII. 99

KÜHLMANN, CHARGÉ D'AFFAIRES IN LONDON, TO THE GERMAN
FOREIGN OFFICE, *August 18th*, 1909

Cipher telegram.

Sir E. Grey invited me to come and see him and, in the
course of a long conversation, said that the Turkish Ambassador,
Tewfik Pacha,[1] who came to see him yesterday, had told him
that the troubles caused by Greek agitation in Macedonia [2]
were much more important than the Cretan question. He,
Grey, had advised that before undertaking any hasty step the
Porte should turn to the six Great Powers, and said that it
might be assured that these would insist at Athens on some
reasonable promise of good behaviour in future on the part of
Greece. A recrudescence of activities by Greek bands in
Macedonia must not be permitted. He set store on giving me
this information in order to maintain all possible harmony
between those Powers who had an equal interest in preserving
peace in the Balkans and to ensure speed in the joint action
which might eventually be necessary. The Turkish Ambassador's
language had certainly not pointed to any immediate danger
of war, but there was a danger in the present irritated state of
public feeling.

The hauling down of the flag in Crete by the naval detachment had taken place without incident. The detachment was
remaining on land for the present merely in case of disturbances.

It is my personal impression that Sir E. Grey wished to sound
me as to our attitude towards joint intermediary action by the
Concert of Europe.

XXVII. 100

THE CHANCELLOR, BETHMANN-HOLLWEG,[3] TO KÜHLMANN, IN
LONDON, *August 19th*, 1909

Telegram.

We join with Sir Edward Grey in desiring earnestly to maintain peace and have made emphatic representations in this
sense in Constantinople.

No fresh friendly representations there are possible for us
at present, as the Porte's reply which has been communicated
to you shows.

[1] Cf. G. & T., V, p. 11.   [2] Cf. Grey, I, p. 259.
[3] Cf. Brandenburg, p. 349.

[This was to the effect that the Porte was not thinking of making war on Greece. The German Government considered that a fresh joint protest would do more harm than good.]

Tittoni's communication [1] must refer to Sir Edward Grey's proposal of joint action by the Powers in Constantinople. We cannot estimate at present what Sir Edward would include in such a *démarche*. If, contrary to her constant peaceful asseverations to us, Turkey should really decide on war with Greece—which we do not believe—we consider that intervention by all six Powers would not promise success, unless the Porte clearly understood that the Powers were prepared to take up arms in the cause of peace.[2] Such pressure, however, would seem to us very questionable, as it might cause changes in Turkey much more menacing to the general peace than a Greco-Turkish war.

Please put the foregoing before Sir Edward Grey in a friendly tone.

XXVII. 102

RIEPENHAUSEN, CHARGÉ D'AFFAIRES AT ATHENS, TO THE GERMAN FOREIGN OFFICE, *August 21st*, 1909

Cipher telegram.

The Italian Minister informed me orally that the four Powers intended jointly to advise the Greek Government, in the event of a fresh Turkish *démarche* in Macedonia, to address its complaints to the six Powers. The idea came from England.

He indicated in strict confidence that he personally thought badly of the idea, since a breach of the Treaty of Berlin was not imminent, so that the Signatory Powers, as such, were hardly entitled to take action. But the solidarity which had come into being owing to the Cretan question would scarcely permit his Government to remain aloof from such a *démarche*.

According to his information England had lost much of her influence in Constantinople.

[A personal feud grew up between Isvolsky and Aehrenthal as a result of the way in which the former had been duped in the Bosnia-Herzegovina affair. Isvolsky organised a meeting between the Tsar and the King of Italy, which came to pass at Racconigi, in Piedmont, on October 23rd, 1909. (Cf. G. & T., V, p. 809; Brandenburg, p. 354; Steed, *Through Thirty Years*, I, p. 333.) As a result of this meeting the following Agreement, to which England and France gave their adherence, was signed.]

Russo-Italian Agreement, October, 1909.

1. La Russie et l'Italie doivent s'employer en première ligne, au maintien du statu quo dans la Péninsule des Balkans.

2. Pour toute éventualité qui pourrait se produire dans les

---

[1] Not given. [2] Cf. Brandenburg, pp. 367–8.

Balkans, elles doivent appuyer l'application du principe de nationalité, par le développement des États Balkaniques, à l'exclusion de toute domination étrangère.

3. Elles doivent s'opposer, par une action commune, à tout agissement en sens contraire aux fins ci-dessus ; par ' action commune ' on doit entendre une action diplomatique, toute action d'ordre différent devant naturellement demeurer reservée à une entente ultérieure.

4. Si la Russie et l'Italie voulaient stipuler pour l'Orient Européen des accords nouveaux avec une tierce Puissance, en dehors de ceux qui existent actuellement, chacune d'elles ne le ferait qu'avec la participation de l'autre.

5. L'Italie et la Russie s'engagent à considérer avec bienveillance, l'une les intérêts russes dans la question des Détroits, l'autre les intérêts italiennes en Tripolitaine et Cyrénaïque.

XXVII. 584

BARON VON MARSCHALL, IN CONSTANTINOPLE, TO THE GERMAN FOREIGN OFFICE, *November 6th,* 1909

Cipher telegram.

Question of shipping on the Tigris and Euphrates seems to be assuming a political character. It is known that the British demand a fusion between the Turkish Hamidie Company and that of Mr. Lynch,[1] both of which have hitherto used the Tigris, and the resulting amalgamation is to have a monopoly of the traffic on both rivers.[2] (The EMPEROR : ' *Unheard-of British insolence.*') Various organs of the Press here are protesting against this concession, which has been strongly opposed in the Council of Ministers also. (The EMPEROR : ' *We must stiffen the backs of the Turks! It is against the Bagdad Railway!* ')

To-day's *Agence Ottomane* states that Sir Edward Grey declared to the Turkish Ambassador that three Turkish Ministers had formally promised the concession to Sir Gerard Lowther, and that if the granting of it were refused or postponed Turkey would run the risk of losing British sympathies. (The EMPEROR : ' *Crete! Suda Bay!* ') Tewfik Pacha's telegram on the subject had made a deep impression on the Porte and caused a special meeting of the Council of Ministers. (The EMPEROR : ' *The devil's claws are sticking out! The " sympathy " has business at the back of it!* ')

[1] Cf. G. & T., V, p. 301.
[2] The negociations began in the autumn of 1909. (XXVII. 113.) Cf. also Brandenburg, p. 362. Cf. p. 369.

XXVII. 585

COUNT VON METTERNICH, IN LONDON, TO THE CHANCELLOR, BETHMANN-HOLLWEG, *November 18th*, 1909

Sir E. Grey informed me yesterday that Herr von Gwinner [1] and Sir William Whittall, [2] the well-known Turkophil and merchant in Constantinople, had recently made a statement there about the Bagdad Railway. He, Grey, now wished to discuss that question in more detail and arrive at an understanding with us, if possible. How he conceives an understanding or a basis for one he did not say, and I did not try to find out his views, for I was without instructions ; also it seemed to me that the Minister wanted to let the business people negociate together first. However he expressed a hope that the affair would now get going, notwithstanding the coming Elections and the short time at his and the Cabinet's disposal just now for dealing with foreign questions.

I asked him whether Sir William Whittall's negociations with the Turkish Government about a monopoly of the river traffic in Mesopotamia were completed. He replied that nothing was yet completed as a few side questions had to be settled. I said I was surprised that the British Government, which elsewhere was for the ' open door ', was aspiring to a monopoly in Mesopotamia. Sir E. Grey replied that it was a matter of Mr. Lynch's company in combination with Sir William Whittall having a share in the monopoly owned by the Turkish Government for the navigation of the Tigris and Euphrates. Under the new agreement with Whittall the monopoly would still be Turkish. I replied : ' Only nominally.' The Minister did not contest this and admitted that by their important contribution of capital for the new enterprise Lynch and Whittall would exercise considerable influence in it. In its defence he added that the shipping monopoly would squeeze no one out of his trading position, as hitherto no foreign nation except the British had had a share in the water-borne traffic of Mesopotamia. I said that in the opinion of Sir William Willcocks, the irrigation scheme, which he was planning for Mesopotamia, would take so much water away from the main streams that their navigation would become problematical ; Sir E. Grey answered that this was correct—and the future there belonged to the railway, which would become the more necessary owing to the enrichment of the land by an irrigation system.

[Early in November, 1909, Turkey circulated a Note to the Protecting Powers, requesting a final settlement of the Cretan question. At the same

---

[1] Of the Deutsche Bank.   Cf. p. 370.
[2] British merchant in Constantinople.   Cf. G. & T., VI, pp. 384, 407.

time she asked Germany to throw in a word for her. Aehrenthal urged that Germany and Austria should promise to help Turkey to maintain her sovereign rights, if these were in jeopardy. Germany refused as it would be ' equivalent to renouncing her *désintéressement* ' in the question.]

XXVII. 109

BARON VON MARSCHALL, IN CONSTANTINOPLE, TO THE GERMAN FOREIGN OFFICE, *November 12th*, 1909

From my conversations with my colleagues I gather that the Powers interested in Crete consider the moment highly inopportune for bringing the Cretan question onto the tapis in the sense of the Turkish suggestion. It is feared that in the more or less anarchical state of affairs at Athens any discussion about the island's autonomy would greatly excite the Greeks and lead to a catastrophe. The unreasonableness of the Greeks causes one to think this fear not ill-founded.

Baron Aehrenthal's proposal is quite unacceptable to us. It arises no doubt from motives more personal than material. The Russian Emperor's journey to Racconigi [1] and the choice of route [2] were painfully felt in the Ballplatz, [3] which looks on them as a successful move by Isvolsky against Count [4] Aehrenthal. For this reason alone we are apparently to form a group with Austria-Hungary in Turkey's interests *against* the Powers interested in Crete. If we let ourselves in for this every one would realise at once that we were playing a secondary part in a counter-stroke planned by Vienna against Racconigi. This would deeply, and with good cause, offend the Cretan Powers, and most especially Italy, to whom direct action inspired by Count Aehrenthal would give the impression; which we, after the events of last spring, must avoid giving more than ever— that the centre of influence in the Alliance lies in Vienna and not in Berlin.

A time may come for renouncing our attitude of reserve in the Cretan question in the interests of peace and of preserving the integrity of the Turkish Empire. This could only happen if Italy at least, among the Cretan Powers, is on our side and agrees with whatever we may decide to do. Action by Germany and Austria-Hungary alone is impossible.

XXVII. 114

MEMORANDUM BY BARON VON SCHOEN, IN BERLIN, *November 25th*, 1909

Baron von Marschall is quite right ; our declarations of *désintéressement* in the Cretan question do not go so far as to give

---

[1] Cf. p. 384.
[2] Avoiding Austrian territory. (Cf. Brandenburg, p. 355.)
[3] Vienna Foreign Office.   [4] Created Count on August 17th, 1909.

the Powers interested in Crete the right to cut the bonds uniting the island with the Turkish State. We expressly assured the Sultan that Germany would defend the integrity of his Empire. There is no doubt that this standpoint is familiar to the Cretan Powers. Count Aehrenthal lately took occasion to declare the same to Turkey once again. It may be assumed at once that this unreserved declaration was reported by the Porte to the Cretan Powers. Under these circumstances the *démarche* with the Cretan Powers which Baron von Marschall proposes would be superfluous.

[This was a proposal that Germany should ' declare confidentially to the Powers interested in Crete that we (Germany) still maintain our *désintéressement* in the Cretan question and still allow the four Powers a free hand to control the internal affairs of the island ; but that it is our definite view that separation of the island from the Turkish State in any form can only take place with the consent of all the Signatory Powers of the Treaty of Berlin.' (XXVII. 113.)]

It seems in fact highly objectionable, since it would react unfavourably on our relations with England and would be a fresh inducement to the protecting Powers to try and draw us into the Cretan question.

And yet, for the purpose of strengthening Turkey's resistance in the Lynch affair against the threats probably delivered by England, it might be well to empower Baron von Marschall to make to the Porte the declaration he proposed. As this declaration expressly announces our *désintéressement*, the Turks could not use it to drag us into the Cretan discussions. The Greeks also might find nothing to object to in it, since it does not exclude union of Crete with Greece.

Count Aehrenthal should be informed that we think it right to follow his example and communicate to the Porte through Baron von Marschall the same standpoint which he indicated to the Turkish Ambassador.

May this be acted upon ?

A draft for a telegram[1] to Baron von Marschall is enclosed. (BETHMANN-HOLLWEG : ' *Agreed.*')

German Note.

After the departure of the forces of the four Powers (July 26th, 1909)[2] the provisional Government, then formed, gave place to another in December, when the Cretan Chamber met. It empowered the Government to introduce into the island all Greek laws which it might consider applicable ; on which the Porte protested in a Note to the four Powers on December 8th, 1909. The new Cretan Government was also embarrassed by the question of the oath of allegiance.

---

[1] Not given.   [2] Cf. p. 382.

XXVII. 119

BARON VON SCHOEN TO THE EMPEROR WILLIAM,
January 26th, 1910

The Turkish Ambassador explained the position of the Cretan situation as follows :

The sending of the Cretan politician, Venezelos, to Athens realises the desire of the Cretans that the Elections in Greece (Hellas and Crete) should take place in the autumn. This is also the wish of the league of officers, who want to gain time for military and naval preparations in the hope of solving the Cretan question by force. (The EMPEROR : '*They have no money, no leaders, no Government.*') The King, however, and politicians like Theotokis, who have insight, wish to hold the Elections in March, their idea being that an Election will bring more sensible members into the Chamber than are there at present and that it will thus pave the way for a peaceful solution of the question. The league's wish is to avoid raising a dynastic crisis, as it fears rightly that it would be followed by European intervention. On the other hand there is a fear that the good intentions of the King and Theotokis may come to grief owing to the King's weakness, and that the league may succeed in their idea of postponing the Elections till the autumn and so gain time for arming.

According to Turkish reports the pretension of the Cretans swell even higher. The Turkish Government knows that the Cretan Government has ordered postage stamps in London, overprinted with ' HELLAS '. There are reports also that in certain cases the Cretans are no longer recognising the legal Consular protection for foreigners and so are committing a breach of the Capitulations. There is still some hope that the Cretans may see reason and refrain at the last moment from sending deputies to the Greek Chamber, if the protecting Powers will definitely threaten to send out troops again. (The EMPEROR : ' *No good any more ! That must stop once for all—standing sentry for the Turks !* ') They have long known in Crete and at Athens that Turkey would regard the despatch of Cretan deputies to the Greek Chamber as a *casus belli*. (The EMPEROR : ' *The Turks must get used to the idea of losing Crete ! Crete will get itself annexed to Greece ! If the Turks march into Greece to stop it they will produce European intervention in favour of the Hellenes—a smash up in the Balkans involving trouble with Servians and Bulgarians; and the Britons will appear in Mesopotamia. Result : loss of Crete, Mesopotamia and, in the end, Stamboul. Let Crete go.*')

XXVII. 253

BARON VON MARSCHALL, IN CONSTANTINOPLE, TO THE CHANCELLOR, BETHMANN-HOLLWEG, *May 30th*, 1910

Extract.

In the last century the Turkish Empire maintained itself not by its own strength, but through the mutually divergent interests of the Great European Powers. The competing heirs of the 'sick man' were so powerful and numerous that none of them could venture to hasten the inheritance by force. The most effective rivalry was that between England and Russia. It led to the Crimean War and finally brought about the Treaty of San Stefano.[1] The fact that England was then prepared to draw the sword in order to force Russia to modify her peace conditions with Turkey and that it took all Prince Bismarck's political science (The EMPEROR : ' ? ') to prevent another war (The EMPEROR : ' *He might just as well have let it go on.*') belongs to recent history. And yet to-day it seems like a Saga of the hoary olden time, so vast has been the change in the last thirty years. Soon after those historical events British policy in the East became anti-Turk. The Young Turks attribute this to the hatred of Abdul Hamid's despotism. That is nonsense. The British never pursued a policy of sentiment. (The EMPEROR : ' *True.*') The change was owing to a historical event—the occupation of Egypt. England's policy in the Crimean War and at the Berlin Congress was incompatible with the possession of this country. The future may perhaps bring changes in England's territorial possessions, but as long as she holds India, South Africa and Egypt, she will continue to be a world Empire. (The EMPEROR : ' *Just what Roosevelt said.*') Now I am convinced that the British control of the Nile country has nothing to fear from the Nationalist movement, if not assisted from outside. Whilst a few hundred British soldiers with guns occupy the Citadel in Cairo any serious armed rising is inconceivable. As for the danger from outside, all the Great Powers, with one single exception, have recognised the British control of Egypt. This exception is Turkey, who has all along maintained her protest. Apart from her legal title which hardly counts in political matters, she has the use of two factors of power, which are not to be despised—political, the creed she shares with the Egyptian people, and military, the fact that her army can march to Egypt without interference by the British navy. (The EMPEROR : ' ? ') I know for certain that the possibility of re-conquering Egypt is working in the minds of many serious Turkish statesmen, especially since the Hedjaz

[1] Cf. Vol. I, p. 70.

Railway was built. I find confirmation in the recent opposition of the higher military authorities to the Alexandretta section of the Bagdad Railway, which was to follow the sea-shore for a long distance. The argument was incontestable, continually brought forward without citing examples, that circumstances might arise demanding the assemblage of several Army Corps for combined action ; which would be impossible if any part of the Bagdad Railway were exposed to the fire of a foreign fleet.

However this may be, as against her former policy it is to England's interest, as possessor of Egypt, that Turkey shall be powerless politically and militarily. This put an end to the Anglo-Russian antagonism, and on its ruins is rising an Anglo-Russian community of interests. It would be unjust to reproach England with keeping her cards hidden from her Young Turk friends in this connection. This is absolutely not the case. The schemes planned by England since the Revolution and supported by the London Cabinet directly or indirectly are in tendency and probable result far more destructive to Turkey than any blow struck by Russia at Turkey during the last ten years. I leave on one side the temporarily crippled Mahsussé Company, which placed under British control the transport by sea of Turkish troops, but will merely mention the Lynch concession, with its monopoly of shipping on the Tigris and Euphrates, out of which a British monopoly of trade in that river territory would develop before long, and the Willcocks [1] scheme for Mesopotamia, with a Hindu immigration to follow ; the perpetual obstacles laid by England in the path of our Bagdad Railway, although this, being the connection between the Capital and Mesopotamia and the vilayet of Bagdad, is a question vital to the Turkish control of that territory ; the raising of the Customs, which England is trying to prevent by insisting on impossible conditions, although an increased Customs revenue is absolutely necessary for Turkey. Do not imagine that the Turks do not see these things or fail to draw their conclusions from them. They still talk of their friendship with England, but in reality they have a fear of England scarcely equalled by their fear of Russia at any time. (The EMPEROR : ' Very good.') Since England showed her cards here the Anglo-Russian agreement in Persia, which three years ago was hardly noticed, has been growing in importance in Turkish eyes ; for it is very evident that if the business in Persia is carried through successfully Turkey will have to pay the bill. Perhaps there are already clauses to this effect. The interest taken by M. Mandelstam [2] at the time in the Lynch concession was suspicious.

[1] Cf. G. & T., V, p. 269.
[2] Second Russian Dragoman in Constantinople.

Supposing Russia were able to offer England compensation in
return for her modifying her attitude towards the Straits question ? This question and others are in the air here just now.
The more it is left to Turkey to find the answer and the more
we deny having a direct interest, the more will Turkish policy
come to the conclusion that another regulator must be sought
in place of the broken one which used to determine the balance
of power between nations in this country. Thus the Triple
Alliance will regain the position which the Turkish revolution
destroyed for a moment. . . .

XXVII. 138

BARON VON WANGENHEIM, AT ATHENS, TO THE GERMAN FOREIGN
OFFICE, *June 14th*, 1910

Cipher telegram.

The representative of one of the protecting Powers informs
me confidentially that, without consulting the others beforehand, France recently proposed calling a conference of the four
Powers. Apparently Italy and Russia have consented, whilst
the British reply is still outstanding. In my opinion this indiscretion of the Agencies about the proposal for a conference has
been committed *pour forcer la main à l'Angleterre.*

The same, June 15th, 1910.

Deville, the French Minister, informed Naby Bey of a telegram from Pichon, in Paris, which stated that England had
rejected the conference idea as being premature. M. Deville
added that henceforward England would have to bear the
responsibility for anything that might happen.

XXVII. 139

COUNT VON POURTALÈS, IN ST. PETERSBURG, TO THE CHANCELLOR,
BETHMANN-HOLLWEG, *June 16th*, 1910

Extract.

The British attitude fills my Turkish colleague, Turkhan
Pacha, with the deepest suspicion. (The EMPEROR : ' *Rightly
so.*') His only explanation of it is that there must have been
discussions with the King of Greece during his stay in England,
and that he must have offered Suda Bay to the British in the
event of Crete being annexed.

M. Isvolsky spoke to me with much dissatisfaction at the
newest development in the Cretan question. He thinks the
situation critical and that re-occupation of the island is the sole
means to prevent further complications. (The EMPEROR : ' *and
the British from getting Suda Bay. Isvolsky fears the upset in
the East which England desires. England would then seize Suda*

Bay, Egypt, Arabia, Mesopotamia, and allow Russia to take the Dardanelles. But as Isvolsky knows that Russia at present is entirely unable to fight even the Turks who are in possession at Stamboul with any chance of success, he wishes to postpone parti-tion, and in order to make this possible he wants to keep Russian troops in Crete to prevent England from seizing Suda Bay pre-maturely.')

German Note.

On June 15th, 1910, in reply to Mr. Gibson Bowles, Sir Edward Grey stated that the protecting Powers had addressed an urgent collective Note demanding that the Cretan Government should not attack Musulman officials and deputies and threatening intervention by the protecting Powers. He said that British policy desired to maintain the Sultan's suzerainty, to protect the Musulman population and ensure good govern-ment of the island under an autonomous régime.

XXVII. 140

KÜHLMANN, IN LONDON, TO THE CHANCELLOR, BETHMANN-HOLLWEG, *June 17th*, 1910

Extract.

A person intimate with the Turkish Embassy here said that Sir Edward Grey's speech about Crete would be received with satisfaction in Constantinople. It was as favourable as could be expected under the circumstances.

There could be no question of a change in the British Govern-ment's attitude. For several months Sir Edward had been say-ing to the Turkish representative almost word for word what he had now declared in his great speech. Turkish diplomacy held Sir Edward Grey to be absolutely honest, and believed him when he denied that the King had influenced the course of official policy regarding Crete. It is believed rather, that Sir Arthur [1] Hardinge, who played a large part in the earlier phases of England's Cretan policy, has always aimed at meeting as far as possible the phil-Hellenic sympathies of Alexandra, the Queen-Mother.[2] My informant said that in Turkey the satis-faction was naturally only relative. The only final solution of the question which could really satisfy Turkey would be one which deprived Greece and Crete once for all of any hope of political union. (The EMPEROR : '*This solution will never come! The Turks are bound to lose Crete!*') The objections urged by the British Government against a definite settlement now were strongly opposed both by M. Paul Cambon, who was very keen about the Entente, and by the Marquis Imperiali,[3]

---

[1] *German Note.* Clearly a mistake for ' Charles '.
[2] King Edward died on May 7th, 1910.
[3] The new Italian Ambassador in London.

who wished to take this opportunity of placing himself on a good footing with the British Government; they would there- fore not be very persistent. Up to now the protecting Powers had let the Cretans do as they liked, and it was scarcely probable that they would try any harder in future to nip in the bud the perpetual incidents with which the Cretans were artfully keeping the question of Turkish suzerainty alive. Turkey's requirement was simple and logical, namely, to be freed for good from the irritating Cretan question. If the Powers refused—as they seemed to be doing—to bring about a final solution, they were all the more morally bound to put a stop to these annoying incidents by force. (The EMPEROR: ' *Turkey ought by herself to put the matter in order without the four Powers; that would be far the best.*') Once it was finally settled Turkey was ready to meet any reasonable wishes as far as she could and especially to favour the Cretans in matters of trade, and to recognise any- one, even a Greek, as Commissioner, President, or whatever the Governor of autonomous Crete was to be called, as long as he was not a subject of King George. (The EMPEROR: ' *If he is a Greek he will feel as a Greek.*')

The Turkish diplomats here are not clear as to England's ultimate aims in Crete. (The EMPEROR: ' *Suda Bay.*') As I mentioned, dynastic wishes are supposed to play a part, and it is believed that England will not favour a final settlement until she has formed a definite opinion on the future of the new régime in Turkey. (The EMPEROR: ' *That too is correct.*') If the latter settled down, the end would be autonomy combined with consideration for the Turkish wishes; but if the internal conditions of that Empire turned out badly, phil-Hellenic sym- pathies would win the day. Nothing is known here of any attempt by the British Government to use the Cretan question to bring pressure on the Turkish Cabinet and force its compliance in other questions (Mesopotamia). My informant added that the British Ambassador would have been sure to hint that such interconnection existed. As far as he knew this was not the case. (The EMPEROR: ' *It has been a piece of stupidity that 4 Powers should attempt to produce order in a bit of Turkish territory—whose inhabitants have long wanted to be free of the Turks—because the sovereign Power can't manage it! Since when have foreigners governed by a Commission parts of other States, when these can't manage their refractory subjects? Just as well might Austria and ourselves govern the Poles for the Russians— or Sweden, Denmark and we occupy the Baltic Provinces and Finland in Russia's interests! It would be mad! It is the same with Crete. Either the wretched Young Turks might settle with Crete by landing troops of occupation, when they could dictate to the Cretans and Greeks ; or they could clear out and leave the Greeks and Cretans to get out of their mess themselves. But to trust so many Great Powers to administer Crete for them is simple idiocy ! This way they will lose it !*)

[In view of a boycott declared by Turkey against Greek ships and goods, the British Government proposed that the six Powers should lodge a protest in Constantinople.]

XXVII. 147

MIQUEL, CHARGÉ D'AFFAIRES IN CONSTANTINOPLE, TO THE GERMAN FOREIGN OFFICE, *July 19th*, 1910

Cipher telegram.

Judging from our Consular reports there appears to me to be no need for the *démarche* proposed by England. German interests were scarcely affected and the Jaffa case is settled. Since such a step by the six Powers would certainly offend Turkish susceptibilities and could only be justified by the fear that if the boycott continued Greece might resort to arms. I do not think this risk is a probable one. Even if the boycott continues at Constantinople and Salonika, it is, on the whole, assuming no very stringent form ; no unrest worth mentioning has occurred, although, as M. Gryparis often complained to me, many Greek families have gone bankrupt.

[On July 22nd Count Metternich was instructed to reply to the British Government in the sense of the foregoing.
M. Venezelos became Prime Minister of Greece in 1910.]

XXVII. 150

BARON VON WANGENHEIM, AT ATHENS, TO THE CHANCELLOR, BETHMANN-HOLLWEG, *December 29th*, 1910

The whole story is no testimony that the four Powers were guided by great or wise ideas in their handling of the Cretan question. (The EMPEROR : ' *Certainly not.*') Their attitude was somewhat comprehensible as long as they thought it possible to carry out their plan of gradually separating Crete from Turkey by means of a painless operation and then attaching it to Greece. This period closed at the moment when the Young Turk party declared the Cretan question a matter of national importance. Turkish chauvinism forced the protecting Powers to choose between Greece and Turkey. They decided on the country in which they possessed the greater interests ; so that the annexation question was relegated *ad calendas Grecas*. The only talk regarding Crete which was left to the Powers was to prevent war breaking out between Turkey and Greece on account of it. There is one certain way to attain this—military occupation of the island. This would suit Turkey and force the Greeks and Cretans to stick to the Powers because of their national aspirations. Crete would cease to be a bone of contention between Greece and Turkey. When the change took place in Turkey the Powers were still in occupation. If this had not been so, the altered situation would have made occupation necessary ; instead of which, in July last year the Powers evacuated the island at England's suggestion. *Events have proved that the withdrawal of troops was a grave political error.* The Cretans read it as a success for themselves and an encouragement to continue working for annexation. As this ceased to make progress the Greek dynasty and its advisers were held responsible. Hence the Greek military revolt, hence the tension in Greco-Turkish relations, (The EMPEROR : ' *All England's fault.*') which even now involves a risk of war.

Now the protecting Powers have placed all their hopes in Venezelos. They expect this professional revolutionary to make an end of the revolt in Greece, and they think that the man who has fought for annexation all his life is especially qualified to restore confidence between Constantinople and Athens. Measures which seem paradoxical at first sight are not always unsuccessful. Thus Spain made the railways of Andalusia safe by appointing robber chiefs as stationmasters. (The EMPEROR : ' *In the Tyrol and Styria the poachers end by being made State foresters.*') So it is not impossible that the trial which the Powers are now making with Venezelos may be successful. But they must have a little patience. . . .

CHAPTER XXX

PERSIA, 1909–10

[In 1907 England and Russia signed a Convention by which each nation undertook to confine its political and commercial activities in Persia, Russia to the North, and England to the South of a certain line ; the Persian Gulf was to lie outside the scope of the Convention, as it was admitted that England possessed special interests there.[1] In 1908 a revolution broke out in Persia, culminating by the end of the year in civil war between Royalists and Nationalists. Russian troops took a leading part in the fighting, which ended in the Shah's abdication on July 15th, 1909. (Cf. Brandenburg, p. 361.) The new Shah fell completely under the influence of Russia. (Grey, II, p. 152 et seq.)

These events encouraged the Germans to hope that the Anglo-Russian Entente might be shaken, and at the same time they themselves might acquire a foothold in Persia. They approached the Russian Government with proposals, but although the Russians were ready to discuss, they stood fast to the Entente with England and France. (Cf. p. 301).]

XXVII. 734

TSCHIRSCHKY, IN VIENNA, TO THE CHANCELLOR, PRINCE VON BÜLOW, *February 1st*, 1909

In the course of a long and confidential conversation with Baron Aehrenthal Persian affairs were mentioned. The Minister suggested that considering the growing importance which events there were having for Anglo-Russian relations it might be desirable for Vienna and Berlin to agree on a joint policy. Lately there had apparently been some small differences of opinion between the representatives of either side at Teheran, which, though nothing in themselves, had better be avoided in the interests of our joint general policy. Herr von Rosthorn, the Austrian representative, seemed to have gone too far in favouring the parliamentary party, (BÜLOW : ' *In my opinion we cannot join in that.*') for which he naturally had had no particular instructions.

The Minister said it would be a good thing for me to discuss with Berlin whether it would be wise to combine for a more active policy in Persia, or—as I think—to leave the Russians and British entirely to themselves, as they are already beginning

[1] Cf. Gwynn, *Letters and Friendships of Cecil Spring-Rice*, II, p. 77, et seq.

to quarrel, and to refrain from disturbing them so that they may bite each other all the harder. (BÜLOW : ' *I think the second is just now the only right policy. They must be allowed to stew in their own juice.*') In his opinion Austria and Germany, for whom the Anglo-Russian agreement about Persia was non-existent, ought to take independence of the country and freedom of trade as the solid basis of their policy.

He thought one of the main tasks for Austrian and German policy was to keep the eyes open and see whether weak spots could not be found in the bridges between England and France or between England and Russia, where we might find the right lever for loosening the joints, whether in India, China, or elsewhere in the world. (BÜLOW : ' *Correct.*')

Finally Baron Aehrenthal begged me to forward, more or less as a preparation to Berlin, a draft scheme for an agreement on the joint policy to be pursued in Persia. He would continue to consider the matter and instruct Herr von Szöyény more in detail when the time came for discussing it with Your Highness.

German Note.
The Tsar and Tsarina accompanied by Isvolsky, stayed with the King and Queen August 2nd to 4th. There had been excited demonstrations against receiving them on the part of the Labour Party.

XXVII. 743
COUNT VON METTERNICH, IN LONDON, TO THE CHANCELLOR, PRINCE VON BÜLOW, *July 14th*, 1909

The events in Persia and the Tsar's coming visit to Cowes show how little the rapprochement with Russia, which leading circles here are seeking, has sunk into the consciousness of the British nation. There have been several questions in Parliament, which prove that Russia's advance in Northern Persia is by no means to the taste of many sections in England. Numbers of resolutions, meetings and letters to the papers condemn the official reception of the Tsar by the King of England. Dozens of resolutions pour in daily to Buckingham Palace—this is confidential—and, as far as I know, into the Foreign Office against this reception ; and not only from the Socialists and Labour Party, but also more especially from the Churches, both Church of England and Nonconformist. These manifestations of disagreement with the policy of rapprochement with Russia will make it unpleasant for the Court and the Government, but they are not strong enough to divert Court and Government from their Russophil policy, as these are supported in it by the Conservative Party. The wish to be secured in Europe against the alleged German menace influences leading

circles in England more than any fear of temporary unpopularity
in their own country.

On December 18th, 1909, Count Quadt reported from Teheran that
George Churchill, Oriental Secretary to the British Legation at Teheran,
had announced that England and Russia meant to call in Frenchmen
as administrative advisers to the Persian Government.

XXVII. 750
SCHOEN, IN BERLIN, TO COUNT VON METTERNICH, IN LONDON,
January 1st, 1910

I beg to send for your confidential information a copy of a
report from the Imperial Minister at Teheran, concerning French
advisers for the Persian Government.

If Mr. Churchill's views, as described in the report, correspond with those of the Entente Powers, it would be well as
soon as possible to indicate our objections to this course to the
Cabinets concerned.   The Entente Powers must not be allowed
to assume that we shall let France also be granted a preferential
position in Persia, as against ourselves.   Rather must we naturally insist that, if the Persian Government decides to engage
foreigners, Russia and England must observe complete impartiality regarding eventual appointment of German subjects and
Frenchmen.

XXVII. 752
COUNT VON QUADT, AT TEHERAN, TO THE GERMAN FOREIGN
OFFICE, *February* 16th, 1910

Cipher telegram.

The British and Russian Ministers have just handed the
Persian Government a document containing the following
conditions for an advance of 10,000,000 marks : Financial
control by a committee of seven persons, viz., the Minister of
Finance, two deputies, two officials, the French financial adviser,
Bizot, and the Belgian Director of Customs, Mornard ; also an
executive of seven French finance officials. This condition,
described here as harmless, is an expression of the Anglo-Russian
domination, since these two Powers can bring pressure to bear
regarding the appointments to the control and the executive.
The condition respecting the Russian gendarmerie has been
dropped.   The bulk of the loan is not to be considered before
the administration of the first amount advanced has been settled.

XXVII. 761
The same.   March 17th, 1910

The Turkish Ambassador learns that there is a very secret
further condition :

In the Russian sphere of interests concessions may only be
granted to Russians, in the British sphere only to Englishmen.

Persian subjects may only obtain concessions there, if they can prove that no foreign capital is behind them. . . .

XXVII. 767

TSCHIRSCHKY, IN VIENNA, TO THE CHANCELLOR, BETHMANN-HOLLWEG, *March 25th*, 1910

Cipher. Extract.

. . . Herr von Müller, of the Foreign Office, read me *in strict confidence*, and with a request not to mention it outside, even to Szögyényi, a report by Count Mensdorff about a conversation with Sir Charles Hardinge about the Anglo-Russian Persian Convention, which throws light on Sir Charles's way of thinking and feeling.

He said that England and Russia, being neighbours in Persia, had special interests there, and that they had to overcome great obstacles in defending these legitimate interests. Germany seemed to be hostilely disposed and to be desiring to make the British and Russian task even more difficult. Sir Charles asked Count Mensdorff outright whether the Austrian Cabinet's action in this affair was due to German suggestion. The Ambassador's reply was that he was merely carrying out instructions which he had received ; of their origin he knew nothing. Sir Charles Hardinge then said Germany seemed to be making difficulties on account of the French financial advisers.[1] But no one could suggest to England and Russia to take on Germans as well, since these would be hostile ; whereas France was impartial. If Germany continued her opposition, they would have to take members of some small nation as financial advisers. Count Mensdorff closes his report with the remark that our inquiries were very badly received in London. He adds that Italy also addressed a similar inquiry to the British Government.

[On May 8th, 1910, the Chancellor directed Metternich to urge the British Government to pause before imposing the Anglo-Russian conditions on Persia. ' I cannot hide from myself the fear that, much against our will, this understanding might be prejudiced, if we were obliged to call attention at Teheran to the breach of our most-favoured-nation rights, as secured by treaty. . . .' (XXVII. 786).]

XXVII. 791

COUNT VON METTERNICH, IN LONDON, TO THE CHANCELLOR, BETHMANN-HOLLWEG, *May 13th*, 1910

To-day I spoke to Sir Charles Hardinge in the sense of your telegram of May 8th. The Foreign Secretary will be in the country till after Whitsuntide.

---

[1] Cf. p. 399.

The Under-Secretary insisted that he could return no answer until Sir Edward Grey had conferred with the British Ambassador in Berlin; he denied that the claim for options on railways, means of communication and harbour works meant an attack on our most-favoured nation rights, and also that these rights gave us any pretext for raising objections at Teheran. Finally in a sharp tone he said that the Government was fully occupied with the preparations for burying the late King and was letting politics rest for the present.

I at once replied that we had no wish to open political controversies during the days of mourning for the late King, who was also deeply respected in Germany. But he had always been first and foremost a British King. So if the Government did not desire political discussions during the days of mourning, they ought, above all, to avoid producing, by their political action, a state of affairs in Teheran injurious to the rights of a third Power and obliging that Power to protest. A policy of abstention by Germany could not be made to coincide with one of action against Germany.

The Under-Secretary replied that I was in error, since no instructions for renewed action had recently been sent to Teheran. I replied shortly that he knew the German point of view, and took my leave.

It is not my impression that the British Government is just now trying, by continuous pressure on Teheran, to present us with an unwelcome *fait accompli*. But I do think that they wish to prove in St. Petersburg that Germany's demands in Persia are not to weaken the Anglo-Russian entente. The Under-Secretary's brusque manner is well known. The tone adopted by him does not necessarily represent the attitude the British Government desires to assume. But it is good for him to see that he can't have it his own way; which is why I have also written to Sir Edward Grey.

If, however, contrary to expectation, Anglo-Russian diplomacy did present us with an official *fait accompli*, (SCHOEN: '*First wait and see whether it does happen.*')—it seems that there is already an oral promise by the Persian Foreign Minister— in my humble opinion, we ought, if possible, to get some concessions from the Persian Government and let them know in St. Petersburg that this is a result of the British Government's attitude. I have never believed that in Persia, the most sensitive spot in British policy, we shall get much beside diplomatic worries. But now that we are involved there we must see how we can get free of it with dignity. The British Government would probably oppose, with the force they have at their disposal on the spot, the carrying out of any German concession in

Southern Persia, which England would regard as political; but probably no one is thinking of carrying out concessions of a political nature in Persia at this stage. But perhaps there may be re-consideration of the concession rights which have been secured. Meanwhile it may be best to come to a friendly understanding with the Entente Powers, in accordance with our proposal. Only if this fails should we act independently of them and obtain concessions for ourselves,—in theory, at any rate.

[The Chancellor desired no sort of discussion during the Emperor's visit to England for King Edward's funeral. ' I think it better under the circumstances to have no discussion of political subjects. I have tried to influence the Emperor in this sense, but am not sure if my arguments will produce a lasting impression. . . .' (XXVII. 793.) For an account of the funeral visit, see G. & T., VI.]

XXVII. 800

THE CHANCELLOR, BETHMANN-HOLLWEG, TO THE EMPEROR WILLIAM, IN LONDON, *May 22nd*, 1910

Telegram.

Respectful thanks for the expression of Your Majesty's will regarding the Persian question.

I also think it more tactful to refrain from insisting in London just now. It is made possible for us, since, as we hear from St. Petersburg, Russia and England have agreed, as a result of our representations, not to demand a formal declaration from Persia respecting preferential treatment for Russia and England with regard to loans and concessions, that is, not to create a *fait accompli*. Our last reply to St. Petersburg mentioned the theoretic character of the question and our wish for a friendly understanding.

I have instructed Metternich to let the Persian question rest until further notice. We shall use our influence with the Press.

[Early in November, 1910, the Tsar and Sazonoff visited the Emperor at Potsdam, where Russia was induced to agree to certain German proposals, comprising Persia and the Bagdad Railway. (Cf. Brandenburg, 364 et seq.) Sazonoff persuaded the Tsar to refuse to have anything in writing, for, as Sazonoff told Pourtalès, ' the Tsar objected to an exchange of documents, as these would not remain secret, and the opponents of good Russo-German relations would point out that Germany had desired to embroil Russia with England ' (XXVII. 879).]

German Note. XXVII. 866.

Speaking in the Reichstag on December 10th, 1910, Bethmann-Hollweg said : ' The result of the final interview may be summarised as follows : It was agreed anew that neither Government should enter any combination which contemplated aggression against the other party.' The Emperor's comment on this was : ' I know nothing about this ! Moreover I have neither proposed nor accepted any such engagement. I only know that Russia will not help us if England forces on a war ! '

and on the words 'combination—etc.' he wrote: 'This would mean destruction of the *casus fœderis* with Austria in the event of war with Russia and endanger the main support of the Triple Alliance ! '

THE CHANCELLOR, BETHMANN-HOLLWEG, TO THE EMPEROR,
December 11th, 1910

Your Majesty has been pleased to take exception to the wording of my declaration on our relations with Russia, as reported in the enclosed cutting from the *Lokalanzeiger.* These words of mine were merely a pregnant summary of the declarations exchanged at the Potsdam meeting.

Your Majesty knows that M. Sazonoff then declared that Russia would never consent to hostile suggestions made by England against us. Since we, on our side, had no aggressive schemes to fear, the Russian promise was capable of being summarised in the general form which I used. The Russian Minister, whom I informed confidentially through Count Pourtalès, has declared his agreement with it. (The EMPEROR : ' *I ought to have been told of it in good time ! For I know nothing about it ! a step of such great importance too !*)

Likewise I was justified in including in my general statement our declaration (given with Your Majesty's approval) that we were neither engaged nor prepared to support Austria-Hungary in any schemes of aggression in the Near East. No one in Russia fears that we shall attack her without warning ; but there has been repeated evidence of the fear of our supporting aggressive action by Austria in the Near East, and that, if war broke out with Russia, we might be ready to take part in it. Thus, if we reassured Russia on this point, her policy would have the certainty that we should enter no combination having its point directed against Russia.

We were able to make this declaration without injury to our engagements arising out of the Triple Alliance Treaty, which are purely defensive in character ; and all the more so, since the Austro-Hungarian Government has repeatedly declared to us that it has *no* aggressive plans in the Near East. Count Aehrenthal, whom I informed of our declaration in a private letter, has to-day expressed to me his agreement with our action. (The EMPEROR : ' *I ought to have been told of this also beforehand, since I knew nothing of it ! It is a moment of high political importance, at which the leader of foreign policy, the Sovereign, must not be kept in the dark ! In future, notification is to be given me beforehand of the contents of any proposed declaration and the steps to be taken with foreign Governments.*'[1])

I should take this occasion of informing Your Majesty that,

---

[1] Cf. Brandenburg, p. 366.

according to a telegram which has reached the Wolffs Bureau, the official *Wiener Fremdenblatt* fully approves of my declarations in the Reichstag.

As for Italy, she has always cultivated good relations with Russia. I believe, therefore, that I may assert absolutely that the form given to our exchange of declarations with. Russia will not be objected to by our allies in any way. (The EMPEROR : '*The foregoing report and explanation fully satisfy me.*')

[On December 12th, Count Pourtalès wrote : ' M. Sazonoff wished to deal with the Persian question separately. His draft proposals are meant as a reply to ours of the summer of 1907, and as a continuation of the negociations which were dropped at that time. I fear that the Russian draft will fall behind your expectations in many points.' (XXVII. 877.)]

XXVII. 890

COUNT VON METTERNICH, IN LONDON, TO THE CHANCELLOR, BETHMANN-HOLLWEG, *January 29th*, 1911

Extract. Confidential.

My impression that the Government here are much less disturbed by the Russo-German negociations, than are the French, has been strengthened by a confidential conversation with Count Benckendorff. . . .

I may, in fact, assume that Sir Edward Grey would not be displeased if Russia agreed with us on the questions connected with the Bagdad Railway, because the British Government hope, as I gather from casual utterances by people connected with them, that after our understanding with Russia an understanding with England may become easier. Now that all hope is dead of a *conférence à quatre*, which would have meant for us merely a decision by a majority of votes, more value is being attached to an understanding *à deux*.[1] . . .

[In August, 1911, Russia and Germany did arrive at an understanding comprising Persia and the Bagdad Railway. Cf. Schulthess, *Europaischer Geschichtkalender*, 1911, p. 498 et seq.]

[1] Cf. p. 372.

CHAPTER XXXI

BETHMANN-HOLLWEG AND THE NAVAL NEGOCIATIONS. AUGUST 1909 TO MAY 1911

[After Bethmann-Hollweg succeeded Prince Bülow in the office of Imperial Chancellor (cf. G. & T., VI, p. 283) the Emperor and Admiral Tirpitz became apparently rather more inclined than they had been to listen to proposals for an arrangement with England. Tirpitz produced two draft proposals with distinct modifications of his former programme, which were to be conceded only if accompanied by a general political agreement with England. The British Government, on the other hand, were undesirous of committing themselves to anything which might interfere with the Entente with France and Russia. Negociations dragged on without advancing a single step towards a definite agreement, until July 1911 ; the appearance of the *Panther* at Agadir on that day ended any hope of a reduction in armaments by agreement.

Herr von Bethmann-Hollweg, who on July 14th, 1909, became Imperial Chancellor in place of Prince Bülow, at once set about negociations, first of all through Herr Ballin and Sir Ernest Cassel, and then after a short interval through the official channels. (Brandenburg, p. 349 et seq. ; B. Huldermann, *Albert Ballin*, Chapter VIII.)]

XXVIII. 219

MEMORANDUM BY KÜHLMANN, CHARGÉ D'AFFAIRES IN LONDON,
August 14th, 1909

Arising out of the attempt of certain entirely unauthorised persons to arrange a visit of German parliamentarians to England, which came to nothing because the Foreign Office would not consider it, Mr. Tyrrell discussed Anglo-German relations spontaneously and in detail. He said that such plans and visits, when arranged by people without authority, did harm instead of good. On the whole he was inclined to think that in this direction too much had been done rather than too little. Relations between the two countries would last out better if as little as possible was done or said about them. The change in the leadership of German policy had been welcomed here with satisfaction. They hoped considerably better things from the new Chancellor. Influential circles in England had felt deep mistrust of the ex-Chancellor [1] on account of a series of incidents

---

[1] Cf. Brandenburg, p. 348.

—he would mention only the Yang-tsze Agreement and the attitude taken up against Chamberlain. It had been felt that Prince Bülow had not resisted the pressure of certain chauvinist elements in German public opinion with sufficient determination. The chief question dividing the two nations was that of the Navy. The British public would get used to the Naval Law in its present form and learn to take for granted a German navy of this size. But they would see danger in a strong supplementary programme brought in before the present Naval Law had run off, for this would lead to a vast increase of anti-German agitation. But he was not pessimistic in general about Anglo-German relations ; he hoped in fact for a certain *détente* before long. (SCHOEN : ' *Tyrrell, Sir Edward Grey's secretary, said to be anti-German.*')

[Admiral Tirpitz's Formula for an Understanding regarding new construction of capital ships for 5 years is given below. It received the Emperor's full approval. (XXVIII. 216.)

(1)

| Year. | German Plan. | | British Plan. |
	Present.	Future.	
1910	4	3 (− 1)	4 (the Dreadnoughts for 1909)
1911	4	2 (− 2)	3
1912	2	2	3
1913	2	2	3
1914	2	2	3
	14	11	16

Consequent ratio = 1 : 1·45.

(2) By the above arrangement the strength in modern capital ships under construction from 1905–1914 is as under :

Germany—24, England—32 ; i.e. a ratio of 3 : 4.

(3) Including all the older capital ships completed and under construction in 1904, the numbers are :

Germany—50, England—92 ; i.e., a ratio of 1 : 1·8.

It should be borne in mind that the older German ships are weaker than British ships of similar age.

(4) By such an agreement it will be assured by treaty that Germany introduces no supplementary programme in 1912.[1]]

---

[1] No. 4 added in Tirpitz's own hand.

XXVIII. 222

THE CHANCELLOR, BETHMANN-HOLLWEG, TO THE EMPEROR, AT CRONBERG, *August 21st*, 1909

I beg to report to Your Majesty that, as commanded, I to-day informed Sir Edward Goschen that Your Majesty's Government is prepared to propose a naval agreement to England.[1] I said also that such an agreement must naturally be based on the conviction that England also would not pursue a policy unfriendly or indeed hostile to Germany. An agreement about the building of war-ships could not be concluded between countries which were hostile to each other. I have not told Sir Edward the substance of Admiral Tirpitz's formula, but so far I have merely begged him to let me have an answer from his Government regarding their willingness in principle to enter into negociations to that end. I also begged him to keep the matter strictly secret not only from the Press, but also from the other Powers. I promised equal discretion on our side.

Sir Edward showed pleasure at my communication and agreed personally with my general suggestions, expressing the view that with good will on both sides the difficulties connected with the question might well be surmounted. He means to telegraph to London to-day and to announce to me his Government's reply as soon as possible.

He appeared to know nothing of the unofficial enquiries [2] which went before.

XXVIII. 223

THE EMPEROR, AT MARBURG, TO THE CHANCELLOR, BETHMANN-HOLLWEG, *August 22nd*, 1909

Cipher telegram.

I have received Your Excellency's letter, for which many thanks. Two different individuals have recently assured me that the British wish for an understanding with us. The first was Dr. von Böttinger, a member of the Herrenhaus, and the other was young Goldschmidt-Rothschild of the London Embassy, who had just come from London. Both declared definitely that various tokens pointed to the fact that there is a serious wish for an understanding. So I hope that, if Sir Edward Goschen shows skill in interpretation, the matter will go forward favourably.

[1] Cf. G. & T., VI, 283.   [2] Through Ballin and Cassel.

XXVIII. 224

THE CHANCELLOR, BETHMANN-HOLLWEG, TO COUNT VON METTERNICH, IN LONDON, *August 31st*, 1909

Telegram.

The British Ambassador has informed me in a private letter of Sir E. Grey's satisfaction at our overtures.   Your Excellency will agree with me that we ought to wait for the British proposals in complete calm and not show too much eagerness.   We had better, therefore, merely acknowledge Sir E. Grey's communication and refrain from mentioning the details of our scheme as yet.

XXVIII. 226

SIR EDWARD GOSCHEN TO THE CHANCELLOR, AT HOHENFINOW, *September 2nd*, 1909

Sir Edward Grey [1] has asked me to state that the communication Your Excellency was good enough to make through me has made the most favourable impression upon him and His Majesty's Government.

As regards Naval Expenditure I am to say that His Majesty's Government are not only prepared to discuss it at any time, but would cordially welcome any improvement which such discussions might bring about.

Sir Edward Grey also wishes me to inform Your Excellency that in discussing a general political understanding His Majesty's Government must of course have regard to the friendships they have formed with other Powers, but that any proposals such as you foreshadowed in your conversations with me, which are not incompatible with the maintenance of these friendships, will be received by His Majesty's Government with the greatest sympathy and studied with the utmost care and goodwill.

[In view of the British Government's genuine willingness to negociate Tirpitz proposed a further modification of his plan, whereby Germany should build 8 new capital ships for the years 1909–1014, and England 12, thus making the ratio 2 : 3.   (Cf. Brandenburg, p. 351.)]

XXVIII. 229

ADMIRAL VON TIRPITZ TO THE CHANCELLOR, *September 1st*, 1909

Private letter.   Extract.

. . . So far as the political situation can be judged, the Liberal Cabinet will be very ready to accept the proposal, as it will remove several large obstacles.   On the other hand it is

[1] Cf. G. & T., VI, p. 288.

quite probable that the British Navy, and especially Sir John
Fisher, will be opposed to it.

If this opposition causes the Agreement to fall through, the
position is the more favourable to us, for we are much more
accommodating than in the first formula, and the odium of
rejection would more evidently fall on England.

Under these circumstances, and moreover since there is greater
probability of an agreement being arrived at with England, I
consider it my duty to ask Your Excellency whether it would
not be right to change our Ambassador in London before the
negociations begin.   Under Prince Bülow and the representative
of his policy in London the idea of a naval agreement, which was
put forward by England, was not carried into execution.   Considering the great willingness shown by Your Excellency to the
British Cabinet from the start and proved by the fact of the
foregoing proposal for an Agreement, I think that no misunderstanding could possibly arise in our disfavour owing to the
recall of the German Ambassador in London.   On the contrary
I think that if Your Excellency marked your principle of showing
accommodation by changing the Ambassador it would be more
evidently a point to the good for your *régime*.   A fresh Ambassador would undoubtedly be regarded as your own personal
representative and would derive much more good for his future
task from the negociations which will take place in Berlin,
than one to whom the aftertaste of the old era is sure to cling—
whether he wishes it or not. . . .

[On September 22nd, 1909, Mr. Balfour made a speech at Birmingham
on the Budget, which the Emperor in a telegram to Bethmann-Hollweg
(September 30th) declared to be ' a challenge *pur et simple*, and the Government has accepted it.   It may perhaps mean an Election in the late autumn
or early winter. . . . We must keep clear of the Election campaign and let
the negociations rest until calm is restored again.   Admiral von Tirpitz
is of the same opinion. . . .'   (XXVIII. 234.)

The question of the moment was whether the House of Lords would or
would not throw out Mr. Lloyd George's very drastic Budget.   If they did
so, an immediate Dissolution and an Election were bound to be the result.
The Lords refused to pass the Bill, ' until it should have been submitted
to the judgment of the country ', and the General Election took place in
January, 1910, bringing the Liberals back with a reduced majority.]

XXVIII. 238

MEMORANDUM BY BARON VON SCHOEN, IN BERLIN,
October 12th, 1909

The British Ambassador, who has returned from leave, spoke
to me at the Diplomatic reception and asked whether we were
ready to resume the negociations regarding a Naval Agreement.
Sir Edward Grey set much store on concluding one soon, and
then a political understanding might follow close upon it.

I replied that the Chancellor was looking forward to a discussion of this question with the Ambassador and would most willingly appoint a meeting. I said that in my personal opinion the main question was whether at the present moment, when the internal situation in England was so uncertain, the Government might think fit to negociate on so important a question. Although we were most willing in principle to second the British desire for a Naval Agreement, it did not interest us greatly as our armaments were of purely defensive character. To us a general political understanding seemed the necessary preparation for the influence of a Naval Agreement in bringing peace and reassurance.

Goschen thought both points ought to be discussed together. A friendly settlement was certainly not hard to arrange if we were not out to draw England away from her friendships. The European balance of power—Triple Alliance and Entente—ought not to be set aside. England could not give more to us than to France and Russia, with whom she had no arrangements directed against us.[1] I said that we were far from wishing to disturb the *status quo*. We merely desired a more friendly orientation of British policy in general and an end of the tension between the two nations. For the rest I advised him to discuss the questions with the Chancellor.

XXVIII. 243

COUNT VON METTERNICH TO THE GERMAN FOREIGN OFFICE,
October 26th, 1909

Cipher telegram. Secret.
For the Chancellor.

To-day Sir E. Grey, who had been absent several days, himself began upon the conversation between yourself and the British Ambassador.[2] He means to speak to the Prime Minister soon and wishes to see me again next Thursday. To-day he spoke for himself and not officially as yet, as he had not spoken to Mr. Asquith, but he earnestly desired to begin as soon as possible in spite of the confusion at home, so that no time might be lost. He waits for Your Excellency's further proposals (after discussion with Mr. Asquith and the official reply). He hopes to be able to tell me more about one or two points next Thursday which may help on our mutual confidence (general policy). He realises that the hardest task in finding a formula which would satisfy both parties lies in the naval question.

He evidently desires to obtain for himself and the Liberal Government the credit of having worked hard for a naval under-

[1] Cf. Brandenburg, p. 352.   [2] Not given.

standing with Germany, whatever may be the result of the present political situation and the negociations. He is convinced that Your Excellency seriously wishes and intends to arrive at an understanding.

I am naturally saying no more than Your Excellency has said to Sir Edward Goschen.

Lord [Charles] Beresford's revelations have hit Sir John Fisher hard, and he will scarcely recover from them in spite of royal favour. Nevertheless he may hang on for months, since the Government must protect him to avoid laying themselves open to attack.

German Note.

In the *Times* of October 25th, 1909, Lord Charles Beresford, Lord Fisher's open rival, who commanded the Channel Fleet, published his correspondence with Mr. Asquith, in which he complained that Fisher had intentionally dismissed his, Beresford's, adherents. (Cf. Churchill, *The World Crisis*, p. 72 et seq. ' *The Schism in the Navy.*') Owing to disagreement with the Government's naval policy Sir John Fisher found himself obliged to resign his post as First Sea Lord. He was followed by Admiral Wilson. (Cf. Brandenburg, p. 366; Bacon, *Lord Fisher*.)

General promises of friendship seem to me not to have much value. During the Morocco crisis Sir Edward Grey and his predecessor promised not to attack us without provocation, although there was little doubt that, if there was a war, England would be caught between us and France. It is a matter of interpretation who is the aggressor. Both Sir Edward Grey and Lord Lansdowne repeatedly assured me that the Entente was not directed against us. But what matters is that in future, whatever happens, England shall not be in the camp of our enemies.

In my humble opinion the promise of no supplementary programme for 1912 should not come from us spontaneously, but should only follow on a desire expressed by the British negociators, for up till now the standpoint of the Imperial Government, as made known publicly by your predecessor, has been that the Naval Law meets our requirements, that we should not exceed it (i.e., no supplementary programme), and that our programme would be unaffected if England chose to build 100 Dreadnoughts.

XXVIII. 253

MEMORANDUM BY SCHOEN, IN BERLIN, *November 1st*, 1909

In our view negociations can take place on the political situation, but not on the Naval programme *by itself*. We can at most declare our readiness to discuss both at the same time.

We cannot frame a Naval Agreement without a political under-standing, which latter is a *conditio sine qua non* for us and is bound up inseparably with a Naval Agreement.

A Naval Agreement and the bases for a political under-standing would have to be published.

If, as they maintain, the British desire one, they must pay for it on the political side. We feel no wish for a Naval Agree-ment. Therefore there is no meaning in the assertions of Sir Edward Goschen and Sir Edward Grey that England can promise no more to us than to France and Russia.[1] England wants some-thing from us and must pay for it.

We have no objection to England making promises of neu-trality to France and Russia similar to those which we will and must have from England.

As for the Naval Agreement, we must say firmly that we cannot depart from the Naval Law. Inside this, we are ready to build slower if England also builds slower. We should pro-pose an even more exactly defined ratio between British and German construction for a series of years, if England would agree with these leading principles. At present an exact ratio could not be named.

To come now to Goschen's and Grey's hobby-horse—the giving of information through the Naval Attachés or otherwise. Our reply should be that this year we gave the British Naval Attaché fully detailed information, which McKenna unfortu-nately made no use of ; that we are ready to give further informa-tion still on a promise of reciprocity. Naturally there is a limit which cannot be overstepped, in order to preserve secrecy on technical points ; the Naval Authorities of both countries must agree upon this limitation.

As regards the Bagdad Railway—we should say (but only if Sir Edward Goschen asks the question) that we are ready to negociate, as we declared before. The railway was never thought of as purely German, but as international. When Abdul Hamid was on the throne we were unable to reach an agreement with England about the Bagdad-Persian Gulf section, because Abdul Hamid never permitted it. French capital is already engaged in it, and there is no objection in principle against Russian money. But our treaty must be preserved as it takes proper account of our interests and those of Turkey.

The Congo question is not to be mentioned yet.

We can conclude a special agreement on colonial questions, but not until the Naval Agreement and the one concerning neutrality are settled.

[1] Cf. p. 410.

[Speaking at Hanley December 3rd, 1909, on the eve of the Election, Mr. Balfour warned the country that within four years the nation might have to face a very critical position. It might not necessarily mean war, but absolutely the only way to ensure peace was to provide against the danger of war.

The Election took place in January, 1910, and the Liberals returned to power.

The naval negociations rested for some months and were not resumed in full force until the autumn. (Cf. G. & T., VI, p. 315.)

On May 7th King Edward died, and one of the strongest champions of peace was removed.]

German Note.

Mr. Roosevelt, the ex-President, being on a journey through Europe, arrived in Berlin on May 10th. He was very warmly received and entertained by the Emperor at the Neues Palais at Potsdam, and also by the Chancellor, who gave a large dinner in his honour on the 12th. He had conversations with the Foreign Minister. On the 15th he went on to London.

XXVIII. 322

Memorandum by the Chancellor, Bethmann-Hollweg, *May 14th*, 1910

Each time I met him Mr. Roosevelt discussed the theme of Anglo-German relations. He thinks an armed conflict not likely, but not out of the question, for England, who until '64, '66 and '70 had only been conscious of a feeling of political mistrust of Germany, now suffered from political fear of her which was leading to the most extravagant suggestions. The mood of the British was such that an unforeseen event might lead to war. He criticised very sharply in this connection Mr. Balfour's famous election speech.

When he got to London he intended to speak as follows to the British statesmen : His meeting with the German Emperor and myself had convinced him that Germany only pursued the practical in her policy (*Realpolitik*). Germany had no possible motive for wishing for a war with England. Assuming she won, no German in his senses would contemplate seizing Australia, Canada, South Africa—let alone India. Whereas if England won, she might succeed in severely damaging German trade for two or at most three years, after which Germany's trade and industry would reappear as England's world competitor just as before. What was war for, anyway, except to waste blood and money ? ! England naturally wanted to keep her supremacy of the sea. She ought to build only as many ships as she considered necessary for that purpose ; Germany would do the same in England's place ; but England should not always be saying she is building these ships against Germany or that Germany is an essential factor in the Two-Power Standard.

England must equally include in her calculations the United States Navy just as much as Germany's.

He would like too to tell the British that he could not understand how they could look askance at the prosperity of Germany's African colonies or the expansion of her trade and enterprise in Asia. Both were to England's advantage. In Africa all white men ought to feel they were standing together as against the blacks, whilst in Asia, especially Asia Minor, the Germans formed a very welcome barrier between the British and Russians. Roosevelt considered further that the differences between England and Germany would only settle down very gradually. The policy for the future—a very necessary one—was a combination of America, England and Germany. This would *really* guarantee the world's peace. There was an open racial antagonism between America and Japan, which might one day cause a war. A strong American Navy would be the best assurance for peace. The despatch of the American fleet into the Pacific had served towards this end.

[The Emperor came to London on May 19th for King Edward's funeral. He met Mr. Roosevelt again there.]

XXVIII. 327

THE EMPEROR, IN LONDON, TO THE CHANCELLOR, BETHMANN-HOLLWEG, 7 a.m. 20/v/10

Mr. Roosevelt began the conversation with the words : ' I come to report progress ' ! He told me of the arrangement with Your Excellency as to what he was to say here. He has talked to Lansdowne, Haldane, and the King.   .

Lansdowne was reserved and silent. ' A man who may be efficient in his way and a good diplomatist, but he runs between blinkers, has no broad views.'

Haldane understood him at once and took him up promptly. Londonderry, a former Viceroy of Ireland, was quite without hope regarding general politics, such as the Far East and a combination of the White races. ' This man has no more brains than those of a guinea-pig, he was obtuse as a lamp-post ; I might as well have talked to the chair opposite us. If the hereditary legislators are in the average like him in the House of Lords, then the Lord have mercy on England ! ' The King had been gracious and had listened to him with attention and had agreed with him.

During our conversation one of the gentlemen asked : ' Why do they build a fleet ? ' Roosevelt answered : ' Because every great Power that respects itself cannot afford to be dependent for its existence on the good will or momentary kindly disposition of this or that Power or group of Powers, whether they will attack it or leave it alone ; it must be able to guard itself quite independently of the disposition of the feelings of its neighbours.'

I spoke to Pichon at the dinner in the sense we had arranged.[1] He promised to do all he could and to meet our wishes. . . .

XXVIII. 334

CAPTAIN WIDENMANN, NAVAL ATTACHÉ IN LONDON, TO ADMIRAL VON TIRPITZ, *July 14th*, 1910

At dinner last evening Mr. McKenna told me that he would have to state next day in the House of Commons that by the spring of 1912 Germany would have completed not 13, but 17 Dreadnoughts. I replied that I could not be astonished if Germany were again seized with indignation and amazement at his not merely disregarding, but actually twisting the information supplied officially to the British Government.

In connection with this, when Sir John Jellicoe [2] asked me if I meant to be present at the naval Debate to-day in the House of Commons, I replied that I had no need to, as I knew what McKenna was going to say. Sir John asked in astonishment how I knew it, and I told him of my conversation with Mr. McKenna.

Sir John replied in a very definite tone : ' You will see that Mr. McKenna will not say that.'

On my asking how he knew what Mr. McKenna was going to answer, Sir John said : ' The Board of Admiralty settled this morning what Mr. McKenna was to say, and you may rest assured that he expressed himself to you incorrectly yesterday.'

Sir John Jellicoe is usually very careful in his statements, and I conclude from his manner of saying this to me in front of Captain Madden, the Fourth Sea Lord, that the Sea Lords are at last getting Mr. McKenna to turn over a new leaf and are in a fair way to make their influence felt.

If this is really a fact, it is doubtless due to Arthur Wilson,[3] who follows his convictions as a naval officer, free from Parliamentary influence. Possibly also Sir John Jellicoe may have brought back from his visit to Kiel, where his eyes were opened as to our view of the Anglo-German question, an impression that the lawyer McKenna must be more tightly controlled by the naval members of the Admiralty.

[In the House of Commons on July 14th Mr. Asquith put the British side of the naval question rather strongly. (Cf. *Parliamentary Debates*,

---

[1] About the delay in settling the Morocco crisis. (Not described in this volume.)   [2] Third Sea Lord and Controller of the Navy.

[3] Fisher's successor as First Sea Lord.

1910. Vol. XIX, p. 635 et seq. ; G. & T., VI, p. 495.) This caused some anxiety in Berlin, where they feared the interruptions caused by the General Election and King Edward's death had left the Government in a less conciliatory mood towards Germany then in the previous year. In order to remove this impression a Memorandum, conceived in a conciliatory tone was sent to Sir Edward Goschen, who handed it to the Chancellor on August 14th. (Cf. G. & T., VI, pp. 501, 511 ; Brandenburg, p. 367.) The Emperor's Minute to this Memorandum follows (XXVIII. 353.)

1. Agreement with England very welcome.

2. Political agreement more important and to be concluded first.

3. With a promise of British reciprocity they demand a pause in German ship-building. As Germany is in a way bound by a detailed Naval Law, it means apparently that we must refrain from a supplementary programme.

4. England has no fixed Naval Law and can lay down ships in any number as she requires them. So how is reciprocity possible ?

5. England must first submit to us a programme of construction with an engagement to stick to it ; it must show clearly the future developments in the British Navy.

6. Exchange of information (with proposed limitations) need be no obstacle. The two Admiralties can combine for this. Much more will not come out than it does now through the visits and reports of Attachés and through publication in the daily papers and technical journals.

7. England wants to have the political agreement so that the Powers which are in the Entente with her may be included in it, i.e., so that England may inform them of it at once—to reassure them ! This is where we demand reciprocity, i.e. :

8. The Franco-Russian Alliance is a military alliance first and foremost against us (on the pretence of a threatened German attack). England in 1904–05 joined this notoriously anti-German coalition and offered France military assistance on the Continent. And yet England declares that it is with no intention against us that she entered her Ententes with Powers which are hostile to Germany and that she has no base thoughts. That is a self-deception. From the German standpoint the mere fact of England's entrance into the Franco-Russian alliance is already an unfriendly act from the start. Arrangements in one direction or the other are no good.

9. Therefore if England wants to tell the other Powers of our intended Entente, our first demand is to be taken into her Entente with France and Russia, the conditions of which were not communicated to us beforehand.

10. Basis for an Entente with us—policy on parallel lines in the world. Above all we must combine in guaranteeing the ' open door '. This is taking hold in all commercial circles in England, especially in the City, and it is popular in Germany also.

11. It is possible that later on there may be a question of a guarantee of India, for they care greatly about India in England. Consider a guarantee of Alsace-Lorraine in return and a promise to cover our rear with the fleet, if the case arises.

On August 24th, 1910, Captain Hugh Watson presented to Admiral von Tirpitz Mr. McKenna's proposals in detail for an exchange of information regarding the naval construction in progress in the two countries. (Cf. G. & T., VI, p. 515.) Tirpitz's comment in forwarding the paper to Bethmann-Hollweg was : ' I consider that the matter should be handled dilatorily for the present. An immediate rejection would not be the right course. As a matter of fact I think we might fall in with the British Government's proposals, were it not for the fear that our showing accommodation might be used in England for purposes of agitation and represented as a score over German policy.' (XXVIII. 356.)]

XXVIII. 359

MEMORANDUM BY KIDERLEN, *September 16th*, 1910

Sir Ernest Cassel is here in Berlin and Herr Ballin also. It is probably about Cassel's well-known charity foundation.

Nevertheless Herr Ballin enquired of Geheimrat Hammann about the understanding with England which His Majesty so greatly desired. Sir E. Cassel had told him that the reason why the negociations broke down last year was because we stipulated that England should leave the Triple Entente.

It is curious how little the British Government troubles about secrecy and how dishonestly and (to us) odiously she commits her indiscretions. It would be well to indicate that to Sir E. Goschen when the reply to the proposals is handed to him. (BETHMANN-HOLLWEG : ' *Yes.*')

XXVIII. 361

COUNT VON GÖTZEN, IN THE EMPEROR'S SUITE AT ROMINTEN, *September 25th*, 1910

Cipher telegram.

His Majesty has written the following comment on the article in the *Westminster Gazette* [1] of the 22nd, which was given to him to read :

' To be noted for all negociations with Goschen or London !

[2] ' England always forgets that the Russo-French alliance is a *military* alliance with a *direct anti-German* tendency, with the ultimate intention of smashing Germany. This is known and perfectly understood by the German people and army. The moment any other European country openly joins this group or proclaims that its aims are identical with those of the afore-named alliance, that it sides with it immediately, in the eyes of all knowing Germans, must create the impression of joining the group of anti-German Powers with an anti-German tendency. That is to say in a sense *inimical* to Germany. Therefore England may officially or otherwise declare and protest, as much as it likes, that in joining the Russo-French group it only followed the dictations of its own political interests for its own benefit, no German will believe that. Germany will always look with distrust on the " sider " with its declared enemies, as long as

---

[1] An article commenting on his famous ' shining armour ' speech in Vienna on September 21st.

[2] All English in the text.

England does not come to a clear and loyal political entente
with Germany, with whom she has more identity of common
interests as [than] with the Gallo-Slavish combination.'

XXVIII. 367

MEMORANDUM [1] HANDED BY THE CHANCELLOR TO SIR EDWARD
GOSCHEN, *October* 13th, 1910

The Imperial Government learns with satisfaction from the
British Government's Memorandum that they are prepared to
resume the discussions which, owing to the state of domestic
politics in the United Kingdom, were discontinued for a considerable period.

In order to meet the British Government's wishes the Imperial
Government has again examined the question whether it is
possible to realise the British Government's idea for a reduction
of naval expenditure on the basis of a mutual understanding.

The Imperial Government started by an examination of the
proposal for a periodical exchange of information on the state
of the ship-building of both nations—through the medium of
the Naval Attachés. The Imperial Government finds no objection to offer to this. If it is based on the assumption that the
Imperial Government *binds itself* not to extend the existing
Naval Law, this suggestion could not be entertained before
clearing up the question of what form of reciprocity the British
Government would be ready to offer in return for such a formal
engagement, since—as the British Government themselves argue
—an Agreement of this kind can only rest on the principle of
reciprocity.

But it may be argued here that the Imperial Government
admitted the possibility and signified its readiness in principle
to consider retardation of construction within the limits of the
Naval Law. The stage of discussion by the naval authorities
of both sides of how such retardation was to be carried out has
never yet been reached owing to the pause in the negotiations,
which the British Government desired. .

The Imperial Government again states its conviction that,
seeing that any Naval Agreement touches the armaments of
both countries, it demands an assurance of reciprocity as an
absolute preliminary condition. The Government thinks therefore that a political understanding is desirable. Since, according
to the British Government's declaration, no arrangement concluded by them with any other Power contains anything directed
against Germany, the Imperial Government considers that it
will be possible to find a formula which will meet its wishes
without prejudice to the British Government's arrangements

[1] Cf. G. & T., VI, p. 524.

with other Powers. The Imperial Government hopes therefore that the British Government will recognise the necessity of a simultaneous political exchange of views, which will represent the interests of both parties.

German Note.

The Memorandum [from which the following extracts are taken] was written as a guide for the oral representations with which the Chancellor accompanied the handing of that of October 13th to Sir Edward Goschen . . . (cf. G. & T., VI, p. 564–6 ; Brandenburg, p. 367.)

XXVIII. 370

MEMORANDUM

Extract.

. . . In their Memorandum [1] the British Government repeat their assurance that their arrangements with other countries contain nothing directed against Germany. We are far from underrating the importance of this declaration. . . . But we cannot ignore the fact that the general tendency of British policy is in a contrary direction to that of Germany and is on the side of other Powers in opposition to German policy in questions in which the identity of interests of the two Powers should indicate common action. I might point to the British Government's attitude in opposition to ours on the maintenance of the open door in Morocco and Persia. Just as at Algeciras British policy, regardless of consequences, supported France's schemes for monopolising the trade of Morocco, it now aims evidently, in conjunction with Russia, at stopping all German commercial activities in Persia. A significant expression of this was the attitude adopted by the British Government last spring towards the intention expressed by me to be extremely accommodating in the Persian question. The British Government did not take advantage of our attitude, but preferred to try, in combination with Russia, to impose commercial restrictions on Germany in Persia by bearing heavily on the hard-pressed Persian Government. . . .

The British Government's attitude in the Bagdad Railway question is a further witness to the disinclination of British policy to settle questions in a spirit of sympathy with Germany. My statement that we were prepared in principle to agree with England about the construction of the last section of the railway from Bagdad to the Persian Gulf[2] was answered by the British Government with an attempt to persuade the Ottoman Government to grant a concession for a rival line from Bagdad to the Gulf. They are trying to reach their objective not by way of negociation with us, but by an effort to rob the Ottoman Govern-

---

[1] Cf. p. 416.   [2] Cf. p. 373.

ment of the possibility of performing its duty as guarantor of the Railway. The British Government's opposition to the Bagdad Railway scheme is not, however, hindering them from favouring schemes for connecting the Mediterranean and Persian Gulf by rail, which are in the hands of nationals of other Powers (the Tardieu and Chester schemes). Likewise England has been ready to assist the French aspiration to organise the *Dette Publique*, in which England is interested no less than Germany, and thus to assure a predominant position in Constantinople for the Ottoman Bank, which is under French influence.

In many minor questions also the British Government's dislike of combined political action or even of merely keeping in touch with German policy is evident. The attitude of British representatives abroad is proof of this. Instead of the former friendly co-operation with their German colleagues, a certain reserve has sprung up, and also in personal relationships there is an intention to mark the greater intimacy of British policy with other Powers. It is inevitable that this attitude of British policy must produce ever increasing estrangement between the two countries and contain the seeds of a serious conflict in the future. . . .

In the opinion of the Imperial Government this policy is above all responsible for the anxiety which has seized upon large sections of the British people regarding Germany's naval policy. The indifference with which England regards the rise of the American Navy is a proof that a strong fleet in the hands of a *friendly* Power is not necessarily a subject of anxiety for England. Therefore the Imperial Government is bound to doubt whether the British Government's suggestion of periodical exchanges of information as to the state of naval construction in each of the two countries will lead to the result hoped for by the British Government, unless accompanied by a change in the orientation of British policy. . . .

Now that the British Government have repeatedly stated that their arrangements with other Powers are not directed against Germany, it is inexplicable how they can have come to suspect that we are seeking an understanding with them in order to upset their relations with other Powers. That is far from our purpose. On the contrary, we think that the result of frank discussion and an understanding with the British Government will be that England's relations with her friends will be undisturbed, whilst our relations with those Powers will improve.

German Note. XXVIII. 368.

Sir Edward Goschen received the text of this Memorandum in December. (Cf. G. & T., VI, p. 564.)

XXVIII. 373
COUNT VON METTERNICH, IN LONDON, TO THE CHANCELLOR, BETHMANN-HOLLWEG, *October 12th*, 1910

Mr. Ramsay Macdonald, a Labour Member, spoke on the disarmament problem at Newcastle-on-Tyne ; amongst other things he said that from the depths of his heart he deplored the present Cabinet's foreign policy. There was no doubt that Sir E. Grey was responsible for the present unsatisfactory relations between England and Germany. (The EMPEROR : ' *Undoubtedly correct.*') He had never been able to free himself from the influence of the officials in the Foreign Office, and these were friendly to Russia because they disliked Germany. (The EMPEROR : ' *Correct.*') A political understanding with Germany was the indispensable preliminary condition for any reduction of armaments. (The EMPEROR : ' *Word for word with what I wrote three weeks ago, and what is in our answer.—Bravo !* ')

KIDERLEN : ' *Mentioned to-day by the Emperor in audience with Goschen.*'

[Writing on October 27th, Count Metternich stated that after reading the Memorandum of October 13th ' Sir Edward Grey remarked that he could not regard the reproaches directed orally against British policy in general as being justified. He intended to reply to them in detail.' (Cf. G. & T., VI, pp. 537–8.)

The conversations continued, but with no definite result. At the end of a report of a conversation (cf. G. & T., VI, p. 567) with Sir Edward Grey on December 16th Metternich wrote :]

XXVIII. 388
COUNT VON METTERNICH TO THE CHANCELLOR, BETHMANN-HOLLWEG, *December 17th*, 1910

Extract.

. . . Sir Edward Grey is not a man who, for the sake of an advantage, would try to arouse hopes which he does not believe in himself, or would promise more than he thinks he can perform. Never more than on this occasion has he so clearly shown his wish for a rapprochement. On taking office in 1905 he said to me that the Liberal Government meant to try by their influence in Paris to soften down Franco-German differences so as to make an Anglo-German Entente easier. (BETHMANN-HOLLWEG : ' ? ') The dispute at that time over the Morocco question drove him more and more to the French side and away from us ; yesterday was the first time that he seriously discussed the subject of an Anglo-German rapprochement with me again.

Your Excellency's statement in the Reichstag of December 10th [1] has had a good effect on public opinion, and the moment

[1] Expressing a desire for a friendly understanding. (Cf. G. & T., VI, p. 567.)

is perhaps approaching again when some improvement in Anglo-German relations may be attained. Our concession in the matter of an exchange of naval information, the good effect of which I pointed out several times three years ago, has made a strong impression on the Government here and has been a deciding factor in the present feeling for a rapproachement. The Englishman is most easily caught by an argument which appeals to his sense. Correct reasoning and a suitably chosen form of words for an agreement concerning the exchange of information will remove any character of suspicion from it. (BETHMANN-HOLLWEG : ' *That will be very important. The Admiralty must not be allowed to choose the form of words all by itself.*')

I see no signs that the Russo-German rapprochement which took place at Potsdam [1] is causing the Government here to fear that Anglo-Russian relations may be prejudiced by it.

[The negociations went on indecisively until the late spring of 1911, when Bethmann-Hollweg wrote on May 9th to Count Metternich. (Cf. G. & T., VI, pp. 625–9.]

XXVIII. 412

THE CHANCELLOR, BETHMANN-HOLLWEG, TO COUNT VON METTERNICH, *May 9th*, 1911

. . . The British Government's handling of this affair has made it impossible to carry into actual practice the idea of retarding the rate of our ship-building, seeing that for the coming year the number of the new ships to be built each year of the Dreadnought class is to drop down to two. Considerations of financial policy and also of the German ship-building industry forbid our going below this number. Also we find it impossible to approach the British Government with proposals for an agreement on armaments. We certainly see no method of mutually reducing the expenditure on armaments as desired by the British, without disturbing the provisions of the German Naval Law, which neither should nor shall be altered in any respect—a fact with which the British Government has by now become familiar. . . .

If the British Government is really prepared to place their relationship with us on the same footing as with France and Russia—if they are willing to discuss questions as they arise in the same conciliatory and trustful spirit as with these two other Powers, they cannot hesitate to hold out their hands for agreements of a kind calculated to remove all cause for the British anxiety regarding the dangers with which the German Navy threatens them. There is nothing to hinder the British

[1] Cf. p. 402.

Government from building up their relationship with the two Entente Powers likewise.   We do not seek a preferential position. We only wish to get the political differentiation removed, under which we suffer at present from England in comparison with those Powers. . . .

[Nevertheless on June 1st the Foreign Office in London were able to write that ' His Majesty's Government have learnt with satisfaction that the Imperial Government adhere to the proposal for a periodical exchange of naval information '.   (Cf. G. & T., VI, p. 637.)

The conversations continued, but with a difference.   The difficulties of an agreement were increased by the ' Agadir Incident ', when the *Panther* suddenly appeared in the bay of Agadir on the Moorish coast on July 21st, 1909.   Volume IV will contain an account of its origin and accompanying circumstances.]

INDEX OF PRINCIPAL PERSONAGES

CAMBON, Paul, French Ambassador in Madrid, 1886–91 ; in Constantinople, 1891–98 ; in London, 1898–1920.

CAMPBELL-BANNERMAN, Sir Henry, Prime Minister, 1905–8.

CARNEGIE, Sir Lancelot, in British Embassy in Vienna, 1907–8 ; in Paris, 1908, 1911–13 ; Minister at Lisbon, 1913.

CARTWRIGHT, Sir Fairfax, Ambassador in Vienna, 1908–13.

CASSEL, Sir E., Financier.

CHAMBERLAIN, Sir Austen, Postmaster-General, 1902–3 ; Chancellor of the Exchequer, 1903–5 ; Foreign Secretary, 1924–29.

CHAMBERLAIN, Joseph, Colonial Secretary, 1895–1903.

CHELIUS, Major von, Military Attaché in Rome, 1904–6.

CHIROL, Sir Valentine, in Foreign Office, 1872–6 ; director of Foreign department of The Times, 1899–1912.

CHOATE, Joseph H., American Ambassador in London, 1899–1905.

CHURCHILL, George, Oriental Secretary at Teheran, 1910.

CHURCHILL, Winston Spencer, Board of Trade, 1908–10 ; First Lord of the Admiralty, 1911–15 ; Munitions, 1917–18 ; War, 1918–21 ; Exchequer, 1924–9.

CLEMENCEAU, G., French Prime Minister, 1906–9 ; 1917–20.

CLEVELAND, Major (and Mrs.), Physician to the Amir of Afghanistan, 1904.

CONGER, E., American Minister in Peking, 1898–1905.

COURCEL, Baron a. de, French Ambassador in Berlin, 1882–6 ; London, 1894–8.

CREWE, Earl of, Colonial Secretary, 1908–10 ; India, 1910–16.

CROMER, Earl of, Consul-General in Cairo, 1883–1907.

CROWE, Sir Eyre, Foreign Office, 1885–1925.

CURZON, Marquess, Viceroy of India, 1899–1905 ; Lord Privy Seal, 1915–16 ; Lord President, 1916–19 ; Foreign Secretary, 1919–23.

DANE, Sir Louis, Foreign Secretary to the Indian Government, 1902–8.

DELCASSÉ, French Foreign Secretary, 1898–1905.

DEVONSHIRE, Duke of, Lord President, 1895–1903.

DUCARNE, General, Chief of the Belgian General Staff, 1906.

DURAND, Sir Mortimer, British Ambassador in Madrid, 1900–3 ; Washington, 1903–7.

ECKARDSTEIN, Baron von, German diplomat in London, 1899–1902.

EDWARD VII.

EGERTON, Sir Edwin, Ambassador in Madrid, 1903–4 ; Rome, 1905–8.

ELIOT, Sir Charles, Constantinople, 1893–98 ; British High Commissioner in Samoa, 1899 ; Washington, 1898–1900 ; East Africa, 1900–4 ; Ambassador to Japan, 1919–26.

ELLIOT, Sir Francis, Minister at Athens, 1903–17.

ENVER PACHA, Turkish Military Attaché in Berlin, 1909, 1912–13 ; War Minister, 1914.

ESHER, Viscount.

FALLIÈRES, French President, 1906–13.

FAURE, Felix, French President, 1895–9.

FERDINAND, King of Bulgaria, 1887–1918.

FISHER, Admiral Sir John (Lord), First Sea Lord, 1904–10.

FLOTOW, H. von, German diplomat in Paris, 1904–7 ; Foreign Office, 1907–10 ; Minister at Brussels, 1910–13 ; Ambassador in Rome, 1913–15.

FORGÁCH von Ghymes and GÁCS, Count, Austrian Minister at Belgrade, 1907–11.

KHEVENHÜLLER-METSCH, Count zu, Austrian Ambassador in Paris. 1903–11.

KIAMIL PACHA, Grand Vizir, 1908–9, 1912–13.

KIDERLEN-WAECHTER, German Minister at Bucarest, 1899–1910 ; Constantinople, 1907–8 ; deputy Foreign Minister, 1908.

KITCHENER OF KHARTOUM, Viscount, Commander-in-chief in India, 1902–9; Consul-General at Cairo, 1911–14 ; War Office, 1914–16.

KOESTER, Admiral von, President of the German Navy League, 1908.

KRUGER, Paul, President of the Transvaal Republic, 1883–1900.

KÜHLMANN, R. von, at Tangier Legation, 1904–5 ; Counsellor of the German Embassy in London, 1908–14.

KUROPATKIN, General, Russian War Minister, 1898–1904 ; commanded in Japanese War, 1904.

LAMSDORFF, Count, Russian Foreign Minister, 1901–6.

LANSDOWNE, Marquess of, Viceroy of India, 1888–93 ; War Secretary, 1895–1900 ; Foreign Secretary, 1900–5 ; member of the Government, 1915–16.

LASCELLES, Sir Frank C., Ambassador in Berlin, 1895–1908.

LIANG CHENG, Chinese Minister in Washington, 1903–7 ; in Berlin, 1910–13.

LICHNOVSKY, Prince von, in Berlin Foreign Office, 1899–1904 ; Ambassador in London, 1912–14.

LITTLEDALE, St. George, explorer of Tibet.

LLOYD GEORGE, D., Board of Trade, 1905–8 ; Chancellor of the Exchequer, 1908–16 ; Prime Minister, 1916–22.

LOUBET, Franch President, 1899–1906.

LOWTHER, Sir Gerard, Minister at Tangier, 1905–8 ; Ambassador in Constantinople, 1908–13.

LYNCH, Henry F. B., Chairman of the Euphrates and Tigris Valley Steamship Company.

MACDONALD, J. Ramsay, M.P., leader of the Labour Party ; Prime Minister, 1924, 1929.

McKENNA, Reginald, First Lord of the Admiralty, 1908–11 ; Home Secretary, 1911–15 ; Chancellor of the Exchequer, 1915–16.

MAHAN, Admiral A. T., American writer on naval subjects.

MALLET, Sir Louis, Foreign Office ; Ambassador in Constantinople, 1913–14.

MARCHANT, Colonel ; Fashoda, 1898.

MARSCHALL VON BIEBERSTEIN, Baron A., German Foreign Minister, 1890–97 ; Ambassador in Constantinople, 1897–1912.

MAXSE, Leo, editor of the *National Review*.

METTERNICH, Count Paul von, German Ambassador in London, 1901–12.

MEYER, G. von L., American Ambassador in Rome, 1905–07.

MIDLETON, Earl of (Hon. W. St. John Brodrick), Secretary of State for War, 1900–3 ; India, 1903–5.

MILLERAND, French War Minister, 1912–13.

MOLTKE, General H. von, chief of the German General Staff, 1906–14.

MONSON, Sir Edmund, Ambassador in Paris, 1896–1905.

MONTEBELLO, Comte de, French Ambassador in St. Petersburg, 1891–1903.

MONTS, Count, German Ambassador in Rome, 1902–9.

MUMM VON SCHWARTZENSTEIN, Baron, German Minister in Peking, 1900–6 ; Ambassador at Tokio, 1906–11.

MÜNSTER, Count G. von, Ambassador in Paris, 1885–1900.

MUSURUS PACHA, Turkish Ambassador in London, 1903–8.

SCHOEN, Baron W. von, Ambassador in St. Petersburg, 1905–7; Foreign Office, 1907–10; in Paris, 1910–14.

SCHULENBURG, Count F. von der, German Military Attaché in London, 1902–6.

SELBORNE, Earl of, First Lord of the Admiralty, 1900–5; High Commissioner in South Africa, 1905–10; Board of Agriculture, 1915–16.

SENDEN-BIBRAN, Admiral von, Chief of the German Naval Council, 1890–1906.

SHEVKET PACHA, Mahmoud, General, Turkish War Minister, 1910–13; Grand Vizir, 1913.

SMALLEY, G. W., *Times* correspondent in New York, 1905.

SMITH, Sir H. Babington, director of the National Bank of Turkey.

SOLF, W., German Colonial Secretary, 1911–18.

SOVERAL, Luiz de, Portuguese Minister in London, 1897–1910.

SPECK VON Sternburg, Baron, German Ambassador in Washington, 1903–8.

SPENDER, Harold, English journalist.

SPENDER, J. A., Editor of the *Westminster Gazette*.

SPEYER, Sir Edgar, Financier.

SPRING-RICE, Sir Cecil, in St. Petersburg, 1903–6; Minister at Teheran, 1906–8; Stockholm, 1908–13; Ambassador in Washington, 1913–18.

STEAD, W. T., Editor of the *Review of Reviews*, 1890–1912.

STEED, H. Wickham, *Times* Correspondent in Vienna, 1902–13; Editor, 1919–22; Editor of the *Review of Reviews*, 1923.

STEMRICH, German Minister at Teheran, 1906–7; in Foreign Office, 1907–11.

STUART-WORTLEY, Col. E. J. M. (Major-General).

STUMM, W. von, in German Embassy at St. Petersburg, 1903–5; Madrid, 1905–6; London, 1906–8; Foreign Office, 1908–16.

SZÖGYÉYI-MARICH, Austrian Ambassador in Berlin, 1892–1914.

TALAAT BEY, Turkish Minister of the Interior, 1909–13.

TARDIEU, A., French journalist and deputy. Supporter of Clemenceau.

TATTENBACH, Count von, German Minister at Tangier, 1889–95; Lisbon, 1897–1908; Tangier, 1905; at Algeciras Conference, 1906.

TEWFIK PACHA, Turkish Foreign Minister, 1895–1909; Grand Vizir, 1909; Ambassador in London, 1909–14.

TEWFIK PACHA, General, Turkish Ambassador in Berlin, 1897–1908.

TIRPITZ, Admiral A. von, Secretary to the German Admiralty, 1897–1916.

TITTONI, Italian Foreign Minister, 1903–5, 1906–9.

TOGO, Japanese Admiral, 1904.

TORES, the Sultan of Morocco's Foreign Secretary, 1904–8; at Algeciras Conference, 1906.

TOWER, Charlemagne, American Ambassador in Berlin, 1902–7.

TREITSCHKE, Heinrich von, German political philosopher.

TSCHIRSCHKY, German Ambassador in Vienna, 1907–16.

TWEEDMOUTH, Lord, First Lord of the Admiralty, 1905–8.

TYRRELL, Sir William, London Foreign Office; Ambassador in Paris, 1927–

VASSEL, German Consul at Fez, 1904.

VASSOS, Greek Colonel.

VENEZELOS, Prime Minister of Greece, 1910–15.

VICTORIA, Queen.

VINCENT, Sir Edgar, Chairman of the Ottoman Bank.

VISCONTI VENOSTA, Marquis, Italian Foreign Minister, 1896–8; at Algeciras, 1906.

INDEX